Communications in Computer and Information Science 2513

Series Editors

Gang Li , *School of Information Technology, Deakin University, Burwood, VIC, Australia*
Joaquim Filipe , *Polytechnic Institute of Setúbal, Setúbal, Portugal*
Zhiwei Xu, *Chinese Academy of Sciences, Beijing, China*

AF167719

Rationale
The CCIS series is devoted to the publication of proceedings of computer science conferences. Its aim is to efficiently disseminate original research results in informatics in printed and electronic form. While the focus is on publication of peer-reviewed full papers presenting mature work, inclusion of reviewed short papers reporting on work in progress is welcome, too. Besides globally relevant meetings with internationally representative program committees guaranteeing a strict peer-reviewing and paper selection process, conferences run by societies or of high regional or national relevance are also considered for publication.

Topics
The topical scope of CCIS spans the entire spectrum of informatics ranging from foundational topics in the theory of computing to information and communications science and technology and a broad variety of interdisciplinary application fields.

Information for Volume Editors and Authors
Publication in CCIS is free of charge. No royalties are paid, however, we offer registered conference participants temporary free access to the online version of the conference proceedings on SpringerLink (http://link.springer.com) by means of an http referrer from the conference website and/or a number of complimentary printed copies, as specified in the official acceptance email of the event.

CCIS proceedings can be published in time for distribution at conferences or as postproceedings, and delivered in the form of printed books and/or electronically as USBs and/or e-content licenses for accessing proceedings at SpringerLink. Furthermore, CCIS proceedings are included in the CCIS electronic book series hosted in the SpringerLink digital library at http://link.springer.com/bookseries/7899. Conferences publishing in CCIS are allowed to use Online Conference Service (OCS) for managing the whole proceedings lifecycle (from submission and reviewing to preparing for publication) free of charge.

Publication process
The language of publication is exclusively English. Authors publishing in CCIS have to sign the Springer CCIS copyright transfer form, however, they are free to use their material published in CCIS for substantially changed, more elaborate subsequent publications elsewhere. For the preparation of the camera-ready papers/files, authors have to strictly adhere to the Springer CCIS Authors' Instructions and are strongly encouraged to use the CCIS LaTeX style files or templates.

Abstracting/Indexing
CCIS is abstracted/indexed in DBLP, Google Scholar, EI-Compendex, Mathematical Reviews, SCImago, Scopus. CCIS volumes are also submitted for the inclusion in ISI Proceedings.

How to start
To start the evaluation of your proposal for inclusion in the CCIS series, please send an e-mail to ccis@springer.com

Sebastian Zielinski · Gerald Eichler ·
Christian Erfurth · Günter Fahrnberger
Editors

Innovations for Community Services

25th International Conference, I4CS 2025
Munich, Germany, June 11–13, 2025
Proceedings

 Springer

Editors
Sebastian Zielinski [iD]
LMU Munich
Munich, Germany

Christian Erfurth [iD]
University of Applied Sciences Jena
Jena, Germany

Gerald Eichler [iD]
Deutsche Telekom Technology
and Innovation
Darmstadt, Germany

Günter Fahrnberger [iD]
University of Hagen
Hagen, Nordrhein-Westfalen, Germany

ISSN 1865-0929   ISSN 1865-0937 (electronic)
Communications in Computer and Information Science
ISBN 978-3-031-94262-4   ISBN 978-3-031-94263-1 (eBook)
https://doi.org/10.1007/978-3-031-94263-1

Foreword

In 2025, the International Conference on Innovations for Community Services (I4CS) celebrates its 25th edition, visiting Munich for the second time, after 2007. The goal focuses on attracting a wider audience for this quarter-century celebration.

24 years ago, at the Technische Univertät Ilmenau, Germany, Herwig Unger and Thomas Böhme initiated a Workshop on Innovative Internet Community Systems (IICS) as a platform for publishing project results. This event continued evolving under the revised name I2CS and later I4CS in 2014. The first proceedings appeared in the Springer *Lecture Notes in Computer Science* series (LNCS) until 2005, followed by *Gesellschaft für Informatik e.V.* (GI) in Köllen Verlag and *Verein Deutscher Ingenieure* (VDI) in 2013. I4CS initially collaborated with the *Institute of Electrical and Electronics Engineers* (IEEE) before returning to Springer's *Communications in Computer and Information Science* (CCIS) series in 2016, establishing a permanent partnership in 2018. The unique combination of printed proceedings and the SpringerLink online edition generates remarkable interest among external readers. With approximately 9,900 web accesses last year at SpringerLink, the annual figure has more than doubled.

The selection of conference locations reflects the event's core concept: Members of the Program Committee (PC) propose suitable venues to foster a thriving scientific community. For 2025, the I4CS Steering Committee proudly entrusted organizational responsibility to Sebastian Zielinski at LMU Munich, Germany. Situated on the banks of the River Isar and representing the heart of Bavaria, the location offers proximity to the Alps, "high" lighting this year's motto: "Celebrating I4CS' Quarter-Century."

I4CS takes pride in offering a strong selection of scientific presentations, complemented by a keynote, two invited talks, and a vibrant social program designed to strengthen the cultural and academic community. The proceedings of I4CS 2025 feature seven sessions, covering 21 full papers and three short papers, selected from a record-breaking 55 submissions from authors in 16 countries. Interdisciplinary thinking remains a key success factor for any community. Thus, the conference highlights a blend of academic, scientific, social, and industrial topics, structured into three long-established key areas: Technology, Applications, and Socialization.

Technology: Distributed Architectures and Frameworks

- Data architectures and enablers for community services,
- Cryptography and cryptology,
- 5G/6G technologies and ad-hoc wireless networks,
- Data models, analytics, and big data management,
- Quantum and cloud computing.

Applications: Communities on the Move

- Social networks, open data, and distributed coworking,
- Barrier-free collaboration, publishing, and eLearning,
- Recommender solutions and chat bots,
- Virtual & augmented reality, robotics, and mobile e-sports,
- Intelligent traffic, logistics, and connected cars.

Socialization: Ambient Work and Living

- Distributed work challenges and eHealth-assisted living,
- Machine learning, human-centered AI, and governance,
- Smart home, energy control, and public infrastructure,
- Internet of things and dynamic sensor networks,
- Cyber- and information security.

Many thanks to the 28 active members of the Program Committee for 2025, representing 13 countries worldwide, for their 238 worthwhile reviews! Special thanks go to the conference chairman Christian Erfurth, this year's program chair Sebastian Zielinski, and finally to our publication chair, Günter Fahrnberger, who ensured a very successful cooperation with the Springer publishing board, maintaining the high reputation of I4CS, rated C-level at CORE.

Following the alternation rule, the 26th I4CS will take place outside Germany, probably in Denmark, around June 2026. Please check the permanent conference URL at http://www.i4cs-conference.org/ regularly for upcoming details.

Proposals on new emerging topics, as well as applications from prospective Program Committee members and potential conference hosts and locations remain kindly welcome at request@i4cs-conference.org.

Kind regards on behalf of the entire Steering Committee and the Editors' Board.

June 2025   Gerald Eichler

Preface

Welcome to the 25th International Conference on Innovations for Community Services (I4CS) proceedings, themed "Celebrating I4CS' Quarter-Century," held from June 11 to 13, 2025, at LMU Munich in Munich, Germany. As the Program Chair of this year's conference, I am pleased to introduce this CCIS volume, featuring cutting-edge research and insights into the dynamic field of digital innovation.

In recent years, we have witnessed significant technological developments, especially in quantum computing and artificial intelligence. At I4CS, we focus on combining these technological advancements with community services (e.g., healthcare, education, transportation, and more) to improve people's quality of life. Thus, this year's proceedings contain a wide variety of publications spanning many different research areas, such as quantum computing, artificial intelligence, cloud computing, and cybersecurity, along with publications applying results and techniques from these fields to community services like healthcare, sports, and smart cities. Furthermore, our proceedings volume benefits from keynotes by Sebastian Feld, Thomas Gabor, and Tobias Fertig, who share insights gained from years of cutting-edge research in quantum computing, artificial intelligence, and cybersecurity. Our keynote speakers explore the intricacies of full-stack quantum computing and its potential as a powerful framework for advancing community-centric approaches. They discuss future artificial intelligence capabilities considering intrinsic and emergent goals in optimization and artificial intelligence, while reminding us that cybersecurity transcends technical issues, embodying a shared social responsibility.

We feel honored that LMU Munich was chosen as the venue for the 25th anniversary of the I4CS conference. Founded in 1472, LMU Munich has long stood as a center of excellence in research and innovation across many disciplines. With 15 Nobel prizes to its name, LMU Munich boasts a legacy enriched by the contributions of alumni and professors such as Werner Heisenberg, Max Planck, and Conrad Röntgen, whose work left a lasting impact on history. Additionally, Munich hosts people from 180 different countries, transforming the city into a multicultural hub where diverse ideas and cultural influences drive innovation and shape the future. Thus, LMU Munich aligns perfectly with the I4CS mission: to foster innovation by combining ideas from various research areas and cultures to improve the future.

Finally, I express my deep appreciation to the program committee and external reviewers for their rigorous assessment of the manuscripts. Their dedication and expertise have greatly contributed to maintaining the high standards of our proceedings. I am equally grateful to the authors, keynote speakers, and participants for sharing their insights and fostering new ideas, ensuring the continued growth and impact of our academic community. Furthermore, we thank Springer for their technical support and excellent management of our CCIS publishing project.

June 2025

Sebastian Zielinski
Gerald Eichler
Christian Erfurth
Günter Fahrnberger

Organization

Program Committee

Sebastian Apel	Technical University of Applied Sciences Ingolstadt, Germany
Udo Bub	Eötvös Loránd University, Hungary
Gerald Eichler	Deutsche Telekom, Germany
Christian Erfurth	University of Applied Sciences Jena, Germany
Günter Fahrnberger	University of Hagen, Germany
Andreas Fink	Helmut Schmidt University of the Federal Armed Forces Hamburg, Germany
Hacène Fouchal	University of Reims Champagne-Ardenne, France
Hanno Friedrich	Kühne Logistics University, Germany
Sapna Ponaraseri Gopinathan	i.k.val Softwares LLP, India
Stefan Hofbauer	University of the Bundeswehr Munich, Germany
Mikael Johansson	CSC - IT Center for Science, Finland
Kathrin Kirchner	Technical University of Denmark, Denmark
Udo Krieger	University of Bamberg, Germany
Peter Kropf	University of Neuchâtel, Switzerland
Ulrike Lechner	University of the Bundeswehr Munich, Germany
Andreas Lommatzsch	Technical University of Berlin, Germany
Karl-Heinz Lüke	Ostfalia University of Applied Sciences Wolfsburg, Germany
Raja Natarajan	Tata Institute of Fundamental Research, India
Deveeshree Nayak	University of Washington Tacoma, USA
Dana Petcu	West University of Timisoara, Romania
Frank Phillipson	Netherlands Organisation for Applied Scientific Research, The Netherlands
Joerg Roth	Nuremberg Institute of Technology, Germany
Amardeo Sarma	Society for the Scientific Investigation of Pseudosciences, Germany
Karl Seidenfad	Siemens Erlangen, Germany
Pranav Kumar Singh	Indian Institute of Technology Guwahati and Central Institute of Technology Kokrajhar, India

Julian Szymanski   Gdańsk University of Technology, Poland
Leendert W. M. Wienhofen   City of Trondheim, Norway
Sebastian Zielinski   Ludwig Maximilian University of Munich,
                                     Germany

Additional Reviewers

Grosmann, Marcel
Khodambashi, Soudabeh
Le, Duy Thanh

Invited Talks

What Will Artificial Intelligence Do on Its Own? Intrinsic and Emergent Goals in Optimization and Artificial Intelligence

Thomas Gabor

LMU Munich, Munich, Germany
thomas.gabor@ifi.lmu.de

Abstract. Artificial Intelligence (AI) is becoming a ubiquitous component of everyday complex software applications and services. This also means that AI components are being used in unforeseen, novel situations, some of which will involve other AI components and give rise to complex interactions between unacquainted AI agents. We examine the scope of AI-to-AI interactions, ranging from adversarial learning for better control in industrial settings to diverging conversations between isolated chatbots. We observe that, aside from the specific goals we assign to AI agents, intrinsic goals can develop purely from the setup we choose. These emergent goals present both a danger to the intended outcomes of complex systems and an opportunity to create systems that can surpass their original complexity.

Keywords. Artificial Intelligence (AI) agents · AI-to-AI interactions

Cutting-edge artificial intelligence (AI) is finally on its way into users' hands. After a long series of AI breakthroughs that were mostly focused on very specialized, controlled problems, the advent of large-language models (LLMs) has already had a different kind of impact: not only can LLMs solve or help to solve various of these specialized problems, they also bring with them a new usability for general purposes; this has sparked interest within the tech-savvy public to utilize these capabilities in everyday contexts. In the first wave, LLMs have mostly been delivered as digital assistants that can be called upon by the user, usually through dedicated apps. We have also seen integration with specific, already widespread tools such as code editors or office suites. Currently, major players are working on a deeper integration of LLMs into operating systems, at least from a user perspective.

To get a glimpse into the near future, we must first realize the new advancements that LLMs are bringing to the table — we reckon there are at least two:

- Making human language available for computer interfaces. LLMs offer a practically complete understanding of human language, foreseeably in text and spoken word. This allows for new interface paradigms, like summarizing mails and notifications or asking for arbitrary categories of photos to be searched for. It should be noted that

the potential to use arbitrary machine languages as data types within an application has been explored [7, 8], but not yet generalized to human language.
- Making common human knowledge available to the computer. LLMs also act as foundation models, i.e., they can be (automatically) queried for a vast amount of basic human knowledge. This can be used to access some results directly (i.e., looking up a well-known heuristic instead of searching an exact result algorithmically), but also, again, in conjunction with human-machine interfaces, which are now able to access assumptions that humans might naturally have about certain realities [6].

To some extent, the utilization of both of these capabilities will allow LLMs and thus AI methods to be applied to an even broader range of situations. While current developments are still focused on using AI as a tool to more easily and quickly develop new software and services, deep integration of AI within the end product will allow for more dynamic, accessible, and personalized software [1]; thus we should expect such an environment for future AI applications.

The "AI-fication" of software and services, however, brings us into some uncharted territory. Beyond technical constraints (i.e., high computational effort) and user concerns (i.e., keeping interactions with users safe and within restraints), we can also predict some algorithmic challenges inherent to complex AI-based systems:

- **Meeting in the field.** Future AI systems will interact with other AI systems to a large degree. Since we are naturally unable to predict all possible combinations of AI systems that may be facing each other in the real world, we also cannot specifically prepare for such a scenario. Instead, we might need to call upon more abstract and general mechanisms to make interaction between arbitrary, independent AI systems productive.
- **Converging interactions.** In a system without external input, interactions between AI components will become stale over time. On a small scale, we can observe such a behavior when ongoing chats between chat-bots tend to converge towards certain message patterns [9]. The creativity necessary to break out of such patterns is still missing from current-generation AI.
- **Self-reinforcing behavior.** AI systems might encode certain behavior patterns without having been actually trained to do so. This phenomenon is rather commonly known for bias in data sets, but might also occur for bias in the solution representation or the training mechanism. In fact, certain hyperparameters tend to influence learning processes differently from optimal learning behavior [2].

If we are to tackle these challenges without a fundamental paradigm shift in how we are building AI, a promising candidate is to further enhance the training and learning process. For example, previous research has led us to recognize the following effects, among many other (possible) observations:

- *The Dieselgate Effect.* Named after an incident where a German car manufacturer cheated on emissions test, we also recognize that a powerful AI-based system needs to be trained against an equally powerful AI-based test system. Otherwise, i.e., if the tests are too primitive compared to the system's capabilities, the system is rather incentivized to trick the tests than to actually implement the behavior the tests intend to cover [3, 4].

– *The Exam Effect.* When generating tests for AI-based systems, systems that pass the hardest tests are also likely to pass easier tests. This phenomenon is clear for human learning (and thus forms the basis for focusing on hard questions in exams); but such an effect also seems to occur in machine learning, where it is more untypical (but nonetheless true) that test cases can be trained for without them being present in the training data, when strictly harder test cases are [3, 5].

Although incomplete, these observations can give us some hope that the increasing complexity of open, open-ended, dynamic, and heterogeneous AI-based systems can, in fact, be tackled through algorithmic means and even give rise to more powerful AI.

References

1. Belzner, L., Gabor, T., Wirsing, M.: Large language model assisted software engineering: prospects, challenges, and a case study. In: International Conference on Bridging the Gap between AI and Reality, pp. 355–374. Springer, Cham (2023)
2. Gabor, T., Phan, T., Linnhoff-Popien.: Productive fitness in diversity-aware evolutionary algorithms. Nat. Comput. **20**(3), 363–376 (2021)
3. Gabor, T., et al.: Scenario co-evolution for reinforcement learning on a grid world smart factory domain. In: Proceedings of the Genetic and Evolutionary Computation Conference, pp. 898–906 (2019)
4. Gabor, T., et al.: The scenario coevolution paradigm: adaptive quality assurance for adaptive systems. Int. J. Softw. Tools Technol. Transfer **22**, 457–476 (2020)
5. Jorgensen, S., et al.: Large language model-based test case generation for gp agents. In: Proceedings of the Genetic and Evolutionary Computation Conference, pp. 914–923 (2024)
6. Mirjalili, R., Krawez, M., Burgard, W.: Fm-loc: Using foundation models for improved vision-based localization. In: 2023 IEEE/RSJ International Conference on Intelligent Robots and Systems (IROS), pp. 1381–1387. IEEE (2023)
7. Romera-Paredes, B., et al.: Mathematical discoveries from program search with large language models. Nature **625**(7995), 468–475 (2024)
8. Stenzel, G., Gerner, S., Kölle, M., Zorn, M., Gabor, T.: A general genetic algorithm using natural language evolutionary operators. In: GECCO Companion (2025). To appear
9. Stenzel, G., Zorn, M., Altmann, P., Mansky, M.B., Kölle, M., Gabor, T.: Self-replicating prompts for large language models: towards artificial culture. In: ALIFE 2024: Proceedings of the 2024 Artificial Life Conference. MIT Press (2024)

More than Just Passwords: The Social Impact of Security Awareness

Tobias Fertig

Technical University of Applied Sciences Würzburg-Schweinfurt, Würzburg-Schweinfurt,
Germany
tobias.fertig@thws.de

Abstract. In an increasingly digital society, cybersecurity is no longer just an
IT issue. It is a shared social responsibility. This keynote explores the broader
impact of information security awareness within community services, emphasizing how individuals and organizations play a pivotal role in protecting the
systems that underpin our daily lives. With the EU's NIS2 Directive raising the
bar for cybersecurity risk management and incident response across essential and
important entities, community services must move beyond mere technical compliance. True resilience begins with people. From healthcare providers and local
administrations to educational and social institutions, fostering a culture of awareness is crucial to ensuring service continuity, public trust, and societal well-being.
Through real-world examples and practical insights, this session will demonstrate
how empowering staff and citizens with the right knowledge reduces vulnerabilities, meets regulatory expectations, and ultimately strengthens the social fabric
of digital public services.

Keywords. Information security awareness · Digital resilience · Human factor ·
Social responsibility

Contents

Invited Paper

Full-Stack Quantum Computing and Distributed Systems:
A Community-Centric Approach 3
  Sebastian Feld

Recognition and Verification

A Pluggable Authentication Module for E-Mail as a Secure Additional
Authentication Factor 23
  Günter Fahrnberger

TRYOLO: A Transformer-Based Real-Time Object Detection Model
for UAV Images 36
  Bhimendra Dewangan, M. Srinivas, and R. B. V. Subramanyam

Automated Text Classification in Maturity Models Using Transformer
Architectures: An Encoder-Based Approach 51
  Patrick Seidel and Wesley Preßler

Computational Intelligence

Accelerated VQE: Parameter Recycling for Similar Recurring Problem
Instances 63
  Tobias Rohe, Maximilian Balthasar Mansky, Michael Kölle,
  Jonas Stein, Leo Sünkel, and Claudia Linnhoff-Popien

Fair Benchmarking Combinatorial Optimization Solvers in the Era
of Emerging Computing Paradigms 79
  Frank Phillipson

Artificial Intelligence Application Scenarios Considering Objective
and Subjective Influence Factors for Industrial Solutions in Supply Chain
Management 94
  Karl-Heinz Lüke, Gerald Eichler, and Denis Royer

Data Processing

Real-Time Energy Data Aggregation for Energy Communities 115
  Stefan Linecker, Felix Strohmeier, Peter Dorfinger,
  and Christof Brandauer

On Self-Improving Token Embeddings 126
  Mario M. Kubek, Shiraj Pokharel, Thomas Böhme, Emma L. McDaniel,
  Herwig Unger, and Armin R. Mikler

Data Mesh and Data Space: A Comparative Analysis with a Focus
on Governance 144
  Attila Papp, Udo Bub, Viivi Lähteenoja, Kai Kuikkaniemi,
  Marko Turpeinen, and Sami Jokela

Quantum Computing

Toward Quantum Annealing for Multi-league Sports Scheduling 159
  Orin Pechler and Frank Phillipson

Optimizing Initial Qubit Mappings Under Fixed Gate Error Rates Using
Deep Reinforcement Learning 189
  Rares Adrian Oancea, Stan van der Linde, Willem de Kok,
  Matthia Sabatelli, and Sebastian Feld

Learning QUBO Formulations from Data 209
  Jonas Nüßlein, Sebastian Zielinski, and Claudia Linnhoff-Popien

Public Sector

A Multi-modal Data-Driven Dashboard for Enhanced Public Health
Surveillance and Awareness 231
  Kiana Lesan Pezeshki, Sepinood Haghighi, Farzaneh Jouyandeh,
  Sarvnaz Sadeghi, Pooya Moradian Zadeh, Jackie Fong, Kendall Soucie,
  R. Michael McKay, Kenneth K. S. Ng, Lisa A. Porter, Yufeng Tong,
  and Lawrence Goodridge

The Digital Product Supply Chain: Demonstrating Digital Sovereignty
in Real-World Scenarios 251
  Razvan Hrestic, Manfred Hofmeier, and Ulrike Lechner

Evolution of Affordable Surveillance Systems for Patients: With
the Integration of Smart Health Sensors 269
  Junaeid Ahmed, Marcel Großmann, Udo R. Krieger, and Duy Thanh Le

Serious Games

Bring Your Own Bug: Enabling User-Generated Content in Serious
Games for Industrial Cybersecurity and AppSec Education 289
    Andrei-Cristian Iosif, Ulrike Lechner, and Maria Pinto-Albuquerque

From Paper to Pixel: The Digitalization of a Serious Game 307
    Judith Strussenberg, Karl Seidenfad, Maximilian Greiner, Kevin Riesel,
    Jan Biermann, and Ulrike Lechner

Cities as Innovation Ecosystems – Game to Enhance City Learning
Through Stakeholder Collaboration 330
    Quynh-Lan Nguyen Pham, Pradipta Banerjee, and Sobah Abbas Petersen

Information Security

A Simulation-Oriented Approach to Securing Logistics Processes Based
on the NIST CSF and OODA Loop 353
    Larissa Schachenhofer, Gregor Langner, Gerald Quirchmayr,
    Philipp Wolf, Patrick Hirsch, Stefan Schauer, Ulrike Lechner,
    and Günter Fahrnberger

Designing and Implementing an Educational Game for Cyber Planning
Building on Cyberspace's Layers 377
    Andreas Kornmaier, Marko Hofmann, and Ulrike Lechner

Cybersecurity Awareness Education by Making Ransomware Tangible
Securely: The Beginning 386
    Günter Fahrnberger, Maximilian Greiner, Stefan Hofbauer,
    Ulrike Lechner, Andreas Seiler, Judith Strussenberg, and Philipp Wolf

Community Challenges

MAD-HOT: Mixed Rate DDoS Attack Detection in IEEE 802.15 4e/TSCH
Networks Using Hoeffding Optimized Trees 417
    Pradeepkumar Bhale, Darpan Maurya, Vaibhav Sodhi,
    Tabish Farooqui, Harsh Singh, and Sonam Maurya

Intelligent Vehicle Detection System 437
    Aahan Singh Charak and Imran Shafiq Ahmad

Challenges in Scaling Agile Frameworks and Ways to Address Them
with Scaled Agile Framework (SAFe) and Scrum of Scrums (SoS) 453
  Christoph Eigner and Günter Fahrnberger

Author Index 471

Invited Paper

Full-Stack Quantum Computing and Distributed Systems: A Community-Centric Approach

Sebastian Feld[(✉)] [iD]

Quantum and Computer Engineering & QuTech, Delft University of Technology,
Delft, The Netherlands
s.feld@tudelft.nl

Abstract. Quantum computing is considered a promising future technology for addressing complex societal and technical challenges. However, it is still in an experimental early stage. This article takes a full-stack perspective and advocates for a community-driven, interdisciplinary development of quantum computing. First, the importance of close collaboration across different scientific and technical disciplines is emphasized. It is then shown that long-term scalable quantum computers can only be realized through distributed architectures, and the resulting technical and organizational requirements are discussed. Using concrete application examples from the fields of energy, logistics, mobility, and network analysis, the paper illustrates where quantum computing could create real societal value in the future. Finally, a roadmap is presented with short-, medium-, and long-term actions addressing technological, infrastructural, and educational aspects. At the core of this message is the idea that open communities, transparent standards, and interdisciplinary knowledge exchange are essential for the sustainable development and broad adoption of quantum-based technologies.

Keywords: Full-stack quantum computing · Distributed architectures · Community-driven innovation

1 Quantum Computing as an Interdisciplinary Collaboration

Quantum computing is one of the most promising future technologies, offering enormous potential to address complex technological and societal challenges. However, this technology is still at an early stage of its development cycle. To fully unlock its potential, quantum computing requires close collaboration across multiple scientific and technical disciplines, as well as among research institutions, industry, and educational organizations. The following sections will elaborate that successful progress in quantum computing can only be achieved through interdisciplinary and collaborative efforts. Thus, the core message of this article is: quantum computing is a community-driven journey centered around people.

© The Author(s), under exclusive license to Springer Nature Switzerland AG 2025
S. Zielinski et al. (Eds.): I4CS 2025, CCIS 2513, pp. 3–19, 2025.
https://doi.org/10.1007/978-3-031-94263-1_1

1.1   Interdisciplinarity is Key

Quantum computing is not a field that can develop in isolation. Due to the complexity and multi-layered nature of quantum computer technology, close cooperation among various scientific and technical disciplines is essential. Each discipline involved contributes knowledge and skills crucial for the practical and meaningful use of quantum computing. The following list (see also Fig. 1) is not intended to be exhaustive, but rather serves as a positive example.

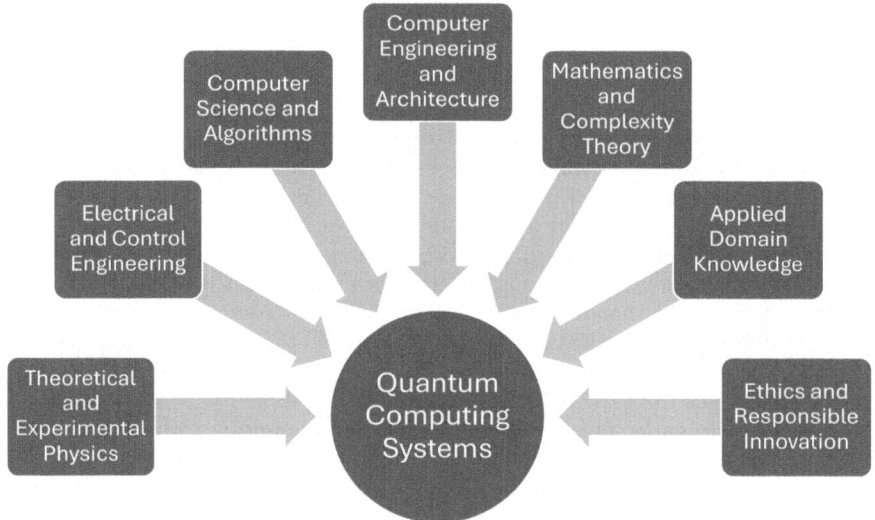

Fig. 1. Interdisciplinary collaboration in quantum computing

Physicists (both theoretical and experimental) lay the foundations for the theory and hardware implementation of quantum computers. They research and develop qubits, improve the stability of quantum states, extend coherence times, and work on realizing and characterizing quantum gates and quantum processors. *Engineers* ensure the reliability, integration, and scalability of the systems. They develop control and cooling technologies, technical infrastructure, and solutions for integrating quantum and classical computing components. *Computer scientists* design and optimize quantum algorithms, software frameworks, middleware, and efficient compiler technologies to maximize the practical usability and performance of quantum hardware. *Mathematicians* develop the theoretical foundations of quantum algorithms and analyze their properties within complexity theory, thereby making the theoretical advantages of quantum-based approaches measurable and understandable. *Domain experts*, such as specialists from chemistry, biology, logistics, the energy industry, and many other fields, ensure the practical relevance of quantum solutions. They define realistic application scenarios and assess the outcomes regarding their actual added value for their specific industry.

Each of these competencies is essential for the practical application of quantum computing. Without physicists, reliable hardware would not exist; without computer scientists, efficient software would be lacking; without engineers, scalable systems would not be achievable; and without domain experts, even the best technological solutions would fail to find practical use.

1.2 Community-Driven Frameworks and Tools

The experience from classical computing communities, especially in the fields of hardware acceleration [50,58] (e.g., GPUs and FPGAs) and distributed systems [82], can provide proven approaches that quantum computing can build upon. Best practices developed over decades, such as those from design automation [76], compiler techniques [1], modularity [66], standardization [26], or software abstraction layers [36], serve as foundations for current quantum computing developments. However, completely "recycling" this knowledge is not possible, as quantum computing has several fundamental differences compared to classical computing [64]. Perhaps the most basic of these differences originate from the underlying physics, such as the No-Cloning theorem [94], which states that it is impossible to copy an unknown quantum state.

Nevertheless, the quantum computing community strongly relies on open and collaborative initiatives. Well-known open-source platforms such as Qiskit (IBM) [45], Cirq (Google) [22], and Pennylane (Xanadu) [9] publicly provide algorithms and simulation tools to promote innovation. The importance of transparency provided by open-source concepts [92] should also not be underestimated. Furthermore, benchmarking – including its standardization – is another essential, community-driven area [12,19,74]. Benchmarking is necessary because quantum hardware significantly differs in underlying technology (e.g., superconducting qubits, photonics, ion traps) and current performance capabilities. This variability not only complicates comparisons between different quantum technologies but also makes evaluating quantum-based solutions against the current state-of-the-art classical computing technologies especially challenging. Such comparisons often seem unfair, given that quantum computers are still at an early stage of development and compete directly against classical systems that have been established and highly optimized for decades. Nonetheless, this comparability is essential for documenting measurable progress and clearly managing expectations. Typical benchmarks range from component-specific tests (e.g., gate error rates), system metrics (e.g., Quantum Volume [19], CLOPS [14]), to application-oriented scenarios [56,57,77], designed to reflect realistic usage scenarios.

1.3 Education and Competence Development

To achieve sustainable success in quantum computing, a broad educational initiative is essential. Just a few years ago, specialized courses existed at individual universities; today, these have evolved into comprehensive, independent degree programs, including specialized Bachelor's and Master's programs. Examples include Quantum Information Science and Technology (TU Delft, University of Leiden, Netherlands) [83], Quantum Science and Technology (TU Munich, LMU Munich, Germany) [62], Quantum Engineering (ETH Zurich, Switzerland) [95], Quantum Technology (RWTH Aachen, Germany) [90], and many others. Additional specialized educational programs exist and continue to emerge globally [79,88,89].

Moreover, there is growing importance of non-commercial, community-driven educational and outreach initiatives, particularly student-led and NGO-managed projects that help "democratize" access to quantum computing. Examples of such initiatives include Quantum Open Source Foundation [31], QWorld [75], Quantum Universal Education [25], as well as initiatives like OneQuantum [65] or Women in Quantum Development [72].

2   Scaling Through Distributed Architectures

In the previous section, we discussed that interdisciplinary collaboration and community-driven efforts are essential prerequisites for sustainable innovation in quantum computing. However, to implement scalable and powerful quantum computers in practice, an additional step is necessary: the explicit transition to distributed architectures.

2.1   Technical Limitations of Monolithic Systems and the Necessity of Distributed Approaches

Current monolithic quantum computers, where a single processor or chip provides all the quantum computing power, face several technical challenges [70]. In particular, high error rates and limited coherence times significantly restrict scalability when increasing the number of qubits [5]. Controlling increasingly large qubit systems also requires complex error-correction procedures, adding further complexity [32]. Additionally, there are physical limitations, for example, in cooling large monolithic quantum processors, especially in superconducting systems. As the processor size increases, demands for cooling power, thermal stability, and mechanical isolation significantly rise, approaching the limits of current technology [51]. Another issue is the complexity of managing the qubits themselves. Centralized control and signal processing of densely integrated qubit systems lead to increasingly complicated electronic control structures, causing issues related to stability, synchronization, and scalability [5].

These challenges alone illustrate that scaling quantum computers to hundreds or thousands of qubits – let alone millions required for fault-tolerant applications – is unlikely achievable using only monolithic architectures. Distributed architectures, where several smaller and more easily controllable quantum processors are interconnected, appear to be a practical approach to achieving true scalability. However, it is not simply a choice between monolithic or modular approaches. Technological advancements will improve both the performance of individual quantum processors and the efficiency of their interconnection. Ultimately, both approaches will be necessary to achieve scalable and powerful quantum computing.

2.2 Local and Global Distribution

To realize distributed quantum architectures, there are essentially two approaches: local and global distribution (see also Fig. 2).

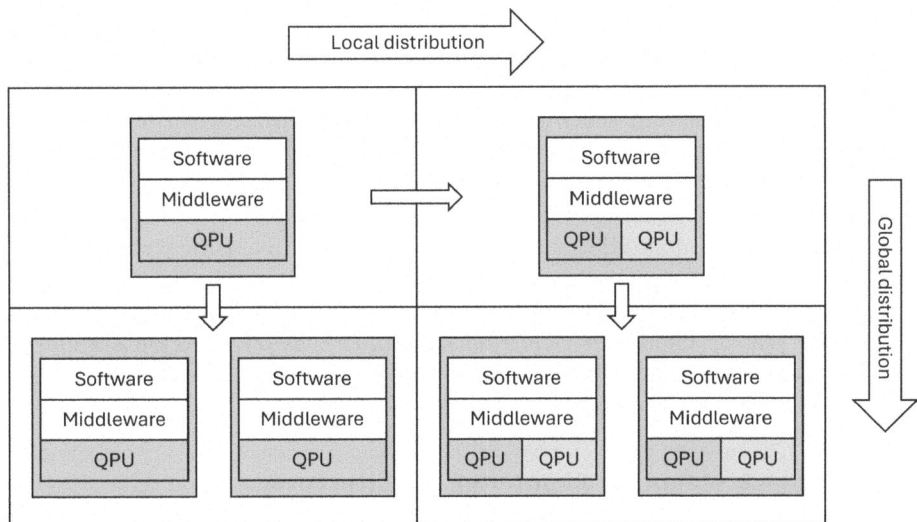

Fig. 2. Local and global distribution approaches

In *local distribution*, multiple smaller quantum processors are closely interconnected within a single location [60]. The central idea is that a quantum computer performs calculations using a "multi-core QPU" (see Fig. 2, the evolution from top-left to top-right, but also in bottom-right). Typical implementations of such systems are based on superconducting qubits that communicate locally through microwave coupling or integrated photonic networks [49].

Key advantages of distributing similar technologies within close proximity include reduced overall system complexity and better controllability, enabling targeted error correction strategies, and reduced communication latency (compared to global distribution, discussed below). Processors that are close together and technologically homogeneous can transfer information quickly and efficiently.

Global distribution is based on geographically separate locations, in which quantum processors (monolithic or locally distributed systems) communicate via photonic connections (see Fig. 2, the evolution from top to bottom). This approach is also referred to as Distributed Quantum Computing [16,55] or Quantum Internet [24,93].

The intended advantages of global distribution differ from those of local distribution. The primary goal here is massive scalability, as geographic separation allows virtually unlimited expandability across multiple locations. It also permits integrating different hardware types, combining the best properties of various technologies (e.g., photonics, superconducting systems, ion traps, and more). Additionally, geographic distribution enhances resilience against local disruptions or technical failures by avoiding dependency on a single central infrastructure.

However, implementing distributed quantum architectures also brings technical challenges. These can be specific to quantum technologies but also resemble challenges encountered in classical distributed systems. Examples include precise synchronization and timing of distributed components, development of scalable resource management and scheduling methods, and error correction over spatial distance and heterogeneous systems [15]. Thus, there is potential to transfer experience from classical distributed systems and high-performance computing infrastructures (HPC) [78]. For instance, research already exists on applying proven communication standards, such as MPI, within quantum systems [40].

Open testing platforms and community-driven benchmarking initiatives also play an essential role in this context. Communities such as the Quantum Internet Alliance [73] or Quantum Benchmarking Initiative [21] develop standards to ensure interoperability, comparability, and ultimately, quality assurance of distributed quantum systems.

2.3   Full-Stack Quantum Computer Architecture

Regardless of the chosen distribution approach, a comprehensive view of all system layers simplifies the successful implementation of (distributed) quantum computer systems. Numerous models and architectures exist for organizing both classical and quantum-based computer systems [6, 20, 34, 43, 47, 59, 91]. The primary goal is always to introduce a certain level of abstraction to simplify system development and operation. Typically, these architectures consist of three main layers.

The *hardware layer* deals with various physical technologies such as photonics, superconducting qubits, ion traps, and neutral atoms. One of the most significant technical challenges here lies in developing standardized interfaces and transmission protocols, such as those needed for transferring entangled quantum states or integrating photonic interfaces [54]. The *middleware layer* primarily handles the efficient distribution and management of quantum-mechanical resources. Challenges at this level include developing distributed compiler technologies, efficient scheduling methods, and robust communication protocols [18]. As previously mentioned, there is potential to adapt established classical methods from distributed systems, such as MPI or containerization. The *software or application layer* often includes frameworks, programming models, and applications explicitly optimized for (distributed) quantum architectures [41]. A major research focus here is minimizing communication overhead and intelligently distributing computations across spatially separated processors.

3   Quantum Computing Empowering Communities

The previous section discussed why distributed architectures are essential for scaling quantum computers. Now, we present specific application scenarios where quantum computing is expected to provide real societal value in the future. The focus is on community services, which is why we take a closer look at use cases in the areas of energy, logistics, mobility, and network or community analysis (see also Fig. 3). At the same time, we apply a clear and deliberately conservative expectation management, as we are still far from practical applicability due to major technical and algorithmic challenges. Nevertheless, it already makes sense to explore – based on the currently available quantum systems – which application domains and optimization problems might offer the most promising potential for quantum-based solutions in the future.

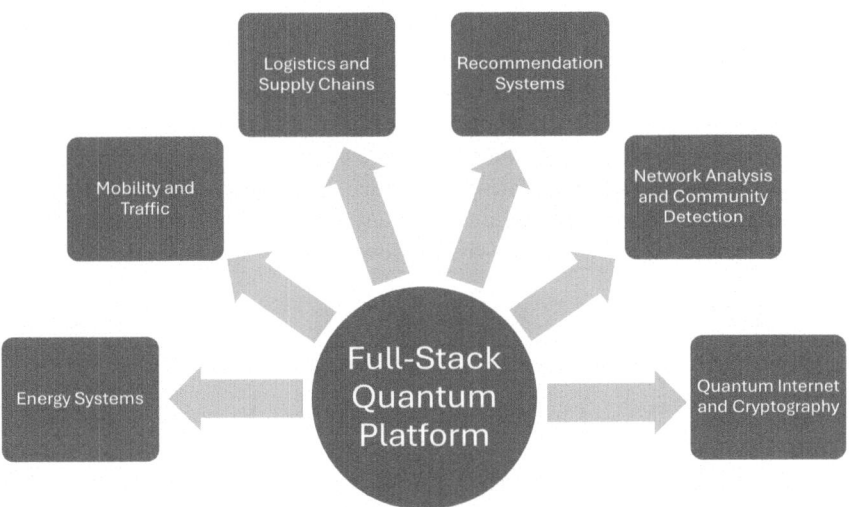

Fig. 3. Potential application areas of quantum computing in the domain of community services

3.1   Quantum-Based Optimization for Energy Systems and Infrastructure

The domains of energy supply and infrastructure planning face numerous complex challenges that could be supported by quantum computing technologies [3,61,67]. In particular, applications involving combinatorial optimization problems may benefit from quantum technologies such as Quantum Annealing [46] or the Quantum Approximate Optimization Algorithm (QAOA) [29]. Both methods aim to find approximate solutions to NP-hard problems, where classical exact algorithms no longer scale efficiently. Beyond these, current research also explores algorithmic strategies such as VQE-based optimization [84], dynamic quantum walks [42], and the Quantum Alternating Operator Ansatz [39], a generalization of QAOA.

In the context of *smart grids* [87], quantum-enhanced algorithms could improve the optimization of electricity distribution in intelligent power networks. Potential applications include load balancing for renewable energy and intelligent battery storage planning. In *energy network resource allocation* [11], quantum optimization might enable more efficient handling of dynamic consumption patterns as well as decentralized energy input (e.g., via solar panels) and storage. The goals are improved energy efficiency and increased resilience of supply networks. In the field of *infrastructure planning* [35], quantum methods could support the selection of locations and capacity planning for critical infrastructure, such as charging stations for electric vehicles or decentralized generation and storage facilities.

Currently, quantum-based approaches in the energy sector are mostly at the level of pilot studies and feasibility analyses, typically based on simplified models with a limited number of nodes. A large-scale deployment of quantum solutions is not yet foreseeable under the current state of technology. Nonetheless, the potential of these technologies should not be dismissed, especially since even minor improvements in optimization can have significant cumulative effects in long-running energy systems. Achieving practical impact, however, will require substantial advances both in algorithm development and quantum hardware capabilities.

3.2   Quantum Technologies for Logistics, Traffic, and Mobility

The domains of traffic and logistics are characterized by complex optimization problems where fast and flexible decision-making is essential [68,81]. In the long term, quantum-based methods could support such processes, provided that scalable algorithms and tight integration with sensor data can be achieved.

One possible application is *adaptive traffic control* [44], where dynamic traffic light coordination and load management could be implemented more efficiently in (near) real time, aiming to reduce congestion and emissions. Another area is *route planning and resource management* [8], particularly in situations involving short-term or critical events such as accidents, traffic jams, or disasters, where quantum-enhanced algorithms may enable faster response and better adaptability.

As in the energy sector, current approaches in logistics, traffic, and mobility are mostly limited to proof-of-concept studies with restricted scope. Initial results suggest promising directions, but practical advantages over established classical methods have not been demonstrated so far. Future progress will strongly depend on advances in quantum algorithm design, hardware capabilities, and integration with classical systems, especially in real-time scenarios.

3.3 Graph-Based Quantum Algorithms for Network Analysis and Community Detection

Many real-world problems from various domains, such as social networks, technological infrastructures, or epidemiological systems, can be modeled using graph-based algorithms [13, 63]. Quantum approaches to graph analysis are currently being explored as potentially promising methods, although their practical applicability is still mostly limited to small or idealized networks.

In the area of *community detection and clustering* [2, 4, 28], quantum algorithms could help accelerate or refine the identification of communities or clusters in large datasets, what is an essential subtask in analyzing social or infrastructure networks. Similarly, *resilience analysis* [33, 86], such as identifying critical nodes in power grids, transportation systems, or communication networks, could become more robust and efficient through quantum-enhanced techniques. This is especially relevant for pattern recognition in dynamic scenarios like epidemics or crisis events.

Although early approaches appear promising, the use of quantum graph algorithms remains largely at a theoretical or early experimental stage. Their practical utility is, for now, mostly demonstrated in simplified models. Achieving real impact in large-scale, real-world networks will require further advancements in both algorithm design and quantum hardware.

3.4 Further Application Areas

The examples discussed so far represent only a subset of the diverse application possibilities of quantum computing. Moreover, the selected examples were deliberately focused on community services. In reality, there are virtually no limits to the imagination when it comes to identifying quantum use cases.

In practice, however, identifying suitable use cases remains an active area of research and development. The "special tool" that is the quantum computer must be carefully tailored to a specific problem domain. Only when the strengths (and weaknesses) of quantum approaches are clearly understood, and the real "pain points" of an application area are well defined, can quantum computing offer concrete added value. At present, hybrid approaches, where quantum algorithms are embedded into classical systems, represent a particularly promising path for combining the best of both worlds [17].

Beyond the areas mentioned so far, additional fields of application are emerging where quantum technologies could also benefit community services. One notable example is the *quantum internet* [24, 93], which is gaining attention as a means for secure communication, for example, through the use of quantum key distribution (QKD) [53]. Closely related is the field of *quantum-based cryptography* [10, 38, 69], which enables secure and decentralized transactions.

Although current hardware resources remain limited, initiatives and research projects in areas such as the quantum internet and quantum cryptography are steadily growing. This trend highlights the strong interest from academic institutions, government bodies, and industry in protecting security-critical infrastructures and driving forward the broader digital transformation.

4   Roadmap for a Sustainable Quantum Computing Ecosystem

The previous section discussed potential application areas of quantum computing in energy systems, logistics, mobility, and network analysis. However, in order for today's still limited and experimental quantum-based solutions to become practically relevant, a number of technical, organizational, and educational challenges must first be addressed. These challenges, along with concrete measures and a corresponding timeline, form the core of the chapter that follows.

4.1   Technical Challenges

Despite significant progress, fundamental technical limitations still persist. The most critical factor remains the limited physical scalability of current systems [52]. The number of reliably controllable qubits is still low, and they continue to suffer from short coherence times and high error rates. However, quantum algorithms operating at realistic problem scales typically require thousands, or even millions, of error-corrected qubits [37]. Another major issue concerns interoperability and interfaces. Different quantum hardware platforms, such as photonic systems, superconducting qubits, or ion traps, require standardized interfaces and protocols to work together efficiently. Lastly, one of the most pressing challenges is the seamless integration of quantum computers into existing high-performance computing (HPC) infrastructures. As a result, hybrid HPC-QC approaches have become an increasingly active area of research [78].

In addition, the development of quantum software remains a key challenge [7,30,80]. Scalable and robust algorithms that can demonstrably outperform optimized classical methods are still rare and require systematic development and validation. This also applies to evaluation and benchmarking efforts [71,85]. Currently, there is a lack of widely accepted standards and methods to objectively assess quantum-based solutions.

These challenges reflect the current state of a still-emerging technology field. The following section outlines a roadmap toward a broadly usable and sustainable quantum computing ecosystem, structured into three successive phases, each with distinct focus areas.

In the *early phase*, the focus is on establishing the fundamental technical and methodological foundations. This includes the development of standardized evaluation frameworks for quantum algorithms and their integration into existing HPC benchmarking suites. In parallel, initial hybrid pilot projects are being implemented (e.g., EuroHPC-Quantum initiatives [27]), in which quantum processors are coupled with classical high-performance computing systems. This phase is characterized by high uncertainty, experimental approaches, and intensive foundational research.

As the technologies mature, the *scaling phase* shifts the focus toward systematic upscaling and industrial testing. Middleware and compiler technologies that enable efficient integration of quantum and classical systems become increasingly important. Concrete application projects emerge in data centers and industrial settings, where quantum solutions are embedded into existing workflows. Interoperability between different quantum platforms becomes a key concern.

In the *established phase*, a stable technological and organizational framework evolves, in which quantum computing becomes an integral part of digital infrastructures. During this phase, global quantum communication networks are established, and quantum processors are integrated as standard resources within supercomputing and cloud platforms.

4.2 Organizational and Infrastructural Challenges

In addition to technical issues, organizational and infrastructural aspects also pose significant challenges on the path toward a functioning quantum computing ecosystem.

One major challenge is the lack of universal standards for evaluating and comparing quantum computing systems. The development of realistic and application-oriented benchmarks, both at the component and system levels, is therefore of central importance. Another important aspect is the creation of collaborative test platforms and supporting structures. International, open testbeds and experimental environments, such as the Quantum Internet Alliance [73], are essential for practically testing and validating distributed and hybrid quantum solutions. The development in this area can also be structured into several successive phases.

In the *early phase*, the focus lies on building foundational structures for collaboration, standardization, and infrastructure development. There is an urgent need for jointly funded, open test platforms that can be shared by research institutions, industry, and public agencies. In parallel, the creation or strengthening of central standardization bodies (e.g., within IEEE, ACM, or ETSI) should be pursued to establish binding evaluation criteria and benchmarking standards for quantum computing systems at an early stage [23].

In the *scaling phase*, international cooperation and the operation of large-scale testbeds become increasingly important. The goal is to provide realistic, scalable, and interoperable quantum infrastructures. At the same time, formal quality standards and certifications for quantum hardware and software can be developed, similar to certification processes in classical IT systems. Institutional collaboration becomes more professionalized, and integration into existing research policies and innovation programs continues to advance.

In the *established phase*, long-term international cooperation structures are set up to secure global standards and ensure long-term interoperability. A stable regulatory and financial framework supports the sustainable development, deployment, and advancement of quantum technologies. Public and private stakeholders routinely access standardized quantum resources that are fully integrated into the broader digital infrastructure.

4.3   Challenges in Education and Skills Development

The long-term success of quantum technologies will depend heavily on broad-based, interdisciplinary skills development. A sustainable integration of quantum computing into science, industry, and society requires not only technological maturity, but also a qualified workforce capable of connecting complex concepts from physics, computer science, and engineering [48]. Once again, this area can be structured into three developmental phases.

In the *early phase*, the focus is on creating low-barrier, accessible educational offerings. These include new certificate programs, hands-on workshops, and the provision of free online courses (e.g., MOOCs) aimed specifically at professionals and decision-makers in industry, government, and research. The goal is to convey basic knowledge and spark broad interest in quantum technologies.

Once foundational knowledge is established, the *scaling phase* involves building structured educational programs with greater academic depth. Interdisciplinary master's and PhD programs involving multiple fields (physics, computer science, engineering, business, and more) are introduced. In parallel, exchange formats and doctoral networks are developed to strengthen knowledge transfer between research and industry.

In the *established phase*, quantum computing becomes an integral part of technical and scientific higher education. Continuing education programs for working professionals are systematically implemented and become a regular component of vocational training and upskilling initiatives.

5   Conclusion

The previous section not only identified challenges but also presented realistic and concrete measures to make quantum computing practically viable in the future. Now we are going to summarize the key contributions of this article.

Section 1 positioned quantum computing explicitly as an interdisciplinary collaborative effort. It became clear that sustainable and practice-oriented quantum computing solutions are only possible when experts from different fields work closely together. In addition, Sect. 2 highlighted that long-term scalable quantum computers can only be realized through distributed architectures. Both technical challenges, such as the physical limitations of monolithic systems, and potential solutions using local and global distributed architectures were discussed. Section 3 used concrete applications, especially in the areas of energy, logistics, traffic control, and network analysis, to illustrate where quantum technologies could potentially address real-world problems. At the same time, realistic expectations were managed by explicitly pointing out the current experimental nature and future potential of these solutions. Finally, Sect. 4 presented practice-oriented recommendations for action. These include short-, medium-, and long-term measures outlining concrete steps toward a sustainable and practically applicable implementation of quantum computing technologies.

The core message of this article is the importance of community: quantum computing is a community-driven journey with people at its center. Open communities, transparent standards, and interdisciplinary collaboration are not only desirable but essential for broad acceptance and sustainable use of quantum-based technologies.

References

1. Aho, A.V., Lam, M.S., Sethi, R., Ullman, J.D.: Compilers: Principles techniques and tools. 2007. Google Scholar Google Scholar Digital Library Digital Library (2006)
2. Aïmeur, E., Brassard, G., Gambs, S.: Quantum clustering algorithms. In: Proceedings of the 24th International Conference on Machine Learning, pp. 1–8 (2007)
3. Ajagekar, A., You, F.: Quantum computing for energy systems optimization: challenges and opportunities. Energy **179**, 76–89 (2019)
4. Akbar, S., Saritha, S.K.: Towards quantum computing based community detection. Comput. Sci. Rev. **38**, 100313 (2020)
5. Arute, F., et al.: Quantum supremacy using a programmable superconducting processor. Nature **574**(7779), 505–510 (2019)
6. Bandic, M., Feld, S., Almudever, C.G.: Full-stack quantum computing systems in the NISQ era: algorithm-driven and hardware-aware compilation techniques. In: 2022 Design, Automation & Test in Europe Conference & Exhibition (DATE), pp. 1–6 (2022). https://doi.org/10.23919/DATE54114.2022.9774643
7. García de la Barrera, A., García-Rodríguez de Guzmán, I., Polo, M., Piattini, M.: Quantum software testing: state of the art. J. Softw. Evol. Process **35**(4), e2419 (2023)
8. Bayerstadler, A., et al.: Industry quantum computing applications. EPJ Quantum Technol. **8**(1), 1–17 (2021). https://doi.org/10.1140/epjqt/s40507-021-00114-x
9. Bergholm, V., et al.: Pennylane: automatic differentiation of hybrid quantum-classical computations. arXiv preprint arXiv:1811.04968 (2018)
10. Bernstein, D.J., Lange, T.: Post-quantum cryptography. Nature **549**(7671), 188–194 (2017)
11. Blenninger, J., et al.: Q-grid: quantum optimization for the future energy grid. KI-Künstliche Intelligenz, pp. 1–11 (2024)
12. Blume-Kohout, R., Young, K.C.: A volumetric framework for quantum computer benchmarks. Quantum **4**, 362 (2020)
13. Boccaletti, S., Latora, V., Moreno, Y., Chavez, M., Hwang, D.U.: Complex networks: structure and dynamics. Phys. Rep. **424**(4–5), 175–308 (2006)
14. Boixo, S., et al.: Characterizing quantum supremacy in near-term devices. Nat. Phys. **14**(6), 595–600 (2018)
15. Briegel, H.J., Dür, W., Cirac, J.I., Zoller, P.: Quantum repeaters: the role of imperfect local operations in quantum communication. Phys. Rev. Lett. **81**(26), 5932 (1998)
16. Caleffi, M., Amoretti, M., Ferrari, D., Illiano, J., Manzalini, A., Cacciapuoti, A.S.: Distributed quantum computing: a survey. Comput. Netw. **254**, 110672 (2024)
17. Callison, A., Chancellor, N.: Hybrid quantum-classical algorithms in the noisy intermediate-scale quantum era and beyond. Phys. Rev. A **106**(1), 010101 (2022)
18. Chong, F.T., Franklin, D., Martonosi, M.: Programming languages and compiler design for realistic quantum hardware. Nature **549**(7671), 180–187 (2017)

19. Cross, A.W., Bishop, L.S., Sheldon, S., Nation, P.D., Gambetta, J.M.: Validating quantum computers using randomized model circuits. Phys. Rev. A **100**(3), 032328 (2019)
20. Dahlberg, A., et al.: A link layer protocol for quantum networks. In: Proceedings of the ACM Special Interest Group on Data Communication, pp. 159–173 (2019)
21. Defense Advanced Research Projects Agency: QBI: Quantum benchmarking initiative (2025). https://www.darpa.mil/research/programs/quantum-benchmarking-initiative. Accessed 30 Mar 2025
22. Cirq Developers: Cirq (2022). https://doi.org/10.5281/zenodo.7465577
23. van Deventer, O., et al.: Towards European standards for quantum technologies. EPJ Quantum Technol. **9**(1), 33 (2022)
24. Dür, W., Lamprecht, R., Heusler, S.: Towards a quantum internet. Eur. J. Phys. **38**(4), 043001 (2017)
25. Quantum universal education. https://www.linkedin.com/company/quantum-universal-education/. Accessed 30 Mar 2025
26. Egyedi, T.M., Blind, K.: The Dynamics of Standards. Edward Elgar Publishing (2008)
27. European High Performance Computing Joint Undertaking: EuroHPC JU: Leading the Way in European Supercomputing. https://eurohpc-ju.europa.eu/index_en. Accessed 30 Mar 2025
28. Faccin, M., Migdał, P., Johnson, T.H., Bergholm, V., Biamonte, J.D.: Community detection in quantum complex networks. Phys. Rev. X **4**(4), 041012 (2014)
29. Farhi, E., Goldstone, J., Gutmann, S.: A quantum approximate optimization algorithm. arXiv preprint arXiv:1411.4028 (2014)
30. Fingerhuth, M., Babej, T., Wittek, P.: Open source software in quantum computing. PLoS ONE **13**(12), e0208561 (2018)
31. Quantum open source foundation. https://qosf.org/. Accessed 30 Mar 2025
32. Fowler, A.G., Mariantoni, M., Martinis, J.M., Cleland, A.N.: Surface codes: towards practical large-scale quantum computation. Phys. Rev. A-Atomic Mol. Opt. Phys. **86**(3), 032324 (2012)
33. Fu, W., Xie, H., Chen, C., Bie, Z.: Quantum-embedded robust optimization for resilience-constrained unit commitment. IEEE Trans. Power Syst. (2025)
34. Fu, X., et al.: A microarchitecture for a superconducting quantum processor. IEEE Micro **38**(3), 40–47 (2018)
35. Ganeshamurthy, P.A., Ghosh, K., O'Meara, C., Cortiana, G., Schiefelbein-Lach, J., Monti, A.: Next generation power system planning and operation with quantum computation. IEEE Access (2024)
36. Garlan, D., Shaw, M.: An introduction to software architecture. In: Advances in Software Engineering and Knowledge Engineering, pp. 1–39. World Scientific (1993)
37. Gidney, C., Ekerå, M.: How to factor 2048 bit RSA integers in 8 hours using 20 million noisy qubits. Quantum **5**, 433 (2021). https://doi.org/10.22331/q-2021-04-15-433
38. Gisin, N., Ribordy, G., Tittel, W., Zbinden, H.: Quantum cryptography. Rev. Mod. Phys. **74**(1), 145 (2002)
39. Hadfield, S., Wang, Z., O'gorman, B., Rieffel, E.G., Venturelli, D., Biswas, R.: From the quantum approximate optimization algorithm to a quantum alternating operator ansatz. Algorithms **12**(2), 34 (2019)
40. Häner, T., Steiger, D.S., Hoefler, T., Troyer, M.: Distributed quantum computing with QMPI. In: Proceedings of the International Conference for High Performance Computing, Networking, Storage and Analysis, pp. 1–13 (2021)

41. Heim, B., et al.: Quantum programming languages. Nat. Rev. Phys. **2**(12), 709–722 (2020)
42. Herrman, R., Humble, T.S.: Continuous-time quantum walks on dynamic graphs. Phys. Rev. A **100**(1), 012306 (2019)
43. Illiano, J., Caleffi, M., Manzalini, A., Cacciapuoti, A.S.: Quantum internet protocol stack: a comprehensive survey. Comput. Netw. **213**, 109092 (2022)
44. Inoue, D., Okada, A., Matsumori, T., Aihara, K., Yoshida, H.: Traffic signal optimization on a square lattice with quantum annealing. Sci. Rep. **11**(1), 3303 (2021)
45. Javadi-Abhari, A., et al.: Quantum computing with Qiskit (2024). https://doi.org/10.48550/arXiv.2405.08810
46. Johnson, M.W., et al.: Quantum annealing with manufactured spins. Nature **473**(7346), 194–198 (2011)
47. Jones, N.C., et al.: Layered architecture for quantum computing. Phys. Rev. X **2**(3), 031007 (2012)
48. Kaur, M., Venegas-Gomez, A.: Defining the quantum workforce landscape: a review of global quantum education initiatives. Opt. Eng. **61**(8), 081806 (2022)
49. Kok, P., Munro, W.J., Nemoto, K., Ralph, T.C., Dowling, J.P., Milburn, G.J.: Linear optical quantum computing with photonic qubits. Rev. Mod. Phys. **79**(1), 135–174 (2007)
50. Kuon, I., Tessier, R., Rose, J., et al.: FPGA architecture: survey and challenges. Found. Trends® Electron. Des. Autom. **2**(2), 135–253 (2008)
51. Ladd, T.D., Jelezko, F., Laflamme, R., Nakamura, Y., Monroe, C., O'Brien, J.L.: Quantum computers. Nature **464**(7285), 45–53 (2010)
52. Lau, J., Lim, K.H., Shrotriya, H., Kwek, L.C.: NISQ computing: where are we and where do we go? AAPPS Bull. **32**(1), 27 (2022)
53. Lo, H.K., Curty, M., Tamaki, K.: Secure quantum key distribution. Nat. Photonics **8**(8), 595–604 (2014)
54. Luo, W., et al.: Recent progress in quantum photonic chips for quantum communication and internet. Light Sci. Appl. **12**(1), 175 (2023)
55. Main, D., et al.: Distributed quantum computing across an optical network link. Nature 1–6 (2025)
56. Martiel, S., Ayral, T., Allouche, C.: Benchmarking quantum coprocessors in an application-centric, hardware-agnostic, and scalable way. IEEE Trans. Quantum Eng. **2**, 1–11 (2021)
57. Mesman, K.J., van der Schoot, W., Möller, M., Neumann, N.M.: QUAS: quantum application score for benchmarking the utility of quantum computers. In: 2024 IEEE International Conference on Quantum Computing and Engineering (QCE), vol. 1, pp. 921–929. IEEE (2024)
58. Mittal, S., Vetter, J.S.: A survey of CPU-GPU heterogeneous computing techniques. ACM Comput. Surv. (CSUR) **47**(4), 1–35 (2015)
59. Mohammadzadeh, N.: Physical design of quantum circuits in ion trap technology-a survey. Microelectron. J. **55**, 116–133 (2016)
60. Monroe, C., et al.: Large-scale modular quantum-computer architecture with atomic memory and photonic interconnects. Phys. Rev. A **89**(2), 022317 (2014)
61. Morstyn, T., Wang, X.: Opportunities for quantum computing within net-zero power system optimization. Joule (2024)
62. Technical University of Munich: MSC in quantum science and technology. https://academics.nat.tum.de/en/msc/qst. Accessed 30 Mar 2025
63. Newman, M.E.: The structure and function of complex networks. SIAM Rev. **45**(2), 167–256 (2003)

64. Nielsen, M.A., Chuang, I.L.: Quantum Computation and Quantum Information. Cambridge University Press (2010)
65. OneQuantum: Onequantum - the leading global community for quantum technology. https://onequantum.org/. Accessed 30 Mar 2025
66. Parnas, D.L.: On the criteria to be used in decomposing systems into modules. Commun. ACM **15**(12), 1053–1058 (1972)
67. Paudel, H.P., et al.: Quantum computing and simulations for energy applications: review and perspective. ACS Eng. Au **2**(3), 151–196 (2022)
68. Phillipson, F.: Quantum computing in logistics and supply chain management an overview. arXiv preprint arXiv:2402.17520 (2024)
69. Pirandola, S., et al.: Advances in quantum cryptography. Adv. Opt. Photonics **12**(4), 1012–1236 (2020)
70. Preskill, J.: Quantum computing in the NISQ era and beyond. Quantum **2**, 79 (2018)
71. Proctor, T., Young, K., Baczewski, A.D., Blume-Kohout, R.: Benchmarking quantum computers. Nat. Rev. Phys. 1–14 (2025)
72. Women in quantum development. https://www.wiqd.nl/. Accessed 30 Mar 2025
73. Quantum Internet Alliance: Quantum internet alliance (2025). https://quantuminternetalliance.org/. Accessed 30 Mar 2025
74. Quetschlich, N., Burgholzer, L., Wille, R.: MQT bench: benchmarking software and design automation tools for quantum computing. Quantum **7**, 1062 (2023)
75. QWorld: Qworld. https://qworld.net/. Accessed 30 Mar 2025
76. Ren, H., Hu, J.: Machine learning applications in electronic design automation. Springer (2022)
77. van der Schoot, W., Wezeman, R., Neumann, N., Phillipson, F., Kooij, R.: Extending the q-score to an application-level quantum metric framework. In: 2024 IEEE International Conference on Quantum Computing and Engineering (QCE), vol. 1, pp. 941–951. IEEE (2024)
78. Schulz, M., Ruefenacht, M., Kranzlmüller, D., Schulz, L.B.: Accelerating HPC with quantum computing: it is a software challenge too. Comput. Sci. Eng. **24**(4), 60–64 (2023)
79. Okinawa Institute of Science and Technology: OIST center for quantum technologies (2022). https://www.oist.jp/ocqt. Accessed 30 Mar 2025
80. Serrano, M.A., Pérez-Castillo, R., Piattini, M.: Quantum software engineering. Springer (2022)
81. Somvanshi, S., et al.: Quantum computing in transportation engineering: a survey. Available at SSRN 5141686 (2025)
82. Tanenbaum, A.S., Van Steen, M.: Distributed systems. CreateSpace Independent Publishing Platform (2017)
83. Delft University of Technology: MSC quantum information science & technology. https://www.tudelft.nl/onderwijs/opleidingen/masters/qist/msc-quantum-information-science-technology. Accessed 30 Mar 2025
84. Tilly, J., et al.: The variational quantum eigensolver: a review of methods and best practices. Phys. Rep. **986**, 1–128 (2022)
85. Tomesh, T., et al.: Supermarq: a scalable quantum benchmark suite. In: 2022 IEEE International Symposium on High-Performance Computer Architecture (HPCA), pp. 587–603. IEEE (2022)
86. Udekwe, D., Ke, R., Lu, J., Guo, Q.W.: Q-restore: quantum-driven framework for resilient and equitable transportation network restoration. arXiv preprint arXiv:2501.11197 (2025)

87. Ullah, M.H., Eskandarpour, R., Zheng, H., Khodaei, A.: Quantum computing for smart grid applications. IET Gener. Transm. Distrib. **16**(21), 4239–4257 (2022)
88. Harvard University: Quantum science and engineering. https://gsas.harvard.edu/ program/quantum-science-and-engineering. Accessed 30 Mar 2025
89. Nanyang Technological University: Nanyang quantum hub. https://www.ntu.edu. sg/nqh. Accessed 30 Mar 2025
90. RWTH Aachen University: Master-studiengang quanten-technologie. https:// www.physik.rwth-aachen.de/cms/physik/studium/im-studium/master-s-program-physics/~dlxbl/quanten-technologie/?lidx=1. Accessed 30 Mar 2025
91. Van Meter, R., Horsman, D.: A blueprint for building a quantum computer. Commun. ACM **56**(10), 84–93 (2013)
92. Von Krogh, G., Von Hippel, E.: The promise of research on open source software. Manage. Sci. **52**(7), 975–983 (2006)
93. Wehner, S., Elkouss, D., Hanson, R.: Quantum internet: a vision for the road ahead. Science **362**(6412), eaam9288 (2018)
94. Wootters, W.K., Zurek, W.H.: A single quantum cannot be cloned. Nature **299**(5886), 802–803 (1982)
95. ETH Zurich: Master in quantum engineering. https://master-qe.ethz.ch/. Accessed 30 Mar 2025

Recognition and Verification

A Pluggable Authentication Module for E-Mail as a Secure Additional Authentication Factor

Günter Fahrnberger[✉][iD]

University of Hagen, Hagen, North Rhine-Westphalia, Germany
`guenter.fahrnberger@studium.fernuni-hagen.de`

Abstract. Anti-hammering mechanisms frequently struggle to manage both Brute Force Attacks (BFAs) and Denial of Service (DoS) attacks effectively, highlighting the need for robust safeguards to counter credential guessing and account lockouts. A pluggable authentication module for e-mail as an additional authentication factor may offer a practical solution but fails to provide an advantage when the same e-mail address resets the primary authentication factor. A thorough literature review reveals no existing module supporting a secondary e-mail address. This technical documentation presents a Lightweight Directory Access Protocol (LDAP)-dependent prototype implemented on a standard Linux Operating System (OS). Each Multi-Factor Authentication (MFA) solution faces inherent vulnerabilities. Therefore, comprehensive threat modeling identifies nine categories of potential weaknesses in the new module, necessitating careful evaluation during deployment.

Keywords: Access Control · Authentication · Authenticity · Information Security · Multi-Factor Authentication (MFA) · One-Time Password (OTP) · Pluggable Authentication Modules (PAM) · Random One-Time Password (ROTP) · Two-Factor Authentication (2FA)

1 Introduction

Application logs and network traces reveal that open ports on public-facing interfaces draw attackers' attention as soon as they emerge. Network scanners locate and probe them, vulnerability scanners determine feasible threat vectors, and BFAs or manual penetration tests attempt to gain initial access to services listening on these open ports [4–6]. Anti-hammering mechanisms, as countermeasures, offer both benefits and drawbacks. They lock out targeted accounts or ban source Internet Protocol (IP) addresses. Beyond permanent lockouts, perpetuated DoS attacks can even exploit temporary lockouts to continuously prevent innocent users from accessing their accounts or to block legitimate requests from shared resources, such as gateways or proxies. For this reason, anti-hammering mechanisms do not always provide a perfect solution. A supplementary approach must effectively counter both credential guessing and account lockouts.

© The Author(s), under exclusive license to Springer Nature Switzerland AG 2025
S. Zielinski et al. (Eds.): I4CS 2025, CCIS 2513, pp. 23–35, 2025.
https://doi.org/10.1007/978-3-031-94263-1_2

Such a remedy already exists by imposing more than one kind of authentication factor, also known as MFA. The often-utilized Two-Factor Authentication (2FA) denotes the imposition of two independent factors. The scientific literature commonly classifies authentication factors into inherence-based (e.g., biometric features), knowledge-based (e.g., passwords), and possession-based (e.g., keys) ones. Fahrnberger proposes Three-Factor Authentication (3FA) for the military domain, consisting of a biometric ElectroCardioGram (ECG), a known password, and a possessed ECG sensor [3]. Such a complex solution might be justified for highly secure use cases, but unreasonable for everyday users.

To avoid cutting a security corner in the name of usability, a doable idea involves applying 2FA by combining the factors of memorizable knowledge and mutable ownership. In simple terms, a user must provide a valid password and an One-Time Password (OTP). Appropriate generators in the user's possession supply such an OTP, also known as a Time-based One-Time Password (TOTP). Compared with a TOTP, the predictability of an instantly conveyed e-mail with a cryptographically secure Random One-Time Password (ROTP) decreases further, reaching virtually zero. This advantage makes ROTP preferable over TOTP. Nowadays, many applications rely on TOTP or ROTP for protection.

The Pluggable Authentication Modules (PAM), the default authentication framework for UNIX derivatives, also support 2FA through TOTP via authenticator apps [1]. The Security Verify Gateway for Linux PAM and Advanced Interactive eXecutive (AIX) PAM from IBM even facilitate 2FA through e-mail [10]. For the sake of secure authentication, e-mail accounts often require 2FA themselves for web access or long Application Programming Interface (API) keys for protocols like IMAP (Internet Message Access Protocol) [12] or POP3 (Post Office Protocol 3) [13].

IBM's Security Verify Gateway relies on a user's e-mail address from an arbitrary identity provider, where a reset portal might send a password reset link for the primary authentication factor. This approach reduces the effectiveness of 2FA via e-mail. No existing deployment includes a pluggable authentication module leveraging a secondary e-mail address as a secure additional authentication factor. An ROTP sent to a secondary e-mail address offers a convenient option that should integrate with PAM.

This treatise details the development and application of such a module to maintain the security of the popular ROTP via e-mail and avoid the need to fall back on a 2FA technique with lower security or convenience. Section 2 reviews relevant literature on PAM and module development. Section 3 delves into the programmatic details of creating a pluggable authentication module based on a secondary e-mail address. Section 4 presents a security analysis of this new module. Finally, Sect. 5 concludes the paper and outlines potential future work.

2   Related Work

No scholarly work examines the use of a pluggable authentication module for an ROTP sent to a secondary e-mail address as a secure additional authentication factor. This section describes PAM and provides guidance on developing new modules.

Samar and Lai developed PAM in 1995 during their employment at SunSoft Inc. It became the standard authentication framework for the Common Desktop Environment (CDE) [14]. PAM should fulfill the following design goals.

- Selectable default authentication mechanism by system administrator(s)
- Configurable user authentication mechanism on a per-application basis
- Support for the display requirements of applications
- Configurable multiple authentication protocols
- No password retyping for already authenticated users
- Easily changeable underlying mechanisms
- Pluggable model for system authentication as well as for password, account, and session management
- Backward compatibility with legacy system-entry services
- API independent of the OS

These objectives have entailed PAM's basic architecture as shown in Fig. 1, which also displays insecure legacy protocols (such as Telnet), the utilization of which nowadays poses a significant danger, making them highly deprecated.

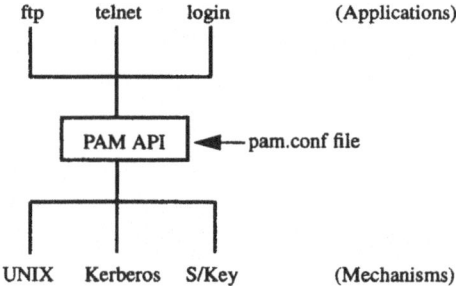

Fig. 1. PAM basic architecture

To accomplish the requirement of a pluggable model for system authentication as well as for password, account, and session management, Samar and Lai differentiate between the four PAM interfaces mentioned below. Geisshirt's guide to PAM does the same but refers to them as management groups [7].

- **auth:** The auth group offers two functions. Initially, it validates the user by confirming authenticity, typically through a username and corresponding password. Subsequently, the auth management group grants credentials, which encompass group membership.
- **account:** Access to a service controlled by the account management group includes limitations such as the frequency of use per week, specific time periods, or account expiration status. PAM enable configuring precise access control settings.

– **session:** The session management group constructs the environment for a given service. Upon a user ceasing to use the service, the session group dismantles the environment. When setting up the environment (or session), necessary data for proper operation gets loaded, such as opening data sources and mounting home directories.

– **password:** The last management group handles passwords and related actions, such as changes and policy enforcement. PAM maintain a separation between the password-changing application and the backend storage.

Each pluggable authentication module may return either success or failure. Some responses hold more importance than others. Thus, the control flags listed below can alter the flow and influence decision-making.

– **requisite:** This control flag stands out as the strongest among all flags. If a PAM configuration file tags a pluggable authentication module as requisite and it fails, PAM will immediately return to the calling application and report the failure.

– **required:** The return code for a required pluggable authentication module gets stored. In the event of failure, execution proceeds to the next module. Once a sequence (stack) of modules has been executed, and at least one required module has failed, PAM will report failure to the calling application. Furthermore, the failure links to the first failing module. The required control flag helps keep unauthorized persons out of your computer, especially since the other modules in the stack also apply. This prevents a cracker from knowing which module caused the failure, leaving many more possibilities of what went wrong.

– **sufficient:** This control flag holds considerable strength. Processing of the stack halts if a pluggable authentication module tagged as sufficient returns success, provided no previous required module has failed. Any required modules following the sufficient modules will not be called.

– **optional:** When a pluggable authentication module receives an optional tag, a failure does not change the stack's execution as it does with a requisite tag. Additionally, the return code gets ignored, and neither failure nor success gets considered.

The sequence of pluggable authentication modules and their control flags holds significant importance. Specifically, the arrangement of modules marked as required and requisite needs attention, as does the order of sufficient and required modules. A stack enforces sequential testing of modules. This process resembles executing a series of steps akin to a procedure or processing firewall rules. Modules can produce side effects, such as printing information on their invocation or failure reasons, or creating/mounting directories. These outcomes could provide attackers with insights to enhance their attacks. In other scenarios, order becomes crucial because one module's effect must precede the correct operation of the subsequent module, such as mounting a home directory before accessing a Secure Shell (SSH) [11,16–19] key.

Speaking of SSH, Binnie elaborates on hardening an SSH server configuration with TCP wrappers, allowing only trusted IP addresses or domain names for login [1]. He also enables the Google Authenticator library to implement 2FA, supporting a range of devices including iPhone, iPod Touch, iPad, and BlackBerry.

Chia et al. address the tightrope walk between password- and hardware token-based authentication via PAM [2]. Easily implementable password-based authentication relies on the strength of the chosen password and has long posed the easiest attack vector. Conversely, small- and medium-sized enterprises struggle to finance all their personnel with more secure hardware tokens for authentication. Hence, the author group raises the research question of finding a method to realize an authentication module for PAM that offers security comparable to state-of-the-art cryptographic methods while remaining low cost, simplistic, and practical. They answer their question positively by proposing identity-based identification schemes and their hierarchical variants in PAM. Their fifth section on design and implementation offers a valuable role model for developing a pluggable authentication module that sends Random One-Time Passwords (ROTPs) to a secondary e-mail address as a secure additional authentication factor.

3   Implementation

This section, the centerpiece of this disquisition, details the architectural nuances of the developed pluggable authentication module responsible for generating and sending ROTPs to a secondary e-mail address and explaining how to integrate it with the SSH Daemon (SSHD) of two common Linux OS families. The authentication process of SSHD depends on several binary and configuration files, five of which require modification or creation. The itemization below represents the chronological sequence in which the modified files get accessed during the authentication process of Debian- and Red Hat-based Operating Systems (OSs).

- /etc/ssh/sshd_config
- /etc/pam.d/sshd
- /etc/pam.d/common-auth (Debian-based), /etc/pam.d/password-auth (Red Hat-based)
- /etc/sssd/sssd.conf
- /usr/lib/x86_64-linux-gnu/security/pam_email.so (Debian-based), /usr/lib64/security/pam_email.so (Red Hat-based)

3.1   /etc/ssh/sshd_config

As Sect. 2 suggests, PAM today form the standard authentication framework for Linux Operating Systems (OSs). This includes core services like SSH. Consequently, SSHD's main configuration file /etc/ssh/sshd_config typically includes a line with the option *UsePAM yes*. If absent or commented out, SSHD defaults to invoking PAM. For example, on Red Hat-based OSs, /etc/ssh/sshd_config may contain a warning against disabling PAM due to potential issues. As an action item, it can be inferred to verify that SSHD employs PAM.

3.2   /etc/pam.d/sshd

Once invoked by SSHD, PAM read the corresponding settings in the configuration file */etc/pam.d/sshd*. Debian-based OSs delegate the authentication process to the central configuration file */etc/pam.d/common-auth* by including the line *@include common-auth*. Similarly, Red Hat-based systems use the directive *auth substack password-auth*, which delegates the authentication process to */etc/pam.d/password-auth*. Either referenced configuration file returns control to */etc/pam.d/sshd* once it completes its tasks. At this point, PAM invoke the new pluggable authentication module for e-mail, *pam_email.so*, as explained in Subsect. 3.5. By utilizing the *sufficient* control flag and the *use_first_pass* option, the password obtained by the variable *PAM_AUTHTOK* from a preceding module in the stack will be reused, respecting the outcomes of all previously integrated modules. This can be achieved by adding the line *auth sufficient pam_email.so use_first_pass*.

3.3   /etc/pam.d/common-Auth (Debian-Based), /etc/pam.d/password-Auth (Red Hat-Based)

An item like *auth sufficient pam_unix.so nullok* in both files */etc/pam.d/ common-auth* and */etc/pam.d/password-auth* prompts for a password to authenticate local users specified in the file */etc/passwd*, verified by their password hashes in */etc/shadow*. The option *nullok* allows users with empty passwords to authenticate. Removing it would require non-empty passwords for authentication, thereby reducing the risk of unauthorized access. Neither */etc/passwd* nor */etc/shadow* can store e-mail addresses of users.

A cumbersome approach would be to rewrite all user management utilities of the OS to incorporate e-mail addresses in an exemplary extra file */etc/email*. A more viable solution utilizes a proven centralized user directory service that inherently supports e-mail addresses in user accounts. For simplicity, the remainder of this document assumes the LDAP as the basis [15]. Consequently, a directly successive line *auth sufficient pam_sss.so use_first_pass* activates authentication via LDAP. As aforementioned in Subsect. 3.2, the option *use_first_pass* reuses the password in the variable *PAM_AUTHTOK* passed from *pam_unix.so* to verify its validity via LDAP.

3.4   /etc/sssd/sssd.conf

pam_sss.so obtains its settings from the file */etc/sssd/sssd.conf*, which could be configured for the domain *example.org* as follows.

– [domain/default]
– auth_provider = ldap
– autofs_provider = ldap
– cache_credentials = True
– chpass_provider = ldap

- id_provider = ldap
- ldap_id_use_start_tls = True
- ldap_search_base = ou=users,dc=example,dc=org
- ldap_tls_cacert = /usr/local/share/ca-certificates/example.org.crt
- ldap_tls_cacertdir = /usr/local/share/ca-certificates
- ldap_tls_reqcert = hard
- ldap_uri = ldaps://ldap.example.org/
- [nss]
- homedir_substring = /home
- [sssd]
- domains = default

3.5   pam_email.so

The novel pluggable authentication module *pam_email.so* resides in the directory */usr/lib/x86_64-linux-gnu/security* on Debian-based and */usr/lib64/security* on Red Hat-based OSs. Figure 2 visualizes the simplified flowchart of *pam_email.so*.

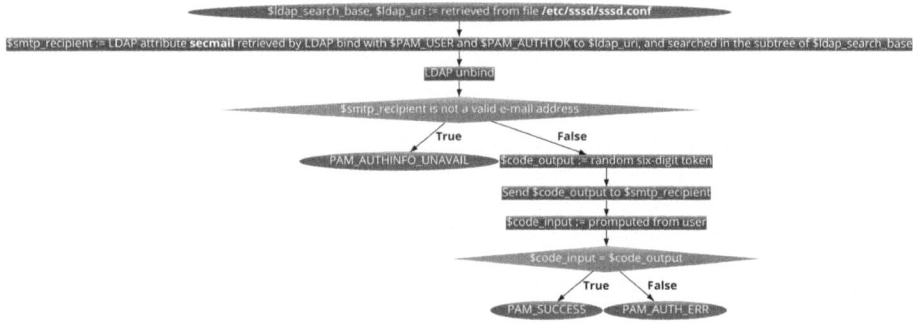

Fig. 2. Flowchart of pam_email.so

Firstly, as previously outlined, *pam_email.so* retrieves the relevant secondary e-mail address from the LDAP service, which has already completed password verification. For this purpose, *pam_email.so* reuses the settings of *pam_sss.so*, i.e., it reads *$ldap_search_base* and *$ldap_uri* from */etc/sssd/sssd.conf* to connect to the LDAP service and fetch the newly introduced *secmail* attribute as the variable *$smtp_recipient*. The LDAP bind works with the credentials *$PAM_USER* and *$PAM_AUTHTOK*, collected by prior modules, usually by *pam_unix.so*. */etc/pam.d/sshd* invokes *pam_email.so* only if *pam_sss.so* succeeds, i.e., terminates with the status code *PAM_SUCCESS*. Therefore, the LDAP bind should also work well. Nonetheless, the retrieval of *secmail* from LDAP could fail, e.g., if a working LDAP account lacks a valid secondary e-mail address. In such a case, *pam_email.so* ends by returning the status code *PAM_AUTHINFO_UNAVAIL*.

Upon successful retrieval of the secondary e-mail address, *pam_email.so* employs the Linux on-board Pseudo Random Number Generator (PRNG) to produce a six-digit ROTP *$code_output*. The module then searches for a local Mail Transfer Agent (MTA), such as Extended Simple Mail Transfer Protocol (ESMTP), Postfix, or Sendmail, to send *$code_output* to *$smtp_recipient*. Afterward, the user receives a message (e.g., *Verification code:*) prompting them to enter the recently dispatched *$code_output*. *pam_email.so* saves the user input in the variable *$code_input* and compares it with *$code_output*. Only a match leads to positive authentication with status code *PAM_SUCCESS*. All other scenarios (such as a mismatch or timeout) result in the termination of the authentication process with status code *PAM_AUTH_ERR*, thereby invalidating *$code_output*.

Section 4 scrutinizes whether an attacker can bypass this 2FA, for instance, by tricking *pam_email.so* into exiting with the status code *PAM_SUCCESS* without being aware of *$code_output*.

4 Security Scrutiny

Once an inventor develops a novel security technique, they must assume an adversarial role to thoroughly understand and patch vulnerabilities in their product. Organizational blindness often impedes this task. Therefore, dedicated security application testers focus on such jobs. In the present 2FA case of a pluggable authentication module for e-mail as an additional authentication factor, Grimes made a name for himself with his article on *The Many Ways to Hack 2FA* [8]. One year later, he imparted even more hacks and solutions against insecure 2FA with his book titled *Hacking Multifactor Authentication* [9]. This section involves self-reflection by leveraging Grimes' extensive best practices to identify and mitigate possible attack vectors against the new pluggable authentication module.

4.1 Man-In-The-Middle (MITM) Attacks

Such a situation occurs when an offender tricks a client into connecting to a malicious node, for example, through phishing, Address Resolution Protocol (ARP) poisoning, or Domain Name System (DNS) poisoning. Phishing rarely targets SSH, as only a few clients understand its locator ssh://. Unbeknownst to a server (with PAM) or a client, an attacker's node functions as a proxy, sitting between them and imitating the server's authentication process. The proxy forwards all commands and content from the client and the server to each other. By offloading and re-encrypting ciphered connections, the proxy can record and/or manipulate any transferred payload. To the client, it seems as though it communicates directly with the server, and vice versa.

An SSH client normally stores fingerprints of trustworthy servers' private keys in its local repository. An unknown fingerprint can indicate an MItM attack and should alert a user immediately.

4.2   Social Engineering Attacks

An individual or entity fraudulently and maliciously impersonates someone or something else to obtain unauthorized information or provoke actions contrary to a victim's or their organization's interests. Often, this occurs in person through phone calls, messaging services, or phishing, similar to MItM attacks. In this publication, an attacker likely attempts to extract a victim's password and gain access to the inbox of their primary and/or secondary e-mail address.

Security awareness training aims to instill a healthy level of skepticism in potential victims, enabling them to recognize, stop, and report social engineering attacks.

4.3   Programming Attacks Against Server Infrastructure

Once an offender acquires control over a server (with PAM) through malware, they can operate with the gained permissions. This does not necessarily entail privilege escalation to superuser rights, administrative access to an LDAP service, or manipulation of PAM options.

Nevertheless, the responsible administrators must ensure comprehensive Endpoint Detection and Response (EDR), stay up-to-date with critical patching, and guard against social engineering attacks.

4.4   Programming Attacks Against Client Infrastructure

Acquiring control over clients (for instance, with malware) yields less benefit compared to gaining control over servers. This task proves more achievable, e.g., due to less protection provided by EDR.

Generally, users should follow the same protective measures for their clients as administrators follow for their servers. Additionally, both factors of 2FA should not store on the same client. If necessary, only a local password manager may retain the first factor (password). E-mails with ROTPs as second factors should remain accessible solely by another device in the client's possession to prevent automatic usage of malware-triggered ROTPs.

4.5   Recovery Attacks

These actions focus on targeting alternative authentication methods provided by vendors for recovering MFA-protected accounts. Risks emerge when a recovery method relies on something less secure than the MFA solution it supports.

The proposal presented in this document assumes users lack the ability to self-enroll in the required LDAP service or modify it, aside from password updates. Administration personnel handle LDAP account management manually. The distinctiveness of both registered e-mail addresses per user in LDAP must undergo technical enforcement. Moreover, both addresses must comply with the security standards of the PAM-secured service. For instance, both addresses must allow access exclusively through MFA. To clarify, the primary e-mail account supports password resets, while the secondary receives ROTPs.

4.6   Brute Force Attacks (BFAs)

BFAs rank among the most basic forms of cyberattacks. Minimal intelligence requires little effort to execute. Attackers repeatedly target a victim, making small adjustments to a single value with each attempt or cycling through all dictionary words until cancellation, exhaustion, or success. Without defensive controls to block excessive attempts, this method guarantees eventual success, though it could take a long time.

A strong password policy must undergo enforcement as a prerequisite. For PAM with SSH, the default SSHD configuration allows only six authentication attempts in a row before terminating the session. Furthermore, this document's author strongly recommends combining the introduced pluggable authentication module with a reliable anti-hammering approach that temporarily blacklists rogue IP addresses. As mentioned in Sect. 1, this policy must maintain strictness while remaining flexible enough to thwart BFAs and prevent excessive lockouts of legitimate users due to DoS attacks. Realtime risk monitoring further enhances security posture [4–6]. For extra security, consider prompting an ROTP via e-mail before requiring the longer-lasting password. This approach would force a brute force attacker to correctly guess the active ROTP again before attempting another password.

4.7   Buffer Overflow Attacks

Such an activity occurs when a program, designed to accept a specific type or range of data, receives input that exceeds the storage capacity allocated for it. The pluggable authentication module expects a six-digit ROTP as input. Instead, a hacker might insert a large amount of binary executable code, which not only overwrites the designated storage area but also affects the current executable code within the program. If this overflow happens smoothly, without causing the module to lock up or terminate, the hacker's executable code may run instead of the original program in the module.

The author of this paper developed a prototype for the proposed pluggable authentication module and conducted buffer overflow attacks against it. All attempts failed because of the module's automatic memory management and extensive bounds checking.

4.8   Side-Channel Attacks

MFA components can unintentionally emit waves, signals, or currents that vary depending on the type of information or activity they handle. A side-channel attack targets these unexpected signals by eavesdropping on them, as they directly relate to operations or stored secrets. These leaks may arise from power consumption, electromagnetic waves, timing, light, temperature changes, and sound. Many devices experience one or more of these unintended emissions.

Effective defenses against side-channel attacks involve thoughtful design, encryption, shielding, jamming, filtering, distancing, and isolation. All relevant devices must include anti-electromagnetic shielding to block wireless side-channel attacks. Additionally, they should incorporate voltage regulators, electrical containment, random signal noise, and jamming measures to reduce the risk of wireless eavesdropping. Encryption algorithms resistant to side-channel attacks should also be employed. While important server infrastructure in data centers benefits from easier shielding, clients exposed to the public face greater challenges.

4.9 Physical Attacks

A significant threat arises when an antagonist gains complete or partial physical control over the client and/or server infrastructure of an MFA solution. At first glance, physical attacks might provide similar opportunities to those offered by programming exploits. However, this assumption holds true only if offenders have already bypassed authentication barriers. Unauthenticated actors can physically damage or destroy hardware, reducing its availability. Extracting data from running or powered-off, hard-to-access computing components, such as Central Processing Units (CPUs), storage media, or Trusted Platform Modules (TPMs), requires sophisticated techniques like electron microscope attacks or cold-boot attacks.

For this reason, any device involved in MFA must resist physical tampering. Additionally, during startup, such devices should perform self-checks for unauthorized modifications.

It can be considered that MFA approaches, including the novel pluggable authentication module for e-mail, face additional attack vectors. Nevertheless, this section aims to cover all currently known threats as thoroughly as possible.

5 Conclusion

Section 1 motivates this scholarly piece, addressing the constraints of anti-hammering mechanisms that often fail to adequately handle both BFAs and DoS attacks. This highlights the need for an effective countermeasure to tackle credential guessing and account lockouts.

Assuming a PAM framework, Sect. 2 reviews its fundamentals while documenting a comprehensive survey of scientific databases. The findings reveal the absence of a pluggable authentication module for e-mail as an additional authentication factor.

To address this gap, Sect. 3 presents a prototype of such a module, implemented on a typical Linux OS. Since Linux omits e-mail addresses by default in its user management, an extended LDAP scheme supporting a second e-mail address per user object for ROTP transmission, along with a related pluggable authentication module, became necessary.

Recognizing that every MFA solution remains vulnerable to attacks, Sect. 4 conducts threat modeling to identify potential vulnerabilities and weaknesses in the novel module. Although not exhaustive, the analysis categorizes nine probable attack vectors.

The ultimate objective involves adoption of the developed module by all major Linux distributors. Future iterations of this work will focus on enhancements to achieve market readiness, including extensive penetration testing based on the established threat model.

Acknowledgments. Many thanks to Bettina Baumgartner from the University of Vienna for proofreading this paper!

References

1. Binnie, C.: Securing SSH with PAM. In: Practical Linux Topics, pp. 51–59. Apress, Berkeley (2016). https://doi.org/10.1007/978-1-4842-1772-6_6
2. Chia, J., Chin, J.J., Yip, S.C.: Pluggable authentication module meets identity-based identification. In: Abdullah, N., Manickam, S., Anbar, M. (eds.) Advances in Cyber Security, pp. 155–175. Springer, Singapore (2021). https://doi.org/10.1007/978-981-16-8059-5_10
3. Fahrnberger, G.: Contemporary IT security for military online collaboration platforms. In: Proceedings of the 18th International Conference on Distributed Computing and Networking, ICDCN 2017, pp. 33:1–33:10. Association for Computing Machinery, New York (2017). https://doi.org/10.1145/3007748.3007754
4. Fahrnberger, G.: Realtime risk monitoring of SSH brute force attacks. In: Phillipson, F., Eichler, G., Erfurth, C., Fahrnberger, G. (eds.) Innovations for Community Services. Communications in Computer and Information Science, pp. 75–95. Springer Cham (2022). https://doi.org/10.1007/978-3-031-06668-9_8
5. Fahrnberger, G.: Bloom filter-based realtime risk monitoring of SSH brute force attacks. In: Krieger, U.R., Eichler, G., Erfurth, C., Fahrnberger, G. (eds.) Innovations for Community Services. Communications in Computer and Information Science, pp. 48–67. Springer Cham (2023). https://doi.org/10.1007/978-3-031-40852-6_3
6. Fahrnberger, G.: Pattern-and similarity-based realtime risk monitoring of SSH brute force attacks with bloom filters. In: 2024 36th Conference of Open Innovations Association (FRUCT), vol. 36, pp. 133–144. IEEE (2024). https://doi.org/10.23919/FRUCT64283.2024.10749895
7. Geisshirt, K.: Pluggable Authentication Modules: The Definitive Guide to PAM for Linux SysAdmins and C Developers: A Comprehensive and Practical Guide to PAM for Linux: How Modules Work and How to Implement them. Packt Publishing (2007). https://www.uploadbag.com/ofiles/5c14a11467c9db666bb31e23df07cba5/Pluggable-Authentication-Modules.pdf
8. Grimes, R.A.: The many ways to hack 2FA. Netw. Secur. **2019**(9), 8–13 (2019). https://doi.org/10.1016/S1353-4858(19)30107-2
9. Grimes, R.A.: Hacking Multifactor Authentication. Wiley (2020). https://doi.org/10.1002/9781119672357
10. Kraft, A.: Municipal Cybersecurity Enhancement (2024). https://www.diva-portal.org/smash/record.jsf?dswid=-8666
11. Lehtinen, S., Lonvick, C.: The Secure Shell (SSH) Protocol Assigned Numbers. RFC 4250 (Proposed Standard) (2006). https://doi.org/10.17487/RFC4250

12. Melnikov, A., Leiba, B.: Internet Message Access Protocol (IMAP) – Version 4rev2. RFC 9051 (Proposed Standard) (2021). https://doi.org/10.17487/RFC9051
13. Myers, J.G., Rose, M.T.: Post Office Protocol – Version 3. RFC 1939 (Internet Standard) (1996). https://doi.org/10.17487/RFC1939
14. Samar, V.: Unified login with pluggable authentication modules (PAM). In: Proceedings of the 3rd ACM Conference on Computer and Communications Security, CCS 1996, pp. 1–10. Association for Computing Machinery, New York (1996). https://doi.org/10.1145/238168.238177
15. Sermersheim, J.: Lightweight Directory Access Protocol (LDAP): The Protocol. RFC 4511 (Proposed Standard) (2006). https://doi.org/10.17487/RFC4511
16. Ylönen, T., Lonvick, C.: The Secure Shell (SSH) Authentication Protocol. RFC 4252 (Proposed Standard) (2006). https://doi.org/10.17487/RFC4252
17. Ylönen, T., Lonvick, C.: The Secure Shell (SSH) Connection Protocol. RFC 4254 (Proposed Standard) (2006). https://doi.org/10.17487/RFC4254
18. Ylönen, T., Lonvick, C.: The Secure Shell (SSH) Protocol Architecture. RFC 4251 (Proposed Standard) (2006). https://doi.org/10.17487/RFC4251
19. Ylönen, T., Lonvick, C.: The Secure Shell (SSH) Transport Layer Protocol. RFC 4253 (Proposed Standard) (2006). https://doi.org/10.17487/RFC4253

TRYOLO: A Transformer-Based Real-Time Object Detection Model for UAV Images

Bhimendra Dewangan, M. Srinivas$^{(\boxtimes)}$, and R. B. V. Subramanyam

Department of Computer Science and Engineering, National Institute of Technology, Warangal, Telangana, India
bd23csm2r06@student.nitw.ac.in, {msv,rbvs66}@nitw.ac.in

Abstract. A fundamental challenge in computer vision is object detection; however, it is still difficult to recognize small things because of their limited pixel representation, size changes, and background noise. In order to tackle these problems, we present TRYOLO, an improved real-time object identification model designed primarily for small object recognition and based on YOLOv11. Two important architectural improvements are included in our model: the DeepFocus Block, which enhances spatial feature extraction by adding more convolutions and residual connections, and the C3XFormer Block, which uses positional embeddings and multi-head self-attention to capture global dependencies and improve contextual understanding. These improvements significantly enhance the accuracy of feature representation and detection, especially for small objects in complicated situations. TRYOLO delivers state-of-the-art performance when we test it on two benchmark datasets, VisDrone-DET2019 and GlobalWheat2020. The validation performance metric shows a +2.4% gain in mAP on VisDrone-DET2019 and a +1.4% improvement in mAP on GlobalWheat2020.

Keywords: YOLO · Object detection · Transformer · CNNs · Aerial images

1 Introduction

One of the fundamental tasks in computer vision is object detection, which involves locating and identifying objects inside pictures or video frames. In contrast to more common classification tasks, which aim to label an image, object detection involves identifying the objects in an image, locating them, and assigning a suitable class label to them. Object detection has a wide range of applications and is essential in many different fields. To ensure safe navigation, autonomous vehicles, for example, multi-object tracking [1], and aerial surveillance [2]. There also exist some other models like Single Shot Multibox Detector (SSD) [21] and RetinaNet which are effective for real-time detection tasks, but

S. Zielinski et al. (Eds.): I4CS 2025, CCIS 2513, pp. 36–50, 2025.
https://doi.org/10.1007/978-3-031-94263-1_3

they often face challenges with handling complex or small objects and achieving high accuracy across a variety of object scales. SSD, for instance, utilizes default bounding boxes of different aspect ratios, which can lead to difficulties in detecting objects at multiple scales, while RetinaNet focuses on addressing class imbalance using a focal loss but still struggles with fine-grained localization.

Conventional techniques like Convolutional Neural Networks (CNN) and CNN-based models frequently rely on designs like Region-based CNNs (R-CNNs) to accomplish object detection because of their capacity to capture precise spatial features [20]. However, on devices with limited computational resources, CNN often has trouble processing huge pictures or managing real-time detection. Because of such a limitation, transformer-based models-which, in contrast to CNNs, are able to evaluate every aspect of visual context at once-have been examined. Transformers have great potential for recognizing complex objects or sceneries with changing sizes because of their capacity to take into account interactions across various parts of an image, which helps them better capture both global structures and fine-grained details.

An important step forward in real-time detection is the YOLO (You Only Look Once) [3, 22–24] family of object detection models, which can predict both object bounding boxes and classifications in a single network run. YOLO models are therefore especially well-suited for time-sensitive applications like drone-based monitoring and autonomous driving. YOLOv7 and YOLOv8 [17] are recent versions that have added architectural enhancements and optimizations that increase performance and accuracy. In YOLOv8, improved detection performance is a result of a simpler design and optimized loss mechanisms. Programmable Gradient Information (PGI) and GELAN modules were added to YOLOv9 [16] to make the model more flexible and improve feature extraction. In YOLOv10 [4], NMS-free training and dual assignments were made better to make detection more reliable. Additionally, to enhance multi-scale detection and computational efficiency, the most recent version, YOLOv11 [5], carries on this trend by integrating sophisticated feature extraction algorithms including the C3k2 block, Spatial Pyramid Pooling - Fast (SPPF), and Parallel Spatial Attention (C2PSA). These improvements ensure increased accuracy without substantially raising the model's complexity, which makes it highly adaptable for a range of computer vision applications. To make the most of both the transformers' deep contextual awareness and YOLO's speed, these hybrid models use both types of backbones. This makes them perfect for real-time settings with limited resources.

Hybrid models that integrate the advantages of transformers and CNNs have been created to further improve object identification capabilities. In these models, transformers give a global context by collecting long-range dependencies over an entire image, while CNNs are excellent at identifying small, detailed characteristics in localized portions of an image. In real-time applications where quick and precise identification is crucial, such as UAV-based surveillance, this hybrid technique has demonstrated great potential. Detecting things at different sizes, inside the same frame is made easier by the Swin Transformer model [25], which splits a picture into smaller windows and focuses attention on different areas of the image. In situations when numerous objects must be detected simultaneously, this multiscale capacity is essential.

Our methodology combines YOLOv11's efficiency with the scale invariance of transformers, particularly when objects appear at different sizes or in complex and cluttered environments. In this work, we propose an enhancement to the YOLOv11 architecture by introducing two key components: the **DeepFocus Block** and the **C3XFormer Block**. The DeepFocus Block is designed to improve feature extraction by aggregating information from multiple input channels, resulting in better feature localization and representation. The C3XFormer Block leverages the self-attention mechanism inherent in transformers and enhances the model's ability to capture long-range dependencies and complex interactions across the image. The DeepFocus Block and the C3XFormer Block improve both the speed and precision of object detection.

2   Related Works

Object identification has been a crucial topic of study in computer vision, and several methods have been developed throughout time to improve efficiency and accuracy. Handcrafted features like Haar cascades and Histogram of Orientated Gradients (HOG) [6] were used in traditional techniques, but they had trouble recognizing small objects and complicated backgrounds. Convolutional Neural Networks (CNNs), a type of deep learning technique, have transformed object recognition by learning hierarchical feature representations.

A multi-scale object detection network called MSODANet was introduced by Chalavadi et al. [7] to enhance detection in aerial photos by employing hierarchical dilated convolutions, which efficiently capture tiny object information at various sizes. YOLOv5, which was presented by Jocher et al. [8], enhanced backbone architectures and real-time object identification with effective anchor-based techniques. To improve tiny item recognition, Li et al. [9] investigated Perceptual Generative Adversarial Networks (PGANs), which produce high-quality feature representations from low-resolution pictures.

Deep learning object detection models [18,19] are powerful frameworks that automatically learn to identify and localize objects within images. Yang et al. [10] addressed issues with object density and size variations in their study of Clustered Object Detection (COD) in aerial images. By combining decoupled heads and sophisticated augmentation techniques, Zheng et al. [11] presented YOLOX, an anchor-free variant of YOLO that outperformed previous YOLO models. In their development of YOLOv7, Wang et al. [12] used trainable "bag-of-freebies" techniques to establish new performance standards for real-time detectors.

In object detection, Transformer models have become popular in addition to CNN-based methods. Through the improvement of feature fusion and the capture of long-range dependencies, Zhang et al. [13] demonstrated the effectiveness of their self-attention steering mechanism with multi-scale feature fusion in

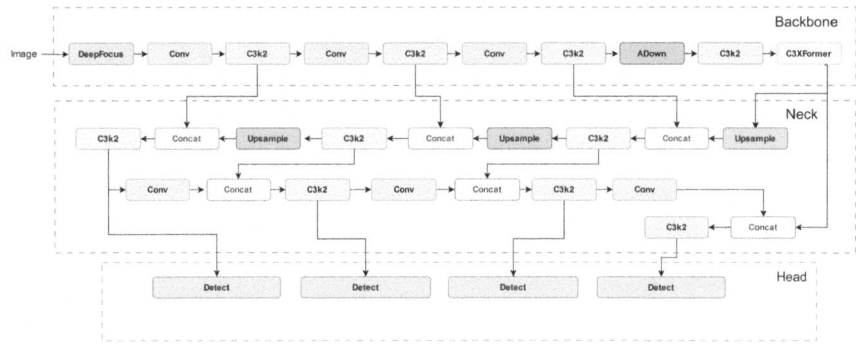

Fig. 1. TRYOLO architecture

UAV-based object recognition. The continuous improvements in object detection methods are demonstrated by these research, especially when it comes to managing small item detection in intricate settings.

3   Proposed Methodology

In this research, we propose a novel methodology named TRYOLO. This model incorporates two key modifications into the backbone network: the DeepFocus Block and C3XFormer Block. The purpose of the DeepFocus Block is to effectively extract and compress spatial information from the feature maps that are supplied. In this block, the channel space is made richer while the spatial resolution is decreased by reordering spatial dimensions and combining characteristics from several input channels. The model can more accurately locate and depict important spatial elements because to this dual functionality, which also guarantees computational efficiency. The DeepFocus Block improves the network's capacity to retain important spatial features, which is crucial for raising the accuracy of object recognition. The C3XFormer Block, which adds sophisticated self-attention mechanisms modeled after transformer designs, complements this. The network's capacity to record intricate feature interactions and long-range dependencies is greatly improved by the C3XFormer Block. Through the use of windowed multi-head self-attention and hierarchical feature extraction, TRYOLO is able to efficiently simulate both fine-grained local features and global context (Fig. 1).

The TRYOLO improves multi-scale detection capability by adding four detection heads. To improve feature extraction depth, it adds more convolutional (Conv), C2f, and concatenation blocks while keeping the architecture of the baseline model.

3.1   DeepFocus Block

The DeepFocus Block (Fig. 2) is a neural network module that transforms spatial information into the channel dimension to improve representation and compu-

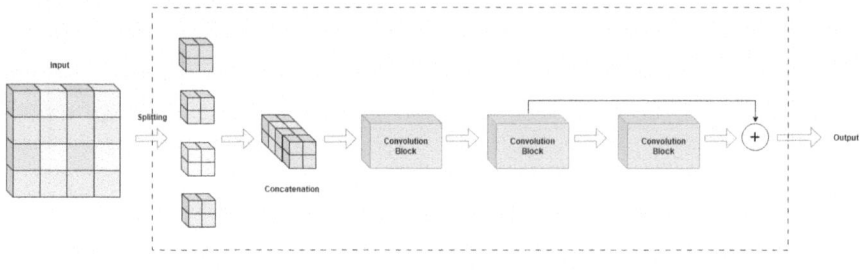

Fig. 2. DeepFocus Block

tational efficiency. It is especially useful for applications like object recognition and image processing since it preserves and concentrates spatial features while lowering the input tensor's spatial resolution. Equation 1 illustrates how the DeepFocus Block divides an input tensor X into quadrants $\{x_1, x_2, x_3, x_4\}$ and then concatenates them into an extended channel space. As seen in Fig. 2, this process quadruples the number of channels while reduces the spatial dimensions.

$$y_i = \text{concat}(x_1, x_2, x_3, x_4) \tag{1}$$

The resultant tensor y_i efficiently lessens the computing load of further operations by preserving rich spatial information in a compact representation. Three convolutional layers are then applied to this altered tensor, improving the representation and customizing it to meet certain learning goals. Equation 2 provides a mathematical definition of the convolutional operation.

$$z_{ij}^{(o)} = \sum_{k=1}^{c_{\text{in}}} \sum_{u=1}^{k_h} \sum_{v=1}^{k_w} W_{o,uvk}^{(o)} \cdot y_{(i+s_u-u)(j+s_v-v)(k)} + b^{(o)} \tag{2}$$

The output tensor element in this equation that corresponds to the spatial position (i, j) in the o-th output channel is represented by $z_{ij}^{(o)}$. The input channel is indicated by the index k, and the spatial coordinates of the kernel are indicated by u and v, which iterate over the kernel's width (k_w) and height (k_h), respectively. The convolutional kernel weights at position (u, v) for the k-th input channel and o-th output channel are represented by the term $W_{o,uvk}^{(o)}$. ($c_{\text{out}}, c_{\text{in}}, k_h, k_w$), where c_{out} and c_{in} indicate the number of output and input channels, respectively, and k_h, k_w represent the height and width of the kernel, are the form of these weights. If bias = True then the bias for the o-th output channel is represented by the term $b^{(o)}$. By adding learnable parameters W and b, this convolutional approach further refines the converted tensor yi to enhance feature representation and capture complex patterns. To reduce the likelihood of vanishing gradients and ensure that the model can learn from both the newly calculated features and the original input features, the Enhanced DeepFocus block includes a residual link. The output of the residual layer is attached to the processed features to promote the flow of unaltered information and aid gradient propagation during training.

3.2   C3XFormer Block

The C3XFormer Block (Fig. 3) integrates convolutional layers, multi-head attention mechanisms, normalization, and residual connections to form a robust framework for feature extraction and representation. The input data, denoted as $X \in \mathbb{R}^{n \times d}$, where n is the number of data points (e.g., time steps or image patches) and d is the dimensionality, is initially processed through a convolutional block (C3). The convolution operation applies a kernel $W_c \in \mathbb{R}^{k \times d}$, resulting in:

$$H_c = \text{Conv}(X, W_c) + b_c,$$

where $H_c \in \mathbb{R}^{n \times h}$ is the output feature map, b_c is the bias, and h is the number of output channels. This operation captures local spatial dependencies, extracting hierarchical features while reducing dimensionality.

The output H_c is flattened and permuted to reshape the feature map into a form suitable for attention processing:

$$H_p = \text{Permute}(\text{Flatten}(H_c)) \in \mathbb{R}^{n \times h}.$$

A linear transformation projects these features into a higher-dimensional space:

$$H_l = H_p W_l + b_l,$$

where $W_l \in \mathbb{R}^{h \times d_a}$ and $b_l \in \mathbb{R}^{d_a}$, allowing the subsequent attention mechanism to operate on enriched features.

The multi-head attention module computes contextual relationships. For each head i, the query, key, and value matrices are defined as:

$$Q_i = H_l W_i^Q, \quad K_i = H_l W_i^K, \quad V_i = H_l W_i^V,$$

where $W_i^Q, W_i^K, W_i^V \in \mathbb{R}^{d_a \times d_k}$. Attention weights are computed using:

$$A_i = \text{softmax}\left(\frac{Q_i K_i^\top}{\sqrt{d_k}}\right),$$

and the weighted value representation is:

$$O_i = A_i V_i.$$

Outputs from all heads are concatenated and linearly transformed:

$$H_{att} = \text{Concat}(O_1, O_2, \ldots, O_h) W^O,$$

where $W^O \in \mathbb{R}^{h \cdot d_k \times d_a}$ and h is the number of attention heads. This mechanism enhances the model's ability to capture global dependencies and contextual relationships across the input sequence. Residual connections are added to preserve

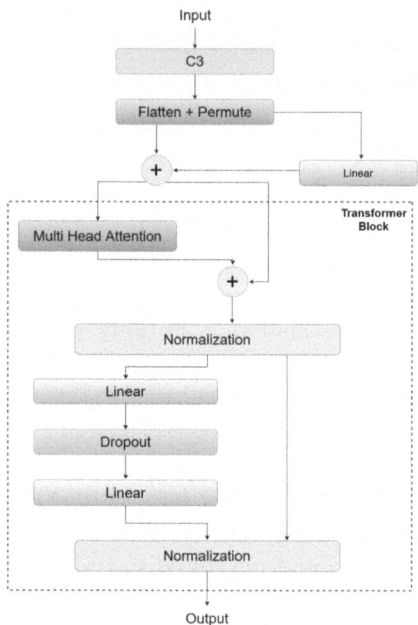

Fig. 3. C3XFormer Block

the original feature information and improve gradient flow. After the multi-head attention, a residual connection combines the input H_l with H_{att}, followed by layer normalization:

$$H_{res1} = \text{LayerNorm}(H_{att} + H_l).$$

The output H_{res1} is then passed through a feedforward network. This consists of a linear transformation with ReLU activation:

$$H_{ff1} = \text{ReLU}(H_{res1}W_{ff1} + b_{ff1}),$$

followed by dropout for regularization:

$$H_{ff2} = \text{Dropout}(H_{ff1})W_{ff2} + b_{ff2}.$$

A second residual connection combines H_{ff2} with H_{res1}, and layer normalization is applied to stabilize training:

$$H_{res2} = \text{LayerNorm}(H_{ff2} + H_{res1}).$$

The final output, $H_{res2} \in \mathbb{R}^{n \times d_a}$, represents a refined and contextually enriched feature embedding that can be used for downstream tasks such as classification or regression.

C3XFormer Block offers a number of advantages. While the multi-head attention captures contextual relationships and global dependencies, addressing long-range patterns, the convolutional block guarantees effective local feature extraction. The concept is scalable to deeper layers because residual connections prevent gradient vanishing and guarantee efficient gradient flow. While dropout lessens overfitting and improves generalization, normalization layers stabilize training and speed up convergence. These elements work together to create a strong foundation for activities requiring contextualized and in-depth feature representations.

4   Experiments and Analysis

4.1   Dataset Description

VisDrone-2017 DET. The VisDrone-2019 DET [26] dataset is a large-scale resource designed for drone-based object detection. It contains a total of 10,209 images, split into 6,471 training samples, 548 verification samples, and 3,190 test samples. The dataset includes a diverse range of 10 categories, such as pedestrian, person, bicycle, car, van, truck, tricycle, awning-tricycle, bus, and motor, with annotations provided in the form of bounding boxes.

GlobalWheat2020. The GlobalWheat2020 [15] dataset consists of over 3,000 training images from regions in Europe (France, UK, Switzerland) and North America (Canada). Additionally, it includes approximately 1,000 test images collected from Australia, Japan, and China.

4.2   Training Setup

A **NVIDIA DGX Station A100** with an 80GB GPU is used to train our model. With a momentum factor of 0.937, the learning rate is set at 0.01. To reduce overfitting, a weight decay factor of 5×10^{-4} is used along with a three-epoch warming phase. With early stopping set to 15, the model is trained from scratch for 300 epochs, guaranteeing ideal convergence while avoiding overfitting. To enable effective data loading, the warmup momentum is also set to 0.8, the warmup bias learning rate is set to 0.1, and there are eight workers. The input image resolution for GlobalWheat2020 is 640×640 with a batch size of 16, while for VisDrone-2019 DET it is 1536×1536 with a batch size of 2. Additionally, the values of Intersection over Union (IoU), a metric that assesses the overlap between predicted and ground truth bounding boxes, are set to 0.4 and 0.7 for VisDrone-2019 DET and 0 for GlobalWheat2020, respectively. Mixup is a data augmentation technique that combines two images and their labels to enhance generalization.

4.3   Evaluation Metrics

Several important indicators are used in this study to assess the model: Precision (P), which evaluates how well the model predicts favorable outcomes, mAP (mean average precision), which is the average precision across all classes with IoU thresholds ranging from 0.5 to 0.95; mAP@50 and mAP@75, which represent the model's performance at IoU thresholds of 0.50 and 0.75 respectively; recall (R), which measures the model's capacity to identify all pertinent objects; and the number of parameters, which denotes the model's complexity.

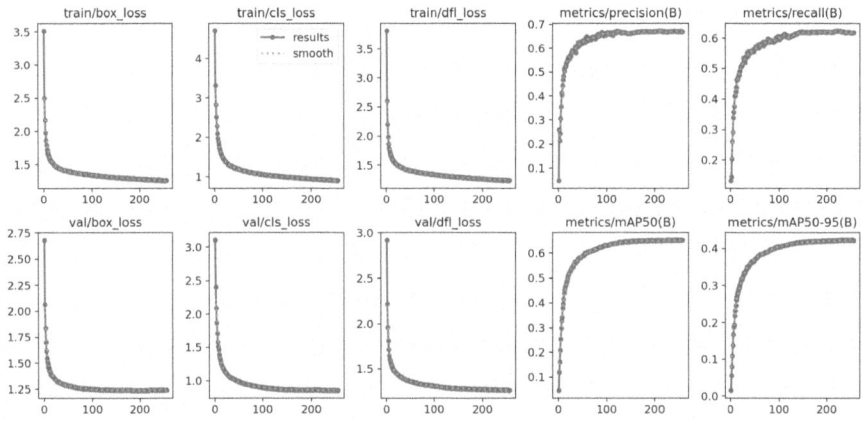

Fig. 4. Intrinsic evaluation metrics

4.4   Experiment Results

A TRYOLO model's training and validation performance metrics are displayed (Fig. 4) over the training epochs in the provided graph. The training losses-box loss, classification loss, and distribution focus loss-are displayed in the top row and exhibit a steady downward trend. This demonstrates how well the model learned bounding box refinement, item classification, and spatial relationships. The validation losses for the same metrics are also displayed in the bottom row, and they again exhibit a steady fall, indicating that the model can successfully generalize to new data.

Based on an evaluation of the VisDrone2019 DET dataset, the results shown in Table 1 demonstrate TRYOLO's superiority over current state-of-the-art object detection methods. Particularly in intricate settings with small objects, traditional CNN-based methods-such as different YOLO versions and MobileNet-based models-find it difficult to capture fine-grained item characteristics. Although some of these models show respectable performance, their dependability in practical applications is limited since they are unable to achieve high

(a)

(b)

Fig. 5. Visualization results on VisDrone dataset

accuracy at more stringent assessment criteria. The inference results in Fig. 5 demonstrate the TRYOLO model's powerful detection capabilities in intricate, real-world aerial scenarios. Vehicles of all sizes and densities, such as automobiles, trucks, buses, motorbikes, people walking, tricycles, and vans, are all correctly detected by the model. TRYOLO maintains distinct object boundaries even in congested traffic flows in Fig. 5(a), correctly identifying and differentiat-

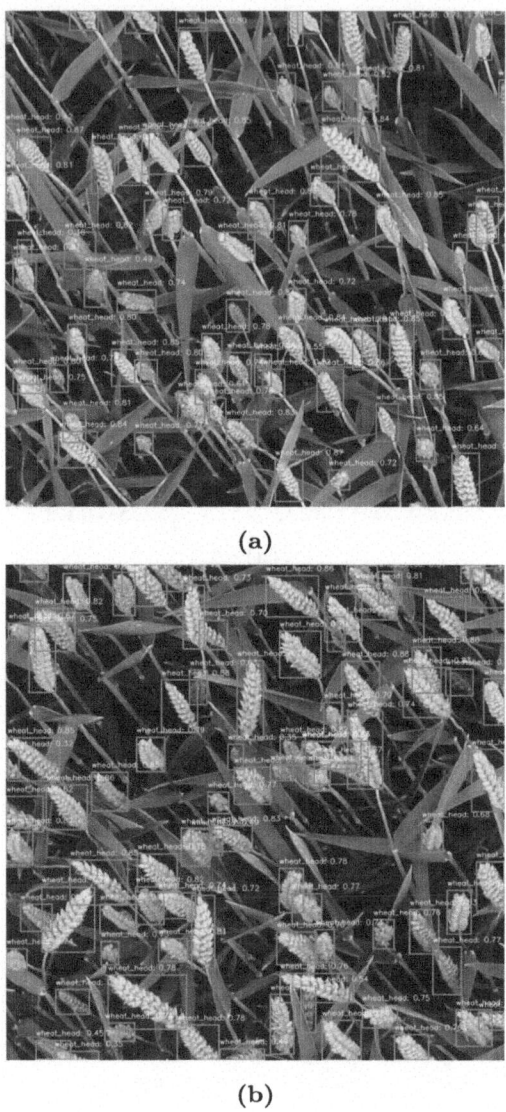

(a)

(b)

Fig. 6. Visualization results on GlobalWheat dataset

ing between several overlapping objects with high confidence despite the highly congested urban road environment. Its capacity to retain robust detection is unaffected by urban clutter, building shadows or green tree cover, highlighting the impact of using attention mechanisms and hierarchical feature extraction, which significantly enhances transformer-based techniques and multi-scale detection models like SGMFNet and mSODANet. The trade-off between accuracy

Table 1. Comparison of different methods based on mAP scores

Method	mAP$_{50}$(%)	mAP(%)	mAP$_{75}$(%)
mSODANet [7]	55.9	36.9	37.4
Yolov5-s [8]	53.7	31.7	31.4
Yolov5-m	58.6	35.4	36.8
DSHNet [9]	51.8	30.3	30.9
ClusDet [10]	56.2	32.4	31.6
Yolox-s [11]	53.5	31.4	31.7
MobileNetv3 [14]	55.4	32.9	32.9
Yolov7-s [12]	57.3	35.6	37.1
SGMFNet-s [13]	60.4	38.2	39.8
SGMFNet-m	62.3	39.5	40.2
Yolov11-m	61.4	39.7	42.0
TRYOLO	**65.0**	**42.1**	**43.2**

and efficiency results from their inability to properly optimist both long-range dependence and local feature extraction, notwithstanding their improvements.

Table 2. Comparative experiments of YOLO-series algorithms

Model	P (%)	R (%)	mAP@0.5 (%)
YOLOv5n	83.5	77.9	84.6
YOLOv6n	76.8	74.6	80.7
YOLOv7t	82.8	79.6	85.3
YOLOv8n	80.4	78.3	85.0
YOLOV11m	96.9	97.0	98.9
TRYOLO	**98.1**	**98.2**	**99.3**

The GlobalWheat dataset was used for all testing, as indicated in Tables 2 and 3. When compared to different YOLO-series algorithms, the results of the experiment in Table 2 show how well the suggested TRYOLO model performs. Figure 6 shows the detection results, which show how well the TRYOLO model can recognize wheat heads in agricultural footage that is packed closely together. Even though the wheat heads and the surrounding leaves appear to be substantially similar, the model reliably and very confidently distinguishes individual heads at different sizes and orientations. Tight bounding boxes are exactly positioned around both noticeable and slightly obscured wheat heads, demonstrating the predictions' high positioning accuracy. The ability of the model to differentiate between tightly crowded wheat structures, even in regions with detailed leaf shadows and lighting swings, demonstrates its resilience in managing overlapping instances and small texture differences, illustrating that the best-performing YOLO version (YOLOV11m) records 96.9% precision, 97.0% recall, and 98.9% mAP@0.5, whereas TRYOLO gets the maximum precision (98.1%), recall (98.2%), and mAP@0.5 (99.3%). These results show a notable increase in detection robustness and accuracy.

Table 3. Comparative experiments on baseline and TRYOLO

Model	Parameter (M)	P (%)	R (%)	mAP (%)	mAP@0.5 (%)	mAP@0.75 (%)
Baseline	20.1	96.9	97.0	77.0	98.9	89.5
TRYOLO	**18.4**	**98.1**	**98.2**	**84.5**	**99.3**	**97.4**

Moreover, TRYOLO exhibits a more effective design in addition to achieving better accuracy when directly compared to the baseline model (Table 3). TRYOLO improves performance on all important measures, including mAP by 8.5% (84.5% vs. 77.0%) and mAP@0.75 by a substantial margin (97.4% vs. 89.5%), even though it has less parameters (18.4M vs. 20.1M). These results demonstrate how well TRYOLO strikes a balance between detection accuracy and computing cost, making it an appealing option for practical object identification problems.

Although the detection architecture becomes more computationally difficult when Transformer blocks are utilized, we reduce this overhead by including a lightweight DeepFocus block that carefully separates the input image into specific regions for attention calculation. This approach substantially decreases insignificant processing by ensuring that the self-attention mechanism is applied only to the most essential spatial areas. Most importantly, the DeepFocus module maintains the efficiency and compactness of YOLO-based designs by not adding more parameters to the model overall. Because of this, the model retains about the same inference performance as the original baseline even with Transformer components included, which makes it ideal for real-time applications. Empirical analysis demonstrates that there are small latency variations and that the inference time stays constant.

5   Conclusion

TRYOLO introduces a novel and efficient architecture that significantly enhances object detection performance, particularly for small and multi-scale objects. The model efficiently compresses spatial dimensions and enriches channel space using the DeepFocus Block, guaranteeing accurate localization and strong spatial feature representation. In addition, the C3XFormer Block overcomes the drawbacks of traditional convolutional techniques by utilizing sophisticated transformer-based self-attention mechanisms to capture complex feature interactions and long-range dependencies. The model is further enhanced in its capacity to learn local and global contextual information by adding the features of multi-head self-attention and hierarchical feature extraction.

References

1. Malagi, V.P., DR, R.B., Rangarajan, K.: Multi-object tracking in aerial image sequences using aerial tracking learning and detection algorithm. Defence Sci. J. **66**(2), 122–129 (2016)
2. Cheng, H.-Y., Weng, C.-C., Chen, Y.-Y.: Vehicle detection in aerial surveillance using dynamic Bayesian networks. IEEE Trans. Image Process. **21**(4), 2152–2159 (2011)
3. Sirisha, U., Praveen, S.P., Srinivasu, P.N., et al.: Statistical analysis of design aspects of various YOLO-based deep learning models for object detection. Int. J. Comput. Intell. Syst. **16**(1), 126 (2023)
4. Wang, A., Chen, H., Liu, L., Chen, K., et al.: YOLOv10: Real-Time End-to-End Object Detection, arXiv preprint arXiv:2405.14458 (2024)
5. Khanam, R., Hussain, M.: YOLOv11: An Overview of the Key Architectural Enhancements, arXiv preprint arXiv:2410.17725 (2024)
6. Pang, Y., Yuan, Y., Li, X., Pan, J.: Efficient HOG human detection. Signal Process. **91**(4), 773–781 (2011)
7. Chalavadi, V., Jeripothula, P., Datla, R., Ch, S.B., et al.: mSODANet: a network for multi-scale object detection in aerial images using hierarchical dilated convolutions. Pattern Recognit. **126**, 108548 (2022)
8. Jocher, G., Stoken, A., Borovec, J., et al.: ultralytics/yolov5: v5.0-YOLOv5-P6 1280 models, AWS, Supervise.ly and YouTube integrations, Zenodo (2021)
9. Li, J., Liang, X., Wei, Y., Xu, T., Feng, J., Yan, S.: Perceptual generative adversarial networks for small object detection. In: Proceedings of the IEEE Conference on Computer Vision and Pattern Recognition (CVPR), pp. 1222–1230 (2017)
10. Yang, F., Fan, H., Chu, P., Blasch, E., Ling, H.: Clustered object detection in aerial images. In: Proceedings of IEEE/CVF International Conference on Computer Vision, pp. 8311–8320 (2019)
11. Zheng, G., Liu, S., Feng, W., Li, Z., Sun, J., et al.: YOLOX: Exceeding YOLO series in 2021, arXiv preprint arXiv:2107.08430 (2021)
12. Wang, C.-Y., Bochkovskiy, A., Liao, H.-Y.M.: YOLOv7: trainable bag-of-freebies sets new state-of-the-art for real-time object detectors. In: Proceedings of the IEEE/CVF Conference on Computer Vision and Pattern Recognition (CVPR), pp. 7464–7475 (2023)
13. Zhang, Y., Wu, C., Zhang, T., Liu, Y., Zheng, Y.: Self-attention guidance and multiscale feature fusion-based UAV image object detection. IEEE Geosci. Remote Sens. Lett. **20**, 1–5 (2023)
14. Koonce, B.: Convolutional Neural Networks with Swift for Tensorflow. Springer (2021)
15. David, E., Madec, S., et al.: Global wheat head detection (GWHD) dataset: a large and diverse dataset of high-resolution RGB-labelled images to develop and benchmark wheat head detection methods. Plant Phenomics (2020)
16. Wang, C.-Y., Yeh, I.-H., Liao, H.-Y.M.: YOLOv9: Learning What You Want to Learn Using Programmable Gradient Information, arXiv preprint arXiv:2402.13616 (2024)

17. Reis, D., Kupec, J., Hong, J., Daoudi, A.: Real-Time Flying Object Detection with YOLOv8, arXiv preprint arXiv:2305.09972 (2024)
18. Srinivas, M., Lin, Y.Y., Liao, H.Y.M.: Learning deep and sparse feature representation for fine-grained object recognition. In: Proceedings of IEEE International Conference on Multimedia Expo (ICME), pp. 1458–1463 (2017)
19. Srinivas, M., Roy, D., Mohan, C.K.: Discriminative feature extraction from X-ray images using deep convolutional neural networks. In: Proceedings of IEEE International Conference on Acoustics, Speech and Signal Processing (ICASSP), pp. 917–921 (2016)
20. Girshick, R., Donahue, J., Darrell, T., Malik, J.: Rich feature hierarchies for accurate object detection and semantic segmentation. In: Proceedings of IEEE Conference on Computer Vision and Pattern Recognition (CVPR), vol. 56, pp. 580–587 (2014)
21. Liu, W.: SSD: single shot multibox detector. In: Proceedings of European Conference on Computer Vision, pp. 21–37. Springer, Cham (2016)
22. Redmon, J., Divvala, S., Girshick, R., Farhadi, A.: You only look once: unified, real-time object detection. In: Proceedings of IEEE Conference on Computer Vision and Pattern Recognition (CVPR), pp. 779–788 (2016)
23. Redmon, J., Farhadi, A.: YOLO9000: better, faster, stronger. In: Proceedings of IEEE Conference on Computer Vision and Pattern Recognition (CVPR), pp. 7263–7271 (2017)
24. Farhadi, A., Redmon, J.: YOLOv3: an incremental improvement, arXiv preprint arXiv:1804.02767 (2018)
25. Liu, Z.: Swin transformer: hierarchical vision transformer using shifted windows. In: Proceedings of IEEE/CVF International Conference on Computer Vision, pp. 10012–10022 (2021)
26. Du, D., Zhu, P., Wen, L., Bian, X., et al.: VisDrone-DET2019: the vision meets drone object detection in image challenge results. In: Proceedings of IEEE/CVF International Conference on Computer Vision Workshops, pp. 213–126 (2019)

Automated Text Classification in Maturity Models Using Transformer Architectures: An Encoder-Based Approach

Patrick Seidel[1]([✉]) and Wesley Preßler[2]

[1] Friedrich Schiller University Jena, 07743 Jena, Germany
`patrick.seidel@uni-jena.de`
[2] Ernst-Abbe-Hochschule Jena, 07745 Jena, Germany
`Wesley.Pressler@eah-jena.de`

Abstract. In recent years, progress in AI and NLP technology has significantly increased. Researchers are exploring various applications of this technology to boost process efficiency. This study examines how encoder-based transformer models can be integrated into sociological maturity models. The process is still largely manual, making it prone to errors and time-consuming. In this scientific paper, we describe how four transformer models were used to assign interview passages to the corresponding categories of a maturity model. It can be observed that two out of four models achieve excellent results and that the leading model correctly assigns 22 out of 23 inputs to a specific class. In this way, transformer models offer an effective method to improve the efficiency of processes in maturity models without compromising the quality of classification. The continuation of the research involves adding additional categories and training the corresponding models to ultimately determine the maturity level using a transformer model.

Keywords: Maturity model · Transformer model · Encoder-based model · Text classification · Semantic analysis

1 Introduction

In recent years, technology in the field of artificial intelligence (AI) and natural language processing (NLP) has advanced significantly. With the help of language models based on encoders, such as bidirectional encoder representations from transformers (BERT) or robustly optimized BERT pretraining approach (RoBERTa), it is possible to process natural language extremely effectively and perform related tasks such as context-dependent classification. This offers numerous opportunities for various industries that work with natural language and need to perform corresponding tasks. One area where such models are used involves the evaluation of natural language through corresponding maturity models to derive appropriate ordinal ratings.

© The Author(s), under exclusive license to Springer Nature Switzerland AG 2025
S. Zielinski et al. (Eds.): I4CS 2025, CCIS 2513, pp. 51–60, 2025.
https://doi.org/10.1007/978-3-031-94263-1_4

The goal of these maturity models is to determine the current process quality in order to assess the extent to which a method or technology is integrated into the corresponding observation environment. There are various ways to evaluate the described quality. There is the possibility to manually categorize these texts, which, however, may take more time. Furthermore, inconsistencies and errors can occur due to the number of data points that need to be categorized. Therefore, the question arises whether encoder-based transformer models can be used to reduce this time effort and ideally improve the accuracy of classifying text segments in maturity models.

Various classification tasks already use encoder-based transformer models, but their application in maturity models represents an innovative approach. One goal of this paper is to conduct basic research and merely indicate some research directions as well as provide initial impulses on how this research field could be further investigated. The research questions are formulated as follows:

- RQ1: Can transformer models like BERT be used for the automated classification of text segments in maturity models for more efficient and precise classification?
- RQ2: Which models are best suited for this type of classification task and which training parameters are most appropriate?

To clarify the aforementioned research questions, a transformer model will be trained, which can then be used for the corresponding classifications. Subsequently, the precision of this model will be verified to enable a comparison with existing methods and technical options. Ultimately, recommendations and best practices should be identified that can be used for future research.

2   Motivation

With the advancement in artificial intelligence, new opportunities are emerging for the analysis and utilization of qualitatively obtained data, including those used for the analysis of maturity models. In this context, large language model (LLM)s like BERT could play a central role in the future. We can use these models to process, classify, and integrate text data into existing maturity models, for example. From the perspective of the ongoing discourse in qualitative research, the use of AI models is, however, controversial. In terms of maturity analysis and the authors' experience, however, the following areas emerge that require closer examination and iterative testing:

1. **Automated Classification of Maturity Levels:** A central use case for LLMs in maturity models is the automated classification of texts. In many cases, maturity analyses are based on qualitative data such as interviews, company reports, or surveys, which have to be manually coded so far. This is not only time-consuming but also prone to inconsistencies and subjectivity. The use of LLMs like BERT can make this process significantly more efficient by automatically semantically analyzing and categorizing text data.

2. **Detection of Development Patterns and Technology Acceptance:** Another advantage of LLMs lies in their ability to recognize patterns in digital transformation. By analyzing large amounts of text data, systematic patterns can be identified that provide insights into technology acceptance, organizational barriers, and social interpretation patterns. This could, for example, be used to identify resistance to digital technologies early on and derive targeted measures to improve technology acceptance.

3. **Continuous Improvement through AI-supported Feedback Loops:** Continuous improvement through AI-supported feedback loops: Traditional maturity models are based on point-in-time assessments conducted at specific intervals. Through the integration of LLMs, such models could, however, be further developed into dynamic systems that continuously evaluate new data and adaptively adjust. This would enable a more agile and data-driven management of digital transformation processes.

The combination of maturity models with LLMs offers a promising opportunity to not only analyze digital transformation more precisely but also to manage it more effectively. The strengths of both approaches complement each other perfectly:

- **Maturity models** provide an established methodological framework for evaluating and managing transformation processes.
- **LLM** enables an automated, more objective, and continuous analysis of text data, making maturity models more dynamic and data-driven.

Through this approach, for example, companies, authorities, and organizations could obtain more precise assessments of their digital maturity and take more targeted measures for further development. Furthermore, societal acceptance processes could be better understood and actively integrated into digital transformation.

3 Theory

3.1 Maturity Model

Digital transformation is a complex and multi-stage process that presents challenges to companies, organizations/institutions, and societal systems. Maturity models offer a structured approach to evaluating and supporting such transformation processes. They enable a systematic assessment of the current state, identification of development goals, and derivation of targeted measures for the improvement and sustainable integration of new technologies [2]. Maturity models were originally developed for process evaluation and organizational development and have now become an established part of transformation research. They follow a systematic structure that progresses in several stages:

1. Assessment of the current state: The current state of an organization or process is analyzed through self-assessment or external evaluation.

2. Goal definition: Based on the results, development goals are set to specifically steer the transformation.
3. Planning and implementation of measures: Strategies to achieve the goals are formulated and implemented.
4. Monitoring and continuous adjustment: Progress is regularly reviewed to ensure sustainable development.

While classic maturity models often focused on technological aspects, current research shows that individual technology acceptance and societal interpretive patterns play a central role in the success of digital transformation. The approach of the interdisciplinary maturity model therefore considers not only technical but also social, cognitive, and organizational dimensions. Aspects such as digital literacy, individual technology acceptance, and socially shared interpretive patterns are crucial for the successful implementation of digital technologies [1,6].

3.2   Transformer Model

In recent years, progress in the field of NLP has significantly increased. One factor for this is the introduction of transformer models by Vaswani et al. in 2017 [9]. The models stand out from conventional RNNs and LSTMs through the use of a so-called "Attention" mechanism. They rely entirely on avoiding recurrence and convolution, which in turn improves parallelizability and reduces the training costs of such models. The distances between the input and output positions remain constant, which makes learning long-term dependencies easier. Furthermore, the use of the "Self-Attention" mechanism fundamentally enables the interpretability of the decisions made by these models, which is not possible with conventional recurrent neural networks (RNN) or long short-term memory networks (LSTM). By using "Attention" mechanisms, each word in the input text receives an individual weighting based on the desired statement. It is therefore possible to ignore unimportant sentence structures and focus on the parts that are important for generating the corresponding output. There is also the possibility of using "multi-head attention", which allows for the simultaneous calculations of attention to generate different representations of text segments. In this way, it is possible to capture and consider a variety of situations, which can lead to a more precise interpretation of natural language.

Through appropriate encoder models, it is possible to interpret natural language based on context. Besides this model variant, there are also decoder models as well as combinations of encoder and decoder. This model combination is versatile for various sequence transduction tasks where one sequence needs to be transformed into another. The encoder transforms the input sequence into a representation form that is used by the decoder to create an output sequence that matches the input. There are also encoder and decoder models that have been developed exclusively for specific tasks due to their specialized architecture. Decoder-only models are particularly well-suited for creating texts that are indistinguishable from natural texts. Encoder-only models are especially adept at text classification because they effectively capture the contextual nuances of words. The focus is primarily on encoder-only models due to the classification and assessment of texts. Decoder-only models are particularly well-suited for producing texts that closely resemble natural texts. However, these models are only partially suitable for text classification, as they cannot develop a comprehensive understanding of the text due to the lack of a bidirectional approach [5]. Encoder models are extremely effective in text classification because they can precisely capture the subtle details of word meaning through their bidirectional approach. Consequently, the focus is primarily on encoder-only models due to their particular suitability for context-sensitive text classification.

3.3   Encoder-Based Models

The language model BERT uses the transformer architecture and is a multi-layer bidirectional transformer encoder [4,9]. As the model name already indicates, it is a bidirectional model, unlike previous RNN/LSTM. Both RNN and LSTM are active in one direction and only take into account the left or right context of a word. In contrast, the BERT model considers the left and right context of a term in all its model layers, thus capturing the context more precisely [4]. As already mentioned, encoder models are well-suited for text classification. Two versions of the BERT model were pretrained using a large amount of unlabeled text. These can be fine-tuned for specific downstream tasks with the corresponding labeled data [4]. Two model variants of BERT were trained for this purpose. These are BERTBASE, which has 12 layers, 768 hidden units, 12 attention heads, and 110 million parameters, and BERTLARGE with 24 layers, 1024 hidden units, 16 attention heads, and 360 million parameters. On this basis, additional improved model variants were developed, such as RoBERTa [4] or DistilBERT [7]. Current progress also indicates further improvements to the original BERT model, which are reflected in ModernBERT [10]. There are various improvements that have been proven to enhance the quality of the model. Therefore, these transformer models are continuously improved and serve as a basis for various tasks in the field of natural language processing, such as text categorization, NER, or sequence tagging [3].

4   Method

4.1   Business Understanding

This research paper uses the CRISP-DM model to ensure a systematic methodology and to prevent potential errors. This section provides a brief explanation of the work's goal. Subsequently, the analysis of the data intended for model training is conducted, followed by the model training phase, and finally, the evaluation of the models. The aim of this scientific paper is to provide a fundamental overview of the use of transformer models in conjunction with maturity models.

4.2   Data Understanding and Data Preparation

The data points used in model training consist of interview excerpts that are assigned to classes in the maturity model. There are the classes "Housing", "Working", "Living", and "Caring". The following values were quantitatively present in the dataset:

- Housing: 452 Entries
- Working: 114 Entries
- Living: 216 Entries
- Caring: 236 Entries

It can be observed that the category "Housing" includes more datasets in the training of the model than the other categories. When evaluating the models, it should be considered whether any of them assign the category "Housing" excessively frequently. The category "Working" has the smallest number of data points, which should be taken into account during the evaluation phase. The number of instances in the classes "Living" and "Caring" is almost identical. The mentioned examples are excerpts from interviews collected as part of a study, as previously mentioned, and are as follows:

- "P1: Und können Sie sich grundsätzlich vorstellen, auch (Ähm) bis ins hohe Alter hier im Quartier zu wohnen, so mit der Ausstattung, die es hier gibt? P3: Ja."
- "Ich gehe gerade mal ganz kurz die Eingänge durch. Wir haben die Gemein-schaftswaschmaschinen Räume, also mit Waschmaschine und Trockner, die man da buchen kann."

This includes both conversation transcripts, as seen in the first example, as well as individual excerpts from residents. To ensure that the trained model can be used not only for revised inputs, these instances are included in the model training unchanged. This also integrates colloquial language into the model and considers potential other syntactic errors that could occur in future applications.

4.3   Modeling

Four different encoder-based transformer models are used for training the model. Each of these models is trained with the aforementioned dataset to then assign text passages to the corresponding categories. There are two different model variants: On the one hand, GottBERT [8], both in the base and the larger variant, and on the other hand, ModernBERT [10], which is also used in the base and larger variant. The foundation of the GottBERT model is the RoBERTa transformer [4], which has already undergone several optimizations and is built on the conventional BERT model. The focus of improving GottBERT is on training with German texts, making it particularly suitable for NLP tasks in the German-speaking area. Therefore, it is particularly suitable for our specific use case. In contrast, ModernBERT was trained on English-language texts, but it is currently the more advanced version of the BERT model and therefore serves as a reference for later evaluation. The models just described have the following parameters:

- GottBERT Base: 12 layers, 125 million parameters
- GottBERT Large: 24 layers, 355 million parameters
- ModernBERT Base: 22 layers, 149 million parameters
- ModernBERT Large: 28 layer, 395 million parameters

We conducted the model training using the following parameters:

- num_train_epochs: 3
- per_device_train_batch_size: 16
- per_device_eval_batch_size: 16
- evaluation_strategy: "steps"
- eval_steps: 100
- save_steps: 100
- logging_steps: 10
- learning_rate: 2e-5
- weight_decay: 0.01

The software was developed using the Python programming language and the Transformer library, which allows for customized training. By using the Python library "Pytorch", the training of the models could be carried out on an Nvidia RTX 4080 Super, leading to a more efficient model training phase. Ultimately, four fine-tuned encoder-based transformer models were developed to assign text inputs to the appropriate categories of the maturity model.

5   Evaluation

The performance of the created models will be analyzed below to ultimately determine which model is best suited for the task. Four encoder-based transformer models were trained for the task of assigning inputs to the classes of a maturity model. Table 1 shows categorizations of responses from conversations that were assigned to the different models. This is the manual evaluation by an expert, called "Classification", which is shown in the first column. This value is used as a guideline to make a more accurate assessment of the final quality of the models. The confidence for each classification indicates the probability of belonging to the respective class. This helps in the more accurate assessment of the model's decision and provides clues when the assignment of a data point is not clear enough.

It can be observed that the model "GottBERT Large" performs the best classification and assigns almost all inputs to the correct class, with one single exception. The smaller model of "GottBERT" assigns some inputs to a different category than those assigned at the expert level. In contrast, the two ModernBERT models make errors in numerous classifications and assign almost all

Table 1. Evaluation classification

Classification	GottBERT L	GottBERT B	ModernBERT L	ModernBERT B
Working	Working (97%)	Working (84%)	Housing (53%)	Housing (82%)
Working	Working (98%)	Working (85%)	Housing (46%)	Caring (41%)
Working	Working (85%)	Working (56%)	Housing (53%)	Caring (42%)
Working	Working (65%)	Working (76%)	Housing (44%)	Caring (57%)
Housing	Housing (92%)	Housing (92%)	Housing (48%)	Housing (72%)
Housing	Housing (97%)	Housing (93%)	Housing (47%)	Housing (86%)
Housing	Housing (97%)	Housing (93%)	Housing (46%)	Housing (57%)
Housing	Housing (96%)	Housing (89%)	Housing (47%)	Housing (60%)
Housing	Housing (92%)	Caring (68%)	Housing (51%)	Housing (40%)
Housing	Housing (97%)	Housing (67%)	Housing (40%)	Caring (36%)
Living	Housing (73%)	Living (69%)	Housing (53%)	Housing (93%)
Living	Living (88%)	Working (50%)	Housing (49%)	Housing (86%)
Living	Living (97%)	Living (90%)	Housing (52%)	Housing (74%)
Living	Living (97%)	Living (92%)	Housing (47%)	Housing (84%)
Living	Living (98%)	Living (92%)	Housing (44%)	Housing (39%)
Caring	Caring (69%)	Caring (66%)	Housing (46%)	Housing (79%)
Caring	Caring (50%)	Caring (76%)	Housing (50%)	Housing (75%)
Caring	Caring (81%)	Housing (59%)	Housing (46%)	Housing (40%)
Caring	Caring (85%)	Caring (83%)	Housing (50%)	Housing (49%)
Caring	Caring (92%)	Caring (87%)	Housing (48%)	Housing (72%)
Caring	Caring (95%)	Caring (90%)	Housing (47%)	Caring (40%)
Caring	Caring (76%)	Caring (63%)	Housing (46%)	Housing (81%)
Caring	Caring (82%)	Caring (84%)	Housing (47%)	Housing (65%)

data points to the "Housing" class. This was already mentioned in the previous chapter and could result from the excessive representation of this category. This may be because these models were trained on English-language data and therefore can only consider the context to a limited extent. It is also important to note that the classification was completed in less than five seconds, which demonstrates a reduction in manual effort, in addition to the quality of the classification. Through the appropriate quality with which the model categorizes the instances, there is the possibility to optimize maturity models and their processes. In summary, it can be noted that the extensively trained GottBERT model delivers the best performance and is therefore the most suitable for this specific use case. The smaller GotBERT model can be optimized in terms of training parameters, which can lead to better performance. The two Modern-BERT models are currently not suitable for use in German-language NLP tasks.

6   Conclusion

The aim of this scientific work was to gain fundamental insights into the application of encoder-based transformer models in maturity models. The data-driven approach model cross industry standard process for data mining (CRISP-DM) was used to ensure a structured approach, and ultimately, four transformer models were trained. As explained in the "Evaluation" section, the two GottBERT models demonstrate the best suitability and achieve an extremely precise classification. Thus, the first research question, whether transformer models like BERT are suitable for such tasks, has been answered. These models achieve high accuracy in classification and require only a fraction of the time for this process. Encoder-based transformer models can understand the context of natural language due to their architecture and use it for the specific NLP task. Furthermore, it has been demonstrated that the language in which the basic training of a model is conducted has a significant impact on the quality of the classification.

The project demonstrates a new approach to accurately categorizing qualitative information into appropriate categories. In this way, the manual and error-prone process can be optimized. It would be advisable to conduct additional investigations, either with more extensive datasets or by using more maturity models with additional categories. It is important to consider that the training time also increases with the amount of data and the complexity of the model. Furthermore, it is only partially possible to trace the internal decision paths in an encoder, which negatively affects the comprehensibility of the model's decisions.

Therefore, the question remains whether and in what way explainable artificial intelligence (XAI) can illustrate the transparency of decisions. This would strengthen trust in such models and therefore promote their everyday application. Future research could continue in a variety of ways. In addition to technical innovations, such as the use of larger datasets and the incorporation of additional maturity models, there are also methodological approaches to advance further research. One possibility would be to use reinforcement learning to avoid errors in classification and improve the models with each input. Another option for improving model quality would be the application of zero-shot or few-shot learning.

Our future research focus is on integrating additional classes into the model and ultimately determining the maturity level. To achieve this, the model should be able to effectively segment qualitative data and classify it at a high level. This study demonstrates that encoder-based transformer models are capable of assigning inputs to the correct class with high accuracy. This provides an option to make the manual process more efficient.

References

1. Datta, P., Walker, L., Amarilli, F.: Digital transformation: learning from Italy's public administration. J. Inf. Technol. Teach. Cases **10**(2), 54–71 (2020)

2. De Bruin, T., Rosemann, M., Freeze, R., Kaulkarni, U.: Understanding the main phases of developing a maturity assessment model. In Bunker, D., Campbell, B., Underwood, J. (eds.) Australasian Conference on Information Systems (ACIS). Australasian Chapter of the Association for Information Systems, CD Rom, 8–19 Conference Name: Australasian Conference on Information Systems (ACIS) Meeting Name: Australasian Conference on Information Systems (ACIS) (2005)
3. Devlin, J., Chang, M.W., Lee, K., Toutanova, K.: BERT: Pre-training of Deep Bidirectional Transformers for Language Understanding (2019). arXiv:1810.04805
4. Liu, Y., et al.: RoBERTa: A Robustly Optimized BERT Pretraining Approach (2019). arXiv:1907.11692
5. Passi, N., Raj, M., Shelke, N.A.: A review on transformer models: applications, taxonomies, open issues and challenges. In: 2024 4th Asian Conference on Innovation in Technology (ASIANCON), pp. 1–6 (2024)
6. Preßler, W., Lucie, S.: Interdisziplinäres Reifegradmodell zur Begleitung nachhaltiger digitaler Transformationsprozesse. Forum Wohnen und Stadtentwicklung (Heft 1/2025 Urbane Räume im digitalen Wandel), pp. 28–32 (2025)
7. Sanh, V., Debut, L., Chaumond, J., Wolf, T.: DistilBERT, a distilled version of BERT: smaller, faster, cheaper and lighter (2020). arXiv:1910.01108
8. Scheible, R., Thomczyk, F., Tippmann, P., Jaravine, V., Boeker, M.: GottBERT: a pure German Language Model (2020). arXiv:2012.02110
9. Vaswani, A., et al.: Attention is all you need. In: Advances in Neural Information Processing Systems, vol. 30. Curran Associates, Inc. (2017)
10. Warner, B., et al.: Smarter, Better, Faster, Longer: A Modern Bidirectional Encoder for Fast, Memory Efficient, and Long Context Finetuning and Inference (2024). arXiv:2412.13663

Computational Intelligence

Accelerated VQE: Parameter Recycling for Similar Recurring Problem Instances

Tobias Rohe$^{(\boxtimes)}$ ⓘ, Maximilian Balthasar Mansky, Michael Kölle ⓘ,
Jonas Stein ⓘ, Leo Sünkel ⓘ, and Claudia Linnhoff-Popien ⓘ

Ludwig Maximilian University of Munich, Munich, Germany
tobias.rohe@ifi.lmu.de

Abstract. Training the Variational Quantum Eigensolver (VQE) is a
task that requires substantial compute. We propose the use of concepts
from transfer learning to considerably reduce the training time when
solving similar problem instances. We demonstrate that its utilization
leads to accelerated convergence and provides a similar quality of results
compared to circuits with parameters initialized around zero. Further,
transfer learning works better when the distance between the source-
solution is close to that of the target-solution. Based on these findings,
we present an accelerated VQE approach tested on the MaxCut problem
with a problem size of 12 nodes solved with two different circuits utilized. We compare our results against a random baseline and non transfer learning trained circuits. Our experiments demonstrate that transfer
learning can reduce training time by around 93% in post-training, relative to identical circuits without the use of transfer learning. The accelerated VQE approach beats the standard approach by seven, respectively
nine percentage points in terms of solution quality, if the early-stopping
is considered. In settings where time-to-solution or computational costs
are critical, this approach provides a significant advantage, having an
improved trade-off between training effort and solution quality.

Keywords: Quantum machine learning · Variational quantum
eigensolver · Quantum optimization · Warm-start · Transfer learning ·
Circuit parameter initialization

1 Introduction

Quantum computing (QC) has applications in chemical simulations [1], machine
learning [2], and optimization [3]. Despite hardware limitations [4], the quantum approximate optimization algorithm (QAOA) [5] and variational quantum
eigensolver (VQE) [6] are promising for noise resilience. While the QAOA is
often used for combinatorial optimization [7–9] and he VQE often for chemical
problems [10–13], also the VQE shows potential for combinatorial optimization (CO) problems [14–17], offering lower circuit depth beneficial in the NISQ
era [18]. Nevertheless, training VQE can be challenging due to issues like barren
plateaus [19].

ⓒ The Author(s), under exclusive license to Springer Nature Switzerland AG 2025
S. Zielinski et al. (Eds.): I4CS 2025, CCIS 2513, pp. 63–78, 2025.
https://doi.org/10.1007/978-3-031-94263-1_5

This paper explores using transfer learning (TL) with VQE for CO problems, a method yet to be investigated [20]. We focus on problems like the capacitated vehicle routing problem (CVRP) [21], which often demands for quick, efficient solutions for similar problem instances in logistics [22,23]. Our study assesses TL's effectiveness and the application of an accelerated VQE process, which reduces training time by 93% while maintaining high solution quality. This approach is advantageous where solutions need rapid, cost-effective resolution and problem instances are similar.

The paper is structured as follows. Section 2 (*Background*) outlines foundational concepts. Section 3 (*Methodology*) details our algorithms. Section 4 (*Results*) presents our findings. Section 5 (*Accelerated VQE*) explores the TL benefits for quick parameter training. Section 6 (*Discussion & Limitations*) examines the study's implications and limits. Section 7 (*Conclusion*) encapsulates the research's main points.

2   Background

2.1   MaxCut Problem

The maximum cut (MaxCut) problem asks for a binary partition of a graphs n vertices, such that the number of edges between the vertices of both partitions is maximized. Identifying the optimal partition for a general graph is NP-hard. We formally write the graph $G = (V, E)$ with n nodes $V = \{0, ..., n - 1\}$ and undirected edges $\{i, j\} \in E$. In our case, the graph is unweighted, each edge has the same weight of $w_{i,j} = 1$. The partitioning of the nodes into the two sets is encoded in binary as $z_i = 1$ for a node i being contained in the first set, respectively $z_i = -1$ for the second set. The corresponding cost function, representing the number of edges that are cut by the partition, is given by:

$$C(z) = \sum_{(i,j) \in E} \frac{1 - z_i z_j}{2} \tag{1}$$

This cost function evaluates the total number of edges that span between the two partitions, thus representing the MaxCut problem. In the following sections, we reformulate this maximization problem as an equivalent minimization problem to leverage specific optimization techniques.

2.2   Variational Quantum Eigensolver

The VQE is a hybrid quantum-classical algorithm, composed of both a classical and a quantum part, applied in a loop. It was first proposed by Peruzzo et al. [6] and is in broad usage since then [24–27]. The quantum part of the algorithm consists of a parameterized quantum circuit (PQC), also known as Ansatz, with parameters $\theta \in \mathbb{R}^m$, described by $f : \theta \mapsto U(\theta) |0\rangle^{\otimes n}$, preparing the quantum state $|\psi(\theta)\rangle := U(\theta) |0\rangle^{\otimes n}$. The prepared quantum state represents the expectation value of the problem Hamiltonian $\hat{H}$, where the problem Hamiltonian can be derived from the underlying problem's cost function. The ground state of the Hamiltonian then represents the optimal solution of the corresponding cost function. This is done by iteratively optimizing the gate parameters θ of the PQC with a classical optimizer in the classical part of the algorithm. The quantum-classical loop is closed after the optimized parameters are returned to the quantum part and the PQC is executed again. The algorithm's execution ends as soon as a predefined convergence criterion is reached, e.g. the expectation value changes are minimal, or the maximum number of loop iterations (`maxiter`) has been reached.

2.3 Transfer Learning in Quantum Computing

While TL is a well-established technique in classical machine learning [28], in quantum machine learning it is just emerging. TL involves the practice of applying pre-trained knowledge, corresponding parameters and weights, to a new, potentially related, task and/or dataset [29]. This approach allows training to commence at a higher accuracy level, leveraging the relevance of the transferred parameters to the problem class. Consequently, for an equivalent number of training steps, a higher accuracy is generally achievable [30].

In the context of QC and TL, an early contribution was made by Brandao et al. in 2018 [31], who explored the QAOA for the MaxCut problem on 3-regular graphs. Their research unveiled that QAOA parameters trained for a random instance also work well for related instances, sampled from the same underlying distribution. In practical terms, once optimal parameters are determined for one instance, these parameters also yield effective results for other similar instances, leading to a significant reduction in the computational overhead for subsequent instances as these pre-trained parameters can be re-used for another QAOA instance [31]. Furthermore, their work posits the feasibility of transferring parameters across problems of varying sizes, especially those requiring more extensive circuits. They call it "leapfrogging" method [31], where parameters optimized for smaller instances can be used as starting points for larger instances. This approach effectively sidesteps the exhaustive search for optimal parameters for every new, but similar problem instance.

Further researchers [32,33] have investigated the transferability of QAOA parameters for 3-regular graphs and broadly confirm the results of Brandao et al. [31]. They highlight the importance of similarity in the instances subgraph decomposition, therefore their local properties, as major factor for the successful application of parameter transfer. These findings are complemented by the work of Wurtz and Love [34], who provide worst case lower bound performance guarantees for uniform 3-regular graphs at particular fixed parameters for $p = 2$ and $p = 3$, as well as upper bounds for all p's. For this so-called fixed angle conjecture numerical evidence for $p < 12$ is provided here [35].

Beside these major contributions, other scientific papers have researched parameter transfer for QAOA, highlighting stable or even improved objective values while drastically reducing training times [36–39]. A dedicated framework

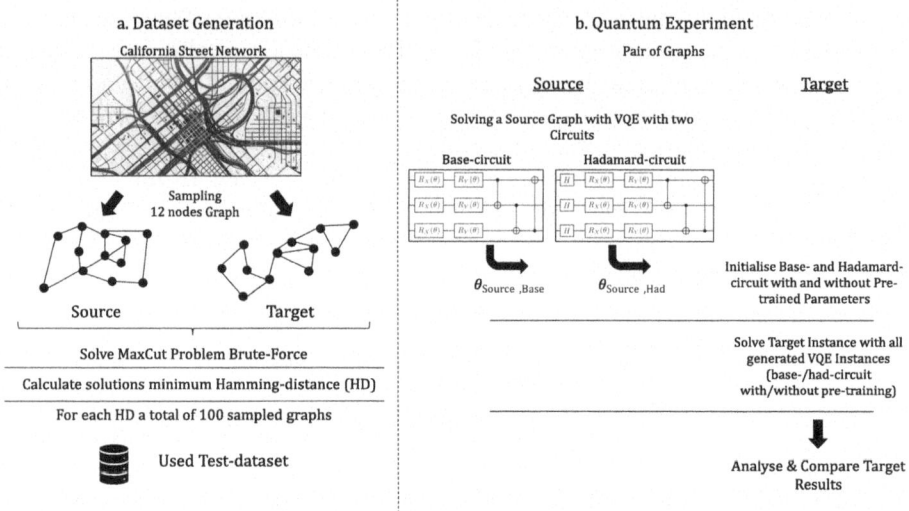

Fig. 1. Overview of the research methodology. Panel (a) on the left illustrates the dataset generation phase, panel (b) on the right depicts the algorithmic setup.

for evaluation is available, containing pre-optimized QAOA parameters and circuits for different instances [40]. Furthermore, pre-optimized QAOA parameters, initially trained on unweighted graphs, can be efficiently applied to weighted graphs upon appropriate rescaling [41].

TL has not been widely applied to VQE algorithms [42], however, the idea has been proposed before [36]. To the best of our knowledge only one paper specifically covers this area of research, while focusing on potential energy surface calculations for molecules [42]. The researchers aim at a faster convergence toward the ground state of the target molecule through initializing the VQE algorithm with the pre-calculated ground state of molecules with similar geometry. The results indicate speedup potential with regards to standard initialization, on condition that a suitable optimization algorithm was used.

A related concept is the so-called warm-starting technique, which also comes from the field of classical machine learning and optimization. Warm-starting uses approximated solutions for initialization to improve the performance of the algorithm used [20]. This is particularly attractive for problems where a good approximation can be efficiently obtained [43–46].

3   Methodology

In the following, we show the methodology, with focus on the dataset creation and the algorithmic setup applied. This is visualized in Fig. 1.

3.1   Dataset Generation

We generated a dataset for parameter pre-training and TL evaluation using the MaxCut problem on undirected, unweighted graphs derived from California's road network, which includes about 1.9 million nodes and 2.7 million edges. Our dataset construction involves sampling graph pairs—source and target—with each graph consisting of 12 nodes selected through a neighborhood expansion algorithm ensuring all nodes and edges are unique and connected.

For each graph pair, we identify optimal MaxCut solutions using brute-force, then calculate the smallest Hamming distance (HD) across all optimal pairings, including symmetrical solutions. HD, ranging from 0 to 6, measures the bit flips required to convert one graph's solution to another's, serving as a metric for solution distance. We sample 10 graph pairs for each HD value to ensure a balanced dataset, facilitating the evaluation of source-target graph distance impacts in our TL study.

3.2   Algorithmic Setup

For evaluation, we use two quantum circuits: the base-circuit and the had-circuit, each featuring rotational X-gates and Y-gates followed by a circular CNOT entanglement, differentiated by an initial layer of Hadamard gates in the had-circuit. Both circuits are illustrated in Fig. 2 and are repeated three times for 12 qubits, serving as a foundation for our proof of concept study, as these architectures can also often be found in literature [48–50].

$$
\begin{array}{llll}
|q_0\rangle & H & R_X(\boldsymbol{\theta_0})R_Y(\boldsymbol{\theta_3}) & 1 \\
|q_1\rangle & H & R_X(\boldsymbol{\theta_1})R_Y(\boldsymbol{\theta_4}) & 1 \\
|q_2\rangle & H & R_X(\boldsymbol{\theta_2})R_Y(\boldsymbol{\theta_5}) & -2
\end{array}
$$

Fig. 2. Schematic illustration of the base- and had-circuits. The Hadamard gates are only present in the had-circuit. For illustrative reasons we only print a three qubit circuit here, the expansion toward a 12 qubit circuit is straightforward. A measurement is carried out at the end of each circuit.

The training consists of two phases. In pre-training, two VQE instances (one with each circuit) are initialized with parameters near zero (range [−0.001, 0.001] [51]) and optimized using the COBYLA optimizer [52] with a maximum of 1000 iterations. The optimized parameters, θ_{pre}, are recorded for the source-graph. Post-training involves using these pre-optimized parameters to initialize the VQE on the target-graph. For comparison, we also train additional VQEs with parameters reinitialized around zero.

We tested our approach with ten different seeds, resulting in a dataset of 700 graph pairs across different HDs, conducted without noise to clearly assess the benefits of our methodology. An additional VQE test with parameters initialized randomly between 0 and 2π served as another baseline, with results detailed in

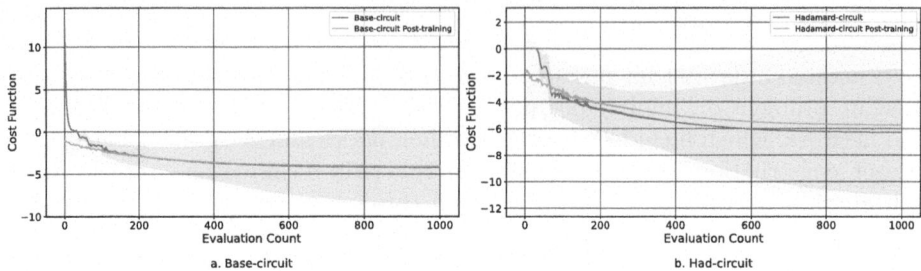

Fig. 3. Convergence of VQE implementations (`maxiter = 1000`). The figure compares the convergence of the (a) base-circuit and the (b) had-circuit, under two initial conditions: near-zero initialization (blue) and pre-trained parameters (orange), averaged over all HD. The variance is visualized as a shaded area. Lower values are better. (Color figure online)

Appendix A. This experiment highlights the drawbacks of non-pre-optimized initialization, as these showed significantly poorer performance, thus omitted from our main findings.

4   Results

In this section, we first analyze the convergence behavior, followed by the solution quality obtained through the various training variants. Finally, we will evaluate the performance based on the distance of the solutions from the source- to the target-graphs, measured as the minimum HD of optimal solutions.

4.1   Convergence Behavior

Throughout the execution, we record the convergence behavior of the different VQE versions, illustrated in Fig. 3. The base-circuit with standard initialization (blue) and the base-circuit with pre-optimized parameter initialization (orange) is depicted in sub-figure a., while the corresponding data for the had-circuit and its two initialization variants is presented in sub-figure b.

Observing Fig. 3(a), we notice that the TL approach curve begins at a significantly lower level compared to the classical initialization approach. The TL version converges more gradually. Moreover, the convergence threshold is observed to be lower in the classical initialization version, wherein its variance is marginally larger.

We interpret this observation as follows: Through the TL, the VQE already represents a state near an optimum of an unknown graph. When this pre-trained instance is applied to a new graph, we can expect that the VQE converges faster since the transferred parameters are closer to a solution of the problem. Rather than starting from scratch, a favorable starting position has already been established, in general, only minor adjustments need to be made to the new solution. Overall, the convergence behavior is relatively similar.

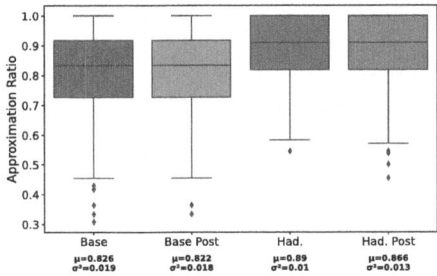

Fig. 4. Approximation ratios of VQE implementations (`maxiter = 1000`). This figure displays the approximation ratios for all four versions of the VQE tested. High values indicate better solution quality, with the best achievable ratio being one.

In Fig. 3(b), which displays the results for the Hadamard-enhanced circuit, we also note a lower starting point for convergence, a more gradual convergence behavior, and a higher convergence limit for the TL approach. Here too, the variance is found to be lower for the standard training. Interestingly, while the TL approach starts at approximately the same energy level as the base-circuit without a ladder of Hadamard-gates, the convergence curve for the standard learning approach, initialized with gate-parameters around zero, begins significantly lower compared to the base-circuit execution. We explain this by the fact that the Hadamard-gates create a superposition of all nodes, effectively simulating each node's presence in both partitions simultaneously. In contrast, the basic circuit's initialization around zero begins as if all nodes were in a single group, yielding the worst possible outcome, zero cuts in the graph. Similar to the base circuit described above, the other observed characteristics – a more gradual convergence, increased variance, and higher convergence level for the TL approach – are also present here.

4.2 Solution Quality

We display the solution quality of the two different circuit-types with the two distinct training approaches in Fig. 4. The boxplot diagram illustrates the average approximation ratios of the various executed VQE instances. The mean values and variances are shown beneath the corresponding boxplots. Two observations can be made. First, the had-circuit outperforms the base-circuit, achieving a higher approximation ratio as well as exhibiting a lower variance in the observations. This becomes particularly clear when the performance of the two circuit types is compared on the graph-level individually. Here, the had-circuit performs better than the base-circuit in 52.3% and 47.7% of all graphs in classical training and post-training respectively. While the had-circuit only provides worse approximation ratios than the base-circuit in 24.9% and 28.7% of all solved graphs. Second, the performance of the two training variants, when compared to each other within the same circuit, is relatively comparable. Although the classical training method slightly performs better then the TL approach, this advantage

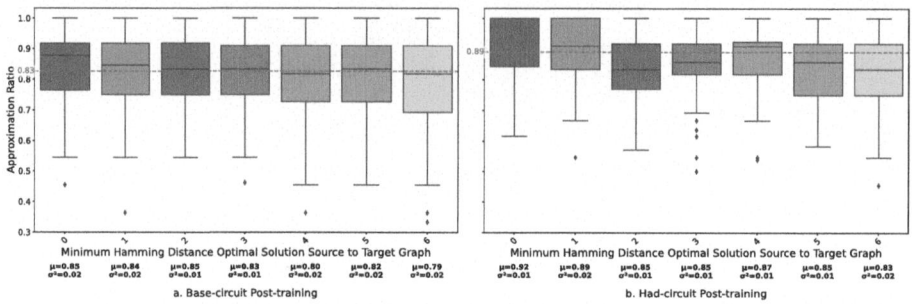

Fig. 5. Approximation ratios of the post-trained VQE instances with regards to the solutions HD (`maxiter = 1000`). The figure illustrates the performance of the post-trained VQE instances ((a) base-circuit, (b) had-circuit) with regards to the minimum HD of the optimal solutions of the underlying source-target graph pairs. High values indicate a better solution quality, with the best achievable ratio being one.

is marginal and therefore insignificant. It cannot be concluded that there is a significant difference in performance between the two circuit initialization variants, leading us to consider the quality of the results as comparable.

4.3   Solution Distance Dependent Analysis

In our study, we assess the impact of the HD between the optimal solutions of source and target graphs on the effectiveness of the TL approach in VQE settings. Our analysis, depicted in Fig. 5, illustrates the approximation ratios for circuits trained with pre-optimized parameters based on the minimum HD between optimal solutions. The data shows that TL-enhanced circuits generally outperform standard initialization for smaller HDs (HD zero to three), indicating a clearer trend in improved performance for closely related graph instances.

For TL applications, smaller HDs correlate with better performance metrics, such as faster convergence and higher solution quality, suggesting that TL is particularly advantageous for problems with similar or closely related instances. These findings, detailed further in Appendix B, underscore the efficiency of the TL approach in achieving rapid convergence and maintaining high solution quality in instances where source and target graphs are similar.

It is critical to note that the HD values were computed based on optimal solutions of the graphs rather than the outcomes of the pre-trained instances, highlighting the strategic application of TL where initial conditions closely mimic optimal solutions, thereby enhancing the overall efficacy of the VQE process. This detailed examination substantiates the TL method's applicability to quantum computing scenarios involving repetitive or similar problem instances, advocating for its broader application in quantum optimizations.

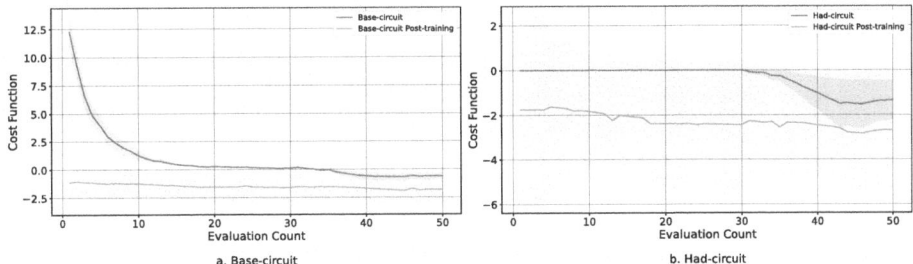

Fig. 6. Convergence of the accelerated VQE implementations (`maxiter` = 50). The figure compares the convergence of the base-circuit (left) and the had-circuit (right), under two initial conditions: near-zero initialization (blue) and pre-trained parameter initialization (orange). Here, the `maxiter` variable was set to 50 iterations. The variance is visualized as a shaded area. Lower values are better. (Color figure online)

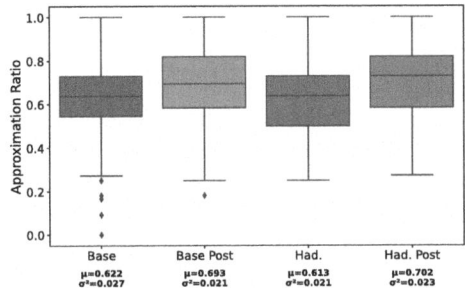

Fig. 7. Approximation ratios of the accelerated VQE implementations (`maxiter` = 50). This figure displays the approximation ratios for all four versions of the accelerated VQE setup tested. High values indicate better solution quality, with the best achievable ratio being one.

5 Accelerated VQE

We have observed rapid convergence behavior in the early training phase of the TL approach, as well as improved approximation ratios for problem instances closely related to those used in training. This has prompted the development of an accelerated training for the VQE, which is not a novel algorithm per se, but rather a specialized application example. The frequency at which problem instances occur can be relatively high, potentially preventing practitioners from conducting extensive optimizations due to the need for solutions in a brief timeframe. For the accelerated VQE we have limited the `maxiter` parameter of the algorithm for all types to 50 iterations (previously 1000), amounting to a reduction of 95% of the training time. With a reduction to 50, the algorithm shows signs that the parameters are being changed, but complete convergence is not possible. However, the parameters on the source-graph, which are subsequently reused, get still trained by a maximum of 1000 iterations.

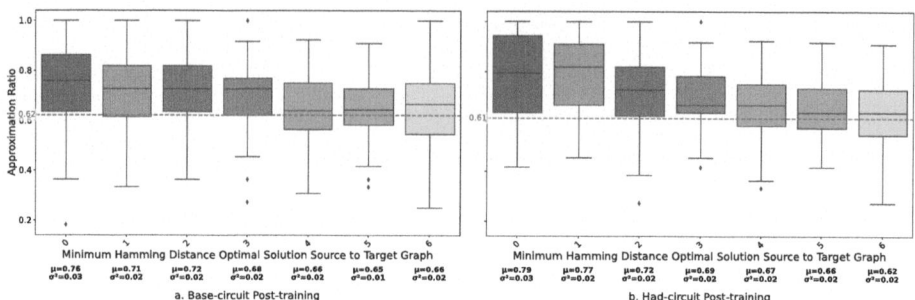

Fig. 8. Approximation ratios of the post-trained accelerated VQE instances with regards to the solutions HD (`maxiter = 50`). The figure illustrates the performance of the post-trained accelerated VQE instances (base-circuit left, had-circuit right) with regards to the minimum HD of the optimal solutions of the underlying source-target graph pairs. High values indicate better solution quality, with the best achievable ratio being one.

Examining the convergence behavior of the executed algorithms in Fig. 6, we do not observe the typical behavior where the algorithm is trained to full convergence. For the base circuit, the TL approach begins at a significantly lower level than the standard initialization approach and converges in a gradual manner, indicating that further convergence could be expected if not through the parameter setup restricted. The base-circuit with classical parameter initialization, exhibits a typical convergence behavior throughout, although the rate of convergence significantly slows in the latter half of the plot. Shifting focus to the right graph, where the had-circuit is depicted, a less stable convergence process is observed. Here again, the expected pattern emerges, with the TL approach starting at a lower level and converging gradually. The classical initialization approach remains stable until the 30th evaluation, after which it rapidly changes. Both graphs suggest a lower energy level for the TL approach, which we will investigate further in the approximation ratios obtained.

To better evaluate the results and relative performance, it is also necessary to consider the corresponding approximation ratios, shown in Fig. 7. Contrary to previous results, we now observe superior approximation ratios for the TL approach for both circuits. The TL approach achieves an around seven to nine percentage points higher approximation ratio compared to the standard initialization approach. Across all 700 instances solved, in an instance by instance comparison, the TL approach outperforms the classical training variant in 55.8% of all instances, achieves comparable results in 15.6%, and under-performs in 28.6% of all instances (for the had-circuit 58.1%, 16.1% and 25.7% respectively). However, this outcome is tempered by the fact that the approximation levels, compared to the `maxiter = 1000` configuration, are significantly lower. The base-circuit loses around 20.4 percentage points, and the had-circuit around 27.7 percentage points, compared to full convergence. The reason our post-trained circuits now perform relatively better is due to the comparatively smaller loss in approximation quality of approximately 12.9 and 16.4 percentage points in the approximation ratio, respectively.

Finally, we also analyze in detail the development of solution quality relative to the distance between the optimal solutions of the source- and target-graph (see Fig. 8). Once again, the data is illustrated in the same manner as before. This time, the average approximation for the classically initialized base-circuits was 0.62, and for the had-circuit, it was 0.61. For both circuits, across every HD in optimal solutions, higher average approximation ratios are achieved with our TL approach. Here too, we observe the trend of decreasing solution quality with increasing distance in the optimal solution partitions of the source- and target-graph, further substantiating our results.

6 Discussion and Limitations

6.1 Transfer Learning in General

Our research demonstrates that initializing VQE parameters with pre-optimized values accelerates early optimization phases and achieves comparable solution quality upon full convergence. Analyzing the distance between optimal solutions of source and target graphs, we found that it is proximity significantly impacts training success, corroborating findings by Galda et al. [33]. Close initial parameters enhance solution quality and convergence, confirming the applicability of TL to VQE and combinatorial optimization. However, the extent to which retraining affects the parameters and solution quality post-initialization remains unclear. We identify this as an area for future research to better understand and improve TL techniques. Additionally, expanding this research to weighted MaxCut problems and other combinatorial challenges could further validate the robustness of the TL approach, as suggested by Sureshbabu et al. [41].

6.2 Accelerated VQE

In our accelerated VQE approach, we apply principles from TL research, notably using the rapid early-phase convergence by setting a reduced `maxiter` parameter, which limits full convergence but starts near the optimal solution. Despite initial doubts about its practicality, the accelerated VQE offers substantial benefits: it reduces circuit evaluations by 93%, significantly lowering resource use, a figure derived from our experiments. This reduction does not achieve the 95% reduction in `maxiter` due to early termination upon meeting convergence criteria.

While there is a noticeable decline in solution quality due to fewer iterations, we interpret this as a favorable trade-off between computational effort and solution quality, especially compared to standard initialization methods. This trade-off offers considerable time and cost savings, making it viable for scenarios needing rapid solutions like last-mile delivery. We believe further enhancements in this trade-off can make our method even more appealing.

Extensive parameter optimization on the source-graph (`maxiter = 1000`) is justified when reusing parameters, suggesting potential cost-effectiveness in repeated applications or evolving problem instances. However, our study does not thoroughly examine scalability due to the limited problem sizes tested, and the gap between source and target graphs remains a concern, as it may lead to suboptimal local minima.

Additionally, our data hint at the potential for defining universal parameter initialization for various graph structures. Early results, indicate that TL-initialized circuits start at a lower convergence point, offering an inherent advantage in final approximation ratios. This suggests that pre-training might establish a generally favorable state for similar graphs, proposing a robust starting point for diverse problems. This hypothesis needs validation across broader applications to confirm its efficacy.

7   Conclusion

We investigated the technique of TL for the VQE algorithm applied to the well-studied MaxCut problem. We have shown that TL also works for this particular combinatorial optimization problem, as convergence behavior and solution quality are comparable. Additionally, we have shown that the distance between source and target graphs' optimal solutions, representing the distance to overcome from the starting point of parameter initialization to the new solution, plays a significant role in the success of the approach execution. A closer optimal solution thereby leads, in general, to better solutions. We have developed the accelerated VQE approach and are able to stop parameter optimization after only 50 iterations, effectively reducing the resource consumption after necessary pre-training by around 93%. Compared to traditional parameter initialization, the solution quality of the pre-trained parameter initialization is seven, respectively nine percentage points higher, giving the TL approach a clear advantage. The proposed technique is particularly suited for problem instances which recur in a similar manner. Also, for use cases where a good solution must be reached quickly and/or inexpensively, this approach might be suitable, thus covering many relevant practical applications. Future research should now investigate the solution adaptation between source and target solutions of the TL approach as well as the scaling characteristics of such a technique with respect to the size of the graph and the variability between these graphs.

Acknowledgments. This paper was partially funded by the German Federal Ministry of Education and Research through the funding program "quantum technologies – from basic research to market" (contract number: 13N16196). J.S. acknowledges support from the German Federal Ministry for Economic Affairs and Climate Action through the funding program "Quantum Computing – Applications for the industry" based on the allowance "Development of digital technologies" (contract number: 01MQ22008A).

Appendix A: Random VQE Initialisation

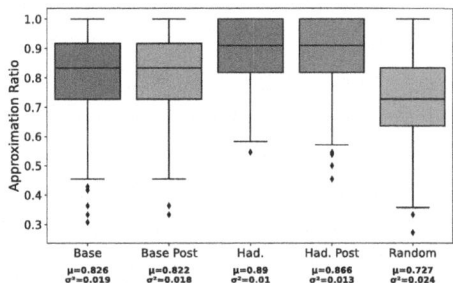

Fig. 9. Approximation Ratios of VQE Implementations with Random Initialised Instance (`maxiter = 1000`). This figure displays the approximation ratios for all four main-versions of the VQE tested. Additionally, a random initialised VQE instance was included. High values indicate better solution quality, with the maximum achievable ratio being one.

We have also introduced a version with randomly initialised gate parameters. The objective was to control for the effect of gates being initialised with values not close to zero. The circuit employed is the base-circuit, as hadamard-gates are not required in this configuration, given that gates are already rotated through random initialisation. We observed significantly inferior results, manifested in a lower average approximation ratio and increased variance in these values. This suggests that a random initialisation does not offer any benefits. Further investigation of this setup was not pursued here.

Appendix B: Convergence Behaviour with Regards to HD

We further assessed the impact of the minimum HD between the source- and target-graphs' optimal partitions on the convergence behaviour. For the sake of clarity, variances have not been presented here. We observe that with increasing HD values, the convergence regarding all three evaluation metrics deteriorates. Specifically, convergence begins at higher values, its slope is flatter, and it reaches a higher level at convergence (indicating poorer performance). The same applies for the had-circuit (not shown here).

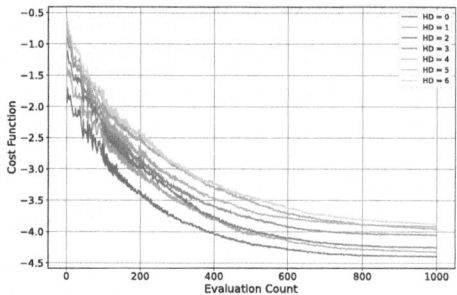

Fig. 10. Convergence of the Base-VQE Implementation depending on HD (`maxiter = 1000`). The figure shows the convergence of the base-circuit as a function of the minimum HD between the source- and target-graphs. Lower values are better.

References

1. Kassal, I., Whitfield, J., Perdomo-Ortiz, A., Yung, M., Aspuru-Guzik, A.: Simulating chemistry using quantum computers. Annu. Rev. Phys. Chem. **62**, 185–207 (2011)
2. Schuld, M., Sinayskiy, I., Petruccione, F.: An introduction to quantum machine learning. Contemp. Phys. **56**, 172–185 (2015)
3. Moll, N., et al.: Others Quantum optimization using variational algorithms on near-term quantum devices. Quantum Sci. Technol. **3**, 030503 (2018)
4. Lubinski, T., et al.: Application-oriented performance benchmarks for quantum computing. IEEE Trans. Quantum Eng. (2023)
5. Farhi, E., Goldstone, J., Gutmann, S.: A quantum approximate optimization algorithm. arXiv Preprint arXiv:1411.4028 (2014)
6. Peruzzo, A., et al.: A variational eigenvalue solver on a photonic quantum processor. Nat. Commun. **5**, 4213 (2014)
7. Khairy, S., Shaydulin, R., Cincio, L., Alexeev, Y., Balaprakash, P.: Learning to optimize variational quantum circuits to solve combinatorial problems. In: Proceedings of the AAAI Conference On Artificial Intelligence, vol. 34, pp. 2367–2375 (2020)
8. Blekos, K., et al.: A review on quantum approximate optimization algorithm and its variants. Phys. Rep. **1068**, 1–66 (2024)
9. Cheng, L., Chen, Y., Zhang, S., Zhang, S.: Quantum approximate optimization via learning-based adaptive optimization. Commun. Phys. **7**, 83 (2024)
10. Lee, J., Huggins, W., Head-Gordon, M., Whaley, K.: Generalized unitary coupled cluster wave functions for quantum computation. J. Chem. Theory Comput. **15**, 311–324 (2018)
11. Grimsley, H., Economou, S., Barnes, E., Mayhall, N.: An adaptive variational algorithm for exact molecular simulations on a quantum computer. Nat. Commun. **10**, 3007 (2019)
12. Blunt, N., et al.: Perspective on the current state-of-the-art of quantum computing for drug discovery applications. J. Chem. Theory Comput. **18**, 7001–7023 (2022)
13. Fedorov, D., Peng, B., Govind, N., Alexeev, Y.: VQE method: a short survey and recent developments. Mater. Theory **6**, 2 (2022)

14. Amaro, D., Modica, C., Rosenkranz, M., Fiorentini, M., Benedetti, M., Lubasch, M.: Filtering variational quantum algorithms for combinatorial optimization. Quantum Sci. Technol. **7**, 015021 (2022)
15. Kolotouros, I., Wallden, P.: Evolving objective function for improved variational quantum optimization. Phys. Rev. Res. **4**, 023225 (2022)
16. Niroula, P., et al.: Constrained quantum optimization for extractive summarization on a trapped-ion quantum computer. Sci. Rep. **12**, 17171 (2022)
17. Liu, X., Angone, A., Shaydulin, R., Safro, I., Alexeev, Y., Cincio, L.: Layer VQE: a variational approach for combinatorial optimization on noisy quantum computers. IEEE Trans. Quantum Eng. **3**, 1–20 (2022)
18. Preskill, J.: Quantum computing in the NISQ era and beyond. Quantum **2**, 79 (2018)
19. Liu, X., Liu, G., Zhang, H., Huang, J., Wang, X.: Mitigating barren plateaus of variational quantum eigensolvers. IEEE Trans. Quantum Eng. (2024)
20. Truger, F., et al.: Warm-Starting and Quantum Computing: A Systematic Mapping Study. arXiv Preprint arXiv:2303.06133 (2023)
21. Ralphs, T., Kopman, L., Pulleyblank, W., Trotter, L.: On the capacitated vehicle routing problem. Math. Program. **94**, 343–359 (2003)
22. Gonzalez-Feliu, J. Models and methods for the city logistics: the two-echelon capacitated vehicle routing problem. (Politecnico di Torino, 2008)
23. Fukasawa, R., et al.: Robust branch-and-cut-and-price for the capacitated vehicle routing problem. Math. Program. **106**, 491–511 (2006). https://doi.org/10.1007/s10107-005-0644-x
24. Cerezo, M., Sharma, K., Arrasmith, A., Coles, P.: Variational quantum state eigensolver. NPJ Quantum Inf. **8**, 113 (2022)
25. Tilly, J., et al.: The variational quantum eigensolver: a review of methods and best practices. Phys. Rep. **986**, 1–128 (2022)
26. Kandala, A., et al.: Hardware-efficient variational quantum eigensolver for small molecules and quantum magnets. Nature **549**, 242–246 (2017)
27. Wang, D., Higgott, O., Brierley, S.: Accelerated variational quantum eigensolver. Phys. Rev. Lett. **122**, 140504 (2019)
28. Zhuang, F., et al.: A comprehensive survey on transfer learning. Proc. IEEE **109**, 43–76 (2020)
29. Mari, A., Bromley, T., Izaac, J., Schuld, M., Killoran, N.: Transfer learning in hybrid classical-quantum neural networks. Quantum **4**, 340 (2020)
30. Torrey, L., Shavlik, J.: Transfer learning. In: Handbook of Research on Machine Learning Applications and Trends: Algorithms, Methods, and Techniques, pp. 242–264 (2010)
31. Brandao, F., Broughton, M., Farhi, E., Gutmann, S., Neven, H.: For fixed control parameters the quantum approximate optimization algorithm's objective function value concentrates for typical instances. arXiv Preprint arXiv:1812.04170 (2018)
32. Galda, A., Liu, X., Lykov, D., Alexeev, Y., Safro, I.: Transferability of optimal QAOA parameters between random graphs. In: 2021 IEEE International Conference on Quantum Computing and Engineering (QCE), pp. 171–180 (2021)
33. Galda, A., et al.: Similarity-based parameter transferability in the quantum approximate optimization algorithm. Front. Quantum Sci. Technol. **2**, 1200975 (2023)
34. Wurtz, J., Love, P.: MaxCut quantum approximate optimization algorithm performance guarantees for p> 1. Phys. Rev. A **103**, 042612 (2021)
35. Wurtz, J., Lykov, D.: The fixed angle conjecture for QAOA on regular MaxCut graphs. arXiv Preprint arXiv:2107.00677 (2021)

36. Shaydulin, R., Safro, I., Larson, J.: Multistart methods for quantum approximate optimization. In: 2019 IEEE High Performance Extreme Computing Conference (HPEC), pp. 1–8 (2019)
37. Shaydulin, R., Lotshaw, P., Larson, J., Ostrowski, J., Humble, T.: Parameter transfer for quantum approximate optimization of weighted maxcut. ACM Trans. Quantum Comput. **4**, 1–15 (2023)
38. Liu, H., Sun, T., Wu, Y., Han, Y., Guo, G.: Mitigating barren plateaus with transfer-learning-inspired parameter initializations. New J. Phys. **25**, 013039 (2023)
39. Montanez-Barrera, J., Willsch, D., Michielsen, K.: Transfer learning of optimal QAOA parameters in combinatorial optimization. arXiv Preprint arXiv:2402.05549 (2024)
40. Shaydulin, R., Marwaha, K., Wurtz, J., Lotshaw, P.: QAOAKit: a toolkit for reproducible study, application, and verification of the QAOA. In: 2021 IEEE/ACM Second International Workshop on Quantum Computing Software (QCS), pp. 64–71 (2021)
41. Sureshbabu, S., et al.: Parameter setting in quantum approximate optimization of weighted problems. Quantum **8**, 1231 (2024)
42. Skogh, M., Leinonen, O., Lolur, P., Rahm, M.: Accelerating variational quantum eigensolver convergence using parameter transfer. Electron. Struct. **5**, 035002 (2023)
43. Egger, D., Mareček, J., Woerner, S.: Warm-starting quantum optimization. Quantum **5**, 479 (2021)
44. Okada, K., Nishi, H., Kosugi, T., Matsushita, Y.: Systematic study on the dependence of the warm-start quantum approximate optimization algorithm on approximate solutions. Sci. Rep. **14**, 1167 (2024)
45. Tao, Z., Wu, J., Xia, Q., Li, Q.: Laws: look around and warm-start natural gradient descent for quantum neural networks. In: 2023 IEEE International Conference On Quantum Software (QSW), pp. 76–82 (2023)
46. Jain, N., Coyle, B., Kashefi, E., Kumar, N.: Graph neural network initialisation of quantum approximate optimisation. Quantum **6**, 861 (2022)
47. Leskovec, J., Lang, K., Dasgupta, A., Mahoney, M.: Community structure in large networks: Natural cluster sizes and the absence of large well-defined clusters. Internet Math. **6**, 29–123 (2009)
48. Ravi, G., et al.: Vaqem: a variational approach to quantum error mitigation. In: 2022 IEEE International Symposium on High-Performance Computer Architecture (HPCA), pp. 288–303 (2022)
49. Gocho, S., et al.: Excited state calculations using variational quantum eigensolver with spin-restricted ansätze and automatically-adjusted constraints. NPJ Comput. Mater. **9**, 13 (2023)
50. Ravi, G., et al.: CAFQA: a classical simulation bootstrap for variational quantum algorithms. In: Proceedings of the 28th ACM International Conference on Architectural Support for Programming Languages and Operating Systems, vol. 1, pp. 15–29 (2022)
51. McClean, J., Boixo, S., Smelyanskiy, V., Babbush, R., Neven, H.: Barren plateaus in quantum neural network training landscapes. Nat. Commun. **9**, 4812 (2018)
52. Powell, M.: A direct search optimization method that models the objective and constraint functions by linear interpolation. Springer (1994)

Fair Benchmarking Combinatorial Optimization Solvers in the Era of Emerging Computing Paradigms

Frank Phillipson[✉]

Maastricht University, Maastricht, The Netherlands TNO,
The Hague, The Netherlands
f.phillipson@maastrichtuniversity.nl

Abstract. As computational needs expand, new computing paradigms such as GPUs, FPGAs, high-performance computing clusters, digital annealers, neuromorphic computing systems, and quantum computers are emerging to complement traditional CPU-based computing models. Each paradigm offers unique capabilities for combinatorial optimization, a field concerned with finding the best solution from a finite set of possibilities. This paper addresses the challenge of fairly benchmarking the performance of combinatorial optimization solvers across these diverse paradigms. We propose a holistic approach to benchmarking that includes recommendations for fair comparisons and the introduction of new metrics. Our findings highlight the need for clear and equitable comparison criteria, particularly when contrasting digital and analogue platforms or different algorithm classes.

Keywords: Combinatorial optimization · Benchmarking · Emerging computing paradigms · Meta-heuristics · Algorithm comparison

1 Introduction

As computational needs expand, new paradigms are emerging to complement the traditional CPU-based computing model [10]. These paradigms include reconfigurable chips such as GPUs and FPGAs, high-performance computing clusters, digital annealers, neuromorphic computing systems, and (digital and analogue) quantum computers. Each offers unique capabilities that make them suitable for specific applications, including combinatorial optimization, a field concerned with finding the best solution from a finite set of possibilities.

Computing paradigms are evolving rapidly, moving beyond the limits of traditional CPU-based systems. Reconfigurable chips, such as GPUs and FPGAs, are designed to handle specialized tasks like matrix computations or machine learning efficiently [28]. High-performance computing clusters use thousands of those processors working in parallel to tackle large-scale problems, pushing parallelism to its limits [25]. Digital annealers [16] simulate quantum annealing processes but operate classically, optimizing problems with a focus on combinatorial challenges. Neuromorphic systems [1] mimic the human brains neural structure, enabling them to process information in a highly parallel and energy-efficient manner, achieving remarkable efficiency in tasks like pattern recognition and decision-making. Finally, quantum computers [9] leverage principles of quantum mechanics, such as superposition and entanglement, to explore solution spaces that are impractical for classical systems. Each paradigm can be categorized as digital or analogue. Analogue and digital computing paradigms represent two distinct approaches to processing information. Analogue computing relies on continuous data, using physical phenomena such as electrical voltage, mechanical motion, or hydraulic pressure to represent and solve problems. It is especially suited for tasks involving natural systems, like modeling weather or fluid dynamics, where precision is approximated. In contrast, digital computing processes discrete data, encoding information in binary (0 s and 1 s) and employing logic-based operations to perform calculations. While systems like GPUs, FPGAs, and HPC clusters are fundamentally digital, neuromorphic systems and quantum computers blur the lines between digital and analogue. These distinctions influence how these systems solve problems, the type of problems they are best suited for, and the way that we can assess their performance.

Combinatorial optimization is a field that seeks the best solution from a finite set of possibilities, often under constraints. These problems are pervasive in both theoretical and practical settings [20]. For example, the Traveling Salesman Problem involves finding the shortest route for visiting a set of cities and returning to the starting point. This type of problem exemplifies the challenges of combinatorial optimization: the solution space grows factorially with the number of cities, making brute-force methods impractical for even moderately sized instances. This hardness makes it so that in practice we are more interested in a good solution quickly than in the best possible solution that would take a lot of time. What 'good' and 'quickly' mean is to be decided by the decision maker in practice. Solving these problems is crucial across various domains, from logistics to network design.

Each of the new computing paradigms offers distinct advantages for tackling combinatorial optimization problems, but their diversity raises an important question: how do we fairly compare their performance? There the area of benchmarking comes into sight. Benchmarking refers to the process of evaluating and comparing the performance of different solvers or algorithms on a standardized set of problems. It is a critical practice for assessing solver efficiency, scalability, and effectiveness across various problem instances and domains. Existing benchmarking methods often favor traditional (computer) architectures, failing to account for the unique characteristics of emerging paradigms. This situation calls for a re-evaluation of how we measure performance to ensure that comparisons are equitable and informative.

The goal of this paper is to address the challenge of fairly benchmarking the performance of combinatorial optimization solvers in the context of the rise of emerging computing paradigms, such as GPUs, FPGAs, high-performance computing clusters, digital annealers, neuromorphic systems, and quantum computers. The paper aims to add to a comprehensive evaluation framework that accounts for the unique characteristics and capabilities of these diverse systems, ensuring that comparisons are equitable and informative. The potential novelty of this work lies in its holistic approach to benchmarking, which includes recommendations for fair comparisons, the introduction of new metrics, and the consideration of end-to-end workflows.

In Sect. 2, we first give a deeper introduction on the computing paradigms. Then, in Sect. 3, the topic of benchmarking is introduced, where the current state of the art and the challenges are presented. In Sect. 4, recommendations can be found for making fair comparisons, the main content of this work. Section 5 gives some conclusions.

2 Computing Paradigms

This section delves into the various emerging computing paradigms that are transforming the landscape of combinatorial optimization and provides an in-depth exploration of configurable chips, neuromorphic computers, digital anneal-ers, and quantum computing. Each section highlights the unique capabilities and applications of these paradigms, illustrating how they differ from traditional CPU-based systems. By understanding these technologies, we can better appreciate their potential to solve complex optimization problems more efficiently and effectively. This chapter sets the stage for a comprehensive discussion on benchmarking these diverse systems, ensuring fair and informative comparisons.

2.1 Configurable Chips

Configurable chips [2,28] are chips whose functionality can be adjusted after manufacturing. GPUs (Graphical Processing Units) and FPGAs (Field Programmable Gate Arrays) are two examples of such chips. GPUs were originally developed for graphics processing, but their ability to perform parallel computations has made them suitable for tasks like deep learning. FPGAs offer fine-grained programmability, allowing users to tailor computational pathways to the demands of specific algorithms. They are used in a wide range of fields, including data streaming, wireless communication, cryptography, network security, multi-media, medical research, bioinformatics, consumer electronics, the automotive industry, and military applications. The reconfigurability of FPGAs enables updates and reuse of hardware designs after deployment and provides advantages over ASICs (Application-Specific Integrated Circuits) in terms of cost, performance, and energy efficiency.

2.2 High-Performance Computing

High-Performance Computing (HPC) clusters represent a powerful computing paradigm designed to tackle large-scale and complex computational problems [6].

These clusters consist of thousands of interconnected processors working in parallel to perform massive computations efficiently. HPC systems are particularly well-suited for tasks that require significant computational power and memory, such as simulations, data analysis, and scientific research.

One of the primary strengths of HPC systems is their scalability. As computational demands grow, additional processors can be integrated into the cluster, allowing the system to handle larger and more complex problems. HPC clusters are designed to achieve high throughput, processing vast amounts of data quickly and efficiently. This capability is crucial for applications in fields such as climate modeling, genomics, and financial modeling. HPC systems often incorporate specialized hardware, such as GPUs and FPGAs, to accelerate specific types of computations. These components enhance the overall performance and versatility of the cluster.

2.3   Neuromorphic Computers

Neuromorphic computing is a type of computer science inspired by the structure and functioning of the brain [7,12,23]. Its goal is to create systems capable of processing information in a manner similar to the efficient, parallel, and adaptive ways the brain operates.

Unlike traditional computers that use digital logic, neuromorphic computers rely on small, distributed computing units analogous to neurons. These neurons are connected in networks and can form new connections or strengthen or weaken existing ones-a process known as synaptic plasticity. This plasticity is crucial for learning and adaptation in neuromorphic systems. The analogue nature of neuromorphic systems makes them much more energy-efficient than traditional digital computers, particularly for tasks like pattern recognition and signal processing. Neuromorphic systems can perform many computations simultaneously, much like the brain, which makes them ideal for real-time applications such as robotics and sensory processing. Furthermore, they can adapt to changing conditions and learn new information through synaptic plasticity.

Neuromorphic computers can be built in several ways. Analogue CMOS circuits mimic the electrical properties of neurons and synapses, with examples including Stanford's Neurogrid and Heidelberg's BrainScaleS. Digital systems use digital logic to simulate neuron and synapse models, as seen in IBM's TrueNorth and Manchester's SpiNNaker. Emerging memory technologies, such as memristors and phase-change memory, enable the creation of artificial synapses capable of altering their conductivity, resembling biological synapses.

Neuromorphic computing has the potential to revolutionize various fields. In artificial intelligence, neuromorphic systems can lead to more efficient, adaptive, and robust technologies. In robotics, they can enable robots to learn from their environment and perform more complex tasks. For sensory processing, these systems can develop efficient and robust sensors for applications like image and speech recognition. Additionally, neuromorphic systems can serve as platforms for better understanding the brain and developing treatments for neurological disorders.

2.4 Digital Annealers

Digital annealing [13,16,18] is a heuristic algorithm inspired by the process of simulated annealing and implemented using digital circuits such as CMOS and FPGAs. Unlike quantum annealing, which leverages quantum effects and is explained in the next section, digital annealing is a fully classical approach. Digital annealers are manufactured using the same fabrication processes as traditional digital circuits, with a focus on creating specialized hardware that efficiently executes the steps of the simulated annealing algorithm.

This approach harnesses the high precision of digital computations while also benefiting from the parallelization capabilities inherent in specialized hardware. Digital annealing can be applied to a wide range of combinatorial optimization problems, including machine learning tasks such as clustering, regression, and classification, as well as challenges in planning, logistics, and finance.

Digital annealers are closely connected to Ising machines because both are designed to solve combinatorial optimization problems. Ising machines in general are specialized hardware or software specifically built to find the ground state of an Ising model.

Advantages of digital annealers over other machines:

– High Precision: Digital annealers benefit from the high precision of digital computations, leading to more accurate solutions.
– Scalability: Digital annealers can be scaled to larger problem sizes relatively easily by adding more digital circuits.
– Connectivity: Digital annealers often support full connectivity between spins, which is advantageous for solving complex problems.

Although digital annealers do not offer the potential speedup advantages of quantum annealers, these benefits make them a promising technology for tackling complex optimization problems.

2.5 Quantum Computing

Quantum computing [9,22,24] is a new computing paradigm that uses the principles of quantum mechanics to perform calculations. Unlike classical computers, which process information as bits (0 or 1), quantum computers use qubits. Qubits can exist in a superposition of states, meaning they can be both 0 and 1 simultaneously. This property, combined with quantum entanglement-where qubits share properties even when physically separated-allows quantum computers to perform certain calculations much faster than classical computers.

There are two main types of quantum computing: digital or gate-based quantum computers (GBCs) and analogue quantum computers, such as quantum annealers (QAs). GBCs operate similarly to current-generation computers, performing operations on specific qubits or multiple qubits simultaneously, enabling programmability. QAs, on the other hand, are single-purpose machines designed to find the minimum value of a specific function encoded in the qubits.

The fabrication of quantum computers is a complex process requiring advanced technology. Qubits can be created using various technologies, such as superconducting circuits, trapped ions, and photonic qubits. The manufacturing process requires extremely low temperatures and precise control to minimize decoherence, a phenomenon where qubits lose their quantum properties.

Quantum computing has a wide range of potential applications, including solving complex optimization problems such as those in logistics and supply chain management, transport network design, and flight route optimization. It can also simulate chemical processes with unprecedented accuracy, which could lead to the development of new materials and drugs. Additionally, it has the potential to enhance machine learning by accelerating algorithms for tasks like clustering, classification, and regression. Furthermore, quantum computing could break modern cryptography using algorithms like Shor's algorithm. Although quantum computing is still in its infancy, it is a promising technology with the potential to revolutionize various industries.

3   Benchmarking

This section provides an overview of the evolving landscape of benchmarking for computational systems, particularly in the context of emerging paradigms. The section begins by exploring the foundations of benchmarking, including the use of standard problem sets and performance metrics like time complexity, solution quality, and wall-clock time. It highlights the limitations of classical benchmarks in capturing the unique capabilities and workflows of new paradigms. Additionally, it examines the challenges in creating fair and transparent benchmarks, emphasizing the importance of reproducibility, end-to-end evaluations, and avoiding misleading practices.

Drawing on recent literature, we identify common pitfalls in current practices and show the proposed solutions. These include focusing on comprehensive workflow evaluations, developing metrics tailored to specific paradigms, and ensuring clarity and transparency in reporting results. Emerging efforts, such as the TAQOS protocol, demonstrate how the field is moving toward more nuanced and robust benchmarking approaches.

3.1   Introduction

Currently, benchmarking for computing systems, including solvers for combinatorial optimization, is primarily designed for traditional digital systems like CPUs and GPUs and is based on classical complexity theory. These benchmarks aim to evaluate algorithm performance or hardware capabilities, but they often fall short when applied to newer paradigms like analogue quantum or neuromorphic computing. When discussing 'time' in computational contexts, especially within complexity theory, it generally refers to the number of computational steps or operations required to solve a problem. This measure, known as time complexity, is abstracted from real-world wall-clock time to focus on the intrinsic computational effort required by an algorithm. Time complexity is measured as the number of fundamental operations (e.g., additions, comparisons, logic gates) an algorithm performs as a function of the input size n, noted as $\mathcal{O}(n), \mathcal{O}(n^2)$, etc. It provides a platform-agnostic way to compare algorithms, independent of specific hardware, implementation details, or system configurations. Assumptions here are that each operation takes a constant amount of 'abstract time' and that parallel or quantum operations may count as a single step if they are simultaneous. The number of steps is determined to come to a (worst-case) formal guarantee of solution quality.

In practice, benchmarks for algorithms focus on solving well-known problems, such as the Traveling Salesman Problem or the Knapsack Problem. Researchers use standard problem sets to ensure comparability. Performance is measured based on metrics like how good the solution is compared to the best-known result, how long it takes to compute (in Wall-Clock time), and how well the algorithm handles larger or more complex problems. These benchmarks emphasize reproducibility by using widely available datasets and algorithms.

Hardware benchmarking, on the other hand, focuses on evaluating the capabilities of the computational systems themselves. This often involves testing how fast a machine can perform certain operations, like matrix multiplications for GPUs or linear algebra for supercomputers. Standard benchmark suites, like LINPACK [5] for supercomputers or SPEC [11] for CPUs, measure raw performance in terms of operations per second or energy efficiency. For newer paradigms specialized metrics are emerging, for example, Quantum Volume [4] is used to evaluate quantum computers, considering factors like qubit coherence and connectivity.

When systems combine traditional and emerging paradigms, such as quantum-classical hybrids, benchmarks often evaluate the entire workflow. For example, in quantum computing, benchmarks might include the time, here Wall-Clock time, taken to prepare the problem on a classical system, compute on a quantum device, and then interpret the results back on the classical system. These end-to-end evaluations are critical for understanding the practical performance of such hybrid systems. An example for this is the Q-Score [15,26], that gives the size of a specific problem, such as MaxCut and MaxClique, that a hardware platform can solve up to some minimal solution quality. An other example is Qoptlib [19], a benchmark designed for quantum computing in combinatorial optimization, featuring 40 instances across four well-known problems: Traveling Salesman Problem, Vehicle Routing Problem, one-dimensional Bin Packing Problem, and Maximum Cut Problem.

3.2 Considerations

Current benchmarking practices face several challenges. They rely heavily on classical (CPU) computing metrics, which are not always relevant to new paradigms. For example, quantum and neuromorphic systems operate on fundamentally different principles, making direct comparisons often unfair. Additionally, many benchmarks evaluate isolated aspects of performance, like raw computational power, without considering how well the system integrates into real-world workflows. Another limitation is the reliance on fixed problem sets, which may not reflect the complexity or variability of real-world applications.

Recent work of McGeoch [17] discusses the reporting of specifically quantum computer performance and how to do so in a fair and accurate manner. It argues that lessons can be learned from earlier discussions on benchmarking in classical computers, particularly David Bailey's "Twelve Ways to Fool the Masses" from 1991 [3]. Based on this, McGeoch proposes four principles to avoid misleading the public when reporting quantum computer performance.

- Principle 1: Do not claim superior performance without specifying runtimes. This is important because quantum heuristics often involve trade-offs between solution quality and computation time. Without runtime information, it is impossible to determine whether superior performance is due to efficiency or simply more computation time.
- Principle 2: Do not report optimized results without disclosing the tuning time required to achieve them. Fair tests require that all solvers receive equal tuning effort or that tuning time is included in the total computation time. Otherwise, reported performance may be an artifact of the chosen test parameters.
- Principle 3: Do not claim faster runtimes for (or compared to) solvers running on hypothetical platforms. Extrapolating runtimes measured on small, existing platforms to large, future platforms is risky, especially since the effects of technological improvements on future quantum hardware cannot be predicted.
- Principle 4: Avoid selective input choices (without justification and qualification). Selecting inputs that consistently favor one solver over another is a pitfall in competitive benchmarks. While selective input choices are not always avoidable, authors should justify their test designs and clearly qualify the scope of their conclusions.

The article provides examples of studies that violate these principles and argues that such practices, even if not intentionally misleading, can lead to mistrust and potentially cause a 'quantum winter'. The author offers suggestions to improve communication between researchers and the general public, including the use of clear language, defining performance metrics, and acknowledging the limitations of results.

3.3 Solution Direction in Literature

Efforts are underway to address these issues. For example, quantum computing researchers are developing benchmarks that evaluate entire workflows rather than just the quantum hardware itself [14]. Neuromorphic systems [27] are being benchmarked for energy efficiency and responsiveness in real-time decision-making tasks, reflecting their unique capabilities. There is also a growing emphasis on end-to-end benchmarks that include all aspects of the computational process, from data preparation to final output, to provide a more complete picture of system performance. An example is the work of [8], that introduces the TAQOS benchmarking protocol, a method for comparing the performance of quantum algorithms, such as Adiabatic Quantum Optimization (AQO) and the Quantum Approximate Optimization Algorithm (QAOA), with classical algorithms. The protocol is designed to provide a fair and robust analysis of quantum systems' performance, emphasizing the need for transparency and accuracy in benchmarking studies. The authors highlight that determining quantum advantage is a complex task and that current benchmarking protocols fall short in terms of problem diversity and their reliance on a single metric to measure solution quality. TAQOS addresses these shortcomings by defining a set of four key metrics:

1. Solution quality: Measured by the ratio between the cost of the best solution found by the quantum computer and a reference cost (e.g., the best-known solution).
2. Time to solution (wall clock time): Includes the entire processing time, from problem formulation to solution extraction, encompassing both classical and quantum processing steps.
3. Energy consumption: While not fully quantified at present, it is a crucial factor for future analyses.
4. Instance set coverage: Evaluates the robustness of the quantum heuristic by analyzing its performance across various types of problem instances.

We can conclude that, while traditional benchmarks have been effective for classical systems, these benchmarks are often inadequate for emerging computing paradigms. New approaches are being developed to provide fairer and more comprehensive evaluations, but fully addressing the diversity of these systems remains an ongoing challenge.

4   New Pathway for Making Fair Comparisons

We think that the direction shown in Sect. 3 is promising; however, there is still room for improvement. When comparing the performance of algorithms across computing paradigms for combinatorial optimization, it is essential to consider the diversity of algorithm classes in this area and their characteristics. We will distinguish four classes [21]:

- Exact Algorithms: These algorithms guarantee finding the optimal solution to a problem by exhaustively exploring all possible solutions. Examples include branch and bound, dynamic programming, and integer programming. They are often computationally expensive and may not be feasible for large-scale problems.
- Approximation Algorithms: These algorithms provide solutions that are close to the optimal, with a guarantee on the quality of the solution (e.g., within a certain factor of the optimal solution). They are particularly useful for NP-hard problems where finding the exact solution is computationally infeasible. Examples include the greedy algorithm for the Set Cover Problem and the Christofides algorithm for the TSP.

- Meta-Heuristics: These are high-level strategies designed to guide other (problem-specific) heuristics to explore the solution space efficiently. They do not guarantee optimal solutions but often find good solutions within reasonable time frames. Examples include genetic algorithms, simulated annealing, tabu search, and ant colony optimization.
- Problem-Specific Algorithms: These algorithms are tailored to exploit the specific structure and properties of a particular problem. They are designed to be highly efficient for the problem at hand but may not be applicable to other problems. Examples include the Dijkstra algorithm for Shortest Path Problems and the Ford-Fulkerson algorithm for Maximum Flow Problems.

Exact algorithms, for example using commercial solvers like CPLEX, Gurobi, LocalSolver/Hexaly and others, guarantee optimal solutions but are often computationally expensive. Approximation algorithms trade off solution quality for efficiency, providing near-optimal results within theoretical bounds. Meta-heuristics, such as genetic algorithms or simulated annealing, offer flexible, problem-agnostic approaches but lack guarantees of optimality. Problem-specific algorithms leverage unique insights into the problem structure to achieve superior performance within a narrow scope. An overview of multiple criteria is given in Table 1.

Theoretical metrics like solution quality, complexity, and preparation (tuning) time are commonly used to evaluate algorithms. However, practical considerations often complicate these evaluations. For instance, real-world data may be incomplete or noisy, necessitating preprocessing. The frequency of solving similar problems can influence the importance of parameter tuning and model reusability. Additionally, the practical usability of a system depends on how much interaction is required from experts or end-users.

Both the work by McGeoch [17] and the work by Gilbert et al. [8] emphasize that wall clock times are important and that for a fair comparison a broader time definition than only running time is needed. McGeoch's 'principle 2' asks for disclosing of the tuning time and Gilbert et al. propose to take the total time for the workflow, including hyperparameter tuning and reduction time to formulate the problem in the required formulation. In their case the latter means the QUBO, quadratic unconstrained binary optimization, problem formulation, which is common for quantum annealing and QAOA approaches.

This is a good first step. Wall clock times will be important when comparing digital to analogue platforms, as operations are harder to define in an analogue world. However, it is recommended to keep the comparison within the algorithms classes or to be clear on, for example, the design time and implementation effort, partly depending on the commercial availability, how easy can you purchase it or download it from an (open source) database, and on the price. It might be fair to compare quantum annealing with simulated annealing or genetic algorithms, as they all fall within the same algorithm type (meta-heuristics) and often regular implementations are available within Python packages. However, the comparison

Table 1. Comparison of algorithm types across various characteristics

Aspect	Exact Algorithms	Approximation Algorithms	Meta-heuristics	Problem-Specific Heuristics
Solution Quality	Optimal (guaranteed)	Near-optimal, with provable bounds	High-quality (not guaranteed, depends on tuning)	High-quality for specific problem instances
Design Time	High: complex to design and prove correctness or Low: incase of standard solvers	Moderate: requires theoretical analysis for bounds	Moderate: general frameworks like GA, SA, PSO	High: tailored to specific problems
Tuning Time	None or Minimal	Minimal: typically no tuning needed	High: requires parameter optimization (e.g., cooling schedules, population sizes)	None or Minimal: this is part of the design time
Running Time	High: exponential or polynomial for simple cases	Moderate: depends on problem and approximation ratio	Low to Moderate: varies widely based on problem size and complexity	Low: efficient due to problem-specific optimizations
Scalability	Poor for large problem sizes	Moderate to Good, depending on approximation ratio	Good: designed for large, complex problems	Good: if problem characteristics dont change
Robustness	High: applicable to all instances of the problem	High: applies broadly but within defined bounds	Moderate: depends on tuning for robustness	Low to Moderate: performance highly instance-specific
Implementation	Difficult: requires deep problem understanding or Easy: in case of standard solvers	Moderate: needs theoretical insight for guarantees	Moderate to easy: general-purpose methods available	Moderate to easy: straightforward for well-understood problems
Availability of the solution	Several commercial optimization solvers available	None - Few	Hardly offered as stand-alone tools - some platforms and libraries offer meta-heuristic implementations	None
Key Strength	Guarantees optimality	Balances solution quality with efficiency	Flexible for various problems	Highly efficient for specific cases
Key Weakness	Computationally expensive for large instances	May not achieve optimality	Requires significant tuning, lacks guarantees	Limited generalizability to other problem types

between quantum annealing and the state of the art problem-specific heuristic might not be fair when the implementation by the user of this algorithm is not taken into account and this algorithm is not available for direct use.

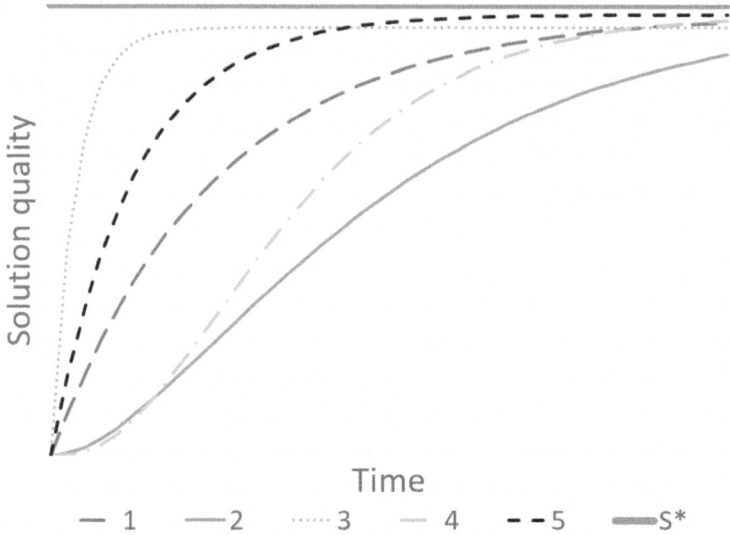

Fig. 1. TS paths for various algorithms (Color figure online)

Another consideration is the availability of intermediate results and the total, so called, Time-Solution quality (TS) path [21]. Some paradigms allow inspection of intermediate states, which can provide valuable insights into the computational process. In Fig. 1, for a number of (fictional) heuristics the course over time through the solution space, so called Time-Solution quality (TS) paths, are shown. The best solution would yield the value indicated by the green line (S^*). This value is usually unknown. All other colors are various different heuristics or heuristic-hardware combinations. The difference between black (5) and yellow (4) is obvious: black gives much faster, much better solutions, although they eventually converge to the same solution, which is not the optimal solution. Gray (3) initially performs even better, but converges to a worse solution. One question now might be, which of these heuristics is preferable. Blue (1) and Orange (2) seem clear losers and Black seems to be preferable to Yellow. The difference between Gray and Black is more subtle and depends, for example, on the time scale on the horizontal axis. If the point where black and gray intersect is after a few seconds or minutes, then Black is probably preferable. If this intersection takes much time to occur, then Gray might be better. You may also wonder whether you can combine Gray and Black.

Of course, these TS-paths hold for a heuristic for specific input (x) and parameters (θ). It is interesting whether the course of the paths for the different input (x, θ) deviates strongly. Interesting for researchers with a more theoretical slant is to prove that a specific heuristic never deviates more than a certain fraction (α) from the best possible answer.

5   Summary and Conclusion

In this article, we explored the evolving landscape of computing paradigms, in particular what that means for benchmarking solution approaches for combinatorial optimization problems. Emerging technologies such as GPUs, HPC clusters, digital annealers, neuromorphic systems, and quantum computers each offer unique advantages and challenges. Traditional benchmarking methods, primarily designed for classical systems, often fall short when applied to algorithms using these new paradigms. Therefore, there is a pressing need for more comprehensive and fair benchmarking practices that consider the diverse capabilities and characteristics of these systems.

To address these challenges, it is essential to develop comprehensive benchmarks that evaluate the entire computational workflow, from algorithm implementation and data preparation to final output. This approach will provide a more accurate representation of system performance. Additionally, incorporating real-world scenarios using problem sets that reflect the complexity and variability of real-world applications will ensure that benchmarks are relevant and practical. Considering energy efficiency by including metrics for energy consumption, especially for neuromorphic and quantum systems, is also crucial, as these systems are known for their energy-efficient operations. Promoting transparency by ensuring that all aspects of the benchmarking process, including tuning times and intermediate results, are transparently reported will help in making fair comparisons across different paradigms. Encouraging collaboration between researchers from different fields to develop standardized benchmarking protocols that can be widely adopted is another important recommendation.

Further research should investigate the performance of hybrid systems that combine traditional and emerging paradigms. Understanding how these systems can complement each other will be crucial for future advancements. Developing benchmarks tailored to specific types of algorithms, such as meta-heuristics or problem-specific heuristics, will provide more nuanced insights into their performance. Conducting studies on the scalability of emerging paradigms, particularly for large-scale combinatorial optimization problems, will help identify the limitations and potential of these technologies. Additionally, further research is needed to quantify the energy consumption of different paradigms accurately, which will be essential for evaluating their sustainability and efficiency. Finally, exploring the applicability of emerging paradigms in real-time decision-making scenarios, such as robotics and sensory processing, will help understand their practical usability.

References

1. Abdallah, A.B., Dang, K.N.: Neuromorphic Computing Principles and Organization. Springer, Cham (2022)
2. Babu, P., Parthasarathy, E.: Reconfigurable FPGA architectures: a survey and applications. J. Inst. Eng. (India): Ser. B **102**, 143–156 (2021)

3. Bailey, D.H.: Twelve ways to fool the masses when giving performance results on parallel computers. Supercomput. Rev. 54–55 (1991)
4. Cross, A.W., Bishop, L.S., Sheldon, S., Nation, P.D., Gambetta, J.M.: Validating quantum computers using randomized model circuits. Phys. Rev. A **100**(3), 032328 (2019)
5. Dongarra, J.J., Luszczek, P., Petitet, A.: The linpack benchmark: past, present and future. Concurrency Comput. Pract. Experience **15**(9), 803–820 (2003)
6. Dongarra, J.J., van der Steen, A.J.: High-performance computing systems: status and outlook. Acta Numer **21**, 379–474 (2012)
7. Furber, S.: Large-scale neuromorphic computing systems. J. Neural Eng. **13**(5), 051001 (2016)
8. Gilbert, V., Louise, S., Sirdey, R.: TAQOS: a benchmark protocol for quantum optimization systems. In: International Conference on Computational Science, pp. 168–176. Springer (2023)
9. Gill, S.S., et al.: Quantum computing: a taxonomy, systematic review and future directions. Softw. Pract. Experience **52**(1), 66–114 (2022)
10. Gill, S.S., et al.: Modern computing: vision and challenges. Telematics Inform. Rep. 100116 (2024)
11. Henning, J.L.: Spec cpu2000: measuring CPU performance in the new millennium. Computer **33**(7), 28–35 (2000)
12. Indiveri, G.: Introducing 'neuromorphic computing and engineering'. Neuromorphic Comput. Eng. **1**(1), 010401 (2021)
13. Komatsu, K., Onoda, M., Kumagai, M., Kobayashi, H.: Investigating the characteristics of ising machines. In: 2023 IEEE International Conference on Quantum Computing and Engineering (QCE), vol. 1, pp. 939–948. IEEE (2023)
14. Lubinski, T., et al.: Quantum algorithm exploration using application-oriented performance benchmarks. arXiv preprint arXiv:2402.08985 (2024)
15. Martiel, S., Ayral, T., Allouche, C.: Benchmarking quantum coprocessors in an application-centric, hardware-agnostic, and scalable way. IEEE Trans. Quantum Eng. **2**, 1–11 (2021)
16. Matsubara, S., et al.: Digital annealer for high-speed solving of combinatorial optimization problems and its applications. In: 2020 25th Asia and South Pacific Design Automation Conference (ASP-DAC), pp. 667–672. IEEE (2020)
17. McGeoch, C.: How not to fool the masses when giving performance results for quantum computers. arXiv preprint arXiv:2411.08860 (2024)
18. Mohseni, N., McMahon, P.L., Byrnes, T.: Ising machines as hardware solvers of combinatorial optimization problems. Nat. Rev. Phys. **4**(6), 363–379 (2022)
19. Osaba, E., Villar-Rodriguez, E.: Qoptlib: a quantum computing oriented benchmark for combinatorial optimization problems. In: Benchmarks and Hybrid Algorithms in Optimization and Applications, pp. 49–63. Springer (2023)
20. Papadimitriou, C.H., Steiglitz, K.: Combinatorial Optimization: Algorithms and Complexity. Courier Corporation (1998)
21. Phillipson, F.: Searching for optimisation (2022)
22. Phillipson, F.: Quantum computing in logistics and supply chain management-an overview. arXiv preprint arXiv:2402.17520 (2024)
23. Rajendran, B., Alibart, F.: Neuromorphic computing based on emerging memory technologies. IEEE J. Emerg. Sel. Top. Circ. Syst. **6**(2), 198–211 (2016)
24. Rawat, M., Mahajan, J., Jain, P., Banerjee, A., Oza, C., Saxena, A.: Quantum computing: navigating the technological landscape for future advancements. In: 2024 International Conference on Trends in Quantum Computing and Emerging Business Technologies, pp. 1–5. IEEE (2024)

25. Robey, R., Zamora, Y.: Parallel and high performance computing. Simon and Schuster (2021)
26. Van der Schoot, W., Wezeman, R., Neumann, N.M., Phillipson, F., Kooij, R.: Q-score max-clique: the first quantum metric evaluation on multiple computational paradigms. arXiv preprint arXiv:2302.00639 (2023)
27. Vogginger, B., et al.: Neuromorphic hardware for sustainable AI data centers. arXiv preprint arXiv:2402.02521 (2024)
28. Wei, S., Lin, X., Tu, F., Wang, Y., Liu, L., Yin, S.: Reconfigurability, why it matters in AI tasks processing: a survey of reconfigurable AI chips. IEEE Trans. Circuits Syst. I Regul. Pap. **70**(3), 1228–1241 (2022)

Artificial Intelligence Application Scenarios Considering Objective and Subjective Influence Factors for Industrial Solutions in Supply Chain Management

Karl-Heinz Lüke[1]([✉]), Gerald Eichler[2] [iD], and Denis Royer[1]

[1] Ostfalia University of Applied Sciences, Siegfried-Ehlers-Str. 1, 38440 Wolfsburg, Germany
{ka.lueke,d.royer}@ostfalia.de
[2] Technology and Innovation, Deutsche Telekom AG, Deutsche-Telekom-Allee 9, 64295 Darmstadt, Germany
gerald.eichler@telekom.de

Abstract. The use and significance of Artificial Intelligence (AI) are widely discussed across various fields, including business and science. AI, a key branch of computer science, enables algorithms to perform tasks that traditionally require human intelligence, such as machine learning, deep learning, and decision-making. AI applications span numerous industries, with Supply Chain Management (SCM) being a particularly relevant domain. AI technologies optimize supply chains by improving inventory planning, demand forecasting, and overall operational efficiency. This includes the planning, management, and control of goods, information, and financial flows along the entire supply chain. An empirical survey of AI use cases in SCM highlights demand forecasting, supply chain traceability and quality management, and inventory management as the most widely accepted and impactful applications.

Keywords: Artificial intelligence · AI governance · Supply chain management · Social influence · Machine and deep learning · UTAUT analysis

1 Motivation and Current Discussion

"Artificial intelligence can become an incredible ally if we join forces to make it a factor of social and economic progress, reconciling productivity and wellbeing at work, to benefit all workers.", emphasized Sana de Courcelles, summit envoy for the future of work at the **Artificial Intelligence (AI) Action Summit** in Paris, February 10 – 11, 2025. Massive investments in research and development on the one hand side and big data centers in all parts of the world on the other, make AI an unpredictable technical, economic, ethical, and political force of the future. It has the potential and risk to challenge a remarkable paradigm shift in our worldwide societies, in how we relate to production and work, knowledge and information, as well as language and culture.

S. Zielinski et al. (Eds.): I4CS 2025, CCIS 2513, pp. 94–112, 2025.
https://doi.org/10.1007/978-3-031-94263-1_7

By appointing thematic envoys to its team, the AI Action Summit spotlighted five key areas of action:[1]

- **Public interest AI:** inequity, actors, and opportunities.
- **Future of work:** labor markets, jobs, and working methods.
- **Innovation and culture:** organizations, sovereignty, and sustainability.
- **Trust in AI:** science, open solutions, and standards.
- **International governance:** worldwide inclusiveness, stakeholders, and partners.

AI presents a multi-dimensional, multi-party challenge, covering scientific, economic, social, governmental and lately high-level political aspects. While AI does not possess individual subjectivity, its responses are nonetheless an extract of human perspective, represented through code and data, reflecting human thought, reverberating within the parameters set by its implemented and trained model.

AI applications are already essential in industrial production and logistics. These include the optimization of the Human Machine Interface (HMI) and predictive maintenance. These applications optimize processes in companies and thus contribute to greater process efficiency [1, 2]. Advances in AI technology and the extraction of knowledge from vast amounts of data are playing a key role in the development of autonomous driving [3].

2   AI Characteristics and Driving Factors

2.1   History of Artificial Intelligence

The term *Artificial Intelligence* was first introduced by John McCarthy during a workshop at Dartmouth College, New Hampshire, in 1955. A fundamental prerequisite for AI is the ability to make everything measurable – commonly referred to as digitalization. Like many technological trends, AI follows cyclical waves of roughly twenty years, marked by periods of enthusiasm and stagnation. Several key domains have influenced perceptions and led to the development of new methods (see Table 1).

In contrast, so-called AI winters refer to periods of reduced funding and waning interest in AI research, such as those between 1974–1980 and 1987–2000 [4]. High-performance computing (HPC) is the trigger for the current developments .

The latest phase of the digital revolution brings governments and governance closer together than ever before, as they seek to manage the accelerating pace of everyday life as well as complex, multi-party trade and industrial processes – characteristic features of integrated Supply Chain Management (SCM). The following literature sources establish a strong connection to production, Industry 4.0, and SCM [1, 2, 5, 6].

Since around 2020, a growing number of scientific publications have focused primarily on the technical aspects of AI, such as machine learning and deep learning [7–11], see Subsect. 3.3.

Recent surveys on AI can be found in the Statista dossiers. In particular, the following surveys should be mentioned [12, 13]. For 2025, a market size of about 222 billion Euro (+31%) is predicted world-wide [14].

---

[1] URL: https://www.elysee.fr/en/sommet-pour-l-action-sur-l-ia/team, accessed February 2025.

Table 1. An AI timeline: characteristics of bi-decades

Decades	Era/epoch	Driving area	Methods	Outcome/usable results
1940/50s	Birth	Curiosity	Math reasoning	Programable computers
1960/70s	Maturation	Medicine	Early deep learning	Algorithms/insights
1980/90s	Boom	Economics	Expert systems	Databases/repositories
2000/10s	Agents	Research	Machine learning	Taxonomies/ontologies
2020s ff	Analytics	Politics	Large models	LLM/generative AI

2.2 A Multi-factor AI Framework

With powerful data centers now available, AI can process a significantly larger number of input parameters in parallel, as required by complex use cases. Human requests are increasingly enriched with environmental data collected by sensor networks, contextual information in space and time, and guided by carefully designed policies and established data-sharing agreements.

These interaction interfaces act as AI controllers, responsible for the system's parametrization. Through AI, the traditional Human-Machine Interface (HMI) is divided into Human-Computer Interfaces (HCI) and Machine-Computer Interfaces (MCI).

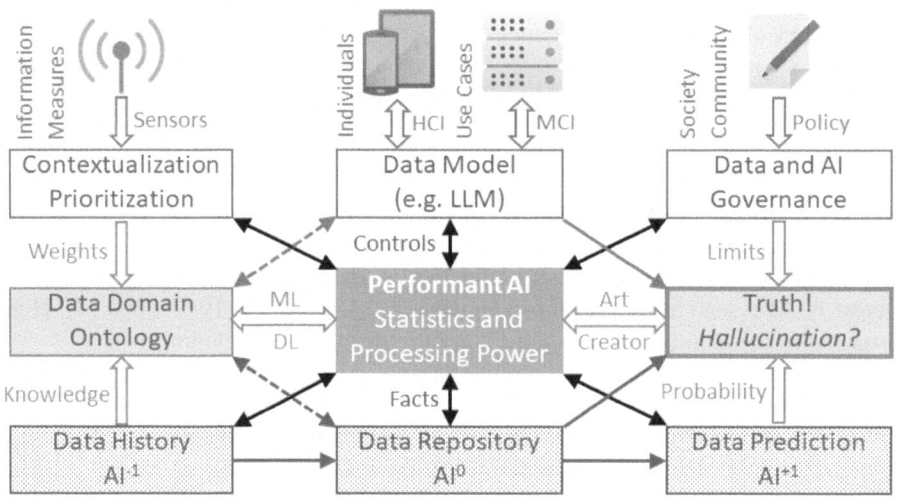

Fig. 1. Interactive enhanced AI framework

Domain knowledge can be organized as a taxonomy when it follows a hierarchical structure. More complex relationships, however, are better represented through an ontology graph, as successfully applied in recommendation services [15].

Effective interaction in AI requires even more: a rich underlying model. This may take the form of a textual model – such as a Large Language Model (LLM) for human communication – a visual model for image recognition and generation, or a feature-based model for audio analysis and composition.

In several cases, a value chain is created by a timeline, having access to a rated history (AI^{-1}). Based on the current data (AI^{0}), high probably future predictions (AI^{+1}) can be derived, as depicted in Fig. 1.

AI is generally expected to always produce a result. Based on extensive training data, learning methods – see Subsects. 3.3 and 3.4 – are applied to continuously improve the underlying data model. In the absence of sufficient or consistent information, however, AI systems may generate artificial content, a phenomenon known as *hallucination*.

Creative outputs, such as those desired in art, fashion, or culture, may be seen as occupying a space somewhere in between factual accuracy and imaginative generation.

The automotive industry, by contrast, relies on clearly defined processes in supply, production, and delivery, which are subject to continuous optimization. The application of innovation management practices is unlocking a new level of AI method exploitation [16].

3   Supply Chain Management Demand for AI Technologies

3.1   Fundamentals of Supply Chain Management

SCM refers to the integrated and process-oriented planning and control of the flow of goods, information and money along the entire value and supply chain, see Fig. 2.

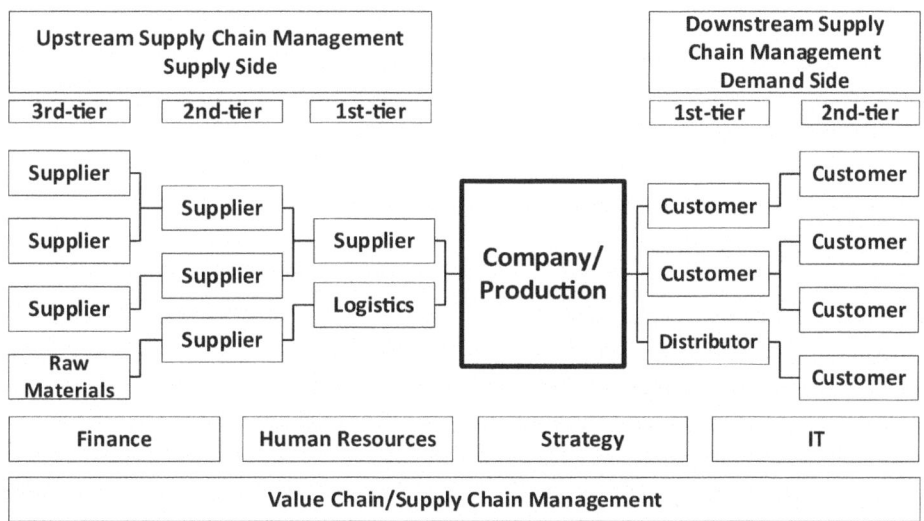

Fig. 2. Supply chain management and value chain [6]

SCM is a management approach concerned with the design, optimization, and control of comprehensive logistics chains. Material and information flows extend from the extraction of raw materials to the delivery of goods to the end customer and encompass all value-creating processes within a company. The overarching goal is to capture and optimize processes across all companies involved along the value chain.

Although the term *Supply Chain Management* is often used synonymously with logistics, it goes far beyond that. SCM plans and controls the value chain across organizational boundaries, with a strong focus on processes. A comprehensive analysis of supplier relationships is essential to ensure the efficient organization and control of goods, cash, and information flows [6, 17].

A frequently observed phenomenon within supply chains is the so-called *bullwhip effect*. This describes a fluctuating demand that becomes increasingly pronounced the further one moves away from the end customer. Various terms for this effect can be found in the scientific literature, including *demand amplification, variance amplification,* and the *Forrester effect*. While this seemingly irrational ordering behavior among supply chain partners has long been known, it has only been studied in greater depth since the late 1990s. A lack of communication and transparency has been identified as a behavioral cause of the bullwhip effect. In the event of supply shortages at the supplier level, the likelihood of repeated orders increases, as ordering entities often lack the necessary information to correctly assess actual product availability. This can result in unexpectedly high follow-up deliveries once the supplier is again able to fulfil orders [18].

Application scenarios play a particularly important role in SCM. AI technologies are being used, for example, to optimize the entire supply chain through improved inventory planning and demand forecasting. This includes the planning, coordination, and control of goods, information, and financial flows along the entire supply chain [5, 6].

The potential of Artificial Intelligence, the resulting business models, and the established processes that may be affected are currently the subject of intensive discussion in both academic and practical contexts [19]. Advances in machine learning and deep learning algorithms are opening up entirely new possibilities – many of which were previously unattainable with earlier technologies [11].

3.2 Fundamentals, Definition and Key Concepts of AI

AI has emerged as a transformative technology in various industries, including SCM. It enables computers to perform tasks that typically require human intelligence, such as pattern recognition, decision-making, and problem-solving. The core of AI in SCM lies in its ability to process vast amounts of data and generate insights that optimize processes like demand forecasting, inventory management, and logistics planning [6, 20].

AI encompasses a range of technologies, including Machine Learning (ML), Deep Learning (DL), and Natural Language Processing (NLP). These technologies allow AI systems to learn from historical data, recognize patterns, and improve decision-making capabilities without explicit programming [11].

AI is primarily focused on **Narrow AI (Weak AI)**, which is designed for specific tasks such as optimizing transportation routes or predicting demand. This contrasts with **General AI (Strong AI)**, which aims to mimic human cognitive abilities comprehensively but remains largely theoretical [21].

3.3 Machine Learning in SCM

ML is a subset of AI that enables systems to automatically learn and improve from experience. ML models analyze historical data to uncover trends and make predictions, reducing human intervention in decision-making processes [8].

Types of ML and potential applications are [8, 22]:

- **Supervised Learning:** The algorithm is trained using labeled datasets, where input-output pairs help the system learn relationships. Example: Demand forecasting models trained on past sales data [23].
- **Unsupervised Learning:** The algorithm identifies patterns in data without predefined labels. Example: Clustering algorithms to segment suppliers based on reliability and cost efficiency [24].
- **Reinforcement Learning**: The system learns by interacting with its environment and receiving feedback. Example: AI-powered warehouse robots optimizing picking and packing strategies based on efficiency rewards [20].

The following applications can successful be exploited in SCM:

- **Demand Forecasting:** ML models analyze market trends, customer preferences, and seasonal variations to predict demand more accurately [6].
- **Inventory Optimization:** AI-driven inventory systems suggest optimal stock levels by considering procurement costs, production constraints, and storage limits [5].
- **Route Optimization:** AI-powered logistics platforms optimize transportation routes based on real-time traffic, weather conditions, and delivery deadlines [20].

3.4 Deep Learning and Its Role in SCM

DL is a specialized form of ML that uses artificial neural networks with multiple layers to process complex datasets. It is particularly effective in tasks involving large-scale data processing, such as image recognition and natural language understanding [1].

Key DL technologies are [9, 11, 25]:

- **Convolutional Neural Networks (CNN):** Used for image recognition in quality control, enabling automated visual inspections of goods.
- **Recurrent Neural Networks (RNN):** Applied in time-series forecasting for demand prediction, considering sequential dependencies.
- **Natural Language Processing (NLP):** Enhances supplier communication through AI-powered chatbots and automated contract analysis.

Applications in SCM include aspects, such as [22, 23]:

- **Demand Forecasting and Inventory Optimization:** AI-powered models enhance the accuracy of demand forecasts by analyzing historical sales data, seasonal trends, and external factors such as weather conditions or economic indicators. This enables more precise inventory planning, preventing overstocking and minimizing the risk of supply shortages.
- **Transport and Route Optimization:** ML helps optimize transportation routes by evaluating real-time traffic data, weather conditions, and freight information. By dynamically adjusting routes, companies can reduce fuel costs, shorten delivery times, and minimize environmental impact.

- **Risk Management and Disruption Detection:** AI-driven systems analyze vast amounts of data from various sources to detect potential disruptions in the supply chain early. This includes geopolitical risks, natural disasters, or supplier bottlenecks. Companies can proactively take mitigation measures, enhancing supply chain resilience.

3.5 Comparing AI with Traditional SCM Approaches

Traditional SCM relies on rule-based systems and mathematical optimization models. While effective in structured environments, these methods struggle with handling dynamic, unstructured, and high-volume data sources [6] (Table 2).

Table 2. Comparing AI with Traditional SCM Approaches, based on [1, 6, 8, 22, 23]

Feature	Traditional SCM Method	AI-driven SCM
Data Handling	Predefined rules and structured data	Learns from unstructured and real-time data
Scalability	Limited to fixed models	Adapts to dynamic conditions
Accuracy	Static forecasting models	Self-improving predictive models
Automation	Manual decision-making	Automated, AI-driven insights

3.6 Future Developments and Challenges

As AI adoption grows, several trends and challenges emerge that impact SCM [1, 11, 21, 23]:

- **Generative AI for Scenario Planning:** AI models generate synthetic data for supply chain simulations, improving resilience planning, but also pose challenges in terms of data reliability and interpretability.
- **Federated Learning:** AI models train across decentralized datasets, enhancing privacy while leveraging collective intelligence, yet requiring strong IT infrastructure and standardized data-sharing frameworks.
- **Ethical and Legal Considerations:** AI decision-making must align with data privacy regulations (e.g. GDPR) and ethical AI principles to prevent biases.
- **Scalability Challenges:** AI adoption in SCM requires robust infrastructure, including cloud computing and edge processing, yet real-time data processing and high implementation costs remain key challenges.
- **Business Models:** AI-driven innovations in SCM enable efficient resource utilization, improved logistics performance, and the development of new business models.

    AI, particularly ML and DL, is revolutionizing SCM by enabling more precise forecasting, improved decision-making, and greater automation. However, organizations must address challenges related to data quality, integration, and trust in AI-driven processes to maximize its potential.

4 AI Application Scenarios in Industrial SCM

4.1 Application Scenario Definition

The definition and selection of application scenarios is of central importance for the SCM analysis to be conducted. AI technologies are used, for instance, to optimize the entire supply chain through enhanced inventory planning and demand forecasting. This includes the planning, management and control of the flow of goods, information, and money along the entire supply chain [5, 6].

An analysis and identification of specific application scenarios (use cases) for AI in SCM is based on suitable literature sources [20, 22–24]. Taking into account industry-specific requirements, eight AI use cases were developed to reflect the particular characteristics of SCM in an industrial context.

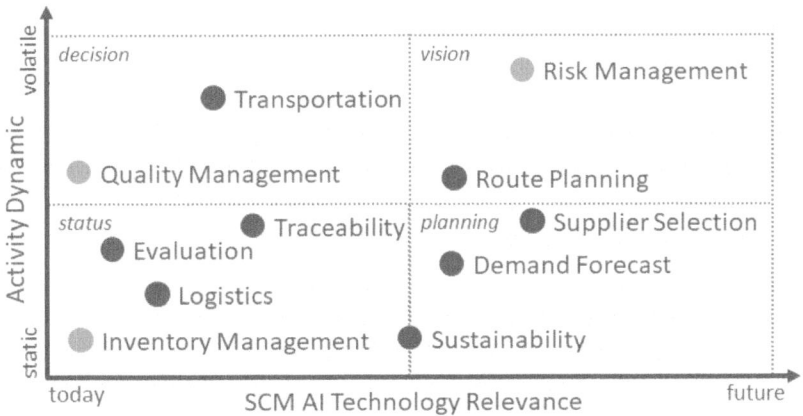

Fig. 3. Relevance and dynamic for AI technology use case topics

On the one hand, these use cases address topics that are relevant both today (analysis) and in the future (planning). On the other hand, some use cases are relatively stable and predictable, while others are subject to external influences that require short- or long-term dynamic responses, as illustrated in Fig. 3. Management actions inherently involve effective control loops.

1. *AI technologies in demand forecasting:* AI in demand forecasting optimizes the prediction of demand volume and behavior by incorporating market trends, customer preferences, and other external factors at an early stage. AI-powered chatbots and virtual assistants process customer inquiries in real time and handle orders efficiently. AI-supported demand forecasting leads to optimized production and delivery processes, reduced inventory levels and stock shortages, and enhanced customer acquisition and retention.

2. *AI technologies in inventory management:* AI-driven systems enhance inventory management across the supply chain by taking into account multiple factors such as

demand volumes, procurement costs, production capacities, warehouse expenses, and supply chain constraints. AI-supported inventory management leads to improved order cycles, optimal batch sizes, and greater accuracy in forecasting inventory shortages or surpluses.

3. *AI technologies in transportation and route planning:* AI algorithms play a crucial role in transportation and route planning by optimizing transport volumes, traffic routes, and the selection of transportation modes. These AI-supported systems effectively reduce delivery times, lower environmental impact, and minimize transportation costs by looking at factors such as traffic volume, weather conditions, road conditions, and delivery priorities.

4. *AI technologies in supplier selection and evaluation:* AI algorithms enhance supplier selection processes by analyzing performance and reliability data from various sources and databases to identify suitable suppliers for the supply chain.
   AI systems also evaluate risks associated with supplier selection, focusing on factors such as financial stability, sustainability, and geopolitical influences.

5. *AI technologies for supply chain traceability and quality management:* AI algorithms enable real-time tracking of the location and condition of goods (e.g., proof of authenticity or maintaining an unbroken cold chain) throughout the entire supply chain. This increases transparency by allowing early detection of faults. Additionally, AI-supported systems use image processing algorithms to perform visual inspections of incoming and outgoing goods and analyze video or sensor data to identify deviations and initiate preventive measures in the event of quality issues.

6. *AI technologies in logistics:* he applications of AI algorithms in logistics are wide-ranging and include the optimization of warehouse processes, monitoring of critical stock levels, and support for warehouse planners in inventory management, picking, and goods transportation. AI systems facilitate the integration of autonomous transport systems into route planning and enable the optimization of dynamic route adjustments, among other functions.

7. *AI technologies in risk management:* AI technologies in risk management identify and assess risks within the supply chain that may disrupt the flow of goods (e.g., delivery delays), financial transactions (e.g., credit risks), or information exchange (e.g., cybersecurity risks). AI systems enhance supply chain resilience by establishing risk assessment metrics, evaluating suitable suppliers, and devising strategies to mitigate potential risks.

8. *AI technologies in sustainability:* AI algorithms play a crucial role in sustainability efforts by reducing CO_2 emissions throughout the supply chain. This is achieved by identifying environmentally friendly transportation and packaging alternatives. AI systems contribute to the evaluation of ecological, social, and economic impacts across the entire supply chain by establishing relevant metrics, selecting alternative suppliers, and determining optimal transportation routes.

4.2   Methodology of the Questionnaire and Evaluation Criteria

The empirical study on AI application scenarios in SCM was conducted between July and September 2024. As part of this online survey, 500 individuals from 483 companies were contacted. In total, 18 completed questionnaires were included as the data basis for this study, corresponding to a low response rate of 3.6%. The survey was carried out using a panel provided by the IPM AG[2].

This panel accurately reflects the composition of representatives from various industrial sectors in middle and upper management positions. Therefore, despite the low response rate typically associated with online surveys, it can be assumed that the use of this panel ensures a representative sample.

1. AI technologies in demand forecasting					
AI in demand forecasting optimises the prediction of demand volume and demand behaviour by considering market trends, customer preferences and other external factors at an early stage. AI-managed chatbots and virtual assistants process customer enquiries in real time and handle orders efficiently. AI-supported demand forecasting results in optimised production and delivery processes, reduced stock levels and stock shortages and improved customer acquisition and loyalty.					
Questions about AI technologies in demand forecasting	do not agree at all	rather disagree	partly/partly	partially agree	fully agree
This AI technology application is already being used in my company.	☐	☐	☐	☐	☐
The (further) implementation of this AI technology application is interesting for my company.	☐	☐	☐	☐	☐
If this AI technology application is available, I can very well imagine (further) implementation in my company.	☐	☐	☐	☐	☐
The implementation of this AI technology application improves company processes.	☐	☐	☐	☐	☐
The integration of this AI technology application simplifies the management of company processes.	☐	☐	☐	☐	☐
My company provides the necessary resources (e.g. financial resources, infrastructure) for the expansion of this AI technology application.	☐	☐	☐	☐	☐
Employees/colleagues inluence me in the use of this AI technology application.	☐	☐	☐	☐	☐

Fig. 4. Questionnaire for Use Case *AI technologies in demand forecasting*

Figure 4 illustrates Use Case 1: AI technologies in demand forecasting. The response scale, ranging from "do not agree at all" (1) to "fully agree" (5), follows the standard approach used for multi-item scales. For further methodological details, see [26]. In principle, it can be assumed that the Likert scale used, which is a form of multi-item scale, sufficiently meets the requirements for interval scaling [26].

User acceptance of the AI application scenarios (use cases) in SCM is analyzed based on the Unified Theory of Acceptance and Use of Technology (UTAUT). The UTAUT model is grounded in an extensive literature review by Venkatesh et al. [27, 28]. It consolidates the most prominent technology acceptance models – such as the Technology Acceptance Model (TAM) – into a comprehensive, redundancy-free framework.

The purpose of the UTAUT analysis is to identify significant influencing factors on behavioral intention and usage behavior. Key constructs include performance expectancy, effort expectancy, social influence, and facilitating conditions.

---

[2] IPM AG, URL: http://www.ipm.ag/, accessed February 2025.

This established method of technology acceptance research is consistently applied in this study to examine the acceptance of AI use cases in SCM. To this end, the significant influencing factors are identified, and a corresponding question is formulated for each factor.

Table 3 presents the key influencing factors from the UTAUT analysis, each represented by a corresponding question applied to all use cases. While it is common to use multiple items i.e., questions, per factor to capture different dimensions of a construct [26], a preliminary review of the questionnaire indicated that, in this case, one item per factor was sufficient to adequately represent each construct.

Table 3. UTAUT analysis: questions and influencing factors [29]

Question	UTAUT factor
The (further) implementation of this AI technology application is interesting for my company	Behavioral intention
If this AI technology application is available, I can very well imagine (further) implementation in my company	Use behavior
The implementation of this AI technology application improves company processes	Performance expectancy
The integration of this AI technology application simplifies the management of company processes	Effort expectancy
My company provides the necessary resources, e.g. financial resources, infrastructure for the expansion of this AI technology application	Facilitating conditions
Employees/colleagues influence me in the use of this AI technology application	Social influence

5   AI Application Scenarios Study Results

5.1   Survey Profile

The detailed profile of the study is shown in Fig. 5. More than 44% of the companies participating in the study have more than 500 employees. Approximately one third of the companies can be classified as Original Equipment Manufacturers (OEMs) in terms of their position in the value chain, while around 44% are categorized as first- and second-tier suppliers. Roughly one third of the participants belong to the automotive industry, whereas about two thirds are part of the electrical and mechanical engineering sectors.

5.2   Specific Evaluation of Application Scenarios

Figures 6, 7, and 8 present the detailed results of the study regarding the questions related to AI use cases in SCM. For each question, a weighted average of all responses

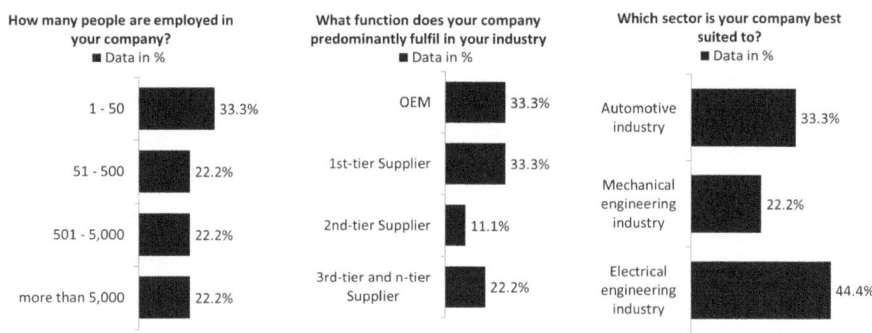

Fig. 5. Profile of the study "AI application scenarios in SCM".

was calculated, taking into account company size (based on number of employees), position within the supply chain, and industry affiliation. The agreement ratings are based on a scale from "do not agree at all" (1) to "fully agree" (5).

Figure 6 (a) shows an example of the ranking of use cases in response to the question: *"The (further) implementation of this AI technology application is of interest to my company."* From this, the following statements can be derived:

- *AI technologies in demand forecasting* (3.33) and *AI technologies for supply chain traceability and quality management* (3.22) achieve high approval ratings.
- Low approval ratings can be observed for *AI technologies in transportation and route planning* (2.56), *AI technologies in logistics* (2.56) and *AI technologies in sustainability* (2.56).

As illustrated in Figs. 6, 7, and 8, the survey results pertaining to the distinct domains of the UTAUT analysis are presented. The specific domains encompass behavior intention, use behavior, performance expectancy, effort expectancy, facilitating conditions and social influence [27, 28].

With regard to the UTAUT domains behavioral intention "The (further) implementation of this AI technology application is of interest to my company" and use behavior "If this AI technology application is available, I can well imagine its (further) implementation in my company", it becomes evident that the use cases AI technologies in demand forecasting, AI technologies for supply chain traceability and quality management, and *AI technologies in inventory management* received the highest approval ratings. By contrast, the use cases *AI technologies in sustainability* and *AI technologies in transportation and route planning* received by far the lowest levels of approval.

The use of AI offers significant potential for optimizing demand forecasts in terms of both volume and demand behavior – particularly in the use case of *AI technologies in demand forecasting*. To this end, market trends, customer preferences, and other external factors must be continuously monitored and addressed in a timely manner. In addition, AI-supported chatbots and virtual assistants enable real-time responses to customer inquiries and facilitate more efficient order processing. AI-enabled demand forecasting can lead to optimized production and delivery processes, reduced inventory levels and delivery bottlenecks, and improved customer acquisition and retention.

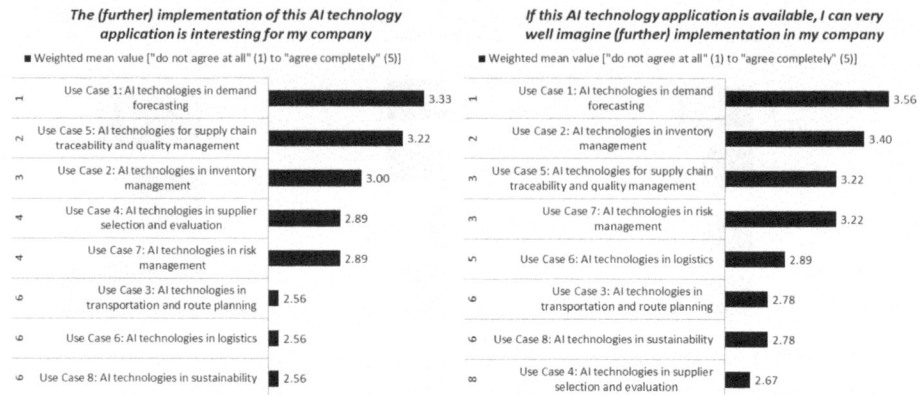

Fig. 6. (a) The implementation of this AI technology application is interesting for my company. (b) If this AI technology application is available, I can imagine implementation in my company.

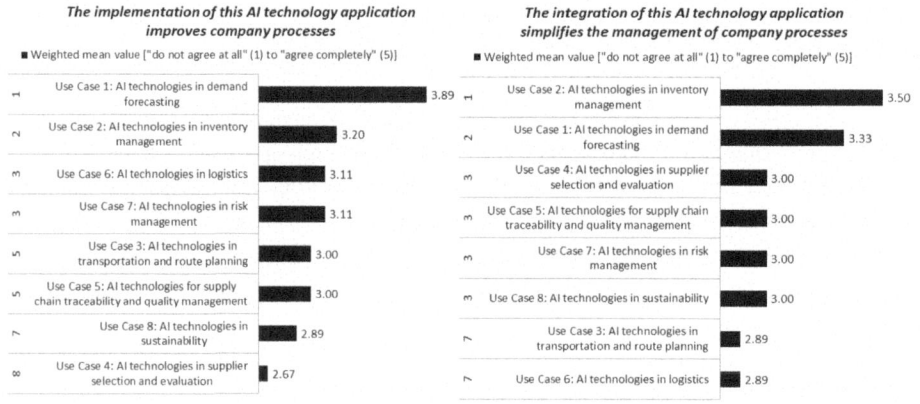

Fig. 7. (a) The implementation of this AI technology application improves company processes. (b) Integration of this AI technology application simplifies management of company processes.

Real-time tracking using AI algorithms (*Use Case: AI technologies for supply chain traceability and quality management*) enables continuous monitoring of the location and status of goods (e.g., proof of authenticity or maintenance of an uninterrupted cold chain) across the entire supply chain. This leads to increased transparency through the early detection of errors.

In addition, AI-supported systems employ image processing algorithms to visually inspect incoming and outgoing goods and to analyze video or sensor data to identify deviations and initiate preventive measures in the event of quality issues.

In the *Use Case: AI technologies in inventory management*, AI-enabled systems enhance inventory management throughout the supply chain by considering various factors such as demand volume, procurement costs, production capacity, warehousing expenses, and supply chain constraints. AI-supported inventory management leads

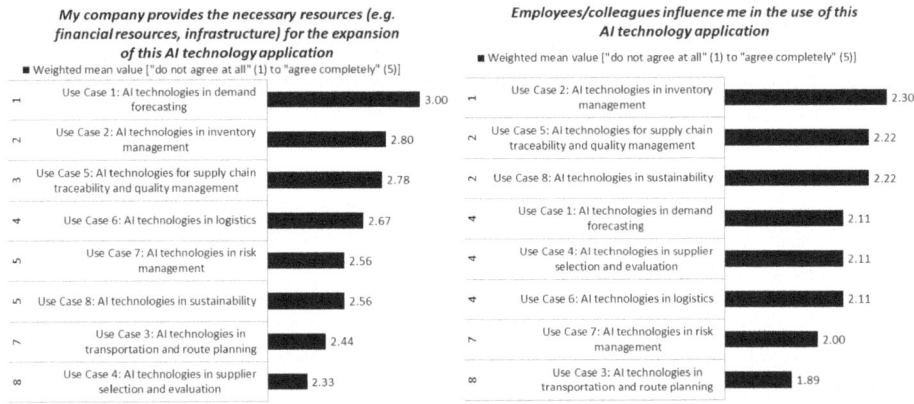

Fig. 8. (a) My company provides the necessary resources for the expansion of this AI technology application. (b) Employees/colleagues influence me in the use of this AI technology application.

to improved order cycles, optimized batch sizes, and greater accuracy in predicting inventory shortages or surpluses.

5.3 Customer-Specific Assessment

In the context of the present survey, where the variables are structured according to a metric system, the implementation of distance measures becomes imperative to facilitate the calculation of both similarities and dissimilarities. A commonly used distance measure within this framework is the Minkowski metric [29, 30]. If the calculated distance between two objects (a, b) is smaller than the distance between another pair of objects (a, c), it can be hypothesized that the former pair exhibits a higher degree of similarity. Conversely, a larger distance indicates lower similarity between the objects in question.

$$
b_{k,l} = \left[\sum_{m=1}^{M} \left| x_{k,m} - x_{l,m} \right|^p \right]^{\frac{1}{p}} \tag{1}
$$

$b_{k,l}$: distance value of the objects k and l
$b_{k,l}^{max} = max\{b_{1,1}, ..., b_{k,l}, ..., b_{n,n}\};$
$b_{k,l}^{min} = min\{b_{1,1}, ..., b_{k,l}, ..., b_{n,n}\}; \forall k \neq l$
$b_{k,l} = b_{l,k}; b_{k,l} = 0 \ \forall k = l$; number of objects $n \ (n = 1, ..., N)$

$x_{k,m}, x_{l,m}$: value of the variable (weighted mean value) m of objects
$k, l \ (m = 1, ..., M)$

A: distance matrix

$$
A = \begin{pmatrix} b_{1,1} & \cdots & b_{1,n} \\ \vdots & \ddots & \vdots \\ b_{n,1} & \cdots & b_{n,n} \end{pmatrix}
$$

p: Minkowski constant ($p \geq 1$), here: $p = 2$

These distance measures clearly indicate the evaluation level of the use cases between the different customer segments. The use case *AI technologies in demand forecasting* is an ideal example of this, as it can be used to examine the customer segments regarding the "position in the supply chain" ("OEM", "1st-tier supplier", etc.) and "company size" (number of employees, "1–50", "51–500", etc.). The Minkowski metric is calculated using the independent variables, see Table 4. The distance matrix A allows us to make the following statements (Table 4 (a) and Table 4 (b)). In Table 4 (a), the 3rd-tier supplier and n-tier supplier customer segments are combined into one, due to differing group sizes in the original survey.

Table 4. Minkowski metric for use case *AI technologies in demand forecasting* in two different customer segments: (a) position in the supply chain, (b) company size

Position	OEM	1st-tier	2nd-tier	3rd-n-tier
OEM	0.00	1.70	1.59	1.94
1st-tier		0.00	1.14	1.70
2nd-tier			0.00	1.94
3rd-n-tier				0.00

Size	1-50	51-500	501-5.000	>5.000
1-50	0.00	5.32	2.74	1.33
51-500		0.00	2.96	4.95
501-5.000			0.00	2.60
> 5.000				0.00

From Table 4, the following conclusions can be drawn:

- Table 4 (a): The customer segments "OEM" with "3rd-n-tier" and "2nd-tier" with "3rd-n-tier" show the highest distance ($b_{k,l}^{max}$) in the evaluation of the AI technologies in demand forecasting use case (1.94). The customer segments "OEM" and "1st-tier" (1.70) as well as "1st-tier" and "3rd-n-tier" (1.70) differ in the evaluation at the same level. The lowest distance $\left(b_{k,l}^{min}\right)$ can be observed between the "1st-tier" and "3rd-n-tier" customer segments (1.14). Overall, there is a positive tendency between the distance level and the position in the supply chain, i.e. the closer the supply levels are aligned, the more similar the evaluation for the use case.
- Table 4 (b): (5.32) is the highest distance level ($b_{k,l}^{max}$) between the customer segments "1–50" and "51–500". If the customer segment "1–50" is compared with " > 5,000", the lowest distance value $\left(b_{k,l}^{min}\right)$ is observed (1.33). It is not quite so clear here that the differences in size (number of employees) between the companies also results in a high distance value.

6   Insights, Trends and Further Research

The increasing adoption of AI in industrial applications, particularly in SCM, presents both opportunities and challenges. This study highlights key insights, combining several UTAUT factors and identifies areas for future application research.

6.1 Strategic Fields of Application

For the strategic analysis of the study results, six central overarching application areas for AI in SCM can generally be identified, as shown in Fig. 9. It can be observed that traditional application fields are ranked higher than emerging.

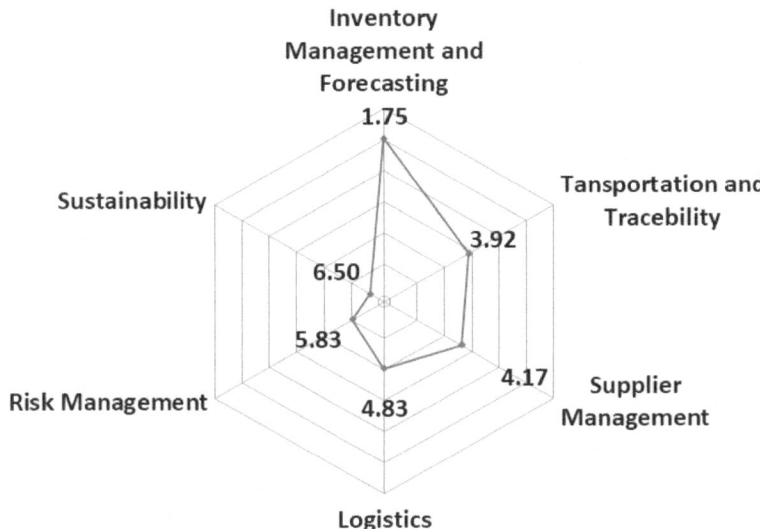

Fig. 9. Strategic fields of application: weighted mean value ranking over all application fields

These are inventory management and forecasting (1.75), transportation and traceability (3.92), supplier management (4.17), logistics (4.83), risk management (5.83), and sustainability (6.50). The calculated rankings of the individual application areas result from the weighted averages of the individual rankings of the UTAUT surveys, which are shown in Figs. 6, 7, and 8. Accordingly, the application area inventory management and forecasting has the highest-ranking value, while sustainability has the lowest ranking value. When developing application solutions, the focus for AI solutions in SCM should therefore initially be on the Inventory Management and Forecasting application area. This field of application includes, for example, AI-supported chatbots and virtual assistants that enable real-time responses to customer inquiries and can ensure more efficient order processing. Furthermore, AI-supported demand forecasts can lead to optimized production and delivery processes.

6.2 Learnings from the SCM Domain

Despite the growing interest in AI applications for SCM, comprehensive studies on real-world implementation remain limited. AI-driven ML, DL, and predictive analytics are proving valuable, yet their integration into supply chains is not solely a technical challenge but also a cultural and strategic one. Key insights from the study include:

- AI improves supply chain efficiency by enhancing demand forecasting, inventory management, and logistics planning.
- Successful implementation depends on both, objective and subjective factors, including data availability, technological readiness, and organizational acceptance.
- Companies must align AI deployment with strategic business goals to fully leverage its potential.
- The introduction of any AI solution requires transparency and clear communication to its users.
- Adoption challenges are not only technical but also include factors such as workforce transformation, transparency in decision-making, and ethical considerations.

6.3 Expectations and Side Conditions

Going forward, organizations and initiatives at the European and international levels are promoting AI adoption while also defining governance structures to ensure ethical AI deployment. Research projects are focusing on scalable AI solutions, interoperability challenges, and sustainability-driven AI applications. Future developments include:

- Regulatory differences between EU's General Data Protection Regulation (GDPR), focused on ethical AI, security, and data protection versus the market-oriented California Consumer Privacy Act (CCPA) pose challenges for global supply chains.
- AI-driven business models are evolving, creating opportunities for process automation, cost reduction, and supply chain resilience.
- Cross-industry AI collaboration is critical for overcoming technical and regulatory hurdles.
- AI governance frameworks must balance innovation with compliance, ensuring both, efficient and responsible AI use.

6.4 Conclusion

AI is poised to fundamentally transform SCM. However, its success depends on a holistic approach that integrates technological innovation with ethical considerations and appropriate regulatory frameworks. Future research should focus on optimizing AI applications, enhancing transparency, and addressing the broader societal impacts of AI-driven automation. As AI continues to evolve, close collaboration between businesses and policymakers will be essential to ensure its responsible and sustainable implementation.

In response to the question *"What is enlightenment?"*, the German philosopher Immanuel Kant (1724 – 1804) famously answered: *"Sapere aude! Have courage to use your own reason!"* (1784). In this spirit, AI must never be allowed to operate independently of human oversight.

References

1. Mockenhaupt, A.: Digitalisierung und Künstliche Intelligenz in der Produktion: Grundlagen und Anwendung, Wiesbaden (2021)
2. Brecher, C., et al.: KI in der Produktion. VDI Verlag, Düsseldorf (2022)

3. Hilbert, M. et al.: KI-Innovation über das autonome Fahren hinaus, in: Buxmann, P., Schmidt, H. (Eds.): Künstliche Intelligenz, pp. 173–185. Springer Gabler, Berlin (2019)

4. Toosi, A., et al.: A brief history of AI: how to prevent another winter (a critical review) PET Clin. **16** 449–469 (2021). https://doi.org/10.1016/j.cpet.2021.07.001

5. Heinrich, C., Stühler, G.: Die Digitale Wertschöpfungskette: Künstliche Intelligenz im Einkauf und Supply Chain Management. In: Gärtner, C., Heinrich, C. (Eds.): Fallstudien zur Digitalen Transformation, pp. 77–88. Springer Gabler, Wiesbaden (2018)

6. Helmold, M.: Digitalisierung und KI-Anwendungen im Supply Chain Management (SCM). Springer Nature, Wiesbaden (2024)

7. Blum, L.B. (ed.): Angewandte Data Science: Projekte, Methoden. Prozesse. Springer, Wiesbaden (2023)

8. Heesen, B.: Künstliche Intelligenz und Machine Learning mit R: Anwendungen im Bereich Business Analytics. Springer, Wiesbaden (2023)

9. Lanquillon, C., Schacht, S.: Knowledge Science – Grundlagen: Methoden der Künstlichen Intelligenz für die Wissensextraktion aus Texten. Springer, Wiesbaden (2023)

10. Matzka, S.: Künstliche Intelligenz in den Ingenieurswissenschaften – Maschinelles Lernen verstehen und bewerten. Wiesbaden (2021)

11. Papp, S., et al.: Handbuch Data Science und KI: Mit Machine Learning und Datenanalyse Wert aus Daten generieren. Hanser, München (2022)

12. Artificial Intelligence: In-depth market analysis. Dossier, Statista (2024). https://www.statista.de/. Accessed Jan 2025

13. Künstliche Intelligenz (KI) (2024), Dossier, Statista (2024). https://www.statista.de/. Accessed Jan 2025

14. Künstliche Intelligenz weltweit, Dossier, Statista, URL: https://www.statista.de/ (2024), accessed March 2025

15. Eichler, G., Lüke, K.-H.: Recommendation as a service (RaaS) - new challenges for, and evaluation metrics of recommender systems. In: Proceedings of 17th International Conference on Intelligence in Next Generation Networks (ICIN), pp. 133–140. IEEE (2013). https://doi.org/10.1109/ICIN31878.2013

16. Lüke, K.-H., Walther, J., Wäldchen, D., Royer, D.: Innovation management methods in the automotive industry. In: Conference Proceedings of Innovations for Community Services (I4CS), pp. 125–141. Springer CCIS, Heidelberg (2019)

17. Becker, T.: Strategische Gestaltung und Digitalisierung der Supply Chain. Springer Nature, Berlin (2024)

18. Gronwald, K.-D.: Globale Kommunikation und Kollaboration. Springer Vieweg, Wiesbaden (2023)

19. Knapp, P., Wagner, C.: Künstliche Intelligenz schafft neue Geschäftsmodelle im Mittelstand. In: Buxmann, P., Schmidt, H. (Hrsg.): Künstliche Intelligenz, pp. 161–172. Springer Gabler, Berlin (2019)

20. Khadem, M., Khadem, A., Khadem, S.: Application of artificial intelligence in supply chain: revolutionizing efficiency and optimization. Int. J. Ind. Eng. Oper. Res. **5**(1), 19–28 (2023)

21. Taulli, T.: Grundlagen der Künstlichen Intelligenz: Eine nichttechnische Einführung Springer Nature, New York (2022)

22. Murrenhoff, A., Friedrich, M., Witthaut, M. (2021): Künstliche Intelligenz in der Logistik, White Paper, Fraunhofer (2021). https://www.iml.fraunhofer.de/. Accessed Jan 2025

23. Thakur, M. et al.: Applications of artificial intelligence and machine learning. In: Supply Chain Management: A comprehensive review. In: Eur. Chem. Bull., 12 (Special Issue 8), pp. 2838–2851 (2023)

24. Edhrabooh, K.M., Al-Alawi, A.I.: AI and ML applications in supply chain management field: a systematic literature review. In: 2024 International Conference in Emerging Technologies for Sustainability and Intelligence Systems (ICETSIS) 2024, pp. 202–206, IEEE (2024)

25. Buxmann, P., Schmidt, H.: Grundlagen der Künstlichen Intelligenz und des Maschinellen Lernens, in: Buxmann, P., Schmidt, H. (Hrsg.): Künstliche Intelligenz, pp. 3–19, Springer Gabler, Berlin (2019)
26. Kuß, A.: Marktforschung, 4th edn. Springer Gabler, Wiesbaden (2012)
27. Venkatesh, V., et al.: User acceptance of information technology: toward a unified view. MIS Q. **27**(3), 425–478 (2003)
28. Venkatesh, V., Davis, F.D.: A theoretical extension of the technology acceptance model: four longitudinal field studies. Manage. Sci. **46**(2), 186–204 (2000)
29. Lüke, K.-H., von Hugo, D., Eichler, G.: 5G network quality of service supporting adequate quality of experience for industrial demands in process automation. In: Conference Proceedings of Innovations for Community Services (I4CS), pp. 201–222, Springer CCIS, Heidelberg (2021)
30. Backhaus, K., et al.: Multivariate Analysemethoden. Springer, Berlin/Heidelberg (2016)

Data Processing

Real-Time Energy Data Aggregation for Energy Communities

Stefan Linecker$^{(\boxtimes)}$ [ID], Felix Strohmeier [ID], Peter Dorfinger, and Christof Brandauer

Salzburg Research Forschungsgesellschaft m.b.H., Jakob-Haringer-Straße 5, 5020 Salzburg, Austria
{stefan.linecker,felix.strohmeier,peter.dorfinger, christof.brandauer}@salzburgresearch.at

Abstract. The number of energy communities in Austria is growing rapidly. Their operation primarily relies on standardized processes for data collection, communication, and billing. Beyond collective accounting within the community, further optimizations—such as maximizing self-consumption and minimizing grid feed-in—are severely limited by the lack of real-time data. Accessing real-time energy data directly via the smart meter customer interface and aggregating it at the community level enables more precise load balancing and better utilization of renewable energy sources. This paper presents the Community Aggregation Tool, a modular software solution designed to collect, harmonize, and aggregate real-time energy data from diverse metering systems and protocols. The tool integrates multiple data sources and leverages existing open-source solutions for its implementation. Initial deployments in selected energy communities demonstrate its potential to address key challenges, such as limited data granularity and the heterogeneity of household devices.

Keywords: Energy communities · Real-time data · Smart meters · Data streaming · Data aggregation

1 Motivation

In Austria, the number of renewable energy communities (EEG – "Erneuerbare-Energie-Gemeinschaften") is growing rapidly. The public register of energy communities lists almost 700 EEGs at the local and regional levels as of early 2025 [2]. According to the Austrian EDA ("Energiewirtschaftlicher Datenaustausch") [3], more than 6500 energy communities exist across all levels (local, regional, and national). For accounting purposes, community members exchange their smart meter data ex post with a delay of up to two calendar days, reporting their energy consumption or supply (in kilowatt-hours) at a 15-min resolution [1].

This non-real-time approach hinders the optimization of load management for flexible consumers, such as water heating systems, electric vehicles, and battery storage systems. The distribution system operator (DSO), acting as a trusted third party, is responsible for gathering the measurements from the smart meters and providing them to the energy communities electronically via the EDA platform. In the best case, data is available with a delay of one day, as collection from smart meters typically happens via powerline communication, and the systems in place were not originally designed for high-frequency data collection. However, energy communities typically aim to maximize self-consumption and local sharing of energy within the community while minimizing energy flows to and from the power grid. Historical data alone, even with good forecasting, will not allow proper balancing of power generation and consumption within an energy community without current data [20].

As an additional driver, dynamic energy prices directly connected to the spot electricity market are now also available for end customers. These prices change hourly and become available 10 to 34 h in advance, as they are published daily at about 2 p.m. at the European Power Exchange [4]. Based on this new flexibility and the dynamic pricing models, shifting loads between 15-min time slots can reduce network loads and save money but requires current data and communication within the community. There are many cases where load shifting can achieve significant energy savings, such as for cooling, heating, hot water, charging, or washing. With smart products entering the market, even autonomous load shifting is possible without compromising living comfort or leading to overcomplicated device management.

To support such flexibility, we present the Community Aggregation Tool (CAT) to enable data transfer within energy communities in this paper. After presenting related work in Sect. 2, we highlight the major challenges of implementing such a system in Sect. 3 and present a prototype implementation in Sect. 4. We conclude the paper with an outlook on future developments in Sect. 5.

2 State-of-the-Art

To address the issue of non-real-time and low-resolution data (with 15-min intervals reported the following day), it is possible to use the smart meter's customer interface ("Kundenschnittstelle") and directly access the metered values with additional hardware. This hardware is available for hobbyists (e.g., accessing the M-Bus interface directly with a USB converter attached to a Raspberry Pi), and there are also commercial off-the-shelf solutions available. The collected data can then be used for household-level optimizations (e.g., in a home energy management system) as well as providing a real-time view of the current energy balance within the energy community to which the household belongs.

The presented Community Aggregation Tool ("CAT") does exactly that. It is a software solution based on open-source tools and standards that collects data from various types of metering equipment (e.g., smart meters) and aggregates the measurements for sharing within an energy community. Before delving into the specifics of the CAT, this section discusses some existing solutions, research, and protocol standards.

2.1 Existing Solutions and Research

The household energy balance has been of interest to tech-savvy individuals for quite some time. In addition to detailed monitoring, self-consumption optimization is a typical use case that requires access to the energy balance in a timely and high-resolution manner. Both inverters and home automation systems often include such capabilities, either via a dedicated second meter or through hardware for interfacing with existing meters.

Alongside commercial offerings, and even before the rollout of smart meters, tin-kerers and the open-source community began developing several approaches for data collection. In Austria, one of the early efforts was "volkszaehler.org" [5]. This initiative published detailed instructions for interfacing with many (including "non-smart") meter types, as well as middleware for data processing and storage, and a frontend application for the user interface.

With the rollout of smart meters in Austria, things have become easier. Several hardware solutions are now available that work with all smart meter vendors in the Austrian market. These devices typically act as bridges from the smart meter's customer interface, such as wired M-Bus, to a local Wi-Fi network. They support widely used protocols like HTTP and MQTT.

As we move from individual households to entire energy communities, a small but dedicated ecosystem of service companies is currently emerging in Austria. The func-tionality of these offerings varies widely. While most focus on management and billing, there are already service providers offering real-time load balancing. Some examples include HivePower [6], Quixotic [7], and SCS [8], an open-source variant.

2.2 Communication Technologies, Protocols and Standards

There are several communication protocols standardized in the context of smart grids and electrical power management. However, most of them are not specific to communication within an energy community:

- OpenADR: A protocol for automated demand response, enabling communities to communicate energy flexibility with DSOs.
- IEEE 2030.5: A smart energy profile for secure communication of distributed energy resources with DSOs. IEEE 2030.5 is the selected standard in the well-known California Rule 21 [6].
- IEC 61850: A standard for seamless integration and management of substation automation and distributed energy systems.
- Modbus TCP/IP: A widely used industrial communication protocol. In the energy world, it is often used with the SunSpec specification.
- EEBus: A framework for integrating smart appliances and energy management systems.
- OCPP: A communication protocol for managing electric vehicle charging stations within energy networks.
- IEC 60870–5: A protocol for telecontrol and data exchange between energy control centers and field devices.
- MQTT: a generic publish/subscribe messaging transport protocol for the Internet of Things (IoT), designed for low-resource devices.

2.3 Commercial Offerings in Austria

The swift integration of energy communities into Austrian legislation has sparked signif-icant interest among both well-established companies in the energy sector and innovative startups. This legislative development has created new opportunities for businesses to offer specialized services tailored to the needs of energy communities. Several vendors, including Energiedigital [10], Neoom [11], and So-Strom [12], have already launched commercial offerings for energy community management.

These services encompass various functionalities such as registration, accounting, and other administrative tasks essential for the smooth operation of energy communities. For more information or additional service providers, we refer to the website of the "Österreichische Koordinationsstelle für Energiegemeinschaften" [13]. This resource serves as a valuable directory for anyone interested in exploring the growing ecosystem of energy community service providers in Austria.

3   Challenges

3.1   Data Privacy

Although energy consumption data, even with high resolution (intervals of 15 min or less), do not fall under the category of personal or sensitive data according to the GDPR, they could still be misused to profile individuals' lives. Therefore, the principles of data minimization and data avoidance should be applied whenever possible. As a result, the community aggregation tool is not designed to create a central, global, single-instance platform, but instead is built to allow for physical separation of data within each energy community.

It can be installed and configured individually, meaning that each community can establish its own rules regarding data sharing, retention, usage, backups, and so on, ensuring that the specific needs of its members are met. For data integration and aggregation at higher levels, the use of data space technologies that support further concepts of data sovereignty is envisioned.

3.2   Installation Requirements and Data Availability

First, smart meters must be installed to electronically read energy consumption and supply in real-time. These meters are equipped with a customer interface that provides this data via wire, such as sending frames with updated meter values every few seconds. The exact interval varies between smart meter types, but it is typically 5 or 10 s. Table 1 provides an example of this data. Depending on the meter used, the data may vary, but typically, the most important information for the CAT includes active energy consumption and generation, as well as active power consumption and generation.

The distinction between power and energy is crucial. Power is an instantaneous value, whereas energy is accumulated over time. When using power for further calculations, the accuracy depends on the sampling interval. Short spikes may be missed, leading to incorrect calculations. By using energy instead of power for calculations and accounting, these sampling issues can be avoided.

The OBIS codes for metering electricity are defined in IEC 62056–6-1:2017, where all codes starting with "1-" represent values for electricity measurements. It should be noted that the exact units (e.g., watts vs. kilowatts) are not defined by the OBIS code but must be taken from the smart meter documentation or encoded in the protocol. Example protocols include DLMS and COSEM, which are part of the IEC 62056 standards family.

Table 1. Datagram example from smart meter

OBIS Code	Example Value	Short Description
0–0:96.1.0	–	Meter number
0–0:42.0.0	–	Logical device name
1–0:32.7.0	239.8	Instantaneous Voltage L1
1–0:52.7.0	239.8	Instantaneous Voltage L2
1–0:72.7.0	240	Instantaneous Voltage L3
1–0:31.7.0	0.19	Instantaneous Current L1
1–0:51.7.0	0.13	Instantaneous Current L2
1–0:71.7.0	0.08	Instantaneous Current L3
1–0:1.7.0	46	Active power consumption
1–0:2.7.0	0	Active power generation
1–0:1.8.0	2357961	Active energy consumption
1–0:2.8.0	0	Active energy generation
1–0:3.8.0	1476	Reactive power consumption
1–0:4.8.0	373125	Reactive power generation
api_version	v1	API Version
Name	–	Name

3.3 Self-consumption Optimization Quality

When optimizing self-consumption within an energy community, several important technical considerations come into play. One factor that eases optimization is that the Distribution System Operator (DSO) calculates the energy mix for community participants based on 15-min intervals (while, within the household and via the customer interface, measurements in intervals of 5 or 10 s are available).

For example, if Household A consumes one kilowatt-hour of energy between 12:00 and 12:15, and Household B has an excess kilowatt-hour of energy during the same interval, the energy is billed as an exchange within the community. The exact power drawn by Household A within that 15-min window does not affect the calculation. For instance, Household A could consume the entire kilowatt-hour in just one minute or distribute it evenly over the entire interval, and the accounting would remain the same. This 15-min accounting interval reduces the need for perfect real-time data, making optimization more feasible.

The benefits of optimization depend on how well consumption and production can be matched. Automation and flexible energy sinks, such as batteries, can significantly enhance control strategies. However, without automation, there is a natural limit to the effectiveness of this optimization. With automation, the optimization gain primarily depends on the quality of the available information.

One factor that makes self-consumption optimization more challenging is the need for data from all involved households. In practice, several issues have been observed. The smart meter is often installed in a metallic box, typically in the basement, which can lead to unstable Wi-Fi connections. Additionally, consumer internet connections may not always be reliable. Some households experience unstable connections, and others turn off their modems at night. A complete and accurate picture of the current power balance within the energy community can only be determined when every household provides up-to-date data. While statistical methods can be used to estimate missing data, this introduces uncertainty. In larger energy communities, the relative error from a single missing household's data becomes smaller, but the likelihood of missing data increases. The impact of a household on the power balance—such as those with significant energy consumption or large photovoltaic systems—makes their data especially important. Therefore, obtaining reliable data from these households is crucial for effective optimization.

3.4 Further Challenges

Another important challenge is trust: when using the Smart Meter Adapter as a data source for optimization, it is crucial to recognize that only the smart meter itself is calibrated ("geeicht"). Any data processing or transmission that occurs after the smart meter can potentially be manipulated or subject to errors. While discrepancies will eventually be identified during the clearing process conducted with the official data collected by the Distribution System Operator (DSO), it is advisable to implement validation measures and plausibility checks to ensure the integrity and accuracy of the data. This proactive approach helps in identifying and rectifying errors promptly, thereby maintaining trust in the optimization process. Without such additional measures, lack of trust also becomes an issue for the CAT.

Another challenge is interoperability. New protocols need to be standardized, or existing semantic standards (such as OBIS) must be used for reliable communication and the harmonization of data streams among various energy communities, also for future cross-border data and energy exchange.

Finally, the management of security and access control is a major challenge. If community members should only receive (anonymized) data they really need for their optimization algorithms, fine-grained access control becomes complex.

4   Solution

The basic idea of the CAT is to assist the operator of an energy community in collecting real-time energy-related data from its members. In the first step, this provides insights into the required and available energy in real-time, which is essential for any serious optimization.

An overview of the components connected to CAT is provided in Fig. 1. As shown on the left side of the figure, data is retrieved from the smart meter using the Smart Meter Adapter (or similar hardware). For data exchange, MQTT is typically used. It is lightweight in terms of memory and CPU requirements, has low communication overhead, and allows secure data transfer over the Internet. To remain compatible with existing and future "Home Automation Systems," the CAT accepts various input protocols. To enable energy data analytics and visualization, CAT generates a common output data stream for time-series databases.

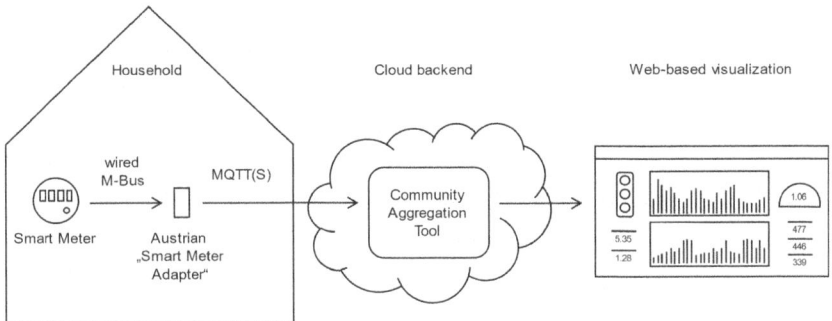

Fig. 1. Components of the community aggregation tool

Given the generic nature of the required functionality—which involves handling input data streams, processing them, and outputting data to a database—we explored existing solutions such as Apache Airflow, Apache NiFi, Spotify's Luigi, and Node-RED as alternatives to developing fully custom Python code. However, while each tool had its strengths, it was difficult to determine whether they could fully meet our requirements without first gaining deep expertise in each. Additionally, these tools are often designed with enterprise-level needs in mind, making them more complex than necessary for our requirements.

4.1 Prototypical Implementation

The architecture, along with its internal components, is shown in Fig. 2. It consists of input modules (on the left), output modules (on the right), and a central block called the "Conversion Engine," which is responsible for unifying the incoming data.

The individual modules are implemented as independent Python services and are only loosely coupled. Unix domain sockets (similar to network sockets but using the file system or an abstract namespace for addressing) serve as the technical foundation for this coupling. There is a Unix domain socket positioned just before the central Conversion Engine and one immediately after it. A simple naming convention is used for the individual services, where the first part of the name indicates the technology on the input side, and the last part refers to the technology on the output side. Consequently, the name of each module to the left of the Conversion Engine ends with "-uds" (for Unix domain socket), while every module to the right of the Conversion Engine begins with "uds-."

The CAT already includes input modules for the Austrian Smart Meter Adapter (SMA) [14], the Loxone Home Automation System [15], and generic UDP and MQTT,

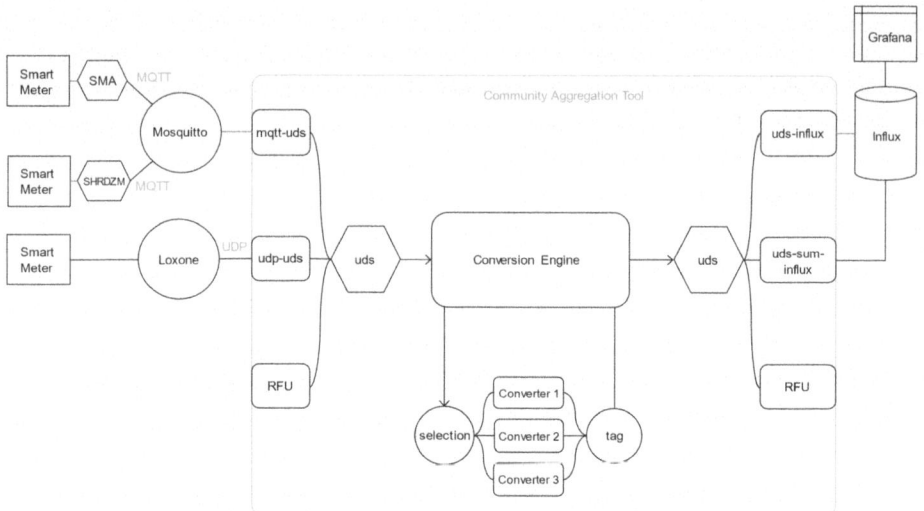

Fig. 2. CAT internal architecture

as provided by various open-source implementations or commercial solutions like "SHRDZM" [16].

Due to its modular design, both input and output modules can be easily added without interrupting the running system (hot-pluggable). Modularity on the input side is necessary to support various input technologies and protocols, while modularity on the output side is not strictly a technical requirement. Instead, it serves as a design feature, allowing distinct functionalities to be separated into independent blocks. For the current output modules, the uds-influx module simply passes the original smart meter data (in a unified format) to the database, while the uds-sum-influx module handles community-wide data aggregation.

The core module of the CAT is the "Conversion Engine." While the input modules handle the diversity of technology and protocols, the Conversion Engine addresses the diversity in data formats. To achieve this, it requires knowledge about the individual participants (such as the expected input format for each participant, and which participants form an energy community, etc.). This information is currently stored in a single configuration file in an easy-to-read JSON format. Based on the participants' configuration, the Conversion Engine selects the appropriate "Converter" for each incoming measurement. After passing through the Conversion Engine, all measurements are standardized in format.

The CAT is built using several open-source services:

- The Mosquitto MQTT Broker as a data sink on the input side (the Austrian Smart Meter Adapter uses MQTT for data transmission).
- The InfluxDB time-series database for storing both the original meter values and calculated values.
- Grafana dashboards for browser-based data visualization.

4.2 Practical Application

The system is currently installed in several communities of varying sizes to gather deeper insights and refine its capabilities. A Grafana dashboard provides multiple views for detailed data visualization, serving as a central repository of valuable knowledge and experience. One view focuses on individual households, showcasing the full range of measurements provided by the smart meters. Another view is geared towards energy communities, displaying aggregated measurements and an initial version of suggestions in the form of a traffic light. Both dashboards allow users to analyze trends, detect anomalies, and optimize system performance. To ensure secure operation, basic security mechanisms have been implemented, including MQTT restrictions based on topics. Additionally, a shared dashboard offers all users access to key data while maintaining controlled visibility and preventing unauthorized modifications.

While both the official EDA portal and third-party service providers offer visually appealing energy consumption charts and production metrics, these services typically provide data on a day-after basis with relatively coarse granularity (one value per quarter-hour). The primary advantage of the CAT is its ability to deliver real-time, high-resolution data (updated every 5 to 10 s), which is essential for use cases such as demand-side management or precise battery dispatch (the practice of using battery storage to capture surplus local generation and dispatching that stored energy when consumption is high, rather than directly shifting the load).

5 Outlook

To further develop the CAT, several considerations have been made. First, a deployment system based on container-based virtualization (e.g., Docker) is planned for easy setup in edge or cloud systems. This system aims to support the wider adoption of real-time data capturing from smart meters and data sharing within energy communities. Additionally, strong security mechanisms and access control features must be supported to ensure the broader acceptance of the CAT.

Secondly, the development of technical and semantic interoperability in the energy domain is currently being addressed by the International Data Spaces Association (IDSA) [18]. As outlined in Subsect. 2.2, several relevant standards are available, but no final semantic standard for the exchange of energy data among energy communities has been defined. However, the concept of dataspace technology, which is expected to become a common foundation across various domains, presents a promising approach. Consequently, we will investigate the compatibility of the data models used in the CAT with upcoming dataspace connectors, such as the EDC [19].

Third, while the CAT is currently tailored to Austria, expanding to other EU countries requires ensuring compatibility with different smart metering infrastructures and data exchange frameworks. Interoperability with existing energy management systems and dataspace technologies to support broader adoption will be explored.

Finally, many active developments are underway in various energy management systems, including new approaches for controlling energy devices and battery charging systems [17]. With the CAT, we can provide valuable real-time data at different aggregation levels (households and energy communities), enabling a loosely coupled optimization beyond individual energy communities.

Acknowledgements. This research was funded by CETP, the Clean Energy Transition Partnership under the 2023 CETP joint call for research proposals, co-funded by the European Commission (GA N° 101069750) and with the funding organizations detailed on https://cetpartnership.eu/fun ding-agencies-and-call-modules.

References

1. Langthaler, O., Kazmi, J., Linecker, S.: Elicitation and formalization of local energy community stakeholder requirements in Austria. In: 18. Symposium Energieinnovation (EnInnov 2024) (2024)
2. Austrian Coordination Site for Energy Communities, „Landkarte Erneuerbare-Energie-Gemeinschaften und Bürgerenergiegemeinschaften." https://energiegemeinschaften.gv.at/lan dkarte/. Accessed 21 Feb 2025
3. Energiewirtschaftlicher Datenaustausch, „Fakten zu Netzbetreibern und Lieferanten." https://www.eda.at/fakten. Accessed 21 Feb 2025
4. EPEX SPOT, "European Power Exchange" https://www.europex.org/members/epex-spot/. Accessed 21 Feb 2025
5. Volkszähler.org, "Das Smart Meter für Jeden" https://volkszaehler.org/. Accessed 21 Feb 2025
6. HivePower GmbH, "Energy Communities" https://www.hivepower.tech/flexo/energy-com munities. Accessed 21 Feb 2025
7. QUIXOTIC, "DSOs Integrations and aggregation" https://www.quixotic.energy/solutions/dso-integration-agregation. Accessed 21 Feb 2025
8. SCS, "Smart Meter Toolkit" https://www.scs.ch/projekt/smart-meter-toolkit/. Accessed 21 Feb 2025
9. Kum, G.: "California Use Case for IEEE2030.5 for Distributed Energy Renewables" https://smartgrid.ieee.org/bulletins/december-2016/california-use-case-for-ieee2030-5-for-distributed-energy-renewables Accessed 21 Feb 2025
10. ed-energiedigital GmbH, "Plattform energiedigital.at" https://www.energiedigital.at/. Accessed 21 Feb 2025
11. neoom international gmbh, "Energiegemeinschaft Österreich: Jetzt starten" https://neoom.com/loesungen-eeg?sector=private. Accessed 21 Feb 2025
12. So-Strom GmbH. "Energiegemeinschaften einfach verwalten und abrechnen": https://www.so-strom.at/. Accessed 21 Feb 2025
13. Austrian Coordination Site for Energy Communities, "Dienstleistungsanbieter für Energiegemeinschaften" https://energiegemeinschaften.gv.at/dienstleister-in-oesterreich/. Accessed 21 Feb 2025
14. Österreichs Energie, "Technische Leitfäden" https://oesterreichsenergie.at/smart-meter/tec hnische-leitfaeden. Accessed 21 Feb 2025
15. Loxone, "Wie funktioniert Home Automation?" https://www.loxone.com/dede/smart-home/hausautomation/. Accessed 21 Feb 2025
16. SHRDZM IT Services e.U. https://www.shrdzm.com/. Accessed 21 Feb 2025
17. Hallmann, M., Pietracho, R., Komarnicki, P., et al.: IKT-Konzepte zur Digitalisierung von MicroGrids und deren Betriebsführung. HMD 61, 855–873 (2024). https://doi.org/10.1365/s40702-024-01075-2

18. Jimenez, S.: Interoperability Framework in Energy Data Spaces, International Data Spaces Association (2023). https://doi.org/10.5281/zenodo.10117882, White Paper, 2023
19. Eclipse Foundation, "Eclipse Dataspace Connector," GitHub. https://github.com/eclipse-edc/Connector. Accessed 21 Feb 2025
20. Mischos, S., Dalagdi, E., Vrakas, D.: Intelligent energy management systems: a review. Artif. Intell. Rev. **56**(10), 11635–11674 (2023). https://doi.org/10.48550/arXiv.2206.03264

On Self-Improving Token Embeddings

Mario M. Kubek[1]($\boxtimes$)(ORCID), Shiraj Pokharel[1](ORCID), Thomas Böhme[2](ORCID),
Emma L. McDaniel[1](ORCID), Herwig Unger[3](ORCID), and Armin R. Mikler[1](ORCID)

[1] Georgia State University, Atlanta, GA, USA
{mkubek,emcdaniel10,amikler}@gsu.edu
[2] Ilmenau University of Technology, Ilmenau, Germany
thomas.boehme@tu-ilmenau.de
[3] University of Hagen, Hagen, Germany
herwig.unger@fernuni-hagen.de

Abstract. This article introduces a novel and fast method for refining pre-trained static word or, more generally, token embeddings. By incorporating the embeddings of neighboring tokens in text corpora, it continuously updates the representation of each token, including those without pre-assigned embeddings. This approach effectively addresses the out-of-vocabulary problem, too. Operating independently of large language models and shallow neural networks, it enables versatile applications such as corpus exploration, conceptual search, and word sense disambiguation. The method is designed to enhance token representations within topically homogeneous corpora, where the vocabulary is restricted to a specific domain, resulting in more meaningful embeddings compared to general-purpose pre-trained vectors. As an example, the methodology is applied to explore storm events and their impacts on infrastructure and communities using narratives from a subset of the NOAA Storm Events database. The article also demonstrates how the approach improves the representation of storm-related terms over time, providing valuable insights into the evolving nature of disaster narratives.

Keywords: Natural Language Processing · Evolving word embeddings · Context-dependency · Topic shift · Storm events · Corpus exploration · Large Language Models

1 Motivation

The assignment of meaningful representations to words and tokens is a crucial activity in many natural language processing (NLP) applications. Using the self-attention mechanism, large language models (LLMs) based on the Transformer architecture, such as BERT [1], assign high-dimensional real-valued embedding vectors, usually referred to as word or token embeddings (hidden states), to input tokens. These hidden states are influenced and modified by the information of the surrounding tokens or text and represent an essential component

S. Zielinski et al. (Eds.): I4CS 2025, CCIS 2513, pp. 126–143, 2025.
https://doi.org/10.1007/978-3-031-94263-1_9

of information processing in the Transformer network[1]. While they are propagated through the network, they are subject to constant changes in the multiple layers of the Transformer models, for example through the aforementioned self-attention mechanism and feed-forward networks. This approach is essential in order to capture subtle linguistic nuances, but it also means that the embeddings are highly contextualized due to these local influences and will result in very different hidden states even for thematically similar words (not just homonyms).

In some applications, however, it is desirable to seek a more stable word and token representation, especially if the surrounding context is a thematically homogeneous document whose thematic orientation does not change. This could be the case in information retrieval systems that aim to semantically transform large collections of documents, in which the thematic orientation remains consistent across documents. Similarly, it can be relevant in document classification tasks in which documents belong to distinct categories, each with consistent thematic content.

To this end, it would make sense to calculate so-called static word embeddings using Word2Vec [2], FastText [3], or GloVe [4] for the document set in question. While this approach is certainly feasible, its computational and time requirements vary depending on the size of the corpora. Furthermore, the generated word embeddings are uncontextualized, unlike those generated by an LLM. An alternative is the use of pre-trained word embeddings such as the vectors [5] calculated from the Google News Dataset. These embeddings cover three million words in the English language. However, the problem is that these embeddings stem from general-language sources, so that even and especially ambiguous terms are only assigned a single embedding that combines several contextual influences. This problem is exacerbated by the fact that word embeddings are often dominated by a word's most frequent meaning. The reason is that the frequency of word senses typically follows a power law [6], with one dominant sense and several less frequent, rarer meanings. However, within a specific domain, words typically appear in one single meaning. Therefore, many ambiguities can be avoided by selecting domain-specific texts.

Consequently, the out-of-the-box use of general language embeddings is not useful if terms in highly specialized or technical language documents are to be assigned a suitable representation. Even so, these general-language embedding vectors may provide a useful starting point for assigning stable and thematically oriented word embeddings to such terms in specialized documents and corpora.

In this article, the authors present a novel and fast approach to assign topic-specific word embeddings by iteratively refining pre-trained word embeddings using contextual information in topically oriented documents and corpora. The

---

[1] In technical contexts, the term 'token' refers to individual units of text, such as words, punctuation marks, or subword units that are processed by a model. 'Word', on the other hand, typically refers to a semantic unit used in natural language. In this article, the authors will use the terms 'word embedding' and 'token embedding' interchangeably, treating them as representations of these textual units regardless of their precise technical distinction.

resulting word embeddings aim to better capture the document- and corpus-specific peculiarities and word usage patterns. In order to speed up their computation, this method does not rely on shallow or deep neural networks. This makes it possible to apply it in a real-time setting in which streams of textual data need to be processed as fast as possible. The authors regard this iterative refinement process as "self-improving," since the embeddings evolve with each contextual update and increasingly reflect the semantics of the domain-specific corpus without requiring model retraining.

In Sect. 2, the fundamentals of this method are introduced, with references to relevant literature. Section 3 then details its mathematical and technical aspects. Section 4 describes the experimental setup and presents the initial results. In Sect. 5, the method's potential fields of application are discussed. Finally, Sect. 6 summarizes the article and explores the implications for future research and applications of the proposed method.

2   Fundamentals

The principle of distributional semantics, rooted in the theory of linguistic structuralism, suggests that words appearing in similar contexts have similar meanings. Embedding techniques like Word2Vec leverage this principle to create embeddings for words, tokens, and (sub)tokens [7]. These high-dimensional real-valued vectors represent such linguistic units in a way that their geometric relationships in the vector space capture – among other aspects – semantic similarities and differences.

In this space, words with similar meanings are located close to each other, reflecting the underlying distributional properties learned from large text corpora. Typically, a single embedding is assigned to a word, although it would be more sensible to assign polysemous and homonymous words different embeddings reflecting their diverse semantic orientations and word senses.

Furthermore, static embeddings can only represent words that were present in the training corpus. Words that did not appear during training (out-of-vocabulary words) cannot be represented effectively per se. Thus, a model generated by Word2Vec, for example, is confined to the world of the given training data. This problem has been alleviated by using subword information in models like FastText [3], which breaks words into character n-grams, allowing the representation of unseen words based on their constituent parts. Another solution called à la carte embedding [8] is able to induce embeddings for previously unseen words by relying on a linear transformation that is efficiently learnable using existing pre-trained word vectors and linear regression.

When working with thematically homogeneous texts and corpora, as mentioned in Sect. 1, the out-of-the-box use of pre-trained word embeddings is only of limited help because they do not adequately represent the meanings of (possibly technical) terms, which are influenced and shifted by their specific contexts and the topical orientation in the actual documents at hand. It is therefore of particular interest to technically determine the degree of these shifts in meaning (especially with respect to the terms' pre-trained general-language embeddings) and the extent to which they capture the document- or corpus-related characteristics of the content.

In the literature, there are various useful solutions for constructing representations of larger textual structures, including methods like text-representing centroid terms (TRCs) [9], Doc2Vec [10], and sentence transformers such as SBERT [11], which aim to provide meaningful representations at this level.

In contrast, the approach discussed herein works at the term level and is aimed at supporting the exploration of content relationships in thematically homogeneous corpora.

3 Computing Topic-Specific Embeddings

3.1 Preliminary Considerations

The method's general goal is to iteratively update embeddings of words and tokens based on their contextual usage. At the same time, the approach aims to capture the evolving meanings of words by keeping a history of the updated embeddings. The method relies on the existence of a set of general-language pre-trained word embeddings such as the vectors [5] calculated from the Google News Dataset.

Since these pre-defined embedding vectors are contextually adjusted by the method, this can be considered a specific case of transfer learning. However, while the use of pre-trained embeddings is not strictly necessary, as the desired word embeddings could also be generated through randomized initialization and iterative updates, reliance on this resource is still preferred. This allows these embeddings to transfer their pre-trained syntactic and semantic knowledge from large amounts of readily available and unlabeled data to other representations, tailored to local contexts. As such, the pre-trained embeddings are used during the initial look-up of a word that appears in the input text.

3.2 The Working Principle

The general working principle of the method is as follows: The words, or more precisely tokens, of a text or corpus D are extracted as part of a tokenization process and filtered according to a predefined part of speech list. Optionally, stop words should be removed and lemmatization can be performed.

The method employs a fixed general context window that remains constant throughout the update process. This window size s is determined based on the specific application requirements. Each target token, whose updated embedding is sought, can appear in a set of context windows C_t. Although only one context window is moved over the list of input tokens, which could be restricted to the necessary criteria (e.g., parts of speech, lemmata), this window covers s positions in the list at each time step. It is therefore justified to speak of different windows here. Generally, all tokens can become a target token.

Within a specific context window c, the most current word embeddings are extracted for each target token t (in the middle of the current context window c, denoted as $e_{t_{current}}$), and its neighboring tokens n in c, denoted as $e_{n_{current}}$. Then, for each context window c, the target token's embedding e_t is updated using learning rate α (hyperparameter) as shown in (1).

$$e_{t_{new}} = e_{t_{current}} + \alpha \sum_{n \in c} e_{n_{current}} \tag{1}$$

The resulting embedding vector should additionally be normalized, as shown in (2):

$$e_{t_{new}} = e_{t_{new}} / \|e_{t_{new}}\| \tag{2}$$

As mentioned before, not only the most recent embedding vector of target token t should be stored, but its update history as well. This will enable a more comprehensive analysis of its topical development.

In case the token's embedding is updated for the first time, its current embedding $e_{t_{current}}$ used will point to the pre-trained embedding vector in case it exists. If it does not, a zero vector will be used as a placeholder. In this case, the initial update will assign a token embedding that is induced by the (existing) neighboring token embeddings in the current context window. The method can therefore compensate for missing embeddings by data imputation, too. The strength of the embedding adjustment therefore depends in particular on the parameter α and the size of the context window.

3.3   Conceptual Influences

As previously mentioned, the embedding vector of a target word is updated with each occurrence by combining its current embedding vector with the embedding vectors of its neighboring words within the respective context. This approach was partly inspired by the graph-based method of evolving text centroids presented in [12], which generalizes and extends the concept of text-representing centroid terms (TRCs) [9]. Centroid terms are single, meaningful words that semantically and topically characterize text documents, thereby serving as compact symbolic representations in automated text processing tasks.

The study demonstrated that such characteristic terms can be identified through a continuous and incremental adjustment of their positions within a large, general-purpose knowledge graph, tailored to the specific circumstances of the analyzed text. This process naturally forms traces of centroids (centroid trails), representing the thematic evolution of these terms until their final centroid terms are established. In contrast, the method described herein leverages word embeddings and is designed to quickly and continuously update the representations of potentially all terms in the given texts. Even so, it is not intended to produce a comprehensive document representation, as it operates solely at the term level. However, it retains the update history of a word's representation, thereby enabling an exploratory analysis of a term's topical shifts, similar to what can be achieved with centroid traces.

This approach also shares similarities with the self-attention mechanism found in Transformer-based neural network architectures to some extent. The similarity arises from the way both methods dynamically adjust representations based on the surrounding context. In the self-attention mechanism, the model computes attention scores that weigh the importance of each word relative to others in the sequence, allowing it to capture contextual relationships effectively. Similarly, in the method discussed here, the embedding of a target word is updated by incorporating information from its neighboring words, ensuring that its representation is continuously adapted to reflect the context it appears in. This iterative, context-driven adjustment of representations helps capture nuanced semantic shifts in a way that is conceptually akin to how self-attention works in Transformers. Both techniques aim to enhance the understanding of word meanings by accounting for their immediate linguistic environment, with the key difference residing in the underlying operations used to achieve this context-dependent adaptation.

4   Experimental Results

To demonstrate the usefulness of the method presented, a series of experimental results will be presented in this section. First, it will be shown that the method using pre-trained general language word embeddings can be applied to compute semantically meaningful adapted word embeddings for terms in thematically homogeneous texts and corpora, which are significantly more expressive than the original embeddings. Additionally, it is demonstrated that the method consistently generates embeddings that align closely with the topical area of the corpus.

All of the following results are based on the "GoogleNews-vectors-negative300" general-language dataset [5], which contains 300-dimensional, pre-trained embedding vectors derived from the Google News dataset using Word2Vec [2]. The plain text of the documents was extracted and tokenized, whereby only the parts of speech adjectives, adverbs, nouns, proper nouns, and verbs were allowed for the analysis (general-language stop words were removed, too). Also, all tokens, except proper nouns, were converted to lowercase, and lemmatization was performed. In case of multi-word expressions, only the individual components were extracted, not the multi-word expressions (connected with e.g. an underscore) as a whole.

4.1   A First Example

To illustrate the method's working principle qualitatively, the result of the analysis of the Wikipedia article "abuse case" [13] in the topical area of secure software engineering and threat modeling will first be interpreted. To parameterize the method, the size s of the context window was set to 19 (the article's mean sentence length is 19.76) and the learning rate α to 0.01. The method was executed twice in succession (2 epochs).

Table 1. Most similar terms to 'abuse' and their similarity scores

Presented method	Score	Orig. pre-trained vectors	Score
case	0.98	sexual_abuse	0.76
use	0.96	Abuse	0.67
diagram	0.94	abusers	0.63
UML	0.88	abuses	0.63
security	0.87	abused	0.63
requirement	0.86	abuser	0.62
system	0.86	mistreatment	0.61
misuse	0.85	abusing	0.61
behaviour	0.82	maltreatment	0.61
term	0.73	sexual_misconduct	0.57

Table 2. Cosine similarity values between updated embedding vectors for the terms most similar to 'abuse' and their respective original pre-trained vectors after the latest update

Updated Term Vector	Cosine Similarity
case	0.33
use	0.68
diagram	0.61
UML	0.13
security	0.63
requirement	0.75
system	0.69
misuse	0.78
behaviour	N/A
term	0.82

The resulting Table 1 distinctly illustrates the divergence in the lists of terms considered most similar to the query term 'abuse' based on the presented method's modified word vectors and the original pre-trained vectors. Similarity scores, truncated to two decimal places, were determined using cosine similarity. The method's results are influenced by the specific context of the analyzed dataset, leading to terms that reflect that context. Conversely, the original pre-trained vectors did not yield comparable results, which suggests a focus on terms related to more general associations with 'abuse'. In addition, many of these terms are syntactically similar to the query term. These desired, context-specific results demonstrate how the method can yield relevant semantic relationships tailored to the specific dataset.

Furthermore, Table 2 shows cosine similarity values between updated embedding vectors for the terms most similar to 'abuse' and their original pre-trained vectors. Low cosine similarity values for terms such as 'case' (0.33) and 'UML' (0.13) indicate significant changes in their embeddings, which reflect considerable shifts from the original vectors. Notably, the term 'behaviour' (British spelling variant) is marked as N/A because it was not found in the pre-trained model. For the term 'abuse' (not included in the table) itself, the same calculation was performed. Here, the cosine similarity value obtained was 0.40, which also indicates a significant shift in its term vector.

4.2   Analyzing Storm Events in the US

The NOAA Storm Events Database [14] is a comprehensive collection of severe weather events documented by the National Oceanic and Atmospheric Administration (NOAA) in the United States. It provides detailed information on various types of extreme weather occurrences, such as tornadoes, hurricanes, floods, thunderstorms, and winter storms. Of particular interest are the often included event narratives, which offer detailed descriptions of the weather phenomena, impacts, and local conditions associated with a particular event. These narratives are particularly well-suited for methods that aim to extract key terms and uncover significant patterns in textual disaster records, as demonstrated by recent work on unsupervised key term extraction [15]. Due to their topical directedness, these event narratives are an interesting subject of analysis for the presented method, too. Therefore, as an example, combined narratives of storm events from 1993 were analyzed.

After pre-processing, the token list to analyze contained 3,466 unique tokens (out of the original 141,206) elements from 4,418 documents (out of the original 8,664) in the dataset that actually contain storm event narratives. Notably, only 2,872 of those unique tokens have a representation in the set of the original pre-trained vectors used. This clearly shows that the mentioned out-of-vocabulary problem is indeed to be addressed. The method's parameters were set as follows: the size s of the context window was set to 13 (aligned with the corpus' mean sentence length of 14.72), and the learning rate α was set to 0.01, 0.075, and 0.15 respectively. The method was executed twice in succession (2 epochs).

Figures 1, 2, and 3 illustrate the transformation of the embedding vector for the term 'thunderstorm' into a two-dimensional space using Principal Component Analysis (PCA). Principal Component 1 (on the x-axis) captures the primary direction of variation in the token embeddings, representing differences between words associated with natural phenomena, such as thunderstorms, earthquakes, or floods. As a result, the embedding for 'thunderstorm' will be positioned along the Principal Component 1 axis, close to other climate-related terms. Principal Component 2 (on the y-axis) represents a more specific direction of variation in the embeddings. This component captures finer distinctions, such as the intensity of the terms. For instance, 'thunderstorm' would be placed closer to terms like 'tornado' or 'avalanche' and farther from milder weather terms like 'breeze.'

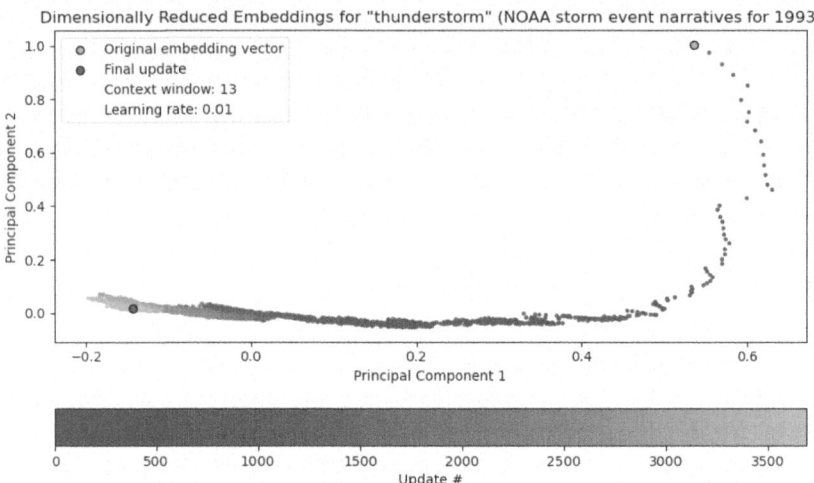

Fig. 1. Two-dimensional representation of the evolving embedding vector for the term 'thunderstorm' with learning rate 0.01 and context window size of 13

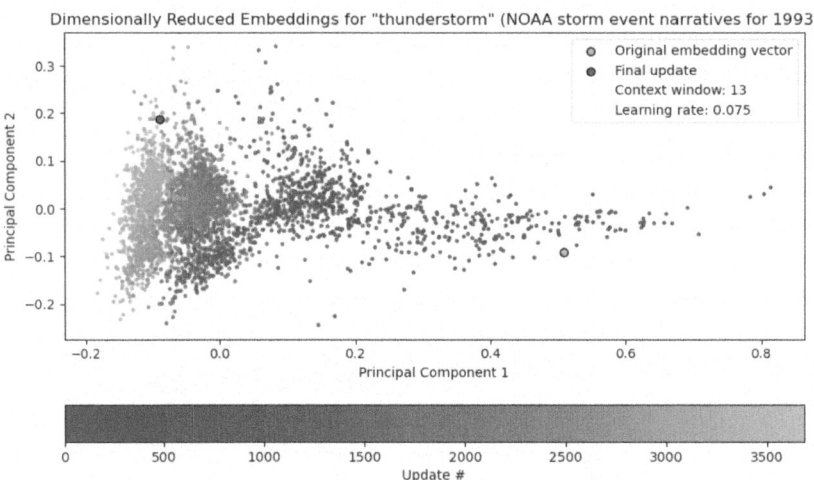

Fig. 2. Two-dimensional representation of the evolving embedding vector for the term 'thunderstorm' with learning rate 0.075 and context window size of 13

Additionally, the figures demonstrate how the embedding vector evolves relative to its original representation from the pre-trained dataset as more text is processed. Specifically, 3,686 embedding vectors were generated from 1,843 occurrences of the term 'thunderstorm' extracted from the corpus. The influence of different learning rates on the stability of these embeddings is clearly observable, with varying rates affecting how the vector shifts over time.

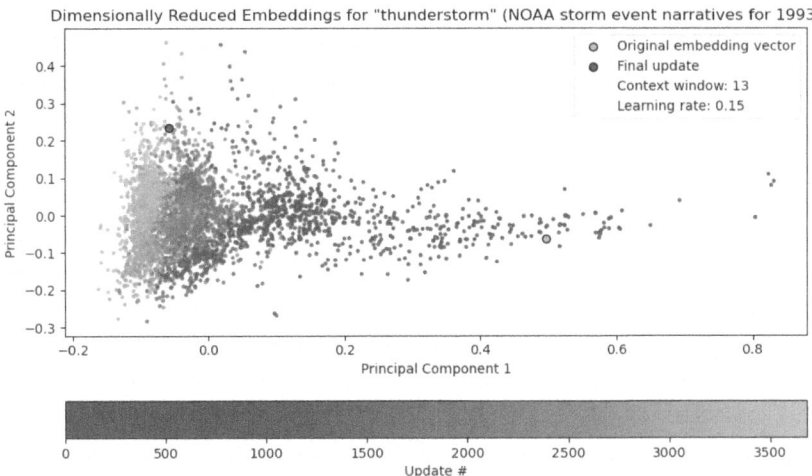

Fig. 3. Two-dimensional representation of the evolving embedding vector for the term 'thunderstorm' with learning rate 0.15 and context window size of 13

A learning rate α of 0.075 and 0.15 results in significant fluctuations influenced by the local context of the term. This observation aligns with the behavior of neural networks during gradient descent, where large learning rates lead to instability. Conversely, a much smaller learning rate α of 0.01 leads to embedding vectors with less fluctuation, a behavior consistently observed across various experiments and datasets. Therefore, a smaller learning rate is recommended, as it leads to a more stable representation of the term in the embedding space. It is worth noting that the method's efficiency, attributed to the application of linear algebra operations, ensures rapid corpus processing. On an i7-12650H processor, the analysis of the 1993 storm event narratives corpus will take approximately four seconds.

To qualitatively assess the results of the presented method, Table 3 lists the five terms most similar to the query terms 'thunderstorm', 'tornado', and 'emergency' for both the presented method and the originally pre-trained vectors. It can be observed that the word embeddings returned by the method are more meaningful, specific, and representative of the given topically homogeneous corpus. For example, the most similar embedding vectors represent terms that point to the impacts and accompanying characteristics of storm events and related terms.

In contrast, the terms most similar to the original vectors are more general and primarily indicate syntactically similar expressions which do not support deeper topic analysis. Hence, even though the original vectors are employed, for the purpose of corpus exploration, the method's returned and modified word embeddings are better suited as they properly capture the underlying documents' topical directions. Furthermore, while the method shares some resemblance with

Table 3. Most similar terms to 'thunderstorm', 'tornado', and 'emergency' according to the embeddings created by the presented method (top) and the original pre-trained vectors (bottom)

Presented method		
thunderstorm	tornado	emergency
storm	crop	management
cluster	public	office
mph	baseball	barn
spotter	school	department
limb	thunderstorm	roof
quarter	lightning	county
time	windshield	afternoon
fence	farmstead	community
outbuilding	ground	Lubbock
sign	police	Skywarn

Orig. pre-trained vectors		
thunderstorm	tornado	emergency
thunderstorms	twister	Emergency
severe_thunderstorm	tornadoes	emergencies
severe_thunderstorms	tornados	emer_gency
rainstorm	twisters	emegency
thundershower	F3_tornado	emergeny
thunder_storms	EF3_tornado	nonemergency
heavy_rain	funnel_cloud	ambulance
downpour	F2_tornado	nonemergencies
rain	tornado_touched	technician_Tim_Rujan
Thunderstorms	EF5_tornado	EMERGENCY

the graph-based and symbolic method of evolving centroid terms [12], the resulting embedding vectors can more accurately capture the syntactic and semantic nuances of the terms. In the analyzed corpus, the average cosine similarity of 0.56 for the mentioned 2,872 unique tokens' embeddings to their original embeddings suggests that the method generates embeddings that greatly differ from the original ones.

Figure 4 presents six 3D PCA projections of the temporal evolution of embeddings for term pairs, each representing 'thunderstorm' and a manually selected comparison term. The key parameters of the method were set to a context window size of $s = 13$ and a learning rate of $\alpha = 0.01$. The first four selected

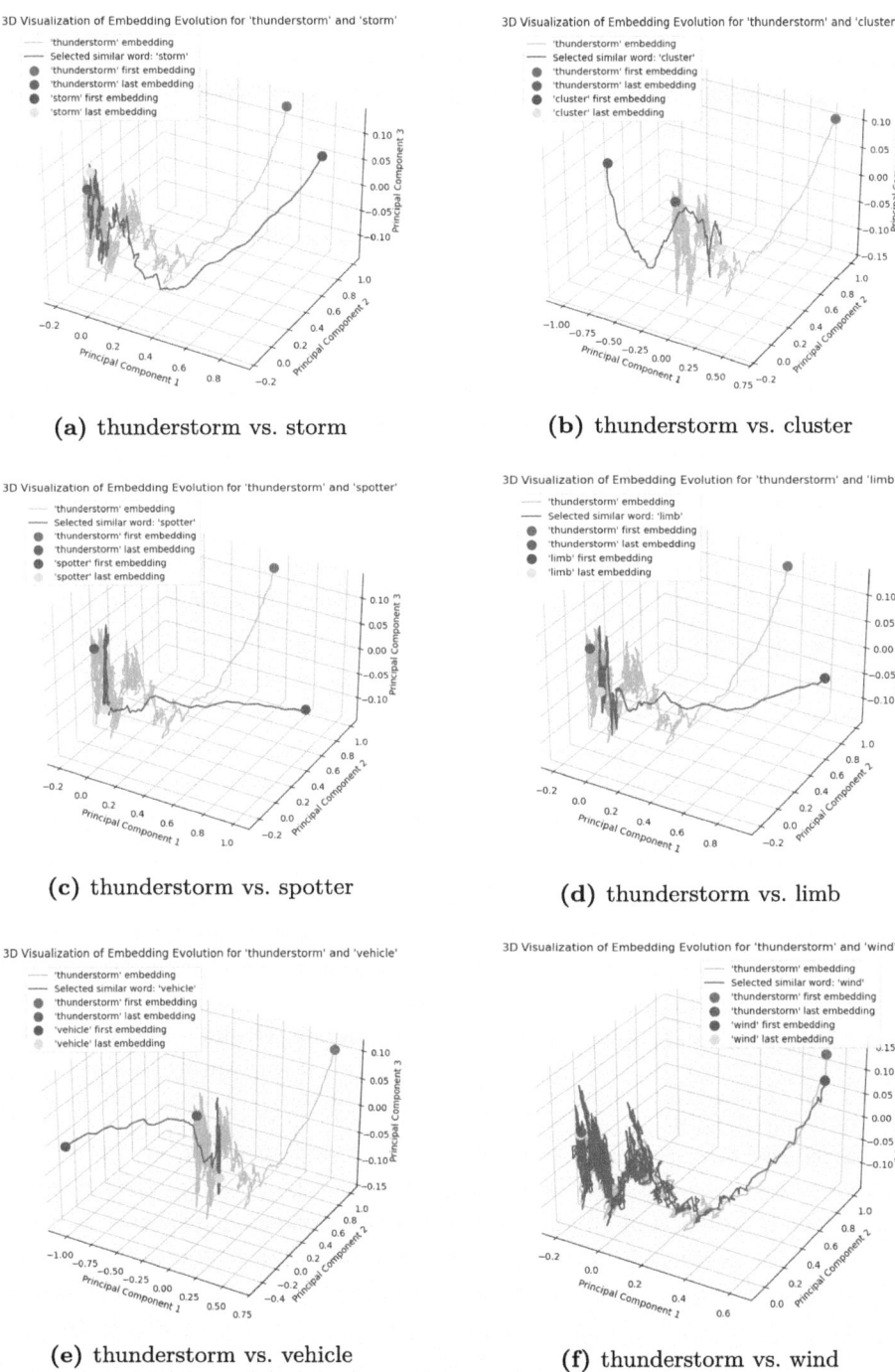

Fig. 4. 3D Visualization of the temporal evolution of word embeddings for selected term pairs using 'thunderstorm' as a reference

terms – 'storm,' 'cluster,' 'spotter,' and 'limb' – are among the most similar to 'thunderstorm' after applying the method. The embeddings for 'vehicle' and 'wind', as represented in Figs. 4e and 4f, exhibit distinct characteristics, which are explained below.

These embeddings evolve over time as they are updated based on storm-related event descriptions extracted from the NOAA Storm Events Dataset [14]. The principal components in the plots capture the most significant variance in the embedding space after dimensionality reduction. Each subplot uses color-coded trajectories and markers to indicate:

- The trajectory of 'thunderstorm' (orange) and that of a given selected word (blue).
- The initial embedding position (red for 'thunderstorm,' purple for the selected word).
- The final embedding position after all updates (green for 'thunderstorm,' yellow for the selected word).

Figure 4a illustrates that the embedding for 'storm' remains closely aligned with 'thunderstorm' throughout the updates, with both trajectories evolving in parallel. The initial positions (red for 'thunderstorm,' purple for 'storm') are already close, and the final positions (green for 'thunderstorm,' yellow for 'storm') remain in proximity, which indicates strong semantic stability. The closely aligned trajectory suggests minimal divergence and reinforces that 'storm' consistently co-evolves with 'thunderstorm' in the dataset. It also suggests that these terms are used interchangeably in the given storm event descriptions.

Figure 4b shows that the embedding for 'cluster' starts farther from 'thunderstorm' than 'storm' but gradually shifts closer over time. While the initial positions (red for 'thunderstorm,' purple for 'cluster') indicate a considerable semantic distance, the final positions (green for 'thunderstorm,' yellow for 'cluster') show increased proximity. This change suggests that 'cluster' becomes more contextually associated with 'thunderstorm' as updates are applied, likely due to its frequent co-occurrence in storm-related reports where storm clusters are described.

Figures 4c and 4d present the temporal evolution of the embeddings for 'spotter' and 'limb', each in relation to 'thunderstorm'. Both exhibit similar trajectories. The embeddings start farther from 'thunderstorm' compared to more directly related meteorological terms like 'storm', and their movements indicate a weaker but still notable semantic association. While both words shift closer to 'thunderstorm' over time, their final positions remain relatively distant, which indicates a more indirect contextual relationship. 'Spotter' is linked to storm observation and reporting, while 'limb' may appear in contexts describing storm-related impacts such as damage or injuries. The observed embedding shifts reflect how these terms interact with storm descriptions in the dataset without being core meteorological concepts.

Figure 4e shows that the embedding for 'vehicle' initially lies in a semantically distant region from 'thunderstorm', which reflects their distinct meanings. Over time, however, their embeddings shift closer together, suggesting an increasing contextual association. This shift is likely driven by their frequent co-occurrence in descriptions of storm impacts, particularly damage to vehicles caused by thunderstorms. While 'vehicle' does not inherently belong to meteorological terminology, its embedding adapts to reflect its relevance in the given corpus, where storm-related damages and disruptions play a significant role.

In Fig. 4f, the embedding for 'wind' initially occupies a position very close to 'thunderstorm', and their trajectories remain nearly identical throughout the updates. This strong alignment indicates a stable semantic relationship, likely due to the intrinsic connection between wind and thunderstorms in meteorological contexts. Unlike other words, which undergo noticeable shifts, 'wind' and 'thunderstorm' evolve in parallel. This pattern indicates that their contextual association is well-established in the dataset and remains consistent over time.

A key observation is that while some words, such as 'wind', remain semantically close to 'thunderstorm' from the beginning and exhibit nearly identical trajectories, others, like 'cluster' and 'vehicle', start from more distant regions and gradually shift closer due to their contextual co-occurrence with storm-related events. This effect is particularly pronounced in homogeneous corpora, such as the analyzed storm-related reports, where words related to storm impacts (e.g., 'vehicle,' 'limb') or observation ('spotter') undergo embedding adjustments due to their frequent co-occurrence with 'thunderstorm' in descriptive contexts.

These results reinforce the idea that word embeddings capture not only static semantic relationships but also context-dependent shifts driven by corpus updates. This study provides insights into how specialized vocabulary in domain-specific datasets stabilizes over time and reflects both inherent semantic relationships and contextual shifts.

5   Applications

The following applications are hypothetical examples from research and practice. They illustrate how the proposed method aligns with various requirements and objectives in different contexts. Future work will investigate these solutions in detail to evaluate their effectiveness and optimize their implementation.

5.1   Corpus Exploration: Term Clustering and Topic Tracking

The method of self-improving embeddings holds significant benefits for corpus exploration, particularly in tasks involving term clustering and the temporal tracking of topics or terms. By maintaining a history of embedding updates, this approach enables researchers and practitioners to observe how the semantic representations of terms evolve across a corpus or over time. This, in turn, allows for the derivation and investigation of new research questions and hypotheses.

Term Clustering. Through iterative refinement, the embeddings generated by this method naturally group semantically or topically related terms in the vector space. This facilitates the identification of term clusters that reveal underlying themes or concepts within a corpus. For example, in a dataset of research articles, terms related to a specific scientific field can converge into cohesive clusters, enabling an automated exploration of thematic patterns.

Topic and Term Evolution. The ability to retain and analyze embedding history adds a unique dimension to topic tracking. By examining changes in the embeddings of specific terms, it becomes possible to monitor shifts in their contextual usage. This is particularly valuable in longitudinal studies, where the emergence or evolution of topics can be traced across different time periods. For instance, in social media analysis, this technique can help capture how the usage of trending terms adapts to evolving public discourse.

In both applications, the context-dependent adjustment of embeddings ensures that the resulting representations are finely tuned to the corpus-specific semantics. This adaptability, combined with the method's computational efficiency, makes it a suitable tool for exploring large, diachronic and topically homogeneous text corpora.

5.2   An Interactive Q&A Chatbot Built on a Local Knowledge Base

Providing effective employee support through a generative AI-powered chatbot requires more than just retrieving documents based on keywords; it necessitates a nuanced understanding of the organization's internal knowledge base. This is especially challenging when the knowledge base consists of diverse file formats like Word, Excel, PDF, and PowerPoint, each tailored to specific organizational purposes. General-purpose embeddings, utilized via an enterprise-licensed or open-source vector database, do not adequately capture the domain-specific nuances embedded within such documents. These static embeddings are trained on fixed datasets, making them ill-suited to adapt to evolving organizational knowledge and contexts. Consequently, responses based on these embeddings risk being generic or outdated, which can diminish user engagement.

The presented method addresses these limitations by continuously refining embeddings based on the content and context of the internal knowledge base. This ensures that the chatbot can dynamically adapt to changes in organizational knowledge, enabling it to offer responses that are precise, context-aware, and tailored to employee queries.

Conceptual Search Through Semantic Transformation. By mapping a document's terms and the document itself into a high-dimensional semantic vector space, a semantic transformation is performed. This allows the chatbot to conduct conceptual searches by gaining a deeper understanding of the textual content. In this space, relationships between words, concepts, and themes are encoded, enabling the chatbot to identify and retrieve relevant information.

Although a semantic transformation does not necessarily require symbolic methods like TF-IDF (term frequency-inverse document frequency) [16], incorporating term weights can improve the process by highlighting domain-specific terms while downweighting common, less-informative ones (e.g., 'the' or 'system'). This hybrid approach merges the symbolic precision of TF-IDF with the rich contextual understanding of word embeddings, empowering the chatbot to uncover both explicit and implicit connections within the knowledge base. Key benefits of this approach include:

- **Context-Aware Retrieval:** Instead of merely identifying documents containing the queried keywords, the chatbot retrieves documents that are conceptually aligned with the query. By leveraging refined embeddings and semantic mapping, the chatbot ensures its responses reflect the broader meaning and relevance of the query.

- **Conceptual Queries with Weighted Embeddings:** Using weighted combinations of word embeddings, powered by techniques like TF-IDF, the chatbot can process complex queries involving multiple terms or themes. For example, a search for 'increasing revenue streams' might retrieve documents discussing profitability, growth strategies, or competitive analysis, even when the exact term 'revenue' is absent.

Through conceptual search, the chatbot not only finds documents that match a query explicitly but also identifies those that share a deeper semantic alignment. This makes it a powerful tool for exploring and navigating the organization's internal knowledge base with greater precision and insight. Beyond internal use cases, such capabilities are highly relevant for community services as well, where public-facing chatbots or local information platforms can benefit from context-sensitive, continuously adapting embeddings – e.g., to support emergency response, citizen inquiries, or evolving municipal knowledge bases that require up-to-date information representation.

Adapting to Evolving Knowledge. By analyzing query logs and iteratively updating embeddings, the chatbot ensures that its semantic space evolves alongside the knowledge base. This dynamic adaptation captures emerging trends and updates domain-specific embeddings, keeping the chatbot relevant and effective over time. With this approach, the generative AI chatbot transitions from a static query-response system to an intelligent assistant capable of conceptual understanding, empowering employees with precise and insightful answers.

5.3   Continuous Deployment and Integration of Data Pipelines

As new word embeddings are generated, they can be directly integrated into existing data pipelines without downtime. A versioning system can ensure that the data pipeline can check-point to previously used embeddings if new updates do not work as expected. A/B testing can be performed to compare the performance of the old and new embeddings on a subset of organizational use cases involving queries, ensuring that updates improve the data pipeline's overall performance without introducing performance degradation.

Once the updated embeddings are deployed, real-time monitoring can assess the pipeline's improved performance. Metrics such as response accuracy, user satisfaction ratings, and query resolution time should be tracked.

6   Conclusion

In this article, the authors presented a novel and fast method for deriving topic-specific word embeddings. It captures the terms' topical directions in topically homogeneous corpora by considering their individual contexts. Designed to continuously update these word representations, it also enables the analysis of topic shifts. In the context of the showcased storm event analyses, it was demonstrated that this feature supports the dynamic assessment of the impacts and risks of these events for specific locations, providing a comprehensive understanding of their evolving effects. Furthermore, the applicability of the proposed method to evolving language data and task-specific requirements was highlighted. For instance, the authors showed that this approach allows embeddings to incrementally improve, resulting in more robust NLP systems capable of handling complex linguistic and contextual variations. This makes the method particularly valuable for real-time, community-centered applications such as local information services, emergency coordination, or public knowledge platforms. Future research work will investigate how the method can be combined with symbolic knowledge representations or lightweight neural models to support structured reasoning and domain adaptation, and to enable integration into large-scale, multilingual, and dynamic information systems that rely on interactive and agent-based components as core elements.

Acknowledgments. The authors sincerely thank Mr. Chandra Kiran Guntupalli, Master's student in Computer Science at Georgia State University, Atlanta, GA for his invaluable efforts in the preparation and interpretation of the 3D visualizations, which have greatly contributed to this work.

References

1. Devlin, J., Chang, M.-W., Lee, K., Toutanova, K.: BERT: pre-training of Deep Bidirectional Transformers for Language Understanding. In: Proceedings of the 2019 Conference of the North American Chapter of the Association for Computational Linguistics: Human Language Technologies, Volume 1 (Long and Short Papers), pp. 4171–4186. Association for Computational Linguistics, Minneapolis, Minnesota (2019). https://doi.org/10.18653/v1/N19-1423
2. Mikolov, T., Sutskever, I., Chen, K., Corrado, G.S., Dean, J.: Distributed representations of words and phrases and their compositionality. In: Advances in Neural Information Processing Systems, vol. 26. Curran Associates, Inc. (2013). https://doi.org/10.5555/2999792.2999959
3. Bojanowski, P., Grave, E., Joulin, A., Mikolov, T.: Enriching word vectors with subword information. Trans. Assoc. Comput. Linguist. **5**, 135–146 (2017). https://doi.org/10.1162/tacl_a_00051

4. Pennington, J., Socher, R., Manning, C.D.: Glove: global vectors for word representation. In: EMNLP, vol. 14, pp. 1532–1543 (2014). https://doi.org/10.3115/v1/D14-1162

5. Google: GoogleNews-vectors-negative300.bin.gz: Pre-trained Word Vectors (2013). https://code.google.com/archive/p/word2vec/. Accessed 26 Jan 2025

6. Kilgarriff, A.: How dominant is the commonest sense of a word? In: Sojka, P., Kopeček, I., Pala, K. (eds.) TSD 2004. LNCS (LNAI), vol. 3206, pp. 103–111. Springer, Heidelberg (2004). https://doi.org/10.1007/978-3-540-30120-2_14

7. Biemann, C., Heyer, G., Quasthoff, U.: Wissensrohstoff Text: Eine Einführung in das Text Mining. Springer Fachmedien Wiesbaden (2022). https://doi.org/10.1007/978-3-658-35969-0

8. Khodak, M., Saunshi, N., Liang, Y., Ma, T., Stewart, B., Arora, S.: A la carte embedding: cheap but effective induction of semantic feature vectors. In: Proceedings of the 56th Annual Meeting of the ACL (Volume 1: Long Papers), pp. 12–22. Association for Computational Linguistics, Melbourne, Australia (2018). https://doi.org/10.18653/v1/P18-1002

9. Kubek, M.M., Unger, H.: Centroid terms as text representatives. In: Proceedings of the 2016 ACM Symposium on Document Engineering, DocEng 2016, pp. 99–102. Association for Computing Machinery, New York, NY, USA (2016). https://doi.org/10.1145/2960811.2967150

10. Le, Q., Mikolov, T.: Distributed representations of sentences and documents. In: Proceedings of the 31st International Conference on Machine Learning ICML 2014, vol. 32, pp. II-1188-II-1196. JMLR.org, Beijing, China (2014). https://doi.org/10.5555/3044805.3045025

11. Reimers, N., Gurevych, I.: Sentence-BERT: sentence embeddings using siamese BERT-networks. In: Proceedings of the 2019 Conference on Empirical Methods in Natural Language Processing and the 9th International Joint Conference on Natural Language Processing (EMNLP-IJCNLP), pp. 3982–3992. Association for Computational Linguistics, Hong Kong, China (2019). https://doi.org/10.18653/v1/D19-1410

12. Unger, H., Kubek, M.: On evolving text centroids. In: Unger, H., Sodsee, S., Meesad, P. (eds.) IC2IT 2018. AISC, vol. 769, pp. 75–82. Springer, Cham (2019). https://doi.org/10.1007/978-3-319-93692-5_8

13. Wikipedia contributors: Abuse case. (2025). https://en.wikipedia.org/wiki/Abuse_case. Accessed 26 Jan 2025

14. National Oceanic and Atmospheric Administration (NOAA): Storm Events Database (2025). https://www.ncdc.noaa.gov/stormevents/. Accessed 26 Jan 2025

15. McDaniel, E.L.: Student research abstract: unsupervised key term extraction of disaster records. In: Proceedings of the 38th ACM/SIGAPP Symposium on Applied Computing (SAC 2023), pp. 653–656. ACM, New York (2023). https://doi.org/10.1145/3555776.3577211

16. Salton, G., Yang, C.S.: On the specification of term values in automatic indexing. J. Documentation **29**(4), 351–372 (1973)

Data Mesh and Data Space:
A Comparative Analysis with a Focus
on Governance

Attila Papp[1]([⊠])[iD], Udo Bub[1,2][iD], Viivi Lähteenoja[3][iD], Kai Kuikkaniemi[4][iD],
Marko Turpeinen[2][iD], and Sami Jokela[2]

[1] Faculty of Informatics, Eötvös Lóránd University (ELTE), Pázmány Péter sétány
1/C, Budapest 1117, Hungary
{attila.papp,udobub}@inf.elte.hu
[2] 1001 Lakes Oy, Porkkalankatu 5, 00180 Helsinki, Finland
{marko.turpeinen,sami.jokela}@1001lakes.com
[3] Faculty of Social Sciences, University of Helsinki, Fabianinkatu 33, 00014 Helsinki,
Finland
viivi.lahteenoja@helsinki.fi
[4] Cadentia Technologies Oy, Siltasaarenkatu 12 A, 00530 Helsinki, Finland
kai.kuikkaniemi@cadentia.ai

Abstract. In this paper, we describe and compare the emergent data
mesh and data space paradigms. These socio-technical approaches aim
to facilitate data sharing, but both of them has unique governance
structures. We rely on design science research methodologies, including a structured literature review subsequently complemented by expert
interviews, to highlight their idiosyncrasies, synergies, and differences.
While data mesh primarily focuses on domain-oriented decentralization
within a single organization, data space, by contrast, addresses inter-
organizational data exchange, emphasizing data sovereignty. In this comparative analysis, we show how each approach offers distinct strategies
for addressing data-sharing challenges, supporting their potential to converge and complement each other. These insights inform practitioners
and researchers about best-fit scenarios, guiding adoption decisions. Ultimately, we propose a foundation for future studies to investigate the
governance models further, elaborate on emerging convergences, explore
technical connection points and refine guidelines for choosing the most
effective paradigm.

Keywords: Data space · Data mesh · Data architecture · Data
management · Data governance · Data sovereignty · Literature review ·
Interview

1 Introduction

Data mesh and data space have been concepts in modern data sharing and management for a few years. Despite their similar goals of enabling data ecosystems,

ⓒ The Author(s), under exclusive license to Springer Nature Switzerland AG 2025
S. Zielinski et al. (Eds.): I4CS 2025, CCIS 2513, pp. 144–156, 2025.
https://doi.org/10.1007/978-3-031-94263-1_10

little research has been done on their idiosyncrasies, synergies, and differences. This study aims to investigate and identify the key aspects worth further attention and remedy a lack of scientifically founded guidance in deploying these paradigms.

The fundamental idea for both data mesh and data space approaches is quite simple: someone has access to data that someone else wants or needs to use, and both parties agree that this data should be shared - preferably in a mutually beneficial, repeatable, reliable, and secure manner. The simple use case of sharing one specific set of data from one particular party with another specific party in this way is relatively trivial. It does not require or warrant a data mesh or a data space. However, as soon as any one element in the use case multiplies, these data governance models become necessary and/or desirable. More sophisticated data-sharing concepts become indispensable once there are multiple data sets, multiple parties with access to data, and multiple parties who need or want the data. Both data mesh and data space approaches can be applied to enable the conditions of mutual benefit, repeatability, reliability, and security.

In the existing literature, data mesh, and data space are well defined from a situational and projectable solution perspective; however, the literature lacks a comparison. Although the fundamentals for both look uncannily similar at first glance, the concepts these two terms denote have differences. Therefore, data mesh and data space are new paradigms that tackle the same problem, but the differences are unclear. Our main goal is to answer the following research question:

RQ. What are the idiosyncrasies, synergies, and differences between data meshes and data spaces?

Literature gaps were also found in governance [9]; therefore, we conducted an in-depth examination of governance.

After describing the scientific methodology applied, this paper first takes a look at the problem space from a high level and then focuses on the solution space by comparing two existing projectable solutions: data meshes and data spaces. Finally, governance is compared for both approaches.

2   Scientific Methodology

2.1   Design Science Research Approach

The insights presented in this paper are embedded in our more comprehensive research activities to develop a scientifically grounded yet practically significant guideline for system design decision support for data sharing. Offermann et al. [14] have identified eight artifact types in information systems research, including the type of "guideline". They define a guideline as a "suggestion regarding behavior in a particular situation (if in situation X do Y)".

We use the Design Science Research (DSR) approach, as described, e.g., by Hevner et al. [8], ensuring scientific rigor and practical relevance for our research approach. Offermann et al. [15] have developed a DSR process that we apply to concrete artifact development. It structures the research process into three major phases: Problem Identification, Artifact Design, and Artifact Evaluation. For the process step of Problem Identification, a comprehensive literature review and interviews with experts are foreseen.

The following phase for the iterative artifact design of the guideline is ongoing but has already yielded useful partial results. This paper presents the stable results of these first two phases, as they provide the community with timely and useful insights that are valuable in their own right. In this paper, we share these results with a focus on data-sharing governance for data mesh and data spaces, as these are the important industrial trends for data-sharing concepts [17].

2.2   Literature Review

In order to find relevant literature on data mesh and data space comparison, the suggested procedure by Brocke et al. [1] for conducting structured and systematic literature reviews was followed. The scope of the literature review was narrowed, as Brocke et al. suggested [2], to focus on research outcomes by comparing data mesh and data spaces. As these data-sharing concepts are relatively new, the literature review focused on understanding the status quo, synergies, and idiosyncrasies in research and compiling existing findings. The review covered the relevant literature as comprehensively as possible to meet this goal.

A systematic database search was performed in October 2024 and repeated in January 2025 to find relevant literature to answer the RQ. Since the data mesh and data space concepts are new paradigms, scientific journals and the proceedings of renowned conferences were searched, as suggested by Brocke et al. [1]. Upon heuristic high-level literature search, it was found that data sharing is an interdisciplinary topic that is not only considered by researchers but also practitioners and is covered not only in computer science (e.g., IEEE Xplore, ACM) but in IS (AIS Library) as well as the fields of management (e.g., Elsevier Science Direct, EBSCO). To further improve the exhaustiveness of the search, Google Scholar was included - with careful consideration to avoid duplicates. The final set of databases searched are IEEE Xplore, ACM Digital Library, Springer Nature, Elsevier ScienceDirect, AIS eLibrary, EBSCO, Elsevier Scopus, and Web of Science. To search the databases, the data mesh and data space keywords were aggregated together to the following applied search string: "data mesh*" AND "data space*". To find relevant literature for discussing governance for each in general, the same databases were searched with the following search string for a second time: "data mesh governance" OR "data space governance".

The search string was applied in both cases without restrictions on publication date, but it was limited to English-language literature exclusively. Additionally, some practitioner publications (e.g., Poikola et al. [17]) were included in the search since they provide valuable insights as common practice in IS research.

The combined search resulted in 388 hits altogether. All hits underwent title screening, and 53 publications were included in the abstract screening. Some duplications were found; after duplicates were removed, 43 relevant publications remained. Sixteen of them were full-text screened and used for this article. The backward search yielded two more additional publications.

Expert interviews subsequently complemented the outcome of the literature review.

2.3   Expert Interviews

Having found that the literature on data mesh and data space comparison is limited, we conducted expert interviews to gather rich information and help identify new aspects. The interviews were exploratory and semi-structured. Questions asked included:

– What is the scope of data mesh and data space?
– What sort of objectives and challenges are targeted by these solutions? Do you see an overlap?
– How would you compare data mesh to data space from a high level?
– How does governance work in your experience in a data [mesh/space] setting?
– Do you see any potential for these data-sharing concepts to converge? If yes, when? If not, why?

All respondents are experts in their field and have experience with either of these two concepts. They not only participated in an interview but also made substantial contributions and reviewed the manuscript critically, and therefore qualified as co-authors of this publication (Table 1).

Table 1. Respondents and their perspectives

Role/Title	Perspectives
Technical lead	Data mesh, data sharing concepts, governance, and data products
Chief Product and Strategy Officer	Data ethics, policy, and governance
Senior Data Strategist, Senior Advisor	Data ethics, policy, and governance
Co-founder and Head of Product, Senior Advisor	Data mesh and data space, data products
Chief Executive Officer	Data sharing, ethics, and governance
Chairman, Chief Technology Officer	Data space implementation

3   Results

3.1   Overview and Comparison

The problem space for both solutions involves data-sharing challenges from different perspectives. The initial problems data meshes ought to solve would be bottlenecks introduced by centralized data management, which leads to a lack of domain ownership resulting in data silos - within a single organization.

Data spaces aim to solve data-sharing challenges across organizational boundaries while maintaining data sovereignty and trust. Fragmented data ecosystems, governance, and interoperability are the key challenges.

Despite having different motivators, both holistically viewing address the problem of efficiently managing and sharing data.

Describing Data Mesh. Data mesh is a projectable solution for data sharing and could be defined as a new generational distributed data platform paradigm aiming to democratize data at scale. Proceeding the first generation of data architectures (data warehouses) and the second generation (data lakes), the third and current generation of enterprise data platforms in the form of data meshes rely on the four following principles:

- **Domain-oriented decentralized data ownership and architecture:** Essentially, it brings back the responsibility of analytical data production to the teams where the operational data originates. By doing this, the ecosystem of data producers and consumers can scale out as the number of sources and destinations required. Think of autonomous nodes in a mesh.
- **Data as a product:** treating analytical data in a way that data users can quickly discover, understand, and securely consume them. Data is distributed across many domains.
- **Self-serve data infrastructure as a platform:** domain teams can create and consume data products autonomously using the platform abstractions, hiding the complexity of building interoperable data products.
- **Federated computational governance:** Data users can get value from the aggregation and correlation of data products. The mesh behaves as an ecosystem following global interoperability standards baked computationally into the platform. We will discuss this in more detail in the following sections.

These principles have been extracted from Dehghani Z.'s definition [4] and widely adopted in various industry settings. For more information, see Dehghani, Z. book [5] and Goedgebuure et al.'s literature review [7].

Describing Data Space. Data space is an interoperable framework based on common governance principles, standards, practices, and enabling services that enable trusted data transactions between participants [6]. It can be considered as a projectable solution for data sharing.

Data spaces have the following key concepts as per the Data Spaces Support Centre's definition [3]:

- **Governance framework:** includes a structured set of principles, processes, and practices that guide and regulate the governance, management, and operations within a data space.
- **Rulebook:** the documentation of the data space governance framework for operational use.

- **Governance authority:** participants committed to developing, maintaining, and enforcing the governance framework.
- **Participants:** parties committed to the governance framework of a data space and have a set of rights and obligations stemming from this framework.
- **Roles:** a distinct and logically consistent set of rights and duties (responsibilities) within a data space required to perform specific tasks related to a data space functionality. Performed by participants.
- **Functionality:** A specified set of tasks that are associated with roles.
- Infrastructure: components and services that enable data transactions to be performed within one or more data spaces.
- **Services:** functionalities for implementing data space capabilities are offered to participants of data spaces.
- **Data transactions:** interaction between data space participants for providing/using a data product.
- **Data product:** a data sharing unit, bundling resources (data and data services), and metadata that describes the license terms, the resources, and other information in a machine-readable way.
- **Use case:** a specific setting where two or more participants use a data space to create value from data sharing.

A practical approach in the form of Gaia-X provides the infrastructure and framework for developing European data spaces. Jeffar, F. & Plebani, P. [11] noted a noticeable resemblance and convergence between Gaia-X and data mesh, which further supports the argumentation that data mesh and data space concepts might converge.

Comparing Data Spaces and Data Meshes. The following comparison is from the literature review and the expert interviews. References are provided for all relevant studies that passed the full-text screening and were deemed relevant to our RQ. Combining these insights aims to provide a more comprehensive understanding of data mesh and space comparison. This topic gives rise to points of convergence and tension in different ways, affecting these approaches as governance models. Before comparing these two approaches in governance, we discuss some observable points of commonalities and differences overall. A summary is included in Table 2.

Origin. Data mesh: Mainly US enterprise architecture. Data space: Mainly EU, ecosystem governance.

Scope. The data mesh emerged from an intra-company setting, while the data space moves inter-company-wise. Data mesh: Intra-organizational/single organization or strictly defined set of partner organizations (for example, a 'digital' twin). In a data mesh setting, an actor is likely a cross-functional domain-oriented team within an organization. Data space: Inter-organizational/multi-organization ecosystem or domain. An actor is likely to represent the entire organization in a data space.

Objectives. Mutual benefit, repeatability, reliability, and security in both. Data-sharing agreements are being implemented on both sides. Data mesh governance focuses on efficiency and practicality. Data space governance focuses on sovereignty, which refers to the "self-determination of individuals and organizations with regard to the use of their data" [10], and transparency across organizational boundaries. It targets a legal and auditable basis to enforce it.

Problem to be Solved. Data mesh: Overcoming limitations of centralized data architectures within large enterprises. Data meshes are adopted to solve challenges faced by traditional centralized architectures, such as data lakes, to prevent bottlenecks imposed by central data lake teams. Data spaces: Overcoming limitations of centralized ecosystem architectures such as platform-based systems. Secure, trusted, and regulated data exchange.

Value to be Gained. Data mesh: Scaling and improving agility and data democratization efforts within an organization. [7] Governance-driven adoption (ESG, CSRD efforts, top-down). Data space: Collaborative goals, industry standards, potential regulations, and data sovereignty [16]. For data spaces, we observe a focus on trusted and regulated data exchange and industry standards, which emphasize data sovereignty and value creation through collaboration. Corporate Sustainability Reporting Directive (CSRD) and the whole supply chain of an industry are significant use cases for the first operational Data Spaces.

Prerequisites. A data mesh implementation apart from the technical know-how requires an organizational change, or at least an organization to be ready for domain-driven design, and a data mesh platform team develops and maintains the mesh, creates blueprints, and supports producers and consumers in their data journey. Machado I. A. et al. [13] and Dehghani Z. [4,5] highlight organizational change, domain-driven design, and platform thinking. Data space: Standardization to enable interoperability on the different levels of the ecosystem (legal, organizational, semantic, and technical), participant maturity in internal data governance, clear use case(s) where inter-organizational data sharing is essential, governance frameworks like rulebooks.

Decentralization. Both solutions aim to move away from centralized data management and towards a more distributed approach. For a data mesh, that means empowering domain-oriented teams within an organization. Data spaces aim to extend a similar decentralization across organizational boundaries.

Domain-Orientation. Both respect the importance of aligning data management with business domains. Data meshes inherently organize data ownership around domains within an organization, while data spaces also focus on specific sectors or domains.

Interoperability. Both approaches are designed with interoperability in mind. In a data mesh setting, governance teams (local and global) collaborate to define standards for data modeling, exchange protocols (output ports), and metadata management. Data spaces aiming for cross-organizational collaboration often prioritize interoperability as a core requirement.

Data Discoverability. Tools to make data findable, tangible ("ownable"), and easier to govern. Some standard tools are shared by both solutions, such as data discovery (data catalog). Some tools have partial overlap, such as data pipelines vs. connectors data sharing access control, and some are unique, such as data marketplaces that apply mainly only to data spaces.

Data Product Thinking. Data mesh thinking approached the "data product" primarily from a data governance perspective and as a data management unit. Secondarily, data meshes use a "business data view", i.e., identifying and treating data as a business object beyond its technical implementation. Data spaces adopted this from Data mesh. Data spaces (currently) approach the term "data product" primarily from an economic perspective and a unit of data monetization. Secondarily, "data product" is a technical term that describes a unit of data sharing that fulfills specific criteria regarding metadata, delivery mechanism, etc. While data spaces will not always explicitly consider treating data as a product, the concept remains: participants need to clearly define, document, and potentially monetize the data they offer within the ecosystem. For a more thorough overview, refer to Kuikkaniemi K., Guggenberger T. [12], and Otto, B. et al. [16].

Technology. From an architectural perspective, both approaches are considered decentralized. They are in sharp contrast with centralized, monolithic data architectures to enable data management scalably by avoiding a central data store. In the case of data spaces, this is driven by data sovereignty and trust [16], whereas, with data meshes, the primary motivation is preventing bottlenecks [4]. Due to their collaborative nature, toolset-wise data spaces tend to employ more open-source components (OSS). While a data mesh can also be built with OSS approaches, most successful implementations are either boxed solutions (e.g., Databricks Unity Catalog, AWS DataZone) or are based on a combination of existing services on a cloud platform. However, with the emergence of open table formats and approaches like Iceberg Catalog, we see a potential for broader open-source data mesh collaboration. The recent OSS release of the Polaris Catalog further supports this potential. Therefore, we see strong potential for data mesh and data space convergence from a technological perspective.

Differences in governance are explored in detail in the following section.

3.2   Governance

Data Mesh Governance. Data Meshes use a decentralized governance model on a "local" level in the sense that teams have the freedom to govern their own (analytical) data products since the original (operational) data is also managed by them (e.g., APIs or their databases). However, to establish interoperability between various teams within the enterprise, an overarching set of governance activities is centralized on a "global" level. Thus, a federated computational governance framework is established in data mesh settings, distinguishing between decentralized local and centralized global governance. [7] The computational

Table 2. Comparative view of data mesh and data space approaches

	Data Mesh	Data Space
Origin	Mainly US.	Mainly EU.
Scope	Intra-organizational data sharing.	Inter-organizational data sharing.
Driving forces	Efficiency and practicality.	Sovereignty, transparency, fairness, and enforceability.
Problem to be solved	Centralized data architectures resulting silos and bottlenecks; data democratization.	Limitations of centralized ecosystem architectures and silos.
Value to be gained	Scaling, agility, data democratization.	Collaborative goals, industry standards, and potential regulations, data sovereignty.
Prerequisites	Technical know-how, organizational change, a data mesh platform team.	Standardization, participant maturity, clear use case(s), governance frameworks.
Decentralization	Empowering domain-oriented teams within an organization.	Empowering data (rights) holders such as companies and individuals.
Domain-orientation	Domains within an organization.	Domains of industry or society.
Interoperability	Teams within an organization.	Cross-organizational collaboration.
Data discoverability	Tools like data catalog, data sharing access control tools, and data pipelines.	Tools like data catalogs, data sharing access control tools, connectors, and data marketplaces.
Data Product thinking	Primarily from a data governance perspective and as a data management unit; secondarily, it is the usage of a "business data view".	Primarily from an economic perspective and as a unit of data monetization, and secondarily as a technical term to describe a data sharing unit that fulfills specific criteria.
Technology	Decentralized architecture and open-source toolset	Decentralized architecture and both boxed solutions and open-source tools.

nature of governance comes from having the global interoperability-related standards baked into the platform computationally (enforced automatically). [4]

Local governance involves the duties performed by the teams on the local level. Either the data product owner (could be the product owner of the team) or the data domain steward (or architect for a specific domain) is responsible for the following governance activities:

– Managing the data product schema: The team knows its data best, so managing and then versioning the schema is best placed on a local level.
– Managing data access (e.g., access policies within a data sharing agreement): Data sharing agreements for specific use cases are usually established on a domain level with the oversight of the data domain stewards. Within such use cases, access policies are created. These policies are approved or denied by the product team responsible for the overall use case. Such policies can involve conditions (e.g., expiry or column or row-level filters) where it makes sense. The policies are rolled out and enforced by automation.
– Ensuring compliance with guidelines defined at the global level.
– Ensuring acceptable data quality, data health, and other Service Level Objectives.

Global governance refers to the activities a central governance team performs on a data mesh level. These governance activities are:

– Defining and enforcing organization-wide standards, such as using certain file formats, naming conventions, a glossary of common terms, security requirements, data modeling aspects, data lineage considerations (aka. family tree for data), and more.
– Providing guidelines for the governance of access management policies.
– Developing a methodology for managing data quality.
– Monitoring the availability of the data catalog, data products, and other subsequent systems involved in operating the data mesh.
– Designing gamification or other incentive models for joining the mesh.

It is often allowed that different data domains within an enterprise use different core technologies. For example, Data Domain "A" uses AWS, where "B" uses Azure or C uses "SAP DWC". In such settings, it is crucial that the standards defined on a global level can be adopted by different technological implementations so that interoperability is ensured, and such standards are automatically enforced. For example, a specific data format (e.g., Apache Iceberg) should be mandated globally. Of course, deviations from this may be necessary to cater to the organization's particular needs, but these should always consider their impact on interoperability.

Data Space Governance. Data spaces are a mechanism to implement and support data ecosystems. They define the technology and the business process that enable trusted data sharing as a foundation for data-driven communities, business models, and ecosystems (Table 3).

Table 3. Data space governance levels

Level	Governance
Ecosystem	A collection of actors and activities governed by relevant local and regional laws and regulations as well as market and societal conditions and considerations.
Data space	A defined system with a governance framework that is documented in a rulebook and managed by a Governance authority.
Use case	Two or more participants sharing one or more data product(s) to jointly create value for themselves (and so for the data space and the ecosystem).
Participant	An organization committed to the governance framework of a data space and with a business incentive to participate in one or more use cases.
Data product	A unit of data sharing, governed by a team in a participant organization, is shared with other participants in the context of one or more use cases.

A Data Space Governance Authority governs a data space. It can be represented by one or more parties that establish, govern, manage, and enforce the rules and policies of a data space. The Governance Model is a tool to define a contractual arrangement or a legal entity to set up the Data Space Governance Authority.

Each governance level focuses on several areas, as defined by Hutterer, A., & Krumay, B. [9].

Comparison of Key Governance Concepts. While both concepts, data spaces, and data mesh, target the same goal of enabling data sharing, they originate from different guiding principles that eventually lead to differences in implementation, mainly in governance and architecture.

The concept of data spaces stems from data sharing across organizational boundaries. In this context, data sovereignty is the guiding principle, i.e., every participant in the sharing process should not only be transparently informed of what happens with the data but also be able to control the form of data usage. This principle is not limited to organizational participants but also includes private persons. Trust and legal compliance are further resulting elements, especially in European Union legislation. Both governance and architecture are flat and distributed, and central governance elements are usually established via a consensus-finding process. A governance is set up that can be legally enforced. The transaction is executed in a peer-to-peer mechanism, i.e., no central data platform is established. The governance hierarchy is flat because the highest decisions are deferred to an inter-organizational body where participants have equal rights. The architecture is highly decentralized, typically based on open-source components that allow data exchange from peer to peer according to agreed rules. On the contrary, Data Mesh originates from ideas to share data within a company, e.g., using an existing common cloud framework. Driving forces are practicality and efficiency in the realization. While governance is also decentralized, it has local and global elements that form a hierarchy and potentially a decision structure that reflects the hierarchy in the company.

Both data space and data mesh define data-sharing frameworks with different origins and characteristics that overlap various aspects. One of those aspects is the problem of how to technologically enable data sharing while keeping sovereignty and safety under control - a balance needs to be found between disruption and correct regulation, as highlighted by van den Broek, T., & van Veenstra, A. F. [18]. Data meshes lean toward their technologically advanced, disruptive nature, whereas data spaces rely on regulation, e.g., governance spanning multiple levels.

4   Conclusion

The emergence of modern data-sharing paradigms such as data mesh and data space highlights a clear need for data democratization. Sharing data in a mutually beneficial, repeatable, reliable, and secure manner intra- or inter-organizations is a complex endeavor, and further research is needed to understand better which solution is best fit for which use case. More importantly, there is a potential for data mesh and data space concepts to converge, and both could be improved by taking inspiration from the other.

In this article, we answered the RQ by uncovering data mesh and data space similarities and differences by providing a comparative overview and then focusing on the respective governance concepts.

In our further work, we would like to focus on building on these findings, researching convergence points, and distilling guidelines as well as comparing more thoroughly from a technological perspective.

In this work, we provide three main contributions: conceptual clarity and comparison of data mesh and data space; delineate each approach's governance model; and highlight potential convergences by offering a base for subsequent investigative work.

References

1. Brocke, J.V., et al.: Reconstructing the giant: on the importance of Rigour in documenting the literature search process. In: ECIS 2009 Proceedings, pp. 2206–2217 (2009)
2. Brocke, J.V., Simons, A., Riemer, K., Niehaves, B., Plattfaut, R., Cleven, A.: Standing on the shoulders of giants: challenges and recommendations of literature search in information systems research. Commun. Assoc. Inf. Syst. **37**(1) (2015)
3. Data Spaces Support Centre. Core Concepts. https://dssc.eu/space/Glossary/176554052/2.+Core+Concepts. Accessed 24 Nov 2024
4. Dehghani, Z.: Data Mesh Principles and Logical Architecture. https://martinfowler.com/articles/data-mesh-principles.html. Accessed 27 Oct 2024
5. Dehghani, Z.: Data Mesh: Delivering Data-Driven Value at Scale. O'Reilly Media (2022)
6. European Committee for Standardization CEN Workshop Agreement Trusted Data Transaction. https://www.cencenelec.eu/media/CEN-CENELEC/CWAs/RI/2024/cwa18125_2024.pdf. Accessed 27 Oct 2024
7. Goedegebuure, A., et al.: Data mesh: a systematic gray literature review. ACM Comput. Surv. (2024)
8. Hevner, A.R., March, S.T., Park, J., Ram, S.: Design science in information systems research. MIS Q. 75–105 (2004)
9. Hutterer, A., Krumay, B.: Scopes of governance in data spaces. In: Australasian Conference on Information Systems 2024, Canberra (2024)
10. Jarke, M., Otto, B., Ram, S.: Data sovereignty and data space ecosystems. Bus. Inf. Syst. Eng. **61**, 549–550 (2019)
11. Jeffar, F., Plebani, P.: Federated data products: a confluence of data mesh and Gaia-X for data sharing. In: Monti, F., et al. (eds.) Service-Oriented Computing - ICSOC 2023 Workshops. ICSOC 2023. LNCS, vol. 14518. Springer, Singapore (2024)
12. Kuikkaniemi, K., Guggenberger, T.: Data products in mesh and space. DSSC. https://dssc.eu/space/News/blog/108199969/Data+Products+in+Mesh+and+Space. Accessed 26 Oct 2024
13. Machado, I.A., Costa, C., Santos, M.Y.: Data mesh: concepts and principles of a paradigm shift in data architectures. Procedia Comput. Sci. **196**, 263–271 (2022)

14. Offermann, P., Blom, S., Schönherr, M., Bub, U.: Artifact types in information systems design science - a literature review. In: Proceedings of the International Conference, DESRIST, St. Gallen (2010)
15. Offermann, P., Levina, O., Schönherr, M., Bub, U.: Outline of a design science research process. In: Proceedings of the International Conference, DESRIST, Malvern, PA (2009)
16. Otto, B., Hompel, M., Wrobel, S.: Designing Data Spaces: The Ecosystem Approach to Competitive Advantage, p. 580. Springer, Cham (2022)
17. Poikola, A., Takanen, V., Laszkowicz, P., Toivonen, T.: The Technology Landscape of Data Spaces. SITRA (2023). https://media.sitra.fi/app/uploads/2023/10/sitra-technology-landscape-of-data-spaces.pdf. Accessed 06 Jan 2025
18. van den Broek, T., van Veenstra, A.F.: Governance of big data collaborations: How to balance regulatory compliance and disruptive innovation. Technol. Forecast. Soc. Chang. **129**, 330–338 (2018)

Quantum Computing

Toward Quantum Annealing
for Multi-league Sports Scheduling

Orin Pechler[1] and Frank Phillipson[1,2(✉)]

[1] Maastricht University, Maastricht, The Netherlands
f.phillipson@maastrichtuniversity.nl
[2] TNO, The Hague, The Netherlands

Abstract. This paper introduces the use of quantum annealing for the
Multi-League Scheduling Problem, under the main assumption that all
leagues contain the same even number of teams. In this problem, a schedule of matches has to be found for several leagues consisting of multiple teams and clubs, a particularly relevant issue in amateur and youth
sports. For this scheduling problem, the main goal is to develop a so-
called QUBO formulation, which is the main type of formulation for a
quantum annealer. Four different techniques are used to develop such
QUBOs. These are then solved for various instances using D-Wave's current Advantage System. The technique called domain-wall encoding is
found to outperform the other three implemented techniques in terms of
solution quality, providing empirical support for this approach. However,
this technique also has the highest running time, whereas the relatively
new technique called unbalanced penalization achieves the lowest running time, with a solution quality that is only marginally worse than
that of domain-wall encoding. Although currently quantum annealing
does not perform as well as the classical approaches, it is expected that
in the future quantum computers will become a superior alternative.

Keywords: Multi league sports scheduling · Quantum annealing ·
Simulated annealing · QUBO modeling

1 Introduction

Every sports league needs a schedule that indicates when and where each team
plays another team. Such a schedule should respect the number of matches, the
number of teams, the venue capacities, and more. When looking at professional
leagues within a country, there are usually only a few leagues and clubs, with each
club having its own venue. Scheduling all games for those professional leagues
can already be a complex matter [3]. Now, when considering amateur leagues,
the complexity of the problem amplifies. Instead of a few leagues, hundreds
of leagues have to be scheduled, each with various clubs and teams. Another
important difference is that some of these teams are part of the same club, and
therefore a venue has to be shared between those teams. At the same time, these

teams are usually also part of different leagues. This creates capacity problems at clubs and inter-dependencies between leagues [13].

This Multi-League Scheduling Problem (MLSP) is bound to have capacity violations at some club at some point in time, due to the vast amount of matches to be scheduled. A desirable schedule would minimize the total amount of these capacity violations. Davari et al. [13] formulated an exact polynomial-time algorithm to give such a schedule under certain assumptions. Namely, each league uses the popular double round robin tournament (DRR) format, where each team plays another team twice, once at home and once away. Moreover, matches are grouped into rounds, every team can only play once per round, and the matches of a league are scheduled using the minimum number of required consecutive rounds. Finally, they assume that each league has the same even number of teams, and all leagues start in the same round. The algorithm presented creates a schedule based on the assignment of Home and Away Patterns (HAP), which will also be used throughout this paper and will be further discussed in Subsect. 4.1.

In this paper, we show how quantum annealing (QA) can solve the MLSP with equal league sizes and examine whether it offers advantages over classical approaches. To use QA for the MLSP, we need to formulate the problem as a Quadratic Unconstrained Binary Optimization (QUBO) problem that quantum annealers are able to solve. We translate a mixed integer linear program for the MLSP into a QUBO, addressing inequalities and discrete variables in various ways, resulting in four different QUBO formulations. These QUBOs are implemented using D-Wave's Ocean Development Toolkit in Python and solved using both simulated annealing and QA on the D-Wave Advantage system.

Quantum computers are still developing and can only solve relatively small problems. To validate the QUBO formulations, simulated annealing is used for larger instances that current quantum annealers cannot handle. While quantum computers currently have limitations and may not yet outperform classical computers, further development is expected to make QA a superior method in the coming years [18].

The structure of the remainder of this paper is as follows. Section 2 reviews the current related literature. Then, in Sect. 3, a background on QA is provided, together with a brief introduction on QUBO formulations. Thereupon, Sect. 4 will give a formal problem description of the MLSP, and Sect. 5 will provide the four different QUBO formulations for this problem. In Sect. 6, the process of generating data for MLSP is described, and the penalty values to be used for the respective QUBOs are discussed. Then, the results and conclusions are presented in Sect. 7.

2   Related Literature

A lot of research has been conducted regarding the scheduling of sports, where only one or few leagues are considered. Bartsch et al. [3] considered the professional soccer leagues in Germany and Austria. They gave a more precise schedule corresponding to the specific needs of the leagues, but at the same time only had to schedule one or two leagues. Lim et al. [20] researched the scheduling of sport competitions at multiple venues, which are shared by all teams in a league. They presented a beam search and simulated annealing algorithm to tackle this problem, where again only one league had to be considered. Li et al. [19] provided a more extensive review on the current state of research on sport scheduling with one or few leagues.

Although, sports scheduling is a well-researched topic, there is limited research focused on the scheduling of multiple leagues, and those available are often based on some assumptions and generalizations. As mentioned before, Davari et al. [13] have developed an exact polynomial-time algorithm for the scheduling of multiple leagues, under the main assumption that leagues have the same even number of teams. They also considered two generalizations of this problem. One of which is where teams from the same club have to play in their league according to the same HAP. The other generalization looks at how matches should be scheduled if the venue capacities of clubs might differ throughout the season. They gave an exact (polynomial-time) algorithm for the latter, under the condition that the number of teams in a league and within a club both are equal to two. It was also shown that if the number of teams in a league is greater than four, the problem becomes NP-hard.

Although two generalizations of the described problem were investigated, the paper's applicability is limited, due to the assumption that every league has the same even number of teams. As multiple leagues were considered (possibly hundreds), it is unlikely that this assumption is met. Hence, Li et al. [19] provided an algorithm to a more realistic scenario, where league sizes are allowed to be different from each other. Moreover, they also relaxed the assumption that all leagues start in the same round, and hence allowed the leagues to have different starting rounds. For this problem, they provided a heuristic, which is substantially faster than solving the problem exactly using a mixed integer linear program. However, for large instances, the heuristic still takes considerable time. The algorithm starts with a feasible initial solution, which is improved upon using local search and perturbation components. It faces challenges on deciding how to choose a feasible initial solution, as the final solution's quality will greatly depend on this choice.

QA may provide some potential advantages for the MLSP. Indeed, for other optimization problems, it has proven to be useful at times, including in finance [15], material science [5], logistics [14,26,29,31], smart city planning [8], telecommunications [28], healthcare [21,25], energy networks [10], and many more.

Implementations of QA usually lead to the conclusion that the time necessary for computation is significantly less than the time taken by classical computers. However, quantum computers are not always reliable yet. Yarkoni et al. [34] found that the empirical performance of QA is highly dependent on the problem being solved. Besides, so far, quantum computers can only efficiently handle relatively small problem sizes. Quantum computing is thus still a growing field and future only will tell how powerful the use of QA algorithms will become.

3   Quantum Annealing

Optimization problems seek the best possible solutions, often using linear programs or algorithms. These problems can be translated into energy minimization problems, leveraging the principle that systems tend to their minimum energy state, a rule true in quantum physics [12]. Quantum annealers utilize this principle to find low-energy states.

Quantum computers store information in quantum bits, or qubits. Unlike classical bits, qubits can be in state 0, state 1, or a superposition of both. During QA, qubits collapse from superposition to either 0 or 1, with probabilities controlled by a programmable bias. This bias affects an external magnetic field, increasing the likelihood of the qubit falling into the lower energy state.

Qubits can also be entangled, influencing each other via a coupler. The coupler can be programmed with a weight to affect the final states of the qubits, forming an energy landscape that the quantum annealer explores to find the minimum energy state [12]. Problems are implemented as either Ising or Quadratic Unconstrained Binary Optimization (QUBO) models, which are equivalent except that Ising variables take values of -1 or 1, and QUBO variables take values of 0 or 1 [22].

In this paper, QUBOs are formulated for the MLSP. The general form of such a QUBO is

$$\min y = \boldsymbol{x}^t Q \boldsymbol{x}, \tag{1}$$

where $\boldsymbol{x}$ is a n-dimensional binary vector and Q a $n \times n$ dimensional matrix [27]. Here, the goal is to minimize the objective value using only binary variables. Another general way to formulate a QUBO, which will also be used throughout this paper, is

$$\min H = A \cdot H_A + B \cdot H_B + ..., \tag{2}$$

where H_A and H_B are penalty functions, and A and B are their weights.

When transforming a linear program to a QUBO, some penalty functions represent constraints or objectives. If a constraint is met, its penalty is zero or low; if not, the penalty increases the objective value, enforcing feasible solutions indirectly [1]. There is extensive research on QUBO and Ising formulations for optimization problems [16,22].

After formulating a QUBO, it can be implemented on a quantum annealer or solved using simulated annealing, a probabilistic optimization method [17]. This paper uses both the quantum and simulated annealers from D-Wave, which support QUBO formulations. D-Wave's current Advantage system, with over 5000 qubits and 35000 couplers, uses the Pegasus layout, allowing each qubit to couple with 15 others. This system outperforms its predecessor, the D-Wave 2000Q, in speed, success rate, and problem size handling [33].

While QA offers potential advantages like faster computation and more reliable solutions, it currently has limitations in the problem sizes it can handle. D-Wave is developing a new system with the Zephyr architecture, promising greater qubit connectivity and the ability to solve larger problems [12]. The future impact of quantum computing remains to be seen.

4   MLSP Description

Before a QUBO can be formulated, the problem in consideration needs to be defined. Hence, in this section, the MLSP is described in detail with all necessary variables. Moreover, a mixed integer linear program (MILP) is provided for this problem. This MILP will make use of HAPs that first have to be discussed (see Subsect. 4.1). After getting an understanding of HAPs, variables will be introduced in Subsect. 4.2, which are necessary for the MILP formulation in Subsect. 4.3. The description, variables and MILP presented in this paper is borrowed from Davari et al. [13] and summarized in Table 1.

Table 1. Definitions of Variables

Variable	Definition and Semantics
L	Set of leagues
C	Set of clubs
T	Set of teams
R	Set of rounds
$\mathcal{H}$	HAP set
m	Number of leagues
n	Number of teams
k	Number of teams per league
δ_c	Capacity of club c

4.1   Home and Away Patterns

As stated, to solve the MLSP, Home and Away Patterns (HAPs) are used. The matches of a league need to be scheduled in rounds, where each team plays at most one match per round. As mentioned before, this paper only considers even number of teams in a league, say k. Thus, the minimal number of rounds necessary to schedule a DRR is equal to $2(k-1)$. If this number is attained, it is referred to as a compact DRR.

If a HAP is assigned to a team, it will determine in every round whether the team plays at home or away. In a HAP there are $k-1$ 'H' symbols and $k-1$ 'A' symbols, resulting in a vector consisting of $2(k-1)$ symbols, which corresponds to a compact DRR. A HAPset is a set of HAPs, with one for each team in a league. Such a set is said to be feasible if there exists a schedule of matches that corresponds with the HAPset. Moreover, two different HAPs h and h' are said to be complementary if whenever the team assigned to HAP h plays away, then the team assigned to h' plays at home and vice versa. Then, a HAPset is called complementary if it only consists of complementary pairs of HAPs. It will be assumed that, as all leagues to be scheduled have the same number of teams, the same complementary HAPset is used for every league.

The choice of a particular HAPset is irrelevant and does not affect the number of violations [13]. Table 2 shows a simple example of a feasible, complementary HAPset for a league consisting of 4 teams.

Lastly, throughout this paper, only compact DRR are considered for an even number of teams, resulting in all leagues being played simultaneously and each team playing either at home or away. In Table 3, a compatible schedule is given to the HAPset in Table 2. Note that determining such a compatible schedule from the assignment of HAPs will not be considered, as there is already sufficient research on that topic available [13].

Table 2. Feasible, complementary HAPset for a league of four teams

HAPs	Rounds					
	r_1	r_2	r_3	r_4	r_5	r_6
h_1	H	H	A	A	H	A
h_2	A	H	A	H	H	A
h_3	A	A	H	H	A	H
h_4	H	A	H	A	A	H

Table 3. Compatible schedule with the HAPset in Table 2, where team i is assigned to HAP h_i, for $i = 1, .., 4$

Rounds					
r_1	r_2	r_3	r_4	r_5	r_6
1 vs 2	1 vs 4	3 vs 1	2 vs 1	1 vs 3	4 vs 1
4 vs 3	2 vs 3	4 vs 2	3 vs 4	2 vs 4	3 vs 2

4.2 MLSP Sets and Variables

For the MLSP, a set L of leagues, a set C of clubs, and a set T of teams are given. Here, $n = |T|$ denotes the number of teams and $m = |L|$ denotes the number of leagues. For the set of teams, there are also two different partitions given. One partitions the set into a subset which indicates which teams belong to which club and the other specifies which teams belong to which league, $\{\hat{T}_1, ..., \hat{T}_{|C|}\}$ and $\{\bar{T}_1, ..., \bar{T}_m\}$ respectively. As it is assumed that every league has the same even number (k) of teams, we have $|\bar{T}_l| = k$ for each $l \in L$. Moreover, $n_c = |\hat{T}_c|$ denotes the number of teams that are part of club c. Each club also has a fixed capacity δ_c, which is equal to the maximum number of matches it can host in each round. Finally, k HAPs are given and together form a feasible, complementary HAPset $\mathcal{H}$. Each HAP has $2(k-1)$ symbols, such that there is a symbol for each round, where R denotes the set of rounds ($\{r_1, r_2, ..., r_{2(k-1)}\}$).

Now, when scheduling the matches, it might occur that more matches are scheduled to take place at a certain club c in round r than allowed by its capacity

δ_c. This is called a capacity violation and the goal of the MLSP is to find an assignment of teams to HAPs, which minimizes the total amount of violations. The discrete variable $z_{c,r}$ will measure the number of violations for club c in round r. This variable is equal to zero if there is no capacity violation, or equal to the difference between the number of teams that play at home in that round and the club's capacity δ_c, if there is a violation. In addition, a binary variable needs to be introduced to assign teams to HAPs:

$$x_{t,h} = \begin{cases} 1 & \text{if team } t \text{ is assigned to HAP } h \\ 0 & \text{otherwise} \end{cases} \quad \forall\, t \in T, \ h \in \mathcal{H}. \tag{3}$$

Also, for each HAP a parameter $U_{h,r}$ is computed, which is equal to one if HAP $h \in \mathcal{H}$ states that the team assigned to it will play at home in round $r \in R$ and zero if the team will play away. Now, using this parameter,

$$\sum_{t \in \hat{T}_c} \sum_{h \in \mathcal{H}} (x_{t,h} U_{h,r}) - \delta_c \tag{4}$$

measures the difference between the number of teams playing at home at club c in round r and the club's capacity. Then,

$$z_{c,r} = \max\{0, \sum_{t \in \hat{T}_c} \sum_{h \in \mathcal{H}} (x_{t,h} U_{h,r}) - \delta_c\} \quad \forall\, c \in C, r \in R. \tag{5}$$

This observation serves as the foundation for the QUBO formulations in Sect. 5. For these formulations further auxiliary and binary variables will be needed. However, these variables will be specific to each different QUBO formulation and hence will be introduced prior to each specific formulation.

4.3   Formulation of MILP for MLSP

Using the variables and sets described, the mixed integer linear program for the MLSP is presented below [13]. As mentioned before, the MILP aims to minimize the total amount of capacity violations to occur at clubs.

In this MILP, (7) and (8) enforce the assignment of teams to HAPs. In particular, (7) ensures that only one team in league l is assigned to HAP h and (8) states that each team $t \in T$ has to be assigned to exactly one HAP (not more or less). Equations (9) and (10) calculate the number of violations corresponding to the assignment of teams to HAPs. Finally, (11) states that $x_{t,h}$ is a binary variable.

This MILP serves as a basis for the formulation of the QUBOs. These formulations are introduced under the same assumptions as before. Observe that deviations from the MLSP can be considered using the MILP. For example, Li et al. [19] introduced a modified MILP, which allows for different league sizes and different starting rounds. This, in turn, can also be used for the QUBO formulations. However, this is out of the scope for this paper and is recommended for further research.

The model can now be given by:
minimize:

$$\sum_{c \in C} \sum_{r \in R} z_{c,r} \tag{6}$$

subject to:

$$\sum_{t \in \bar{T}_l} x_{t,h} = 1 \qquad\qquad \forall\, l \in L,\ h \in \mathcal{H} \tag{7}$$

$$\sum_{h \in \mathcal{H}} x_{t,h} = 1 \qquad\qquad \forall\, t \in \bar{T}_l,\ l \in L \tag{8}$$

$$z_{c,r} \geq \sum_{t \in \hat{T}_c} \sum_{h \in \mathcal{H}} (x_{t,h} U_{h,r}) - \delta_c \qquad\qquad \forall\, c \in C,\ r \in R \tag{9}$$

$$z_{c,r} \geq 0 \qquad\qquad \forall\, c \in C,\ r \in R \tag{10}$$

$$x_{t,h} \in \{0, 1\} \qquad\qquad \forall\, t \in T,\ h \in \mathcal{H} \tag{11}$$

5   QUBO Formulations for MLSP

Now, using the mixed integer linear program for the MLSP, four different QUBO formulations will be developed. These QUBOs will all include the same penalty function for the equality constraints in the MILP. The derivation of these penalty functions is described in Subsect. 5.1. The main issue with developing a QUBO for the MLSP lies within the construction of penalty functions for (9) and (10), due to the discrete variable and the inequality in the constraints. In order to deal with this, a penalty function will be developed using different techniques, where a direct penalty will be imposed on the QUBOs in the occurrence of capacity violations. For this, (5) serves as a foundation. The used techniques can be clustered into two groups, one of which uses auxiliary variables to model discrete values. This group consists of one-hot encoding (Subsect. 5.2), domain-wall encoding (Subsect. 5.3), and binary encoding (Subsect. 5.4). The other group consists only of the technique called unbalanced penalization (Subsect. 5.5), which applies an approximate penalty for capacity violations.

5.1   Dealing with the Equality Constraints

Deriving a penalty function for (7) and (8) is relatively straightforward. As these are equality constraints, quadratic penalties can be used, where the penalty is determined by the difference between the left-hand side and the right-hand side of the equality [16]. Then, for example, the first equality constraint is defined for all $l \in L$ and $h \in \mathcal{H}$. To include this in the QUBO, the penalty function is summed over all $l \in L$ and $h \in \mathcal{H}$.

This leads to the following penalty function for (7):

$$H_1 = \sum_{l \in L} \sum_{h \in \mathcal{H}} \left(1 - \sum_{t \in \bar{T}_l} x_{t,h}\right)^2, \tag{12}$$

where in the QUBO a penalty coefficient λ_1 is multiplied with H_1 to give an even higher penalty to solutions that do not satisfy the constraint. The value of this coefficient (and other penalty coefficients) needs to be determined before the full QUBO can be implemented. This will be examined later on in Sect. 6. A penalty function for (8) is derived similarly.

$$H_2 = \sum_{l \in L} \sum_{t \in \tilde{T}_l} (1 - \sum_{h \in \mathcal{H}} x_{t,h})^2 \tag{13}$$

5.2 QUBO 1: One-Hot Encoding

In the QUBO formulation, (9) is used to create a function that penalizes violations directly. This function gives a penalty value that is positive if there are violations and zero otherwise:

$$H = \sum_{c \in C} \sum_{r \in R} (y_{c,r} + (\sum_{t \in \hat{T}_c} \sum_{h \in \mathcal{H}} (x_{t,h} U_{h,r}) - \delta_c))^2, \tag{14}$$

with $y_{c,r} \geq 0$ ($\forall\ c \in C,\ r \in R$), which offsets any negative values for (4). To model $y_{c,r}$, which is an integer valued variable, we use auxiliary variables. The first way to encode this is by using one-hot encoding [9]. Using this technique, binary variables are used that are equal to 1 if a certain (discrete) value is needed. This gives the following expression:

$$\sum_{v=0}^{\delta_c} y_{c,r,v} \cdot v + \sum_{t \in \hat{T}_c} \sum_{h \in \mathcal{H}} (x_{t,h} U_{h,r}) - \delta_c \qquad \forall\ c \in C,\ r \in R, \tag{15}$$

now with $y_{c,r,v}$ binary, encoding the offsets. This expression can be forced to be non-negative by using it properly as a penalty function. For this, it needs to be ensured that $y_{c,r,v}$ takes on 1 for only one value $v \in \{0, ..., \delta_c\}$ for each $c \in C$, $r \in R$, i.e.

$$\sum_{v=0}^{\delta_c} y_{c,r,v} = 1 \qquad \forall\ c \in C,\ r \in R. \tag{16}$$

This leads to the penalty functions:

$$H_3 = \sum_{c \in C} \sum_{r \in R} (\sum_{v=0}^{\delta_c} y_{c,r,v} \cdot v + (\sum_{t \in \hat{T}_c} \sum_{h \in \mathcal{H}} (x_{t,h} U_{h,r}) - \delta_c))^2, \tag{17}$$

$$H_4 = \sum_{c \in C} \sum_{r \in R} (1 - \sum_{v=0}^{\delta_c} y_{c,r,v})^2. \tag{18}$$

These functions together with H_1 and H_2 form the first QUBO formulation that can be used to find a feasible schedule, while minimizing the number of violations. The complete formulation can be found below:

$$\text{minimize } \lambda_1 H_1 + \lambda_2 H_2 + \lambda_3 H_3 + \lambda_4 H_4. \tag{QUBO 1}$$

Observe that for each penalty function, there is also a penalty coefficient included. The number of variables in this QUBO is equal to $\sum_{c \in C}((\delta_c + 1) \cdot |C| \cdot |R|) + |T| \cdot |\mathcal{H}|$.

5.3 QUBO 2: Domain-Wall Encoding

Another technique that can be used, to obtain the same effect as in (15), is the so-called domain-wall encoding, which has been proposed by Chancellor [6]. By using domain-wall encoding instead of one-hot encoding, one fewer qubit is necessary to describe the same set of values and less interactions between qubits are necessary [7].

Using the same penalty structure as before, a new penalty function is obtained and presented below.

$$H_5 = \sum_{c \in C} \sum_{r \in R} (\sum_{i=1}^{\delta_c} y_{c,r,i} + (\sum_{t \in \hat{T}_c} \sum_{h \in \mathcal{H}} (x_{t,h} U_{h,r}) - \delta_c))^2 \qquad (19)$$

Here, we use the auxiliary variable $y_{c,r,i} \in \{0,1\}$ ($\forall\, c \in C,\, r \in R,\, i \in \{1, ..., \delta_c\}$) to implement the domain wall encoding. In order to ensure that these binary variables take on values that are valid according to this technique, a second penalty function is necessary. The following penalty function, similar to the one presented by Codognet [9], tries to enforce a valid domain-wall encoding:

$$H_6 = \sum_{c \in C} \sum_{r \in R} (\sum_{i=1}^{\delta_c - 1} (y_{c,r,i+1} - y_{c,r,i+1} \cdot y_{c,r,i})). \qquad (20)$$

Together with the usual penalty functions H_1 and H_2, these form a QUBO that can be used for the MLSP and is presented below:

$$\text{minimize } \lambda_1 H_1 + \lambda_2 H_2 + \lambda_5 H_5 + \lambda_6 H_6. \qquad \text{(QUBO 2)}$$

The corresponding penalty coefficients are included as well. The total variables used in this equation is equal to $\sum_{c \in C}(\delta_c \cdot |C| \cdot |R|) + |T| \cdot |\mathcal{H}|$, which is less than the variables necessary for one-hot encoding. It is expected that this QUBO will outperform QUBO 1, as empirical results have shown before that domain-wall encoding typically outperforms one-hot encoding [7].

5.4 QUBO 3: Binary Encoding

In this QUBO formulation, binary encoding will be used [30]. The structure of the QUBO is similar to QUBO 1 and 2, where binary variables are used to offset negative values. For this, the same slack variables as before are used ($y_{c,r,i}$). However, i will now vary from 1 to M_c instead of δ_c, with $M_c = \lceil log_2(\delta_c + 1) \rceil\ \forall\, c \in C$. Note that the number of binary variables necessary depends on the respective capacities of the clubs. The following penalty function is constructed for capacity violations:

$$H_7 = \sum_{c \in C} \sum_{r \in R} \left(\sum_{i=1}^{M_c} 2^{i-1} y_{c,r,i} + \left(\sum_{t \in \hat{T}_c} \sum_{h \in \mathcal{H}} (x_{t,h} U_{h,r}) - \delta_c \right) \right)^2. \qquad (21)$$

The full QUBO formulation is presented below:

$$\text{minimize } \lambda_1 H_1 + \lambda_2 H_2 + \lambda_7 H_7. \qquad \text{(QUBO 3)}$$

This includes H_1, H_2, H_7 and their respective penalty coefficients. The number of variables used is significantly less than compared with QUBO 1 and 2. In total, there are $\sum_{c \in C} (M_c \cdot |C| \cdot |R|) + |T| \cdot |\mathcal{H}|$ binary variables. Moreover, QUBO 3 also only includes only one penalty function next to the usual two functions, resulting in less couplers needed to embed the problem.

5.5 QUBO 4: Unbalanced Penalization

The QUBO presented here differs a lot from the previous formulated QUBOs and is also a relatively new technique. So far, auxiliary variables were necessary to introduce in order to obtain a penalty function. Using unbalanced penalization this is unnecessary. This technique gives rather an approximate penalty for capacity violations. The general form of this penalty, given by Montañez-Barrera et al. [24], is

$$\zeta(x) = -\alpha_1 h(x) + \alpha_2 h(x)^2. \qquad (22)$$

Here, α_1 and α_2 are penalty coefficients and $h(x)$ is a function representing the inequality constraint. This penalty penalizes negative values for $h(x)$ a lot more than positive values.

In our case, positive values should be penalized, as they imply capacity violations, whereas negative and zero values should not be penalized. In the case of unbalanced penalization, it can not be ensured that negative values will not be penalized. However, using

$$h(x) = -\left(\sum_{t \in \hat{T}_c} \sum_{h \in \mathcal{H}} (x_{t,h} U_{h,r}) - \delta_c \right) = \delta_c - \sum_{t \in \hat{T}_c} \sum_{h \in \mathcal{H}} (x_{t,h} U_{h,r}), \qquad (23)$$

positive values will be penalized a lot more. Observe that for this formulation, it is not needed to define any new variables, which results in a more efficient QUBO, as less qubits are needed. On the other hand, by using this technique only an approximate penalty can be obtained, as desirable values for (9) will still get a small penalty.

Combining (22) and (23) yields the following two penalty functions that will form the new QUBO together with the usual functions:

$$H_8 = -\sum_{c \in C} \sum_{r \in R} \left(\delta_c - \sum_{t \in \hat{T}_c} \sum_{h \in \mathcal{H}} (x_{t,h} U_{h,r}) \right), \qquad (24)$$

and

$$H_9 = \sum_{c \in C} \sum_{r \in R} \left(\delta_c - \sum_{t \in \hat{T}_c} \sum_{h \in \mathcal{H}} (x_{t,h} U_{h,r}) \right)^2. \tag{25}$$

Note that, as (24) is already taken to be negative, the corresponding penalty coefficient will be positive. The total formulation is now:

$$\text{minimize } \lambda_1 H_1 + \lambda_2 H_2 + \lambda_8 H_8 + \lambda_9 H_9. \tag{QUBO 4}$$

The number of variables needed for this new QUBO is equal to $|T| \cdot |\mathcal{H}|$, which is significantly less compared to the other three QUBOs. Indeed, when embedding this onto the D-Wave architecture, it will most likely be more efficient, but it has to be seen whether or not QUBO 4 will also lead to relatively good solutions. Nevertheless, this method seems promising, as Montañez-Barrera et al. [23] found that unbalanced penalization outperforms methods using slack variables for the traveling salesman problem.

6   Implementation

6.1   Generating Instances

In order to evaluate the performance of the QUBO formulations, various instances are needed. Unfortunately, for the considered problem, there are very limited public instances available. In [19] instances for the MLSP are provided, however, these instances are not based on the assumption that all leagues have the same even number of teams. Instead, the league sizes vary in these provided instances. Hence, an instance generator is developed that creates artificial instances, which do comply with the assumptions made throughout this paper.

This generator takes as input the number of leagues ($|L|$), the league size (k), the number of clubs ($|C|$), the number of teams ($|T|$) and the number of rounds ($|R| = 2(k-1)$). From this, it generates an artificial instance. First, the teams are assigned to leagues. For each team, a random league is chosen and is assigned to this league if the league does not already contain k teams, until all leagues have the same even number of teams (k).

For each league l and its participating teams, a set of eligible clubs is defined, which are the clubs that do not yet contain a team that is part of league l. Obviously, when no team from a league has yet been allocated to a club, all clubs are eligible. Then, a random (eligible) club is chosen for each team in a particular league, after which the club is made ineligible for any other team in that same league. This procedure is executed for all teams and randomly creates all clubs. Observe that in order to generate clubs that do not contain teams part of the same league, the number of clubs must be greater than the league size. Otherwise, it will be impossible for the instance generator to provide such artificial clubs. The club sizes (n_c for $c \in C$) follow directly from the assignment of teams, as it is equal to the number of teams that are part of the club. Using this value, a random capacity is also drawn for each club in the range $\{\max(\lfloor n_c/2 \rfloor - 2, \ 1), \ \dots \ , \ \min(\lfloor n_c/2 \rfloor + 2, \ n_c)\}$, also used by Li et al. [19] in their instance generator. Finally, the parameter U has to be generated, which is created from [19]. Together with the generated clubs and leagues, they form one artificial instance.

In total, 21 different sets of instances are generated, where league sizes vary from 4 to 16, with 3 different sets for each league size: small, medium and large scale. Throughout these sets, the number of leagues varies from 3 to 270, the number of clubs from 5 to 300, and the number of teams from 12 to 4320. Each of these sets includes five versions of the instance set using the same input parameters, resulting in 105 different instances on which the QUBO formulations can be tested on. The instances are named after the properties given to them by the input parameters:

[league size] − [number of leagues] − [number of clubs] − [instance index].

For example, an instance with a league size of 4, number of leagues equal to 3, and number of clubs set to 5, is named as "4-3-5-A".

6.2   Penalty Values

Before the generated instances can be solved, the penalty coefficients of the QUBO formulations have to be set. Setting weights to obtain both a feasible and (close to) optimal solutions is not an easy task. High values for the penalty functions that mimic the constraints, will lead more often to feasible solutions. However, setting these values too high will lead to solutions that do not typically perform well regarding the objective [2]. On the other hand, weights that are too small are undesirable as they will lead to infeasible solutions. This creates a trade-off when deciding on the penalty coefficients in the four different QUBO formulations. It is desired that the weights for the penalty functions that mimic (7) and (8), namely H_1 and H_2, are high enough to obtain feasible solutions, but also as low as possible to ensure a better solution quality. From now on, these two functions will be referred to as the "feasibility penalties". Also (16) and (19) are counted to this group as these also are needed to obtain feasible solutions.

Next to the feasibility penalties, the QUBO formulations all contain a component that penalizes high values of capacity violations. This component induces the QUBOs to favor a solution with a lower amount of capacity violations. For these we choose: $\lambda_3 = \lambda_5 = \lambda_7 = \lambda_8 = \lambda_9 = 1$.

Now, for each QUBO, the feasibility penalties are each as important, as these are the penalties that mimic constraints on our models. Hence, they have been set equal to each other in each QUBO. This means that the coefficients have been taken as: $\lambda_1 = \lambda_2 = \lambda_4 = \lambda_6$, where the lambdas still have to be set to some value. A formula is derived for this, based on empirical results when solving the QUBOs using various values for the penalty coefficients. For details the reader is referred to Appendix A. We will use

$$A = \alpha \cdot \max_{c \in C}(n_c - \delta_c)^2 \tag{26}$$

for the first three QUBO formulations and

$$B = \beta \cdot \max_{c \in C}(n_c)^2 \tag{27}$$

for the fourth. The scalars α and β can be used to tune these penalties in an easy way. These values will be reported with the results in the next section.

7   Results and Conclusions

At this point, the QUBO formulations can be implemented, using the coefficients calculated by the suggested penalty formulas. The quantum annealer provided by D-Wave currently can only solve relatively small problems, due to the fact that there are only limited amount of qubits available. This means that not every instance can be solved by the quantum annealer. In order to still get an idea of performance differences of the QUBO formulations, simulated annealing is used for all instances. The solutions found by using simulated annealing can then be compared with the exact approach, obtained using CPLEX in Java. After this, the results are discussed of the instances that were solved by the quantum annealer. Both the process of simulated and QA is applied using D-Wave's Ocean Development Toolkit in Python, on a computer with an Intel(R) Core(TM) i5-8365U CPU 1,6 GHz processor, with 4 cores, 1896 MHz, and 8 logical processors. CPLEX was run on a computer with a 13th Gen Intel Core i5-1345U 1,6 GHz processor, with 16 GB RAM.

7.1   Results Using Simulated Annealing

We run simulated annealing using 100 samples. We improved for each instance the result by further re-scaling the penalty coefficients. The detailed results can be found in Appendix B. From the tables in the appendix, it can be observed that for the smaller instances, the simulated annealer is very much capable to find optimal solutions. On the other hand, when looking at instances with more teams and leagues, it becomes more difficult to find optimal solutions. This is an obvious result of the fact that the simulated annealer is not an exact solver, but rather an approximation tool.

The summary of the results are shown in Table 4. Here, Best Quality Count is the number of times a certain QUBO formulation outperforms (or performs as good as) the other QUBOs. Similarly, the Optimality Count is equal to the amount of instances a QUBO could solve to optimality, i.e. it has been able to find a solution that gives the same number of violations as the optimal solution found using CPLEX. The Solution Gap refers to how much worse the solution found by the QUBO is as compared to the optimal solution, and is measured in percentages. Then, the Max Solution Gap is equal to the largest approximation error over all instances, whereas the Mean Solution Gap shows the average error. Note that, the smaller instances influence this average a lot, while the smaller instances do not as closely represent a real-life scenario as compared to the bigger instances, where a league consists of at least 10 different teams. This is then also precisely why the Mean Solution Gap is also reported for those instances where $k \geq 10$. For the same reasons, the Best Quality Count and the Optimality Count is also reported for $k \geq 10$.

Table 4. Summarized results from simulated annealing

	QUBO 1	QUBO 2	QUBO 3	QUBO 4
Best Quality Count	32	63	51	50
Optimality Count	29	35	36	32
Max Solution Gap	14%	11%	12%	13%
Mean Solution Gap	4%	3%	3%	3%
Best Quality Count ($k \geq 10$)	5	31	19	16
Optimality Count ($k \geq 10$)	4	10	10	6
Mean Solution Gap ($k \geq 10$)	7%	5%	5%	5%

First of all, it can be immediately deduced that QUBO 2, which uses domain-wall encoding, performs the best. It outperforms the other QUBOs and solving it often leads to an optimal solution, even when looking only at instances that have at least a league size of 10. Moreover, the largest approximation error is also the lowest for this QUBO formulation. QUBO 3 and 4, which use binary encoding and unbalanced penalization respectively, perform very similar when looking at the same metrics. Notable is that QUBO 1, which uses one-hot encoding, performs a lot worse in comparison to the other formulations. In general however, it can be concluded from the Solution Gap metrics that the QUBO formulations perform quite well using simulated annealing, which is a promising sign for the use of QA on this scheduling problem.

Purely looking from a performance perspective, QUBO 2 should be preferred, which also shows support for the technique of domain-wall encoding. However, the quality of the solution does not tell the whole story. The reason why QA is such an interesting development is primarily by the potential speed at which it can compute solutions. On that account, the running times of each QUBO is also an important consideration and these values can be found in detail in Appendix B and summarized in Table 5. When comparing the different QUBO formulations, it can be seen that QUBO 4 is substantially faster than all the other formulations. This follows most likely as a result of the fact that less variables are necessary when implementing unbalanced penalization. Moreover, QUBO 2, which performed best in terms of quality of the solution, now performs the worst in terms of running time.

Table 5. Comparison of CPLEX and QUBO/SA results on calculation time (in seconds)

Data File	CPLEX	QUBO 1	QUBO 2	QUBO 3	QUBO 4
4-3-5	0.022	0.173	0.151	0.147	0.080
4-10-12	0.015	0.489	0.426	0.416	0.203
4-100-50	0.065	6.178	5.490	4.913	2.652
6-3-7	0.013	0.416	0.357	0.326	0.162
6-5-10	0.011	0.678	0.597	0.564	0.264
6-25-30	0.040	3.941	3.516	3.230	1.591
8-3-10	0.036	0.864	0.748	0.710	0.303
8-50-40	0.240	27.966	31.345	26.417	11.657
8-75-80	0.506	27.256	27.546	22.356	11.980
10-5-15	0.024	2.432	2.516	2.224	0.999
10-40-50	0.448	26.110	27.157	22.077	11.766
10-150-200	1.077	180.393	187.314	143.461	67.413
12-6-15	0.055	4.970	5.194	4.564	2.198
12-50-80	1.400	74.933	70.974	56.410	26.631
12-200-250	3.000	3863.923	4870.380	3065.369	1643.681
14-6-20	0.057	7.445	7.715	6.892	3.201
14-70-100	2.753	229.039	261.452	190.821	101.436
14-300-300	1586.123	-	-	-	-
16-8-25	0.189	12.934	13.695	12.477	6.698
16-70-100	4.823	2861.976	3577.134	2580.331	1302.131
16-270-300	3440.647	-	-	-	-

7.2   Results Using Quantum Annealing

As stated before, the quantum annealer only has a set number of qubits available, on which a problem can be embedded. For that reason, not every generated instance can be solved by the quantum annealer (yet). Hence, only the instance sets are considered that are small enough to be embedded onto the QPU. The best found solutions and the average over 10 runs for those instances can be found in Table 6. For each solution, the scalar that was used on the quantum annealer is also given in brackets. These scalars are the values for the corresponding α and β in the penalty formulas.

Just as for the simulated annealer, the number of samples again have to be specified. Besides that, on the quantum annealer it is also possible to change the annealing time, which is 20 microseconds by default. For the smallest set of instances, i.e. 4-3-5, it was sufficient to use 100 samples and the default annealing time. However, when extending the use of the quantum annealer to relatively bigger instances, it was necessary to increase the number of samples to a range of 1000 to 2000, and set the annealing time to a range of 100 to 200 microseconds, in order to obtain feasible solutions. A further increase in these parameters is not possible due to the limitation set by D-Wave. We used the SteepestDescent-Solver [11] as post-processing of the solutions. This solver is the discrete analogue of gradient descent, but the best move is computed using a local minimization rather than computing a gradient. At each step, it determines the dimension along which to descend based on the highest energy drop caused by a variable flip. This post-solver did not give any better results for the Simulated Annealing approach.

Table 6. Best and average found solutions using the quantum annealer (in brackets is given the scalar used in the respective penalty formula, which is used to calculate the penalty coefficient)

Data File	CPLEX	QUBO 1	QUBO 2	QUBO 3	QUBO 4
4-3-5-A	6	6 (1)	6 (1)	6 (1)	6 (1)
4-3-5-B	6	6 (1)	6 (1)	6 (1)	6 (1)
4-3-5-C	3	3 (1)	3 (1)	3 (1)	3 (1)
4-3-5-D	3	3 (1)	3 (1)	3 (1)	3 (1)
4-3-5-E	3	3 (1)	3 (1)	3 (1)	3 (1)
4-10-12-A	9	10/13.9 (1)	9/9,9 (1,5)	10/11.2 (1)	9/9.6 (0,25)
4-10-12-B	9	9/11.7 (1.8)	9/9 (1,5)	9/9.3 (1,1)	9/9.1 (0,6)
4-10-12-C	9	9/10.7 (2)	9/9 (1,5)	9/9.4 (1)	9/9.2 (0,6)
4-10-12-D	18	18/22 (1.5)	18/18.3 (2)	18/19.7 (1,5)	18/19.1 (0,25)
4-10-12-E	9	10/12.2 (1.5)	9/9 (2)	9/10 (1)	9/9.6 (0,5)
6-3-7-A	15	15/16 (3)	15/15 (3)	15/15.3 (3)	15/15 (1,5)
6-3-7-B	10	10/10 (3,2)	10/10 (3)	10/10 (3,1)	10/10 (1,5)
6-3-7-C	15	15/15.1 (3,2)	15/15 (3)	15/15 (3,1)	15/15 (1,5)
6-3-7-D	5	5/7.5 (3,3)	5/5 (3)	5/5.8 (3,1)	5/5 (1,25)
6-3-7-E	15	15/16.7 (3,2)	15/15 (3)	15/15.1 (3,1)	15/15 (1,5)
6-5-10-A	10	11/13.3 (3)	10/10 (3)	10/10.9 (3)	10/11.1 (2,8)
6-5-10-B	20	21/23.5 (3)	20/20.3 (3)	20/20.2 (3)	20/21 (3,5)
6-5-10-C	10	12/14.8 (3)	10/11 (3)	10/12.3 (3)	10/11.4 (4,1)
6-5-10-D	25	26/28.5 (3)	25/25.2 (3)	25/26 (3)	25/25.8 (3,6)
6-5-10-E	20	20/22.2 (3)	20/20.1 (3)	20/20.8 (3)	20/20.7 (4)
8-3-10-A	7	8/11.5 (4)	7/7 (4)	7/8.7 (4)	7/9.6 (4)
8-3-10-B	21	21/21.5 (4)	21/21 (4)	21/21.2 (4)	21/21 (4)
8-3-10-C	7	7/8.6 (4)	7/7 (4)	7/7.4 (4)	7/7.1 (4)
8-3-10-D	21	21/22.3 (4)	21/21 (4)	21/21.7 (4)	21/21.2 (4)
8-3-10-E	14	14/14.7 (4)	14/14 (4)	14/14.2 (4)	14/14 (4)

It can be immediately observed from the table that the scalars necessary to calculate these solutions are much higher than the values that were used for the simulated annealer. When comparing the performances of the QUBOs, it is clear that QUBO 2 obtains the best solutions again overall. QUBO 1 gives the worst results. QUBO 3 and QUBO 4 are close together, but slightly worse than QUBO 2.

The running times of the QUBOs on the quantum annealer can be found in Appendix C, which also reports those values for the instances where it was not possible to obtain a feasible solution. There are no surprises here, with again QUBO 4 being able to find solutions much faster than the other formulations.

It can also be seen that even the fastest QUBO requires a running time between 6 and 70 s, depending on the instance. Of course, this is still a lot larger than the exact solver. Most of the time, however, is spend on finding an embedding of the problem onto the QPU and connecting with the quantum computer, which is based in Canada. The process of finding an embedding is automated by D-Wave's Ocean software, but can still take up a fair amount of time depending on the size of the problem. The actual process of QA only takes around 0,002 to 0,4 s depending on the choice of number of samples and annealing time.

Obviously, these running times do not yet show the power of the quantum computer, as for these small instances, the classical approach is still superior in terms of both running time and solution quality. Nonetheless, when even larger instances, than the ones in this paper, are considered, the running time of CPLEX becomes enormous due to the exponential increase to problem size. QA might provide an advantage for those larger problems in the future, but the benefit in running time is still highly dependent on the problem being considered [32]. It could be that in some cases the running time scales (nearly) linearly. Indeed, for example, Lidar and Bauza [4] found that in their case the quantum annealer nearly reaches linear running time, when allowing for approximate solutions. Hopefully, in a few years time, the quantum computer has seen substantial advances in technology and consequently might play an important role for larger instances for the MLSP, as the results from the simulated annealer do show promising signs on solution quality.

7.3   Conclusion

In this paper, it has been studied how a QUBO can be formulated for the Multi-League Scheduling Problem. The formulations presented in this paper were created by translating constraints from the MILP to penalty functions. The main issue with this translation was that some of the constraints included a discrete variable and an inequality. To overcome this, four different techniques have been used, namely: one-hot encoding, domain-wall encoding, binary encoding, and unbalanced penalization. After formulating these QUBOs, penalty coefficients have been suggested for each respective QUBO.

The QUBOs were then implemented using the current state of the art Ocean software provided by D-Wave. Using simulated and QA, various instances for the MLSP were solved, resulting in approximate solutions for those instances. Moreover, using CPLEX, exact solutions were also obtained for these instances, which were used to benchmark the performance of the respective QUBOs. Then, based on the empirical results, it was determined how the current generation of quantum annealers compares in performance with an exact solver, and how the different QUBOs compare in terms of performance and running time.

Specifically, it has been found that domain-wall encoding performed the best in terms of solution quality, both using the simulated and quantum annealer. On the other hand, when using this technique, the time necessary to compute a solution was considerably larger than for the other three techniques. Using unbalanced penalization, the time necessary to compute was actually the lowest, both on the simulated and quantum annealer, while also achieving a solution quality that is only marginally worse than that of the domain-wall encoding. Besides, the faster speed at which the QUBO, using unbalanced penalization, can compute, is beneficial for larger instances. As this will allow in general the user to scale the penalty coefficients of the QUBO more efficient, such that a better solution quality can be achieved.

Currently, the classical approach is still superior to the quantum annealer, in terms of both running time and solution quality. However, the results from the simulated annealer showed promising signs for the quantum annealer that once they are fully developed, they might be able to give relatively good approximate solutions. In addition, the running times of the quantum annealer could potentially scale favorable in problem size, in contrast to the exponential increase for the exact solver.

Throughout the implementation of the QUBOs, the results have been benchmarked using CPLEX. However, as stated in the review on the current literature, Davari et al. [13] already provided an exact polynomial-time algorithm that solves the MLSP considered in this paper. This means that this paper gives a first step in the direction of solving the problem with varying league sizes, where such an (exact) algorithm does not exist. Li et al. [19] has provided a heuristic for this problem, which performs quite well. Nonetheless, if the QUBO formulations provided in this paper are extended to also allow for different league sizes, the quantum annealer might prove to be superior. In the future, when quantum computers are further developed, they might be able to find solutions to the MLSP faster and more reliable. Before that time, it is important to already have a considerable amount of research available that indicates the best techniques for the use of the quantum annealer.

Acknowledgement. This work was supported by the Dutch National Growth Fund (NGF), as part of the Quantum Delta NL program. The work is based on the bachelor thesis of the first author.

A   Appendix: Penalty Values

Using simulated annealing, the minimum required penalty is found for each QUBO, for a subset of the generated instances. That is, the minimum value for λ_1, λ_2, λ_4, and λ_6 to obtain a feasible solution in each respective QUBO. This feasible solution does not have to be optimal, it only has to satisfy the necessary constraints. From these results, it is found that the required penalty value increases as the league sizes increase. Moreover, as more teams and clubs are considered in the instance, it is necessary to further increase the penalty coefficients.

Now, Fig. 1 plots the minimum required penalty for each QUBO, for a subset of the instances. Next to this a line is plotted, which is the result of the following penalty formula:

$$A = \alpha \cdot \max_{c \in C}(n_c - \delta_c)^2, \tag{28}$$

where α is a positive scalar, which is set to 1 in the plot, and A depends on the characteristics of the instance. From the figure, it can be seen that this formula would work well for QUBO 1, 2, and 3, as it generally takes on a sufficient high value for a feasible solution. Moreover, taking $\alpha \in [0, 1]$, allows the calculated value to be scaled downwards, such that a potentially better solution can be obtained.

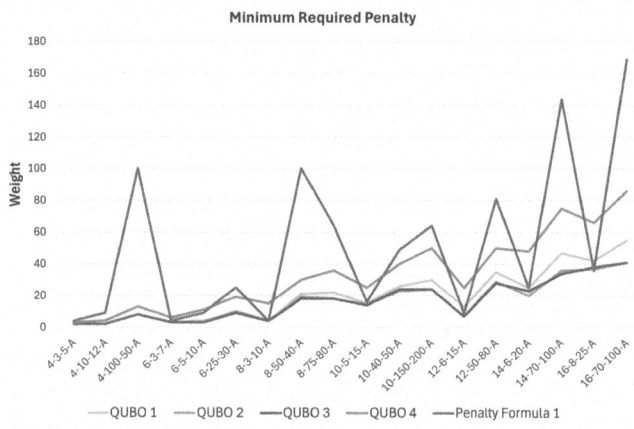

Fig. 1. Minimum required penalty for each QUBO and penalty formula 1

The intuition behind the formula is as follows. The third penalty function of QUBO 1, 2, and 3, for a fixed club $c \in C$ and round $r \in R$, should never give a higher penalty than $\max_{c \in C}(n_c - \delta_c)^2$. This is due to the reasoning that the auxiliary variables are only activated if (4), which measures the difference between scheduled matches at a club in a certain round and the capacity, is negative. If the expression is positive or equal to zero, these auxiliary variables should not be activated as this would only increase the penalty given to the QUBO.

Having a penalty from one of the feasibility penalties, i.e. a violation in one of the constraints, might lead to a lower penalty from the third penalty function depending on the instance. Hence, when minimizing the QUBO, it might give infeasible solutions. Thus, having a violation in one of the constraints should be at least as unattractive as the savings that could be made by having such a violation. This leads to the suggested formula for the penalty coefficients. Note that, so far the savings have been treated for a fixed club and round. However, for larger files, it might be the case that these savings accumulate over multiple rounds. Then, a larger coefficient for the feasibility penalties is necessary, which can be achieved by up-scaling the penalty value with $\alpha > 1$. As will be seen in the results, this was indeed necessary for larger instances.

Finally, in Fig. 1, it can also be seen that QUBO 4 requires higher penalty values in order to find feasible solutions, as compared to the other three formulations. Besides, the suggested penalty formula does not always suffice for this QUBO. Hence, a different formula is used to calculate penalty coefficients for the QUBO using unbalanced penalization:

$$B = \beta \cdot \max_{c \in C} (n_c)^2, \tag{29}$$

where β is again a scalar. This formula leads to higher penalty values and as can be seen in Fig. 2 yields sufficiently high values for feasible solutions. Again, using the scalar, the calculated weights can be scaled downwards to obtain better solutions.

To sum up, the penalty coefficients are used as follows. All penalty functions, which are not part of the feasibility penalties, are given a coefficient equal to 1. For QUBO 1, 2, and 3, the feasibility penalties are multiplied by a weight calculated by (28), whereas in QUBO 4 the feasibility penalties are given a weight calculated by (29). In general, scalars α and β are set to 1. However, if using this term, an infeasible solution is found, the total penalty weight is increased by up-scaling the respective scalar. Moreover, if a feasible solution is found which potentially can be improved upon, the scalar is set to a value between 0 and 1.

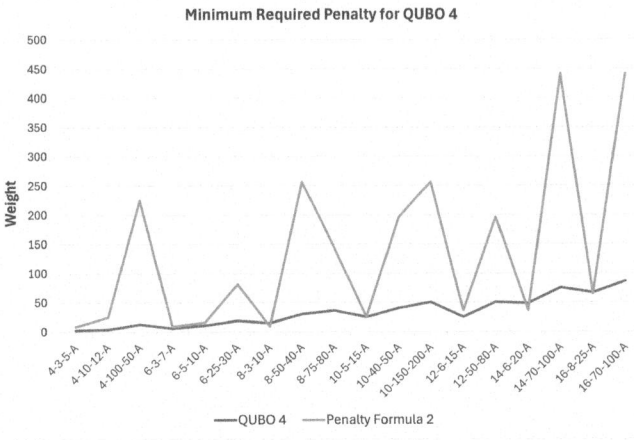

Fig. 2. Minimum required penalty for QUBO 4 and penalty formula 2

Note that, in the case of unbalanced penalization, it has been chosen to set λ_8 and λ_9 both equal to 1. However, (24) and (25) together behave differently depending on the combination of penalty coefficients chosen, as can be seen in Fig. 3. Hence, the choice for λ_8 and λ_9 needs to be justified.

First of all, in Fig. 3, five different series are plotted. Each of them corresponds to the penalty value obtained from (22) with $h(x)$ corresponding to (23), using each respective combination of penalty coefficients. For this penalty value, one club and one round stays fixed, rather than summing over all clubs and rounds as in (24). The combinations of penalty weights are formatted as (λ_8, λ_9), where λ_8 is set to 1 and λ_9 takes on different values. Besides, observe that $h(x)$ is equal to the difference between a club's capacity and the number of matches scheduled at that club in a particular round. This means that $h(x)$ could take on any integer value between $\delta_c - n_c$ and δ_c, as the maximum number of matches scheduled at a club can not exceed the number of teams part of that club and the minimum is obviously zero. For that reason, to represent as many combinations of n_c and δ_c, it has been chosen to let $h(x)$ take on values in the range $\{-20, -19, ..., 19, 20\}$.

As stated before, it is needed that negative values for (23) are penalized more than positive values. It would be even better to not penalize positive values for $h(x)$ at all, which would lead one to think it would be best to use combination $(1, 0.10)$, as positive values are barely penalized. However, using this combination, the penalty value is very low when $h(x)$ takes on a value between -1 and -5. Here, negative values for $h(x)$ correspond to capacity violations at a club, and especially those low number of violations occur often. As the penalty value for these low number of violations would be very low, it might become too attractive for the quantum annealer to have some violations at clubs in multiple rounds. This in turn would lead to a higher amount of violations in total. This problem would not occur if the combination $(1, 1)$ is taken, as even for low number of violations, the penalty value increases quickly.

Moreover, the high penalty values for positive values of $h(x)$ should not pose a problem depending on the other two penalty weights chosen for λ_1 and λ_2. If these weights are set high enough, then regardless of the other penalty for positive values of $h(x)$, it would not be attractive to violate one of the constraints. Indeed, as will be seen in the results, QUBO 4 is perfectly able to find feasible solutions with the $(1, 1)$ combination. In addition, after solving some of the instances with both the $(1, 1)$ and $(1, 0.10)$ combination, it was found that minimizing QUBO 4 with the former combination, led in general to better solutions in terms of number of violations. This all justifies the choice of setting λ_8 and λ_9 equal to 1.

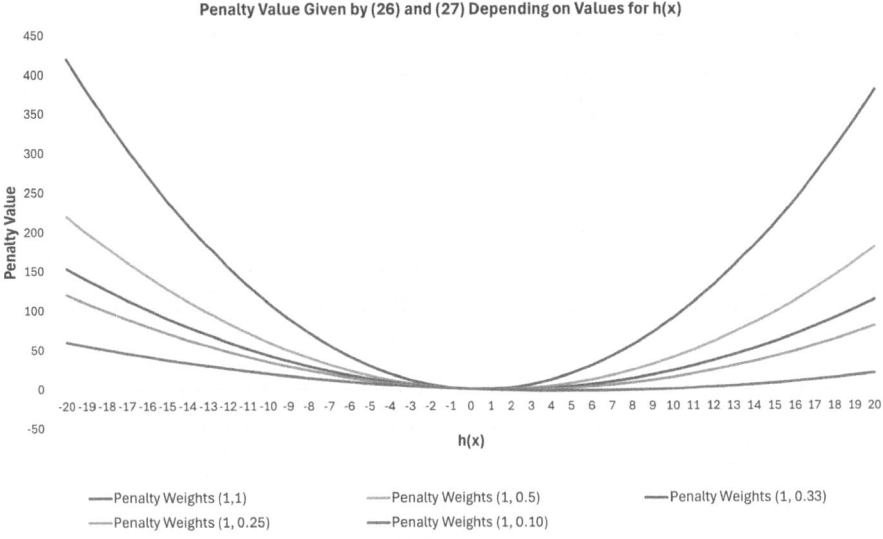

Fig. 3. Penalty values obtained from (24) and (25) together using different combinations for the respective penalty coefficients, depending on values for (23)

B Appendix: Simulated Annealing Results

B.1 Solutions Using Simulated Annealing

In Tables 7 and 8 the objective value of the solutions, i.e. the number of violations, are given for CPLEX and the QUBO formulations, for all the generated instances. Note that all solutions given are indeed feasible. For the QUBO formulations, the best solution is given with next to it in brackets the scalar used in the corresponding penalty formula. That is the penalty coefficient used, can be calculated by the corresponding penalty formula and the scalar given in brackets. Moreover, for each process of simulated annealing, a total of 100 samples is used. (As stated before, the values for the two biggest files: 14-300-300 and 16-270-300, are not obtained.) See next two pages for the tables.

B.2 Running Times Using Simulated Annealing

In Tables 9 and 10, the running times are given for CPLEX as well as all QUBOs (all in seconds).

Table 7. Best solutions found using simulated annealing (in brackets is given the scalar used in the penalty formula)

Data File	CPLEX	QUBO 1	QUBO 2	QUBO 3	QUBO 4
4-3-5-A	6	6 (1)	6 (1)	6 (1)	6 (1)
4-3-5-B	6	6 (1)	6 (1)	6 (1)	6 (1)
4-3-5-C	3	3 (1)	3 (1)	3 (1)	3 (1)
4-3-5-D	3	3 (1)	3 (1)	3 (1)	3 (1)
4-3-5-E	3	3 (1)	3 (1)	3 (1)	3 (1)
4-10-12-A	9	9 (0,5)	9 (1)	9 (1)	9 (0,5)
4-10-12-B	9	9 (1)	9 (1)	9 (1)	9 (1)
4-10-12-C	9	9 (1)	9 (1)	9 (1)	9 (1)
4-10-12-D	18	18 (1)	18 (1)	18(1)	18 (1)
4-10-12-E	9	9 (1)	9 (1)	9 (1)	9 (1)
4-100-50-A	270	274 (0,09)	271 (0,08)	274 (0,08)	273 (0,06)
4-100-50-B	174	182 (0,13)	177 (0,12)	179 (0,12)	176 (0,07)
4-100-50-C	204	212 (0,11)	206 (0,1)	208 (0,1)	207 (0,09)
4-100-50-D	174	178 (0,17)	176 (0,16)	177 (0,17)	178 (0,08)
4-100-50-E	246	248 (0,11)	250 (0,11)	249 (0,1)	248 (0,06)
6-3-7-A	15	15 (1)	15 (1)	15 (1)	15 (1)
6-3-7-B	10	10 (1)	10 (1)	10 (1)	10 (1,5)
6-3-7-C	15	15 (1)	15 (1)	15 (1)	15 (1,5)
6-3-7-D	5	5 (1)	5 (1)	5 (1)	5 (1,5)
6-3-7-E	15	15 (1)	15 (1)	15 (1)	15 (1,5)
6-5-10-A	10	10 (1)	10 (1)	10 (1)	10 (1)
6-5-10-B	20	20 (1)	20 (1)	20 (1)	20 (1)
6-5-10-C	10	10 (1)	10 (1)	10 (1)	10 (1)
6-5-10-D	25	25 (1)	25 (1)	25 (1)	25 (1)
6-5-10-E	20	20 (1)	20 (1)	20 (1)	20 (1)
6-25-30-A	105	106 (0,42)	106 (0,4)	106 (0,4)	105 (0,27)
6-25-30-B	70	76 (0,24)	72 (0,22)	73 (0,22)	73 (0,15)
6-25-30-C	135	136 (0,26)	136 (0,25)	135 (0,3)	136 (0,25)
6-25-30-D	125	128 (0,38)	127 (0,36)	126 (0,36)	126 (0,21)
6-25-30-E	100	105 (0,2)	101 (0,17)	102 (0,2)	105 (0,19)
8-3-10-A	7	7 (0,95)	7 (1)	7 (1)	7 (2)
8-3-10-B	21	21 (1,5)	21 (1)	21 (1)	21 (2)
8-3-10-C	7	7 (0,95)	7 (1)	7 (1)	7 (2)
8-3-10-D	21	21 (1,5)	21 (1)	21 (1)	21 (1)
8-3-10-E	14	14 (1,5)	14 (1)	14 (1)	14 (2)
8-50-40-A	392	414 (0,25)	406 (0,2)	405 (0,18)	406 (0,14)
8-50-40-B	357	383 (0,28)	373 (0,23)	372 (0,32)	371 (0,16)
8-50-40-C	644	670 (0,24)	659 (0,19)	659 (0,19)	662 (0,12)
8-50-40-D	413	436 (0,16)	429 (0,17)	427 (0,17)	423 (0,09)
8-50-40-E	420	448 (0,27)	443 (0,24)	436 (0,24)	440 (0,18)
8-75-80-A	735	789 (0,33)	776 (0,3)	770 (0,3)	784 (0,27)
8-75-80-B	735	767 (0,34)	759 (0,29)	761 (0,29)	769 (0,22)
8-75-80-C	672	725 (0,35)	717 (0,3)	716 (0,3)	714 (0,14)
8-75-80-D	756	804 (0,39)	790 (0,3)	779 (0,29)	777 (0,22)
8-75-80-E	791	837 (0,3)	836 (0,25)	830 (0,25)	822 (0,2)
10-5-15-A	108	108 (0,95)	108 (1)	108 (1)	108 (1,5)
10-5-15-B	72	78 (1,01)	72 (0,85)	72 (0,9)	72 (1,3)
10-5-15-C	72	72 (1,2)	72 (1)	72 (1)	72 (1,2)
10-5-15-D	36	36 (1,2)	36 (1)	36 (1)	36 (1)
10-5-15-E	45	45 (1,1)	45 (1)	45 (1)	46 (1,2)

Table 8. Best solutions found using simulated annealing (in brackets is given the scalar used in the penalty formula)

Data File	CPLEX	QUBO 1	QUBO 2	QUBO 3	QUBO 4
10-40-50-A	639	683 (0,65)	656 (0,48)	658 (0,48)	663 (0,24)
10-40-50-B	792	819 (0,38)	816 (0,35)	813 (0,35)	813 (0,25)
10-40-50-C	522	582 (0,5)	556 (0,37)	549 (0,37)	554 (0,25)
10-40-50-D	567	614 (0,55)	592 (0,5)	596 (0,48)	597 (0,25)
10-40-50-E	522	551 (0,55)	553 (0,5)	553 (0,48)	566 (0,25)
10-150-200-A	2223	2415 (0,5)	2361 (0,4)	2380 (0,4)	2401 (0,21)
10-150-200-B	2286	2465 (0,25)	2413 (0,23)	2437 (0,25)	2432 (0,2)
10-150-200-C	2385	2597 (0,35)	2539 (0,28)	2557 (0,28)	2564 (0,17)
10-150-200-D	2277	2440 (0,35)	2421 (0,35)	2439 (0,35)	2455 (0,2)
10-150-200-E	2484	2670 (0,32)	2616 (0,25)	2637 (0,25)	2693 (0,22)
12-6-15-A	22	25 (1,5)	22 (0,7)	22 (1)	22 (0,85)
12-6-15-B	99	102 (1,5)	99 (1,1)	99 (1,1)	103 (1,2)
12-6-15-C	88	94 (1,25)	91 (1,1)	88 (1,1)	92 (1,2)
12-6-15-D	121	127 (1,3)	125 (1,25)	126 (1,25)	122 (0,95)
12-6-15-E	132	142 (1,25)	136 (1,5)	139 (1,5)	136 (1,1)
12-50-80-A	990	1095 (0,45)	1069 (0,4)	1079 (0,4)	1087 (0,3)
12-50-80-B	1001	1095 (0,5)	1104 (0,37)	1097 (0,37)	1077 (0,26)
12-50-80-C	1056	1128 (0,48)	1123 (0,37)	1128 (0,37)	1135 (0,35)
12-50-80-D	1111	1213 (0,4)	1182 (0,32)	1197 (0,32)	1212 (0,26)
12-50-80-E	1408	1506 (0,48)	1478 (0,37)	1475 (0,37)	1479 (0,27)
12-200-250-A	4620	4917 (4)	4914 (4)	4924 (4)	4980 (4,5)
12-200-250-B	3608	4049 (4)	3992 (4)	4057 (4)	4082 (4,5)
12-200-250-C	3806	4133 (5)	4072 (4)	4080 (4)	4114 (4,5)
12-200-250-D	3773	4149 (4)	4093 (4)	4152 (4)	4178 (4,5)
12-200-250-E	4136	4439 (4)	4437 (4)	4498 (4)	4486 (4,5)
14-6-20-A	91	98 (1,3)	93 (0,95)	94 (0,95)	95 (1,75)
14-6-20-B	156	160 (1,2)	158 (1)	164 (1)	170 (1,5)
14-6-20-C	130	133 (1,5)	132 (1,25)	130 (1,25)	130 (1,3)
14-6-20-D	91	92 (1,2)	91 (1)	91 (1)	93 (1,25)
14-6-20-E	104	106 (1,6)	104 (1,25)	107 (1,4)	108 (1,5)
14-70-100-A	2093	2308 (0,4)	2251 (0,25)	2231 (0,25)	2254 (0,2)
14-70-100-B	2041	2259 (0,5)	2218 (0,4)	2211 (0,4)	2202 (0,25)
14-70-100-C	1859	1975 (0,45)	1973 (0,35)	1971 (0,35)	1971 (0,3)
14-70-100-D	1729	1907 (0,5)	1871 (0,4)	1860 (0,4)	1888 (0,3)
14-70-100-E	2158	2330 (0,5)	2285 (0,4)	2303 (0,4)	2297 (0,25)
14-300-300-A	6292	N/A	N/A	N/A	N/A
14-300-300-B	5226	N/A	N/A	N/A	N/A
14-300-300-C	6292	N/A	N/A	N/A	N/A
14-300-300-D	5252	N/A	N/A	N/A	N/A
14-300-300-E	6487	N/A	N/A	N/A	N/A
16-8-25-A	585	589 (1,5)	585 (1,5)	589 (1,5)	591 (1,25)
16-8-25-B	435	452 (1,5)	447 (1,5)	443 (1,5)	441 (0,9)
16-8-25-C	525	540 (1,5)	541 (1,5)	536 (1,5)	535 (1,5)
16-8-25-D	315	321 (1,4)	321 (1,3)	321 (1,3)	319 (1,5)
16-8-25-E	570	594 (1,2)	598 (1,2)	589 (1,2)	593 (1,2)
16-70-100-A	2250	2450 (6)	2435 (5)	2433 (5)	2419 (5)
16-70-100-B	2325	2557 (6)	2491 (5)	2505 (5)	2523 (5)
16-70-100-C	1890	2126 (6)	2049 (5)	2054 (5)	2079 (5)
16-70-100-D	2655	2865 (6)	2859 (5)	2840 (5)	2853 (5)
16-70-100-E	3105	3294 (6)	3240 (5)	3265 (5)	3221 (5)
16-270-300-A	6900	N/A	N/A	N/A	N/A
16-270-300-B	6570	N/A	N/A	N/A	N/A
16-270-300-C	7845	N/A	N/A	N/A	N/A
16-270-300-D	7215	N/A	N/A	N/A	N/A
16-270-300-E	6750	N/A	N/A	N/A	N/A

Table 9. Running times for simulated annealer and CPLEX solver (in seconds)

Data File	CPLEX	QUBO 1	QUBO 2	QUBO 3	QUBO 4
4-3-5-A	0,069	0,179	0,145	0,140	0,078
4-3-5-B	0,009	0,168	0,146	0,141	0,075
4-3-5-C	0,01	0,168	0,151	0,138	0,080
4-3-5-D	0,011	0,178	0,162	0,169	0,086
4-3-5-E	0,01	0,172	0,152	0,147	0,079
4-10-12-A	0,031	0,476	0,404	0,398	0,216
4-10-12-B	0,011	0,496	0,427	0,428	0,208
4-10-12-C	0,011	0,528	0,467	0,431	0,196
4-10-12-D	0,01	0,475	0,416	0,396	0,195
4-10-12-E	0,01	0,468	0,419	0,427	0,201
4-100-50-A	0,088	5,812	6,148	5,056	2,756
4-100-50-B	0,077	6,247	4,982	4,960	2,670
4-100-50-C	0,083	6,254	4,956	4,862	2,572
4-100-50-D	0,04	6,521	6,078	4,885	2,564
4-100-50-E	0,035	6,056	5,284	4,801	2,696
6-3-7-A	0,02	0,402	0,322	0,325	0,167
6-3-7-B	0,01	0,446	0,385	0,348	0,166
6-3-7-C	0,011	0,417	0,351	0,321	0,161
6-3-7-D	0,014	0,425	0,377	0,322	0,167
6-3-7-E	0,01	0,391	0,349	0,316	0,149
6-5-10-A	0,016	0,742	0,644	0,613	0,265
6-5-10-B	0,012	0,664	0,589	0,523	0,259
6-5-10-C	0,01	0,684	0,598	0,570	0,266
6-5-10-D	0,01	0,596	0,536	0,503	0,264
6-5-10-E	0,008	0,705	0,616	0,610	0,263
6-25-30-A	0,038	4,075	3,726	3,106	1,567
6-25-30-B	0,03	4,011	3,117	3,599	1,668
6-25-30-C	0,026	3,958	3,546	2,979	1,547
6-25-30-D	0,033	3,546	3,356	2,927	1,556
6-25-30-E	0,075	4,115	3,834	3,540	1,615
8-3-10-A	0,025	0,887	0,766	0,691	0,299
8-3-10-B	0,016	0,832	0,728	0,682	0,291
8-3-10-C	0,063	0,934	0,781	0,743	0,302
8-3-10-D	0,063	0,811	0,699	0,704	0,331
8-3-10-E	0,012	0,856	0,764	0,729	0,291
8-50-40-A	0,263	31,684	28,431	25,904	15,983
8-50-40-B	0,249	29,730	20,380	26,669	10,102
8-50-40-C	0,237	35,279	36,354	23,550	9,102
8-50-40-D	0,212	21,472	33,233	25,353	12,680
8-50-40-E	0,239	21,664	38,325	30,611	10,416
8-75-80-A	0,526	26,963	25,877	21,779	11,677
8-75-80-B	0,438	27,850	26,708	22,037	11,785
8-75-80-C	0,555	29,274	28,991	24,509	12,478
8-75-80-D	0,525	25,759	27,765	21,492	11,867
8-75-80-E	0,488	26,435	28,390	21,966	12,094
10-5-15-A	0,027	2,182	2,015	1,921	0,983
10-5-15-B	0,024	2,236	2,207	2,085	0,974
10-5-15-C	0,016	2,518	2,824	2,207	1,021
10-5-15-D	0,036	2,547	2,676	2,618	1,015
10-5-15-E	0,016	2,674	2,859	2,289	1,001

Table 10. Running times for simulated annealer and CPLEX solver (in seconds)

Data File	CPLEX	QUBO 1	QUBO 2	QUBO 3	QUBO 4
10-40-50-A	0,327	26,691	27,491	21,833	11,696
10-40-50-B	0,430	24,284	25,220	20,973	11,608
10-40-50-C	0,437	26,498	29,201	21,825	11,823
10-40-50-D	0,449	26,034	25,582	24,170	11,810
10-40-50-E	0,595	27,043	28,291	21,583	11,894
10-150-200-A	0,946	183,594	167,203	140,008	64,620
10-150-200-B	1,135	181,599	216,399	147,075	64,374
10-150-200-C	0,710	176,524	182,521	136,256	66,306
10-150-200-D	1,521	194,278	198,038	148,228	76,134
10-150-200-E	1,075	165,972	172,409	145,738	65,632
12-6-15-A	0,023	5,781	6,279	5,426	2,250
12-6-15-B	0,065	4,910	5,235	4,462	2,186
12-6-15-C	0,026	4,936	5,129	4,429	2,191
12-6-15-D	0,059	4,655	4,812	4,381	2,215
12-6-15-E	0,102	4,569	4,514	4,123	2,147
12-50-80-A	1,611	78,421	74,895	55,725	26,721
12-50-80-B	1,741	73,709	62,982	57,139	26,333
12-50-80-C	1,265	77,459	80,706	56,800	26,529
12-50-80-D	1,259	76,404	79,646	57,861	26,478
12-50-80-E	1,122	68,670	56,640	54,530	27,094
12-200-250-A	3,371	3735,544	4660,985	2855,063	1593,728
12-200-250-B	2,753	3993,802	4894,699	3104,615	1627,983
12-200-250-C	3,231	3763,838	5020,771	3110,483	1643,741
12-200-250-D	2,897	4071,487	4876,719	3136,091	1646,363
12-200-250-E	2,726	3754,944	4898,727	3120,591	1706,590
14-6-20-A	0,041	7,512	7,085	6,994	3,222
14-6-20-B	0,089	7,044	7,174	6,529	3,202
14-6-20-C	0,056	7,501	8,040	7,036	3,217
14-6-20-D	0,037	7,589	8,149	7,026	3,201
14-6-20-E	0,06	7,580	8,128	6,877	3,163
14-70-100-A	2,871	229,234	264,879	192,676	101,677
14-70-100-B	3,227	227,874	252,710	185,806	101,025
14-70-100-C	2,124	231,737	261,437	188,296	100,239
14-70-100-D	2,665	232,502	262,096	188,699	97,972
14-70-100-E	2,877	223,848	266,137	198,626	106,270
14-300-300-A	158,914	N/A	N/A	N/A	N/A
14-300-300-B	2644,025	N/A	N/A	N/A	N/A
14-300-300-C	3020,453	N/A	N/A	N/A	N/A
14-300-300-D	665,713	N/A	N/A	N/A	N/A
14-300-300-E	1441,511	N/A	N/A	N/A	N/A
16-8-25-A	0,139	12,502	13,181	12,049	6,605
16-8-25-B	0,255	13,449	14,599	13,182	6,753
16-8-25-C	0,212	12,607	13,087	12,169	6,609
16-8-25-D	0,105	14,186	15,657	13,271	6,676
16-8-25-E	0,233	11,927	11,950	11,712	6,846
16-70-100-A	4,539	2812,535	3482,553	2588,668	1297,817
16-70-100-B	4,920	2958,303	3573,247	2590,456	1262,907
16-70-100-C	4,718	2957,133	3832,043	2634,108	1326,598
16-70-100-D	5,382	2846,541	3625,403	2554,825	1329,382
16-70-100-E	4,556	2735,368	3372,425	2533,599	1293,951
16-270-300-A	2493,823	N/A	N/A	N/A	N/A
16-270-300-B	3067,386	N/A	N/A	N/A	N/A
16-270-300-C	3576,27	N/A	N/A	N/A	N/A
16-270-300-D	5184,67	N/A	N/A	N/A	N/A
16-270-300-E	2881,084	N/A	N/A	N/A	N/A

C   Appendix: Quantum Annealing Running Times

In Table 11, the running times are given for each QUBO using QA (in seconds). Note that the star indicates that the reported running time is measured for the calculation of an infeasible solution.

Table 11. Running times for the quantum annealer and CPLEX solver (in seconds)

Data File	CPLEX	QUBO 1	QUBO 2	QUBO 3	QUBO 4
4-3-5-A	0,069	5,369	7,580	8,732	6,445
4-3-5-B	0,009	3,029	8,454	7,070	6,253
4-3-5-C	0,010	3,484	7,664	7,797	5,83
4-3-5-D	0,011	7,563	8,297	12,475	8,774
4-3-5-E	0,010	3,345	7,0995	7,415	6,056
4-10-12-A	0,031	21,363	21,763	23,249	16,255
4-10-12-B	0,011	28,839	24,037	28,032	13,774
4-10-12-C	0,011	34,791	30,0367	20,937	15,870
4-10-12-D	0,010	26,776	24,011	23,084	15,745
4-10-12-E	0,010	28,940	34,938	28,362	16,346
6-3-7-A	0,020	57,120	38,421	32,360	12,544
6-3-7-B	0,010	56,883	46,063	30,492	23,134
6-3-7-C	0,011	46,991	50,710	29,765	17,257
6-3-7-D	0,014	36,381	46,433	40,931	21,367
6-3-7-E	0,001	41,738	29,874	58,095	16,747
6-5-10-A	0,016	61,096*	41,112*	46,727*	32,620
6-5-10-B	0,012	55,850*	64,426*	38,924*	25,371
6-5-10-C	0,010	30,592*	45,548*	33,850*	49,788
6-5-10-D	0,010	43,154*	60,784*	47,357*	28,775
6-5-10-E	0,008	75,632*	38,789*	35,220*	32,315
8-3-10-A	0,025	76,126*	98,893*	76,853*	68,001*
8-3-10-B	0,016	104,163*	87,693*	73,955*	64,951*
8-3-10-C	0,063	88,140*	152,215*	93,963*	57,678*
8-3-10-D	0,063	78,336*	67,237*	70,952*	39,174*
8-3-10-E	0,012	153,965*	99,702*	73,795*	41,431*

References

1. Aguilera, E., de Jong, J., Phillipson, F., Taamallah, S., Vos, M.: Multi-objective portfolio optimization using a quantum annealer. Mathematics **12**(9) (2024)
2. Ayodele, M.: Penalty weights in QUBO formulations: Permutation problems. In: Pérez Cáceres, L., Verel, S. (eds.) Evolutionary Computation in Combinatorial Optimization, pp. 159–174. Springer, Cham (2022)
3. Bartsch, T., Drexl, A., Kröger, S.: Scheduling the professional soccer leagues of Austria and Germany. Comput. Oper. Res. **33**(7), 1907–1937 (2006)
4. Bauza, H.M., Lidar, D.A.: Scaling advantage in approximate optimization with quantum annealing. arXiv preprint arXiv:2401.07184 (2024)
5. Camino, B., Buckeridge, J., Warburton, P., Kendon, V., Woodley, S.: Quantum computing and materials science: a practical guide to applying quantum annealing to the configurational analysis of materials. J. Appl. Phys. **133**(22) (2023)

6. Chancellor, N.: Domain wall encoding of discrete variables for quantum annealing and QAOA. Quantum Sci. Technol. **4**(4), 045004 (2019)
7. Chen, J., Stollenwerk, T., Chancellor, N.: Performance of domain-wall encoding for quantum annealing. IEEE Trans. Quantum Eng. **2**, 1–14 (2021)
8. Chiscop, I., Nauta, J., Veerman, B., Phillipson, F.: A hybrid solution method for the multi-service location set covering problem. In: Krzhizhanovskaya, V.V., et al. (eds.) ICCS 2020. LNCS, vol. 12142, pp. 531–545. Springer, Cham (2020). https://doi.org/10.1007/978-3-030-50433-5_41
9. Codognet, P.: Comparing QUBO models for quantum annealing: integer encodings for permutation problems. Int. Trans. Oper. Res. (2024)
10. Colucci, G., van der Linde, S., Phillipson, F.: Power network optimization: a quantum approach. IEEE Access **11**, 98926–98938 (2023)
11. D-Wave: D-wave ocean software documentation (2024). https://docs.ocean.dwavesys.com/en/stable/docs_samplers/. Accessed Sept 2024
12. D-Wave: Getting started with D-Wave solvers (2024). https://docs.dwavesys.com/docs/latest/doc_getting_started.htmlDa
13. Davari, M., Goossens, D., Beliën, J., Lambers, R., Spieksma, F.C.: The multi-league sports scheduling problem, or how to schedule thousands of matches. Eur. J. Oper. Res. **48**(2), 180–187 (2020)
14. Domino, K., Koniorczyk, M., Krawiec, K., Jałowiecki, K., Deffner, S., Gardas, B.: Quantum annealing in the NISQ era: railway conflict management. Entropy **25**(2), 191 (2023)
15. Egger, D.J., et al.: Quantum computing for finance: state-of-the-art and future prospects. IEEE Trans. Quantum Eng. **1**, 1–24 (2020)
16. Glover, F., Kochenberger, G., Du, Y.: Quantum Bridge Analytics I: a tutorial on formulating and using QUBO models. 4OR - Q. J. Oper. Res. **17**, 335–371 (2019)
17. Guilmeau, T., Chouzenoux, E., Elvira, V.: Simulated annealing: a review and a new scheme. In: 2021 IEEE Statistical Signal Processing Workshop (SSP), pp. 101–105 (2021)
18. Jünger, M., et al.: Quantum annealing versus digital computing: an experimental comparison. ACM J. Exp. Algorithmics **26**(1.9) (2021)
19. Li, M., Davari, M., Goossens, D.: Multi-league sports scheduling with different leagues sizes. Eur. J. Oper. Res. **307**(1), 313–327 (2022)
20. Lim, A., Rodrigues, B., Zhang, X.: Scheduling sports competitions at multiple venues - revisited. Eur. J. Oper. Res. **175**(1), 171–186 (2005)
21. Lin, M.M., Shu, Y.C., Lu, B.Z., Fang, P.S.: Nurse scheduling problem via pyqubo. arXiv preprint arXiv:2302.09459 (2023)
22. Lucas, A.: Ising formulations of many NP problems. Front. Phys. **2** (2014)
23. Montañez-Barrera, J.A., van den Heuvel, P., Willsch, D., Michielsen, K.: Improving performance in combinatorial optimization problems with inequality constraints: An evaluation of the unbalanced penalization method on D-Wave Advantage. In: IEEE International Conference on Quantum Computing and Engineering (QCE), vol. 1, pp. 535–542 (2023)
24. Montañez-Barrera, J.A., Willsch, D., Maldonado-Romo, A., Michielsen, K.: Unbalanced penalization: a new approach to encode inequality constraints of combinatorial problems for quantum optimization algorithms. Quantum Sci. Technol. **9** (2024)
25. Nazareth, D.P., Spaans, J.D.: First application of quantum annealing to IMRT beamlet intensity optimization. Phys. Med. Biol. **60**(10), 4137 (2015)
26. Neukart, F., Compostella, G., Seidel, C., Von Dollen, D., Yarkoni, S., Parney, B.: Traffic flow optimization using a quantum annealer. Front. in ICT **4**, 29 (2017)

27. Phillipson, F., Chiscop, I.: Multimodal container planning: a QUBO formulation and implementation on a quantum annealer. In: Paszynski, M., Kranzlmüller, D., Krzhizhanovskaya, V.V., Dongarra, J.J., Sloot, P. (eds.) ICCS 2021. LNCS, vol. 12747, pp. 30–44. Springer, Cham (2021). https://doi.org/10.1007/978-3-030-77980-1_3

28. Phillipson, F.: Quantum computing in telecommunication-a survey. Mathematics **11**(15), 3423 (2023)

29. Phillipson, F.: Quantum computing in logistics and supply chain management-an overview. arXiv preprint arXiv:2402.17520 (2024)

30. Phillipson, F., Bontekoe, T., Chiscop, I.: Energy storage scheduling: a QUBO formulation for quantum computing. In: Krieger, U.R., Eichler, G., Erfurth, C., Fahrnberger, G. (eds.) Innovations for Community Services, pp. 251–261. Springer, Cham (2021)

31. Phillipson, F., Chiscop, I.: Multimodal container planning: a qubo formulation and implementation on a quantum annealer. In: International Conference on Computational Science, pp. 30–44. Springer, Cham (2021)

32. Rajak, A., Suzuki, S., Dutta, A., Chakrabarti, B.K.: Quantum annealing: an overview. Philos. Trans. R. Soc. A: Math. Phys. Eng. Sci. **381**(2241) (2022)

33. Willsch, D., Willsch, M., Gonzales Calaza, C.D., et al.: Benchmarking advantage and D-Wave 2000Q quantum annealers with exact cover problems. Quantum Inf. Process. **21**(141) (2022)

34. Yarkoni, S., Raponi, E., Bäck, T., Schmitt, S.: Quantum annealing for industry applications: introduction and review. Rep. Progress Phys. **85**(10) (2022)

Optimizing Initial Qubit Mappings Under Fixed Gate Error Rates Using Deep Reinforcement Learning

Rares Adrian Oancea[1] , Stan van der Linde[1] , Willem de Kok[1] ,
Matthia Sabatelli[2] , and Sebastian Feld[3(✉)]

[1] The Netherlands Organisation for Applied Scientific Research (TNO),
Oude Waalsdorperweg 63, 2597 AK The Hague, The Netherlands
[2] University of Groningen, Nijenborgh 7, 9747 AG Groningen, The Netherlands
[3] QuTech, Delft University of Technology, Mekelweg 5, 2628 CD Delft,
The Netherlands
s.feld@tudelft.nl

Abstract. Quantum computing promises to execute some tasks exponentially faster than classical computers. Quantum compilation, which transforms algorithms into executable quantum circuits, involves solving the initial mapping problem, crucial for optimizing qubit assignment and minimizing gate error rates. This study explores Deep Reinforcement Learning (DRL) for initial mapping across various qubit topologies, considering fixed gate error rates. Previous DRL approaches have succeeded but didn't account for fixed error rates, used only one algorithm (PPO), and focused on a single topology with 20 qubits. The trial-and-error nature of Reinforcement Learning makes it ideal for initial mapping. DRL agents, using multiple policy gradient algorithms (A2C, PPO with and without action masking, and TRPO), compute high-quality mappings for small- and medium-scale quantum architectures. While effective, their efficiency decreases with larger systems, necessitating further optimization. Fine-tuning hyperparameters and action masking prevent illegal actions and enhance accuracy. Although currently not surpassing tools like Qiskit or achieving scalability for larger systems, this study highlights DRL's potential for initial mapping in quantum computing, encouraging further innovation and refinement.

Keywords: Quantum compilation · Deep reinforcement learning

1 Introduction

In quantum computing, gate-based quantum computers execute a series of gates on qubits to perform computations, which are believed to efficiently handle [10,12] tasks that are otherwise intractable for classical computers [17]. Algorithms for these systems are often designed using a quantum circuit representation, specifying which gates are applied to which qubits and in what sequence. Although this representation is hardware-agnostic, executing arbitrary quantum circuits on actual hardware is complex. Furthermore, the high-level design of

S. Zielinski et al. (Eds.): I4CS 2025, CCIS 2513, pp. 189–208, 2025.
https://doi.org/10.1007/978-3-031-94263-1_12

a quantum circuit often does not take into account the restrictions imposed by the physical quantum hardware [30]. This process, known as quantum compilation [2], involves converting the circuit into a hardware-specific executable algorithm [20]. Among numerous compilation steps and possible optimization passes [19], quantum compilation [15] generally includes steps like qubit routing [7] and initial mapping [30], both recognized as NP-hard optimization problems [27]. The main roadblock which restricts the execution of quantum algorithms on quantum computers is given by the manner in which qubits are connected on the hardware. Depending on how the qubits are connected on the target architecture, some of the gates on the circuit may not be executable on the quantum computer, due to the connectivity constraints of the hardware.

This concept is illustrated in Fig. 1, which shows the interaction graph representation of a quantum circuit, with virtual qubits, on the left, and the connectivity scheme of some quantum hardware on the right, denoted as the "connection graph", with physical qubits. The connection graph represents the physical qubits and their connections on the hardware. In contrast, the interaction graph represents the virtual qubits and their interactions within the circuit. The challenge is to map each virtual qubit to a physical qubit in a way that minimizes the difference between the logical interactions and the available physical connections. More formally, we define a connection graph $G_C = (V, E_C)$, where the vertices $v \in V$ represent the physical qubits of the hardware and the edges $(v, u) \in E_C$ represent the qubit connections. Next, we define an interaction graph $G_I = (V, E_I)$, with vertices $v \in V$ the virtual qubits of the circuit and the edges $(v, u) \in E_i$ the interactions in the circuit. In the initial mapping problem, the objective is to find a bijection $f : V \rightarrow V$, which maps every virtual qubit to a physical qubit such that some cost function on the mapped edges E_M is minimized, where $E_M = \{(f(v), f(u)) : (v, u) \in E_I\}$. In some cases, a perfect mapping might exist where $E_M \subset E_C$. However, this is not always the case, and the objective should be some cost function of $E_M \backslash E_C$, i.e., a cost function of connections that exist in the mapped interaction graph, but not in the connection graph.

The graph at the bottom of the figure shows the manner in which the virtual qubits on the circuit were mapped to the quantum computer. For example, virtual qubits 0 and 2 from the circuit were mapped to physical qubits A and B from the hardware. This connection can be executed, as there is a connection between A and B in the connectivity scheme. On the other hand, the mapping of qubits $0 - A$ and $1 - E$ leads to a connection which can not be executed, since there is no link between qubits physical A and E in the connection graph. In this example, it is easy to see which connections can and can not be executed, and why the mapping proposed in Fig. 1 does not enable the compilation of the algorithm on the example hardware. However, this setting can get much more complex, with almost endless possibilities to customize the algorithms, both in terms of qubit and gate count. Furthermore, quantum computers have evolved significantly, with current architectures featuring 53 [11], 97 [1] or even 127 qubits [4].

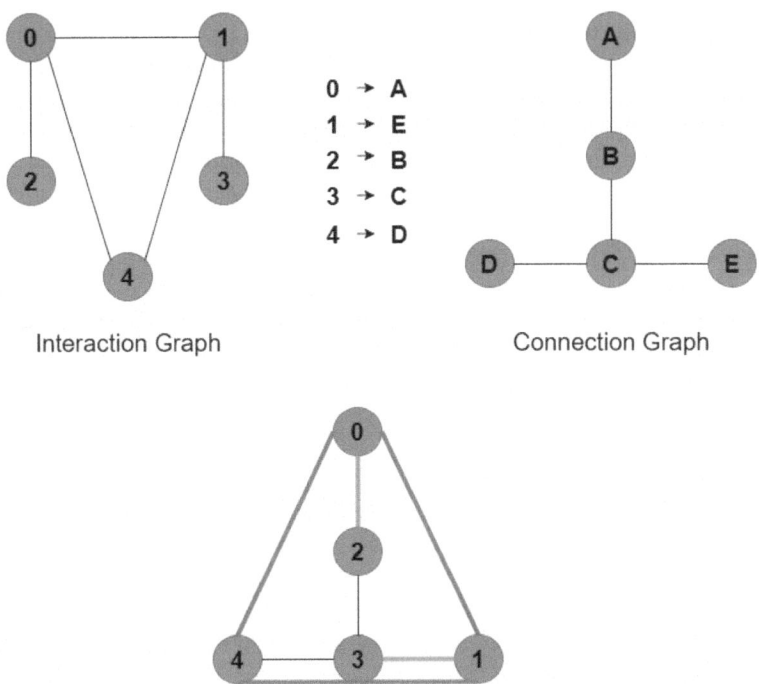

Interaction Graph Mapped Onto Connection Graph

Fig. 1. Process of mapping an interaction graph (a compressed representation of a quantum circuit, on the left) to a connection graph (a representation of the quantum hardware, on the right). The proposed qubit mapping leads to two executable connections ((0, 2) and (3, 1)) and three non-executable connections ((0, 4), (0, 1) and (4, 1)).

High-quality compilation strategies are essential components to allow for this computational advantage over classical computers [22], because in the current Noisy Intermediate-Scale Quantum (NISQ) era, hardware is prone to noise [18]. The compilation influences the resulting fidelity of running the circuit on the actual hardware in many ways, such as by increasing the circuit depth and by determining which qubit connections are used for which multi-qubit gates [13]. If there are bad qubits or bad connections, it is crucial to avoid using them, generally achieved by routing a mapped circuit, to ensure optimal performance.

One task in the compilation step is to relate every virtual qubit in the circuit to a physical qubit in the hardware in such a way that all gates can be operated. Ideally, this should be done to minimize the total noise of running the whole circuit [13]. Similarly to the situation portrayed in Fig. 1, a high quality mapping would result in as few non-executable interactions as possible. This task is not obvious, as quantum hardware topologies are not all-to-all connected. In practice, the task is split into two steps that both are NP-hard [6]. Firstly, as already mentioned, initial mapping relates every virtual qubit to a physical qubit. Secondly, the routing stage involves changing the assignment of virtual qubits to physical qubits to enable the execution of gates that could not be executed under the initial mapping. This process effectively moves quantum information and can be technically realized in different ways, such as using SWAP, Hadamard [29] or BRIDGE gates. The initial mapping is a crucial step as it affects the total noise of the final executable circuit in two ways. Namely, it can alter the amount of SWAP and BRIDGE gate insertions in the routing stage, and it influences which qubits and qubit connections are used for which gates. Finding a good initial mapping is challenging because the routing process changes the qubit assignments dynamically. The initial mapping is not static; it serves as a starting point, and the mapping changes at each time step as the quantum information is moved.

This research focuses on improving the initial mapping step, a crucial task in quantum computing. Initial mapping involves assigning virtual qubits to physical qubits, and this step directly influences all subsequent activities, including the routing of qubits and execution of quantum gates. Making optimal decisions at this stage is essential, as it can reduce the number of adjustments during routing, reduce error rates, and ultimately achieve a higher-quality execution of quantum algorithms [18]. By optimizing this process, we aim to enhance the overall performance and reliability of quantum computations. The task at hand will tackle a modified version of the initial mapping problem, which will incorporate the problem description described above, as well as various hardware constraints. The previously described problem is a generalization of the subgraph isomorphism problem, which is a NP-complete problem [6]. The version of the problem considered for this project will consider various hardware constraints imposed by the target hardware. One such constraint is that of gate error rates, which in this context translates to the quality of qubits or of the connections between qubits. This added layer of difficulty increases the overall complexity of the problem. Notably, since the graph isomorphism problem is a special case of this problem, it can be classified as NP-hard.

With this objective in mind, this paper proposes a Deep Reinforcement Learning (DRL) based approach to compute initial mappings for given quantum circuits and topologies. This branch of Artificial Intelligence has gained significant interest within the quantum community, and previous research has shown promising results within the compilation process as well [9,14]. However, they do not take into account gate error rates, and they do not show the scalability of proposed RL approaches. To this end, several policy gradient DRL methods (Advantage Actor-Critic (A2C) [16], Proximal Policy Optimization (PPO) [24], Trust Region Policy Optimization (TRPO) [23], and PPO with action masking) will be employed to investigate whether high quality initial mappings can be computed for various qubit connectivity schemes which feature varying degrees of error rates on their connections. Furthermore, a database of quantum computer connectivity schemes is introduced to facilitate benchmarking and analysis of DRL agents on various quantum compilation steps.

The remainder of the paper is structured as follows. Section 2 provides an overview of previous attempts to solve the initial mapping problem using DRL. Section 3 details the workings of the environment and the specific DRL algorithms employed in this research. Section 4 presents findings from experiments conducted on three simulated quantum devices. Finally, Sect. 5 summarizes the study's key findings and their implications.

2   Related Work

The goal of the initial mapping step is to obtain a mapping which (heuristically) minimizes the need for later adjustments imposed by hardware connectivity limitations and gate error rate variations. Previous research has investigated whether RL agents are able to successfully compute high quality initial mappings. In this section, a comprehensive overview and discussion of this previous work is provided.

Huang et al. [9] separate qubit mapping into two separate subproblems, namely discovering high quality initial mappings and minimizing SWAP insertion, respectively. The authors start by proposing a RL-based approach which uses a self-attention model to extract features from a circuit and formulate initial mapping as a sequence to sequence learning task. The neural architecture includes three encoders: two that process distinct aspects of the input data, and one dedicated to feature extraction. Each encoder incorporates multi-head attention mechanisms [28]. Afterwards, a RL algorithm makes use of these mechanisms to compute high quality initial mappings. The method employed by [9] is the REINFORCE algorithm [31] with baseline algorithm, which is a policy gradient algorithm. This policy gradient algorithm takes the extracted features as input and outputs the probabilities of mapping virtual to physical qubits. The baseline, which usually comes in the form of a function or even a constant, as long as it is independent of the actions, is used to stabilize the learning procedure. The second step, namely the qubit routing stage, involves a novel Dynamically Extract and Route (DEAR) framework, which extracts circuits iteratively and uses the A* algorithm to determine when and where it is necessary to insert SWAP gates. Their results show that method REINFORCE with baseline architecture obtains initial mappings that require 12% fewer gate insertions when used in combination with DEAR for qubit routing. This comparison was made against a nearest neighbor transformation approach [5] and a dynamic look-ahead heuristic [32]. The RL architecture was trained using 140 circuits from the IBM QX set, with 19 circuits used for testing. The target hardware that the circuits were mapped to is the IBM QX20 architecture.

Another recent attempt to tackle the qubit mapping problem with a RL approach was made by Li et al. in [14]. The authors divided the task similarly to Huang et al. in [9], however, the key difference is that they employed an RL-based architecture for the routing stage, using an isomorphic graph search algorithm for initial mappings. Li et al. [14] adopted a value-based approach, specifically the Dueling Deep-Q Network, to minimize the number of SWAP gate insertions. The B131 circuit set was used for training and testing the RL model, targeting the IBM QX20 architecture. Li et al. [14] reported 63% fewer SWAP gate insertions compared to simulated annealing and heuristic search.

2.1   Limitations

Previous research in tackling either initial mapping or qubit routing using various RL techniques has shown that RL agents are indeed capable of both computing high quality initial mappings and reducing the number of SWAP gate insertions, for a 20 qubit topology. The studies conducted by Huang et al. [9] and Li et al. [14] have investigated the application of RL agents in mapping circuits to a hardware topology with 20 qubits, displaying promising results in this field.

Meanwhile, larger and more complex architectures have been developed, with quantum computers featuring up to 127 [4] qubits. The increase in scale goes hand in hand with an increase in the complexity of the initial mapping problem. Therefore, the demand for efficient and high quality initial mapping techniques grows. However, aforementioned research only focused on quantum architectures featuring up to 20 qubits.

Furthermore, the two-qubit gate error rates were not taken into account in the previously discussed research, while this is a crucial aspect of the compilation process. Some connections may have a poorer quality than others, which can severely impact the quality of the mapping and also lead to a higher error rate of the final circuit.

Thus, our proposal applies DRL models across various quantum architectures with different qubit connectivity schemes. A distinguishing feature is the inclusion of fixed gate error rates, allowing to test model scalability under diverse conditions.

3   Methodology

We use the QGYM library [27] to investigate whether the application of DRL agents can result in high quality initial mappings for various quantum computer topologies with incorporated gate error rates. The package functions in a manner similar to the well known GYM package [3], in the sense that it provides a number of environments on which RL agents can be applied. The main purpose of QGYM is to provide environments which represent various stages of the quantum compilation process, including those for the initial mapping, qubit routing, and scheduling stages.

In the following, Subsect. 3.1 provides a detailed explanation of the environment's functionality. Next, Subsect. 3.2 discusses the characteristics of the DRL algorithms. Subsection 3.3 then outlines the topologies employed and their integration into the experiments. Finally, Subsect. 3.4 offers insights into the development of the experiments.

3.1   Environment Functionality

We focus on experiments within the "Initial Mapping" environment from QGYM, which involves mapping virtual qubits of a quantum circuit to physical qubits on quantum hardware. In this environment, both the quantum circuit and hardware topology are represented as graphs. The quantum circuit is represented by a graph after reduction to an interaction graph, where virtual qubits are vertices, and two-qubit gates are represented by edges (i.e., Fig. 1). This representation omits single-qubit gates, gate types, gate order, and the amount of two-qubit gates between qubits. This reduction improves the training and evaluation times of the RL agent (i.e., the agent efficiency), while neglecting some aspects that do impact the overall performance (e.g. the gate error rates) of the compiled circuit. This trade-off between agent efficiency and compiled circuit performance can be tweaked by including edge weights to account for aspects like the number of gates between qubits and/or the order of gate execution in the original circuit. The quantum hardware is represented by a connection graph, with vertices representing physical qubits and edges indicating hardware connections. The edges can be weighted between 0 and 1 to reflect the gate error rates of the hardware connections, with 1 indicating perfect qubit connection reliability and 0 no reliability.

The logic for transposing the initial mapping problem to a reinforcement learning setting goes as follows. The setup begins with a fixed connection graph, static across all episodes. Each episode introduces a novel interaction graph for the agent to observe, alongside an initially empty mapping. At every step, the agent can map a virtual qubit to a physical qubit until the mapping is fully established. In theory, this process enables the training of agents that are capable of managing various interaction graphs on a predetermined hardware layout. The process of mapping an interaction graph to a connection graph is depicted in Fig. 2. At each step, a virtual qubit is mapped to a physical qubit, until a complete mapping is obtained (i.e., every virtual qubit is mapped to a physical qubit).

In this work, we want to optimize the initial mapping on its own, whereas more commonly the initial mapping is optimized together with the routing compilation step. In the combined setting the optimization target often is minimization of the total CNOT-, T- or gate count or the overall gate error rate of the mapped and routed circuit. These targets make sense as they all contribute in a clear manner to the optimization of the full quantum compilation pipeline. However, what this means for the optimization target of the initial mapping step is not self-evident. Nonetheless, we propose an optimization metric for the initial mapping which aims to anticipate minimizing the routing while also taking into account the gate error rates of the hardware connections. Roughly speaking, the metric tries to minimize the "mismatch" between the interaction graph and the connection graph and utilize the connections with highest reliability (i.e., lowest error rate). This optimization is done in the training phase, via the reward function r. The reward function emits reward signals $R(a)$ to the DRL agent, guiding its training process and policy.

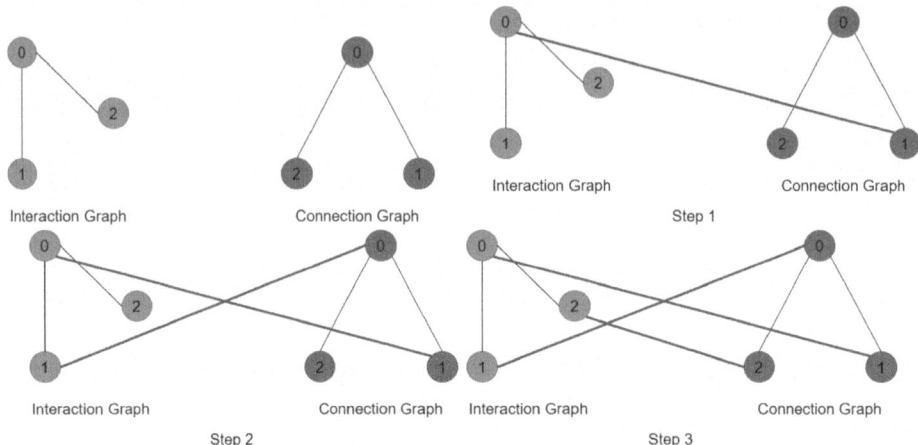

Fig. 2. Process of mapping an interaction graph to a connection graph. At each step, a virtual qubit is mapped to a physical qubit.

The reward is computed based on the previous state, the action chosen by the agent, and the new state after the action has been executed. Besides these three preset rewarder types, the design of QGYM is focused towards customization, and as such new rewarders can be implemented. A visual representation of what it means to have a "good" or "bad" mapped edge can be seen in Fig. 1. The figure displays an interaction graph on the left, and a connection graph on the right, each with five nodes. In the middle, the mappings between logical and physical qubits can be observed, and the mapped connection graph is found at the bottom of the image. In this picture, virtual qubits 0 to 4 are mapped to physical qubits A, E, B, C and D, respectively. This qubit mapping results in two good edges, namely edge $(0,2)$ and edge $(3,1)$ in the mapped connection graph at the bottom of the image. Furthermore, the obtained mapping leads to three bad edges, $(0,4)$, $(0,1)$ and $(4,1)$.

The agents that will be trained on the environment can also perform legal or illegal actions. A visual representation of how an agent can select illegal actions in the environment is shown in Fig. 3. In this example, if the agent first maps virtual qubit 0 in the interaction graph to physical qubit 0 in the connection graph, it can not map the same virtual qubit to another physical qubit. In a similar manner, if any virtual qubit is mapped to physical qubit 0, it will not be allowed to map another virtual qubit to the same physical qubit.

The reward signal is computed as follows. First, a partial reward function is precomputed. This reward function $r(q_{i,p}, q_{j,p})$ defines a reward for an edge in the interaction graph that is mapped to the physical qubits $q_{i,p}$ and $q_{j,p}$ based on the error rates of the connection graph. Specifically, the reward function is defined as follows:

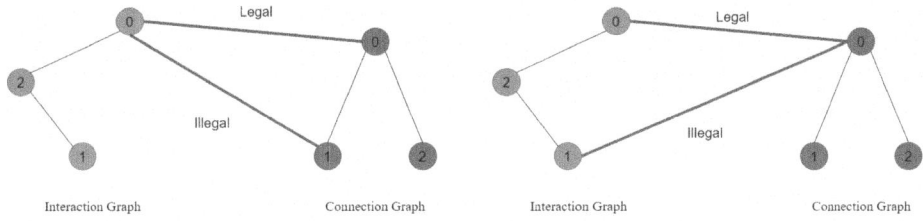

Fig. 3. Figure depicting the difference between legal and illegal actions. An action is illegal if a virtual qubit is mapped to two physical qubits or if two virtual qubits are mapped to the same physical qubit.

$$r(q_{i,p}, q_{j,p}) = \min_{P \in \mathcal{P}(q_{i,p}, q_{j,p})} \left(\prod_{e \in P} (1 - \text{err}(e)) \right)^{-1}, \tag{1}$$

where $\mathcal{P}(q_{i,p}, q_{j,p})$ is the set of all simple paths from $q_{i,p}$ to $q_{j,p}$ in the connection graph. Note that r uses the path with the lowest combined error rates. This concept simulates the introduction of SWAP and/or BRIDGE gates in the routing step of the compilation process. This partial reward can then be used to compute a score for a completed mapping M

$$S(M, E_I) = \sum_{\{q_{i,v}, q_{j,v}\} \in E_I} r(M(q_{i,v}), M(q_{j,v})). \tag{2}$$

The reward signal for the agent is then constructed as follows:

$$R(a) = \begin{cases} -0.2, & \text{if } a \text{ is illegal} \\ 0, & \text{if } a \text{ does not complete the mapping} \\ \exp\left((S(M, E_I))^{-1} \right), & \text{if } a \text{ completes the mapping} \end{cases} \tag{3}$$

where M is the mapping from virtual qubits to physical qubits build by the agent. Note that only the last action in an episode gives a reward and that all other actions give no reward or a negative reward in the case of an illegal action.

3.2 DRL Algorithms

To address the initial mapping problem, three policy gradient DRL algorithms were implemented: Proximal Policy Optimization (PPO) [24], Trust Region Policy Optimization (TRPO) [23], and Advantage Actor-Critic (A2C) [16]. The main reason for choosing these algorithms comes from their availability, provided through the STABLE BASELINES 3 library [21]. This package facilitates their implementation, as well as thorough customization of hyperarameters and architecture depth. PPO stabilizes training by clipping the probability ratio during policy updates, allowing for controlled changes and balancing exploration and exploitation, which is essential for complex tasks like initial mapping, in the context of quantum compilation. TRPO maximizes a surrogate objective while constraining the Kullback-Leibler divergence between policies, ensuring stable updates and reducing performance collapse, making it reliable for precise mapping tasks. A2C combines policy learning (actor) and value estimation (critic) with an advantage function to improve the accuracy of the value estimate, contributing to more stable learning and making it well-suited for the complexities of initial mapping.

Additionally, a variant of PPO with illegal action masking will be applied to handle complex topologies with many qubits, where the probability of selecting illegal actions increases. This masking aims to prevent such actions, improving learning efficiency [26].

These DRL models are implemented using the STABLE BASELINES 3 library [21]. PPO and A2C are directly supported by the library, while TRPO and Maskable PPO are implemented using the STABLE BASELINES 3 CONTRIB package.

3.3   Target Topologies

The four DRL models were trained to compute initial mappings for various target topologies from the leading superconducting devices, provided by vendors such as IBM, Rigetti and Google. An example showing some topologies that were used in the experiments can be seen in Fig. 4, showing the qubit connectivity schemes for the Rigetti Aspen, IBMQ Tokyo and Google Sycamore devices. All topologies are represented as NETWORKX graphs, with random edge weights in the range of $[0.85, 1]$, different hardware qubit connectivity schemes, and qubit counts. The edge weights were set in the range $[0.85, 1]$ because values lower than 0.85 would denote poor qubit connection qualities. Having edge weights close to, or lower than 0.5 for instance, would indicate two-qubit gates that are only corrected half the time. For this, we developed a dataset of quantum computer qubit connectivity schemes with connections encoded as lists of tuples, to be retrieved for the connection graph before training. Each tuple denotes a bidirectional connection between two qubits.

The dataset includes connectivity schemes with 5 to 8 qubits, such as IBMQ Athens or Rigetti Agave; architectures with 15 to 20 qubits from IBMQ Melbourne, QuTech Surface17, IBMQ Tokyo, and Almaden; and 27 to 28 qubits from IBMQ Kolkata, Falcon, and Cambridge devices. To explore mappings for larger topologies, the dataset includes IBMQ Rochester and Google Sycamore (both 53 qubits), IBMQ Manhattan (65 qubits), QuTech Surface97 (97 qubits), and IBMQ Washington (127 qubits). These qubit connectivity schemes can be loaded into the connection graph component and used in the QGYM Initial Mapping environment to train DRL agents.

3.4   Experimental Setup

The learning rate α and discount factor γ are key hyperparameters in Deep Reinforcement Learning, influencing the speed of learning and the balance between immediate and future rewards. The learning rate determines the magnitude of

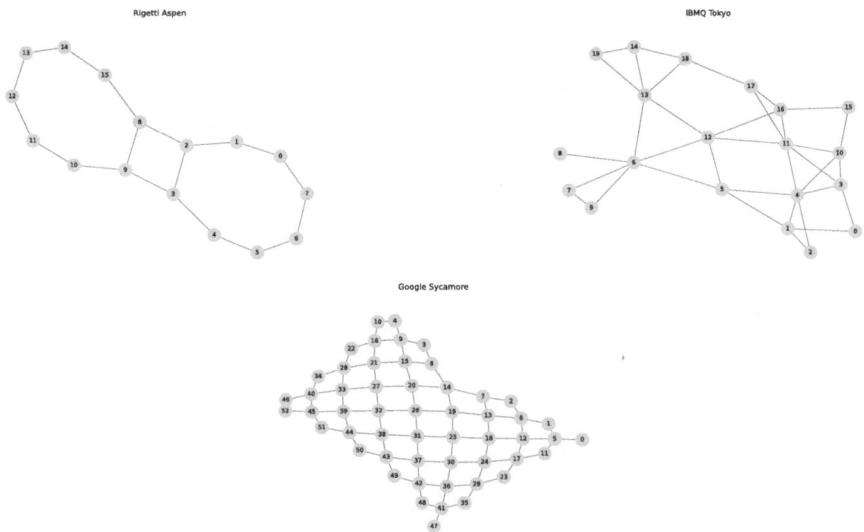

Fig. 4. Examples of quantum computer qubit connectivity schemes, for the Rigetti Aspen (16 qubits), IBMQ Tokyo(20 qubits) and Google Sycamore (53 qubits) devices

adjustment to the weights of our network with each step during the learning process. The discount factor regulates the importance assigned to future rewards compared to obtaining more immediate rewards. A grid-search procedure will optimize these parameters using PPO (with action mask), TRPO, and A2C on two small-scale architectures: IBMQ Casablanca and CC Light. The best performing values, determined by the average rewards achieved, will guide agent training across all topologies in the database. Fine-tuning was conducted for all four DRL models on these 7-qubit devices, and parallelization was employed to enhance computation efficiency. The procedure took approximately one week using 8 CPUs. Each training procedure will consider $400,000$ training steps, with $\gamma \in \{0.8, 0.85, 0.9, 0.95, 0.99\}$ and $\alpha \in \{0.0003, 0.0001, 0.003, 0.001, 0.1\}$.

The best performing hyperparameter values determined during fine-tuning will be used in the training of the DRL algorithms on each of the 25 topologies in the database. The number of timesteps for each training session will depend on the number of qubits in the topology, with larger qubit counts requiring more training time to ensure that the neural network in the DRL algorithm learns an effective policy for the given environment. The relationship between the number of timesteps (i.e., interactions between the DRL agent and the environment) and number of qubits in the target topology is assumed to be quadratic, beginning at $200,000$ timesteps for topologies with 4 qubits. The reason for this design choice is that, for training and evaluating the DRL agent on a simple, four qubit topology, $200,000$ training steps were sufficient to obtain high quality mappings, hence it was considered to be a good starting point. The exact number of training timesteps allocated, given the number of qubits, can be seen in Fig. 5. Given that the number of environment interactions varies according to the number of qubits in the target topology, so does the number of interactions graphs used during training. As the agents are tasked with mapping interaction graphs to connection have that contain a greater number of qubits, the agents will require more training time, and consequently more interaction graphs in order to converge to an optimal solution. When dealing with larger connection graphs, the agent needs to be exposed to more interaction graphs during training because the number of possible interaction graphs increases significantly with the number of qubits. This ensures the agent can effectively learn and adapt to the expanded range of interactions. Table 1 shows the number of interaction graphs that were used throughout the training procedure, for each number of qubits facilitated by the hardware.

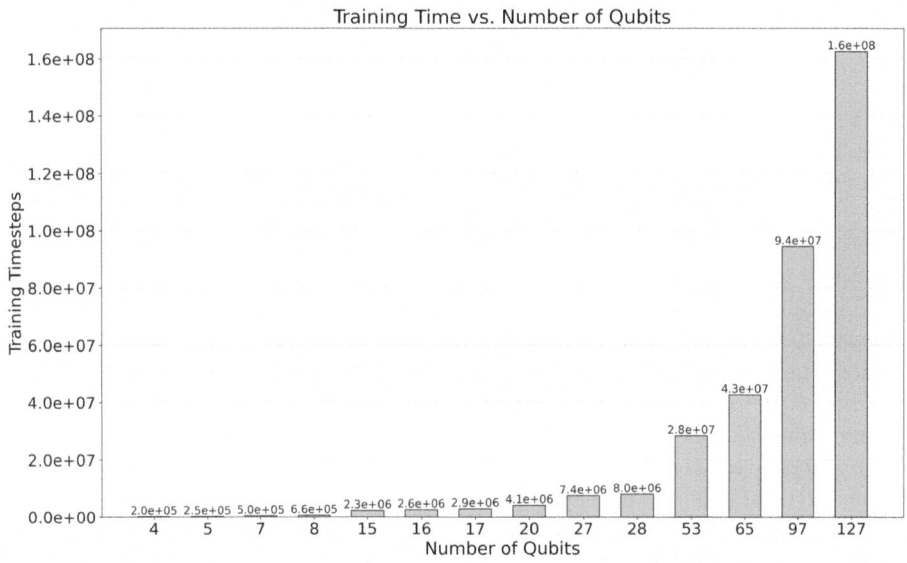

Fig. 5. Training timesteps required for different number of qubits

Similarly, as the complexity of the quantum computer architecture increases, the number of hidden layers in the neural networks will be expanded to better capture the intricate patterns and dependencies within the data. Deeper networks with more hidden layers can model more complex relationships, enabling the agent to make more informed decisions in challenging environments. This increase in network depth helps to ensure that the model has sufficient capacity to learn and generalize effectively from the higher-dimensional feature space associated with more complex topologies.

Table 1. Number of interaction graphs used in training

# Qubits in Target Hardware	# Interaction Graphs
4	50, 000
5	50, 781
7	71, 540
8	81, 920
15	152, 473
16	162, 500
17	172, 977
20	203, 125
27	273, 509
28	284, 388
53	534, 618
65	655, 060
97	973, 038
127	1, 279, 527

During evaluation, trained DRL agents map, in a greedily manner by following the policies learned during training, interaction graphs generated using the Erdős-Rényi model [8], where each pair of nodes is connected with a probability $p = 0.5$. Null graphs (no edges) are excluded. The RL paradigm is generally a data hungry approach, and agents do not receive information from a fixed dataset. Instead, they receive information by continuously interacting with the environment [25]. The information that reinforcement learning agents receive from the environment keeps changing over the course of the learning process because of this continuous cycle of interaction of obtaining feedback. This eventually results in a substantial number of interactions for long simulations, resulting in often sample-inefficient solutions. For this reason, both training and evaluation data comes in the form of randomly generated graphs, not from an actual dataset of quantum circuit qubit connectivity schemes.

Performance is assessed over ten runs, each with 100 unique graphs, with the mean reward and a gate error rate-aware distance metric:

$$D = \frac{S}{|E_I|} \geq 1, \tag{4}$$

where S the sum mentioned in (2), and $|E_I|$ is the number of edges in the interaction graph. This metric is such that a value of 1 indicates an optimal mapping and higher values indicate worse mappings. A distance valued to 1 indicates that all mappings are executable on the hardware. Values larger than 1 denote that not all mappings and executable, and modifications need to be done to the obtained initial mapping in the routing stage. This approach helps to evaluate the agents' ability to learn mappings with an uniform metric that is scalable between different topology sizes as well. Finally, the models will be compared against a random policy and a random mapper in terms of rewards obtained during the training procedure, and will also be compared to the random mapper distance-wise. These two metrics were chosen because the reward provides insight into how the agent develops during the training procedure, while the distance portrays the performance during evaluation, during which no learning takes place. The random policy will perform actions completely at random, both legal and illegal, while the random mapper will only perform random, legal actions.

4   Results

In this section we provide the performance comparison of the DRL models when applied to three quantum architectures, the IBMQ Casablanca, Tokyo and Kolkata devices (7, 20, 27 qubits). These architectures were chosen, as their results show a trend, displaying the evolution of the performance of the DRL agents as the complexity (i.e., the number of qubits) of the topologies increases. We also provide the hyperparameters obtained during the finetuning procedure, visible in Table 2.

Table 2. Learning rates and discount factors for different models

Model/Parameters	α	γ
PPO	0.0003	0.8
A2C	0.0003	0.85
TRPO	0.001	0.8
PPO with invalid action mask	0.0003	0.99

The choice of parameters for the PPO algorithm balances learning stability with moderate emphasis on future rewards. The configuration of the A2C model uses the same learning rate as PPO but has a slightly higher discount factor, indicating a greater focus on future rewards. The optimal learning rate indicated by the finetuning procedure for TRPO reflects the method's capability for stable policy updates despite faster learning. Its discount factor is similar to PPO's. When it comes to the variant of PPO with an invalid action mask, the results from finetuning indicated that a lower learning rate with a significantly higher discount factor would be optimal. This configuration is particularly useful in environments with numerous invalid actions, ensuring that long-term rewards are heavily prioritized.

The evaluation results for the IBMQ Casablanca device (7 qubits) can be seen in Fig. 6(a) shows the four DRL models having similar median rewards around 0.15 and similar IQR spreads. It is TRPO that shows the presence of some

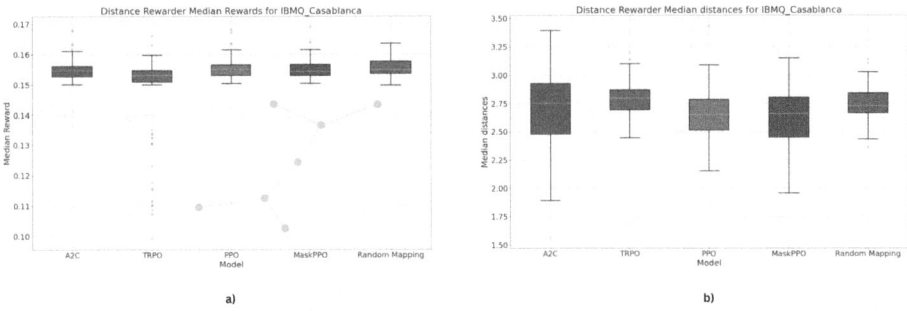

Fig. 6. Median rewards and distances for the IBMQ Casablanca device

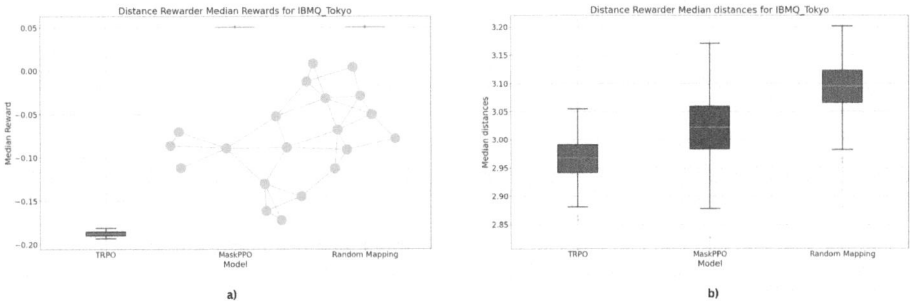

Fig. 7. Median rewards and distances for the IBMQ Tokyo device

outliers reaching towards the median reward of 0.1. In Fig. 6(b), it is shown that that PPO, along with its illegal action masking variant, have a smaller median distance compared to the other models, around 2.65. TRPO has the highest median distance value above 2.75, while A2C has an exact median distance of 2.75. MaskPPO was an IQR spread in the range $[2.5, 2.75]$, A2C an IQR spread in the range $[2.5, 2.9]$, whereas random mapping and TRPO have the smallest IQR spreads out of all four. A2C has the highest spread, with the whiskers of the boxplot having their minimum value towards 1.75.

For the IBMQ Tokyo device (20 qubits, Fig. 7), only TRPO and Maskable PPO have finished the evaluation procedure. In Fig. 7(a), PPO with invalid action masking and random mapping have a median reward of 0.05, while TRPO displays a median reward just above -0.2. Maskable PPO and TRPO outperform the random mapping technique in terms of mapping quality Fig. 7(b). Random mapping has a median distance of 3.1, PPO with invalid action masking displays a median distance between 3.0 and 3.05, whereas TRPO has a slightly lower median distance, between 2.95 and 3.0.

Moving on to a more complex architecture, Fig. 8 displays the results for the IBMQ Kolkata device, which features 27 qubits. For this device, the A2C and PPO with invalid action masking models are evaluated. In Fig. 8(a), it can

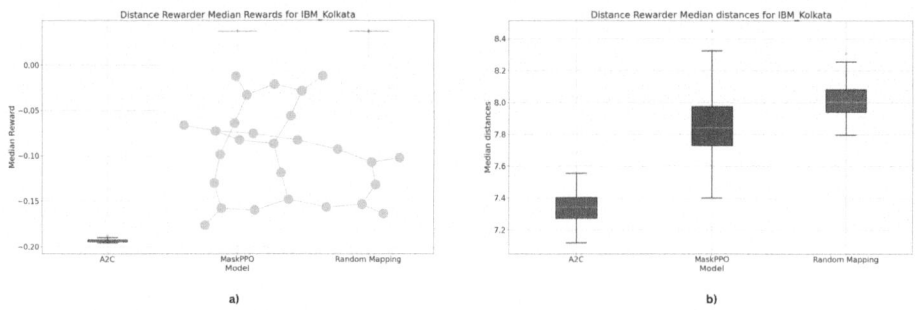

Fig. 8. Median rewards and distances for the IBMQ Kolkata device

be seen that Maskable PPO and random mapping achieved a median reward around 0.05, with A2C around −0.20. For this 27 qubit quantum device, Fig. 8(b) portrays the fact that the two DRL models outperform the random mapping approach. In terms of the quality of the obtained mappings, the random mapping has a median distance of 8.0, Maskable PPO a median distance just above 7.8, and A2C a median distance just below 7.4.

4.1   Discussion

Across the various quantum architectures tested, the performance of the Deep Reinforcement Learning (DRL) models, A2C, TRPO, PPO, and MaskPPO was consistent for small qubit topologies but varied significantly as the complexity of the topologies increased. For topologies featuring 5 qubits, such as the IBMQ Casablanca, all four DRL models displayed relatively similar median rewards and median distances, indicating comparable performance. However, the MaskPPO variant, which incorporates invalid action masking, slightly outperformed other models, particularly in avoiding illegal actions and achieving more stable median rewards. As we moved to more complex topologies however, such as the IBMQ Tokyo or Kolkata devices, with 20 and 27 qubits, the differences between models became more pronounced. While MaskPPO continued to perform well, the other algorithms started to display inconsistencies.

One key observation across all topologies is the relationship between the median distance achieved by the models and the number of qubits in the device. For smaller topologies, the DRL models typically achieved distances close to the optimal value 1. For these devices, all DRL models had median distances around 1.5 to 1.6, which aligns with what is expected for small circuits. This proves that Deep Reinforcement Learning agents are capable of computing high quality optimal initial mappings for small scale quantum computer architectures. For devices with 20 qubits, such as the IBMQ Tokyo, the DRL models continued to show an upward trend in median distances, reaching values around 4.9 and 5.5. The random mapping approach, in these scenarios, often produced results comparable to the DRL models, indicating that the complexity of larger devices limited the ability of DRL models to uncover high quality mappings. For topologies with more than 20 qubits, such as the IBMQ Kolkata, the upward trend in median distance continued. For example, on the IBMQ Kolkata device, A2C and MaskPPO models displayed median distances between 7.4 and 7.8, which are somewhat higher distances than those observed in the smaller, previous topologies. The random mapping approach, for this quantum computer architecture, yielded a median distance of around 8.0, which shows that DRL models, though slightly better on this occasion, are having a harder time achieving distances that are close to the optimal value.

4.2   Limitations

One limitation of this project is the design of the fine-tuning procedure for the DRL models, which was focused on small-scale topologies. This approach may lead to suboptimal values for the learning rate (α) and discount factor (γ) when applied to more complex topologies. Expanding the fine-tuning process to include a wider range of qubits could improve generalization and performance but would require significantly more computational resources.

Furthermore, the failure of PPO to complete the evaluation procedure, due to convergence to a suboptimal policy, suggests a need for tuning the policy's entropy coefficient to promote more diverse action sampling and avoid premature convergence. This issue indicates that the agent may have become trapped in a local optimum or not explored the action space sufficiently, leading to suboptimal performance. Another limitation involved TRPO's application to large-scale quantum devices, which revealed challenges related to the exploding gradient phenomenon. The complexity of the task-mapping virtual qubits onto physical qubits-further compounds this issue, as it involves satisfying various constraints such as connectivity and gate error rates, leading to steep gradients in the loss landscape.

These challenges highlight the need for network architectures with deeper layers or specialized structures to capture intricate dependencies, along with optimization techniques to ensure stability and effective learning for complex quantum topologies. Addressing these limitations would likely involve more sophisticated fine-tuning procedures, tailored reward mechanisms, and advanced optimization strategies to enhance the robustness and scalability of DRL models for quantum computing applications.

5   Conclusion

In this study, we evaluated the performance of four policy gradient DRL models (A2C, PPO with and without action masking, and TRPO) on the task of computing high-quality initial mappings between virtual qubits of quantum circuits and physical qubits of various quantum computers. The analysis focused on two metrics, namely the median rewards and median distances. The findings reveal that policy gradient DRL models can generate high-quality initial mappings across small to medium hardware topologies.

For smaller topologies with up to 20 qubits, such as IBMQ Casablanca and Tokyo, the algorithms achieved near-optimal mappings in terms of distance, with consistent performance. However, as the scale increased to larger devices like the IBMQ Kolkata (27 qubits), the DRL agents had a harder time learning optimal policies. PPO with action masking demonstrated the highest adaptability and consistency, effectively balancing scalability and gate error rate considerations, and minimizing distances in complex scenarios. This demonstrates that DRL approaches, particularly PPO with action masking, are capable of effectively solving the initial mapping problem across a wide variety of quantum computer architectures.

The results indicate that, while DRL models can generate high-quality initial mappings for small to moderately sized architectures, they require careful calibration to perform effectively on larger systems. For complex topologies, some DRL models, mostly PPO, but occasionally TRPO and A2C, failed to train properly, preventing successful evaluation. This highlights the effectiveness of action masking (as used with PPO), which improves performance, especially in larger topologies. Although numerical improvements in median distances were modest, they could lead to reduced error rates and enhanced reliability for qubit connections in quantum computations.

The main bottlenecks for scaling DRL models to larger qubit systems include increased complexity in control systems and computational bottlenecks requiring more complex calibration procedures. Implementing multi-core architectures can help distribute the computational load and manage larger qubit counts more effectively. Leveraging advanced accelerated computing technologies, such as GPUs and AI-driven techniques, can significantly reduce computational time and cost for optimization tasks, such as the one tackled in this study. Fine-tuning DRL models on more complex architectures before training and evaluation can also lead to better performance.

Future research could look into comparing the performance of these trained RL agents to some well-known mappers, such as those from Qiskit. A proper benchmark against these other mappers would require some extra translation methods, as our agents work with interaction graphs instead of quantum circuits. Moreover, generating useful random circuits is a non-trivial task. Fine-tuning the models first on more complex architectures (i.e., more than 20 qubits), which is a resource-intensive task itself, could lead to improved performance during evaluation and result in higher quality mappings.

Acknowledgments. We thank QuTech and TNO for their support in realizing this research.

Disclosure of Interests. The authors have no competing interests to declare that are relevant to the content of this article.

References

1. Bandic, M., Almudever, C.G., Feld, S.: Interaction graph-based characterization of quantum benchmarks for improving quantum circuit mapping techniques. Quantum Mach. Intell. **5**(2), 40 (2023)
2. Bandic, M., Feld, S., Almudever, C.G.: Full-stack quantum computing systems in the nisq era: algorithm-driven and hardware-aware compilation techniques. In: 2022 Design, Automation & Test in Europe Conference & Exhibition (DATE), pp. 1–6. IEEE (2022)
3. Brockman, G., et al.: OpenAI gym. arXiv preprint arXiv:1606.01540 (2016)
4. Cheng, C.Y., Yang, C.Y., Wang, R.C., Kuo, Y.H., Cheng, H.C., Huang, C.Y.: Qubit mapping toward quantum advantage. arXiv preprint arXiv:2210.01306 (2022)
5. Cheng, X., Guan, Z., Zhu, P.: Nearest neighbor transformation of quantum circuits in 2D architecture. IEEE Access **8**, 222466–222475 (2020)
6. Cook, S.A.: The complexity of theorem-proving procedures. In: Logic, Automata, and Computational Complexity: The Works of Stephen A. Cook, pp. 143–152 (2023)
7. Cowtan, A., Dilkes, S., Duncan, R., Krajenbrink, A., Simmons, W., Sivarajah, S.: On the qubit routing problem. arXiv preprint arXiv:1902.08091 (2019)
8. Erdos, P., Rényi, A., et al.: On the evolution of random graphs. Publ. Math. Inst. Hung. Acad. Sci **5**(1), 17–60 (1960)
9. Huang, C.Y., Lien, C.H., Mak, W.K.: Reinforcement learning and dear framework for solving the qubit mapping problem. In: Proceedings of the 41st IEEE/ACM International Conference on Computer-Aided Design, pp. 1–9 (2022)
10. Karuppasamy, K., Puram, V., Johnson, S., Thomas, J.P.: A comprehensive review of quantum circuit optimization: current trends and future directions. Quantum Rep. **7**(1), 2 (2025)
11. Kharkov, Y., Ivanova, A., Mikhantiev, E., Kotelnikov, A.: Arline benchmarks: automated benchmarking platform for quantum compilers. arXiv preprint arXiv:2202.14025 (2022)
12. Kwon, S., Tomonaga, A., Lakshmi Bhai, G., Devitt, S.J., Tsai, J.S.: Gate-based superconducting quantum computing. J. Appl. Phys. **129**(4) (2021)
13. Lao, L., Van Someren, H., Ashraf, I., Almudever, C.G.: Timing and resource-aware mapping of quantum circuits to superconducting processors. IEEE Trans. Comput. Aided Des. Integr. Circuits Syst. **41**(2), 359–371 (2021)
14. Li, Y., Liu, W., Li, M.: Deep reinforcement learning for mapping quantum circuits to 2D nearest-neighbor architectures. Adv. Quantum Technol. **7**(2), 2300289 (2024)
15. Maronese, M., Moro, L., Rocutto, L., Prati, E.: Quantum compiling. In: Quantum Computing Environments, pp. 39–74. Springer, Cham (2022)
16. Mnih, V., et al.: Asynchronous methods for deep reinforcement learning. In: International Conference on Machine Learning, pp. 1928–1937. PMLR (2016)
17. Nielsen, M.A., Chuang, I.L.: Quantum Computation and Quantum Information. Cambridge University Press, Cambridge (2010)
18. Preskill, J.: Quantum computing in the NISQ era and beyond. Quantum **2**, 79 (2018)
19. Quetschlich, N., Burgholzer, L., Wille, R.: Compiler optimization for quantum computing using reinforcement learning. In: 2023 60th ACM/IEEE Design Automation Conference (DAC), pp. 1–6. IEEE (2023)
20. Quetschlich, N., Burgholzer, L., Wille, R.: MQT predictor: automatic device selection with device-specific circuit compilation for quantum computing. ACM Trans. Quantum Comput. **6**(1), 1–26 (2025)

21. Raffin, A., Hill, A., Gleave, A., Kanervisto, A., Ernestus, M., Dormann, N.: Stable-baselines3: reliable reinforcement learning implementations. J. Mach. Learn. Res. **22**(1), 12348–12355 (2021)
22. Rattacaso, D., Jaschke, D., Ballarin, M., Siloi, I., Montangero, S.: Quantum circuit compilation with quantum computers. arXiv preprint arXiv:2408.00077 (2024)
23. Schulman, J., Levine, S., Abbeel, P., Jordan, M., Moritz, P.: Trust region policy optimization. In: International Conference on Machine Learning, pp. 1889–1897. PMLR (2015)
24. Schulman, J., Wolski, F., Dhariwal, P., Radford, A., Klimov, O.: Proximal policy optimization algorithms. arXiv preprint arXiv:1707.06347 (2017)
25. Sutton, R.S., Barto, A.G.: Reinforcement Learning: An Introduction. MIT Press, Cambridge (2018)
26. Tang, C.Y., Liu, C.H., Chen, W.K., You, S.D.: Implementing action mask in proximal policy optimization (PPO) algorithm. ICT Express **6**(3), 200–203 (2020)
27. Van Der Linde, S., De Kok, W., Bontekoe, T., Feld, S.: qgym: a gym for training and benchmarking RL-based quantum compilation. In: 2023 IEEE International Conference on Quantum Computing and Engineering (QCE), vol. 2, pp. 26–30. IEEE (2023)
28. Vaswani, A., et al.: Attention is all you need. In: Advances in Neural Information Processing Systems, vol. 30 (2017)
29. Wille, R., Burgholzer, L., Zulehner, A.: Mapping quantum circuits to IBM QX architectures using the minimal number of swap and h operations. In: Proceedings of the 56th Annual Design Automation Conference, pp. 1–6 (2019)
30. Wille, R., Hillmich, S., Burgholzer, L.: Efficient and correct compilation of quantum circuits. In: 2020 IEEE International Symposium on Circuits and Systems (ISCAS), pp. 1–5. IEEE (2020)
31. Williams, R.J.: Simple statistical gradient-following algorithms for connectionist reinforcement learning. Mach. Learn. **8**, 229–256 (1992)
32. Zhu, P., Guan, Z., Cheng, X.: A dynamic look-ahead heuristic for the qubit mapping problem of NISQ computers. IEEE Trans. Comput. Aided Des. Integr. Circuits Syst. **39**(12), 4721–4735 (2020)

Learning QUBO Formulations from Data

Jonas Nüßlein[(✉)], Sebastian Zielinski, and Claudia Linnhoff-Popien

LMU Munich, Munich, Germany
jonas.nuesslein@ifi.lmu.de

Abstract. Quadratic Unconstrained Binary Optimization (QUBO) is a fundamental framework for solving combinatorial optimization problems, with significant applications in quantum computing. Many real-world optimization tasks can be naturally expressed as QUBOs, making them well-suited for quantum annealing, a promising paradigm for harnessing quantum hardware to find optimal solutions efficiently. A key challenge in utilizing QUBO models effectively is the formulation of an appropriate QUBO matrix Q that correctly encodes a given problem p, ensuring that the optimal solution x^* of p corresponds to the minimum value of $x^T Q x$.

In this paper, we propose an algorithm for learning QUBO formulations from data, enabling automated discovery of problem encodings that align with optimal solutions, reducing the need for manual problem modeling and enhancing adaptability to diverse optimization tasks. Experimental results show that our learned QUBO formulations yield accurate representations of the underlying problems, paving the way for more effective problem encoding strategies in quantum computing applications.

Keywords: Machine learning · Quantum computing · Quadratic Unconstrained Binary Optimization (QUBO) · Quantum annealing · Ising

1 Introduction

Many real-world prediction tasks require solving NP-hard problems where the goal is to map an input instance $x \in \mathcal{X}$ to its optimal solution $y \in \mathcal{Y}$ [2]. Examples include finding the maximum clique in a graph [8], selecting items for a knapsack [11], or solving a Sudoku puzzle [5]. In these settings, the underlying function $f : \mathcal{X} \to \mathcal{Y}$ is inherently combinatorial and computationally intractable for conventional learning methods.

A promising strategy for tackling such NP-hard prediction tasks is to leverage the Quadratic Unconstrained Binary Optimization (QUBO) framework [9]. In a QUBO formulation, the optimization task is expressed as minimizing a quadratic function:

$$y^* = \arg \min_{y \in \{0,1\}^n} y^T Q y, \tag{1}$$

© The Author(s), under exclusive license to Springer Nature Switzerland AG 2025
S. Zielinski et al. (Eds.): I4CS 2025, CCIS 2513, pp. 209–227, 2025.
https://doi.org/10.1007/978-3-031-94263-1_13

where Q is a symmetric matrix that encodes the structure of the problem. This formulation is particularly attractive because it can represent a wide range of combinatorial problems and is amenable to both classical heuristics and emerging quantum annealing technologies.

However, a significant bottleneck remains: the manual derivation of an appropriate QUBO matrix Q for each problem instance. Traditional methods depend heavily on expert knowledge and intricate, problem-specific modeling, limiting their applicability in dynamic environments where the problem instances change frequently. Moreover, directly learning the mapping $f : \mathcal{X} \to \mathcal{Y}$ is challenging due to the combinatorial explosion of potential solutions and the non-linear, discrete nature of these problems.

Motivated by these challenges, we propose a novel, data-driven approach that learns QUBO formulations from a set of problem-solution pairs. Instead of directly predicting the optimal solution y from x, our method introduces an intermediate mapping:

$$g : \mathcal{X} \to Q, \tag{2}$$

which automatically constructs a QUBO matrix tailored to each input instance. The optimal solution is then recovered by solving:

$$y^* = \arg\min_y \; y^T Q y. \tag{3}$$

This intermediate representation leverages robust clause-based formulations inspired by Max-SAT approaches, enabling the learned QUBO to tolerate moderate perturbations in clause weights while still preserving the optimal solution.

Our framework is particularly well-suited for NP-hard prediction tasks, where the relationship between x and y is complex and non-linear [7]. By automating the generation of QUBO formulations, we not only alleviate the need for manual problem encoding but also enhance the integration of machine learning with both classical and quantum optimization techniques. In summary, our contributions are as follows:

1. We introduce an algorithm for learning QUBO formulations from data, effectively automating the translation of NP-hard prediction tasks $f : \mathcal{X} \to \mathcal{Y}$ into a QUBO framework.
2. We develop a robust learning approach that employs clause-based representations and a tailored loss function to ensure that the learned QUBO matrix retains the optimal solution despite moderate perturbations.
3. We validate our method on benchmark problems-including maximum clique, knapsack, and Sudoku-demonstrating that our learned QUBO formulations not only capture the underlying problem structure but also enhance the performance of subsequent optimization routines.

The remainder of the paper is organized as follows. Section 2 reviews the necessary background in QUBO formulations and supervised learning. Section 3 discusses related work on automated QUBO generation and differentiable optimization approaches. Section 4 details our algorithm for learning QUBO formulations from data, and Sect. 5 presents extensive experimental evaluations.

Finally, Sect. 6 concludes with a discussion of future research directions and potential applications.

2 Background

In this section, we review the key concepts that underpin our approach to learning QUBO formulations from data for NP-hard prediction tasks. We first introduce the QUBO framework and its role in formulating combinatorial optimization problems. We then discuss common NP-hard problems that have been successfully cast into QUBO form, followed by an overview of supervised learning techniques that enable us to learn mappings from problem instances to their corresponding QUBO matrices.

2.1 Quadratic Unconstrained Binary Optimization (QUBO)

The QUBO framework [9] provides a unified formulation for a wide range of combinatorial optimization problems. A standard QUBO problem is defined as:

$$\min_{y \in \{0,1\}^n} \quad y^T Q y, \tag{4}$$

where $Q \in \mathbb{R}^{n \times n}$ is a symmetric matrix encoding the structure of the problem. This formulation is particularly attractive for several reasons:

- It is sufficiently expressive to model many NP-hard problems.
- It serves as a common interface for both classical solvers (such as tabu search or simulated annealing) and emerging quantum optimization technologies (like quantum annealing).
- It allows the incorporation of constraints via penalty terms. For example, a constraint $g(y) = 0$ can be enforced by adding a term $\lambda\, g(y)^2$ to the objective.

The flexibility of QUBO formulations makes them a natural target for our data-driven approach. Rather than manually crafting Q for each problem, we aim to learn a mapping from an input instance $x \in \mathcal{X}$ to a QUBO matrix Q that encodes the corresponding NP-hard prediction task [1].

2.2 QUBO Formulations for NP-Hard Problems

Many classic NP-hard problems can be reformulated as QUBOs [12,13]. Below, we highlight a few representative examples that also serve as benchmarks in our experiments.

Maximum Clique. Given an undirected graph $G = (V, E)$, the maximum clique problem seeks the largest subset $S \subseteq V$ where every pair of vertices is connected. By introducing a binary variable y_i for each vertex $i \in V$, the problem can be cast as:

$$\min_{y \in \{0,1\}^{|V|}} \quad -\sum_{i \in V} y_i + \lambda \sum_{(i,j) \notin E} y_i y_j. \tag{5}$$

Here, the first term encourages the selection of many vertices, while the second penalizes the simultaneous selection of non-adjacent vertices.

Knapsack. In the knapsack problem, each item i has a value v_i and a weight w_i, and the goal is to select items to maximize total value without exceeding a weight limit W:

$$\min_{y \in \{0,1\}^n} \quad -\sum_{i=1}^{n} v_i y_i + \lambda \left(\sum_{i=1}^{n} w_i y_i - W\right)^2. \tag{6}$$

The quadratic penalty term ensures that the weight constraint is approximately satisfied.

2.3 Max-K-SAT

Max-k-SAT is a canonical NP-hard problem where the goal is to find an assignment $y \in \{0,1\}^n$ to Boolean variables that maximizes the number of satisfied clauses in a Boolean formula in conjunctive normal form (CNF) [6,22]. In the CNF, each clause C_j is composed of exactly k literals:

$$C_j(y) = l_{j1} \vee l_{j2} \vee \cdots \vee l_{jk}, \tag{7}$$

where each literal l_{ji} is either a variable y_i or its negation $\overline{y}_i = 1 - y_i$.

A natural way to penalize an unsatisfied clause is to assign a penalty when all literals in the clause evaluate to false. To formalize this, define for each literal in clause C_j the function:

$$\ell_{ji}(y) = \begin{cases} y_i, & \text{if } l_{ji} = y_i, \\ 1 - y_i, & \text{if } l_{ji} = \overline{y}_i. \end{cases} \tag{8}$$

Then, the penalty function for clause C_j can be written as:

$$P_{C_j}(y) = \prod_{i=1}^{k} (1 - \ell_{ji}(y)). \tag{9}$$

Notice that $P_{C_j}(y) = 1$ if and only if all literals in C_j are false (i.e., the clause is unsatisfied), and $P_{C_j}(y) = 0$ otherwise.

The overall objective of a weighted Max-k-SAT problem is to minimize the total penalty:

$$\min_{y \in \{0,1\}^n} \sum_{j=1}^{m} \lambda_j P_{C_j}(y), \tag{10}$$

where $\lambda_j > 0$ is the penalty weight assigned to clause C_j. Since $P_{C_j}(y)$ is a polynomial of degree k, it is not directly in the quadratic form required by QUBO [3]. To reduce the polynomial unconstrained binary optimization (PUBO) problem to a QUBO, auxiliary binary variables are introduced to represent intermediate products. For instance, for a clause with $k = 3$, one common technique is as follows:

$$z_j \equiv (1 - \ell_{j1}(y))(1 - \ell_{j2}(y)). \tag{11}$$

Then, the clause penalty can be approximated by:

$$P_{C_j}(y) = (z_j - (1 - \ell_{j1}(y))(1 - \ell_{j2}(y)))^2 \\ + (z_j(1 - \ell_{j3}(y)) - (1 - \ell_{j1}(y))(1 - \ell_{j2}(y))(1 - \ell_{j3}(y)))^2. \tag{12}$$

By carefully choosing penalty coefficients for these additional quadratic terms, one can enforce that the auxiliary variable z_j correctly models the product $(1 - \ell_{j1}(y))(1 - \ell_{j2}(y))$, and subsequently, the clause penalty $P_{C_j}(y)$ is accurately represented in a quadratic form.

In the general case, the conversion of a degree-k term into a quadratic function involves recursively introducing auxiliary variables for each multiplication step and adding penalty terms to enforce the correct relationships. The resulting QUBO formulation for the Max-k-SAT problem then takes the form:

$$\min_{y,z} \; y^T Q y + \sum_{j=1}^{m} \phi_j(y, z), \tag{13}$$

where z collects all auxiliary variables and each $\phi_j(y, z)$ is a quadratic penalty term ensuring that the auxiliary variables correctly capture the products needed for clause C_j [6].

This QUBO formulation for Max-k-SAT serves as a critical intermediary in our framework. By learning a mapping from problem instances to QUBO matrices Q that inherently encode these clause-based representations, our approach ensures that the optimal solution y^* is recovered by solving:

$$y^* = \arg\min_{y} \; y^T Q y, \tag{14}$$

even if the ideal binary clause weights are slightly perturbed. This robustness is particularly valuable in real-world NP-hard prediction tasks, where exact modeling may be infeasible and approximations are necessary.

In another line of work, Zielinski et al. investigated an approximate QUBO encoding for 3-SAT problems that does not require auxiliary variables [26] by devising a novel penalty function that captures the logical structure of each clause solely with quadratic terms, thereby eliminating the need for extra variables.

3   Related Work

There has been a surge of interest in automating the process of mapping classical combinatorial optimization problems into QUBO formulations suitable for quantum annealers and other quantum devices [25]. In this section, we review a broad range of contributions that are relevant to our work, spanning data-driven QUBO generation, automated problem reformulation, hybrid quantum-classical methods, and differentiable optimization approaches that integrate optimization as part of the forward pass in neural networks.

3.1 Data-Driven QUBO Generation and AutoQubo

The idea of automatically generating QUBO formulations from problem instances has been explored in several recent works [3,14]. One notable approach is the *AutoQubo* framework [14] and its recent extension *AutoQubo v2* [27], which learns a mapping $f : p \rightarrow Q$ from a set of training instances. The method minimizes a loss function that measures the discrepancy between the cost function of the original problem and the corresponding QUBO representation. This approach has been extended by several works that incorporate regularization techniques [15] and even reinforcement learning to adjust QUBO parameters dynamically [16].

3.2 Automated Problem Reformulation

The automated reformulation of combinatorial problems into QUBO or Ising models has a long history. Early work by Lucas [12] provided Ising formulations for many NP-complete problems, establishing a mathematical foundation that links various optimization challenges with spin glass models. Subsequent research has built on these ideas by developing systematic methods for embedding constraints as quadratic penalty terms:

$$\min_{x \in \{0,1\}^n} x^T Q x + \lambda\, g(x)^2, \tag{15}$$

where $g(x) = 0$ represents the set of constraints. Other contributions include studies on minor embedding techniques for mapping dense problems onto hardware with limited connectivity [17] and algorithmic strategies for automated parameter tuning [4].

3.3 Integration of Machine Learning with Quantum Optimization

Machine learning techniques have been integrated with quantum optimization to both enhance performance and automate model generation. For example, supervised learning has been utilized to predict optimal QUBO parameters from historical data:

$$\min_{\theta} \frac{1}{N} \sum_{i=1}^{N} \mathcal{L}\big(g(p^{(i)}; \theta), Q^{(i)}\big), \tag{16}$$

where $g(p^{(i)}; \theta)$ is the QUBO predicted by a neural network with parameters θ and $Q^{(i)}$ is the target QUBO matrix for problem instance $p^{(i)}$ [18].

3.4 Hybrid Quantum-Classical Algorithms

Several works have focused on hybrid algorithms that combine the strengths of classical optimization with quantum annealing. Venturelli et al. [19] proposed methods that integrate classical pre-processing steps with quantum post-processing to refine solutions obtained from a quantum annealer. Similarly,

Benedetti et al. [20] developed quantum-assisted learning techniques where a classical machine learning model iteratively updates a QUBO formulation based on feedback from quantum hardware. Such hybrid approaches address limitations of current quantum devices, such as noise and limited qubit connectivity [10].

3.5 Differentiable Optimization Approaches

An emerging line of research seeks to integrate optimization solvers directly into neural network models as differentiable layers, enabling optimization to be performed as a forward pass. These approaches allow gradients to flow through optimization problems, thereby unifying discrete or continuous optimization with end-to-end learning.

OptNet. Amos and Kolter [24] introduced *OptNet*, which embeds a quadratic program (QP) as a differentiable layer. A standard QP in OptNet is formulated as:

$$\min_{z} \quad \frac{1}{2}z^T Q z + c^T z,$$
$$\text{subject to} \quad Az = b, \tag{17}$$
$$z \geq 0.$$

By differentiating through the Karush-Kuhn-Tucker (KKT) conditions of the QP, OptNet enables the backpropagation of gradients with respect to the parameters Q, c, A, and b.

SATNet. In a related approach, *SATNet* [21] integrates a differentiable satisfiability solver into neural network architectures. SATNet relaxes the discrete Boolean constraints into a continuous domain, allowing the network to learn logical relationships by optimizing a continuous surrogate of the original SAT problem.

CombOptNet. Paulus et al. [23] extend these ideas to combinatorial optimization by developing *CombOptNet*. This framework incorporates combinatorial constraints and graph-based structures into the differentiable optimization layer, enabling the network to solve combinatorial subproblems as part of its forward computation.

These differentiable optimization frameworks share a common goal with our approach: to incorporate the power of optimization into the learning process in a seamless, end-to-end differentiable manner. In our work, we leverage a similar philosophy by learning QUBO formulations that enable optimization within the forward pass of a neural network, thereby bridging the gap between discrete optimization and gradient-based learning.

4   Learning QUBO Formulations from Data

In this section, we present our method for learning QUBO formulations from a set of problem-solution pairs. Rather than directly learning the mapping

$$f : p \mapsto x, \tag{18}$$

where p is a problem instance (e.g., a graph for maximum clique) and x is its optimal solution, we introduce an intermediate step by learning a function

$$g : p \mapsto Q, \tag{19}$$

which produces a QUBO matrix $Q \in \mathbb{R}^{n \times n}$ such that the solution

$$x^* = \arg \min_{x \in \{0,1\}^n} x^T Q x \tag{20}$$

corresponds to the optimal x. Inspired by Max-SAT formulations, we define an ideal clause weight vector $w^* \in \{0,1\}^{N_c}$ for each instance, where each clause C_j satisfies

$$w_j^* = \begin{cases} 1, & \text{if } C_j \text{ is satisfied by } x, \\ 0, & \text{otherwise.} \end{cases} \tag{21}$$

In our formulation, the QUBO objective is derived from these clauses, such that

$$x^T Q x = \sum_{j=1}^{N_c} \lambda_j \, P_{C_j}(x), \tag{22}$$

with $P_{C_j}(x)$ representing the penalty for clause C_j (e.g., for a clause with k literals, $P_{C_j}(x) = \prod_{i=1}^{k} (1 - \ell_{ji}(x))$).

Even if some weights deviate (i.e., some w_j^* flip), our analysis studies the tolerance τ such that

$$\tau = \#\{j : \hat{w}_j \neq w_j^*\}, \tag{23}$$

and x remains optimal as long as τ is below a threshold. This robustness is critical for our learned QUBO to reliably encode the NP-hard prediction task. Thus, our method learns the mapping g so that the QUBO formulation

$$x^* = \arg \min_{x \in \{0,1\}^n} x^T Q x, \tag{24}$$

with

$$Q = Q(\hat{w}) \quad \text{and} \quad \hat{w} = g(p), \tag{25}$$

preserves the optimal solution x despite moderate clause weight perturbations.

4.1   Detailed Algorithm Description

Our approach consists of the following steps:

1. **Input Preparation:**
   (a) Receive a dataset of problem-solution pairs $\{(p^{(i)}, x^{(i)})\}_{i=1}^{N}$. The problem instance p is represented in a suitable feature space (e.g., graph features), and x is encoded as a binary vector.
   (b) For each problem, precompute a collection of clauses based on a chosen clause size k. Let n be the number of output variables; then the number of distinct clauses is

$$b = \binom{n}{k}, \tag{26}$$

   and by defining

$$a = 2^k, \tag{27}$$

   the total number of clauses is given by

$$\text{numClauses} = a \cdot b. \tag{28}$$

2. **Learning the QUBO Mapping:**
   (a) Build a deep neural network that takes as input the problem instance p and outputs a vector in $[0, 1]^{\text{numClauses}}$. This output is interpreted as a set of clause weights that define the QUBO matrix Q since we can transform any Max-SAT instance into a QUBO form [6, 22].
   (b) The network consists of several fully connected layers with nonlinear activations (e.g., ReLU), and its final layer uses a Sigmoid activation to ensure the output is bounded between 0 and 1.
3. **Constructing the Ideal Clause Weights:**
   (a) For each training pair $(p^{(i)}, x^{(i)})$, determine the ideal clause weight vector w^* as follows:

$$w_j^* = \begin{cases} 1, & \text{if clause } j \text{ is satisfied by } x^{(i)}, \\ 0, & \text{otherwise.} \end{cases} \tag{29}$$

   (b) Optionally, different penalty values can be assigned to clauses depending on whether they are satisfied or unsatisfied, reflecting the sensitivity of the QUBO's optimality to deviations.
4. **Loss Function Computation:**
   (a) For each x compute the number of flips from $0 \rightarrow 1$ and $1 \rightarrow 0$. They define a point p_x, in a 2-dim map (see Sect. 5). Now we can compute the distance d from this point to the curve defined by:

$$\texttt{offset} = b\left(1 - \frac{1}{\texttt{output\_dim}}\right), \tag{30}$$

$$\texttt{slope} = \frac{\texttt{offset}}{\frac{14}{25} \cdot (a-1) \cdot b}. \tag{31}$$

   This curve was empirically derived on a large set of randomly generated problem instances (see Sect. 5 for more details).

(b) Scale the distance d by a predefined threshold $d_{threshold}$ using a sigmoid function:

$$\ell = \sigma\left(\frac{\texttt{scaling} \cdot (d - d_{threshold})}{d_{threshold}}\right), \tag{32}$$

where $\sigma(z) = \frac{1}{1+e^{-z}}$. This value ℓ serves as the loss for the sample.

5. **Optimization:**
   (a) Update the network parameters using a gradient-based optimizer (e.g., Adam) to minimize the average loss over the training dataset.
   (b) Employ early stopping based on validation performance to save the best model.

6. **Inference and Post-Processing:**
   (a) For a new problem instance p, compute the predicted clause weight vector $\hat{w}$ using the trained network.
   (b) Use any SAT-to-QUBO transformation algorithm for converting $\hat{w}$ into the QUBO matrix Q.
   (c) Solve the QUBO using a combinatorial optimization routine (e.g., via tabu search, or another heuristic) to obtain the solution

$$x^* = \arg\min_x \; x^T Q x. \tag{33}$$

4.2   Discussion

This algorithm integrates the structure of Max-SAT formulations into a differentiable learning framework. By training a neural network on a dataset of problem-solution pairs, we learn a mapping from problems to QUBO matrices that inherently encode the optimal solution x as the minimizer of $x^T Q x$.

The use of weighted clause errors and a scaled sigmoid loss allows the network to tolerate a limited number of clause weight deviations, which we further investigate in our experiments. This method bridges continuous learning and discrete optimization, paving the way for efficient QUBO formulations that can be deployed in both classical and quantum optimization settings.

A key advantage of our approach compared to other differentiable optimization algorithms such as SATNet, OptNet, and CombOptNet is that, during training, we do not require solving any optimization problem. In these alternative methods, incorporating an optimization layer into the network often necessitates solving a discrete or continuous optimization problem in every forward pass, which can be computationally expensive and prone to instability. In contrast, our framework circumvents this bottleneck by directly learning the QUBO matrix from the data. This not only makes the training process much faster but also enhances its stability, as the network can be optimized using standard gradient-based methods without the overhead of embedded solvers. Consequently, our method offers a more efficient and robust pathway for integrating combinatorial optimization within a deep learning paradigm.

4.3   Pseudocode Summary

The following pseudocode summarizes the algorithm:

Algorithm 1. Learning QUBO Formulations from Problem-Solution Pairs

---

1: **Input:** Dataset of problem-solution pairs $\{(p^{(i)}, x^{(i)})\}_{i=1}^{N}$, hyperparameters $k, \text{scaling}, \text{penalty}, d_{threshold}$
2: Precompute the set of clauses based on k and calculate numClauses $= 2^k \cdot \binom{n}{k}$
3: Construct a deep neural network f_θ mapping p to a clause weight vector $\hat{w} \in [0, 1]^{\text{numClauses}}$
4: **for** each training sample (p, x) **do**
5:    Compute the ideal clause weight vector w^* where:

$$w_j^* = \begin{cases} 1, & \text{if clause } j \text{ is satisfied by } x, \\ 0, & \text{otherwise} \end{cases} \tag{34}$$

6:    Compute the elementwise error: $\Delta = |\hat{w} - w^*|$
7:    Apply penalty weights to obtain $\Delta_{\text{weighted}} = \Delta \odot \text{penalty}$
8:    Compute the distance d of the point p_x to the curve defined by:

$$\text{offset} = b \left(1 - \frac{1}{\text{output\_dim}} \right), \tag{35}$$

$$\text{slope} = \frac{\text{offset}}{\frac{14}{25} \cdot (a - 1) \cdot b}. \tag{36}$$

9:    Scale d using the sigmoid function:

$$\ell = \sigma \left(\frac{\text{scaling} \cdot (d - d_{threshold})}{d_{threshold}} \right) \tag{37}$$

10: **end for**
11: Update network parameters θ to minimize the average loss using Adam
12: **Output:** Trained network f_θ such that for any problem instance p:

    1. Compute $\hat{w} = f_\theta(p)$
    2. Construct QUBO matrix Q from $\hat{w}$
    3. Solve $x^* = \arg\min_x x^T Q x$

---

5   Experiments

We evaluate our approach on a collection of benchmark problems. Our experiments are designed to address the following key questions:

1. Can the learned QUBO formulation consistently yield the optimal solution x for a given problem p by ensuring that

$$x = \arg\min_x x^T Q x, \tag{38}$$

even when the learned clause weights deviate from the ideal binary setting?

2. How robust is the QUBO with respect to bit-flips in the clause weights? In other words, how many weight perturbations (from 1 to 0 or vice versa) can occur before the optimal solution x is no longer preserved?

3. How does our approach compare to other differentiable optimization methods such as SATNet, OptNet, and CombOptNet, which are known to quickly converge to local optima?

5.1   Empirical Analysis of QUBO Robustness via Weight Flips

In our first set of experiments, we investigate the robustness of a QUBO formulation derived from a weighted Max-SAT instance with respect to perturbations in the clause weights. The central question we address is: *How many weight flips (i.e., changes of a clause weight from 1 to 0 or vice versa) can be introduced before the optimal solution x is no longer the global minimum of the QUBO?*

To this end, we consider the following experimental setting:

– Let x be a fixed, random binary assignment of dimension `output_dim` (e.g., `output_dim` $= 6$).
– Let k be the clause size (e.g., $k = 3$); then we define

$$a = 2^k \quad \text{and} \quad b = \binom{\texttt{output\_dim}}{k}, \tag{39}$$

so that the total number of clauses is `num_clauses` $= a \cdot b$.

– By construction, exactly $(a-1) \cdot b$ clauses are satisfied by x and the remaining b are not. In the ideal weighted Max-SAT formula, each clause c_i is assigned a weight

$$w_i = \begin{cases} 1, & \text{if } c_i \text{ is satisfied by } x, \\ 0, & \text{otherwise.} \end{cases} \tag{40}$$

Under these conditions, x is guaranteed to be the global minimizer of the QUBO formulation associated with the Max-SAT formula.

In our experiment, we perturb the clause weights by flipping a controlled number of bits:

– For clauses originally assigned weight 0 (unsatisfied), we randomly flip a specified number (`unsat_flip_nr`) to 1.
– For clauses originally assigned weight 1 (satisfied), we similarly flip a specified number (`sat_flip_nr`) to 0.

The experimental procedure is as follows:

1. For a fixed precision (number of iterations), and for each combination of a given number of unsatisfied flips (ranging from 0 to b) and satisfied flips (ranging from 0 to $(a - 1) \cdot b$), we:

(a) Randomly select an assignment x and generate all clauses for the given `output_dim` and k.

(b) Compute the initial weight vector by checking clause satisfaction for x.

(c) Randomly choose indices corresponding to unsatisfied clauses and satisfied clauses to flip their weights.

(d) Solve the resulting weighted Max-SAT instance using a tabu search routine to obtain the candidate optimal assignment x_{best}.

(e) Record a success if $x_{\text{best}} = x$; otherwise, note a failure.

2. The success rates are aggregated over multiple iterations and stored in a heatmap, where the axes represent the number of weight flips from 1 to 0 and 0 to 1, respectively.

Figure 1 (a) shows the resulting heatmap from one experiment (with `output_dim` $= 6$, $k = 3$, and precision of 50 iterations). The color scale indicates the fraction of times the original assignment x remained optimal despite the weight flips. A value of 1.0 (or 100%) indicates that the solution x was preserved in every iteration for that combination of flips, while lower values indicate degradation in the ability of the QUBO formulation to maintain x as the optimum.

The overlaid gray curve in the plot provides an empirical boundary showing the expected tolerance threshold for weight perturbations. In our experiments, the empirical threshold line is computed as follows:

$$\texttt{offset} = b \left(1 - \frac{1}{\texttt{output\_dim}} \right), \tag{41}$$

$$\texttt{slope} = \frac{\texttt{offset}}{\frac{14}{25} \cdot (a - 1) \cdot b}. \tag{42}$$

In summary, this experiment not only validates that our constructed weighted Max-SAT formula yields x as the optimal solution under ideal conditions but also quantifies the resilience of the QUBO formulation. The results offer insights into how many clause weight flips can be tolerated before the integrity of the solution is compromised, a critical factor for applications in noisy or approximate optimization settings. In this experiment, we derived the empirical threshold curve that we will use in all other experiments.

5.2 Loss Map Visualization

In addition to assessing the robustness of the QUBO formulation via weight flips, we analyze the behavior of the loss function over a range of perturbations through a loss map. The loss map provides a visual representation of how the network's loss changes as a function of the number of weight flips in two directions: from 1 to 0 and from 0 to 1.

In our implementation, the loss for a given configuration of weight flips is computed as follows. For each combination of unsatisfied flips (number of clauses originally set to 0 that are flipped to 1) and satisfied flips (number of clauses

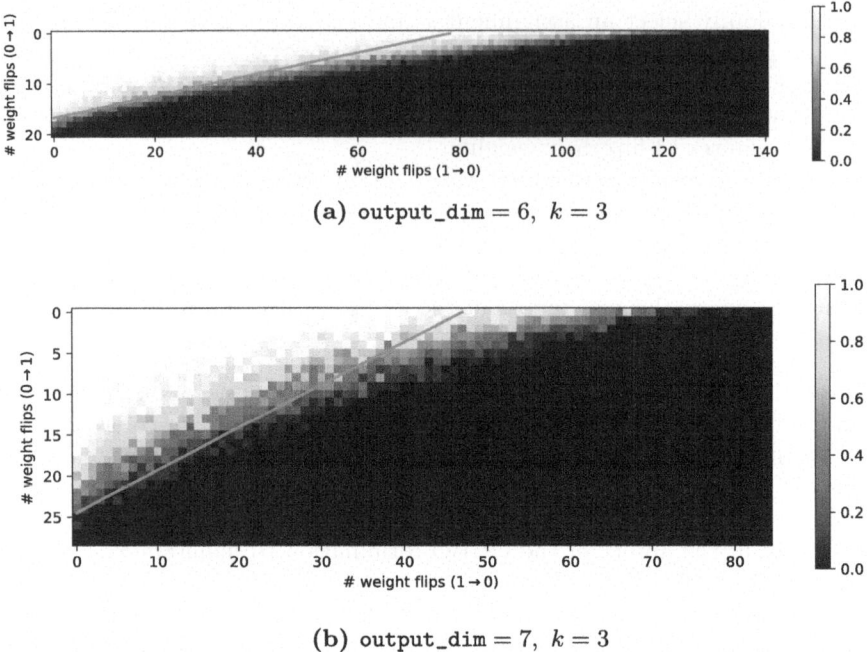

(a) `output_dim = 6`, $k = 3$

(b) `output_dim = 7`, $k = 3$

Fig. 1. Combined robustness heatmaps for different configurations. Each subfigure displays the success rate (fraction of iterations in which the original assignment x remains optimal) as a function of the number of weight flips from 1 to 0 (horizontal axis) and from 0 to 1 (vertical axis). The gray curves indicate the empirically derived tolerance thresholds.

originally set to 1 that are flipped to 0), the distance of this point p_x to the gray line can be computed. This distance is then transformed into a loss value using a scaled sigmoid function:

$$\text{loss} = \sigma\left(\frac{\texttt{scaling} \cdot \left(\text{d} - d_{\text{threshold}} \right)}{d_{\text{threshold}}} \right) \quad \text{with} \quad \sigma(z) = \frac{1}{1 + e^{-z}}, \qquad (43)$$

where $d_{\text{threshold}}$ is the empirically determined distance from the origin to the threshold line. This transformation converts the raw distance into a loss value between 0 and 1.

The resulting loss values are stored in a 2D array (heatmap) whose dimensions correspond to the range of unsatisfied and satisfied flips. A lower loss indicates that the QUBO formulation is closer to preserving the optimal solution x, while a higher loss signals that the perturbations are likely to lead to a suboptimal solution.

Figure 2 displays the loss map for a configuration with `output_dim = 6` and $k = 3$. The color scale represents the loss values, and the overlaid gray curve represents the empirical threshold line.

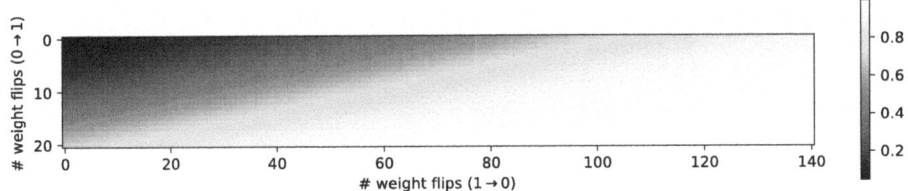

Fig. 2. Loss map for `output_dim` $= 6$ and $k = 3$. The heatmap shows the loss values (computed via a sigmoid transformation) as a function of the number of weight flips from 1 to 0 (horizontal axis) and from 0 to 1 (vertical axis). The gray curve indicates the empirical threshold line given by $y = \texttt{offset} - x \cdot \texttt{slope}$, with $\texttt{offset} = b \left(1 - \frac{1}{\texttt{output\_dim}}\right)$ and $\texttt{slope} = \frac{\texttt{offset}}{\frac{14}{25} \cdot (a-1) \cdot b}$.

In summary, the loss map visualization not only reinforces our understanding of the network's performance under varying degrees of perturbation but also quantifies the resilience of the QUBO formulation. The empirical threshold line serves as a clear indicator of the transition region beyond which the loss increases significantly, thus marking the boundary where the optimality of the solution x is at risk.

5.3 Maximum Clique Dataset Evaluation

We further validate our approach using a maximum clique dataset. In this dataset, we generated 600 training examples and 20 validation examples, where each example represents a graph with 6 nodes. For each graph, we computed the corresponding optimal binary vector y indicating the maximum clique. This results in a training set of (x, y) pairs, where x encodes the graph and y is the binary maximum clique vector.

To evaluate the effectiveness of our QUBO learning framework, we computed the position of each data point in the loss map, which reflects the robustness of the corresponding QUBO formulation. These positions indicate how many weight flips (from 1 to 0 and from 0 to 1) are needed for the loss to increase significantly. We perform this analysis both before and after training our network.

Figure 3 shows the distribution of loss map positions for both the training and validation data prior to training. In contrast, Fig. 4 presents the loss map positions after training. As observed, post-training the data points shift toward the region corresponding to lower loss values, indicating that the learned QUBO formulations are more robust and closer to the ideal weighted Max-SAT representation.

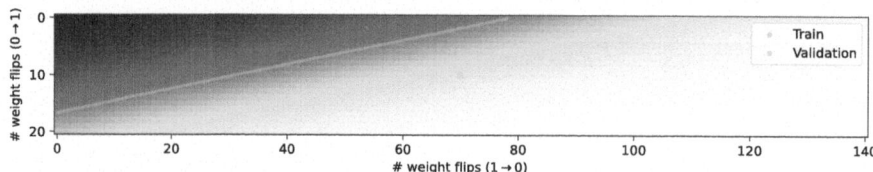

Fig. 3. Loss map positions for the maximum clique dataset (training and validation) before training.

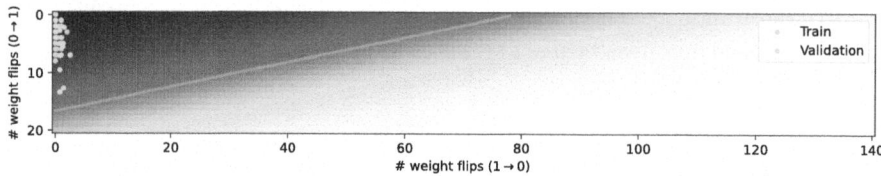

Fig. 4. Loss map positions for the maximum clique dataset (training and validation) after training.

In summary, this experiment confirms that our method successfully learns to map problem instances to QUBO formulations that preserve the optimal solution. The shift of data points toward lower-loss regions in the loss map, observed in both the training and validation sets post-training, demonstrates the increased robustness of the learned QUBO representation—a critical factor for applications in noisy or approximate optimization settings.

5.4 Comparison of Approaches

To evaluate the effectiveness of our method in predicting the optimal binary vector y for a given problem instance x, we compare our approach (DeepSAT) against several related methods, including SATNet, OptNet, CombOptNet, and a standard feed-forward network (FF). The evaluation covers three distinct problem classes: Maximum Clique, Knapsack, and 4×4 Sudoku.

For the Maximum Clique problem, we consider graphs with 7 nodes; for Knapsack, we use problem instances with 7 items; and for Sudoku, we focus on 4×4 puzzles. Table 1 summarizes the results across these problem classes, with each row corresponding to a problem type and each column reporting a performance metric (e.g., prediction accuracy). As shown, DeepSAT outperforms the competing methods, achieving significantly higher accuracy in predicting y from x.

In these experiments, DeepSAT was trained on a Nvidia H100 GPU. Results are reported on a held-out test set of size 50. Overall, the results clearly indicate that DeepSAT provides a robust and effective framework for mapping problem instances to optimal solutions in NP-hard prediction tasks, bridging the gap between discrete optimization and continuous learning.

Table 1. Performance comparison across problem classes

Problem	DeepSAT	SATNet	OptNet	CombOptNet	FF
Max Clique (7 nodes)	**0.92**	0.65	0.70	0.72	0.33
Knapsack (7 items)	**0.88**	0.34	0.55	0.51	0.18
4 × 4 Sudoku	**0.99**	0.72	0.34	0.67	0.11

6 Conclusion

In this work, we introduced a novel, data-driven approach for learning QUBO formulations directly from problem-solution pairs, effectively bridging the gap between discrete combinatorial optimization and continuous machine learning. Rather than directly predicting optimal solutions, our method learns an intermediate mapping from a problem instance to a QUBO matrix, which inherently encodes the combinatorial structure of NP-hard tasks. By leveraging clause-based formulations inspired by Max-SAT, our framework is able to tolerate moderate perturbations in clause weights while preserving optimality, leading to robust performance even in noisy settings.

Our extensive experiments demonstrate that the learned QUBO formulations not only capture the underlying problem structure for benchmark tasks such as Maximum Clique, Knapsack, and 4 × 4 Sudoku, but also outperform alternative approaches like SATNet, OptNet, CombOptNet, and standard feed-forward networks. Notably, our approach achieves superior prediction accuracy while significantly reducing the computational overhead by avoiding embedded optimization steps during training.

In future work, we plan to extend this framework to larger and more complex problem instances, explore adaptive mechanisms for penalty tuning, and investigate integrations with emerging quantum annealing hardware. Overall, our results suggest that learning QUBO formulations from data is a promising direction for automating the translation of NP-hard prediction tasks into optimization problems that can be efficiently solved using both classical and quantum techniques.

Acknowledgement. This publication was created as part of the Q-Grid project (13N16179) under the "quantum technologies – from basic research to market" funding program, supported by the German Federal Ministry of Education and Research. The authors acknowledge funding from the German Federal Ministry of Education and Research under the funding program "Förderprogramm Quantentechnologien - von den Grundlagen zum Markt" (funding program quantum technologies - from basic research to market), project BAIQO, 13N16089.

References

1. Bucher, D., et al.: Dynamic Price Incentivization for Carbon Emission Reduction using Quantum Optimization, 2023. arXiv preprint arXiv:2309.05502

2. Milan, A., Rezatofighi, S., Garg, R., Dick, A., Reid, I.: Data-driven approximations to NP-hard problems. In: Proceedings of the AAAI Conference on Artificial Intelligence, vol. 31, no. 1, February 2017

3. Zielinski, S., Nüßlein, J., Stein, J., Gabor, T., Linnhoff-Popien, C., Feld, S.: Pattern QUBOs: algorithmic construction of 3SAT-to-QUBO transformations. Electronics **12**(16), 3492 (2023)

4. Roch, C., Ratke, D., Nüßlein, J., Gabor, T., Feld, S.: The effect of penalty factors of constrained Hamiltonians on the eigenspectrum in quantum annealing. ACM Trans. Quantum Comput. **4**(2), 1–18 (2023)

5. Lynce, I., Ouaknine, J.: Sudoku as a SAT Problem. In: AI&M (January 2006)

6. Nüßlein, J., Gabor, T., Linnhoff-Popien, C., Feld, S.: Algorithmic QUBO formulations for k-SAT and hamiltonian cycles. In: Proceedings of the Genetic and Evolutionary Computation Conference Companion, pp. 2240–2246, July 2022

7. Guo, H., Hsu, W.H.: A machine learning approach to algorithm selection for-hard optimization problems: a case study on the MPE problem. Ann. Oper. Res. **156**(1), 61–82 (2007)

8. Bomze, I.M., Budinich, M., Pardalos, P.M., Pelillo, M.: The maximum clique problem. In: Handbook of Combinatorial Optimization: Supplement, Volume A, pp. 1–74 (1999)

9. Glover, F., Kochenberger, G., Du, Y.: A tutorial on formulating and using QUBO models, 2018. arXiv preprint arXiv:1811.11538

10. Nüßlein, J., et al.: Reducing QUBO Density by Factoring Out Semi-Symmetries, 2024. arXiv preprint arXiv:2412.17841

11. Salkin, H.M., De Kluyver, C.A.: The knapsack problem: a survey. Nav. Res. Logist. Q. **22**(1), 127–144 (1975)

12. Lucas, A.: Ising formulations of many NP problems. Front. Phys. **2**, 5 (2014)

13. Nüßlein, J., et al.: Towards less greedy quantum coalition structure generation in induced subgraph games. In: 2024 IEEE International Conference on Quantum Computing and Engineering (QCE), vol. 2, pp. 28–33. IEEE, September 2024

14. Moraglio, A., Georgescu, S., Sadowski, P.: AutoQubo: data-driven automatic QUBO generation. In: Proceedings of the Genetic and Evolutionary Computation Conference Companion, pp. 2232–2239, July 2022

15. McCormick, T.M., Osborn, B.R., Angle, R.B., Streit, R.L.: Implementation of a multiple target tracking filter on an adiabatic quantum computer. In: 2022 IEEE Aerospace Conference (AERO), pp. 1–14. IEEE, March 2022

16. Zhang, Y., Gong, Y., Fan, L., Wang, Y., Han, Z., Guo, Y.: Quantum-assisted online task offloading and resource allocation in mec-enabled satellite-aerial-terrestrial integrated networks. IEEE Trans. Mob. Comput. (2024)

17. Choi, V.: Minor-embedding in adiabatic quantum computation: I. The parameter setting problem. Quantum Inf. Process. **7**, 193–209 (2008)

18. Biamonte, J., Wittek, P., Pancotti, N., Rebentrost, P., Wiebe, N., Lloyd, S.: Quantum machine learning. Nature **549**(7671), 195–202 (2017)

19. Venturelli, D., Mandrà, S., Knysh, S., O'Gorman, B., Biswas, R., Smelyanskiy, V.: Quantum optimization of fully connected spin glasses. Phys. Rev. X **5**(3), 031040 (2015)

20. Benedetti, M., Realpe-Gómez, J., Biswas, R., Perdomo-Ortiz, A.: Quantum-assisted learning of hardware-embedded probabilistic graphical models. Phys. Rev. X **7**(4), 041052 (2017)

21. Wang, P.W., Donti, P., Wilder, B., Kolter, Z.: Satnet: bridging deep learning and logical reasoning using a differentiable satisfiability solver. In: International Conference on Machine Learning, pp. 6545–6554. PMLR, May 2019

22. Nüßlein, J., Zielinski, S., Gabor, T., Linnhoff-Popien, C., Feld, S.: Solving (max) 3-SAT via quadratic unconstrained binary optimization. In: International Conference on Computational Science, pp. 34–47. Springer Nature, Switzerland, Cham (2023)
23. Paulus, A., Rolínek, M., Musil, V., Amos, B., Martius, G.: Comboptnet: fit the right np-hard problem by learning integer programming constraints. In: International Conference on Machine Learning, pp. 8443–8453. PMLR, July 2021
24. Amos, B., Kolter, J.Z.: Optnet: differentiable optimization as a layer in neural networks. In: International Conference on Machine Learning, pp. 136–145. PMLR, July 2017
25. Farhi, E., Goldstone, J., Gutmann, S.: A quantum approximate optimization algorithm, 2014. arXiv preprint arXiv:1411.4028
26. Zielinski, S., Nüßlein, J., Kölle, M., Gabor, T., Linnhoff-Popien, C., Feld, S.: Solving Max-3SAT using QUBO approximation. In: 2024 IEEE International Conference on Quantum Computing and Engineering (QCE), vol. 1, pp. 681–691. IEEE, September 2024
27. Pauckert, J., Ayodele, M., García, M.D., Georgescu, S., Parizy, M.: Autoqubo v2: towards efficient and effective QUBO formulations for ising machines. In: Proceedings of the Companion Conference on Genetic and Evolutionary Computation, pp. 227–230, July 2023

Public Sector

A Multi-modal Data-Driven Dashboard for Enhanced Public Health Surveillance and Awareness

Kiana Lesan Pezeshki[1]([✉]), Sepinood Haghighi[1], Farzaneh Jouyandeh[1],
Sarvnaz Sadeghi[1], Pooya Moradian Zadeh[1,7], Jackie Fong[2,7], Kendall Soucie[3,7],
R. Michael McKay[4], Kenneth K. S. Ng[5,7], Lisa A. Porter[2,7], Yufeng Tong[5,7],
and Lawrence Goodridge[6]

[1] School of Computer Science, University of Windsor, Windsor, ON, Canada
{lesanpe,haghigh7,jouyand,sadeghi4,pooya}@uwindsor.ca
[2] Department of Biomedical Sciences, University of Windsor, Windsor, ON, Canada
{jackie.fong,lporter}@uwindsor.ca
[3] Department of Psychology, University of Windsor, Windsor, ON, Canada
ksoucie@uwindsor.ca
[4] Great Lakes Institute for Environmental Research, University of Windsor,
Windsor, ON, Canada
robert.mckay@uwindsor.ca
[5] Department of Chemistry and Biochemistry, University of Windsor, Windsor, ON,
Canada
{kenneth.ng,yufeng.tong}@uwindsor.ca
[6] Canadian Research Institute for Food Safety, Department of Food Science,
University of Guelph, Guelph, ON, Canada
goodridl@uoguelph.ca
[7] WE-SPARK Health Institute, University of Windsor, Windsor, ON, Canada

Abstract. Effective public health responses require timely access to diverse information and a holistic understanding of the situation. This paper describes a community-centered framework for developing a multi-modal visualization and analytical tool that integrates disparate data sources such as epidemiological data, wastewater surveillance data, and social media sentiment analysis into a unified platform. Our focus is on creating a user-friendly experience that empowers both the public and experts to monitor, analyze, and respond to public health events. We also present the results of our initial evaluation, including an effectiveness and usability assessment based on a survey of over 1,600 participants, demonstrating the platform's potential to enhance public health communication, decision-making, and overall situational awareness.

Keywords: Data analytics · Health informatics · Multi-modal data

K. Lesan Pezeshki, S. Haghighi, F. Jouyandeh and S. Sadeghi—These authors contributed equally.

1   Introduction

In today's digital age and interconnected world, we are surrounded by a vast and ever-expanding stream of information from diverse channels ranging from news and online platforms to personal interactions. This information spans a broad spectrum of topics, shaping our awareness of global and local issues and influencing public opinion and responses on matters such as public health, economic stability, environmental challenges, and social dynamics. As the volume and complexity of data continue to grow, the need to understand, interpret, and act on this information becomes increasingly paramount.

One of the most creative and effective ways to utilize these data and information is through digital dashboards. These tools can transform vast, scattered datasets into clear, interactive visualizations that help people track trends, identify risks, and make informed decisions. Over the last decade, dashboards have become essential across industries, from finance and business analytics to disaster response and public health.

In recent years, especially during the COVID-19 pandemic, dashboards have become a critical source of information for both policymakers and the general public. Google Trends data on dashboards [10], as shown in Fig. 1, illustrates the growing public interest in these tools over time, especially between 2020 to 2022. In fact, at the height of the pandemic, a vast amount of information was flooding in from various directions, including new case numbers, hospitalizations, testing rates, government policies, and personal experiences shared online. It was easy to feel lost in the flood of data. This is where dashboards played a critical role by providing a clear and organized representation of the situation for their audiences. One notable example is the Johns Hopkins COVID-19 Dashboard, which accumulated millions of views and served as a key information hub for accessing real-time data during the COVID-19 pandemic [8].

This widespread reliance on dashboards highlights the growing demand for solutions that can seamlessly integrate, combine, and interpret data from various sources into a cohesive, unified platform, thereby enabling more informed decision-making based on a complete picture.

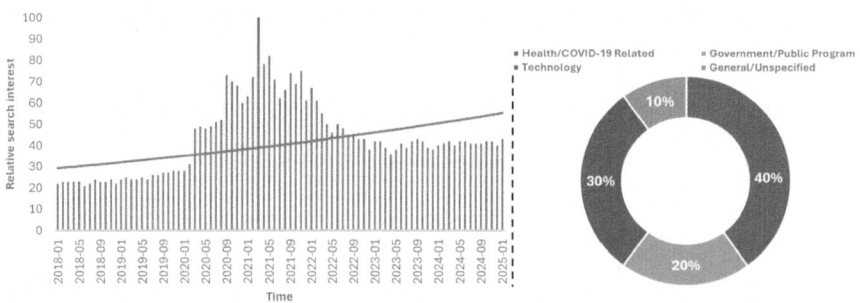

Fig. 1. Evolution of interest in dashboards over time, based on Google Trends data.

While the use of dashboards in health surveillance systems has grown significantly, many public health dashboards still focus primarily on presenting data from single centralized official sources, such as case numbers, hospitalizations, or test results from designated testing centers. However, there is significant potential to enhance these platforms by incorporating additional data, particularly from local sources. By including more community-specific information, dashboards can provide insights that are more relevant and actionable for local audiences. Although broad data help to track trends and understand the overall situation, localized information can offer immediate, context-rich insights that empower individuals to make more informed decisions in their daily lives.

Our research aims to fill this gap by proposing a framework for a comprehensive dashboard that integrates epidemiological data, wastewater surveillance, health-related news trends, and social media sentiment analysis. This approach allows us to go beyond just tracking disease cases to understanding the broader social and environmental context of public health trends.

Wastewater surveillance, for instance, can potentially detect rises in viral infections before they are reflected in clinical reports and provide an early warning system for disease outbreaks [1,6,21]. Meanwhile, social media sentiment analysis provides valuable insights into how people are reacting to health or societal crises and can reveal their concerns and emotional responses [13,25,27]. By examining patterns in online posts, we can assess public sentiment, whether it is fear, uncertainty, or optimism, regarding specific events. This approach also helps spot early warning signs that may not yet appear in clinical data, such as growing anxieties about a disease or emerging issues like vaccine hesitancy, long before these trends are reflected in official statistics. Complementing these, news trend analysis tracks how health issues are covered in the media, revealing changing narratives that influence public perception and policy decisions.

By integrating these various data streams, our proposed dashboard offers a multilayered, real-time view of public health, blending both the biological and social dimensions of disease outbreaks. This comprehensive approach enables policymakers, healthcare professionals, and researchers to not only access raw data but also understand the context surrounding those data-an essential tool for making informed, effective decisions.

The remainder of this paper is organized as follows. Section 2 provides a brief review of related work in the field. Section 3 outlines our proposed framework for data collection, processing, and visualization. Section 4 presents the implementation and key features of the dashboard, while Sect. 5 examines its impact and functionality. In Sect. 6, we conclude with a discussion of future directions.

2 Literature Review

The development and use of health dashboards have evolved significantly in recent years, largely due to advancements in data visualization, interactive interfaces, and the integration of artificial intelligence. These innovations have expanded the capabilities of health dashboards, enabling them to address a wide range of public health needs, from raising awareness of specific health issues to enabling real-time data monitoring and supporting personalized health interventions. In this section, we briefly review some of the research directions that are shaping the development and application of health dashboards.

Traditionally, dashboards have been primarily designed as analytical tools for experts and researchers, helping them interpret complex data and make informed decisions [22]. However, in recent years, particularly during and after the COVID-19 pandemic, their role has expanded significantly. Today, dashboards are no longer exclusive to academia and policymakers; they are increasingly designed for public use, offering intuitive interfaces and accessible visualizations that empower individuals to stay informed [28]. These tools now serve a variety of purposes, functioning as communication platforms for public health updates, hubs for raising awareness about emerging health issues, decision-support systems for both individuals and organizations and even educational resources that enhance data literacy among the general population [28]. This shift reflects the growing demand for transparent, real-time data that empowers both experts and the public to make informed decisions in an increasingly data-driven world.

For example, platforms like the Johns Hopkins COVID-19 Dashboard became invaluable tools, not only for experts but also for the general public, offering real-time case counts, and other key health metrics [7,8]. Similarly, the World Health Organization (WHO) Dashboard has played a pivotal role in providing real-time information about global health trends, outbreaks, and country-specific data, thus aiding in international health coordination and policy-making [30].

Additionally, some health dashboards have gone beyond traditional data sources by incorporating data from wastewater surveillance programs [12,19]. These programs are increasingly being used as early warning systems for tracking the spread of infectious diseases, as wastewater can provide early indications of virus prevalence in the community [5,20]. These dashboards can offer timely insights into potential outbreaks and help public health authorities respond more swiftly and efficiently [20].

Moreover, public health data transparency has been enhanced through the development of numerous regional and country-specific surveillance dashboards and tools. A representative example is the Ontario Respiratory Virus Tool [23], which provides comprehensive epidemiological information on respiratory virus activity within Ontario, encompassing SARS-CoV-2, influenza, RSV, and other respiratory viruses. The dashboard facilitates analysis of case trends, health outcomes (e.g., hospital and ICU bed occupancy, mortality rates), laboratory testing capacity, and outbreak dynamics. However, health dashboards are not solely focused on pandemic response. In fact, they serve a broad range of public health purposes, such as infectious diseases, chronic conditions, environmental risks, healthcare system performance, and behavioral health trends [22,29].

The growing use of health dashboards has also driven a parallel increase in research evaluating their impact and effectiveness. Some researchers have proposed frameworks and approaches to assess the performance of these tools, offering suggestions for their design and development. In [2], the authors conducted a case study to assess the usability of public health data dashboards. Their research highlighted several key design considerations that could enhance the effectiveness of these dashboards. These included the need for intuitive, well-labeled charts, the incorporation of contextual information to aid in data interpretation, and a consistent layout to streamline navigation. Additionally, they emphasized the importance of clearly communicating the limitations of the data and providing clear guidance to assist users in interacting with the dashboard efficiently.

In another study [16], the authors aimed to identify the top attributes of effective healthcare dashboards by surveying 218 individuals across the U.S. They identified 15 key features, including easy navigation, simplicity in design, and clear descriptions. The authors also highlighted the importance of mobile compatibility, compliance with the Americans with Disabilities Act, and the use of predictive analytics. They concluded that these findings could contribute to standardizing dashboard design, improving accessibility, and empowering the public with better health data for informed decision-making.

In [4], the authors have conducted a systematic review of 144 dashboards in order to identify their patterns and design practices. They documented 42 design patterns, organized into 8 categories, to guide design decisions. In [31], the authors proposed a framework to evaluate healthcare dashboards, consisting of seven distinct scenarios grouped into three evaluation themes. These scenarios assess various aspects of dashboard functionality and effectiveness, including task performance, behavior change, interaction workflow, perceived engagement, potential utility, algorithm performance, and system implementation.

On the other hand, some studies have explored the integration of AI into health dashboards. In [26], the authors proposed and studied a conversational dashboard for the COVID-19 pandemic that leverages Natural Language Processing (NLP) for interaction via speech or text while guiding users through conversational onboarding. Meanwhile, advances in data analytics have enabled social media platforms to serve as real-time public health monitoring tools for disease tracking and crisis management [17]. For instance, the WHO's EARS project [15,24] leverages social listening and AI to track public sentiment, generating rapid insights into potential health trends and public concerns that can inform health interventions through predictive analytics.

3 Proposed Framework

As shown in Fig. 2, our proposed framework consists of four layers designed to systematically collect, process, analyze, and visualize data. These layers, Data Ingestion, Data Connection, Business Model, and Visualization, function in an integrated manner to transform raw data into structured outputs that support public health monitoring and decision-making. Each layer plays a distinct role in the overall system and ensures a seamless flow of information from data acquisition to final representation.

The ingestion layer defines the data sources feeding our dashboard. Guided by pre-defined Key Performance Indicators (KPIs) and aligned with project

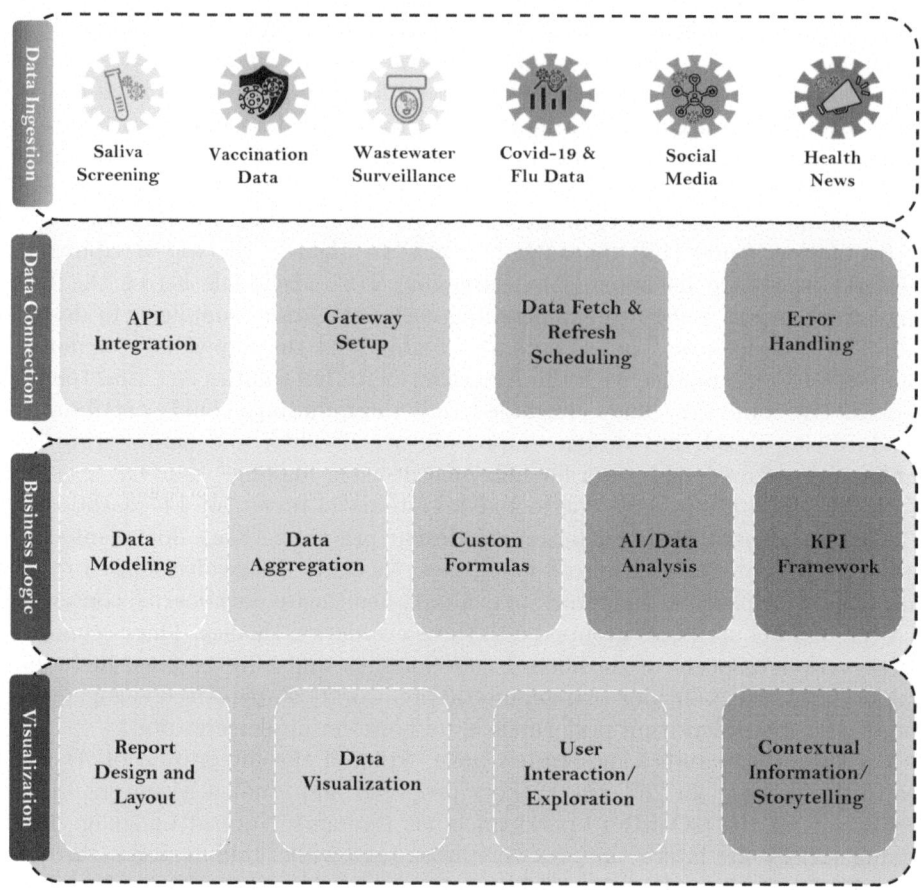

Fig. 2. Multi-modal data-driven dashboard framework.

objectives, this layer integrates diverse data streams to provide a multi-faceted perspective on viral activity and community health. Specifically, the framework incorporates data on individual and community-level viral presence, traditional epidemiological indicators, vaccination data, social media insights, and related health news.

Initially and during the pandemic, one key source of local infection data was received from the University of Windsor COVID Screening Platform, which is accessed via the REDCap API [11]. Participants in this initiative self-administered saliva specimen collection at a designated site at the University of Windsor [14]. The samples were analyzed using low-cost, high-throughput qPCR screening, a method capable of detecting SARS-CoV-2 in both symptomatic and asymptomatic individuals. Anonymized results were securely recorded on the REDCap platform and made available via the API.

Complementing individual screening, data from the Wastewater Surveillance initiative provides a community-level indicator of viral activity and serves as a potential early warning system for outbreaks. Wastewater-based epidemiology (WBE) was established at the University of Windsor to monitor SARS-CoV-2 RNA in wastewater samples collected three times per week starting in February 2021 [9]. For this project, we used aggregated data from multiple treatment plants throughout Windsor-Essex. Following the pandemic, the monitoring program was expanded to include influenza and RSV. The results of these analyses were recorded on REDCap and shared via the secure API.

In addition to these surveillance data sources, the framework incorporates established epidemiological indicators, including case counts, hospitalizations, and mortality rates, sourced from Ontario Public Health at both local and provincial levels. This allows for the assessment of disease burden and trends within specific geographic areas and across the province. Furthermore, comprehensive COVID vaccination data and associated metadata are integrated to analyze vaccination uptake and its correlation with other epidemiological indicators. This was one of the critical factors in assessing public health during the pandemic.

To further enhance situational awareness, the framework integrates real-time social media insights and related health news. Public social media posts are analyzed to identify emerging health concerns and shifts in public sentiment, offering valuable context to complement epidemiological data. Additionally, health-related news articles, sourced from platforms such as Google News, provide timely updates on evolving health threats, policy changes, and global disease trends. By incorporating these data streams, we aim to enhance real-time monitoring capabilities and enable a more proactive and informed response to public health challenges.

The data connection layer is responsible for securely collecting data from predefined sources and integrating it into the system through an automated pipeline. This process is facilitated through API interactions, which enable the retrieval of data from external sources while ensuring structured and standardized access to the data sources. API interactions are performed using RESTful endpoints and the data returned from the API is parsed and standardized according to the predefined schema (e.g., CSV, JSON).

A key element of this layer is the gateway setup, which enables secure data transmission between on-premises data sources and cloud-based services. This mechanism ensures that reports and dashboards are regularly updated with the latest available data. To maintain synchronization with real-time data, a fetching and refresh schedule governs the frequency of data retrieval. In fact, daily data fetches are scheduled, with the process occurring at a specific times and if the system detects changes in the dataset, it updates the reports accordingly.

To ensure data integrity, an error handling system is implemented to identify failed API calls, missing values, and inconsistencies. Automated validation procedures are employed to identify and rectify anomalies, ensuring that only accurate and complete data are processed in subsequent analytical sections.

Following data acquisition and integration, the business logic layer performs data structuring and processing to generate actionable analytical outputs. Initially, raw datasets are transformed into structured formats, such as relational tables or multidimensional arrays, optimized for querying, aggregation, and advanced computations. This structured data facilitates efficient storage and access for subsequent analytical tasks.

To facilitate comparative assessments, the system applies data aggregation techniques that consolidate information across various dimensions, such as temporal intervals, geographic regions, and demographic categories, through methods like grouping, summarization, and pivoting. These techniques enable the extraction of high-level trends while preserving the necessary granularity for detailed analysis at more specific levels (e.g., by geographic zone or time period). The aggregation process typically involves the application of functions like sum, mean, and weighted averages according to the characteristics of the data and the analytical objectives.

The framework also supports the definition and application of custom formulas to calculate key epidemiological or public health metrics. For instance, formulas for positivity rates and vaccination coverage are implemented using statistical methodologies, such as logistic regression or other relevant techniques, to derive accurate estimates based on evolving data.

The AI/Data Analysis component enhances analytical capabilities by integrating sentiment analysis and predictive modeling. Using NLP techniques, it extracts public sentiment from social media sources, identifying key concerns and shifts in community perception regarding health trends. Additionally, it leverages historical and real-time epidemiological data to model infection trajectories and assess potential outbreak risks, applying statistical and machine learning techniques to improve forecasting accuracy.

To ensure consistency in monitoring and evaluation, a KPI framework is integrated, systematically defining a set of metrics that track infection trends, intervention effectiveness, and regional health disparities. Our KPIs include metrics such as incidence rates, hospitalization trends, mortality rates, outbreak frequencies, and vaccination coverage, among others. These indicators provide a structured approach for evaluating the impact of public health interventions and guiding decision-making.

The final layer is the visualization layer, which presents the analytical outputs in a structured, interactive format. The report design and layout component ensures that insights are displayed in a clear and accessible manner, with an emphasis on logical organization and readability. A range of data visualization techniques are employed, including time-series graphs to track infection trends, geospatial mapping to illustrate regional variations, and comparative charts for assessing differences across population groups. The system also includes user interaction and exploration capabilities, allowing users to apply filters, zoom into specific data points, and dynamically explore case trajectories.

To enhance interpretability, the visualization layer integrates contextual information, such as explanatory annotations and comparative benchmarks. This ensures that data is not only displayed but also framed within a meaningful analytical context.

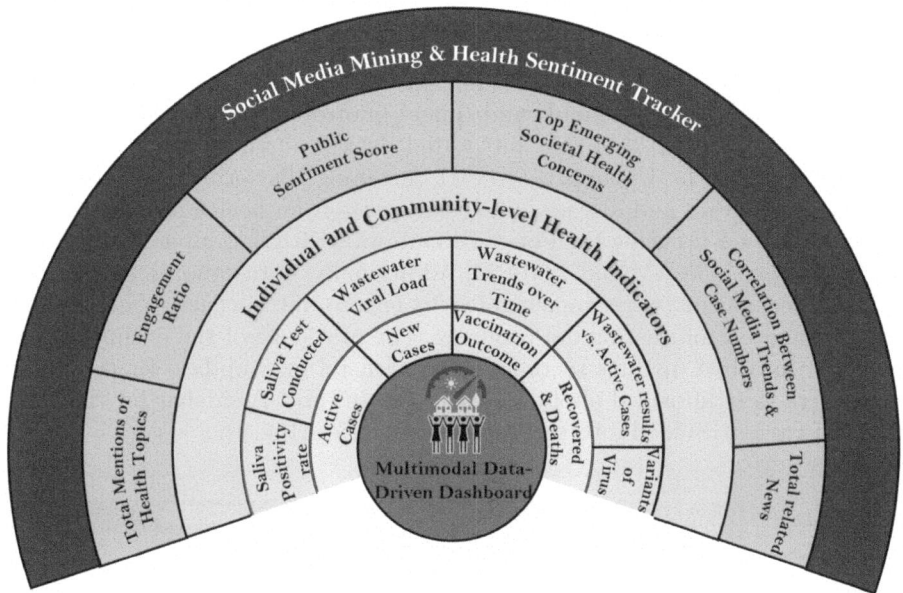

Fig. 3. Key metrics of our health surveillance and community sentiment dashboard.

4   Implementation

We have implemented a Power BI dashboard based on the proposed framework in two distinct phases. The first phase was developed and launched during the pandemic, with a focus on monitoring local wastewater surveillance and saliva-based COVID-19 screening. The main objective of the project was to provide real-time insights into viral activity within the community. Building upon lessons learned during the pandemic, the second phase of development focuses on enhanced readiness and preparedness. The resulting dashboard expands capabilities to address a broader range of health and societal challenges. Our key metrics and objectives are shown in Fig. 3.

For both phases of the project, we formed a team to analyze existing health dashboards with similar objectives and identify key metrics essential for public decision-making and addressing community concerns. To inform this process, we reviewed over 30 different dashboards from around the world and explored publicly available official data sources. Each source was technically assessed to ensure accessibility and integration with our framework.

Usability, accessibility, and meaningful data representation were the focal points of our design process. The color scheme was chosen to reflect the University of Windsor's branding and the regional context of the dashboard.

4.1 Phase 1: COVID-19 Surveillance Dashboard

In response to the COVID-19 pandemic, this dashboard was developed to provide the community with reliable and timely information. Its primary aim was to create an interactive tool that integrated data from the local saliva screening initiative (i.e., the UWindsor COVID Screening Platform), the wastewater surveillance program and disease outbreak reports from health authorities. The dashboard was set up using the Power BI Gateway, with data updates scheduled twice per day at 8:30 AM and 2:00 PM. Additionally, data validation and error-handling mechanisms were implemented to ensure data accuracy and provide alerts in the event of missing data sources. The first page of the dashboard was structured into five distinct sections, each with its own update timestamp to ensure users were informed about the last update time. A sidebar provided key numerical values, divided into three main categories (Fig. 4):

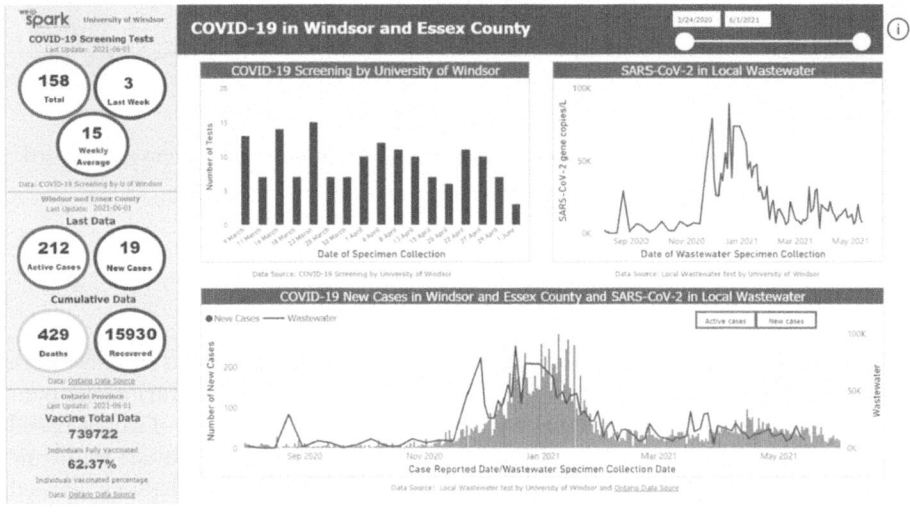

Fig. 4. The landing page of the COVID-19 surveillance dashboard (phase one).

COVID-19 Saliva Screening Tests: This category included a range of metrics, such as the total number of tests conducted, the tests performed within the past week, the weekly average, and the count of positive results. These figures were designed to provide an overall snapshot of testing activity, while also allowing for easy comparison of trends on a week-over-week basis.

Windsor-Essex County Epidemiological Data: This category displayed key COVID-19 metrics, including active cases, new cases, deaths, and recoveries in the region, based on data obtained from Ontario health officials. It provided both a broad overview and a detailed analysis, allowing users to track the evolving epidemiological situation in Windsor and Essex County.

Ontario Vaccination Rates: This category highlighted vaccination statistics, including the percentage of individuals fully vaccinated and those who have received at least one dose.

In the main content area of the dashboard, we used line and stacked charts to visualize trends over time. It displayed data from the Saliva Screening Initiative and the SARS-CoV-2 presence in wastewater samples to help visitors identify potential outbreaks. A slicer filter was also integrated to allow users to explore and analyze historical data.

It also featured a mixed chart to visualize the volume of the virus found in wastewater alongside either confirmed active cases or new cases. This chart was designed to highlight the potential relationship between the virus detected in wastewater and the confirmed COVID-19 cases identified through lab tests. By displaying both data sets together, the chart aimed to demonstrate how the presence of the virus in wastewater can serve as an early indicator of increased community transmission.

On the second page, we retained the sidebar and slicer filter, while shifting the focus to tracking different SARS-CoV-2 variants detected in wastewater and monitoring outbreak trends within the region. This page was designed to provide insights into the spread of emerging variants in the community and their contribution to evolving outbreak patterns.

4.2   Phase 2: Multi-modal Dashboard

After the pandemic, and based on the lessons learned and feedback gathered through surveys and direct interactions, we formed a group to reimagine the role of dashboards in the post-pandemic era. Our primary goal was to create a tool that could provide informative, comprehensive insights for both the public and researchers. While we retained certain functionalities, we made strategic changes to the data sources. Some data sources were removed either because they were no longer available or because they were not as relevant to the daily needs of the community. Our focus shifted towards preparedness and readiness indicators, which could help forecast and respond to future health challenges.

For instance, we introduced social media data and Google News as new sources of real-time information to capture public sentiment and emerging trends. As part of this transition, we discontinued data inputs related to the Saliva Screening Initiative and vaccination rates, as these were no longer a primary concern for daily public health activities. Additionally, we included influenza and RSV as new data sources to ensure the system could track a broader range of health risks, complementing our new focus on general health preparedness and monitoring. Similar to the previous version, this dashboard integrates and manages data using Power BI and is set to update daily.

To enhance the dashboard's usability and expand its analytical capabilities, we studied various health and wastewater monitoring dashboards in Canada and the USA. As a result, we have developed a new version containing a few main sections, which are Summary, Trends, and Social Media. The sections are organized into tabs within the dashboard to optimize the user navigation experience.

We have also refined the color scheme while maintaining the previous yellow and blue tones. The new design featured more vibrant hues to enhance readability and engagement. Additionally, the page length has been extended to accommodate more data, and an information window was added to clarify data sources and last update timestamps.

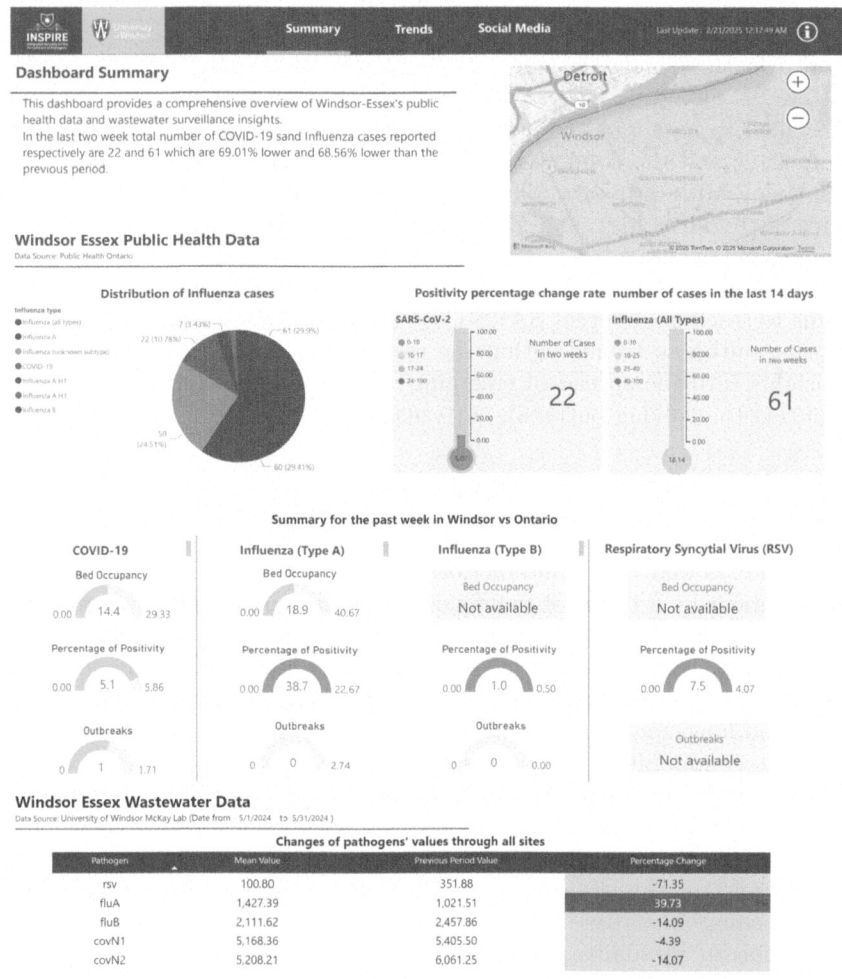

Fig. 5. The sample landing page of the multi-modal dashboard (phase two).

Since we are working with multiple datasets, we established appropriate relationships between them using Power BI's Data Model. To ensure consistency in time-based analysis, we created a Date Table and linked all datasets to it. This approach enables unified filters and time slicers, allowing seamless cross-filtering and consistent time-based comparisons across reports.

To enhance data processing and analysis, we leveraged Measures in Data Analysis Expressions (DAX) to perform dynamic calculations and transformations. Measures allow us to generate KPIs, aggregations, and other computed values efficiently without modifying the original dataset. For example, to calculate the latest number(in the last two weeks) of influenza cases in the city, we used the following command.

```
CALCULATE([total cases], DATESINPERIOD( 'Cases_Data'[Week end date], MAX(
    'Cases_Data'[Week end date]), -14, DAY ))
```

For predictive analytics in Power BI, we implemented time series forecasting using line charts [18]. This technique analyzes historical trends to predict future values with exponential smoothing (ETS) to identify patterns and seasonality. To ensure forecasts remain responsive to current trends, this approach weights recent data more heavily than older data in the model. The model was trained on all available historical data and generated forecasts for up to three months with a 95% confidence level.

Additionally, we utilized Copilot AI within Power BI to generate summaries and insights [18]. It analyzes the related dataset and provides natural language summaries of key findings, trends, and anomalies. This AI-driven feature enhances data storytelling by offering insightful interpretations. It enables us to provide an updated summary of the data efficiently.

As partially shown in Fig. 5, the landing page of our dashboard provides an overall summary of key health indicators. It features a small map of the city, with a color-coded status representing the current health situation, where red indicates heightened alert and green signaling a normal situation.

A stacked bar chart visualizes pathogen levels in wastewater, while another chart highlights the distribution of influenza subtypes, with color-coded indicators displaying the percentage of positive cases. To facilitate comparative analysis, we use gauge charts to compare bed occupancy, positivity rates, and outbreak statistics between the province and the city. In the case of unavailable data, alert messages are displayed on the dashboard. Additionally, a summary of the percentage changes in pathogen levels across various locations is provided, with color-coded indicators highlighting potential outbreaks. We have also incorporated a live news feed from Google News RSS Feed that lists recent articles on respiratory disease.

To provide more details about our data indicators, we have created a separate set of visualizations and analyses, which are available under the "Trends" tab. This section serves two key audiences: the general public and health experts. In that section, we present a detailed comparison and analysis of case counts, outbreaks, and lab data from both our region and the province. This helps identify variations and track the evolution of changes in disease dynamics using our historical data. The second set of analyses, intended for experts, focuses on wastewater data. Accessible only to authorized users, this section details pathogen trends across multiple monitoring sites, including site-specific and aggregate overviews. Cross-border comparisons are also presented, currently using publicly available data from Michigan, with the potential for expansion to other regions. A couple of sample diagrams are provided in Fig. 6.

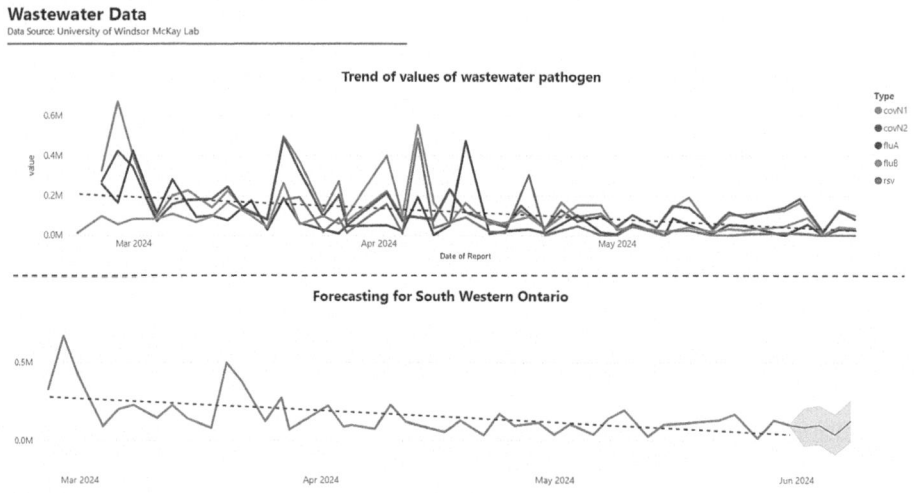

Fig. 6. Illustrative examples of wastewater data visualization: (a) Time series plot of historical pathogen trends; (b) showing short-term forecasted pathogen level.

To better understand community needs and concerns, we have integrated a social media sentiment analysis section. Currently, we aggregate data from the AskPolly AI platform, which collects information from various social media sources [3]. We have designed different scenarios to analyze public sentiment on key topics related to the pandemic, including employment, social behavior, technology adoption, the healthcare system, public health policies, community support, and symptoms.

Additionally, we included the overall engagement data as reflected in the Google Trends dashboard, providing a summary of public interest in health-related topics. This helps contextualize how public engagement fluctuates over time in response to health events and trends.

One of our indicators here is the overall sentiment of public opinion, ranging from very negative to very positive, over time. The data are processed and visualized using a ribbon chart, where color gradients distinguish between sentiment categories. We also capture and highlight the sentiment values for each of our key topics (e.g., Community Support, Education, Public Health, etc.) using a bar chart with filtering options for detailed exploration. Additionally, the system captures engagement levels associated with these topics and displays them in a time-series chart to monitor fluctuations over time. For example, Fig. 7 represents a sample chart from our dashboard, illustrating social media engagement visualization related to the pandemic.

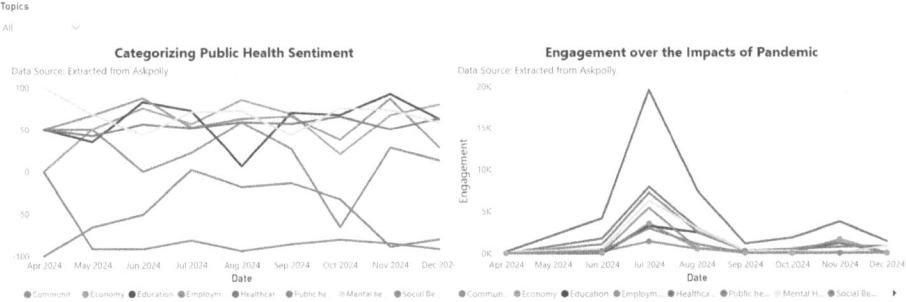

Fig. 7. Sample charts of pandemic-related social media engagement.

5   Evaluation

To evaluate the effectiveness and usability of the dashboard in its first phase, we gathered feedback from University of Windsor campus community members about their experiences. The goal was to evaluate its impact, identify strengths and weaknesses, and explore areas for improvement. As part of this effort, participants were asked the following questions:

– Have you visited the University of Windsor COVID-19 dashboard?
– Do you find it effective? (If not, please explain what makes it ineffective.)
– Do you find it user-friendly? (If not, please explain what makes it difficult to use.)
– What additional information would you like to see on the dashboard?
– How often do you anticipate using this tool to monitor the COVID-19 situation? (Response options: Daily, Weekly, Monthly, Once in a while)

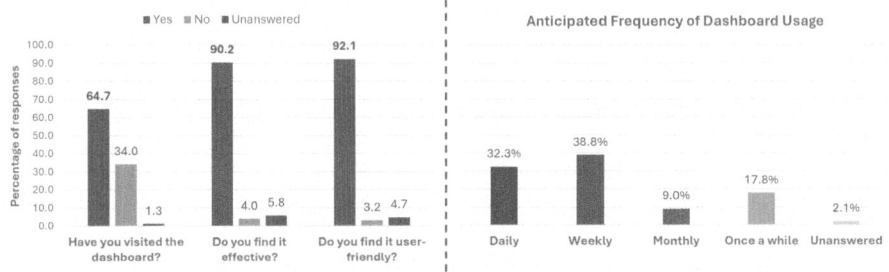

Fig. 8. Summary of survey responses (N = 1642).

From a total of 1856 survey participants, we obtained 1642 complete responses for analysis. 214 responses were incomplete and excluded.

One of the key goals of this initiative was to create a widely used and effective information resource for our community. As shown in Fig. 8, the survey results indicate significant progress toward this goal: 1,063 respondents ($\approx$65%) reported having visited the dashboard. Among them, 90% found the dashboard effective, and 92% found it user-friendly. Meanwhile, the majority of people indicated they plan to visit the tool daily or weekly. These data suggest that the dashboard is meeting the informational needs of most visitors in terms of both functionality and ease of use.

We also analyzed comments from participants who did not perceive the tool as effective. We have reviewed the comments and categorized them into 7 distinct subjects. A summary of their main concerns is provided in Fig. 9.

Around 15% of the participants had indicated their concerns regarding accessibility and awareness. They noted that the dashboard could benefit from increased visibility and regular updates. They suggested enhancing communication through email announcements, social media posts, or even integrating the dashboard's information into existing community channels in order to make it easier for users to stay informed. Clarity and usability, along with content quality, were other areas of concern, each representing nearly 18% of the feedback. Participants recommended simplifying the language used and clarifying terms and processes. Some of the comments also emphasized the need for more precise data on vaccination status and highlighted the importance of addressing the evolving understanding of COVID-19 transmission.

Additionally, comments regarding Design/UI and the overall effectiveness of dashboards emerged as two key areas in the received feedback. Participants suggested a simpler design, easier navigation, and a more focused presentation of information to improve usability. The remaining comments were mainly centered on general opinions about the dashboard and suggestions for improvement, such as including more detailed data on positive cases and utilizing email or social media for greater reach of updates.

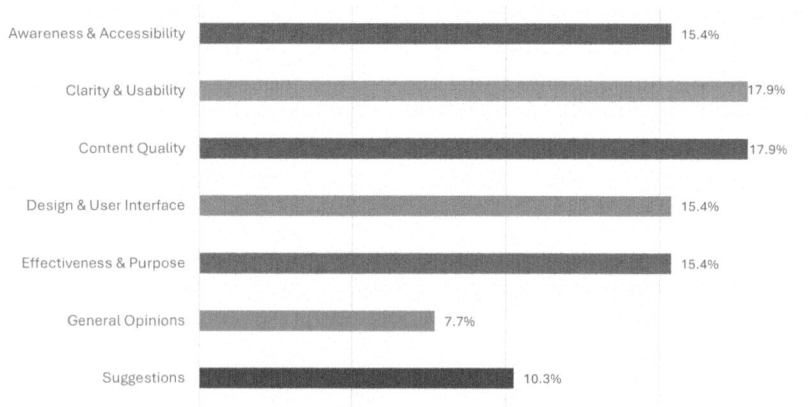

Fig. 9. Main user concerns regarding tool effectiveness and usability.

We have also reviewed and explored the suggestions and comments received in response to the fourth question. After data cleaning, 177 suggestions were analyzed and clustered into seven key themes, as shown in Fig. 10.

The majority of responses consisted of general comments, including feedback on satisfaction with the dashboard and suggestions related to pandemic prevention strategies. Another key theme of suggestions was to enhance epidemic tracking by providing more detailed data, such as more comparative charts, daily discharge rates, current hospitalizations (including ICU cases), recovered patient numbers, and global trends.

Participants also recommended adding vaccination indicators, such as vaccine type and patient vaccination status. Additionally, many suggested incorporating sections to clarify pandemic-related policies, guidelines, and educational resources to enhance public understanding.

The results show that many participants are interested in learning more about local and community health trends. They recommended adding new data representations, such as a breakdown of positive test cases by group and geotemporal data. Additionally, air quality, especially inside buildings, was highlighted as a key local data point. Suggestions also included improving the dashboard's design and navigation for better user experience, along with incorporating community engagement and mental health support resources.

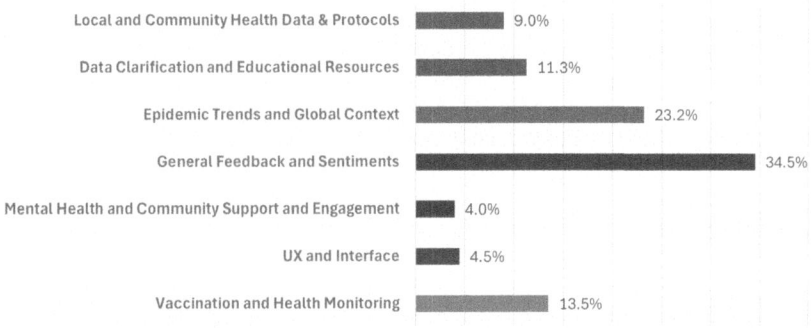

Fig. 10. Insights from participants organized into seven key themes.

5.1 Discussion

The development of this public health surveillance dashboard represents a significant step towards a more proactive and data-driven approach to community health management. By consolidating diverse data sources, we have laid the foundation for a system capable of not only monitoring current health trends but also predicting future outbreaks and potential resource shortages. The initial evaluation confirms the dashboard's effectiveness in raising public awareness, indicating a positive direction for its future development and potential impact. There are, however, challenges and opportunities that require further discussion.

One of the major challenges we encountered and anticipate will persist is our dependence on external data sources, including government health agencies and official news outlets. These sources are often outside of our control, and changes in their API access, data formats, or reporting policies can disrupt data flow and impact the dashboard's functionality. Therefore, a flexible and adaptive design, along with proactive maintenance, is needed to ensure the system can adapt to evolving external data sources and maintain long-term reliability.

Data heterogeneity and integration were other key challenges in the development of this project. Specifically, data heterogeneity such as variations in data formats, reporting units, and time stamps (e.g., reported date vs. test date) required extensive data cleaning, standardization, and harmonization. To address this, we employed a range of techniques, including data mapping, format conversion, and timestamp alignment. Careful attention was paid to preserving data integrity throughout this process.

From another perspective, while social media can provide valuable insights into public sentiment and emotions, its interpretation must be approached with caution. Social media data is often noisy, biased, and prone to misinformation. Thus, further investigation are needed to filter out noise, identify misinformation, and address biases, ensuring the analysis remains accurate and reliable.

Looking ahead, we envision this project as a platform for community engagement, empowering individuals to access information, understand community concerns, and actively participate in public health initiatives. Although still in its early stages, further development is needed to fully realize this potential. Whereas the current evaluation has focused mainly on public awareness and effectiveness, future work will prioritize research on the dashboard's impact on public health decision-making and health outcomes. Although the worst of the COVID-19 pandemic has passed, history and biology suggest future health challenges from emerging pathogens will likely disrupt society again. Critically evaluating tools like dashboards for data gathering, analysis, and communication provides a foundation for preparing society and government for future public health challenges, including pandemics.

6   Conclusion

This paper proposes a framework and holistic approach for developing a more comprehensive public health surveillance dashboard. It has the potential to integrate diverse data sources, including regional and national data, locally administered tests, wastewater surveillance, social media, and official news outlets.

We believe this scalable and reliable system can be used not only during crises but also as a tool to predict and mitigate the potential negative impacts of major health issues within communities. Evaluation of the dashboard's first phase confirms its effectiveness in raising public awareness.

Our future research will explore the tool's impact on a wider range of health outcomes. We also plan to integrate additional data sources, including supply chain data, and conduct further analysis to uncover correlations that can support data-driven decision-making.

Acknowledgement. This work was supported by the WE-SPARK Health Institute at the University of Windsor, Canadian Institutes of Health Research (#177776), the New Frontiers in Research Fund (#NFRFR-2022-00416), and the INSPIRE project, which is funded through the Canada Biomedical Research Fund Stage 2 (#CBRF2-2023-00008).

References

1. Ahmed, W., et al.: Sars-cov-2 rna monitoring in wastewater as a potential early warning system for COVID-19 transmission in the community: a temporal case study. Sci. Total Environ. **761**, 144216 (2021)
2. Ansari, B.: Evaluating the usability of public health data dashboards as information sources for professionals and the public: findings from a case study with domain experts. Health Inf. Libr. J. (2024)
3. AskPolly AI: AI-Powered Social Media Listening and Analysis (2024). https://www.askpolly.ai/. Accessed 03 Feb 2024
4. Bach, B., et al.: Dashboard design patterns. IEEE Trans. Vis. Comput. Graph. **29**(1), 342–352 (2022)
5. Corchis-Scott, R., et al.: Actionable wastewater surveillance: application to a university residence hall during the transition between delta and omicron resurgences of COVID-19. Front. Public Health **11**, 1139423 (2023)
6. D'Aoust, P.M., et al.: Catching a resurgence: increase in sars-cov-2 viral rna identified in wastewater 48 h before COVID-19 clinical tests and 96 h before hospitalizations. Sci. Total Environ. **770**, 145319 (2021)
7. Dong, E., Du, H., Gardner, L.: An interactive web-based dashboard to track COVID-19 in real time. Lancet Infect. Dis. **20**(5), 533–534 (2020)
8. Dong, E., et al.: The johns hopkins university center for systems science and engineering covid-19 dashboard: data collection process, challenges faced, and lessons learned. Lancet Infect. Dis. **22**(12), e370–e376 (2022)
9. D'Aoust, P.M., et al.: Sars-cov-2 viral titer measurements in ontario, canada wastewaters throughout the covid-19 pandemic. Scientific Data **11**(1), 656 (2024)
10. Google: Google Trends. https://trends.google.com/trends/. Accessed 31 Jan 2025
11. Harris, P.A., et al.: The redcap consortium: building an international community of software platform partners. J. Biomed. Inform. **95**, 103208 (2019)
12. Hill, D., Dunham, C., Larsen, D.A., Collins, M.: Operationalizing an open-source dashboard for communicating results of wastewater-based surveillance. MethodsX **11**, 102299 (2023)
13. Kaur, S., Kaul, P., Zadeh, P.M.: Study the impact of COVID-19 on twitter users with respect to social isolation. In: 2020 Seventh International Conference on Social Networks Analysis, Management and Security (SNAMS), pp. 1–6. IEEE (2020)
14. LaBute, B., et al.: Evaluating and optimizing acid-ph and direct lysis rna extraction for sars-cov-2 rna detection in whole saliva. Sci. Rep. **14**(1), 7017 (2024)
15. Mahajan, A., et al.: Advances in real-time social listening for an adaptive public health response: WHO's EARS platform. Eur. J. Public Health **31**(Supplement_3), ckab164–501 (2021)
16. Malkani, M., et al.: Rank ordered design attributes for health care dashboards including artificial intelligence: usability study. Online J. Public Health Inform. **16**(1), e58277 (2024)
17. Martín-Corral, D., García-Herranz, M., Cebrian, M., Moro, E.: Social media sensors as early signals of influenza outbreaks at scale. EPJ Data Sci. **13**(1), 43 (2024)
18. Microsoft: Power BI Documentation. https://docs.microsoft.com/en-us/power-bi/. Accessed 31 Jan 2025
19. Naughton, C.C., Holm, R.H., Lin, N.J., James, B.P., Smith, T.: Online dashboards for sars-cov-2 wastewater data need standard best practices: an environmental health communication agenda. J. Water Health **21**(5), 615–624 (2023)

20. Naughton, C.C., et al.: Show us the data: global COVID-19 wastewater monitoring efforts, equity, and gaps. FEMS Microbes **4**, xtad003 (2023)
21. Peccia, J., et al.: Measurement of sars-cov-2 rna in wastewater tracks community infection dynamics. Nat. Biotechnol. **38**(10), 1164–1167 (2020)
22. Preim, B., Lawonn, K.: A survey of visual analytics for public health. In: Computer Graphics Forum, vol. 39, pp. 543–580. Wiley Online Library (2020)
23. Public Health Ontario: Ontario respiratory virus tool. Public Health Ontario (2025). https://www.publichealthontario.ca/en/Data-and-Analysis/Infectious-Disease/Respiratory-Virus-Tool. Accessed 31 Jan 2025
24. Purnat, T.D., Wilson, H., Nguyen, T., Briand, S.: Ears– a WHO platform for ai-supported real-time online social listening of COVID-19 conversations. In: Public Health and Informatics, pp. 1009–1010. IOS Press (2021)
25. Rafi, A.M., Rana, S., Kaur, R., Wu, Q.J., Zadeh, P.M.: Understanding global reaction to the recent outbreaks of COVID-19: insights from instagram data analysis. In: 2020 IEEE International Conference on Systems, Man, and Cybernetics (SMC), pp. 3413–3420. IEEE (2020)
26. Ruoff, M., Gnewuch, U., Maedche, A., Scheibehenne, B.: Designing conversational dashboards for effective use in crisis response. J. Assoc. Inf. Syst. **24**(6), 1500 (2023)
27. Salaris, S., Ocagli, H., Casamento, A., Lanera, C., Gregori, D.: Foodborne event detection based on social media mining: a systematic review. Foods **14**(2), 239 (2025)
28. Sarikaya, A., Correll, M., Bartram, L., Tory, M., Fisher, D.: What do we talk about when we talk about dashboards? IEEE Trans. Vis. Comput. Graph. **25**(1), 682–692 (2018)
29. Schulze, A., Brand, F., Geppert, J., Böl, G.F.: Digital dashboards visualizing public health data: a systematic review. Front. Public Health **11**, 999958 (2023)
30. World Health Organization: WHO COVID-19 dashboard. https://covid19.who.int/. Accessed 31 Jan 2025
31. Zhuang, M., Concannon, D., Manley, E.: A framework for evaluating dashboards in healthcare. IEEE Trans. Vis. Comput. Graph. **28**(4), 1715–1731 (2022)

The Digital Product Supply Chain: Demonstrating Digital Sovereignty in Real-World Scenarios

Razvan Hrestic[(✉)] [ID], Manfred Hofmeier[ID], and Ulrike Lechner[ID]

University of the Bundeswehr Munich, Neubiberg, Germany
{Razvan.Hrestic,Manfred.Hofmeier,Ulrike.Lechner}@unibw.de

Abstract. Digital sovereignty is a concept usually found on the political agenda and one increasingly present in research. But can it also be seen as a desirable and quantifiable dimension in supply chain management for products and services? And if so, which factors can influence this dimension? The concepts in this paper address this topic and related issues including risks to digital sovereignty, decision support enhanced by distributed ledger technology in procurement and supply chain management for cyber-physical systems. The concepts are explored by means a scenario of a vacuum cleaner robot and a proof-of-concept software tool for integrating the concepts into procurement and management of the supply chain. An evaluation of design and implications for decision making concludes the article.

Keywords: Digital sovereignty · Digital product supply chain · Distributed ledger technology · Scenario · Supply chain management

1 Introduction and Motivation

When looking at Digital Sovereignty (DS) there are multiple meanings in the literature and several layers of abstraction. Digital sovereignty is an important goal on the political agenda and potentially also on the agenda of individuals or organizations. How to achieve digital sovereignty? How to build the products and services to make individuals, organizations, and nation states digitally sovereign? This article is part of a larger research initiative LIONS that aims to make the concept of digital sovereignty tangible and that develops models and concepts to raise the level of digital sovereignty.

This article takes the organizational perspective of product owners, products, their manufacturers and supply chains. A customer wants to use a product and service in a sovereign way: the functionality of the product and service should be available, and there should be neither surprises nor hassles in terms of unwanted functionality or conflicts with regulations. Procurement, that is, the buy decision, determines the level of sovereignty a customer enjoys and this level of sovereignty also depends on the sovereignty of the supplier and the supply chain. Our research interest is to make the concept of Digital Sovereignty

S. Zielinski et al. (Eds.): I4CS 2025, CCIS 2513, pp. 251–268, 2025.
https://doi.org/10.1007/978-3-031-94263-1_15

tangible as a topic of procurement, risk management, and supply chain management and to demonstrate with a proof of concept the management of digital sovereignty at this level.

The research questions address the management of digital sovereignty at the level of a supply chain:

RQ1: How can digital sovereignty be quantified and measured?

RQ2: What factors influence digital sovereignty at the organizational level?

RQ3: What are specific risks in the digital supply chain and how to mitigate them?

RQ4: How can the use of blockchain technology contribute to digital sovereignty goals and which other trade-offs does it offer?

RQ5: Which choices of strategy are possible when considering their effects on digital sovereignty?

We employ a Design Science research approach and design a scenario and a demonstrator as proof-of-concept tool to explore digital sovereignty for customers, products, services, manufacturers, and the supply chain. Our approach has been crafted in a dialogue between a research team and a systems house that brings together research on blockchain as an instrument to increase visibility in the supply chain and contract management to ensure security and resilience of the supply chain. Our research is centered on the digital supply chain of Internet-of-Things (IoT) devices as bundles of software, hardware, tangible products and services. This involves perspectives on digital risks and supporting procurement in the effort to manage or raise the level of digital sovereignty.

This article is organized as follows. We present an analysis of related work (Sect. 2) as well as research design (Sect. 3). We have two results sections with the description of the scenario (Sect. 4) and the presentation of the demonstrator (Sect. 5). We follow this with design knowledge (Sect. 6) and conclude the paper with a discussion and an outlook.

2   Related Work

As stated above, what is considered digital sovereignty is dependent on the perspective – such as state (or supranational institution), organization or the individual [7].

Much existing research focuses on the narrower concepts of "data sovereignty" (partly motivated by the concepts of Industry 4.0 [16] and 5.0) and "technological sovereignty" [17] and [22], promoting a high degree of autarky. However, other concepts are emerging which emphasize the complex systemic nature of technological sovereignty, such as the competence-based approach in [19].

Regarding individuals, digital sovereignty is partly understood as competencies (such as in [18]) and partly as informational self-determination in the sense of data protection. Globalization and economies of scale drive organizations to outsource, often to opaque multinational providers [24,28]. This can undermine an organization's control over data and privacy.

Other authors also address the question of technological dependence (especially for key technologies) as a possible impediment to states being able to act independently in a sovereign manner and identify a gap regarding DS quantification [12]. This gap is confirmed by [10]. Dependency issues also apply to work on and with open source projects [14].

Digital supply chains are increasingly featured as research objects. Some authors focus on supply chain design to specific objectives (e.g., performance, resilience in dynamic ecosystems and competitiveness in [21]). Other aspects of increasing supply chain resilience to geopolitical risks have also been considered [8].

For organizations, the discussion is focused on technological standards and freedom of choice (technological sovereignty) for software, tools, cloud providers. This is illustrated by projects such as the Sovereign Cloud Stack [3]). A special case is Data Sovereignty [1].

Regarding the use of Blockchain Technology(BT), in Supply Chain Management, this research area has been growing since 2016 as remarked by [9] and [25]. Blockchain applicability has been seen to extend outside of existing finance/cryptocurrency use cases. In Supply chain Management, use cases such as increased traceability across supply chains and information transparency among supply chain participants and consumers have been investigating. Increasingly there more specialized use cases from agricultural [5,13,27] to automotive [4,26] supply chains and indeed cybersecurity [20]. First approaches also address the hardware/electronics supply chains specifically issues such as asset and tracking of manufacturing chain [6], traceability of specific IC properties [30] or software patching and provenance tracing for the energy sector [23]. Our approach uses private permissioned BT to not only address the information sharing problem about cyber-physical products and their components, but also address trust establishment in such supply chains through reputation information and custom metric models to increase digital sovereignty.

Only technological sovereignty in the sense of autarky is not enough - Other analyses [15] highlight different factors e.g. encouraging freedom of choice through sovereign supply chains for digital products, rethinking partnerships and the ability of an organization of thinking strategically about actions in the digital sphere.

3   Research Design

The research described in this paper follows the Design Science method according to Alan Hevner [11]. Two artifacts are the results of the design research endeavor: a scenario and a software demonstrator. The scenario is centered on a robot vacuum cleaner and its supply chain. The management of the level of sovereignty is captured in a demonstrator, and this demonstrator takes the perspective of procurement. This demonstrator allows to capture and analyze risks to digital sovereignty and changes in the level of digital sovereignty. It allows an organization and its risk management or supply chain management to manage the level of digital sovereignty. Goal of the research is to make the abstract notion of digital sovereignty tangible in terms of quantification of the level of sovereignty, management of the level of sovereignty, and to demonstrate that digital sovereignty can be increased in a way that is compatible with many organizational processes. The focus was on IoT devices, that is, bundles of software, hardware, product, and services.

This research was carried out in cooperation between the research teams and a small IT software company specialized in products and services with high level of security risks as part of a larger research project. The researchers brought their ideas of a blockchain for risk management of IT-security related risks. The system house brought their ideas on contract and service management for management of resilience and sovereignty in case of an incident. The cooperation was done in the form of a fixed price project, and this format encouraged researchers and practitioners to reduce the ideas to a relevant and demonstrable kernel. This cooperation was done in the form of an agile design and development process to discuss, refine, and implement ideas. The scenario was created first, then the demonstrator as the second artifact. Research was carried out mainly in the years 2023 and 2024. Researchers and practitioners communicated their findings to communities of practitioners and the research community.

4   Results - The Robot Vacuum Cleaner Scenario

Making Digital Sovereignty manageable describes our research interest. The first artifact designed in our research approach is a scenario of an IoT product, its supply chain, and its risks. IoT devices and cyber-physical systems in general are part of everyday life of consumers and of critical infrastructures alike. They are exposed to security risks and need to be available.

The research on the scenario is guided by the scenario technique [29] and was done in the years 2022 and 2023. We also follow the research by Fries et al. [7] on the notions of digital sovereignty.

In the research process of designing our scenario, we had initial expectations: the scenario should be relatable to the general public, should have a reasonable size, and it should have hardware, software, physical components, and a service interface. The vacuum cleaner robot is the result of a three-step process where we identified a set of initial scenarios, prioritized and eliminated two of them, remaining as the winning scenario. One of the reasons for selecting it was that household IoT devices and in particular vacuum cleaning robots have had critical press coverage regarding security and privacy issues.

4.1   Scenario Description: The Vacuum Cleaning Robot and Its Supply Chain

This vacuum cleaner robot is a fairly simple IoT product, and in our scenario, we assume a small digital supply chain and ecosystem (cf. Fig. 2). We introduce a fictional organization (HHH) as the robot producer. This organization develops parts of the software in-house, but specifies and outsources the construction of

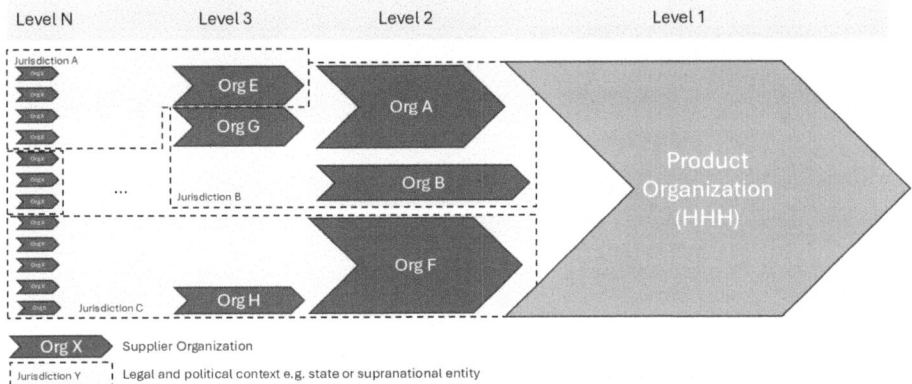

Fig. 1. Supply chain composition within the layered model with multiple layers and suppliers shows not only supply chain depth but also the organizational relation to the legislative domain.

hardware and other pieces of software for its product. The robot has different hardware components and software components, each of the components having a different supplier. For software in our scenario we further differentiate between off-the-shelf components (including open-source) and custom software projects.

For the real-world problems described in the SSR42 scenario we define two objectives of a solution:

1. Show a useful practical method to empower organizations (procurement, supply chain management, and other roles) to implement and track measures for more digital sovereignty.
2. Show the real-world impact of Distributed Ledger Technology (DLT) usage in supply chain scenarios with high information transaction costs / coordination costs w.r.t. digital sovereignty and supply chain resilience

The scenario itself was designed to represent a general version of a Digital Product Supply Chain. It would thus apply according to our working definition to all software or cyber-physical systems with several components in transnational and complex supply chains.

4.2 Considerations on Digital Sovereignty

Vacuum cleaner robots were chosen for their relatively clear value proposition. They are purchased to clean the rooms with minimal human intervention over the upcoming years. Spare parts for wearing parts, IT updates - everything that is necessary to maintain the functionality - has to be available such that the core functionality of cleaning the floor remains available. Digital sovereignty in this context means having the functionality available and, moreover, that there are no privacy or security concerns with this robot.

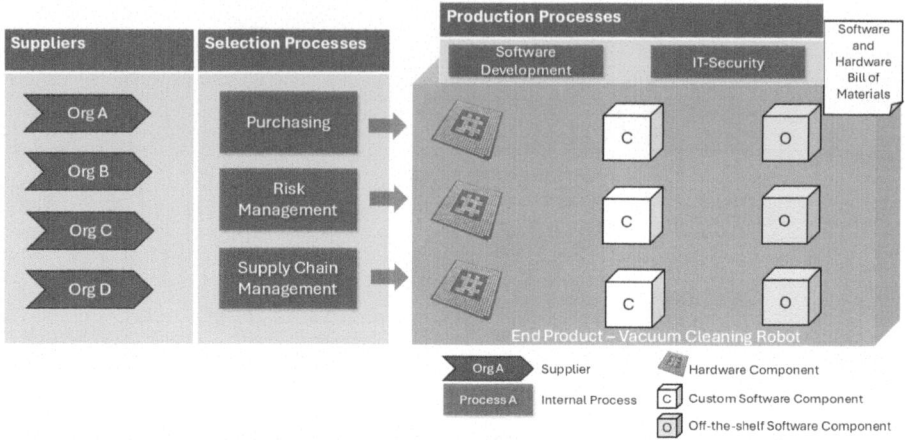

Fig. 2. The vacuum cleaner robot scenario illustrates the product supply chain, including suppliers, processes, components, and actors. It serves as a starting point for modeling the application domain of the demonstrator.

In general, even for a simple IoT product over a couple of years, many security and optimization updates may occur, and wearing parts will be exchanged. At the point of purchase, the customer wants to be sure that the company producing the robot ensures that it can do the necessary work to meet compliance, security, and functionality requirements.

We identify risks to the sovereignty of the product, the manufacturer, and the supply chain:

Risk 1: Key components in the supply chain depend on few or even single suppliers.

Risk 2: Key components in the supply chain are not well understood or checked by the producing organization because of missing capabilities or personnel (e.g., skills, specific qualifications, etc.).

Risk 3: Gathering data e.g. the full bill of materials for software and hardware components or security findings is difficult or time-consuming to gather across systems and thus not used as a decision basis for the product itself.

Risk 4: When data is available, it is usually difficult to anonymize and prepare for usage for the entire supply chain or even outside it. Information e.g. about a compromised component is thus not conveyed in a timely manner. Also nobody else outside the data producing organization may use the data to e.g. gain and share insights that might help improve the product.

Risk 5: When suppliers do not get data on e.g. how they rank in good security practices compared to others, they do not have as much incentive to improve their practice. This can lead to overall less secure products of lower quality.

Risk 6: Global supply chains are affected by global crises and geopolitical tensions. Should a component become unavailable because of e.g. technology embargo, bankruptcy, sabotage etc. and there is no alternative, the entire product availability is at stake.

Generally, we can state that being resilient to the above type of risks correlates with increased digital sovereignty. This is why in the remaining of this paper we discuss digital sovereignty and implicitly mean resilience as well. IT security weaknesses and supply chain risks decrease digital sovereignty. In the next section we present the demonstrator for the management of digital sovereignty.

Digital sovereignty also means that IT security and privacy risks can be mitigated throughout the planned lifetime of the device. We identify a set of security and privacy requirements:

- The robot must not violate privacy by recording voice or images and transferring them online to other parties,
- The robot must not accept a command to harm furniture, pets, or people.
- End customers and organizations want to be able to apply updates or develop functionality further (e.g., improved algorithms for navigation, scheduling and orientation, IT-security updates) or to integrate with smart home appliances. It must be possible to update the night sleep time or schedule a recharge when electricity is cheapest.
- End customers and organizations want to apply updates to keep the robot and its services compliant with regulation.

4.3   Examples of Threats for DPSCs

To make the threats more clear, we illustrate them with an example. We assume that a security vulnerability for a software library is exploited e.g. at level 3 in the supply chain (refer to Fig. 1). What happens then? This depends on the security detection capabilities of either a) the suppliers and integrators at higher levels or b) those belonging to the product organization. With low detection capabilities and tools, the exploit may be discovered too late, thus delaying remediation. This means in the worst case, that customers use a vulnerable version of the product for a longer time. Also, the quality of information chains regarding security-related incidents determines how (and if) such information is passed along up to other supply chain members. However, if there was a system which stores and disseminates such security-critical events in a secure way e.g., even without disclosing the identity of the exploited party, then this would mean low dependency on ad-hoc communication procedures. Basing the design on decentralized systems such as distributed ledgers further increases reliability. We used this premise in designing the SSR42 demonstrator, which we describe in the next section.

5   Results - The SSR42 Demonstrator

A team of researchers and a system house designed and developed the demonstrator, working according to agile principles.

After a series of initial meetings, we documented design principles and functionality in two documents. The first document describes the stakeholder roles (cf. Table 1) (e.g., supply chain manager), implementation goals, and the general roadmap while the second document delineates requirements in the form of user stories and technological decisions such as which development stack to use. A general overview of the architecture is given below in Fig. 3. In a productive scenario this system would integrate with existing infrastructure and tools so that no unnecessary duplication of functionality is created.

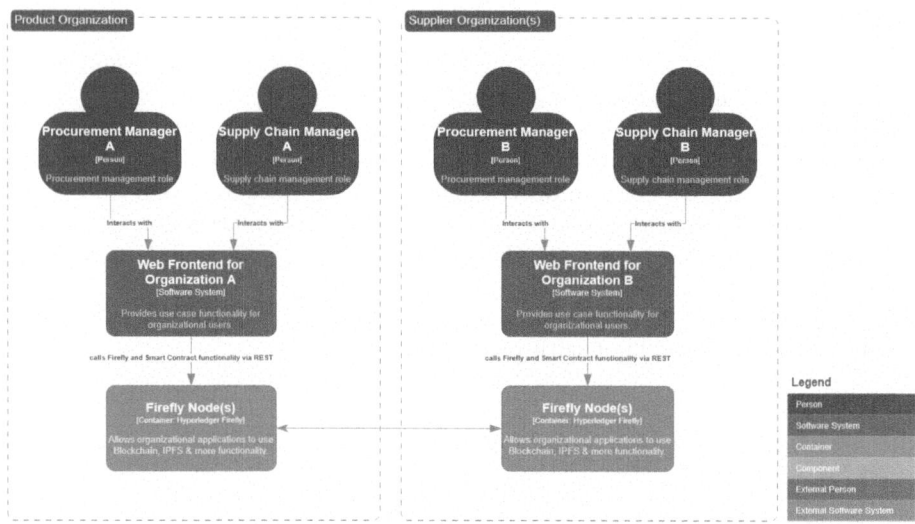

Fig. 3. C4 System Context Diagram of the Demonstrator shows the two of many possible participants in the proposed consortial structure.

5.1   Main Functionality

The following key functions were implemented: supplier and component risk analysis, smart contracts for supply chain components, integration of oracles (open vulnerability databases), geopolitical risk assessment. Figure 4 presents the main screen with various functionalities.

Subsequently, we describe the various functions and how they relate to the presented perspective on the DPSC and digital sovereignty.

Table 1. Description of organizational roles who derive benefits from functions implemented in this demonstrator

Role Name	Role Description
Procurement	Is responsible for finding and purchasing appropriate suppliers and components for the SSR42. Includes other subfunctions such as contract management
Supply Chain Management(SCM)	Is responsible for assessing suppliers and components at the supply chain level so that the entire product creation process corresponds to organizational goals
Risk Management	Is responsible for assessing and managing organizational risks
Interested Actors	Have an interest in using the data generated in the market for one or more supply chains. These could be e.g., consulting firms, governmental and non-governmental organizations etc.

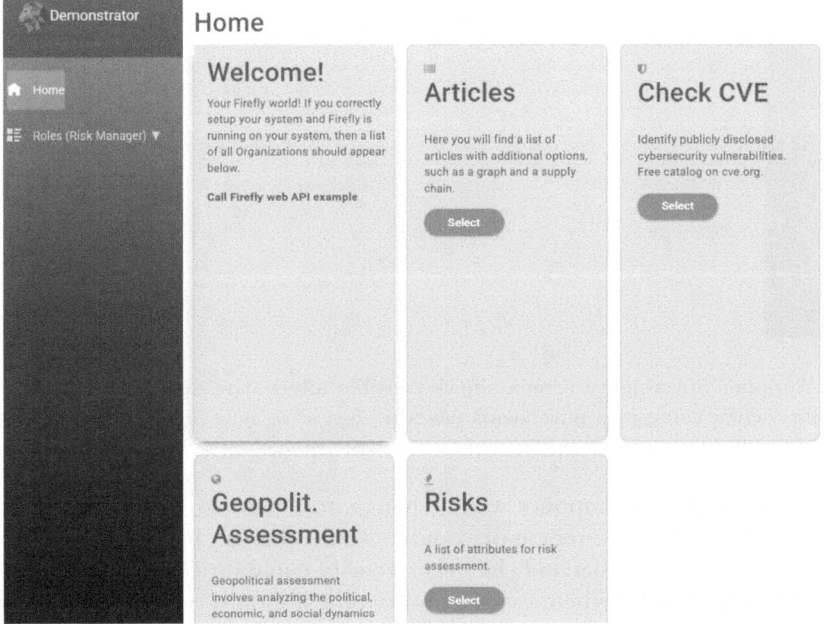

Fig. 4. Main screen from a Supply Chain Management perspective to navigate between major functionality blocks.

5.2   Supplier Sovereignty and Component Risk Analysis

The sovereignty of a producing organization is influenced by the sovereignty of the suppliers i.e., how much freedom do they have in the economic and digital product space within a specific supply chain. A limited number of potential suppliers would increase dependency and reduce the level of digital sovereignty. For this part of the functionality, we first collect data on risks 1, 2, 3 and 6. Secondly, using this functionality procurement can compare suppliers, allowing it to make an informed choice in the procurement process and select suppliers not only by using established criteria (price, certifications), but also according to the desired level of sovereignty (see Fig. 5).

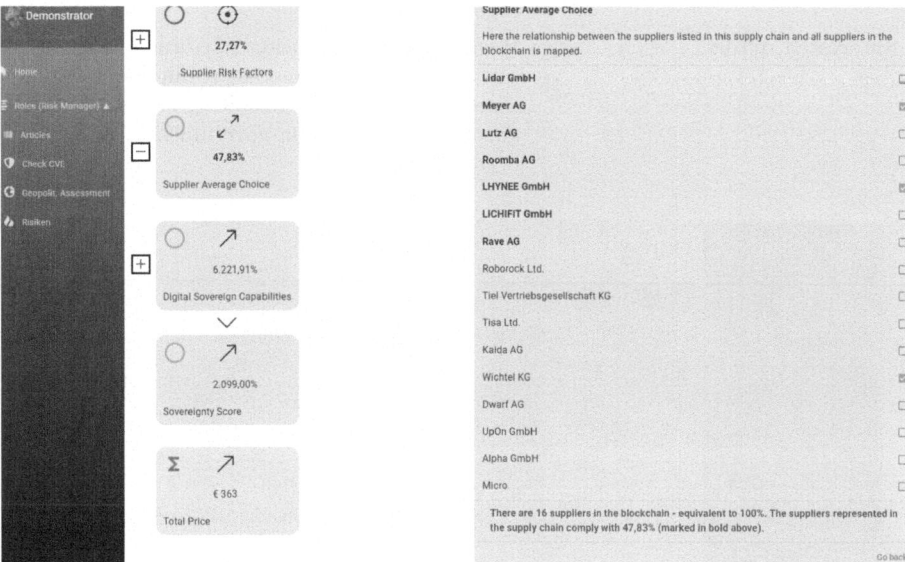

Fig. 5. Supplier Sovereignty screen shows possible alternative suppliers and relative availability when using own purchasing criteria.

The sovereignty of a supplier would change, for example, when the geopolitical risk assessment of the region or country would change. It would also change with the cybersecurity risks and the cybersecurity capabilities of the supplier. In the case of our scenario, when a vulnerability of a standard component procured from a supplier is exploited, the manufacturers need to get this information and a security patch. The sovereignty of the manufacturer depends on the ability of the supplier in cybersecurity and incident response and this is captured in this module.

A supplier with the necessary IT-security capabilities and a proper information flow contributes to sovereignty, lack of capabilities or a lag in information flows decreases sovereignty.

Regarding component risk analysis, this function allows scenario roles to view suppliers and software/hardware component metrics available in the system (see Fig. 6). The Purchaser, Risk Manager or Supply Chain Manager are able to specifically see metrics related to digital sovereignty which they can further evaluate and integrate in their decision-making processes.

Further details regarding the metrics can be found in Subsect. 5.6.

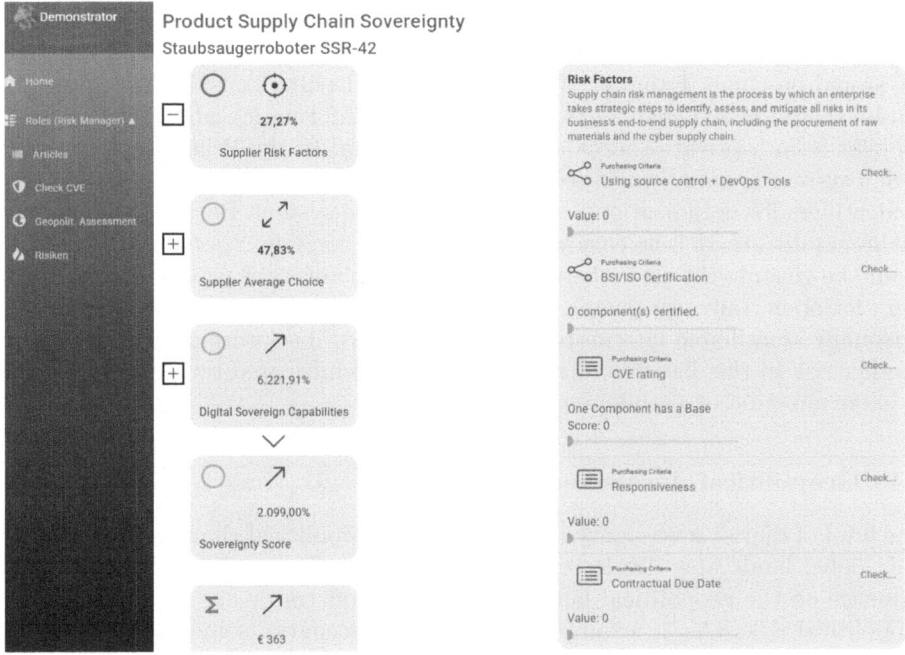

Fig. 6. Supply Chain Sovereignty Dashboard for SSR42 robot displays the risk score component of the sovereignty index. Several criteria such as certifications, timely contract fulfillment and more can be considered.

5.3 Smart Contracts for Supply Chain Components

The contracts run as Chaincode on a private-permissioned blockchain platform, Hyperledger Fabric, and integrate with the Web3 framework Hyperledger Firefly. Their purpose is to gather and store metrics for different systems and interactions in an immutable distributed ledger shared by DPSC participants. Our data model focuses on the *Component* object as a main part of the software supply chain. Thus it is possible to store metadata related to components such as name, version, security ratings etc. Technically the Firefly nodes and underlying systems (Fabric, IPFS) are running as containers inside an OpenShift bare-metal cluster which we designed for large scale blockchain infrastructure operations in a research context. Using the Firefly architecture, it is possible to change the underlying blockchain technology with Ethereum implementations already available.

This functionality relates to risks 4 and 5. Through blockchain technology it is possible to share metric data which can be used by all participants in the supply chain as a basis for their assessments. Participants can choose what they share up to a certain governance threshold - a minimal set of metrics must be shared as tuples $\langle id, value \rangle$, also possible as time-series. Metric data can be shared with all organizations using the same channel, with specific organizations (via private data/gossip protocol) or be made private. As a good practice only data identifiers are stored on-chain. Example: Penetration Test Results for SSR42 components can be shared in the channel to all participants, information about the Camera supplier from a private source are stored off-chain. In the When implementing such a system in a real-world scenario it is important to decide upon which type of identifiers for organizations can be stored in the system. Because blockchains are immutable, there is no easy way to reverse this decision. Special consideration should be given to the case where suppliers are freelancers or private contributors (e.g., for open source projects). In that case company data may be identical to personally identifiable information (PII). Unwanted disclosure of PII introduces another risk in the distributed system and can be mitigated by techniques such as anonymization or pseudonymization.

5.4   Geopolitical Assessment

The level of digital sovereignty is influenced by geopolitical changes in the political, global landscape. Trade restrictions, tariffs or free trade agreements have influence on the geopolitical landscape. The demonstrator has one view on the geopolitical risks. As an example in our SSR42 scenario, some critical components (camera, sensors etc.) may be produced in a land where political turmoil causes a regime change and the producer is forced to introduce spyware in their products. The Geopolitical assessment screen is depicted in Fig. 7

The purpose of this module is the ability to combine risk assessment with the results of the geographical analysis as seen in Fig. 7. Changes in digital sovereignty can be triggered by changes in political alliances and relations, changes in nation capabilities to mitigate cyber-risks, in changes of leadership or economic factors in countries. Climate change and risks to supply chains also affect this score.

These data can be part of the internal risk assessment for the organization, a score (probability) can be assigned to each combination of land and risk type. This view can be updated as result of a regular or periodic risk analysis of the organization or a specialized information broker or triggered by sudden changes.

The geopolitical assessment data go into the digital sovereignty index of the organization.

Land	Bemerkung	Bewertung1	Auswahl Risiken		Bewertung2	Score	Add	
Land R	CR	Cyber-Attacken mit gravi	Cyber-Attacken mit gravierenden Auswirkungen	⌄		Very High	Sele	x
Land G	CG		none	⌄		Low	Sele	x
Land H	CH		none	⌄		Low	Sele	x
Land S	CS		none	⌄		Low	Sele	x
Land D	CD		none	⌄		Low	Sele	x
Land T	CT		none	⌄		Low	Sele	x
Land U	CU		none	⌄		Low	Sele	x
Land C	CC		none	⌄		Low	Sele	x
Land A	CA		none	⌄		Low	Sele	x
Land B	CB		none	⌄		Low	Sele	x
Land F	CF		none	⌄		Low	Sele	x

Fig. 7. Geopolitical assessment screen allows risk adjustment and weighing per supplier with respect to geography.

5.5   Integration of Oracles

The demonstrator includes functionality to query external data sources, e.g., the MITRE Corporation Common Vulnerabilities and Exposures (CVE) web service for information regarding software vulnerabilities. This service was embedded into the demonstrator as seen in Fig. 8. Linking existing and trusted data sources is an important requirement for building reputation information. However, the level of integrity of such systems must be ensured. Data coming from sources outside a blockchain is not cryptographically related to existing data (off-chain), so that the integration of any such system is an instance of the oracle problem [2]. Smart contracts need information from the real world to be able to feasibly function and provide trusted computing functionality.

Fig. 8. CVE assessment screen shows the possibility of integrating external data sources and generation of Software-Bill-of-Materials for use in other systems.

5.6   Metrics and Computation of the Digital Sovereignty Index

For demonstrator purposes we use rather basic metrics to illustrate potential
use. We chose to focus on a) the number and severity of software vulnerabilities,
b) a subjective rating metric (e.g., responsiveness) and c) industry-relevant certifications (e.g. BSI/ISO certification). The customizable metric model however,
allows for introduction of further metrics. It is important to note that chang-
ing/adding metrics to be stored on-chain needs to be agreed upon among the
participants. Hyperledger Fabric supports the ability of participants to install
and use varying versions of specific smart contracts. Alternatively the new metric can be deployed as a separate smart contract. If different supply chains are
represented in separate channels (i.e., the have separate ledgers per channel)
then it is possible to deploy metric sets at that level.

To illustrate how the index works, we compare two fictional supply chains:
that of the SSR42 robot and the competing model RRS51. The general formula
for calculating the Sovereignty Score is:

$$\frac{\text{Supplier Risk Factor} \times \text{Supplier Average Choice} \times \text{Digital Sovereign Capabilities}}{3}$$

The data model allows organizations to specify critical components, i.e., components which need to be available without which the product cannot be built.
We compute for each critical component the

$$\frac{\text{number of available suppliers per component}}{\text{total number of suppliers}}$$

Thus, if RRS51 has more available suppliers for critical components, it will get
a higher component score for Supplier Average Choice. SSR42 has few suppliers
in geopolitically unstable regions, which results in a higher Supplier Risk Factor score and thus to a higher overall score value. Finally, the SSR42 product
team has invested heavily in automated vulnerability detection tooling and hired
penetration testers for their critical components. These measures also have individual ratings in the systems and add up to a higher score for Digital Sovereign
Capabilities. Thus, SSR42 receives an overall higher score than RRS51. The balance of individual factors can be fine-tuned by adjusting weight values in the
system to align with management and procurement requirements.

6   Design Knowledge

Considering the levels of complexity attached to managing multi-level digital
product supply chains, focusing on key enabling aspects has been a particular
challenge. The processes of scenario design, followed by demonstrator design and
implementation allowed us to iteratively refine and reflect upon these challenges.

From the design process we extract the following findings:

- Digital sovereignty can be managed, tracked and implemented in purchasing
  decisions.

- Systems which support decision making should integrate with existing systems, concepts and frameworks to avoid high switching costs.
- Our data model has practical implications. A low amount of changes in current practice result in awareness of the topic.
- Focusing on a single supply chain role, in this case the purchasing perspective, allows for clearer modeling of threats such as supply chain attacks and interruptions.
- Future views on supply chain through the lens of digital sovereignty.
- The roles of capabilities - e.g., detect, remedy and prevent software and hardware security issues - is as important as that of risk management.
- Affordances for organizations to assess how good they are in detecting and remedying risk.
- Decentralized decision support information through distributed ledger with higher digital sovereignty concerning control over shared information.
- Governance constraints are necessary, requiring preliminary coordination among participants - How much can each participant decide and which information is required at a minimum?
- Increasing sovereignty of individual participants also increases supply chain sovereignty. Participants also gain the ability to share supply chain data in a more secure and controlled manner.
- Using techniques described here allows individual participants to consider future decisions in the supply chain context which could also benefit multiple other members (positive feedback loop).

In real-world business contexts, the topics of contract management and risk management are central to supply chain operations. These aspects were included in our scenario and adapted to focus on DPSC specific risks. Furthermore we used a blockchain system design that allows integration with existing systems through a Web3 framework as an overlay. From a product supply chain perspective, it also made sense to embed a non-prescriptive reputation system which allows for individual weighting but is based on facts stored in an immutable ledger.

With respect to research question 1 we demonstrate quantification from an intuitive perspective of risk management. We also offer a possible answer to the question of how concrete risks (1–6) influence the level of digital sovereignty. Research question 2 addresses factors influencing digital sovereignty, and we address aspects such as security tools, certifications, etc. embedded in a category within the digital sovereignty index. Regarding specific risks mentioned in research question 3, we address these at the purchasing decision point in time. We provide appropriate information to avoid risks, e.g. of geopolitical nature - where are critical components sourced? Each information type can be represented as part of the index. To answer research question 4, we implemented smart contracts for quantification and analysis, as well as critical data dissemination, e.g., vulnerability information. As an example, the Software/Hardware Bill of Materials (SBOM/HBOM) can thus be represented and linked to specific vulnerabilities per component as one of many possible measures. Finally, our visualization and decision support in the form of a flexible metric system allows for more grounded strategic choice and thus answers research question 5.

As we strive for a balance between accurate representation of real-world issues and a useful mode, not all aspects could be considered. We explicitly took another digital sovereignty perspective than autarky. Due to the focus on the single organization, our group strongly emphasizes risk management. We believe this to be only a partial aspect of modern DPSCs which require intensive coordination and collaboration. We also excluded other levels of digital sovereignty such as the individual level, with minor exceptions such as awareness aspects. Regarding the digital sovereignty score we can say that the initial version allows an even weighting of the three score factors. This may not always be appropriate, and fine tuning of the score model is needed in real-world implementations.

7   Conclusions, Discussion and Limitations

Coordination in DPSC to increase digital sovereignty can only work when the systems and the concepts are in place due to complexity and thus the presence of multiple risk factors. Digital sovereignty is thus not only limited to a political context, but also plays an important role within modern supply chains. With the demonstrator, we show an approach on how these concepts could be implemented by using scenario modeling of important characteristics of the DPSC, metric models targeting digital sovereignty risks and involved roles specifically, decentralized decision support through appropriate technology and architecture and how to avoid introducing new dependencies which in turn could lower digital sovereignty.

In its current state our prototype has been so far only validated through presentations and demonstrations in scientific venues such as the LIONS symposium and talks with practitioners at security-related trade fairs such as the it-sa in Nuremberg. However, improvements are necessary and further validation in cooperation with organizations producing cyber-physical systems. One hindering factor could be a limited level of awareness with respect to digital sovereignty in organizations or an autarky-centered understanding. Also by necessary assumptions to base our scenario upon, we may have adopted models which do not align in all real-world scenarios or for other roles. By focusing on the organizational perspective we automatically take that focus away from the individual and national or supranational actors which have different priorities. However, we attempted to compensate for this focus shift by integrating concepts from the DS layered model.

As digital products (cyber-physical systems) become more complex, especially when combined with enhanced techniques such as Machine Learning, it is clear that their producing supply chains must also increase in complexity. This increases pressure on organizations in the context of digital transformation but also presents an opportunity to build or expand supply chains with digital sovereignty in mind.

Acknowledgments. This work originates from the LIONS research project. LIONS is funded by dtec.bw – Digitalization and Technology Research Center of the Bundeswehr, which we gratefully acknowledge. dtec.bw is funded by the European Union – NextGenerationEU.

We thank our research partner itWatch GmbH for the collaboration in the design of the supply chain demonstrator.

Disclosure of Interests. The authors have no competing interests to declare that are relevant to the content of this article.

References

1. AISBL, G.X.E.A.f.D., Cloud: Gaia-X Dataspaces (2025). https://gaia-x.eu/what-is-gaia-x/. Accessed 29 Mar 2025
2. Albizri, A., Appelbaum, D.: Trust but verify: the oracle paradox of blockchain smart contracts. J. Inf. Syst. **35**(2), 1–16 (2021)
3. Alliance, O.: Sovereign Cloud Stack Initiative (2024). https://scs.community/index.html. Accessed 27 Jan 2025
4. Alsadi, M., Arshad, J., Ali, J., Prince, A., Shishank, S.: Trucert: blockchain-based trustworthy product certification within autonomous automotive supply chains. Comput. Electr. Eng. **109**, 108738 (2023)
5. Chandan, A., John, M., Potdar, V.: Achieving UN SDGs in food supply chain using blockchain technology. Sustainability **15**(3), 2109 (2023)
6. Cui, P., Dixon, J., Guin, U., Dimase, D.: A blockchain-based framework for supply chain provenance. IEEE Access **7**, 157113–157125 (2019)
7. Fries, I., Greiner, M., Hofmeier, M., Hrestic, R., Lechner, U., Wendeborn, T.: Towards a layer model for digital sovereignty: a holistic approach. In: Hämmerli, B., Helmbrecht, U., Hommel, W., Kunczik, L., Pickl, S. (eds.) Critical Information Infrastructures Security (LNCS), pp. 119–139. Springer Nature Switzerland, Cham (2023)
8. Gervais, E., Sprecher, B., Nold, S., Brailovsky, P., Kleijn, R.: Tracing the propagation of disruptions in supply chain scenarios: a case study of photovoltaics diversification. Resour. Conserv. Recycl. **212**, 107948 (2025)
9. Gurtu, A., Johny, J.: Potential of blockchain technology in supply chain management: a literature review. Int. J. Phys. Distrib. Logist. Manag. **49**(9), 881–900 (2019)
10. Hellmeier, M., von Scherenberg, F.: A delimitation of data sovereignty from digital and technological sovereignty. In: Proceedings of the European Conference on Information Systems (ECIS) (2023)
11. Hevner, A.R., March, S.T., Park, J., Ram, S.: Design science in information systems research. MIS Q. 75–105 (2004)
12. Kaloudis, M.: Sovereignty in the digital age-how can we measure digital sovereignty and support the EU's action plan? New Glob. Stud. **16**(3), 275–299 (2022)
13. Kamilaris, A., Fonts, A., Prenafeta-Boldύ, F.X.: The rise of blockchain technology in agriculture and food supply chains. Trends Food Sci. Technol. **91**, 640–652 (2019)
14. Klare, M., Lechner, U.: Digital sovereignty: affordances in open source projects. In: Papatheocharous, E., Farshidi, S., Jansen, S., Hyrynsalmi, S. (eds.) 15th International Conference on Software Business (ICSOB 2024). LNBIP, vol. 53, pp. 20–34. Springer, Cham (2025). https://doi.org/10.1007/978-3-031-85849-9_2
15. Klare, M., Verlande, L., Greiner, M., Lechner, U.: How blockchain and artificial intelligence influence digital sovereignty. In: European, Mediterranean, and Middle Eastern Conference on Information Systems, pp. 3–16. Springer (2022)

16. Lasi, H., Fettke, P., Kemper, H.-G., Feld, T., Hoffmann, M.: Industry 4.0. Bus. Inf. Syst. Eng. **6**(4), 239–242 (2014). https://doi.org/10.1007/s12599-014-0334-4
17. Lass, S., Bender, B.: Dedicated data sovereignty as enabler for platform-based business models. ESSN: 2701-6277 (2021)
18. Leipold, B., Haunschild, I.M.: Soziale Mediennutzung und digitales Sicherheitsverhalten bei Berufstätigen: Die Rolle motivationaler Variablen. In: Individuen in digitalen Arbeitswelten: Interdisziplinäre Perspektiven auf Individuum und Organisation, pp. 265–282. Springer (2024)
19. March, C., Schieferdecker, I.: Technological sovereignty as ability, not autarky. Int. Stud. Rev. **25**(2), viad012 (2023)
20. Mylrea, M., Gourisetti, S.N.G.: Blockchain for supply chain cybersecurity, optimization and compliance. In: Resilience Week (RWS), pp. 70–76. IEEE (2018)
21. Nuerk, J., Dařena, F.: Systems engineering methodology for digital supply chain business models. Syst. Eng. (2025)
22. Otto, B., Hompel, M.t., Wrobel, S.: International data spaces: reference architecture for the digitization of industries. Digit. Transform. 109–128 (2019)
23. Pan, B., Zhang, L., Li, C., Chen, L.: Supply chain management system's cybersecurity based on blockchain technology. Int. J. Sci. Adv. Technol. **11** (2023)
24. Posch, R.: Digital sovereignty and IT-security for a prosperous society. In: Informatics in the Future: Proceedings of the 11th European Computer Science Summit (ECSS 2015), pp. 77–86. Springer International Publishing, Cham (2017)
25. Queiroz, M.M., Telles, R., Bonilla, S.H.: Blockchain and supply chain management integration: a systematic review of the literature. Supply Chain Manag. Int. J. **25**(2), 241–254 (2020)
26. Reddy, K., Gunasekaran, A., Kalpana, P., Sreedharan, V.R., Kumar, S.A.: Developing a blockchain framework for the automotive supply chain: a systematic review. Comput. Ind. Eng. **157**, 107334 (2021)
27. Seidenfad, K., Hoiss, T., Lechner, U.: A blockchain to bridge business information systems and industrial automation environments in supply chains. In: Proceedings of Innovations for Community Services: 21st International Conference, I4CS 2021, Bamberg, Germany, 26–28 May 2021, pp. 22–40. Springer, Cham (2021)
28. Thieulin, B.: Towards a European digital sovereignty policy. Opin. Paris France Econ. Soc. Environ. Counc. **13** (2019)
29. Weidenhaupt, K., Pohl, K., et al.: Scenarios in system development: current practice. IEEE Softw. **15**(2), 34–45 (1998)
30. Xu, X., Rahman, F., Shakya, B., Vassilev, A., Forte, D., Tehranipoor, M.: Electronics supply chain integrity enabled by blockchain. ACM Trans. Des. Autom. Electron. Syst. (TODAES) **24**(3), 1–25 (2019)

Evolution of Affordable Surveillance Systems for Patients
With the Integration of Smart Health Sensors

Junaeid Ahmed, Marcel Großmann$^{(\boxtimes)}$ (iD), Udo R. Krieger, and Duy Thanh Le

Fakultät WIAI, Otto-Friedrich-Universität, An der Weberei 5,
96047 Bamberg, Germany
{marcel.grossmann,duy-thanh.le}@uni-bamberg.de

Abstract. Along with the rise of the Internet of Things, smart health sensors are transforming patient monitoring by facilitating continuous, economical surveillance. Our research dives into the creation of an economical patient monitoring system that integrates intelligent health sensors. Based on their data, real-time video streaming on cost-effective devices let the medical representative connect to the patient. Our objective is to improve patient oversight by utilizing intelligent sensors for vital sign monitoring, while facilitating continuous, real-time visual evaluation via WebRTC, so guaranteeing a dependable and user-friendly experience for healthcare professionals. We utilize essential supporting technologies to retrieve sensor data and enable low-latency WebRTC video transmission to be able that medical representatives can diagnose patients early. Furthermore, we focus on interoperability and scalability by utilizing container technology, while suggesting methods to enhance system efficiency and cost-effectiveness. All in all, we combine WebRTC-enabled video streaming with smart health sensors to enhance remote healthcare, minimize hospital visits, and improve patient outcomes in a cost-effective and accessible way.

Keywords: WebRTC · MQTT · Sensors · eHealth · Surveillance

1 Introduction

Technological breakthroughs have transformed conventional approaches, leading to significant changes in healthcare systems. These advancements have improved the efficiency, accessibility, and capacity for remote healthcare treatment and provide the foundation for immediate surveillance. Telemedicine has emerged as a crucial instrument for addressing the increasing need for customized and timely healthcare solutions. The rise of chronic illnesses, aging populations, and the need for emergency interventions underscore the importance of efficient and scalable systems that provide continuous monitoring and care. Despite the growing availability of telemedicine solutions, their adoption encounters significant challenges. Many modern solutions need significant costs, proprietary systems, and intricate implementation conditions, hence restricting their availability, especially in

S. Zielinski et al. (Eds.): I4CS 2025, CCIS 2513, pp. 269–286, 2025.
https://doi.org/10.1007/978-3-031-94263-1_16

resource-limited settings and among small healthcare practitioners. These issues highlight the urgent need for economical and adaptable solutions applied in various settings without compromising quality or security.

Real-Time Communication (RTC) revolutionizes contemporary healthcare systems, particularly in telemedicine and monitoring applications. The capacity to convey speech, video, and data with little delay is essential for efficient patient monitoring and prompt actions. Web Real-Time Communication (RTC) is a secure, open-source, low-latency framework for real-time communication that is rapidly becoming a fundamental technology. WebRTC improves security and responsiveness by including encryption in Peer-to-Peer (P2P) communication [20, 22, 25].

1.1 Related Work in the Healthcare Video Surveillance Realm

El Jaouhari et al. [12] present an enhanced healthcare architecture utilizing secure WebRTC/Web of Things (WoT) with access control. WebRTC facilitates multimedia communication through native APIs implemented in browsers, utilizing P2P connections. It also offers a real-time video and data exchange capability, making it suitable for applications necessitating live interaction and monitoring. This architecture improves security in real-time systems by incorporating mechanisms such as authentication, integrity, and data confidentiality. Implementing a Role-Based Access Control (RBAC) architecture guarantees that only authorized individuals can access critical resources. WebRTC's encryption protocols, such as Datagram Transport Layer Security (TLS) for signaling and secure Real-Time Transport Protocol (RTP) for media, provide security for sensitive data streams, ensuring confidentiality and resilience against interception. The proposed architecture highlights WebRTC's integration capabilities with other frameworks. Based on this, it displays the potential to enhance secure, scalable, and interoperable systems. Our goal of developing a real-time monitoring and surveillance system meets with the facilities provided by the WebRTC features.

Namee et al. [20] utilize WebSocket and WebRTC for video conferencing in telemedicine during the COVID-19 pandemic. The effectiveness of WebRTC for real-time video communication was highlighted during the COVID-19 pandemic, in situations where low latency and dependability were critical. This technology is essential for effective video transmission in remote consultations and real-time monitoring applications. WebRTC facilitates seamless video conferencing through P2P communication, reducing reliance on centralized infrastructures. Significant findings indicate efficient network utilization with WebRTC, facilitating real-time streaming despite limited bandwidth constraints. Nonetheless, WebRTC has problems, such as elevated memory consumption, necessitating optimization for multi-camera systems or continuous streaming services. The study emphasizes WebRTC's effectiveness in live monitoring and surveillance systems, where quick video transmission and real-time interaction are crucial. The context is dedicated telemedicine, with similar principles applicable to our camera-based surveillance systems, facilitating scalable and responsive frameworks for real-time monitoring.

"Mimic" by Crandall et al. [9] is an innovative implementation of WebRTC technology for live video streaming. Mimic illustrates how WebRTC facilitates continuous communication between devices via video by converting a smartphone into a webcam without requiring supplementary software installations. This feature offers a user-friendly and accessible alternative to conventional video streaming methods by employing the browser-based WebRTC API. The principles exhibited by Mimic, particularly employing WebRTC for device interoperability and real-time video streaming, align strongly with the requirements of camera-based surveillance systems. WebRTC improves flexibility by linking cameras to a monitoring system and simplifying system design. Scalable surveillance systems that prioritize resource efficiency and usability must be versatile.

Alshammari [6] presents a healthcare monitoring system utilizing the Message Queue Telemetry Transport (MQTT) protocol within the Internet of Things (IoT) for effective and prompt data transmission in a real-time monitoring system. MQTT guarantees minimal latency and dependable communication through the publisher-subscriber paradigm, rendering it appropriate for real-time applications. The system's principal objective is to guarantee flawless signal transmission, minimize latency, and secure data transfer between devices. Within the realm of IoT, MQTT is particularly advantageous for facilitating communication in resource-constrained contexts. Assessments of MQTT-based systems have revealed their resilience, indicating potential for scalability and interaction with alternative frameworks. The work presented below emphasizes patient monitoring; nonetheless, the principles of MQTT, including efficient data interchange and low-overhead communication, are directly applicable to video streaming and device synchronization in systems analogous to our proposed framework in this paper. This framework achieves improved real-time performance, a streamlined communication architecture, and reduced complexity by leveraging data exchanges between cameras and subscribers.

Deshmukh et al. [10] developed video conferencing via WebRTC. Their Media Engine oversees the capture, processing, and rendering of audio and video streams. It employs essential APIs, such as the Media Stream API and Audio/Video Processing APIs, to provide superior media transmission quality. This framework employs WebRTC for media streaming and data transmission. The P2P network connects endpoints and facilitates media stream transmission. It utilizes fundamental protocols such as Interactive Connection Establishment (ICE) for network traversal and sRTP to guarantee safe media delivery. The Signaling Protocol is essential for establishing and terminating connections, as well as for sending the metadata required for communication, including the Session Initiation Protocol (SIP) and bespoke protocols designed for certain applications. Our paper identifies WebRTC as a fundamental technology for the video streaming framework, utilizing its P2P networking and secure data exchange functionalities. Employing tailored protocols for signaling guarantees adaptability to the system's particular needs.

Thorat and Bhute [24] created "SquashCord", a video conferencing application based on WebRTC. Their project employs WebRTC, Node.js, and MQTT for providing a callable video streaming and conferencing solution. The integration of MQTT with WebRTC's robust API eliminates the necessity for additional plugins or proprietary software. This functionality guarantees smooth video and audio transmissions with little latency. This method ensures scalability and adaptability, assuring dependable real-time data delivery. WebRTC improves video transmission quality by enabling P2P connections, thus minimizing latency and overhead. Although Docker-assisted virtualization simplifies the deployment process, it enhances the security of communication protocols. Our system offers a comprehensive real-time video communication and monitoring solution applicable to various domains, including healthcare monitoring, conferencing, and surveillance, through the integration of these technologies.

Islam et al. [17] inspect dynamic service deployment in local IoT edge computing for the healthcare use case. Their research presented a nanoservice architecture to enhance resource allocation and service deployment on limited IoT devices. This system provides remote monitoring, with the Docker containerization deployment of the nanoservices improving the resources efficiently with auto-scaling and the ability to roll back changes. Although containerization resulted in a slight delay increase (1–1.5 s), the benefits of scalability and fault tolerance were considered worthwhile. This corresponds with our objective of utilizing containerized microservices for scalable and modular deployment. The study highlighted the necessity for systems that can operate under uncertain network conditions, guaranteeing the local continuity of essential services, a premise reflected in your utilization of MQTT for efficient and dependable communication among components. Notwithstanding these constraints, the findings of this study provide substantial insights into the advancement of modular, resource-efficient designs in healthcare applications.

1.2 Our Proposal for a Real-Time Surveillance System

Our paper presents a cost-efficient surveillance system that addresses several challenges through the application of modern deployment and communication technologies. Based on open-source containerized applications, the system utilizes, inter alia, the MQTT protocol and WebRTC to create a versatile architecture that enables efficient message transmission, real-time video collaboration, and swift deployment processes. This approach ensures that, especially in resource-limited environments, healthcare practitioners have an extensive and adaptable solution for real-time observation and engagement. The suggested healthcare support system, which is published under the Github repository `uniba-ktr/e-health-rtc` [2], employs advanced technology to enhance RTC and accessibility. It decreases expenses, enhances scalability, guarantees real-time engagement, and streamlines deployment. The system is intended for applications such as geriatric care, postoperative surveillance, and teleconsultations, and can be combined with IoT sensors and physiological data acquisition systems.

Our paper is organized as follows: First, we find out more about the applications that can be used in a healthcare environment in Sect. 2. Subsequently, we will provide a concise summary of the technological underpinnings that are discussed in Sect. 3. Here, we analyze a WebRTC framework that is built on Python, assess the effectiveness of the MQTT protocol for IoT connections, and illustrate the reasons why virtualization is extremely important in the healthcare information technology sector as well. On the basis of these foundations, we develop our system in Sect. 4, which is where we demonstrate our reference architecture. As part of this design, we highlight the interactions between microservices, which include the publish-subscribe paradigm being implemented within the context of real-time video communication. In particular, the interactions of the new mediator, the SyncMate Representational State Transfer (REST) API, are detailed, as well as the manner in which a client acquires the knowledge that corresponds to those interactions. When conducting the evaluation of Sect. 5, we make a comparison between existing frameworks and applications to our newly developed prototype. Finally, we conclude our work in Sect. 6, where we also illustrate which future steps can be realized.

2   Applications in Healthcare

RTC, particularly WebRTC, has revolutionized healthcare by enabling innovative applications that enhance patient care, remote collaboration, and medical education. These enhancements leverage WebRTC's capabilities to address challenges with accessibility, efficiency, and accuracy in various healthcare settings, such as:

- **Telemedicine Consultations**: WebRTC has been effectively employed in healthcare for remote consultations, diagnostics, and continuous monitoring. It facilitates the transmission of medical images, remote evaluations of old or handicapped patients, and hands-free communication for paramedics using devices like Google Glass. WebRTC-based solutions demonstrated adaptability and efficacy across many healthcare settings by enhancing RTC and data transfer, managing essential scenarios, and facilitating diverse monitoring applications, including tele-home and telecommuting exercise platforms [23].
- **Remote Patient Monitoring**: In the healthcare sector, the WoT/IoT enables clinicians to remotely monitor patients' medical devices, providing ongoing and up-to-date health information. WoT/IoT delivers real-time data, facilitating patient relationships and improving care for elderly or disabled patients. Moreover, as the elderly population expands, such technologies facilitate intervention and tailored treatment strategies [13].
- **Surgical Collaboration**: Kwabla et al. [18] present a cloud-based system for surgical simulations using haptic devices via WebRTC. The system operates on Google Cloud, enabling remote, high-fidelity simulations that are accessible through web browsers on inexpensive devices. It diminishes hardware expenses, addresses platform reliance, and facilitates remote oversight,

alleviating the responsibilities of attending surgeons and enhancing training for fellows and residents. The model prioritizes remote collaboration, fostering skill development and allowing developers to improve simulation realism without hardware constraints [18].

- **Healthcare Training**: RTC-Medical Representative (MR) [15] utilizes WebRTC in mixed reality settings, particularly with HoloLens 2^{TM}. This device provides natural interaction via gestures and eye-tracking, features a broad 52° field of view, and delivers 2K resolution for each eye. It facilitates accurate and intricate images, which are crucial for healthcare and industrial applications necessitating precision. Mixed reality experiences limited support and documentation for MR devices, a challenge that RTC-MR has mitigated with the incorporation of WebRTC. This diminishes the obstacles to entry for developers. It functions as a crucial resource for developing bespoke MR solutions with RTC, aiding in the resolution of issues commonly linked to the use of WebRTC in MR settings [15].

The integration of WebRTC into healthcare applications advances the business by enhancing patient outcomes, facilitating remote collaboration, and equipping healthcare personnel with sophisticated training tools.

3   Foundations for a Surveillance System

At this point, we would like to investigate already existing technologies, which will serve as the foundation for a surveillance system. First we show, how a Python-based framework facilitates IoT applications to communicate via WebRTC in Subsect. 3.1. A publish-subscribe model utilizing MQTT is employed for communication among all microservices, with an emphasis on transmission fundamentals in Subsect. 3.2. Consequently, a virtualization approach is essential for the provision of all our services, as seen in Subsect. 3.3.

3.1   A Python-Based WebRTC Library

The Python package "aiortc" [1] supports WebRTC and the ICE protocol, enabling developers to construct WebRTC-based apps in Python. It is lightweight, asynchronous, and versatile, rendering it optimal for Python-based systems. The library provides features including media management, data transmission, and cross-platform interaction, rendering it a vital resource for WebRTC-based applications. It enables the streaming, processing, and manipulation of audio and video data, facilitating RTC. It facilitates P2P data transmission, audio for customized signaling, metadata exchange, and application-specific protocols. Furthermore, aiortc is interoperable with WebRTC implementations across other programming languages, allowing for simple integration into various systems and providing cross-platform capabilities.

The healthcare monitoring system with WebRTC capabilities was essential for this paper because of its lightweight, asynchronous design, which guarantees efficient RTC and data integrity. The basic aspects cover two items:

- **Video Streaming**: The suggested architecture of Amezcua Aragon [7] employs adaptive streaming and WebRTC to deliver high-resolution video across various devices and networks, ensuring scalability, low latency, and flexibility, hence facilitating smooth streaming for different audiences and novel content distribution opportunities [7].
- **Video Surveillance**: Our former surveillance system [16] aimed to develop an IoT-enabled video surveillance system employing WebRTC. We evaluated video streaming on Single Board Computers (SBCs) to identify the ideal configurations for a standardized, scalable, and efficient framework. An effective design pattern ensures that the solution is efficient, browser-independent, and maintained, with outcomes assessed against predefined standards [16].

3.2   Message Queue Telemetry Transport for IoT Communications

MQTT is a lightweight messaging protocol intended for low-resource environments, such as IoT networks. A centralized broker can establish an indirect client connection via a publish-subscribe architecture. MQTT is an ideal choice for IoT applications in healthcare, where the continuous and efficient transmission of data is essential, particularly for the real-time transmission of critical signals such as blood pressure and heart rate, owing to its architecture [5,19].

MQTT is a publish-subscribe protocol engineered for efficient, scalable, and reliable communication among IoT systems. It employs a publish-subscribe model, enabling devices to communicate without direct connections. The broker functions as a mediator, facilitating reliable communication between publishers and subscribers. The modular architecture of MQTT enhances scalability and adaptability, while the preservation of session information guarantees seamless reconnection for devices with sporadic connectivity. This straightforward and resilient architecture facilitates scalable and adaptable IoT systems, especially in instances of intermittent connectivity.

MQTT provides three Quality of Service (QoS) levels for dependable message transmission: QoS 0 guarantees messages are delivered at most once, and is appropriate for non-essential updates; QoS 1 guarantees messages are sent at least once, suitable for standard health monitoring applications; and QoS 2 guarantees messages are delivered precisely once, eliminating duplicates and maintaining data integrity, and is crucial for patient information and emergency alerts.

MQTT is a vital technology in healthcare IoT systems, safeguarding patient data through the implementation of various security measures. Authentication, TLS encryption, and access control mechanisms safeguard sensitive data between clients and the broker. MQTT transforms healthcare applications by enabling dependable alarm systems, continuous data transmission, and immediate communication. Its lightweight form renders it optimal for IoT-based healthcare systems, facilitating timely interventions and improving patient outcomes.

Remote patient monitoring is enabled by MQTT, allowing wearable devices to transmit real-time health data to healthcare providers. This instantaneous data transmission facilitates proactive patient management and diminishes response times in crucial scenarios. MQTT enhances interoperability across healthcare IoT ecosystems by enabling data exchange among diverse platforms and devices. It integrates cloud middleware, IoT technologies, and biometric sensors to improve telemonitoring, refines clinical decision-making, and advocates for standardized solutions for enhanced patient care.

In summary, MQTT provides healthcare providers with efficient, dependable, and scalable solutions by facilitating remote patient monitoring and enhancing interoperability among healthcare IoT networks.

3.3   Application Virtualization in the Healthcare Sector

Regarding virtualization, we chose Docker, which is a robust platform for containerizing applications, guaranteeing uniform deployment across diverse environments. It enhances the administration of intricate microservices in the healthcare sector by enclosing them within portable containers, facilitating deployment across many Operating Systems (OSs) and infrastructures without compatibility challenges. Docker enhances modularity, scalability, and integration by encapsulating applications along with their dependencies within containers [8]. The principal advantages encompass portability, scalability, isolation, ease of deployment, resource efficiency, and streamlined upgrades and maintenance. Docker's lightweight virtualization guarantees that each container functions within its distinct environment, hence preventing interference with others. It enhances resource efficiency by enabling several containers to operate on a single host machine, hence decreasing infrastructure expenses while preserving optimal performance. Docker's benefits render it an essential instrument for contemporary healthcare systems, allowing providers to meet changing requirements while ensuring reliability, high performance, and security standards.

The telemedicine system, originally implemented locally, can be effortlessly migrated to a cloud platform without necessitating reconfiguration of dependencies or software [11,21]. Containerized applications can augment video conferencing functionalities, facilitating enhanced remote consultations during pandemics such as COVID-19. This enables healthcare providers to accommodate heightened demand without experiencing system downtime or performance degradation [14].

4   System Design of Our Patient Surveillance System

Our system architecture, depicted in Fig. 1, employs a modular approach, with the Publisher Module serving as the principal service. It collects data from several modules and transmits it to services such as Publisher Manager and Video Stream Subscriber. The MQTT broker functions as a message center, facilitating communication between publishers and subscribers. The SyncMate Server oversees user authentication, retains camera and publisher data, and transmits tokens to the SyncMate client. The architectural design facilitates flexibility and maintenance by enabling each service to operate independently. This modularity method facilitates dynamic scaling, enabling the incorporation of new publishers and subscribers without disrupting the system. The MQTT broker oversees several interactions, such as video stream transmission, heartbeat monitoring, and metadata exchange. The system's modular strategy guarantees efficient message transmission and dynamic scalability.

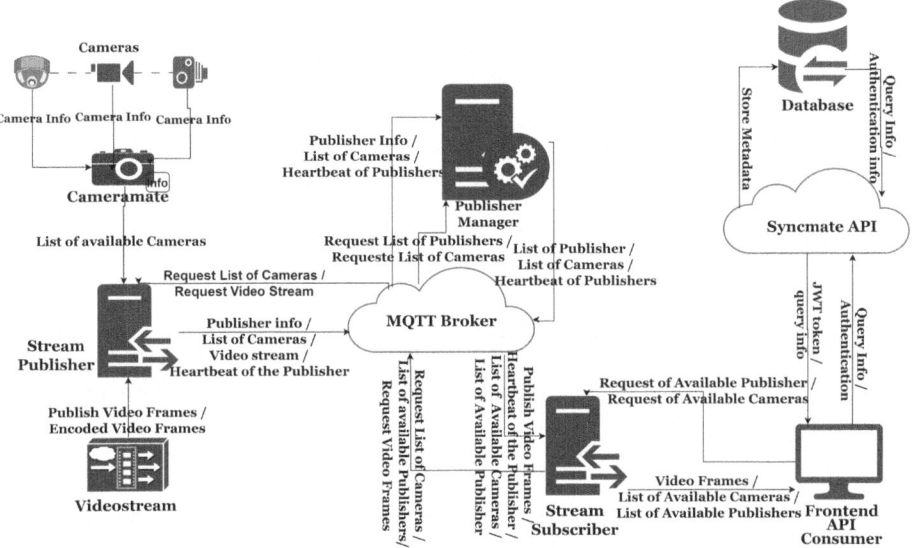

Fig. 1. System design of smart health integration into a surveillance system

The healthcare surveillance system is executed through various essential phases, commencing with the Video Stream Module. This module captures real-time video with the OpenCV library [4] and encodes the frames for transmission over aiortc [1], a Python-based WebRTC framework. The Camera Module acquires camera data and produces metadata for system integration. Error handling techniques are implemented to address camera malfunctions, with automatic reconnection capabilities guaranteeing uninterrupted video transmission. The Publisher module collects data and transmits it to the MQTT broker. The subsequent phase is the Messenger, enabling subscribers and publishers to transmit data over MQTT. The publisher service catalogs accessed cameras and transmits video frames to designated topics. QoS standards are defined for bandwidth-limited environments to guarantee reliable message transmission.

The frontend and backend development aims to deliver an intuitive interface for healthcare professionals. TypeScript facilitates the regulation of live video stream access, camera data, and access tokens. The Python-based backend manages user authentication, server data storage, and video input encoding.

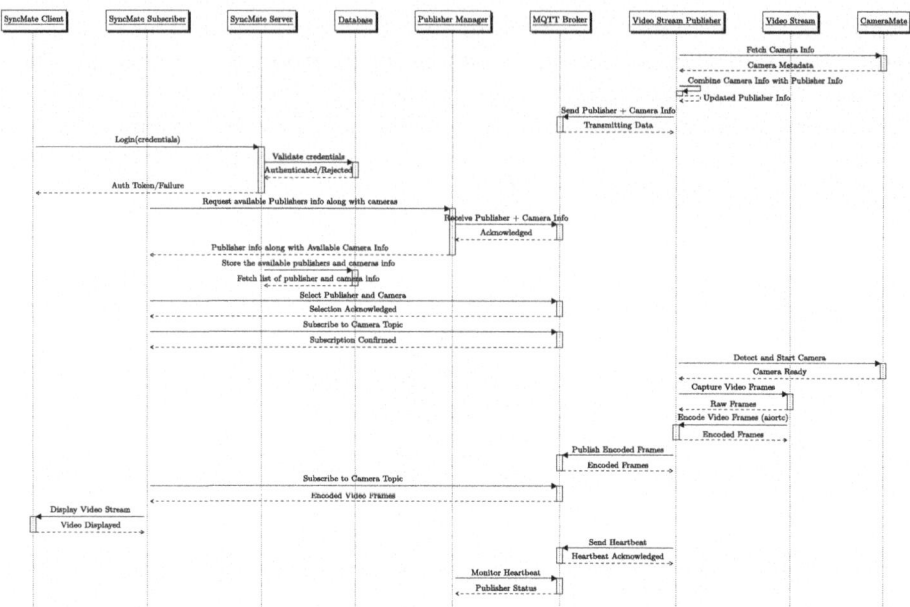

Fig. 2. Workflow of the real-time video streaming system with SyncMate subscriber handling streaming

The connection to the MQTT broker facilitates seamless interactions between the user interface and system components, enabling real-time patient monitoring. Docker streamlines deployment by encapsulating each service into a Docker container, hence enabling system deployment across many environments.

4.1   Microservice Interactions

The suggested healthcare surveillance system has a modular architecture for real-time video monitoring, secure communication, and scalability. It is constructed with WebRTC, MQTT, and Docker for simplified deployment and enhanced performance. The system comprises of the SyncMate Frontend, SyncMate REST Application, Publisher Manager, Publisher Module, Camera Module, Subscriber Module, and MQTT Broker as shown in Fig. 2. The SyncMate Frontend serves as the primary interface for healthcare professionals, facilitating authentication, access to publications and cameras, and the monitoring of real-time video transmissions. The SyncMate REST App manages user authentication, verifies authorization, and sustains the API. The Publisher Manager supervises publishers and their metadata, tracks publisher availability, and gathers information regarding cameras associated with these publishers. The Publisher Module oversees real-time video transmission via WebRTC and the Python-based aiortc library. The Subscriber Module acquires video feeds from the MQTT broker and transmits them to the Frontend for visualization. Docker containerization guarantees consistent data delivery across environments. The system initiates when a healthcare practitioner signs into the SyncMate Frontend, authenticates using the SyncMate REST App, and selects a camera.

4.2   The SyncMate REST API

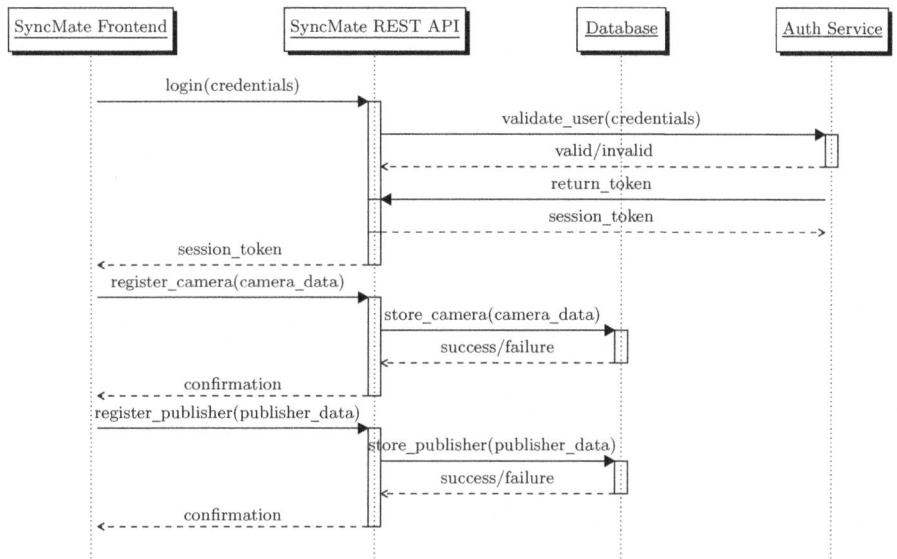

Fig. 3. SyncMate REST API workflow

We will further depict the central element of our deployment, the SyncMate REST API. It is the central element of our system, facilitating the effective control of publishers, cameras, and user authentication. It guarantees secure operations via role-based access control and connects smoothly with all other modules.

The SyncMate Server delivers information about camera utilization and publications, employing metadata to establish a strong and scalable framework. The API employs secure authentication methods such as OAuth2 and JSON Web Token (JSON) for user authentication and role management, enabling users to authenticate using API endpoints that produce a role-based session token. The API provides a secure JWT token for different user categories, including normal users and administrators.

The API supervises publisher management, facilitating the connection of cameras to the system. Core functionalities are the registration of publishers, retrieval of publishers, and management of cameras. The camera module enables the registration and retrieval of publishers, providing extensive metadata, usage monitoring, and integration with other system modules, including the video streaming application.

The API provides secure authentication, keeps metadata of the publisher and a list of cameras in the database, is user-friendly, and provides scalable and efficient system operations.

The workflow description of Fig. 3 delineates the authentication, registration, and integration protocols inside the healthcare surveillance system, highlighting the SyncMate REST API's function in enabling seamless interaction across components. The system employs a session token to authenticate user roles and authorizes access to endpoints. The registration process guarantees accurate data management and seamless integration of publications and cameras, ensuring consistency and reliability. The SyncMate REST API interfaces efficiently with system components including the MQTT Broker, Video Stream Subscriber Module, and Admin Tools, enabling communication and supplying metadata for live video streaming. This workflow enhances authentication, registration, and system module integration, guaranteeing strong, secure, and efficient operations that meet both user and administrative needs. The modular architecture facilitates seamless interaction with MQTT and WebSocket components, while upholding robust authentication and data integrity. The versatility and extensibility of the SyncMate REST API render it a crucial element of the system.

4.3   The SyncMate Client

The SyncMate API interface is an essential element of the surveillance system, facilitating user engagement with the backend system. It amalgamates real-time video transmission, camera data gathering, and user identification, offering an effective interface for monitoring surveillance activities. The system's fundamental components are safe authentication, rapid access to camera data, and seamless live video streaming.

User authentication facilitates system access via verification, with a session token generated and retained for future utilization upon successful authentication. Camera information retrieval uses the MQTT protocol to obtain publisher and camera data from the broker management server, stores it in the backend server, and displays it in an organized fashion on the frontend. The inclusion of live video streaming enables users to choose publications and cameras, facilitating dynamic and expandable video surveillance.

The system provides a cohesive and scalable solution through the integration of secure user authentication, organized camera management, and real-time video streaming. To mitigate latency difficulties and provide a direct connection to the streaming service, the system integrated the SyncMate REST API with the MQTT protocol, where the interactions are depicted in Fig. 4.

The user authentication process entails completing a login form with necessary information, after which the API client submits a POST request containing the credentials. Upon successful validation, the server generates a session token for safe connectivity. The camera information workflow commences by selecting the "Fetch Cameras" option in the frontend interface, while the SyncMate client establishes a connection to the MQTT protocol to retrieve data about available publications and cameras.

The live video streaming procedure entails transmitting designated camera information via MQTT to the MQTT broker, which subsequently acquires stream data through a MQTT topic from the broker. The API client acquires video frames from the broker and transmits them to the front end for prompt presentation.

Integrating the SyncMate API client with essential system components guarantees a cohesive and efficient workflow, encompassing secure authentication, extensive camera management, and seamless real-time video streaming capabilities.

5   Evaluation of Our Proposed Prototype

The analysis in Table 1 indicates that the suggested prototype successfully mitigates scalability, integration, and deployment constraints, while enhancing efficiency and flexibility in RTC contexts.

The suggested architecture seeks to deliver a thorough, scalable, and robust solution for IoT-enabled video surveillance and healthcare monitoring. It improves scalability by dynamically adjusting to various cameras, publications, and subscribers, facilitating the utilization of the MQTT protocol for efficient multi-device communication and Docker-orchestrated microservices for seamless growth.

The system effectively connects IoT and RTC by utilizing aiortc [1], a Python-based WebRTC module, for asynchronous and efficient video streaming. It integrates MQTT for device communication and WebRTC for real-time streaming, guaranteeing low-latency performance and compatibility with diverse IoT protocols. This guarantees protocol interoperability and minimal latency.

The deployment procedure resembles current systems, utilizing dockerized services for platform freedom, dynamic role-based access control, and camera metadata management. The SyncMate REST API simplifies the system by consolidating information in a single location.

The suggested system consists of a server and a communication protocol, providing adaptability and security through the integration of a SyncMate Server to oversee device metadata, user roles, and permissions. The MQTT topic-based communication facilitates configurable data streams, accommodating distinct healthcare and surveillance contexts. This facilitates solutions for various healthcare and monitoring requirements, particularly for the senior population.

Advanced security features incorporate an access control system utilizing SyncMate and MQTT for TLS, while rival systems rely on rudimentary security measures such as SDP and intermittent messages. The MQTT protocol utilizes TLS to enhance security, allowing subscribers and publishers to communicate via encrypted channels while maintaining publisher connectivity. Role-based access control via SyncMate prevents unwanted access to sensitive streams and data.

Table 1. Comparison of WebRTC-based frameworks and applications

Aspect	SquashCord [24]	IoTRTC [16]	Performance Evaluation Framework [23]	Mimic [9]	E-Health Framework [12]
Core Technology	WebRTC	WebRTC, Docker, Node-RED	WebRTC	WebRTC, Python, Tkinter	WebRTC, IoT
Main Components	STUN/TURN, RTCDataChannels, MediaStreams	Dockerized camera nodes, signaling server	RTP/UDP, RTCStatsReport API	Graphical UI (UI), WebRTC peer connection	WebRTC client, Gateway, IoT
Communication	P2P via Session Description Protocol (SDP) and ICE	AppRTC rooms, Web Push API	P2P with limitations	WebRTC, Heartbeat messages	Gateway mediates client and IoT
Signaling Mechanism	STUN/TURN setup	Node.js signaling server	RTCStatsReport API	WebRTC data channels	Node.js gateway
Integration	JavaScript API	Docker, Node-RED	Dummynet for testing	QR code-based access	IoT protocols (Wi-Fi, Bluetooth)
Scalability	P2P only	Multiple cameras/users	Two-peer connection	Desktop-mobile connection	Scales for multiple devices
Use Case	Video conferencing	Surveillance	Performance testing	Virtual webcam	E-health monitoring
Customization	Add custom MediaStreams	Configure with Node-RED	Modify network tests	QR-code camera access	Diverse IoT devices
Strengths	Simple APIs, real-time media	Easy deployment, compatibility	Detailed metrics, testing	GUI ease of use, QR codes	Interoperable, IoT-focused

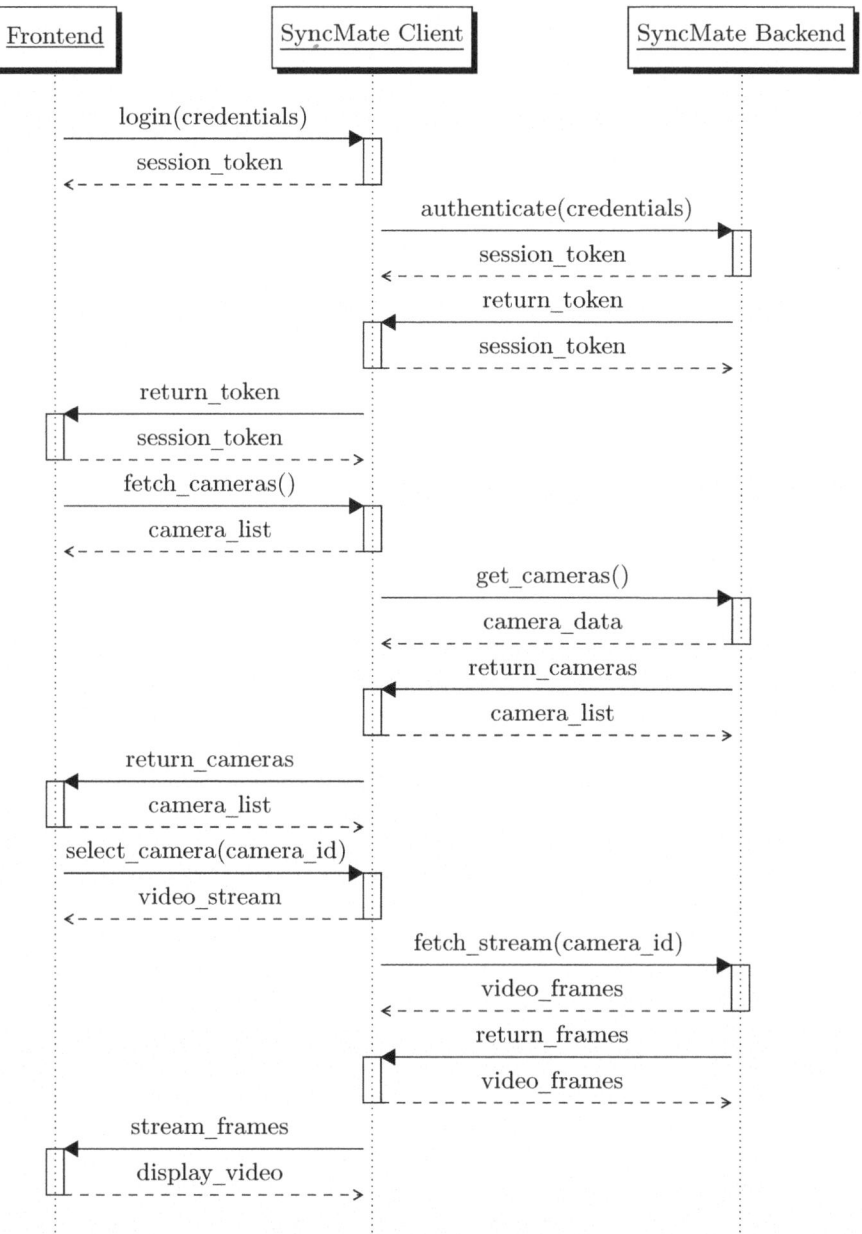

Fig. 4. Interactions of the SyncMate client

The integration of aiortc, a lightweight real-time streaming service utilizing MQTT for resource management, enhances performance and resource efficiency, similar to Node-RED [3] and IoTRTC [16], which depend on Docker. The proposed prototype surpasses Docker and NodeRED-based IoTRTC in resource efficiency and performance by employing lightweight aiortc for streaming and MQTT to reduce protocol overhead.

The architecture's enhanced use case support encompasses multi-camera, multi-user surveillance for security and healthcare applications, in addition to e-health monitoring (E-Health Framework [12]) and video conferencing (Squash-Cord [24]). MQTT ensures interoperability with low-power IoT devices, catering to various industrial and healthcare monitoring needs.

The assessment and examination of the suggested architecture alongside existing frameworks underscores its advantages in providing performance and scalability in real-world scenarios. The system attains substantial enhancements in scalability, modularity, deployment efficiency, and security with the integration of sophisticated technologies like aiortc, MQTT, and Docker containerization.

6   Conclusion and Future Work

The paper presented the planning, execution, and assessment of a real-time healthcare monitoring system by investigating MQTT, WebRTC, Docker, and other innovative technologies. These technologies facilitate the provision of efficient healthcare solutions from a distant location. The proposed prototype tackles real-time video streaming, secure data transmission, and streamlined deployment across diverse contexts. The framework comprises Publisher Service, Publisher Manager, Subscriber Service, MQTT Broker, SyncMate Server, and SyncMate Client application, while remaining a modular and scalable solution. These components facilitate the system's ability to capture, transmit, and display live video streams, while also assuring security and reliability. Docker containerization further optimizes the deployment procedure. It simplifies the deployment location and ensures consistency across deployment environments, facilitating seamless growth. Due to its low latency, MQTT is optimized for lightweight and efficient message handling, rendering it particularly ideal for healthcare environments and P2P video tracking. The assessment of this framework indicates that the architecture can accommodate several cameras and publishers while sustaining latency and performance across diverse workloads. Docker facilitates the evaluation of the framework within a simulated network environment, hence assessing the system's resilience and adaptability. Single host constraints and network bottlenecks were recognized; nonetheless, they do not impede the system's efficacy in fulfilling the fundamental requirement for real-time healthcare surveillance. WebRTC, MQTT, and Docker establish a foundation for future enhancements and applications in various healthcare settings, allowing telemedicine to respond to changing requirements. The healthcare sector may implement efficient, reliable, scalable, and secure real-time monitoring systems using the presented prototype.

Our suggested prototype seeks to enhance the functionality, security, scalability, and user experience of a healthcare support system. Due to its containerization it can also encompass multi-host deployment through Kubernetes, adaptive streaming techniques, automated performance assessment, security features, integration with motion sensors, real-time notifications, increased sensor compatibility, improved user interface, Artificial Intelligence (AI), comparative performance benchmarking, and mobile platform support. The system is provided as a multi-host microservice architecture to enhance fault tolerance, optimize load balancing, and facilitate horizontal scaling. Adaptive streaming will alleviate latency and frame disruptions resulting from network connectivity and capacity limitations. Automated performance testing will diminish the duration of manual testing and guarantee compliance with regulations. The REST API enables a future development of a mobile application, improving accessibility for healthcare providers and patients. The system's scalability is essential for its adaptability and durability. Cutting-edge technology such as edge computing, adaptive streaming, and AI-driven analysis will foster innovation. The use of third-party technology and mobile platforms will enhance the systems functionality across diverse healthcare environments. The prototype demonstrates the functionalities of tailored video tracking and containerization technologies, including WebRTC for video streaming, MQTT for scalability and encoded message transmission, and Docker for deployment.

References

1. aiortc: Webrtc and ortc implementation for python using asyncio. https://github.com/aiortc/aiortc
2. Github repository uniba-ktr/e-health-rtc. https://github.com/uniba-ktr/e-health-rtc
3. Node-red: Low-code programming for event-driven applications. https://nodered.org
4. Opencv - open computer vision library. https://opencv.org
5. Akram, P.S., Ramesha, M., Valiveti, S.A.S., Sohail, S., Rao, K.T.S.S.: Iot based remote patient health monitoring system. In: 2021 7th International Conference on Advanced Computing and Communication Systems (ICACCS), vol. 1, pp. 1519–1524, IEEE (2021)
6. Alshammari, H.H.: The internet of things healthcare monitoring system based on MQTT protocol. Alex. Eng. J. **69**, 275–287 (2023)
7. Amezcua Aragon, L.: Real-time neural network based video super-resolution as a service: design and implementation of a real-time video super-resolution service using public cloud services (2022)
8. Costa, J.: Microserviced etl system in a healthcare environment (2022)
9. Crandall, L., Roberts, M., Cheng, E.: Mimic: a remote webcam device over webrtc. In: 2021 International Conference on Computational Science and Computational Intelligence (CSCI), pp. 1355–1359. IEEE (2021)
10. Deshmukh, R., Nand, N., Pawar, A., Wagh, D., Kudale, A.: Video conferencing using webrtc. In: 2023 International Conference on Sustainable Computing and Data Communication Systems (ICSCDS), pp. 857–864. IEEE (2023)
11. DesLauriers, J., et al.: Cloud apps to-go: Cloud portability with TOSCA and MICADO. Concurrency Comput. Pract. Experience **33**(19), e6093 (2021)

12. El Jaouhari, S., Bouabdallah, A., Bonnin, J.M.: A secure webrtc/wot-based health-care architecture enhanced with access control. In: 2018 International Conference on Information Networking (ICOIN), pp. 182–187. IEEE (2018)
13. El Jaouhari, S., Bouabdallah, A., Bonnin, J.M., Lemlouma, T.: Toward a smart health-care architecture using webrtc and wot. In: World Conference on Information Systems and Technologies, pp. 531–540. Springer (2017)
14. Gabriela, P., Lee, D., Van Tu, N., Hong, J.W.K.: Machine learning-based auto-scaler for video conferencing systems. In: 2021 IEEE 7th International Conference on Network Softwarization (NetSoft), pp. 142–150. IEEE (2021)
15. García, F.M., Schez-Sobrino, S., Glez-Morcillo, C., Castro-Schez, J.J., Albusac, J.A., Vallejo, D.: Rtc-mr: a webrtc-based framework for real-time communication in mixed reality. Softw. Impacts **23**, 100727 (2025). ISSN 2665-9638
16. Großmann, M., Klinger, L., Krolikowsky, V., Sarkar, C.: Efficient internet of things surveillance systems in edge computing environments: accessible via web based video transmissions from low-cost hardware. In: International Conference on Innovations for Community Services, pp. 292–311. Springer (2023)
17. Islam, J., Kumar, T., Kovacevic, I., Harjula, E.: Resource-aware dynamic service deployment for local IoT edge computing: healthcare use case. IEEE Access **9**, 115868–115884 (2021)
18. Kwabla, W., et al.: Evaluation of webrtc in the cloud for surgical simulations: a case study on virtual rotator cuff arthroscopic skill trainer (vircast). In: International Conference on Human-Computer Interaction, pp. 127–143. Springer (2023)
19. Maqbool, S., Iqbal, M.W., Naqvi, M.R., Arif, K.S., Ahmed, M., Arif, M.: IoT based remote patient monitoring system. In: 2020 International Conference on Decision Aid Sciences and Application (DASA), pp. 1255–1260. IEEE (2020)
20. Namee, K., Sawatdee, P., Promsorn, N., Chinchua, S., Meny, A., Kulchan, S.: Applying of websocket and webrtc for video calling in telemedicine during covid-19 pandemic. In: 2023 International Conference on Information Networking (ICOIN), pp. 340–346. IEEE (2023)
21. Soltanmohammadi, E., Hikmet, N.: Optimizing healthcare big data processing with containerized PySpark and parallel computing: a study on ETL pipeline efficiency. J. Data Anal. Inf. Process. **12**(4), 544–565 (2024)
22. Suciu, G., Stefanescu, S., Beceanu, C., Ceaparu, M.: Webrtc role in real-time communication and video conferencing. In: 2020 Global Internet of Things Summit (GIoTS), pp. 1–6. IEEE (2020)
23. Tarim, E.A., Tekin, H.C.: Performance evaluation of webrtc-based online consultation platform. Turk. J. Electr. Eng. Comput. Sci. **27**(6), 4314–4327 (2019)
24. Thorat, A., Bhute, A.: Squashcord: video conferencing application using webrtc. In: High Performance Computing and Networking: Select Proceedings of CHSN 2021, pp. 425–436. Springer (2022)
25. Vidul, A., Hari, S., Pranave, K., Vysakh, K., Archana, K.: Telemedicine for emergency care management using webrtc. In: 2015 International Conference on Advances in Computing, Communications and Informatics (ICACCI), pp. 1741–1745. IEEE (2015)

Serious Games

Bring Your Own Bug: Enabling User-Generated Content in Serious Games for Industrial Cybersecurity and AppSec Education

Andrei-Cristian Iosif[1,2](✉) iD, Ulrike Lechner[2] iD,
and Maria Pinto-Albuquerque[3] iD

[1] Siemens AG, Munich, Germany
andrei-cristian.iosif@siemens.com
[2] University of the Bundeswehr Munich, Neubiberg, Germany
{andrei.iosif,ulrike.lechner}@unibw.de
[3] University Institute of Lisbon, Lisbon, Portugal
maria.albuquerque@iscte-iul.pt

Abstract. This work investigates the integration of User Generated Content in a Serious Game for cybersecurity education and training in the industry. This Serious Game deals with security code reviews as part of an industrial software lifecycle, and players are invited to review vulnerable snippets to gain awareness of secure coding. We design and implement a way to include User Generated Content contributions into the Serious Game and we evaluate how this approach in cybersecurity education opens a path for a community-driven initiative to gather and share security knowledge. We develop an open contribution pipeline that allows developers to submit security-relevant code snippets in the Serious Games challenge collection, for players of the game to review, and present the technical design choices behind it: automating the integration of content, acceptance quality gates, and the potential for custom data analytics from recorded player interactions. Furthermore, we explore the voluntary contributors' perceptions of the ease of contribution (with respect to our proposed convention for challenge snippets) and also investigate the characteristics of what is considered an effective educational snippet.

Keywords: Code review · Secure coding · Cybersecurity · Education · Awareness · Information systems · User-generated content

1 Introduction

As industrial sectors increasingly integrate digital technologies, this trend has given cybersecurity increasing importance. Furthermore, regulatory pressure, such as the European Union's Cyber Resilience Act (EU CRA, Regulation 2024/2847) [6], has transformed cybersecurity into one of the central requirements for market entry.

S. Zielinski et al. (Eds.): I4CS 2025, CCIS 2513, pp. 289–306, 2025.
https://doi.org/10.1007/978-3-031-94263-1_17

Code review is one of the essential practices in cybersecurity for critical infrastructures, i.e., in the software lifecycle of producing products and services for critical infrastructures and other customers [2]. Detecting weaknesses as early as possible in the software lifecycle is the best and most cost-effective way to mitigate software-related risks [1]. Static and dynamic code analysis can help speed up the process with automation. Still, manual review remains necessary for dealing with false positive results from the tools and for many software vulnerability classes, e.g. business logic flaws [18]. A proper manual security review methodology is a skill that needs to be trained and practiced.

To this end, the authors have designed and developed a Serious Game for security code review in the industry, the DuckDebugger. The game is actively used and continuously developed within the industrial environment for which it was designed, with the goal of empowering developers to learn to spot security weaknesses in code and know how to mitigate them.

Raising the level of ambition in secure coding faces several challenges. A challenge is the lack of engagement and adaptability in traditional training methods. Research finds that a viable approach to security awareness is to employ Serious Games, as they improve learning retention and better simulate real-world scenarios [20]. However, we face more challenges in making our Serious Game a useful education and training tool. One challenge is to find training material, i.e. code weaknesses suitable for training. In addition, software development requires multiple frameworks, platforms, tools, and languages. Thus, a diverse training set with a collection of weaknesses is desired for different work contexts. A centralized approach with one game designer or team is potentially always limited to a few languages and frameworks, therefore providing limited insights into the weaknesses arising from the practices used by a specific team or business unit. A game designer and an initial game design can provide a collection of good weaknesses for training purposes. Software developers have the best understanding for their languages, tools, frameworks and software development approach, including typical and unique vulnerabilities that are relevant to them. User Generated Content promises scalability in terms of number and variety. Soliciting User Generated Content is the game design step that we report in this paper.

In this work, we explore the concept of *crowdsourcing* for the content used in our Serious Game and ask the following central research question: Can we show that sourcing User Generated Content (UGC) for Serious Games in cybersecurity education is feasible? To this end, we: develop a way to enable UGC to be included in the collection of code review challenges of the DuckDebugger; design and implement a pipeline for User Generated Content for the DuckDebugger; provide results on the feasibility of this approach aimed at engaging industrial software developers to contribute content for the Serious Game.

The DuckDebugger has been successfully adopted within its industrial context, demonstrating the viability of Serious Games for security education.

The paper focuses on the educational benefits of the technical design of enabling User Generated Content in DuckDebugger, positioning it as a platform for a community of industrial software developers.

The main contributions of this work are:

- A technical design spotlight of the user contribution ingestion pipeline
- Quantitative assessments about the ease of contribution via our proposed pipeline, based on the collected contributors' impressions
- Insights into what potential contributors consider to be an educational bug
- Exploring the proactiveness of respondents in our UGC pilot, with results indicating a potential for incorporating UGC within the DuckDebugger.

This paper extends previous work on the design of the DuckDebugger Serious Game and evaluations of the game [10,12,13] with the new concept or design of the User Generated Content pipeline and its evaluation.

The paper is structured as follows. Section 2 reviews related work on Serious Games, User Generated Content, and empowerment in software development. Section 3 presents the DuckDebugger game, the UGC ingestion pipeline, and the survey methodology. Section 4 reports results from our industrial evaluation. Section 5 discusses the findings and their implications. Section 6 concludes the paper and outlines directions for future work.

2   Related Work

To contextualize our research, we first explore the related work on Serious Games (SGs) as a tool for cybersecurity education and training, outlining their benefits and limitations. Next, we examine the role of User Generated Content (UGC) in fostering engagement and scalability in digital learning environments. We then discuss how empowerment theory informs secure software development and code review practices. Finally, we connect these themes by discussing previous research on our industrial Serious Game for code review. This lays the theoretical groundwork for our exploration the feasible integration of UGC in SGs and the implications thereof.

Dörner et al. define a Serious Game (SG) as *"a game that is designed with a primary goal other than pure entertainment"* [5]. SGs provide an educational *simulation*, which distinguishes them from the concept of gamification, which encompasses the inclusion of elements of the game in everyday activities. An experience report by Namin et al. [23] and a literature review by Hendrix et al. [8] have shown that SGs effectively communicate key lessons to their players.

Roepke et al. offer a comprehensive analysis of cybersecurity-focused SGs, investigating the availability of games designed for end-users without prior knowledge and assessing whether these games facilitate long-term learning and skill acquisition [21]. Their findings suggest that, despite the increasing number of cybersecurity SGs, many lack relevant content, often prioritizing factual knowledge over contextual understanding.

Svábensky et al. explore how the creation of Serious Games improves cybersecurity education by fostering adversary thinking and practical skills [27]. By adopting an attacker's perspective, students develop adversary thinking, which helps them anticipate threats and design effective defenses. Through project-based learning, they engage in hands-on problem solving, applying cybersecurity concepts while building and refining their games.

User Generated Content (UGC) has a long tradition in computer science and software engineering. Think of the first online forums of the World Wide Web, the open-source communities, and communities like Wikipedia, LINUX and Apache that build essential parts of the digital infrastructure, or ad-hoc peer support communities such as Stack Overflow. The paradigm of Interactive Innovation or Open Innovation [7,9] leverages user contributions and skillful processes and setups to engage users in creating products and services of all kinds and to empower them to contribute. Scalability and specificity of the results, as well as raising awareness for a product and service, short time-to-market, and high user acceptance are attributed to open innovation approaches. UCG has been widely explored in the context of information quality, participatory design, and conceptual modeling. The following works provide insights relevant to integrating UGC into a cybersecurity education platform.

The review of the literature by Naab et al. examines research on User Generated Content, identifying key developments and gaps in the field [19]. It highlights diverse scholarly approaches, the potential for interdisciplinary collaboration, and challenges posed by UGC's evolving nature.

Sina et al. demonstrate a scalable approach to UGC integration in Serious Games using crowd-sourced contributions, automated processing, and quality validation mechanisms [24]. While their focus is on narrative-based training, their structured pipeline automates content integration, enforces quality gates, adapts scenarios based on user data, and analyzes player interactions. These aspects parallel the challenges of incorporating user-submitted security challenges in a cybersecurity SG, offering a structured framework applicable to cybersecurity SGs.

Lukyanenko et al. [17] demonstrate that fixed classification structures in structured UGC can restrict data quality, leading to information loss, while free-form data entry and instance-based modeling improve accuracy and completeness. In [15], they examine participatory design in UGC, highlighting challenges related to motivation, usability, and alignment with organizational needs, and propose distributed design methods such as interactive prototyping, virtual collaboration, and aggregate feedback. In [16], they propose guidelines for conceptual modeling in UGC that balance flexibility and structure, such as prioritizing instance-based representation, allowing user-defined attributes, and incorporating unstructured data to enhance usability and capture diverse contributor perspectives.

Weir et al. highlight secure development as a *dialectic*, i.e. a process of learning through challenging interactions [26]. They emphasize a *challenging dialogue*, where developers actively question and are questioned by security experts, tools, or peers. Among six assurance techniques identified as dialectic counterparts, they include code review for the following reason: unlike traditional security approaches based on checklists, review fosters critical thinking and proactive problem-solving.

This active engagement enhances developers' technical skills while also fostering empowerment – boosting confidence in security-conscious decision-making and increasing ownership over software security. Dorner et al. [4] find that code reviews function as an effective communication network, enabling information to reach up to 85% of participants in smaller reviews and as many as 11,000 in larger systems within a few weeks. Their study further shows that knowledge typically propagates within five hops and five days, reinforcing the role of code review in enhancing team awareness and cross-boundary information flow. As such, we posit that exploring the concept of *empowerment* can be beneficial to code review practices and the design of our game.

Tessem et al. highlight that knowledge in software development emerges through social interaction and shared experiences [25]. Developers acquire and refine expertise not only through formal instruction but also by engaging with peers, exchanging insights, and collaboratively solving problems. Furthermore, the authors emphasize that empowerment is a key factor in enhancing job satisfaction and motivation, particularly in agile teams where developers have greater autonomy and decision-making power. They claim that the arisen sense of ownership over one's work fosters deeper engagement and encourages proactive participation in knowledge-sharing practices.

The seminal work by Seibert et al. [22] seeks to explore the antecedents and consequences of psychological and team empowerment in organizations. The authors identify a positive correlation between team empowerment and team performance, indicating that the benefits of empowerment extend beyond the individual level to influence team outcomes.

Empowerment can be understood through structural, psychological, and resource empowerment [14]. Structural empowerment refers to the environmental factors and organizational structures that facilitate or inhibit individuals' access to resources, information, and opportunities to participate in meaningful ways, while psychological empowerment fosters confidence and ownership. Resource empowerment ensures access to necessary tools and support.

Key outcomes of empowerment include: shared identification, where individuals align with collective goals and values, collaborative control, which distributes decision-making authority among members of a group, and collective participation, ensuring inclusive engagement in processes that impact outcomes [14].

Tessem [25] highlights that empowerment in software teams is driven by autonomy, competence, and meaningful participation, leading to higher engagement and ownership over security practices. This aligns with Lukyanenko et al.'s findings that UGC platforms benefit from flexible, contributor-driven content, as overly rigid structures reduce engagement and data quality [17].

In previous works, the authors explored their industrial Serious Game for security code review, *DuckDebugger*, from multiple perspectives. Prior research has examined its effectiveness in raising awareness of secure code review practices, its role in cybersecurity awareness training and developer empowerment, and how gameplay analytics inform design improvements [10–13]. The game will be further covered in Subsect. 3.1.

Prior work has not addressed structured UGC integration in serious games for industrial code review training. We close this gap by designing a UGC pipeline and evaluating its feasibility through an industry-focused survey.

3 Experimental Setup

In this section, we briefly present the DuckDebugger Serious Game, present the data pipeline which enables User Generated Content submissions, and cover the options which contributors can choose when authoring a new challenge for our platform.

To evaluate the feasibility of enabling User Generated Content in DuckDebugger, we conducted a structured online survey targeting industry practitioners. The survey employed a mixed-methods approach, combining multiple-choice questions, Likert-scale items, and open-ended responses. Participation was voluntary and anonymous. The instrument aimed to gather quantitative and qualitative insights into contributors' understanding, preferences, and willingness to engage with the proposed content submission pipeline.

3.1 Serious Game for Security Code Review: DuckDebugger

The game's interface is shown in Fig. 1 as a mock-up, and consists of three columns: Comment, Code, and Solution. The vulnerable code appears in the 2nd column (Code). Players are first shown a brief instructions pop-up and are then invited to add review comments in the first column (Comment) to highlight the vulnerabilities which they claim to spot. Players receive help in the means of a generic security review checklist, and findings from Static application security testing (SAST) tools for the snippet, which can both be consulted alongside the code. This setup aims to educate developers in observing *false positives/negatives*, and illustrate when automated security evaluation can be augmented by human insight.

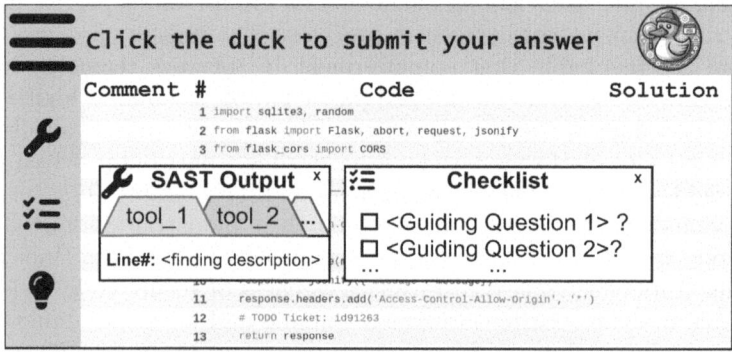

Fig. 1. DuckDebugger serious game

To complete a challenge, players must find at least 50% of vulnerabilities in a snippet. This threshold is based on previous work, where authors found that developers typically identify half the vulnerabilities which experts find, following the participation a secure coding workshop [10]. Upon submitting a review above this threshold, the full solution is displayed in the 3rd column, as a means to foster learning and reflection.

3.2 Data Pipeline

The creation of new challenges and the updating of existing challenges is implemented as a data pipeline which takes a code snippet, annotated with comments, as input. The solution to the challenge must be specified inline, by means of code comments. The solution-related comments must follow a writing convention proposed by the authors, which we explain in full in Subsect. 3.3. The pipeline is presented in Fig. 2.

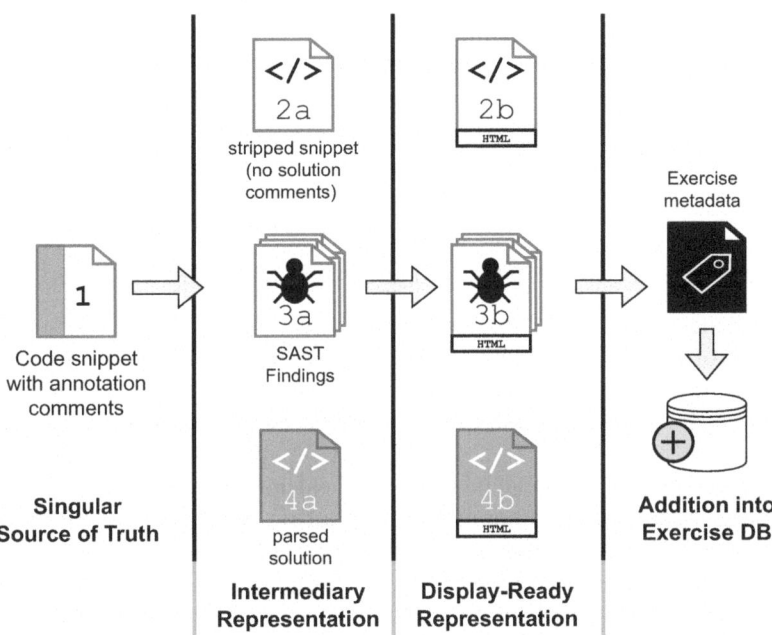

Fig. 2. Snippet ingestion pipeline

Upon submitting a challenge snippet into the DuckDebugger, the platform extracts and processes the comments, and runs SAST analysis against the snippet. This process yields in three results: the *stripped* snippet (i.e. without the solution comments), aggregated findings from tools, and the solution itself. An intermediary step processes the results further, in a display-ready format.

The data pipeline rests on a proposed comment convention, to be introduced in the next Section, and language-specific tool orchestration; the remaining intermediary steps involve transformations to generate display-ready formats and to separate solution data in accordance with the game's content architecture.

3.3   Challenge Structure and Comment Convention

Favoring extensibility and flexibility, we opt for a *single-source-of-truth* approach for our exercises. Specifically, we build a pipeline to ingest code snippets and output a challenge – this requires orchestrating SAST tools and converting everything (snippet, SAST results) into content to be rendered to the user in the browser.

By implementing a single-source-of-truth approach for security review challenges, our pipeline allows developers to contribute without requiring centralized oversight or learning another tool or language, promoting autonomy and self-directed learning. This aligns with structural empowerment principles, where individuals are given the tools and authority to influence their work environment, as seen in software development empowerment research.

This approach simplifies the creation of a challenge and enables easy content updates for existing challenges. Furthermore, this approach enables the tagging/labeling of individual weaknesses, which can be done independently of data collection, including post-facto.

Concretely, each item in the master solution is appended as a comment into the code snippet (on the offending line), and has the following structure:

```
!! master_solution_text @@FIELD1 v1_1 v1_2 @@FIELD2 v2_1 ...
```

The beginning marker (!!) allows for comments unrelated to the solution to still be part of the challenge and be displayed to players of the game for realistic context. Fields can be: keywords to match against, relative line numbers or ranges to consider valid, or mappings to other standards or internal company guidelines.

It is important to note that neither the field names nor their corresponding value(s) are hard-coded in our approach. Opting for a *single source of truth* (i.e. the code snippet, following the comment structure convention) ensures that updating a challenge's metadata (solution, tags) does not introduce neither breaking changes nor incongruences across files. This makes our approach highly flexible and unlocks potential for further studies on the same collected data.

Solution comments also allow additional options, apart from text related to vulnerability pertaining to the problematic line(s) in the snippet, to be specified inline. Contributors to the platform have multiple options for what they can choose to include in their solutions. Below, we present the features supported by the DuckDebugger's platform:

– **Simple Comments** - The minimum requirement for a solution comment is for it to include text relevant to the vulnerability it aims to highlight on the line of code it pertains to. Furthermore, Markdown syntax is supported, as it is an established and widely adopted markup convention which allows including links and images.

- **Complex Comments** - Apart from text, solution comments can be augmented with additional data to enhance the game experience:

  - Extending the matching lines for a weakness (NUMS field): Some code vulnerabilities can span across multiple lines, or can be mitigated at different locations in the code. Furthermore, reviewers can have different comment styles (before/above the offending line, etc.). Accordingly, we add this field so challenge developers can address these nuances in review and security. *Example:* For a vulnerability on line **7** (arbitrary line number), a contributor may specify, after the solution text: "@@NUMS -1 +1 10-12 15". Support is thus enabled for: relative numbering, line ranges, and additional individual values.

  - Keyword matching (KWORDS field): A space-separated list of keywords can be provided to ensure that the comment pertains to the vulnerability (user solutions must match at least one regex pattern). *Example:* For an injection-type vulnerability, a contributor may specify "@@KWORDS inject input sanitiz escap". Words are truncated so the pattern-matching algorithm can be more permissive towards correct grading of user solutions, e.g. *sanitize* and *sanitization* both get matched against the specified *sanitiz* keyword.

- **Custom Fields** - as previously mentioned, none of the field names are hard-coded (except for NUMS and KWORDS). As such, challenge creators can directly specify their own arbitrary fields in the code snippet, with any number of values, and in any order. This is particularly useful if operators of the Duck-Debugger, i.e. trainers and educators, want to collect data and have it mapped to categories from e.g. a standard or an internal guideline. This approach is one of the design cornerstones of the game, ensuring the platform maintains flexibility during development and use.

3.4   Survey Design

In order to evaluate the feasibility of crowdsourcing new challenges for the Duck-Debugger, we employed an anonymous and voluntary online survey, consisting of multiple-choice questions, Likert-like answers and free-form feedback. Data was collected exclusively from industry practitioners working in Europe.

The survey was structured as follows:

- **Introduction:** First, the DuckDebugger game was presented (what a player's task is, what help they get, what reward is received for solving), mentioning its intended audience (developers, testers) and goal (awareness and empowerment in cybersecurity practices).

- **Background Information:** Age group, years of experience in software development and cybersecurity and Self-assessed familiarity with cybersecurity concepts and secure coding techniques.

– **Challenge Structure Preferences:** Programming languages for security
   code review exercises, the number and visibility of security bugs, and the
   realism of vulnerabilities.
– **Comment Convention Evaluation:** Understanding and appeal of the simple and complex comment conventions.
– **Educational Aspects:** Perceived value of @@NUMS, @@KWORDS, and
   optional custom tags in security learning.
– **Optional User Contributions:** Willingness to submit security-challenged
   code snippets, with or without solutions, and/or openness to contributing
   security challenges in the future.

4   Results: DuckDebugger UGC in Industrial Trials

In total, our survey received input from 23 respondents. Their demographics are
presented in Fig. 3.

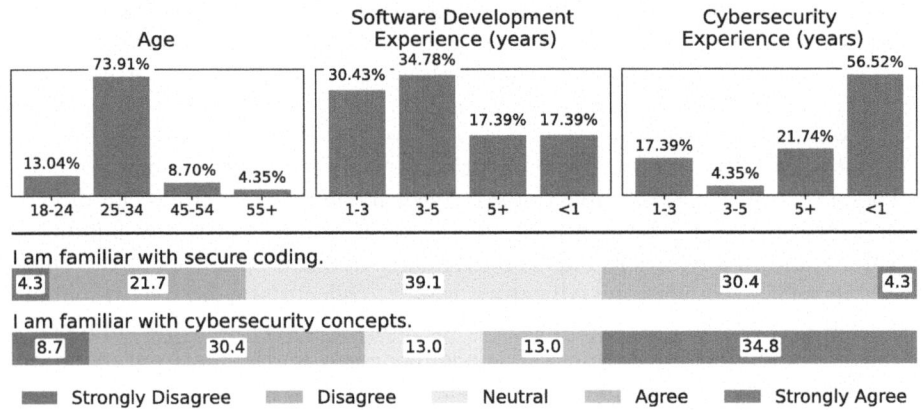

Fig. 3. Respondent demographics

It is important to note that overall, people rate their cybersecurity knowledge higher than their knowledge of secure coding. We observe that a growing
awareness of cybersecurity risks correlates with lower self-ratings in secure coding
ability, and that software development experience and cybersecurity knowledge
are the only two factors which display inverse correlation.

However, this finding aligns with previous research in learning models, such as
Burch et al. work [3], as it may reflect the transition from unconscious incompe-
tence, where they are unaware of their lack of knowledge, to conscious incompe-
tence, recognizing their deficiencies. This increased awareness may lead to more
accurate self-assessments and a commitment to improving their secure coding
practices (aligned with the culture of the industrial context of the study) and
requires further investigation.

4.1   Impressions About Proposed Comment Convention

Figure 4 reflects the respondents' impressions to the clarity and appeal of the proposed comment conventions.

We can observe that the appeal of *inline solutions* that are self-contained in the challenge snippet is overwhelmingly positive (87% above neutral). Similarly, the simple comment convention is considered clear by 91.3% of respondents. The complex convention, however, shows a lower approval rating (65.2%). It is nonetheless encouraging to see that none of the respondents exhibit strong disagreement towards the proposed schema.

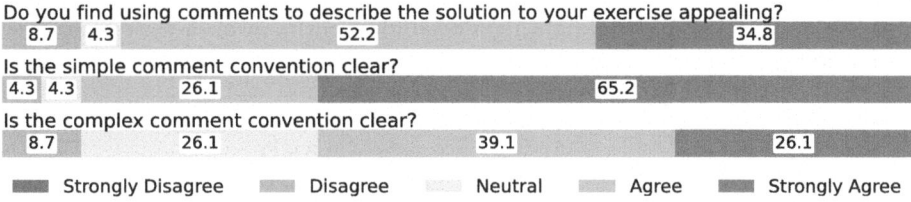

Do you find using comments to describe the solution to your exercise appealing?

| 8.7 | 4.3 | 52.2 | | 34.8 |

Is the simple comment convention clear?

| 4.3 | 4.3 | 26.1 | 65.2 |

Is the complex comment convention clear?

| 8.7 | 26.1 | 39.1 | 26.1 |

■ Strongly Disagree   ■ Disagree   Neutral   ■ Agree   ■ Strongly Agree

Fig. 4. Comment convention: clarity impressions

Figure 5 portrays the responses related to possible tags in the complex comment convention.

Are @@NUMS tags valuable for learning? (as a player/user)

| 4.3 | 13.0 | 21.7 | 39.1 | 21.7 |

Are @@KWORDS tags valuable for learning? (as a player/user)

| 4.3 | 8.7 | 26.1 | 30.4 | 30.4 |

Is support for optional custom tags valuable? (as a developer/data scientist/manager)

| 4.3 | 8.7 | 13.0 | 30.4 | 43.5 |

■ Strongly Disagree   ■ Disagree   Neutral   ■ Agree   ■ Strongly Agree

Fig. 5. Complex comments: perceived value of tag categories

Respondents consider extended line numbering (NUMS) and keywords (KWORDS) valuable for players of our Serious Game, with a 60.8% positive rating for both. There is stronger agreement towards keywords, requiring further insight. Furthermore, the optional custom tags garner the most agreement. This can be likely attributed to our demographics: we ask if the fields are valuable for *developers, data scientists, and managers*, which overlaps with our survey sample.

4.2   Opinions on Security Bug Characteristics

Part of the survey questions were aimed to assess what expectations in terms of content would potential contributors have. The collected results in this subsection serve as our respondents' views of what the characteristics an *educational vulnerable code snippet* could be.

The language preferences from survey respondents are as follows (cf. Fig. 6): Python (17 mentions), C (9), Java (7), JavaScript (6), and C++ (6), with additional interest in C# (2), SQL (2), Go (2), Rust (1), PL/SQL (1), TypeScript (1), Shell (1), and Scripting (1). The presence of JavaScript, SQL, and scripting languages suggests a focus on web security, while Go and Rust indicate growing attention to secure coding in modern environments. Responses also included Ansible (1) and Bash (1), highlighting a need for security awareness to also cover automation and infrastructure as code.

Fig. 6. Desired programming languages for security review challenges

It is important to note that, when we conducted this design and evaluation research, the DuckDebugger already includes challenges in 75% of the programming languages mentioned in the responses.

Respondents were asked if their snippets would involve just one single security bug. 43.5% responded yes, while 56.5% answered negatively. When asked if the introduced security bug should be *obvious*, the majority of respondents (82.6%) answered positively, with only 17.4% considering that spotting the bug should be straightforward. Lastly, when asked if the bug should be inspired by a real-life vulnerability, the immediate response was positive. These findings are presented visually in Fig. 7.

4.3   Measuring Engagement

The survey assesses the feasibility of the approach and indicates the degree of interactivity and engagement to expect from the industrial software developers. Figure 8 presents the overall engagement of the N=23 respondents.

Of the respondents, 5 out of 23 (21.73%) contributed a code snippet, and 7 (30,43%) said they will contact the authors for a later contribution. Across code contributions, collaborators unanimously chose not only to annotate the

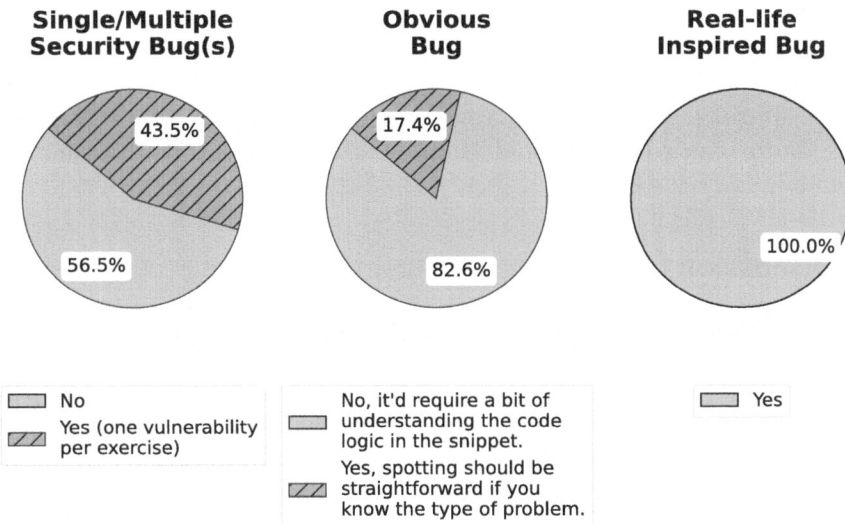

Fig. 7. Responses: educational bug characteristics

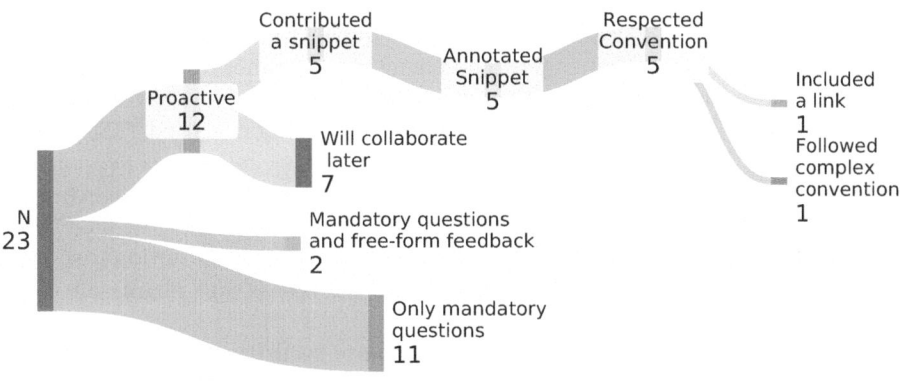

Fig. 8. Funnel of engagement

snippet but also to follow the comment convention. Furthermore, a respondent chose to include a link for further information, and another followed the complex convention, including the NUMS and KWORD tags.

In freeform responses, survey participants remarked the following:

- *"It might be the case that a security issue is not covered by a single script but might require multiple classes/scripts to be shown to the user."*
- *"Give concrete (maybe simplified) examples of the outcome of the vulnerability or the vulnerability being exploited"*

In total, we have received 5 vulnerable snippet contributions. Their representation with respect to programming language is as follows: JavaScript (1),

Rust (1), C (1), Python (1), Java (1). Following expert review in the industrial context of one the authors, based on input from two cybersecurity professionals, the following point was concluded: 80% of challenges included bugs which pertain to categories from well established standards, such as OWASP Top10 and CWE Top25. The average snippet length was 12.8 lines of code, containing 1–3 vulnerabilities (1.4 average).

5   Discussion

Overall, we have observed an encouraging amount of proactive respondents (52.17%, or 12/23), cf. the Sankey diagram presented in Fig. 8. In total, we received 5 code contributions and 7 responses indicating interest in participating in crowdsourcing content. Of the received snippets, all contributors annotated their snippet and followed the indicated convention. Furthermore, one respondent included a link and another respondent followed the complex comment convention, with all options. We consider this a positive result, indicating that the proposed simple comment convention is very approachable and that the complex convention can also be followed by users with receiving minimal onboarding about the UGC pipeline.

These results show a positive potential to enable User Generated Content for our Serious Game, DuckDebugger. The engagement funnel results also confirm previous results that the comment convention is clear enough to be followed with minimal onboarding. We currently consider the sourcing of varied challenges to be the primary bottleneck in extending the platform's challenge collection, and as such, consider following the simple comment convention to suffice for this purpose. A manual quality gate instrumented by manual review of UGC challenges can further augment crowd-sourced content to include optional solution tags (NUMS, KWORDS) and ensure the general correctness and alignment of the content with the industrial guidelines.

By allowing developers to submit and validate security challenges, DuckDebugger functions not just as an educational tool but as an artifact of empowerment. Tessem [25] notes that psychological empowerment is driven by autonomy, competence, and meaningful work, all of which are reinforced when developers actively contribute to a security training platform. This shift from passive learning to active content creation aligns with the principles of structural empowerment, where individuals gain decision-making power and influence over shared knowledge. Furthermore, as contributors see their submissions adopted, they gain a sense of impact, reinforcing ownership over security best practices.

However, the success of UGC in cybersecurity education depends on both technical and human factors. Maintaining submission quality requires a balance between automated validation and human oversight, ensuring that the challenges contributed are educationally valuable and security relevant. Since UGC is only as effective as its contributors and curators, designing clear contribution guidelines and lightweight moderation mechanisms is crucial to sustaining high-quality content.

Further research would be required to explore how to maximize willingness to contribute and mechanisms for content curation, but these initial results are nonetheless optimistic, given that the premise of the survey was first of all to assess the clarity of the comment convention, rather than to receive snippets.

6   Conclusion and Future Work

This work investigated the feasibility of integrating User Generated Content (UGC) in the DuckDebugger Serious Game for industrial cybersecurity education and training. We designed and implemented a content ingestion pipeline, allowing developers to contribute security-relevant code snippets. Our study evaluated the technical design choices, contributor perceptions, and the characteristics of effective educational security challenges.

Our findings indicate that UGC is a viable approach for expanding the game's repository of security flaws. The comment convention received high clarity ratings, particularly for the simple comment format (91.3% positive), while extended tagging options (NUMS, KWORDS, custom fields) were also valued by participants. The study revealed a high degree of proactiveness among industry practitioners, with 21.73% submitting a challenge and 30.43% expressing interest in future contributions. Contributions adhered to the prescribed format, demonstrating the feasibility of a structured crowdsourcing approach.

Beyond its technical contributions, this study demonstrates that UGC fosters empowerment among developers, turning DuckDebugger into an empowering artifact for cybersecurity education. By allowing practitioners to contribute and refine security challenges, the game shifts control from a centralized development team to the developer community, fostering structural empowerment through decision-making autonomy and knowledge-sharing.

Furthermore, psychological empowerment is reinforced by the meaningfulness, competence, and impact contributors experience when engaging with security education through active participation. The ability to define, share, and validate security vulnerabilities mirrors participatory decision-making in agile teams, increasing motivation and ownership of security best practices.

This aligns with prior research highlighting that empowered individuals exhibit higher engagement, job satisfaction, and a stronger security mindset.

In future work, the authors would like to explore scaling UGC contributions by improving automation in content validation and streamlining the submission process. Sustaining long-term contributor engagement is critical and merits future exploration; however, the transient nature of industrial settings constrains repeatability and reliable access to participants, owing to the fluidity of organizational structures and personnel. Ensuring high-quality, security-relevant challenges requires automated filtering mechanisms to enforce alignment with industry standards (e.g. OWASP Top 10, CWE Top 25) while keeping the contribution process intuitive and accessible. Additionally, refining moderation workflows and providing structured templates can enhance submission quality and encourage broader participation. Crowdsourcing security challenges may risk redundancy through recurring or overly familiar content, or introduce complexity that exceeds players' understanding. Additionally, contributors may submit misleading examples that require unrealistic assumptions or span multiple files, reducing their educational value.

Further work should explore UGC integration into real-world security practices to ensure relevance across different software development workflows. Expanding the DuckDebugger's crowdsourcing model to other industries, such as finance, healthcare, and industrial control systems, could help tailor cybersecurity training to sector-specific threats. By refining the UGC pipeline and fostering cross-industry adoption, DuckDebugger can evolve into a scalable, community-driven platform for security education and knowledge-sharing, further empowering developers to shape their own peers' cybersecurity training.

Acknowledgment. This research task was partially supported by the Fundação para a Ciência e a Tecnologia, I.P. (FCT) through ISTAR projects UIDB/04466/2020 and UIDP/04466/2020. Ulrike Lechner acknowledges funding for project CONTAIN by the Bundesministerium für Bildung und Forschung (FKZ 13N16581). Andrei-Cristian Iosif acknowledges the funding provided by the Bundesministerium für Bildung und Forschung (BMBF) for the project CONTAIN with the number 13N16585.

References

1. Allen, J.H., Barnum, S., Ellison, R.J., McGraw, G., Mead, N.R.: Software Security Engineering: A Guide for Project Managers. Addison-Wesley, Boston (2008)
2. Bosu, A., Carver, J.C.: Impact of peer code review on peer impression formation: a survey. In: 2013 ACM / IEEE International Symposium on Empirical Software Engineering and Measurement, pp. 133–142. IEEE (2013). https://doi.org/10.1109/esem.2013.23
3. Burch, N.: The four stages for learning any new skill. Gordon Training International, CA (1970)
4. Dorner, M., Mendez, D., Wnuk, K., Zabardast, E., Czerwonka, J.: The upper bound of information diffusion in code review. Empirical Softw. Eng. **30**(1) (2024). https://doi.org/10.1007/s10664-024-10442-y
5. Dörner, R., Göbel, S., Effelsberg, W., Wiemeyer, J.: Serious Games: Foundations. Springer International Publishing (September, Concepts and Practice (2016)
6. Regulation 2024/2847 of the European Parliament and of the Council of 23 October 2024 on horizontal cybersecurity requirements for products with digital elements (Cyber Resilience Act). `bit.ly/eu-cra` (2024). Accessed 18 Dec 2024
7. Faber, M.J.: Open Innovation Ansatz von Reichwald/Piller, pp. 45–65. Gabler, Wiesbaden (2009). https://doi.org/10.1007/978-3-8349-8027-4_4
8. Hendrix, M., Al-Sherbaz, A., Bloom, V.: Game based cyber security training: are serious games suitable for cyber security training? Int. J. Serious Games **3**(1) (2016). https://doi.org/10.17083/ijsg.v3i1.107
9. von Hippel, E.: Democratizing Innovation. The MIT Press, Cambridge (2005). https://doi.org/10.7551/mitpress/2333.001.0001
10. Iosif, A.C., Espinha Gasiba, T., Lechner, U., Albuquerque, M.P.: Raising awareness in the industry on secure code review practices. In: 8th International Conference on Cyber-Technologies and Cyber-Systems, pp. 62–68. IARIA (2023)

11. Iosif, A.C., Lechner, U., Pinto-Albuquerque, M., Espinha Gasiba, T.: Code review for cybersecurity in the industry: insights from gameplay analytics. In: Santos, A.L., Pinto-Albuquerque, M. (eds.) 5th International Computer Programming Education Conference (ICPEC 2024). Open Access Series in Informatics (OASIcs), vol. 122, pp. 14:1–14:11. Schloss Dagstuhl – Leibniz-Zentrum für Informatik, Dagstuhl, Germany (2024). https://doi.org/10.4230/OASIcs.ICPEC.2024.14

12. Iosif, A.C., Lechner, U., Pinto-Albuquerque, M., Espinha Gasiba, T.: Cybersecurity awareness training for industrial software developers via a serious game for code review. In: Wirtschaftsinformatik 2024 Proceedings. No. 60 in 19 (2024). https://aisel.aisnet.org/wi2024/60

13. Iosif, A.C., Lechner, U., Pinto-Albuquerque, M., Gasiba, T.E.: Serious game for industrial cybersecurity: experiential learning through code review. In: 36th International Conference on Software Engineering Education and Training (CSEE&T), pp. 1–6. IEEE (2024). https://doi.org/10.1109/cseet62301.2024.10663058

14. Leong, C., Pan, S., Ractham, P., Kaewkitipong, L.: ICT-enabled community empowerment in crisis response: social media in thailand flooding 2011. J. Assoc. Inf. Syst. 16(3), 174–212 (2015). https://doi.org/10.17705/1jais.00390

15. Lukyanenko, R., Parsons, J., Wiersma, Y., Sieber, R., Maddah, M.: Participatory design for user-generated content: understanding the challenges and moving forward. Scandinavian J. Inf. Syst. 28(1) (2016)

16. Lukyanenko, R., Parsons, J., Wiersma, Y., Wachinger, G., Huber, B., Meldt, R.: Representing crowd knowledge: guidelines for conceptual modeling of user-generated content. J. Assoc. Inf. Syst. 18(4), 297–339 (2017). https://doi.org/10.17705/1jais.00456

17. Lukyanenko, R., Parsons, J., Wiersma, Y.F.: The IQ of the crowd: understanding and improving information quality in structured user-generated content. Inf. Syst. Res. 25(4), 669–689 (2014). https://doi.org/10.1287/isre.2014.0537

18. McGraw, G.: Software Security: Building Security In. Addison-Wesley Professional, Boston, MA (2006)

19. Naab, T.K., Sehl, A.: Studies of user-generated content: a systematic review. Journalism 18(10), 1256–1273 (2016). https://doi.org/10.1177/1464884916673557

20. Prümmer, J., van Steen, T., van den Berg, B.: A systematic review of current cybersecurity training methods. Comput. Secur. 136, 103585 (2024). https://doi.org/10.1016/j.cose.2023.103585

21. Roepke, R., Schroeder, U.: The problem with teaching defence against the dark arts: a review of game-based learning applications and serious games for cyber security education. In: Proceedings of the 11th International Conference on Computer Supported Education. SCITEPRESS - Science and Technology Publications (2019). https://doi.org/10.5220/0007706100580066

22. Seibert, S.E., Wang, G., Courtright, S.H.: Antecedents and consequences of psychological and team empowerment in organizations: a meta-analytic review. J. Appl. Psychol. 96(5), 981–1003 (2011). https://doi.org/10.1037/a0022676

23. Siami Namin, A., Aguirre-Muñoz, Z., Jones, K.: Teaching cyber security through competition an experience report about a participatory training workshop. In: 7th Annual International Conference on Computer Science Education: Innovation & Technology (CSEIT 2016). CSEIT, Global Science & Technology Forum (GSTF) (2016). https://doi.org/10.5176/2251-2195_cseit16.39

24. Sina, S., Rosenfeld, A., Kraus, S.: Generating content for scenario-based serious-games using crowdsourcing. In: Proceedings of the AAAI Conference on Artificial Intelligence, vol. 28, no. 1 (2014). https://doi.org/10.1609/aaai.v28i1.8790

25. Tessem, B.: Individual empowerment of agile and non-agile software developers in small teams. Inf. Softw. Technol. **56**(8), 873–889 (2014). https://doi.org/10.1016/j.infsof.2014.02.005
26. Weir, C., Rashid, A., Noble, J.: Challenging software developers: dialectic as a foundation for security assurance techniques. J. Cybersecur. **6**(1) (2020). https://doi.org/10.1093/cybsec/tyaa007
27. Švábenský, V., Vykopal, J., Cermak, M., Laštovička, M.: Enhancing cybersecurity skills by creating serious games. In: Proceedings of the 23rd Annual ACM Conference on Innovation and Technology in Computer Science Education. ITiCSE 2018, ACM (2018). https://doi.org/10.1145/3197091.3197123

From Paper to Pixel: The Digitalization of a Serious Game

Judith Strussenberg$^{(\boxtimes)}$ ⓘ, Karl Seidenfad ⓘ, Maximilian Greiner ⓘ,
Kevin Riesel, Jan Biermann ⓘ, and Ulrike Lechner ⓘ

University of the Bundeswehr Munich, Neubiberg, Germany
Judith.Strussenberg@unibw.de

Abstract. *A Question of Security* is a serious game that aims to enhance cybersecurity awareness and incident response preparedness. Its current tabletop format presents several limitations that may restrict its scalability and adaptability. In this article, we present the integration path for the Miroⓒ digital whiteboard platform. Using a Design Science Research approach, we outline the transformation from a physical tabletop format to a digital game. We start by explaining the concept of *A Question of Security* to make both the digital implementation and our design decisions understandable. Then, we show where and how elements could be adopted for digital use and where there were challenges and considerations that must have been taken into account. We would not have designed a digital version if digitization had not offered us interesting and promising opportunities and possibilities to further develop the game. As a result, the digital version of the game provides an interactive, scalable, and engaging platform for participants. The game now allows remote teams to participate from anywhere, eliminates the need for physical presence, and enables simple modifications to the scenario to reflect emerging cybersecurity threats. The digital format ensures that cybersecurity education remains interactive and accessible to a broader audience, making it a resource for organizations seeking to strengthen their security awareness and response strategies.

Keywords: Serious games · Digitalization · IT security ·
Cybersecurity · Awareness

1 Introduction

Cybersecurity incidents, particularly ransomware attacks, pose a growing threat to individuals and organizations, requiring rapid and effective responses [19]. Although technical solutions play a crucial role in mitigating risks, the human factor remains a critical element to ensure the resilience to cybersecurity [17,20]. Employees must be equipped with decision making skills and awareness to respond effectively when faced with an attack. Traditional cybersecurity training methods often lack engagement, leading to limited retention and practical application [8]. To address this, serious games can be used as an effective tool for interactive learning and scenario-based training, allowing participants to

S. Zielinski et al. (Eds.): I4CS 2025, CCIS 2513, pp. 307–329, 2025.
https://doi.org/10.1007/978-3-031-94263-1_18

explore real-world cybersecurity challenges in a controlled and risk-free environment [2]. Especially in cybersecurity incidents, collaboration and communication are important for successfully responding to threats [28].

This paper builds on *A Question of Security*, a serious game designed to train non-experts in incident response strategies for ransomware attacks [30]. Originally developed as a tabletop game, it simulates the experience of dealing with a compromised smartphone used for both business and personal purposes. The round-based structure of the game encourages players to identify risks, make critical decisions and reflect on the impact of their actions, fostering a deeper understanding of cybersecurity best practices. While effective in small groups, the physical format presents limitations, such as restricted participant numbers, logistical constraints, and limited adaptability to new scenarios.

To overcome these challenges, our goal is to migrate *A Question of Security* to a Miro virtual whiteboard, expanding its scalability, accessibility, and flexibility. Using a Design Science Research (DSR) approach, we design a digital version to enable remote collaboration, making the game more inclusive for hybrid and distributed teams. Additionally, the transition allows for real-time interaction, automated event triggers, and scenario customization, ensuring that the game remains engaging and adaptable to evolving cybersecurity threats.

We further explore the design process, gameplay mechanics, and benefits of the Miro-based version of *A Question of Security*. We discuss how this digital transformation enhances engagement, accessibility, and scalability, addressing the limitations of traditional tabletop training. Furthermore, we examine the potential for artificial intelligence integration, where a large language model (LLM) could replace the human game leader, making the game more cost-effective and available on demand. The findings contribute to the growing body of research on serious games for cybersecurity training, demonstrating how digital and gamified approaches can strengthen cybersecurity awareness and incident response preparedness.

The paper is structured as follows. It begins with an overview of the theoretical background in Sect. 2, covering serious games, IT security, cybersecurity awareness, and the digitalization of learning tools. The research design is then presented in Sect. 3, followed by a detailed description of the physical tabletop game *A Question of Security* and its limitations in Sect. 4. In Sect. 5, the virtual adaptation is introduced, highlighting its structure and functionality. The results in Sect. 6 explore the digital implementation, the participant experience, and the navigation within the platform. A discussion in Sect. 7 follows, comparing the traditional and digital formats. In Sect. 8, the paper concludes with key findings and future research directions.

2   Theoretical Background

This theoretical background introduces the interdisciplinary foundations for employing serious games as effective educational tools. It outlines how serious games merge learning objectives with engaging gameplay to enhance motivation, knowledge retention, and practical skills—especially in contexts like incident management and cybersecurity. Furthermore, it discusses the evolving concept of IT security awareness, emphasizing the cognitive and behavioral dimensions required for secure practices, as well as the challenges and benefits of digitizing serious games. Together, these perspectives provide a comprehensive framework for understanding the design, application, and impact of serious games in both training and real-world scenarios.

2.1   Serious Games

Serious games integrate educational or training content with game-based elements, creating learning experiences beyond entertainment [5,7,14]. In this regard, these games have demonstrated effectiveness in enhancing motivation, engagement, and knowledge retention in various domains, including education, healthcare, and business [10,12,27]. Successful serious games balance educational objectives with engaging gameplay elements. Research suggests that incremental difficulty levels, real-time feedback, and opportunities for reflection enhance learning effectiveness [23]. Immersive, scenario-driven game designs further boost engagement and knowledge retention. They can also raise awareness, empathy and lead to social change [18]. Moreover, collaboration within serious games strengthens team coordination and communication skills [1].

In the context of incident management, serious games offer an ideal opportunity to simulate real-life scenarios. Players can master realistic situations, such as dealing with security incidents, in a protected environment [14]. This method not only promotes awareness of risks and challenges, but also helps to understand decisions and consequences and reflect on their own actions [5,12]. By repeating these scenarios, participants can continuously develop and internalize the skill [14]. Collaborative approaches can also promote teamwork and communication [27]. Learning content and game mechanics must be combined in such a way that they are fun, motivating and effective at the same time [14]. In this context, learning approaches with increasing levels of difficulty have proven to be useful [12]. Regular feedback and the opportunity for reflection are key components to support the learning process and enable skills to be improved [27]. An immersive and realistic design of the game environment increases engagement and makes learning sustainable. To enable players to concentrate fully on the learning content, the design should be intuitive and user-friendly [14]. Serious games therefore represent an innovative and effective method for teaching complex content and content and sustainably promote practical skills in areas such as incident management sustainably.

2.2   IT Security and Cybersecurity Awareness

Information security awareness describes the degree of sensitization to information security. The term has thus also found its way into the German-speaking world, also in the form security awareness or awareness for short. There are different views in research on the question of what exactly is meant by awareness in the context of IT security [25,32]. Richter et al. [25] suggest reading the term information security awareness as the conscious handling of information that considers the security risks regardless of its medium. This definition illustrates the problem with the German term Sensibilization, which is used as an alternative to awareness: Understood in this way, awareness is a state, while sensitization describes a process. According to Weber's [32] understanding, security awareness is a cognitive and affective construct that encompasses all factors that lead to information security-compliant behavior. Specifically, these are behavioral intention, knowledge, salience, and/or habit. In practice, IT security awareness is often equated with training and education, where the outcome is to make employees' behavior more secure. Weber argues that although this approach serves the knowledge factor, it ignores the aforementioned essential factors of human behavior formation and can therefore be doomed to failure [31]. If attempts are made to achieve the desired result, namely compliance with a company's information security guidelines, through coercion and negative consequences, this can lead to the opposite effect [4]. In order to create a positive, motivating version of awareness creation, a serious game was developed that deals with ransomware.

Ransomware is a form of malware that is designed to generate economic profit through blackmail. It blocks access to systems or encrypts files in order to subsequently demand a ransom from the affected users [16,22,33]. The literature distinguishes between two or three forms of ransomware. 'Locker ransomware', which blocks access to a system without encrypting data and 'Crypto ransomware', which encrypts files and provides victims with the decryption key only against payment [33]. The third type combines the first two types and is therefore called the 'Hybrid Type' [3,13]. Ransomware can be spread via different attack vectors, with phishing and social engineering playing a central role. Here, victims are sent manipulated emails to open malicious attachments or links that contain and execute malicious code [16,22,33]. Newer ransomware variants can simultaneously exfiltrate data in addition to encrypting it in order to gain access to sensitive information. This is done to add additional pressure on victims by threatening to publish sensitive information [16].

2.3 Digitalization of Serious Games

Dörner et al. [6] cite several reasons for the digitalization of serious games. Main arguments are that fun increases motivation, promotes goal achievement, and enables immediate feedback so that users can evaluate their progress. Digital games are also easier to adapt. At the same time, there are challenges: A serious game might offer too little entertainment, which makes immersion more difficult. Larsson and Ekblad [15] note that digital tabletop games often fail to achieve the social interaction and engagement of physical variants. Especially, games with incomplete information mechanics benefit from physical implementation. Nevertheless, there are exceptions, especially in games with high social connectivity. Overall, digital games were only rated slightly better in terms of usability. In addition, they often restrict social interaction, for example, through limited means of communication such as prefabricated messages and emojis [15]. When switching from digital to physical versions, tester perceptions of rules and mechanics changed, although similar digital implementations were deliberately chosen. Kaufman [11] compared analog and digital versions of a public health game in terms of perception, attitude and cognition. Players of the digital version showed no significant change in attitude or improvement in systems thinking, but perceived the game as more complicated. Although both versions were nearly identical, digitization led to significant differences. Kaufman [11] suggests that analog and digital games create different mindsets and expectations, which may influence their effect on learning and attitude.

Only a few approaches can be found in the literature in which a Miro board is explicitly used to implement a serious game [26,29]. Stals et al. [29] describe the use of Miro to co-create a serious game via software development with the help of the Serious Slow Game Jam (SSGJ) method. *Breaking the Silos* is a serious game designed to help various stakeholders such as policy makers, risk managers and researchers to understand and manage the complexity of DRR000 measures in a multi-hazard environment. What both games have in common is that the COVID-19 pandemic has made it difficult to play them in person, so making a digital version of each became necessary.

Although serious games have shown promise in enhancing cybersecurity awareness, their digital adaptation, especially for non-expert incident response training, remains underexplored. Existing research highlights challenges in maintaining engagement and collaboration in virtual formats. This paper addresses this gap by examining how a physical tabletop game can be effectively transformed into a scalable, interactive digital version using Miro.

3   Research Design

Our research procedure follows the DSR approach according to Hevner et al. [9] to develop and evaluate an innovative artifact - the digitalization of the serious game *A Question of Security*. This research is part of a larger project with several iterative design cycles. The first design cycle includes the design, development, execution, and refinement of the physical tabletop game *A Question of Security*. In this paper, we present the foundation for the second design cycle, which involves the digitalization of the game. Therefore, we draw on the reflection and learning of the first cycle to provide our problem space by describing our game scenario and the limitations of the physical tabletop game. The primary artifact of this work is the digital version of the game, which retains its core cybersecurity education objectives while incorporating structured digital interactions and automated facilitation. This transformation addresses the problem of limited scalability and accessibility in traditional tabletop games used for cybersecurity training.

The design process begins with the conceptual transformation of the physical tabletop game into a digital format, requiring a systematic analysis of the game mechanics, user interactions, and technical requirements. This involves mapping existing game components to digital equivalents, selecting appropriate platforms, and designing an interactive interface that preserves the educational and engagement goals of the game. The development process follows an iterative prototyping approach. In doing so, the focus is on the virtual game board, the interactive elements, remote collaboration and accessibility, and customization and expansion. In addition, a refinement phase takes place where post-game reflection and learning leads to the final result. The study employs a comparative ex-post evaluation, contrasting the digital version with the physical game to assess learning outcomes and engagement differences [21]. The methodological rigor is ensured through a structured development-evaluation cycle, where theoretical insights from game-based learning and cybersecurity education inform design decisions, while empirical validation iteratively refines the artifact.

4   Scenario Outline

4.1   The Tabletop Game Design *A Question of Security*

The serious game *A Question of Security* is a tabletop turn-based game designed to educate players on ransomware incident response [30]. It is structured to simulate a real-life ransomware attack on a smartphone used for both business and personal purposes, helping players develop the necessary questions and actions to mitigate such an incident effectively. The game encourages players to think critically, collaborate, and learn best practices in cybersecurity without requiring prior technical expertise. The game's setup and structure is characterized as follows (see Fig. 1):

- The game is designed for three to eight players working together as a team.
- It consists of five structured rounds, each taking 10–15 min.
- Players interact with playing cards, a dice, a scoreboard, and game figures.
- A game leader (facilitator) guides the game, acting as a quiz master and storyteller, providing responses to players' questions about handling ransomware incidents.

The gameplay revolves around progressive problem-solving through a ransomware crisis on a smartphone. The goal is to restore the ability to work by regaining access to a smartphone with its services while minimizing damage to data, privacy, and business operations. Unlike other games, the game rounds here differ in terms of the process and the object of consideration (see Fig. 2). In round 1, the focus is on the fears and anxieties of the affected individual with regard to the incident. Rounds 2 to 4 work according to the same game principle and focus on solving the incident with the aim of restoring the ability to work as well as on the options for action and possible resources that the person affected has here. The last round opens up the view from the individual smartphone user to the other stakeholders, such as family, friends, and colleagues, the IT security officer, the data protection officer, or security authorities.

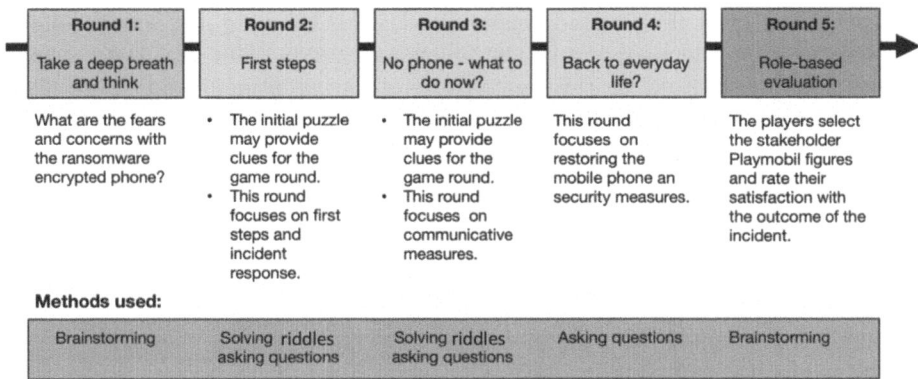

Round 1:	Round 2:	Round 3:	Round 4:	Round 5:
Take a deep breath and think	First steps	No phone - what to do now?	Back to everyday life?	Role-based evaluation
What are the fears and concerns with the ransomware encrypted phone?	• The initial puzzle may provide clues for the game round. • This round focuses on first steps and incident response.	• The initial puzzle may provide clues for the game round. • This round focuses on communicative measures.	This round focuses on restoring the mobile phone an security measures.	The players select the stakeholder Playmobil figures and rate their satisfaction with the outcome of the incident.

Methods used:

Brainstorming	Solving riddles asking questions	Solving riddles asking questions	Asking questions	Brainstorming

Fig. 1. Conceptual overview of *A Question of Security*, outlining its core mechanics, round-based structure, and educational objectives in cybersecurity awareness and incident response.

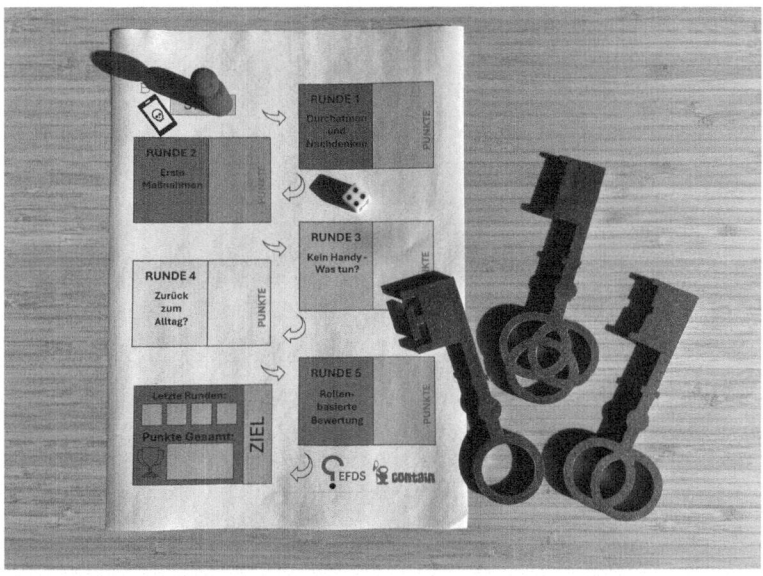

Fig. 2. Overview of the tabletop version of *A Question of Security*, depicting the physical components, player roles, and structured gameplay mechanics.

Round 1: Take a Deep Breath and Think. In Round 1, players are introduced to the ransomware scenario where their smartphone, used for both business and personal purposes, has been encrypted. They reflect on the immediate consequences of the attack, such as potential data loss, financial risks, and work interruptions. Players write down their fears and concerns on premade cards, addressing issues like labor law implications, lost backups, or inability to access transportation apps. This round encourages critical thinking and sets the stage for structured problem-solving in the following rounds. The goal is to engage players emotionally and to raise awareness of the emotional and operational impact of a ransomware incident.

Round 2: First Steps. In Round 2, the players begin to formulate initial response actions to the ransomware attack. They write down critical questions such as:

- Who should I inform?
- Should I disconnect from the internet?
- How do I document the incident?

The game leader provides responses based on best practices, emphasizing informing IT security, preserving evidence, and avoiding hasty actions that could worsen the situation. Players roll dice, introducing random events that simulate real-life disruptions. The round concludes with players handing over their infected phone to IT for recovery, reinforcing the importance of proper incident reporting and containment.

Round 3: No Phone What to Do Now? In Round 3, players navigate the challenges of working and communicating without access to their smartphone. They brainstorm and write down questions like:

- How can I continue working without my phone?
- What alternative communication methods are available?
- How do I inform colleagues, clients, and family?

The game leader provides guidance on temporary solutions, such as using backup devices, secure communication alternatives, and adjusting workflows. A puzzle challenge, inspired by escape rooms, provides hints for key questions in round 2 and 3. This round highlights the organizational and personal impact of ransomware and the importance of preparedness and contingency planning.

Round 4: Back to Everyday Life? In Round 4, players focus on restoring normal operations while strengthening security to prevent future ransomware incidents. They consider questions such as:

- How can I securely restore my smartphone?
- What security measures should I implement to prevent future attacks?
- Should I change passwords or enable multi-factor authentication (MFA)?

The game leader provides insights into safe device recovery, data restoration, and best security practices. This round emphasizes long-term improvements, including backup strategies, software updates, and cybersecurity policies. The goal is to transition from reactive recovery to proactive security enhancements for better incident preparedness.

Round 5: Role-Based Evaluation. In Round 5, players assess the effectiveness of their incident response by adopting different stakeholder perspectives, such as the CEO, IT security, data protection officers, employees, and family members. Each role evaluates how well the situation was handled and identifies strengths and weaknesses in the response.

Players use Playmobil figures (see Fig. 3) to represent the affected parties during the incident and discuss their satisfaction levels with the recovery process. The game leader facilitates reflection on crisis communication, organizational policies, and lessons learned. This round helps players understand the broader impact of ransomware incidents, the different focuses of the individual stakeholders, and reinforces collaboration in cybersecurity resilience.

Fig. 3. Playmobil figures used in Round 5 to symbolize different stakeholder perspectives in the role-based evaluation phase. Players use these figures to analyze various viewpoints and assess the effectiveness of their ransomware response.

4.2 Limitations of the Tabletop Game Design

While *A Question of Security* is an effective serious game for cybersecurity awareness and incident response training, its current tabletop format presents several limitations that may restrict its scalability and adaptability.

First, the number of participants is highly limited. The game is designed for three to eight players, making it challenging to accommodate larger groups in a single session. Organizations with many employees would need to conduct multiple game sessions, which may be time-consuming and resource-intensive.

Second, the game requires the physical presence of all players, which can be a barrier in remote or hybrid work environments. As modern workplaces increasingly adopt remote collaboration, the necessity of gathering all participants in one location reduces the game's accessibility and flexibility.

Third, the static nature of the physical game components makes it difficult to modify the storyline or integrate entirely new scenarios. While the game is designed to simulate a ransomware attack, expanding it to cover other cybersecurity threats—such as phishing, insider threats, or cloud security issues—would require significant redesign of physical materials. A digital version of the game could offer greater adaptability by allowing easy updates, new narratives, and customizable experiences for different user groups and organizational needs.

Future developments could explore digital adaptations to overcome these limitations, enabling larger-scale participation, remote accessibility, and enhanced scenario customization while maintaining the game's core educational and engagement value.

5   A *Question of Security* as a Virtual Tabletop Game

To overcome the limitations of the physical tabletop format, *A Question of Security* can be adapted to digital whiteboard platforms such as Miro [24]. These platforms provide an interactive and collaborative environment that can effectively simulate gameplay while allowing remote participation, scalability, and easy scenario customization. The fact that several players can edit the board at the same time promotes the interactive character of Serious Games. In addition, external media such as images, videos, and links can be integrated to improve the gaming experience and create a more immersive feeling. Errors can also be easily corrected, which creates a risk-free teaching environment.

5.1   Channels of Interaction

While the interactive and visual components of the serious game can be mapped well in Miro, an auditory channel is missing here, which is essential for the success of the serious game in the current version. Accordingly, an additional video conferencing tool is needed to cover this part of the requirements. Seeing the players and interacting with them gives the game master additional information about the interest of the players, whether they are attentive or tired, which can be very helpful in making a game successful and fun for everyone involved. Therefore, in this article we present the integration path for the Miro digital whiteboard platform.

5.2   Platform Features and Game Structure

To implement *A Question of Security* on Miro, the game board needs to be recreated in a digital format while maintaining the structure of the physical tabletop version. The first step here is to consider the functions and features to be used. The free version includes many basic functions such as creating boards, placing sticky notes or inserting images and texts, but there are still some restrictions that affect the gameplay. A distinction must be made between functions that make the gameplay more enjoyable for the game master, so that he can pay more attention to the players, and functions that have a direct influence on the game. For example the locking of objects in the free version is only possible to a limited extent, which can lead to game content being moved or changed unintentionally. The paid version also makes it possible to better guide players through individual rounds, making the process more structured and more predictable. This not only makes it easier for the moderator to control the game but also ensures a smoother gaming experience. The timer, which is used for time-limited game rounds, is available only in the paid version. The timer proved to be an important feature in the course of the analog game rounds, as it is very well suited to simulating the time pressure that would also arise in such a situation in reality.

Depending on the application scenario, it should therefore be weighed up whether the free version is sufficient for the implementation of the game or whether the use of the paid version to support the game mechanics and moderation even more. Through the targeted use of these functions, the original game is enhanced by the digital possibilities of a paid Miro version. The interactive elements promote collaboration, while the clear structure ensures that players can find their way around at all times. Players can find their way around at any time. This enables a modern and effective implementation of the serious game that is both playful and educational.

5.3   Creating the Virtual Board Setup

With this in mind, let us dive into the creation of the board itself: The board can be divided into five sections, one for each round, with designated areas for questions, answers, decision-making, and puzzles. Players interact with digital sticky notes or text boxes to write down their questions, simulating the physical cards used in the original game. The game leader has a hidden area where response cards are stored and revealed progressively as the game advances.

A drag-and-drop system can be implemented, where players move their question cards into the response area, allowing the game leader to provide structured feedback. Additionally, a collaborative notepad or comment section can be used for players to document key decisions, insights, and strategy discussions.

To enhance engagement, color-coded elements can differentiate game stages, and connectors/lines can visually link questions to answers. Pre-designed templates ensure that each game session follows a structured format, making the game easier to facilitate.

By setting up the game board digitally, players can collaborate remotely, and the game can be easily adapted or expanded for different cybersecurity training needs.

A useful element for getting started with the game is an area where players can first practice using the selected tool correctly and familiarize themselves with how to use it, e.g. dragging and labeling cards, zooming or navigating through the tool. This is not necessary with the analog version, as the game materials are usually used intuitively and correctly. When designing the virtual game board, care must be taken to create a navigation system that offers players intuitive guidance between the individual game elements such as the game board, rounds and events. This should fit into the action as organically as possible without interrupting the flow of the game.

6   Results

The *A Question of Security* serious game has been successfully implemented on a Miro virtual whiteboard, providing an interactive, scalable, and engaging platform for participants. The Miro implementation retains the game's round-based structure while incorporating new interactive elements such an event wheel, an additions in the use of point and dynamic transitions, and a clear user journey. Figure 4 depicts an overview of the whiteboard implementation with details for each figure. Another point that can increase the accessibility of the game is the chosen language. Care has already been taken to avoid technical IT terms wherever possible or to explain them so that users without in-depth technical knowledge can also participate and develop a better understanding of what is happening. However, German as the chosen language limits the target group, so consideration should be given to developing an English-language version in the future.

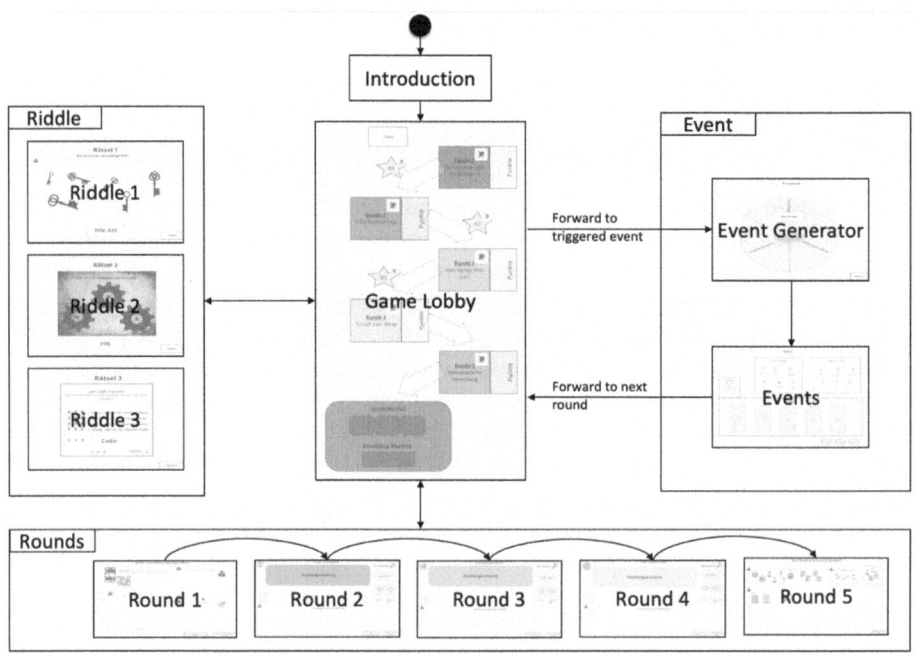

Fig. 4. Overview of the *A Question of Security* implementation in Miro, displaying all game components and user navigation paths. The connection lines illustrate the structured journey between different game stages.

The overview of the *A Question of Security* implementation in Fig. 4 displays all components of the game on the Miro whiteboard. The connection lines illustrate the users' journey across various game stages, ensuring a seamless progression between rounds and additional activities. The implementation of links and buttons is crucial for a good user experience, because otherwise you can easily loose track over the variety of elements on the Miro board.

The game lobby in Fig. 5 acts as the central hub, offering players entry points to each game round. The lobby also tracks progress by showing the number of remaining rounds, gained points and keeping participants engaged and motivated. The feedback from former participants has shown that an additional motivating factor for the players is when they can compare their score, i.e. the total number of points collected, with those of the previous teams. This feedback led to the introduction of the lower field on the game plan, which contains the last results in addition to the player's own result.

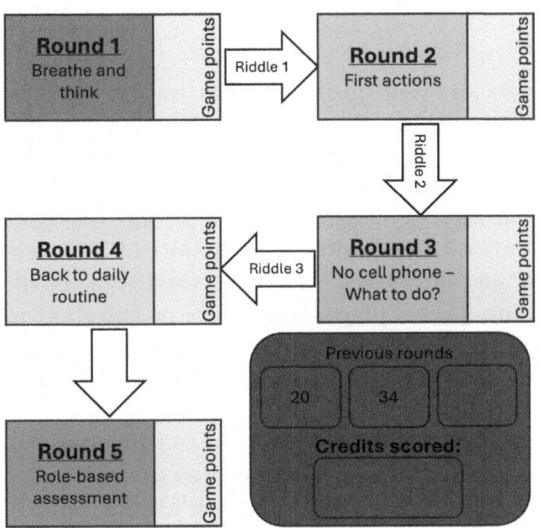

Fig. 5. The game lobby in Miro, serving as the central hub with entry points to each round.

The first round in Fig. 6, 'Take a Deep Breath and Think,' introduces the ransomware scenario. Participants identify their fears and concerns. The analog version is limited to these questions, which help you to better empathize with the situation. The digital version expands this setting to include the perspective of the attacker and also asks about the attack vectors and methods as well as the goals that are to be achieved with the attack.

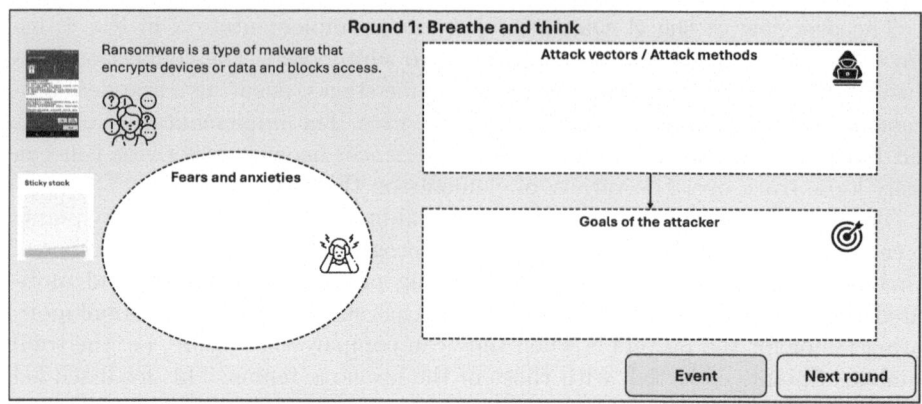

Fig. 6. Representation of Round 1, 'Take a Deep Breath and Think', where players analyze the ransomware scenario, identify potential attack vectors, and reflect on their immediate concerns.

Figure 7 highlights an event during the first round. Designed as a side quest, it provides players with an engaging mini-challenge that enriches the gameplay experience. Turning the event wheel initiates small side quests during the course of the game, which simulate interruptions typical of work in most offices. Depending on the result, positive or negative events or quiz questions follow. Players can gain or lose points or time and also win points by answering quiz questions correctly. The event wheel replaces the analog version of the dice roll, which the game master randomly asks a player to do once or twice per round.

The second round in Fig. 8, 'First Steps,' focuses on initial actions such as notifying IT security and preserving evidence. Players write down their strategies and discuss the best course of action. In the analog version, questions are formulated and written on cards, which are assigned to the recommended measures at the end of the round. This task can be translated directly by using digital sticky notes. So that the players do not have to search for the event wheel or the game board for a long time, they are guided to these elements on the Miro board via the buttons in the bottom right-hand corner. In the top right-hand field, you can see an element that has been newly developed in the digital version: For every two points, players can choose to buy a minute of extra time or a clue.

The third round in Fig. 9, 'No Phone – What to Do Now?' emphasizes maintaining workflows without smartphone access. Participants brainstorm alternative solutions and effective communication methods. In addition to the question of how to communicate, the reference process also includes informing superiors or colleagues about the incident and urging them to be more vigilant if the affected smartphone or the access and data on it are to be used for further attacks. The provision of relevant information for the information security officer or data protection officer also falls into this category. The aim is to show the players that they can contribute a great deal to successfully overcoming such a situation, even or especially in such a situation.

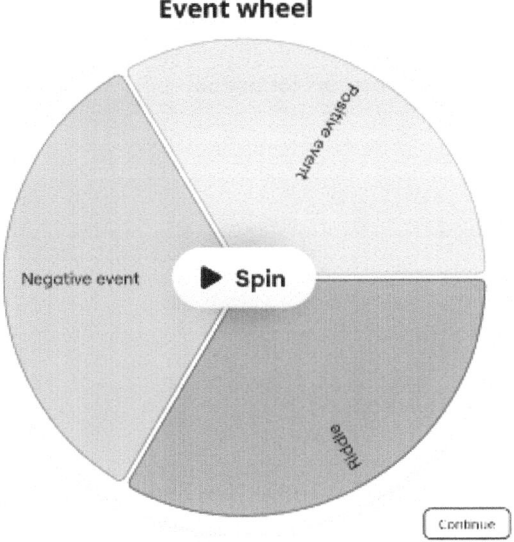

Fig. 7. The event wheel used in Round 1, introducing randomized side quests that simulate real-world workplace interruptions. Depending on the outcome, players face positive or negative events, quiz questions, or time penalties.

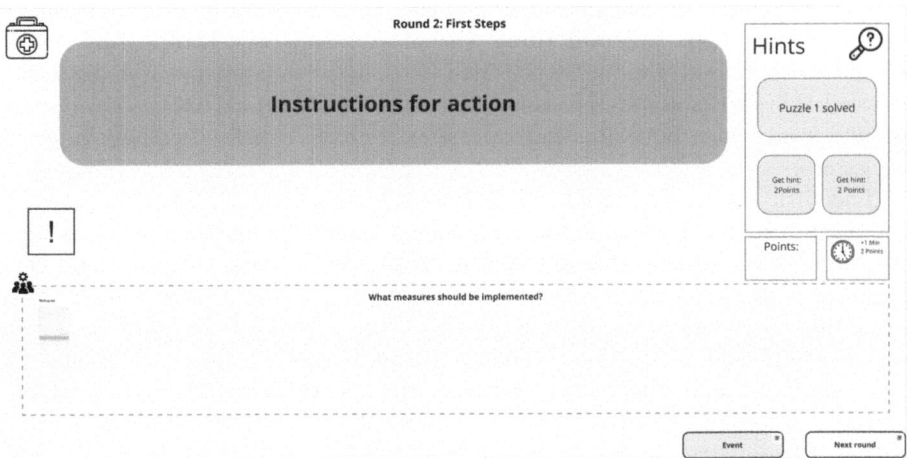

Fig. 8. Visualization of Round 2, 'First Steps', where players determine initial response actions, such as informing IT security, documenting the attack, and preserving evidence.

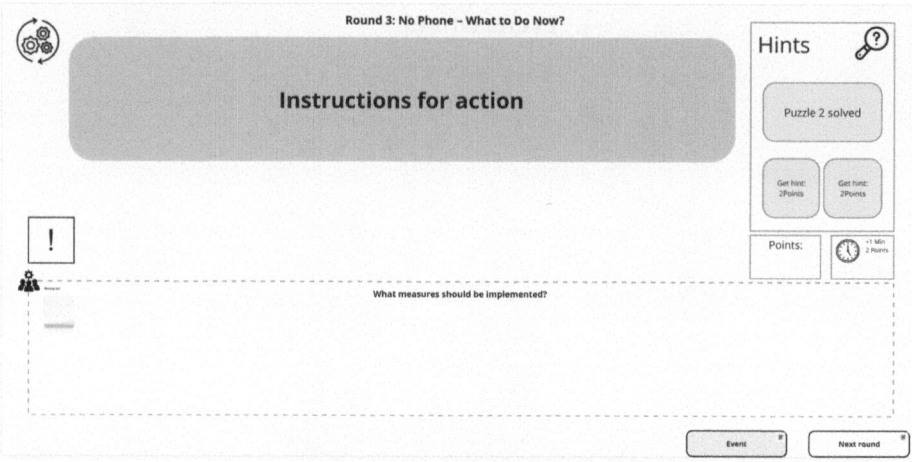

Fig. 9. Round 3, 'No Phone – What to Do Now?', focuses on maintaining workflows without smartphone access. Players brainstorm alternative communication methods and consider how to inform stakeholders about the incident.

The fourth round in Fig. 10, 'Back to Everyday Life,' explores restoring normal operations securely and strengthening long-term security measures. Players focus on recovery and prevention strategies. As this round is structured in the same way as rounds two and three, the players can concentrate fully on the content. The shared gaming experience and the associated natural discussion between the participants creates good conditions for an exchange on an equal footing, from which both amateurs and experts have benefited equally in previous games.

The fifth round in Fig. 11, 'Role-Based Evaluation,' shifts perspective to assess the response from different stakeholder roles. The participants first identify the relevant stakeholders for this incident. Afterwards, they evaluate their points of view and learn from the outcomes. In the past, these have differed depending on the group and company size. Typically mentioned are, for example, superiors and colleagues, friends and family, the IT department and the data protection and information security officers. However, the Federal Office for Information Security (BSI), law enforcement agencies, the legal department and the PR department have also been mentioned. To do this, the participants select a graphic symbolizing the role from the graphics at the top left and a field for labeling from the top middle box. On the red and green digital sticky notes in the central box, the participants write the positive and negative points that the stakeholders could make when assessing the ransomware incident. These elements are then grouped together in the central box, as shown in the example in the top right-hand box. Each figure adds a unique element to the game design, enhancing interactivity and player engagement. These features make the Miro implementation of *A Question of Security* an effective tool for remote and hybrid teams, allowing for flexible and immersive cybersecurity training.

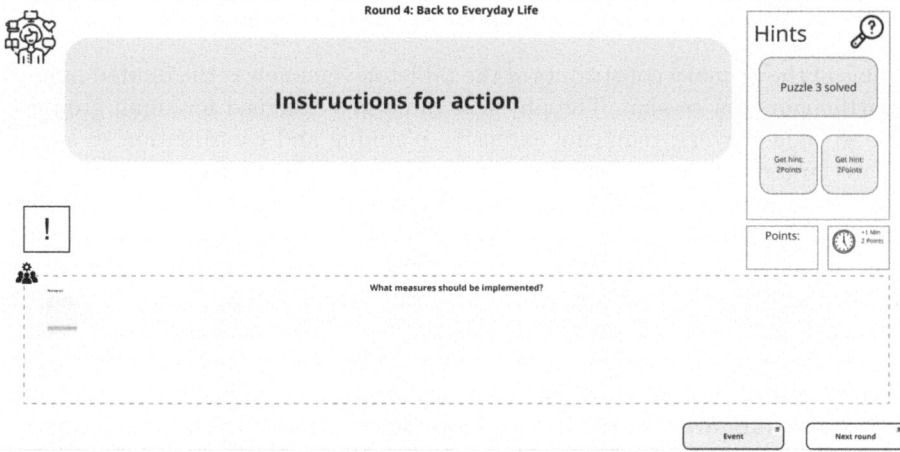

Fig. 10. Representation of Round 4, 'Back to Everyday Life', where players explore strategies for securely restoring operations and implementing long-term cybersecurity measures.

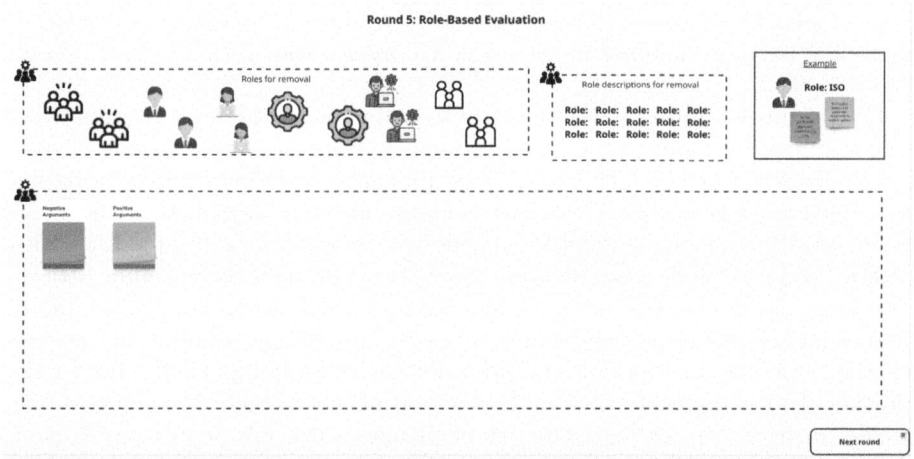

Fig. 11. Round 5, Role-Based Evaluation, where players assess the effectiveness of their response by adopting different stakeholder perspectives.

7   Discussion

Revisiting the three types of limitations identified in a physical tabletop game in Subsect. 4.2, the advantages of our chosen approach for designing a virtual tabletop game are discussed in light of the following limitations.

- Limited number of participants and planning efforts.
- Missing inclusion of hybrid work environments.

– Absence of a flexible game design and adaptability to new scenarios.

One of the primary constraints of the tabletop version was the limited number of participants per session. The physical game was designed for small groups of three to eight players, requiring extensive planning and coordination to accommodate larger audiences. This limitation made it difficult for organizations to integrate the game into large-scale training programs. Our Miro-based implementation has eliminated this issue by allowing multiple teams to play simultaneously within a shared digital workspace. By duplicating game boards, organizations can facilitate parallel sessions, ensuring that more employees can participate in cybersecurity training without logistical constraints. Additionally, the elimination of physical materials reduces preparation efforts, making it easier for organizations to schedule and conduct game sessions on demand.

A second limitation of the physical format was its lack of support for hybrid and remote work environments. Many modern organizations operate with distributed teams, making it impractical to gather all participants in a single physical location. The Miro adaptation directly solves this challenge by enabling remote collaboration. Players can join from any location, interacting with the game board in real time while communicating via integrated video conferencing or chat tools. This ensures that cybersecurity training is no longer restricted by geographic barriers, making it accessible to organizations with hybrid or fully remote teams.

The third key limitation was the rigid structure of the tabletop version, which made it difficult to modify or expand the game to cover new cybersecurity threats or organizational needs. The physical components—such as printed cards and pre-defined game scenarios—restricted adaptability. In contrast, the Miro-based version introduces a highly flexible game design, allowing for quick modifications, scenario updates, and customization. New threats, such as phishing attacks, insider threats, or cloud security breaches, can be easily integrated by modifying game elements or adding new question-answer cards. This adaptability ensures that the game remains relevant and up-to-date with evolving cybersecurity risks. Additionally, the digital format enables organizations to tailor the game to their specific security policies and industry challenges, ensuring contextual learning that is more impactful for participants.

However, implementing a serious game on Miro also poses challenges that need to be considered. The multitude of functions can initially seem overwhelming to new users and require a certain amount of familiarization time. In addition, performance problems can occur with large boards or complex projects, which can affect the user experience. To avoid chaos, it is essential to clearly structure the content and take technical precautions to ensure that it is not accidentally moved or changed. Thoughtful planning and organization are therefore necessary to make the most of Miro's capabilities and ensure smooth implementation of the game process.

When using a tool such as Miro, careful consideration must be given to whether the basic functionality of the free version is sufficient to create a serious game, or whether the game experience and handling by the game master does not increase to such an extent that it is worth using the paid version.

8   Conclusion and Outlook

The successful migration of *A Question of Security* to a Miro virtual whiteboard has significantly enhanced its accessibility, scalability, and adaptability while preserving its structured, round-based gameplay. Originally designed as a physical tabletop game, the serious game educates players on ransomware incident response by guiding them through a series of structured discussions and decision-making exercises. By transitioning to a digital format, the game now allows remote teams to participate from anywhere, eliminates the need for physical presence, and enables easy modifications to the scenario to reflect emerging cybersecurity threats.

The game retains its five-round structure, each of which simulates a different phase of an incident response. In the first round, players reflect on the immediate impact of a ransomware attack on their smartphone, considering risks such as compromised business and personal data, financial consequences, and communication disruptions. The second round focuses on defining the first steps to contain the incident, such as informing IT security, preserving forensic evidence, and preventing further damage. The third round shifts attention to how players can operate without their smartphone, addressing alternative means of communication and maintaining productivity. The fourth round explores recovery and preventive measures, encouraging participants to consider long-term security improvements such as backup strategies and multi-factor authentication. The final round introduces a role-based evaluation, where players assess their response from the perspectives of different stakeholders, such as CEOs, IT security officers, legal teams, and affected employees, allowing them to see the broader implications of their decisions.

Miro's virtual whiteboard functionality enhances the game's interactivity and effectiveness. Players can use digital sticky notes to write and organize their responses, while the game leader, who facilitates the session, can reveal predefined answer cards in real-time, mimicking the physical version's structured guidance. The digital board allows for a seamless, drag-and-drop approach, helping players visualize the progression of their decisions throughout the game. Additionally, integrating dice rolls, quizzes, and puzzles keeps the game dynamic and engaging.

One of the most significant advantages of the Miro version is its flexibility. Unlike the physical tabletop game, which requires fixed materials, the digital version can be easily customized to introduce new cybersecurity threats beyond ransomware, such as phishing, insider threats, or cloud security vulnerabilities. This makes it possible to tailor the game to different industries, ensuring relevance across various organizational contexts. Moreover, organizations can store and revisit game sessions to analyze decision-making patterns, allowing them to refine their real-world incident response strategies based on gameplay insights.

Another benefit of the virtual adaptation is that it fosters collaboration among remote and hybrid teams. By eliminating geographical constraints, it allows larger groups to participate simultaneously, making it an promising cyber-security training tool for modern work environments. Furthermore, post-game reflections can be recorded directly on the board, ensuring that key takeaways are documented for future reference. A digital scoreboard can track team performance, adding a gamified competitive element that increases engagement and motivation.

The transition of *A Question of Security* to Miro has transformed it into a more inclusive, scalable, and adaptable training tool while preserving its core objective of enhancing ransomware incident response preparedness. The digital format ensures that cybersecurity education remains interactive, relevant and accessible to a broader audience, making it a valuable resource for organizations seeking to strengthen their security awareness and response strategies.

The availability of a digital and an analog version of the same game enables further validation for the future as well as the implementation of comparative user studies. Interesting questions can be investigated here, whether with regard to learning outcomes, the game experience or user interaction.

A promising next step for the evolution of *A Question of Security* is the replacement of the human game leader with a Large Language Model (LLM). In the current version, the game leader is typically a cybersecurity expert who facilitates discussions, provides answers to players' questions, and ensures the smooth progression of the game. However, relying on a human expert introduces costs, scheduling limitations, and potential biases, as the facilitator may unconsciously steer the discussion based on their personal experiences and perspectives.

By integrating an LLM-driven game leader, the game could be hosted at any time, allowing participants to engage in cybersecurity training sessions without the need for expert availability. The model could dynamically interpret the players' questions, provide accurate responses based on best cybersecurity practices, and guide teams through the game structure in a way that remains neutral and consistent. Unlike a human facilitator, the LLM would not be influenced by personal biases or organizational constraints, ensuring a standardized experience for all players.

This AI-driven approach would make *A Question of Security* more scalable, cost-effective, and accessible, enabling organizations to offer on-demand cybersecurity training sessions without requiring direct human supervision. Future developments will focus on refining the model's ability to provide real-time contextual feedback and ensuring it maintains the interactive and engaging nature of the game.

Acknowledgments. CONTAIN serves as the name of a bilateral German-Austrian research project. The authors acknowledge funding for CONTAIN from the German Federal Ministry of Education and Research (BMBF) (grant numbers 13N16581-13N16587) as part of the SIFO program, and from the Austrian Research Promotion Agency (FFG) (grant number FO999902707).

References

1. Almås, H., Giæver, F.: The emergence of collaboration in serious games. An exploratory study. Int. J. Serious Games **11**(3), 89–108 (2024). https://doi.org/10.17083/ijsg.v11i3.739
2. Angafor, G.N., Yevseyeva, I., He, Y.: Game-based learning: a review of table-top exercises for cybersecurity incident response training. Secur. Priv. **3**(6), e126 (2020). https://doi.org/10.1002/spy2.126
3. Chen, J., Wang, C., Zhao, Z., Chen, K., Du, R., Ahn, G.J.: Uncovering the face of android ransomware: characterization and real-time detection. IEEE Trans. Inf. Forensics Secur. **13**(5), 1286–1300 (2017). https://doi.org/10.1109/TIFS.2017.2787905
4. Dhillon, G., Abdul Talib, Y.Y., Picoto, W.N.: The mediating role of psychological empowerment in information security compliance intentions. J. Assoc. Inf. Syst. **21**(1), 5 (2020). https://doi.org/10.17705/1jais.00595
5. Djaouti, D., Alvarez, J., Jessel, J.P.: Classifying serious games: the g/p/s model. In: Handbook of Research on Improving Learning and Motivation Through Educational Games: Multidisciplinary Approaches, pp. 118–136. IGI global (2011).https://doi.org/10.4018/978-1-60960-495-0.ch006
6. Dörner, R., Göbel, S., Effelsberg, W., Wiemeyer, J. (eds.): Serious Games. Springer, Cham (2016). https://doi.org/10.1007/978-3-319-40612-1
7. Hamari, J., Shernoff, D.J., Rowe, E., Coller, B., Asbell-Clarke, J., Edwards, T.: Challenging games help students learn: an empirical study on engagement, flow and immersion in game-based learning. Comput. Hum. Behav. **54**, 170–179 (2016). https://doi.org/10.1016/j.chb.2015.07.045
8. He, W., Zhang, Z.: Enterprise cybersecurity training and awareness programs: recommendations for success. J. Organ. Comput. Electron. Commer. **29**(4), 249–257 (2019). https://doi.org/10.1080/10919392.2019.1611528
9. Hevner, A.R., March, S.T., Park, J., Ram, S.: Design science in information systems research. MIS Q. 75–105 (2004). https://doi.org/10.2307/25148625
10. Hofstede, G.J., De Caluwé, L., Peters, V.: Why simulation games work-in search of the active substance: a synthesis. Simul. Gaming **41**(6), 824–843 (2010). https://doi.org/10.1177/1046878110375596
11. Kaufman, G.F., Flanagan, M.: Lost in translation: comparing the impact of an analog and digital version of a public health game on players' perceptions, attitudes, and cognitions. Int. J. Gaming Comput.-Mediated Simul. (IJGCMS) **5**(3), 1–9 (2013). https://doi.org/10.4018/jgcms.2013070101
12. Kerres, M., Bormann, M., Vervenne, M.: Didaktische Konzeption von Serious Games: Zur Verknüpfung von Spiel- und Lernangeboten. MedienPädagogik: Zeitschrift für Theorie und Praxis der Medienbildung, pp. 1–16 (2009). https://doi.org/10.21240/mpaed/00/2009.08.25.X
13. Ko, M.H., Kim, D.: Trends in mobile ransomware and incident response from a digital forensics perspective. J. Inf. Commun. Convergence Eng. (2022). https://doi.org/10.56977/jicce.2022.20.4.280
14. Lameras, P., Arnab, S., Dunwell, I., Stewart, C., Clarke, S., Petridis, P.: Essential features of serious games design in higher education: linking learning attributes to game mechanics. Br. J. Edu. Technol. **48**(4), 972–994 (2017). https://doi.org/10.1111/bjet.12467
15. Larsson, A., Ekblad, J., Alvarez, A., Font, J.: A comparative UX analysis between tabletop games and their digital counterparts. In: Extended Abstracts of the 2020

Annual Symposium on Computer-Human Interaction in Play, pp. 301–305 (2020). https://doi.org/10.1145/3383668.3419899

16. McIntosh, T., et al.: Ransomware reloaded: re-examining its trend, research and mitigation in the era of data exfiltration. ACM Comput. Surv. **57**(1), 1–40 (2024). https://doi.org/10.1145/3691340

17. Nobles, C.: Botching human factors in cybersecurity in business organizations. HOLISTICA J. Bus. Public Adm. **9**(3), 71–88 (2018). https://doi.org/10.2478/hjbpa-2018-0024

18. Ntoa, S., et al.: Serious games beyond entertainment and learning: an evaluation methodology for assessing awareness raising, empathy, and social change. In: International Conference on Human-Computer Interaction, pp. 141–164. Springer (2024). https://doi.org/10.1007/978-3-031-76821-7_11

19. Patterson, C.M., Nurse, J.R., Franqueira, V.N.: Learning from cyber security incidents: a systematic review and future research agenda. Comput. Secur. **132**, 103309 (2023). https://doi.org/10.1016/j.cose.2023.103309

20. Pollini, A., et al.: Leveraging human factors in cybersecurity: an integrated methodological approach. Cogn. Technol. Work **24**(2), 371–390 (2022). https://doi.org/10.1007/s10111-021-00683-y

21. Pries-Heje, J., Baskerville, R., Venable, J.R.: Strategies for design science research evaluation. In: ECIS 2008 Proceedings, vol. 87 (2008). http://aisel.aisnet.org/ecis2008/87

22. Rana, M.U., Shah, M.A., Alnaeem, M.A., Maple, C.: Ransomware attacks in cyber-physical systems: countermeasure of attack vectors through automated web defenses. IEEE Access (2024). https://doi.org/10.1109/ACCESS.2024.3477631

23. Ravyse, W.S., Seugnet Blignaut, A., Leendertz, V., et al.: Success factors for serious games to enhance learning: a systematic review. Virtual Reality **21**, 31–58 (2017). https://doi.org/10.1007/s10055-016-0298-4

24. RealtimeBoard Inc.: Miro - The visual workspace for innovation (2025). https://miro.com/about/

25. Richter, S., Straub, T., Lucke, C.: Information Security Awareness – eine konzeptionelle Neubetrachtung. In: Drews, P., Funk, B., Niemeyer, P., Xie, L. (eds.) Multikonferenz Wirtschaftsinformatik (MKWI) 2018, Data driven X - turning Data into Value, pp. 1369–1380. Leuphana Universität Lüneburg (2018)

26. de Ruiter, M.C., Couasnon, A.A., Ward, P.J.: Breaking the silos: an online serious game for multi-risk DRR management. Geosci. Commun. Discuss. **2021**, 1–21 (2021). https://doi.org/10.5194/gc-4-383-2021

27. Serrano-Laguna, Á., Martínez-Ortiz, I., Haag, J., Regan, D., Johnson, A., Fernández-Manjón, B.: Applying standards to systematize learning analytics in serious games. Comput. Standards Interfaces **50**, 116–123 (2017). https://doi.org/10.1016/j.csi.2016.09.014

28. Solansky, S.T., Beck, T.: Interorganizational information sharing: collaboration during cybersecurity threats. Public Adm. Q. **45**(1), 105–122 (2021). https://doi.org/10.37808/paq.45.1.5

29. Stals, S., et al.: Evaluating serious slow game jams as a mechanism for co-designing serious games to improve understanding of cybersecurity. ACM Games Res. Pract. (2024). https://doi.org/10.1145/3709745

30. Strussenberg, J., Rudel, S., Lechner, U.: How to deal with ransomware on your mobile phone: the serious game 'a question of security' (2025), to be Published at GamiFIN 2025

31. Weber, K.: Mensch und Informationssicherheit: Verhalten verstehen, Awareness fördern, Human Hacking erkennen. Carl Hanser Verlag GmbH Co KG (2024)

32. Weber, K., Schütz, A., Fertig, T.: Grundlagen und Anwendung von Information Security Awareness. Springer (2019)
33. Zimba, A.: Malware-free intrusion: a novel approach to ransomware infection vectors. Int. J. Comput. Sci. Inf. Secur. **15**(2), 317 (2017)

Cities as Innovation Ecosystems – Game to Enhance City Learning Through Stakeholder Collaboration

Quynh-Lan Nguyen Pham$^{(\boxtimes)}$, Pradipta Banerjee$^{(\boxtimes)}$ [ID], and Sobah Abbas Petersen [ID]

Department of Computer Science, Norwegian University of Science and Technology, 7034 Trondheim, Norway
{quynh.l.n.pham,pradipta.banerjee,sap}@ntnu.no

Abstract. This study explores the concept of city learning which views cities as urban innovation ecosystems, emphasising the role of continuous learning and adaptation in addressing complex societal challenges. The main contribution of this paper is a board game to enhance the understanding of city learning, based on a conceptual model, which highlights interactions among key city elements and the processes that drive city learning. The game is designed to reflect real-world decision-making processes, fostering collaboration and experience sharing among the players. The game was evaluated through a focus group workshop using a mixed methods approach. Results indicate that players valued the social interaction, role-playing and collaborative aspects of the game, recognising the complexity of citizen-centric innovation in city transformation. While the physical format of the board game was well received, participants suggested integrating digital elements to enhance engagement, streamline game mechanics, and provide real-time visualisation of urban dynamics.

Keywords: City learning · Board game · Role playing · City ecosystem · Urban transformation

1 Introduction

Cities are socio-technical systems where the functioning of cities depends on interrelated social, ecological, and technological systems [1]. Different service systems are developed for cities to provide services to citizens to meet their needs, such as water, food, health, education, recreation, electricity, communication and transport. Cities and communities within cities continuously evolve as complex ecosystems as a result of the demographic, economic, social and environmental changes taking place in and around them. Due to such evolutionary changes, they face opportunities for innovation and development alongside "wicked problems" [2, 3] such as complex challenges in addressing issues such as climate change, resource scarcity and social inequality.

To achieve this, cities must continuously learn and innovate in response to emerging challenges and opportunities. Technology, particularly Information and Communications Technology (ICT) is a fundamental driver in the transition towards smart cities,

© The Author(s), under exclusive license to Springer Nature Switzerland AG 2025
S. Zielinski et al. (Eds.): I4CS 2025, CCIS 2513, pp. 330–349, 2025.
https://doi.org/10.1007/978-3-031-94263-1_19

serving as a crucial backbone in this transformation [4]. However, many cities attempt to achieve this transition by replicating ICT solutions from highly developed cities [5]. This approach often overlooks the importance of local contextual factors, as it lacks knowledge transfer through interaction and feedback among the city's stakeholders and service providers. Consequently, such replications are insufficient for achieving meaningful outcomes unless they incorporate the human dimension of urban life [6].

Cities function as urban innovation ecosystems, evolving like living organisms by adapting to interactions and feedback from their internal elements and other cities [7]. An ecosystem is described as a dynamic structure of loosely connected social and economic actors who interact through institutions and technology to co-create and exchange value [8]. Each intervention within this system alters its characteristics by integrating the effects of the change, leading to a transformed system [9]. Given this evolving nature, cities must continuously learn from interactions and feedback to address local challenges and opportunities, ensuring that interventions are both effective and contextually relevant.

Concepts of learning in cities such as smart city learning have often been linked to Lifelong Learning [10, 11], where individuals can grow their knowledge [12] through learning anytime and anywhere within a city [10]. Learning across cities, or city-to-city learning, refers to when a city learns from other cities [13, 14]. While the study in [15] highlights that the knowledge generated within a specific city context may transcend the boundaries of the corresponding contextual settings in which the learning takes place, insights from existing literature highlight that there are no one-size-fits-all "best practices" for cities [16]. Developmental practices/policies cannot simply be copied from one city to another without human-centric contextualisation for respective city requirements, resources, challenges and opportunities [17]. For a city to achieve sustainable development across economic, social and environmental dimensions, it is crucial to have an ecosystem view of the city while considering the specific needs of its stakeholders when designing innovations for the city. These innovations should be informed by insights gained through interactions and feedback among various city elements. Without an ecosystem view of a city, one could overlook the underlying interconnected nature of urban systems while innovating them and then end up with undesirable outcomes from city transformations. For instance, roadway planning directly impacts mobility services, while traffic congestion influences air pollution, work-life balance, and education systems while environmental factors play a crucial role in determining public health and overall quality of life. Challenges remain in applying learning to address urban issues, fostering continuous contextual innovation, and enabling a city to learn as a system. While research exists on smart city learning [10], there is a limited exploration of cities as dynamic learning and innovation ecosystems [18, 19].

City learning is an emerging concept described by [20, 21] that conceives the idea of an interactive learning process in which a city, as an ecosystem, can learn relevant information from its elements and other cities for contextual innovations to address emerging challenges or opportunities for achieving sustainable citizen-centric transformations. A city learning from its elements, referred to as "city learning from within itself" and from other cities termed "city-to-city learning" or "learning across cities". A city can participate in the learning process through interactions at the different levels of city elements ranging from individual to institutional and through interactions with other cities [22].

The importance of learning about actions and outcomes within and across communities for better systemic change was highlighted in [23]. Furthermore, scalable and inclusive collaboration among citizens has been identified as an important element of learning.

The study by [20] identifies the relevant city elements and presents a high-level conceptual model of interrelationships and interactions between the city elements that can drive city learning from within and across cities. A conceptual model of a city ecosystem and a set of processes are presented in [21, 24], and describe how learning of contextually relevant knowledge can take place regarding challenges, opportunities and requirements of service systems related to diverse aspects of a city ecosystem, such as business, recreation, comfort, transport, environment, goods availability, medical care and education. How this knowledge could be utilised at a given time for addressing any specific emerging challenge or opportunity through city learning to ensure continuous contextual innovation of cities needs to be understood.

The motivation for this study is to gain insights into how the conceptual model and set of processes that can support city learning, which are derived from theory, [20, 21, 24], could be conveyed to stakeholders such as city administrators, urban researchers, citizens and service providers. Furthermore, how the knowledge captured in the conceptual model and a set of processes, could be utilised for addressing emerging challenges and/or opportunities in cities to ensure continuous contextual innovation of cities needs to be investigated. Games have been identified as a means of supporting learning in a participatory, engaging and motivating way [25]. Therefore, to achieve our objective, we designed a board game based on the understanding of the principles of the conceptual model and processes that can support city learning. Through the board game, the players are engaged in collaborative activities that require them to navigate challenges, share resources and co-develop solutions. By creating a board game based on the conceptual model and a set of processes that can support city learning, this study aims to obtain feedback for the conceptual model for city learning through the game; present insights on the ability of the board game design to utilise the knowledge of the model and processes that can drive city learning; and to reflect on the role of ICT solutions to support city learning.

The main contribution of this paper is a board game that is designed to communicate and facilitate the knowledge and processes described in the conceptual model for city learning. The game was designed using the Design Science Research Method and the game concept was evaluated in a focus group workshop. A mixed methods approach was used to analyse the outcomes of the workshop. The results are discussed in the context of city learning and how the game could be a means of contributing to enhancing knowledge about the important elements and processes for learning and innovation in cities and communities.

The rest of the paper is organised as follows. Section 2 presents an overview of the theoretical background of the conceptual model and set of processes that can support city learning and related work in the context of games. Section 3 presents the overall method of this study. Section 4 presents the design concept of the board game. Section 5 illustrates the game sessions played with the participants and data collection. Section 6 presents the results from the game sessions and Sect. 7 concludes the study presenting the overall discussion and future work.

2 Theoretical Background

This section describes the conceptual model of city ecosystem and processes for city learning developed from theory [20, 21, 24] and provides a brief overview of games and gamified applications that are designed to convey and foster knowledge related to the conceptual model as well as enhance participation, collaboration and interaction among different stakeholders in real-world like situations.

2.1 Conceptual Model of City Learning

A high-level conceptual model, illustrated in Fig. 1, has been introduced by Banerjee & Petersen [20] to represent the interactions and relationships among various city elements that contribute to city learning. This model demonstrates how cities can function as learning ecosystems by integrating perspectives from citizens, society and the environment.

The city ecosystem consists of both internal and external elements. Internal elements include the human-driven environment, technological systems, the built environment, and natural environments, while external elements comprise other city ecosystems or networks. These internal elements are further categorised into three groups. The human-driven environment acts as the driving force of a city ecosystem, responsible for initiating, designing and implementing urban innovations. It consists of key stakeholders actively shaping and transforming the city. Technological systems facilitate communication, enable knowledge transfer within the human-driven environment, and support data collection and analysis related to service systems and the natural environment through sensing mechanisms [26, 27].

The conceptual model in Fig. 1 represents the city as an ecosystem functioning as a large organisational entity, where interactions among internal and external elements at individual, group and organisational levels shape its emergent behaviour. Four key segments within this ecosystem serve as drivers of city learning for innovation: (1) the human-driven environment, (2) technological systems, (3) the natural environment, and (4) other city ecosystems. Banerjee & Petersen [24] expand on this perspective, by defining a city as a system and identifying the core elements and processes that can facilitate city learning, as follows:

- Elements of a city:Individuals, Groups of individuals and institutions, Government, institutions, Academic and research institutions, Private organisations and industries, Other Cities, Technology, Natural environment
- Processes crucial for city innovations through learning: Planning innovations with leadership, Motivation and participation of Citizens, Engagement and empowerment of Citizens, Collection and sharing of information, Sharing ideas and codesigning, Providing feedback, Reflecting on experiences and available contextual information

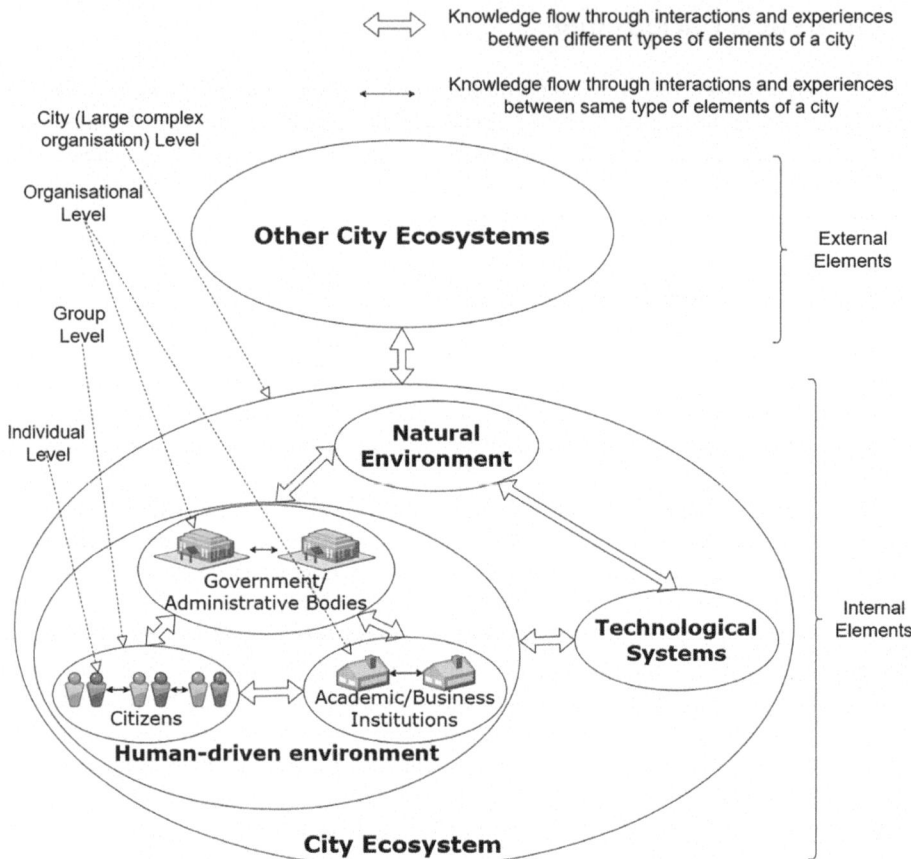

Fig. 1. High-level conceptual model of a city ecosystem [20]

2.2 Related Work

Games emphasise how structured play could transform abstract ideas into accessible, interactive learning experiences. Examples of games in this genre include SWOT in a Box, which supports a SWOT (Strengths, Weaknesses, Opportunities, Threats) analysis and discussions around it in transport planning [25], InnoCards, a game for developing creative solutions [28], and AudaCity, which is a board game for urban design [29]. Studies such as Lanezki et al.'s neighbourhood energy management game [30] demonstrate how gamified applications simplify complex subjects, turning theoretical concepts into tangible experiences. The use of card-based or board games has been praised for simplifying complex topics and broadening the inclusivity of participants from diverse backgrounds. Several games integrate narrative elements, role-playing and stakeholders' perspectives to help participants connect emotionally with complex decision-making scenarios [29, 31]. Several games emphasise the importance of collaboration, and facilitate navigation through trade-offs, stakeholder negotiations and collective problem-solving, reflecting the interdisciplinary nature of urban and environmental challenges [25, 31].

The applicability to real-world contexts is important for innovations in cities and communities and for conveying theoretical models such as the conceptual model for city learning. Games such as AudaCity [29] and Schalbetter et al.'s urban transformation simulations [32] embed players in realistic scenarios where the players must navigate challenges akin to those encountered in actual urban planning or development. This connection to real-life situations enhances the applicability and impact of the games on policy discussions and professional practice.

Another important aspect in addressing city learning is systems thinking and the long-term perspective of actions. Some games, such as Armenia et al.'s board game [33], encourage systems thinking by highlighting the interconnectedness of decisions within economic, social and environmental contexts. Coastal Cities at Risk [34] aim to foster a long-term, systems-oriented perspective, moving beyond immediate decision-making to consider the cascading impacts of actions over time. However, these games do not fully integrate the complexity of these relationships and seem to lack deeper engagement with feedback loops or the cascading effects that characterise real-world urban systems. They struggle to provide a deeper, more comprehensive understanding of real-world urban systems.

Several games rely on digital platforms or require skilled facilitators for implementation, which can present barriers in resource-constrained settings, e.g., [32], may be difficult to deploy on a larger scale due to the need for a skilled facilitator, or in areas that lack the necessary technological infrastructure.

3   Method

The Design Science Research Method (DSRM) was used for the design of the City Learning game [35]. DSRM is an appropriate method for designing new artefacts based on the needs of the context, and as in this case, leveraging on the existing body of knowledge, methods and theory. The method includes three closely related cycles of activities, which are called the relevance, rigour and design cycles. The relevance cycle identifies the environment in which the designed artefact will be applied and the requirements for the designed artefact. The rigour cycle brings existing knowledge, methods and theories into the design cycle and adds the new knowledge generated through the design process. The design cycle is an iterative process that includes the design, development and evaluation of the design artefact until it has reached the desired quality and expectations. Our adoption DSRM is illustrated in Fig. 2.

The designed artefact is a game for supporting learning and knowledge sharing within and across cities. It is based on a conceptual model and set of processes that can support city learning, based on theory. In the relevance cycle, the game was developed by mapping the concepts in the city learning model to elements in the game. In the rigor cycle, the game design was evaluated by university students to play the game and to provide feedback.

The game sessions were conducted as a focus group workshop to obtain structured discussions about the game design and to obtain some qualitative data [36]. A mixed-methods approach was employed, combining qualitative and quantitative data collection techniques. The focus group provided in-depth qualitative insights into participants' experiences and perspectives on the game, while the questionnaire gathered

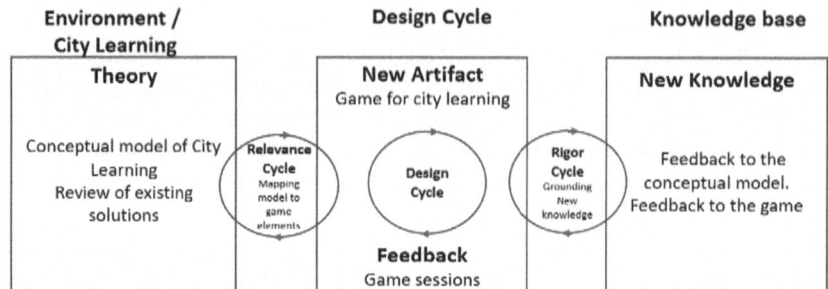

Fig. 2. Design Science Research Method (DSRM), adapted from [35]

quantitative data to assess usability and effectiveness systematically. The feedback from the focus group workshop provides requirements for improving the game design and the conceptual model for city learning.

4   Game Concept

The primary goal of the game is for players to collaborate to overcome challenges and find solutions that affect the city's transformation. Players adopt distinct roles, each with unique resources and solutions, to collectively address urban issues such as air pollution, housing crises and energy sustainability. Through strategic decision-making and resource management, players aim to improve the city's status in multiple areas, reflected in a transformation score, which quantifies the progress of both the city and individual players. The game concept has been inspired by the theoretical model of city learning described in Subsect. 2.1, from [20]. It is a role-playing game, that uses cards to represent the elements of the city learning model. Points are used as feedback to the players, where individual roles are assigned points.

4.1   Mapping Theoretical Model to the Game

The elements of the theoretical model of city learning are mapped to elements in the game as follows:

- **Human-driven environment**: Roles in the game represent key constituents of the human-driven environment, including individuals, NGOs, private organisations and government institutions. These roles are represented as the citizen, environmental advocate, private sector representative and city government official.
- **Natural environment**: This is represented as challenge cards that introduce crises such as water supply shortages. Ecological parameters are visualised using a spider diagram, representing the city's environmental condition.
- **Technological systems**: Technological advancements are integrated into solution cards, featuring ICT-based solutions such as smart devices, IoT systems and sensor technologies that address urban challenges.

- **Other city ecosystems**: The game incorporates the influence of other cities, represented through the external collaborator role. This role introduces solutions from another city, promoting knowledge sharing and regional innovation.

The theoretical background for the city learning model also identifies several processes that are important for cities as learning ecosystems [20, 21]. The processes that the game is designed to support and are integrated into the gameplay are:

- **Sharing ideas**: Encouraging collaboration and solution exchange among all elements in the human-driven environment.
- **Motivation and participation**: Citizens are motivated to engage through their role-specific solution cards and resource cards, promoting active involvement.
- **Engagement and empowerment**: The game empowers citizens by enabling them to contribute resources and solutions, fostering co-creation and collaboration. Their participation in decision-making directly shapes the outcome, reflecting the model's focus on active citizen engagement in urban development.
- **Information collection and sharing**: Roles are encouraged to share information among themselves to strengthen collaboration and develop effective solutions.
- **Reflection on experiences:** Players reflect on strategies and outcomes from previous rounds (game sessions) to adapt and improve future approaches. Transformation Points measure the city's progress, reflecting the cumulative impact of collaborative solutions on urban transformation.

4.2 Game Elements

The main elements of the game are roles, cards, a status overview and transformation points. Each player is assigned a role that represents a key urban stakeholder. The roles are represented as cards through Role Cards; see Fig. 3 (a).

The different types of cards are shown in Fig. 3 and they are described below:

Role Cards: the roles that are included in the game are City Government Official, Environmental Advocate, Private Sector Representative, Citizen and External Collaborator. Role cards contain the name of the role, e.g., City Government Official, an icon to describe the role and a textual description of that role; see Fig. 3(a). Each role has its own unique set of solution cards and resource cards that are associated with the role, which are used during the game to propose and support solutions.

Challenge Cards: challenge cards represent a situation or a challenge that the city faces and needs a solution for. For each round of gameplay, a new challenge card is drawn, presenting the players with a current urban situation (e.g., "Air Pollution Crisis" or "Housing Shortage"). The players must find solutions to these challenges using available resources and solutions cards. Challenge cards contain the specific challenges and the need related to that challenge, an icon to describe the challenge and other information related to the challenge and possible penalties if the challenge is not resolved. An example of a challenge card is shown in Fig. 3(b).

Solution Cards: represent different solutions that could be used to address urban challenges, e.g., "Free Public Transport". Each solution card is categorised by type and has an associated cost that must be covered by the resource cards. In addition, each solution

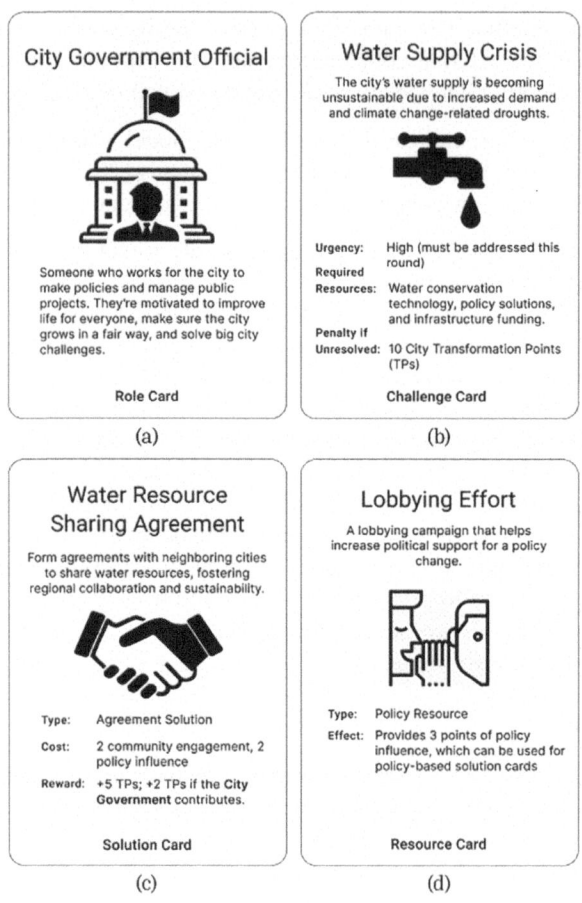

Fig. 3. Types of cards: (a) Role card (b) Challenge card (c) Solution Card (d) Resource card

card has a reward, indicating the number of transformation points granted upon implementation, and additional points earned if a specific role collaborates using a resource or solution card. An example of a solution card is shown in Fig. 3(c).

Resource Cards: represent the resources needed to implement solutions, such as funds, technology, or community networks. Players use these resources to fund the solutions proposed during the game. Some resource cards offer bonus points when used in collaboration with a specific role. An example is shown in Fig. 3(d).

The status of the city is described through key areas such as transportation, ecology, water resources, energy, air quality and the economy. The key areas are:

- Transportation: The efficiency and sustainability of the city's transportation system, including public transit, roads, and environmentally friendly alternatives,
- Ecology: The city's environmental impact and sustainability, including factors like green spaces, biodiversity, and waste management.

- Water resources: The management of water resources, including water supply, quality, and sustainable usage.
- Energy: The city's energy consumption and production, and the transition to more sustainable energy sources.
- Air quality: The cleanliness of the air and the level of air pollution, which affects the health and quality of life of the residents.
- Economy: The city's economic health, including income levels, cost of living, and economic growth.

The status is updated after each round to reflect the impact of the solutions implemented. The status is visualised as a spider diagram as shown in Fig. 4. Each solution card introduces fixed changes to the parameters in the diagram, and the overall status is updated by adding these changes for each implemented solution. The final score at the end of the game session is represented as a Transformation Score, which reflects the overall transformation of the city. This score is calculated by adding the transformation points from the implemented solution cards, and any additional bonus points. Individual transformation scores for each player are calculated by summing only the rewards and bonus points from the cards they contributed to the implementation throughout the game session.

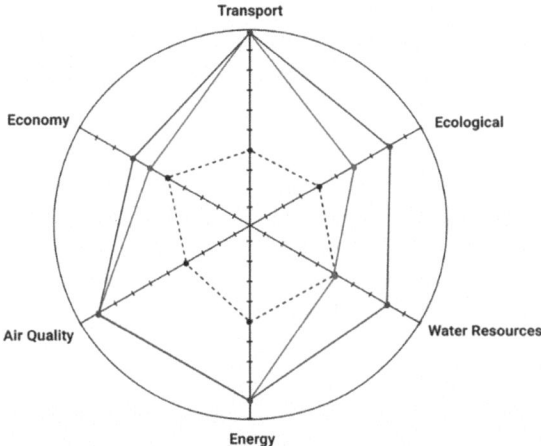

Fig. 4. City Status is visualised as a spider diagram. The dashed line represents the initial state of the city, the red line shows the city's status after the first round, and the blue line shows the city's status after the second round.

4.3 Gameplay

The game begins with each player receiving a role card, along with a separate deck of solution cards and a separate deck of resource cards specific to their role. Solution cards represent possible ways to address in-game challenges, while resource cards provide the necessary tools or assets to implement those solutions. These cards vary based on the player's role, ensuring that each role contributes differently to the game. The spider diagram is placed in the centre of the table, showing the current state of the city. Challenge cards are shuffled and placed in a pile. Each player keeps their solution and resource decks face down to keep them hidden until they are used in the game. The game proceeds in rounds, with each round consisting of several phases:

1. Card Selection Phase: A challenge card is drawn, presenting the current issue the city faces. All players draw one solution card and two resource cards from their respective decks. These are the cards that can be used in the discussion phase.
2. Discussion Phase: Players have 10–15 min to collaborate and discuss how they can combine their available solutions and resources to address the challenge. Each player brings their role-specific knowledge and resources to the discussion, encouraging creative and strategic thinking.
3. Voting Phase: Once the discussion concludes, players vote on which combination of solution and resource cards should be implemented to solve the challenge. A maximum of two solution cards may be chosen collectively per round from all players' proposed solutions to solve the current challenge. If the vote is tied, a random decision (e.g., dice roll) breaks the tie.
4. Update Phase: After the solution is chosen, the spider diagram is updated to reflect the city's progress. The transformation score is calculated to show how the city has improved and is displayed accordingly. The used cards are set aside, while unused cards can be carried over to the next round.
5. Repeat: A new round begins by drawing a new challenge card. Each player draws one new solution card and one new resource card. The round continues with discussion and voting as before.

The game session ends after 5 rounds and the final transformation score of the city is calculated based on the implemented solutions. Each player's individual contribution to the transformation process is also calculated. The game ends with a summary of the city's status across the different key areas that are included in the spider diagram, along with an assessment of the players' collaborative efforts.

5   Evaluation

The design of the game was evaluated in a focus group workshop, by using qualitative and quantitative data. Since the game was designed for citizens and a diverse set of stakeholders in a city, a group of university students were invited to participate in the workshop. Six participants were recruited from among friends and classmates from the authors' university. All participants were male (not intentional), in their twenties, and studying Computer Science. Table 1 shows the background of each participant.

For the evaluation, a game session was conducted with two rounds of gameplay, and the session lasted 40 min. Prior to the game session, the aim of the workshop was presented and the game and the rules of the game were introduced. In addition, the participants received a 2-page textual description of the game elements, the rules of the game (referred to as the rulebook) and instructions on what to do during the focus group workshop. Following the game session, the participants were asked to respond to

Table 1. Overview of focus group workshop participants

ID	Level of Education	Gaming frequency
P1	Bachelors	Hardcore player (more than 10 h per week)
P2	Bachelors	Hardcore player (more than 10 h per week)
P3	Bachelors	Active player (5–10 h per week)
P4	High School	Non-player (I do not play games)
P5	Bachelors	Non-player (I do not play games)
P6	Bachelors	Active player (5–10 h per week)

a questionnaire individually, followed by a focus group discussion, which lasted 90 min altogether.

5.1 Game Sessions

The game sessions followed the sequence of activities described in the subsection on Gameplay. Players were dealt role cards, and each player had a different role. When the number of participants exceeded the available unique roles, multiple players were assigned to the same role (e.g., two citizens). They then drew the solution and resource cards from their role-specific card decks. The players took rounds to inform each other about the resources they had, the costs and the transformation points related to them.

The challenge card for the first game round was related to air quality, depicting a crisis related to poor air quality in the city. The challenge card for the second game round was about a water crisis. The players retained the same roles during both rounds. The players were engaged in the game and there was laughter and lively discussions (Fig. 5). Questions such as how the use of specific resource and solution cards would lead to a successful solution or a higher transformation score, were posed.

Fig. 5. Photos from the game sessions

5.2   Data Collection

During the game sessions, audio recordings were made to capture participant interactions and gameplay strategies for subsequent analysis. The audio recordings were transcribed and analysed. Observations focused on how players navigated the game and collaborated to solve challenges.

Questionnaire. After the game sessions, participants completed a paper-based questionnaire, which consisted of 16 statements. The participants were asked to indicate their level of agreement with the statements using a Likert scale; 1 for strongly disagree and 5 for strongly agreement. The questionnaire was developed using the Usability Heuristics Applied to Board Games framework [37] and evaluated the key usability and design aspects of board games. Most heuristics were represented by two questions each. The questionnaire is shown in Table 2.

Focus Group Discussion. The focus group discussion was driven by a set of questions to trigger discussions. The questions were of six categories: how the game relates to the concept of city learning, game mechanics, game functions, collaboration and discussion, the cards and game objects and the general game experience. The discussions were audio recorded and transcribed. A thematic analysis was conducted following the approach outlined by Braun and Clarke [38], which involved familiarizing with the transcribed data, coding meaningful segments, generating initial themes, and refining them for coherence. Representative extracts were selected to ensure themes accurately captured key aspects, providing deeper insight into participants' perspectives on the game.

6   Results

The results of the evaluation consist of both quantitative and qualitative results from the questionnaire and the discussion respectively.

6.1   Results from the Questionnaire

The analysis of the results from the questionnaire reveals that participants generally perceived the game positively, as reflected in the mean scores ranging between 3.5 and 4.8 in Fig. 6. The highest-rated statement, Q16, achieved a mean score of 4.83, highlighting strong agreement on the game's ability to engage and entertain. In contrast, the lowest-rated question, Q5, with a mean score of 3.67, indicates less agreement about the meaningfulness of choices and decisions during gameplay. Standard deviations (SD) further illustrate the consistency of responses, with questions such as Q16 (SD = 0.41) and Q9 (SD = 0.55) showing low variability, while Q14 (SD = 1.55) exhibited high variability, suggesting differing opinions about the comfort level in teaching the game.

When grouped into heuristic categories, similar trends emerged as shown in Fig. 7. The "Visibility" category scored a mean of 4.08 (SD = 0.86), showing general agreement that the game offers clear signals and status updates. "Real World" integration, which examines the intuitive and relatable nature of the theme and mechanics, achieved a mean score of 4.17 (SD = 0.61). "Control" received a mean of 4.00 (SD = 0.77), indicating

Table 2. Questionnaire Design

Heuristic	ID	Statements
Visibility status	Q1	I could easily understand my current status in the game at all times
	Q2	The game provided clear indicators of progress or objectives
Real-world match	Q3	The game's theme and mechanics felt intuitive and easy to grasp.
	Q4	The game effectively used real-world conventions to simplify understanding
Control and Error Recovery	Q5	I felt I had meaningful choices and decisions to make during gameplay
	Q6	The game allowed me to recover from mistakes without excessive penalties
Error Prevention	Q7	The game rules and components helped prevent errors during gameplay
	Q8	I rarely felt frustrated due to preventable mistakes caused by unclear instructions or design
Recognition/Memory load	Q9	The game minimised the need to memorise rules or complex information
	Q10	Reference materials (e.g., rulebooks, guides, icons) were easy to use and understand
Aesthetic Design	Q11	The game's visual design highlighted essential information effectively
	Q12	The components of the game were attractive and functional
Help Documentation	Q13	The rulebook or other resources were helpful and easy to follow
	Q14	I would feel comfortable teaching this game to others using its provided materials
Fun Engagement	Q15	The game struck a good balance between challenge and enjoyment
	Q16	I felt engaged and entertained throughout the game

moderate agreement on meaningful choices and the ability to correct mistakes, with some variability in responses. Error prevention had a lower mean of 3.83 (SD = 0.52), suggesting that while the game prevents errors to a degree, there is room for improvement. Meanwhile, "Memory Load" was rated highly, with a mean of 4.33 (SD = 0.61), reflecting consistent agreement that the game minimises complex memorisation. Mixed responses were noted in the "Aesthetic Design" category, which scored a mean of 3.83 (SD = 0.88), with significant variability highlighting differences in players' perceptions of the game's visual and component design. The "Help and Documentation" category achieved a mean of 4.17 (SD = 1.03), suggesting that while the written description and

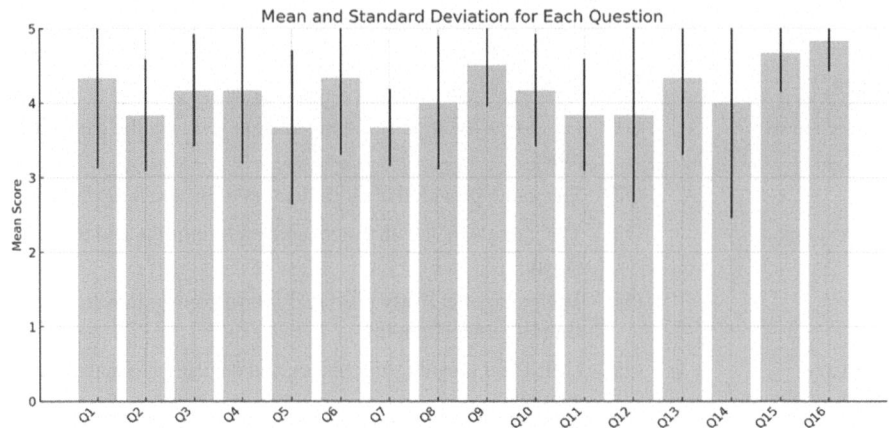

Fig. 6. Mean score and standard deviation for each statement

reference materials were generally helpful, some respondents experienced difficulties. Lastly, "Engagement" scored very positively, with a mean score of 4.75 (SD = 0.42), indicating strong agreement on the game's entertainment value.

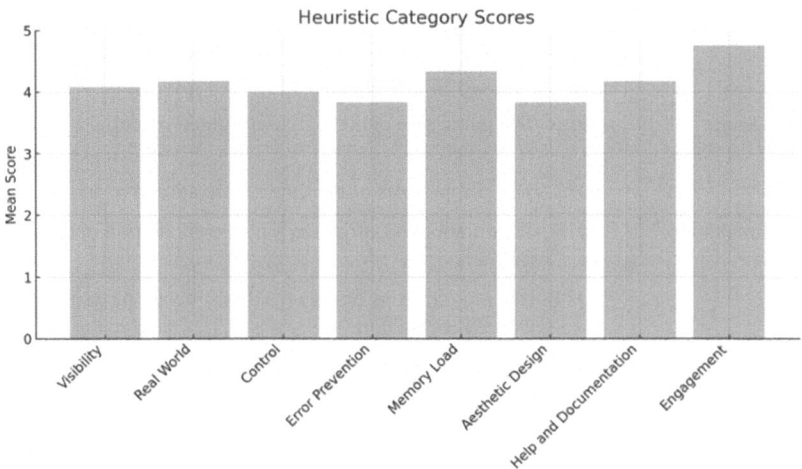

Fig. 7. Mean score for heuristic categories

The reliability of the questionnaire was assessed using Cronbach's Alpha, which yielded a value of 0.79, indicating good internal consistency. However, this result could potentially be improved by addressing high variability in certain questions, such as Q14, or refining questions to reduce overlap in the constructs they measure. For example, questions related to aesthetic design and engagement may benefit from clearer distinctions to ensure each question captures a unique aspect of the game experience.

Overall, the findings highlight the game's strengths, particularly its high engagement, minimal cognitive load, and effective alignment between the theme and game mechanics.

Positive feedback on visibility and real-world relatability further supports the game's appeal. However, areas such as error prevention and aesthetic design require attention to address mixed feedback. Additionally, the relatively lower score for Q5 highlights the need to enhance the meaningfulness of choices and decisions in gameplay, ensuring players feel their actions have significant consequences. Simplifying and clarifying help materials could also reduce variability and improve the overall user experience, especially in teaching the game.

6.2 Results from the Thematic Analysis

The transcriptions of the audio recordings were analysed to identify the themes that emerged from the discussion. The themes that were identified are described below.

Resource Management and Game Mechanics. Participants repeatedly expressed a desire for more complex and limiting resource management. It was suggested that resources should have some negative effects, (e.g., using funds could prevent players from acquiring new resources for some time), to force players to make more strategic decisions. One participant noted, *"Resources should have more negative effects, I think, so you can't just use 10 funding and move to the next."* This feedback highlighted a desire for the game to challenge players more and introduce tougher choices.

Game Format: Digital vs. Physical. The majority of participants preferred the physical card-based format, citing the social aspect of the game and the ease of communication as major benefits: *"I really enjoy physical cards. They help with communication because we have to look at each other"*. However, some suggested a hybrid approach, incorporating digital elements such as a shared screen for feedback while maintaining face-to-face interaction.

Challenge Resolution and Problem-Solving. A recurring theme was the limited variety of solution cards, with players suggesting more diverse options to enhance strategic decision-making. However, there was also a recognition that finding the "best" solution card could be complex and subjective, especially without clear metrics for evaluating outcomes. Some players felt the game could benefit from more realistic mechanisms for solution development, such as requiring more public support or specific resources: *"Some of these solutions should require more collaboration. There should be more emphasis on public support to give the citizen role more influence. Certain other cards should depend on citizen approval, and more of the solution cards should require community backing"*. Participants also expressed a preference for challenges that span multiple rounds, allowing for a sense of gradual progress and escalation. They suggested that this approach would create more engagement and a stronger feeling of narrative continuity: *"For my part, better reflection would come from focusing on problems over several rounds, but then having sudden issues you must handle"*. Unexpected challenges, such as crises, to disrupt long-term planning and force immediate resource reallocation were also welcomed: *"A combination of long-term and sudden challenges would be more exciting and add tension"*. Having decision-based challenges where challenges are directly influenced by the players' prior decisions was also suggested.

Role-Playing and Game Immersion. Several participants enjoyed the role-playing aspect of the game, particularly when they could immerse themselves in the character of their role. However, some felt that the roles, especially the "citizen" role, were too generic and did not offer enough depth to fully engage. Suggestions included providing more detailed backstories or specific interests for each role to encourage players to better engage with the game's narrative. Some suggested that citizens should have more influence on the game, with certain actions requiring community support to reflect the dynamic of urban decision-making: *"I think if citizens had more to say, maybe through supporting certain solutions, it would be more interesting"*. While the game incorporated a variety of roles, participants observed that there was a lack of clear individual goals and meaningful incentives tied to the success or failure of those roles.

General Impressions and Learning Opportunities. The social aspect of the game was one of its most appreciated features, with participants enjoying the discussions and negotiations. However, some felt that the game didn't provide much educational value, particularly when it came to understanding urban systems or the specific roles of different sectors: *"It was a lot of fun, but it was more fun than educational. I didn't really learn anything here."* The game was seen as educational for younger audiences but too simplified for those with prior knowledge of urban planning. Some suggested more complex game mechanics for advanced players. The idea of using the game to better understand collaboration between various roles in a city was seen as a strength. Some felt that it demonstrated the importance of different stakeholders working together to achieve common goals.

Overall, the thematic analysis of the focus group discussions reveals that the players valued the social interaction, cooperation and the role-playing elements of the game. However, they also expressed a need for more balanced and realistic game mechanics. Many participants highlighted the importance of deeper role integration and, as well as for improved resource management systems that could better reflect real-world challenges. The feedback suggests that the players found the game to be fun, but a clearer learning objective could make the game more engaging and strategically robust. While the physical format of the game was favoured, some digital integration could enhance the gameplay without compromising its social dynamics.

7   Discussions and Future Work

The main contribution of this paper is a board game, based on role playing and cards, to engage stakeholders in the transformation of cities. The game represents the elements in the conceptual model and has design elements to support the processes promoted by the model. The game was evaluated in a focus group workshop, which provided relevant feedback to enhance the game to enhance player engagement and deeper insights on learning and innovation in cities through participation and collaboration.

The results indicate a positive experience for the players and reveal that the players valued social interaction and collaboration through the board game and the role-playing elements of the game. However, players also expressed a need for more balanced and realistic game mechanics to better reflect the complexities and the unpredictability in the real-world. Many participants highlighted the importance of deeper role integration and improved resource management systems that could better reflect real-world challenges. The players realised the importance of each role, representing the city elements from the conceptual model, which has been the basis for the game design. Even though improvements have been suggested for the game design, the players provided positive feedback regarding the ability of the game to mimic real-life scenarios. The players realised the complexity of developing citizen-centric innovations for the transformation of cities due to multiple interdependencies and constraints, ensuring the ecosystem view of a city. The feedback from the players also highlighted the importance of the funding aspect for developing innovations suggesting an inclusion of this aspect in the conceptual model. Overall, the game communicated and facilitated the knowledge of the conceptual model and processes that could drive city learning through interactive participation and engagement. The feedback also suggests that the players found the game to be fun, which aligns with the observations of players engaged in lively discussions.

While the physical format of the game was favoured, some digital integration could enhance the gameplay without compromising its social dynamics. The introduction of a hybrid digital-physical solution seems to offer significant potential for improving both the playability and educational value of the game. The integration of a digital display could visualise the city in real time, helping players better understand the urban environment and the impact of their decisions. Visualising aspects like the spider diagram and general city data could provide a clearer picture of how interdependent systems operate and evolve, enhancing engagement and comprehension. The digital component could also handle the calculation of scores and manage the complexity of tracking decisions, reducing the manual work required and ensuring that players can focus on strategic decision-making rather than administrative tasks. Additionally, by storing session history, the system could allow players to review past decisions, their impacts, and how the game progressed, fostering learning about long-term consequences and reinforcing the concept of sustainable city planning. By adopting a hybrid approach, the game could preserve the social interaction and collaborative discussions central to the physical format while offering the computational power of ICT to enhance the sharing and reuse of knowledge and scalability.

Our future work will focus on enhancing the game based on the feedback from the focus group workshop, to better align with the conceptual model and processes that can support city learning. One of the limitations of this work is that the game has not been played by urban stakeholders other than young adults. Hence, we aim to conduct more focus group workshops with different user groups such as urban stakeholders and decision-makers, and younger users as suggested by the participants of the workshop. Based on the feedback, we will enhance the game and make it available to interested stakeholders. We are also working on a hybrid version of the game to support scoring, visualise the status of the gameplay, and facilitate the capture of the different solutions from game sessions.

Disclosure of Interests. The authors have no competing interests to declare that are relevant to the content of this article.

References

1. Krueger, E.H., Constantino, S.M., Centeno, M.A., et al.: Governing sustainable transformations of urban social-ecological-technological systems. NPJ Urban Sustain. **2**(10) (2022)
2. Rittel, H.W., Webber, M.M.: Dilemmas in a general theory of planning. Policy. Sci. **4**, 155–169 (1973)
3. Duckett, D., Feliciano, D., Martin-Ortega, J., Munoz-Rojas, J.: Tackling wicked environmental problems: the discourse and its influence on praxis in Scotland. Landsc. Urban Plan. **154**, 44–56 (2016). https://doi.org/10.1016/j.landurbplan.2016.03.015
4. Giovannella, C., et al.: Smart territory analytics: toward a shared vision (2014)
5. EC: The Making of a Smart City: Replication and Scale-Up of Innovation in Europe. Brussels, Belgium (2017)
6. Oliveira, Á., Campolargo, M.: From smart cities to human smart cities. In: 2015 48th Hawaii International Conference on System Sciences, pp. 2336–2344 (2015)
7. Granstrand, O., Holgersson, M.: Innovation ecosystems: a conceptual review and a new definition. Technovation **90**, 102098 (2020). https://doi.org/10.1016/j.technovation.2019.102098
8. Vargo, S.L., Lusch, R.F.: It's all B2B…and beyond: toward a systems perspective of the market. Ind. Mark. Manage. **40**, 181–187 (2011). https://doi.org/10.1016/j.indmarman.2010.06.026
9. van Geert, P.L.: Dynamic systems, process and development. Hum. Dev. **63**, 153–179 (2019)
10. Gianni, F.V., Divitini, M.: Technology-enhanced smart city learning: a systematic mapping of the literature. IxD&A Interact. Des. Archit. **27**, 28–43 (2015). https://doi.org/10.55612/s-5002-027-002
11. Scott, L.: Learning cities as smart cities: connecting lifelong learning and technology. In: Examining the Socio-Technical Impact of Smart Cities, pp. 68–90. IGI Global (2021)
12. Komninos, N.: Intelligent Cities: Innovation, Knowledge Systems and Digital Spaces. Routledge (2013)
13. de Oliveira, Á., Campolargo, M., Martins, M.: Constructing human smart cities. In: Smart Cities, Green Technologies, and Intelligent Transport Systems, pp. 32–49. Springer (2015)
14. Layte, M., Ravet, S.: Rethinking quality for building a learning society. In: Handbook on Quality and Standardisation in E-learning, pp. 347–365. Springer (2006)
15. Schuurman, D., Baccarne, B., Marez, L.D., et al.: Living Labs as open innovation systems for knowledge exchange: solutions for sustainable innovation development. Int. J. Bus. Innov. Res. **10**, 322–340 (2016). https://doi.org/10.1504/IJBIR.2016.074832
16. Meijer, A.: Smart city governance: a local emergent perspective. In: Smarter as the New Urban Agenda, pp. 73–85. Springer (2016)
17. Calzada, I.: Replicating smart cities: the city-to-city learning programme in the replicate EC-H2020-SCC project. Smart Cities **3**, 978–1003 (2020)
18. Concilio, G., Marsh, J., Molinari, F., Rizzo, F.: Human smart cities: a new vision for redesigning urban community and citizen's life. In: Knowledge, Information and Creativity Support Systems: Recent Trends, Advances and Solutions, pp 269–278. Springer, Cham (2016)
19. Mayangsari, L., Novani, S.: Multi-stakeholder co-creation analysis in smart city management: an experience from Bandung, Indonesia. Procedia Manufact. **4**, 315–321 (2015). https://doi.org/10.1016/j.promfg.2015.11.046
20. Banerjee, P., Petersen, S.A.: Learning in cities from within and across cities: a scoping review. Triple Helix (2023). https://doi.org/10.1163/21971927-bja10044
21. Banerjee, P., Petersen, S.A.: Key elements, processes and research gaps in city learning as an innovation ecosystem: a scoping review. IxD&A 32–58 (2024). https://doi.org/10.55612/s-5002-060-001

22. Seymoar, N.-K., Mullard, Z., Winstanley, M.: City-to-city learning. International Centre for Sustainable Communities: Vancouver, BC, Canada (2009)
23. Kraaij, W., Bouma, G., van der Klauw, M., van Empelen, P.: Better together–empowering citizen collectives with community learning. In: International Conference on Innovations for Community Services, pp. 69–82. Springer (2024)
24. Banerjee, P., Petersen, S.A.: How cities can learn: key concepts, role of ICT and research gaps. In: Dascalu, M., Mealha, Ó., Virkus, S. (eds.) Smart Learning Ecosystems as Engines of the Green and Digital Transition, pp. 53–73. Springer, Singapore (2023)
25. Lyons, G., Paddeu, D., Cragg, S., Wallis, A.: Development and demonstration of a "SWOT in a Box" card game to help socialise triple access planning. J. Transp. Health **38**, 101876 (2024). https://doi.org/10.1016/j.jth.2024.101876
26. Bibri, S.E.: A foundational framework for smart sustainable city development: theoretical, disciplinary, and discursive dimensions and their synergies. Sustain. Cities Soc. **38**, 758–794 (2018)
27. Bouzguenda, I., Alalouch, C., Fava, N.: Towards smart sustainable cities: a review of the role digital citizen participation could play in advancing social sustainability. Sustain. Cities Soc. **50**, 101627 (2019)
28. Tamanini, J.-V., Gorlt, J.: Towards a card game for creative solution ideas: InnoCards. In: REFSQ Workshops (2024)
29. King, C., Cazessus, M.: Teaching with audacity: a board game for urban studies. In: European Conference on Games Based Learning. Academic Conferences International Limited, p. 272 (2014)
30. Lanezki, M., Siemer, C., Wehkamp, S.: "Changing the game—neighbourhood": an energy transition board game, developed in a co-design process: a case study. Sustainability **12**, 10509 (2020). https://doi.org/10.3390/su122410509
31. Sousa, M.: A planning game over a map: playing cards and moving bits to collaboratively plan a city. Front. Comput. Sci. **2** (2020). https://doi.org/10.3389/fcomp.2020.00037
32. Schalbetter, L., Salliou, N., Sonderegger, R., Grêt-Regamey, A.: From board games to immersive urban imaginaries: visualization fidelity's impact on stimulating discussions on urban transformation. Comput. Environ. Urban Syst. **104**, 102003 (2023). https://doi.org/10.1016/j.compenvurbsys.2023.102003
33. Armenia, S., Ciobanu, N., Kulakowska, M., et al.: An innovative game-based approach for teaching urban sustainability (2019)
34. Marome, W., Pholcharoen, T., Wongpeng, N.: Developing and using a board game as a tool for urban and social resilience and flood management planning in the Bangkok metropolitan region. Urbanisation **2**, 28–37 (2017). https://doi.org/10.1177/2455747117708932
35. Hevner, A.R.: A three cycle view of design science research. Scand. J. Inf. Syst. **19**, 4 (2007)
36. Masadeh, M.A.: Focus group: reviews and practices. Int. J. Appl. Sci. Technol. **2** (2012)
37. Sunwall E Usability Heuristics Applied to Board Games. In: Nielsen Norman Group. https://www.nngroup.com/articles/usability-heuristics-board-games/. Accessed 6 Feb 2025
38. Braun, V., Clarke, V.: Thematic analysis. In: Encyclopedia of Quality of Life and Well-Being Research, pp. 7187–7193. Springer (2024)

Information Security

A Simulation-Oriented Approach to Securing Logistics Processes Based on the NIST CSF and OODA Loop

Larissa Schachenhofer[1]([✉]) [iD], Gregor Langner[2] [iD], Gerald Quirchmayr[3] [iD], Philipp Wolf[3,4] [iD], Patrick Hirsch[1] [iD], Stefan Schauer[2] [iD], Ulrike Lechner[5] [iD], and Günter Fahrnberger[6] [iD]

[1] BOKU University, Vienna, Austria
{larissa.schachenhofer,patrick.hirsch}@boku.ac.at
[2] Austrian Institute of Technology, Vienna, Austria
{gregor.langner,stefan.schauer}@ait.ac.at
[3] University of Vienna, Vienna, Austria
gerald.quirchmayr@univie.ac.at
[4] Austrian Armed Forces, Vienna, Austria
philipp.wolf@bmlv.gv.at
[5] University of the Bundeswehr Munich, Neubiberg, Germany
ulrike.lechner@unibw.de
[6] University of Hagen, Hagen, Germany
guenter.fahrnberger@studium.fernuni-hagen.de

Abstract. Integrating simulation techniques with the Observe-Orient-Decide-Act (OODA) loop concept into the cybersecurity of logistics processes offers an innovative solution to address the growing and evolving threats in the digital world. By simulating potential attack scenarios, organizations can identify vulnerabilities in their systems and take proactive measures to mitigate them. Grounded in the principles of rapid decision-making and adaptability, the OODA loop enables decision-makers to respond to threats in real time and implement appropriate countermeasures. Hybrid simulation models, which combine various techniques, represent attack scenarios in logistics processes with a high degree of realism and detail. These models can account for numerous factors, including interactions between different actors in the supply chain, the impact of cyberattacks on operations, and potential financial and operational damage. Additionally, integrating the OODA loop into the simulation process fosters continuous improvement in incident response strategies. In conclusion, combining simulation techniques with the OODA loop concept offers a scientifically novel, robust, and holistic strategy to enhance the security of logistics processes in a complex and ever-changing cybersecurity landscape. By enabling proactive risk mitigation, rapid decision-making, and continuous improvement, organizations can strengthen their cybersecurity posture and safeguard the integrity of their supply chains.

Keywords: Cybersecurity · Decision modeling · Hybrid simulation · Logistics processes · Modeling

S. Zielinski et al. (Eds.): I4CS 2025, CCIS 2513, pp. 353–376, 2025.
https://doi.org/10.1007/978-3-031-94263-1_20

1   Introduction

The security of logistics processes faces growing challenges in an increasingly globalized and digitized world. Rising vulnerabilities to cyberattacks present a significant threat. Hazards such as cyberattacks, physical attacks, and other risks not only threaten financial stability but also jeopardize supply chain integrity and customer satisfaction. While attacks on critical infrastructures have increased for many years, only recently have logistics processes become the focus of targeted cyberattacks. This trend, anticipated for over a decade [8,46,50], has now sparked serious concerns [34]. Numerous examples demonstrate the significant impact of such attacks, while also exposing inadequate cybersecurity management of these processes and their underlying infrastructure [2]. The effects of WannaCry on industry and healthcare, in particular, underscore the urgency of implementing suitable protective measures [3,19].

Particularly when the focus falls on assets, threat modeling offers a method for addressing these challenges [52]. However, a process-oriented approach becomes necessary when prioritizing processes over assets, leveraging proven frameworks like the National Institute of Standards and Technology (NIST) Cybersecurity Framework (CSF) [37] or the OODA loop (see Subsect. 2.3). The aim involves developing a comprehensive, adaptive security strategy for logistics processes. The problem space encompasses the following areas.

- **Cyberattacks and Data Security:** Logistics companies face an increasing number of cyberattacks, including data leaks and ransomware. As a result, protecting sensitive information and ensuring data integrity remains essential.
- **Physical Security:** The physical security of goods and infrastructure, including risks such as theft and natural disasters, remains crucial. Threats that disrupt smooth logistics operations demand robust protection mechanisms.
- **Fast Decision-Making:** In dynamic environments, quick and informed decisions play a key role in responding to security incidents. The OODA loop offers a framework for crafting effective responses to changes.
- **Compliance with Security Standards:** Unstructured and ad-hoc approaches to cybersecurity often lack efficiency and sustainability. Adhering to security standards, particularly the NIST CSF, plays a critical role in enhancing the effectiveness of the security strategy and safeguarding against current and future threats.
- **Simulation-Based Approach:** Its development protects logistics processes by enhancing resilience against security risks while also enabling an adaptable response capability.

Ransomware, Distributed Denial-of-Service (DDoS), and Advanced Persistent Threat (APT) attacks reveal the significant vulnerabilities present in systems, organizational structures, and processes initially developed without adequate cybersecurity measures [33]. Against this concerning backdrop, the continued sophistication of cyberattacks, as documented in various reports [16,29,45], raises serious concerns about the resilience of essential logistics processes. Emerging trends such as Crime as a Service (CaaS) [32], the criminal use of artificial intelligence [25], and increasingly powerful Information Technology (IT) infrastructures accessible to organized crime necessitate a more strategic approach to cybersecurity. This urgency intensifies as the boundaries between state actors and organized crime blur further.

Relying solely on simple system defense measures and closing security gaps proves insufficient. While these measures may effectively counter simpler forms of cyberattacks, they cannot block advanced criminal strategies looming on the horizon. Therefore, the research presented in this paper aims to develop a process-oriented protection approach based on leading European and NIST recommendations, particularly the NIST CSF, as well as the standards published by the German Federal Office for Information Security (BSI). This approach operationalizes the OODA loop, originally rooted in the tactics of air force fighters, along with the established double-loop learning model. This combination serves as the foundation for modeling and analyzing logistics processes under threat conditions through simulation.

Thus, this research contributes to theorizing the application of the OODA loop concept to the simulation approach in a scientifically novel manner. We present the applied simulation technique in the KIRAS research project CONTAIN [26] and explain the components using the OODA loop concept. The focus centers on developing a holistic protection approach that not only incorporates reactive measures but also embraces proactive strategies to effectively counter the continually growing threat of cyberattacks targeting logistics processes.

In Sects. 2 and 3, we present the underlying concepts that shape the development of our approach.

Delving into Sect. 2 reveals the holistic nature of cybersecurity through an examination of strategic approaches, knowledge management, and information sharing in logistics processes, laying the groundwork for integrating simulation techniques with the OODA loop concept.

Moving on to Sect. 3, the OODA loop and its role in decision support for cybersecurity undergoes introduction, emphasizing the application of modeling and simulation for a detailed analysis of potential threats. Subsequently, the process of identifying and categorizing risks unfolds, providing a foundation for effective decision-making. Furthermore, the discussion of protective measures in mitigating cyberthreats utilizes the Network and Information Systems (NIS) 2 framework alongside the BSI Baseline Protection catalog.

In Sect. 4, attention shifts toward the convergence of hybrid simulation modeling and the OODA loop. This integration encompasses incident handling and examines scenarios of attack development. The primary objective involves providing a lifelike and detailed representation of potential cyberthreats to logistics processes.

In Sect. 5, we present an overview of how the proposed concept applies to a real-world example. The use case focuses on the cyber incident involving the shipping company Maersk, which faced the NotPetya malware attack in 2017.

This attack paralyzed all IT systems worldwide and led to significant business interruptions.

This paper concludes by summarizing and discussing the findings in Sects. 6 and 7. In these sections, we derive insights from the integrated approach, underscoring the advantages of combining simulation techniques with the OODA loop. This approach highlights proactive risk mitigation, swift decision-making, and continual improvement. The overarching aim focuses on fortifying cybersecurity in logistics by refining incident response strategies and ensuring the resilience of supply chains against dynamic digital threats.

2   The Holistic Nature Behind Cybersecurity

In the ever-evolving landscape of cybersecurity, advanced attacks play an increasingly significant role, as reported by [48]. A prominent example involves the attack on A. P. Møller-Maersk, where the NotPetya ransomware inflicted substantial financial losses. Additionally, Svitzer Australia, a subsidiary of A. P. Møller-Maersk, experienced a data breach in the same year that involved the forwarding of financially sensitive information through compromised email accounts [12]. These incidents highlight the growing complexity and danger of cyberattacks targeting both large corporations and their subsidiaries.

The current situation in cybersecurity features promising models, guidelines, and standards. For example, the NIST CSF, International Organization for Standardization (ISO) standards, and BSI standards, along with industry-specific recommendations, gain importance as legal obligations in the area of cybersecurity increase. Despite these advances, past experience shows that an organized and strategic approach remains essential for effectively countering the ever-changing threat landscape.

The implementation of appropriate security measures often does not occur voluntarily, contrasting with past practices. Historical cases reveal the necessity for legal obligations, as warnings from experts, institutions, vendors, and the police frequently went unheeded in time or entirely. Ransomware attacks and Advanced Persistent Threats (APTs) demonstrate that neglect and inaction can inflict considerable damage.

The role of decision models in cybersecurity gains increasing recognition. Early applications of the OODA loop and similar models demonstrate promising results. Furthermore, information security culture holds significant importance, as emphasized in works by [14,27,38]. Thus, highlighting that cybersecurity presents not only a technical challenge but also an organizational and cultural one becomes essential. Successful measures necessitate both the implementation of technical solutions and the establishment of a security culture supported by company management and employees.

Overall, current developments in cybersecurity emphasize the necessity for a holistic and proactive approach to effectively counter complex and constantly changing threats.

2.1   NIS 2, Standards, and Recommendations

The newly adopted NIS 2 Directive, which took effect in 2023 and had its enactment by member states scheduled for October 17, 2024, represents a pivotal shift for European cyberspace. By broadening cyber protection obligations to include vital supply chains, it establishes not only a legal framework but also a pressing practical need for adequate cybersecurity measures. Companies now face the dual challenge of meeting regulatory requirements while implementing effective cybersecurity processes across all organizational levels.

While earlier European cybersecurity laws concentrated on safeguarding critical infrastructures, the NIS 2 Directive broadens legal obligations to include supply chains vital for the functioning of these infrastructures. This expansion requires operators of such supply chains to ensure a baseline level of cybersecurity. Consequently, the associated logistics processes and infrastructures demand adequate protective measures to meet these new standards.

The extent these measures need to reach depends on the risk associated with potential disruptions or failures. Cybersecurity standards, particularly the ISO 27000 series, have long provided a foundational framework. Alongside recently updated cybersecurity frameworks and recommendations from international bodies, European institutions, and national agencies, sufficient guidance exists for meeting legal obligations. Key reference sources include the European Union Agency for Cybersecurity (ENISA), the NIST CSF combined with the Special Publication (SP) 800 series, and the German BSI Baseline Protection (IT-Grundschutz) standards [10]. These resources collectively offer a comprehensive foundation for aligning cybersecurity practices with regulatory requirements.

At their core, these sources recommend adopting a risk-based approach to cybersecurity, establishing a governance structure, and implementing a set of coordinated processes.

Following the structure outlined in the NIST CSF [37], the governance of cybersecurity plays a central role in the successful implementation of a framework, providing risk-oriented guidance for Identification, Protection, Detection, Reaction, and Recovery. While Identification, Protection, and Detection can rely on risk assessments and business impact analysis, effective Reaction and Recovery still require a decision model as a foundational element.

Training and simulation exercises play a crucial role in preparing an enterprise for cyberattacks, allowing for the evaluation of implemented measures, the cybersecurity decision-making process, and the supporting model's effectiveness against current and emerging threats.

2.2   The Need for Strategic Approaches to Cybersecurity Governance and Decision-Making

The importance of cybersecurity receives broad recognition from management, yet governance and decision-making in this area present significant challenges for organizations of all kinds. Ensuring a suitable level of cybersecurity across supply chains and coordinating responses to cyberattacks have grown increasingly complex, especially with the involvement of highly distributed supply chains and the participation of Small and Medium Enterprises (SMEs). As attackers become more sophisticated in both their technological capabilities and their planning and execution of attacks, a new approach must be adopted to achieve resilience. In the case of APTs, the tactics used already exhibit military-level precision [35,44]. Ad-hoc and reactive defense measures have reached their limits in terms of effectiveness. For the various organizational and technical measures provided by governments and industries to yield lasting results, cyberthreats need to be addressed strategically. Preventive and defensive actions must align with corporate governance principles, be systematically planned, and executed in a risk-focused manner as outlined by recent legislation. Ultimately, these measures must undergo validation, testing, and auditing to ensure they meet resilience standards.

2.3   Knowledge Management and the Ability to Share Information

Effective cyber defense goes beyond leveraging advanced technologies. It demands a well-structured and flexible strategy. Security measures like Security Information and Event Management (SIEM) tools, Security Operations Centers (SOCs), and standardized information-sharing formats hold immense value. However, to unlock their full potential, these elements must integrate seamlessly into business workflows and organizational culture. This alignment ensures that technical solutions not only function optimally but also support a broader security strategy that anticipates threats and adapts to evolving risks.

While the ISO 27000 series outlines a framework for information security management, implementing it demands more than mere compliance. Effective cyber defense relies on approaching security as a continuous, evolving process rooted in hands-on experience and adaptive strategies. The OODA loop and double-loop learning serve as key elements in this approach, enabling organizations to maintain flexibility and refine strategies based on insights gained from real-world incidents and emerging threats. This mindset encourages proactive adjustments and ongoing enhancements to counteract the shifting nature of cybersecurity risks.

The OODA loop, developed by Colonel John Boyd, presents an iterative decision-making framework designed to facilitate swift and effective responses in rapidly evolving situations [4]. In cyber defense, this approach requires organizations to swiftly observe threats, grasp their potential impact, make well-informed decisions, and translate these decisions into prompt, decisive actions. The OODA loop's focus on continuous monitoring and adaptation ensures that responses remain relevant and timely, allowing defenders to outpace adversaries and adjust strategies as threat dynamics shift. This cycle of observing, orienting, deciding, and acting fosters a proactive stance in combating cyber risks.

The double learning cycle, based on the work of Chris Argyris, emphasizes an organization's capacity to learn not only from actions but also from the underlying assumptions and thought patterns influencing those actions [5]. This approach fosters deep adaptability and continuous improvement in addressing cyberthreats. By reflecting on both outcomes and the rationale behind decisions, organizations can refine their strategies and enhance their resilience against evolving cyber risks. Such a learning-oriented framework encourages a culture of inquiry and growth, crucial for navigating the complexities of the cybersecurity landscape.

Emphasizing that the aforementioned approaches should not exist in isolation remains crucial. The combination of technologies, standards, and adaptive decision-making processes forms a comprehensive foundation for a robust cyber defense strategy. Integrating the OODA loop and double learning cycle into the organizational decision-making process strengthens a company's ability to address current threats while also implementing proactive measures against future attacks. Such a holistic approach fosters resilience and agility, allowing organizations to navigate the complexities of the ever-evolving cybersecurity landscape effectively. Simulation studies focus on a specific use case. Although inherently created processes prove difficult to generalize, they can adapt to other organizations.

3   OODA Loop for Cybersecurity Decision-Support

Recent academic sources highlight the potential of the OODA loop to transform cybersecurity decision-making by offering a structured process and a reliable model for making decisions. With the NIST CSF emerging as a leading standard for organizing cyber defense efforts, mapping core functions to the OODA loop provides a practical approach for integrating this framework within the industry.

Begin by adapting the three-phase model of NIST CSF (see Fig. 1) that includes Preparation, Reaction, and Reflection phases, aligning with the OODA loop's architecture. Next, map the Reaction phase of the OODA loop (see Fig. 2), with the option to construct a secondary OODA loop around the Preparation phase if necessary. Since the adoption of Intrusion Prevention System (IPS) technology, the Identify and Protect elements in the NIST CSF receive comprehensive coverage. With the latest NIST CSF update adding a governance function, risk analysis and treatment now approach a more strategic level.

From a cybersecurity perspective, the most critical steps in the OODA loop involve those linked to situational awareness, specifically Observe and Orient. The Observe step leverages advanced SOC and SIEM technologies, laying a strong foundation. However, the biggest challenge arises in the Orient step, which demands significant effort from an organization's security culture, knowledge base, and ability to analyze and synthesize information during an attack. The adage *know yourself and know your enemy* encapsulates this challenge, emphasizing the importance of understanding systems and the nature of the threats

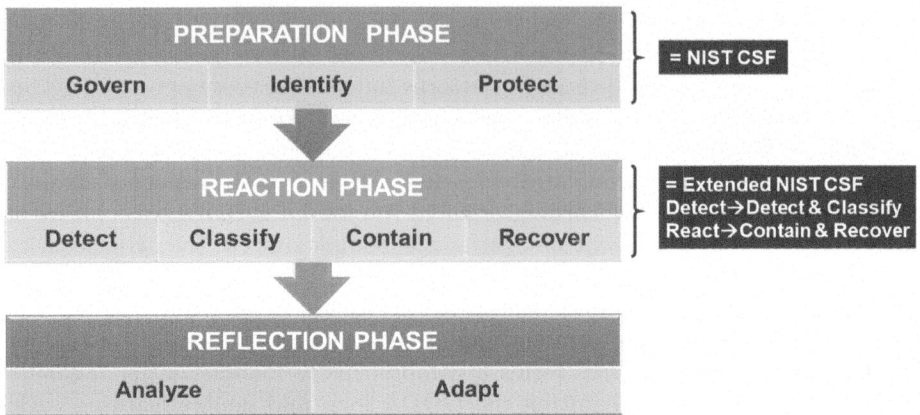

Fig. 1. Three-phase model

faced. Despite the inherent difficulties, widely available knowledge about system vulnerabilities and exploits, along with advanced classification frameworks, facilitate the identification of attack characteristics. Contributions from cybersecurity networks, such as the European Computer Security Incident Response Team (CSIRT), further enhance identification and classification capabilities.

While individual companies may still face difficulties in implementing the Orient step locally, the sharing of expertise and observations within the European Union (EU) now facilitates a more sophisticated approach. The reporting obligations outlined in the NIS 2 Directive establish a foundation for creating an early warning system. However, individual organizations still confront the challenge of processing the available information and adhering to the recommendations. If this coordinated European approach alleviates pressure on organizations as expected, they can focus on mapping the provided information to their own systems (NIST CSF Detect) and to the OODA loop steps Decide and Act during an ongoing cyberattack.

Since the main objective of supply chains and supply chain networks centers on ensuring a steady flow of goods, protection efforts must focus on safeguarding this flow, specifically the underlying processes. The sectors identified in the NIS 2 Directive define the core flows upon which industry and society depend: Material Flow, Energy Flow, Information Flow, and Financial Flow. To illustrate how this protection operates in practice, we examine a logistics flow modeled in the KIRAS research project CONTAIN and demonstrate how to combine the OODA loop with the NIST CSF to achieve this goal.

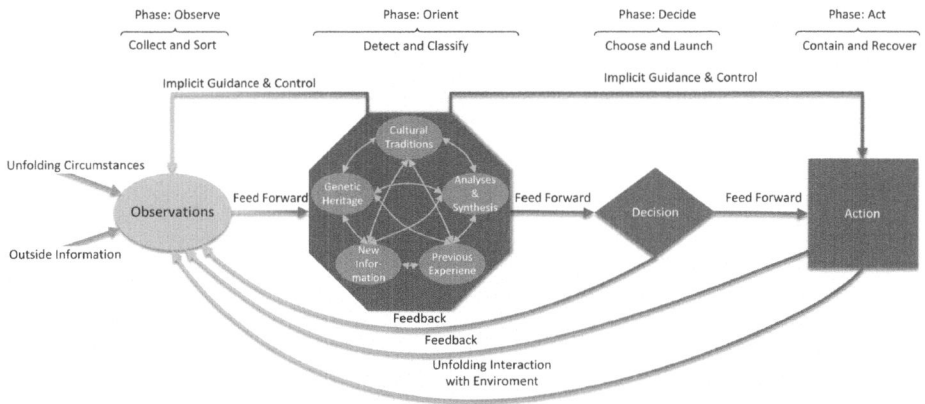

Fig. 2. Mapping the reaction phase on the OODA loop

3.1 Modeling and Simulation-Based Analysis

Modeling approaches divide into System Dynamics (SD), Discrete Event Simulation (DES), and Agent-Based Modeling (ABM) [22]. Forrester developed SD to capture complex system behavior over time, incorporating feedback loops, stocks, and flows [17]. Problematic model behavior may arise from so-called archetypes, as discussed in [31], which suggests various leverage points for addressing them. The SD approach finds application across a wide range of areas. Past research, for instance, modeled the impact of an internet blackout on organizational information flows [41] and assessed threats to Austria's drinking milk supply chain [43].

DES focuses on distinct events occurring sequentially, with each potentially altering the system's state. It supports analyses such as product transitions and has found applications in assessing production systems and logistics processes [24,39]. ABM facilitates the examination of complex systems by simulating the behavior of individual agents, modeled autonomously. The interactions among these agents form multi-agent systems, revealing the system's overall behavior [47,49]. Combining various simulation approaches results in the Hybrid Simulation (HS) method, which merges different modeling techniques [6]. For instance, past studies employed HS to evaluate the resilience of the Austrian pork supply chain during an African swine fever outbreak [28].

3.2 Modeling Logistics Processes for Cybersecurity Analysis and Simulation

Simulation-based analysis and modeling offer diverse applications, as highlighted by the areas covered in previous studies. This methodology proves particularly valuable in critical situations, where various scenarios can be explored without incurring risks. Insights derived from such analyses support enhanced preparedness for potential future disasters. Logistics processes, essential for maintaining the supply of goods to society, benefit significantly from advancements in the Internet-of-Things (IoT). This technology facilitates data collection via sensors, order processing, and automated delivery of materials or products. While automation minimizes human error and boosts efficiency, it also heightens vulnerability to cyberattacks [12]. Consequently, modeling logistics processes for cybersecurity purposes remains essential. Moreover, studies on cybersecurity within the logistics sector remain scarce, as noted by [20].

3.3 Identifying and Categorizing the Risk Related to Logistics Processes

The risks associated with cyberattacks on logistics processes cover a wide range of potential impacts. In traditional logistics settings, such as terminals, Schachenhofer et al. have explored the effects of internet blackouts on organizational information flows [41]. While an internet blackout differs from a cyberattack, both can disrupt information flow in comparable ways. This similarity became evident in the recent cyberattack on DP World Australia, the nation's second-largest port operator, in early November 2023. In response, the company halted operations on November 10 and disconnected from the internet [1]. This containment effort aimed to limit further damage but disrupted import and export activities at the ports of Brisbane, Fremantle, Melbourne, and Sydney [53]. The shutdown led to a backlog exceeding 30,000 containers. Operations resumed on November 13, with the backlog cleared within seven days [1].

Internet disruptions affect various aspects of corporate logistics, including email traffic and other forms of digital communication [41]. Haulers face obstacles in processing or storing new orders, updating reports for hazardous or refrigerated goods, and using location-based services. Terminal operators, who often depend on internet-based systems, struggle with accessing, modifying, or updating stock reports. These disruptions also complicate container issuance, receipt handling, truck and train operations, and customs procedures. The impairments noted during such disruptions show notable similarities to the challenges encountered in the DP World Australia cyberattack.

However, risks associated with logistics processes extend beyond logistics actors. As vital logistics processes underpin numerous critical areas, cyberattack-related threats spread across different sectors. For example, rescue service departments face disruptions in digital data handling, order and status updates, and digital documentation. Hospitals lose access to digital reporting channels and web-based applications essential for medical processes. The inaccessibility of laboratory and hospital information systems halts electronic procurement, leading to significant delays [41]. These examples highlight how disruptions in logistics processes, especially in fields like healthcare, can become critical. When vital medication cannot be ordered through e-procurement and alternative means prove unfeasible, a severe medication shortage may arise.

Building on the model outlined in the previous chapter, the next step involves identifying and categorizing risks linked to this process, along with vulnerabilities that may potentially be exploited.

3.4 Establishing the Necessary Protective Measures Building on NIST CSF and BSI Basic Protection

Establishing essential protective measures, grounded in the NIST CSF and BSI Basic Protection, serves as a cornerstone for a scientific approach to cybersecurity. The NIST CSF offers guidelines and best practices to enhance an organization's cybersecurity posture, encompassing identification, protection, detection, response, and recovery within the realm of cybersecurity events. At a scientific level, this framework draws upon risk management principles and follows a cycle of continuous improvement.

The BSI Basic Protection framework outlines modules and controls addressing various IT security aspects. From a scientific perspective, BSI Basic Protection builds on risk analysis and management principles, providing a structured method for evaluating and addressing security requirements.

Implementing protective measures demands a comprehensive strategy that integrates the principles of both the NIST CSF and BSI Basic Protection. This involves conducting a thorough risk assessment, deploying security controls, maintaining continuous monitoring and improvement, and ensuring regulatory compliance. Scientifically, this approach entails an ongoing feedback loop where data undergoes collection, analysis, and utilization to strengthen security measures over time.

Regulatory compliance holds equal importance to developing incident response and recovery plans, aiming to reduce the impact of cybersecurity incidents. In sum, implementing protections aligned with the NIST CSF and BSI Basic Protection requires a systematic, scientific approach to managing cybersecurity risks. This encompasses risk assessment, deployment of security controls, continuous monitoring, adherence to regulatory standards, and incident response planning to bolster an organization's resilience against cyber threats.

4 Hybrid Simulation: Modeling Meets OODA Loop

Integrating hybrid simulation modeling with the OODA loop offers a robust approach, combining advanced simulation methods with a dynamic decision-making framework. This technique supports various applications, including military operations, emergency management, and the analysis of complex systems such as supply chains.

Hybrid simulation models merge different simulation techniques, such as DES, SD, or ABM in Sect. 3 to achieve a more comprehensive and precise representation of a system. The use of hybrid simulation in operational research dates back to the 1960s, though the term's definition remains ambiguous [9]. Initially, *hybrid simulation* described models that ran simultaneously on digital and analog computers or integrated both discrete and continuous variables. Additionally, models that combined computer simulation with analytical methods like optimization fell under the same category [42]. These models leverage the strengths of individual simulation techniques, making them particularly valuable for analyzing complex systems that involve both discrete events and interactions among agents.

As outlined in Sect. 3, the OODA loop functions as a decision cycle that emphasizes rapid decision-making and adaptability in dynamic, uncertain environments. Integrating this cycle with hybrid simulation models supports detailed analysis of system behaviors, aiding decision-makers in quickly orienting themselves to evolving situations. In supply chains, this combination enhances decision support and adaptive responses. Hybrid simulation models provide accurate representations of complex interactions across production, transport, and distribution. The OODA loop encourages swift decision-making, essential for navigating the fast-changing landscape of supply chain operations. These approaches find practical applications in military operations, where rapid, informed choices influence outcomes, and in emergency management, where they assist in coordinating responses and efficiently allocating resources during crises. In business, organizations apply these methods to model intricate environments and optimize strategic supply chain decisions. Challenges include integrating diverse data sources into simulation models and handling the computational demands linked to hybrid simulations. Despite these hurdles, combining hybrid simulation models with the OODA loop provides a robust framework for analyzing and responding to complex systems across various domains, including supply chains. The major advantage of combining the OODA loop with simulation modeling lies in the risk-free testing of different scenarios using a structured decision-making approach.

4.1 Preparing for Handling Cyberattacks by Initializing the OODA Loop

Adapting the OODA loop for an agile information strategy in cybersecurity, as described in [51], enables defenders to manage the heavy information flow during cyberattacks. The phase following the detection of comprehensive attacks, such as APTs, holds significant importance for adjusting to the current situation and demands decisive action throughout the incident.

By incorporating various information sources, such as Computer Emergency Response Teams (CERTs), the Malware Information Sharing Platform (MISP), and SIEM solutions, defenders must integrate this information into a comprehensive situational report. This approach visualizes the ongoing situation while providing vital information for prioritizing specific capabilities needed to resolve the incident, as depicted in the extended OODA loop in Fig. 3.

Without comprehensive situational awareness, resolving issues can take excessively long and may even fail to remove attacker persistence. Acquiring information not only proves vital during incidents but throughout all operations. Enriching this information through simulations enhances understanding of the potential attack surface and threat landscape, offering deeper insights into the threat actors' intentions. Grasping not only the nature of the attack but also the goals and competence levels of potential threat actors aids decision-making, helps prioritize protective measures, and facilitates effective incident resolution.

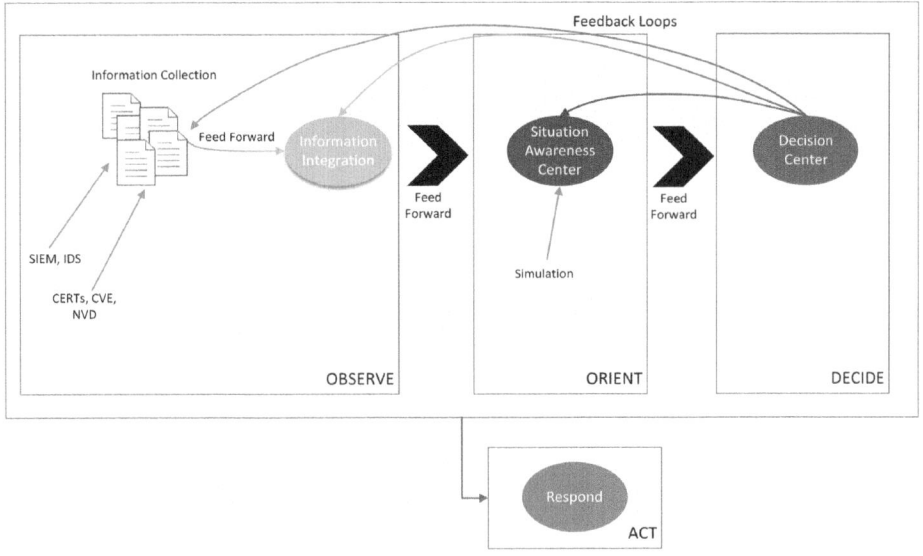

Fig. 3. Extended OODA loop

4.2   Simulating an Attack Development in Logistics Processes

Simulating potential attack vectors in logistics plays a crucial role in under-standing associated hazards. A model of attackers and defenders for cybersecu-rity within logistics management addresses this need [11]. This model suggests assigning a specific security level to assets within a digital logistics network, reflecting their priority for protection during an attack. Such an approach aims to reduce the industry's vulnerability to cyber threats. Current studies on cyber-security in logistics management remain limited, indicating a need for further research to develop more robust strategies [12].

Due to outsourcing logistics to Third-Party Logistics (3PL) partners, com-panies often assume they can transfer the responsibility for cybersecurity risk management onto their 3PL partners as well. However, the effectiveness of this strategy remains unclear. While 3PLs typically handle daily operational risks, their capacity to manage unpredictable and unexpected events varies signifi-cantly and may involve potentially severe consequences for their business part-ners [20]. Most studies on cybersecurity in logistics and supply chain manage-ment reviewed applied qualitative approaches [12].

Cybersecurity data presents challenges in terms of accessibility. The preva-lence of qualitative studies within the academic community indicates a lack of consensus on major concepts in this research field. [13]. However, a noticeable rise in quantitative studies over recent years suggests a growing agreement on certain key aspects of cybersecurity management [12]. Quantitative approaches, including simulation studies, contribute to advancing the maturity of this emerg-ing field, as stated in [18]. In this context, we apply the OODA loop concept to the simulation method by identifying parallels between elements of the strategic framework and the simulation-based approach, as illustrated in Fig. 4.

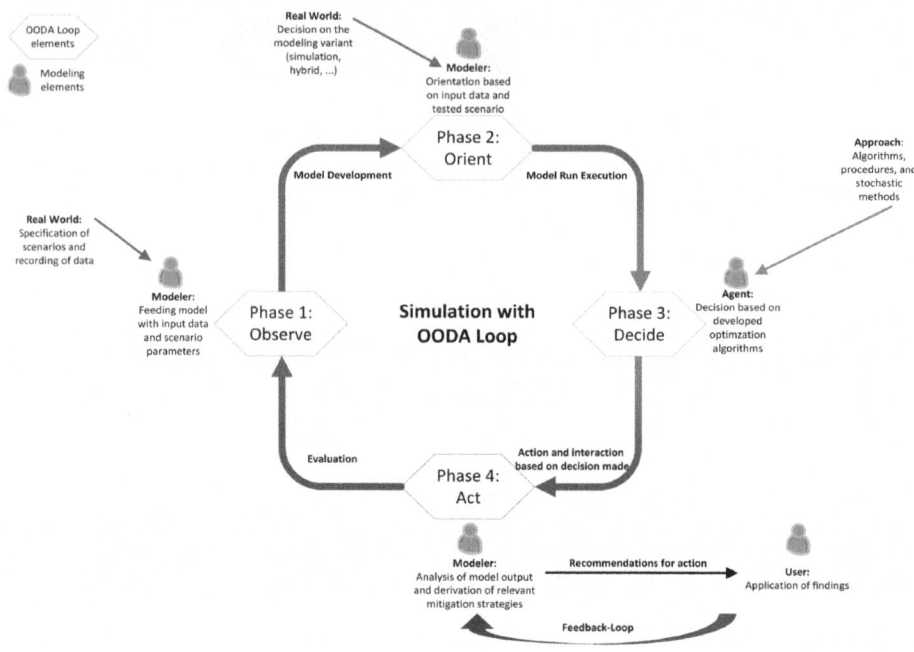

Fig. 4. Similarities between the elements of the OODA loop and the simulation approach

The OODA loop effectively describes incident response processes resulting from abrupt disasters [23]. It encompasses four sequential steps: Observation, Orientation, Decision, and Action.

The first step of the OODA loop, Observe, aligns with examining the simulation data, which serves as a crucial input for setting up the simulation model. The quality of the input data significantly influences the accuracy of the developed model. In the context of the OODA loop, and as noted by [30], this step involves various inputs from both internal and external sources, with external factors forming the foundation of the observation phase. Moreover, tacit feedback elements, such as cultural background and experience, play a critical role in shaping the decision-making process [30].

Based on the observed circumstances, considered equivalent to the simulation data available to the model developer(s), the next step of the OODA loop, Orient, can be undertaken. Orientation involves regaining control over the environment and setting up initial steps to reorganize it according to the pre-disaster conditions [40]. This process depends heavily on both collective and individual factors. Specifically, orientation entails evaluating data gathered through prior observation by the modeler, paving the way for the next step: Decide [30].

When applying the third stage of the OODA loop to the simulation approach, decision-making occurs through the designated agent(s). Depending on whether a single agent or a multi-agent system operates, the decision phase involves one or multiple agents, possibly representing different agent types. Both ABM and HS approaches with ABM elements enable modeling of actions and interactions among various agents and agent types, guided by predefined traits and behavioral rules [7]. Incorporating the OODA loop as a strategic tool for decision support into the behavioral rules governing agent decision-making within a simulation model may enhance incident response effectiveness. Testing across diverse scenarios in the case studies examined within the research project CONTAIN remains necessary.

The fourth and final step of the OODA loop, Act, involves implementing the chosen action(s) [30], carried out by the simulation modeler. At this stage, model outputs inform critical mitigation strategies and specific recommendations for action. Ideally, an iterative learning process enables practitioners to apply and evaluate findings. Practical insights gained can contribute to the model's quality by accurately reflecting the status quo and predicting expected outcomes in specific scenarios.

5   Case Study: Maersk and NotPetya

On June 27, 2017, the shipping company Maersk fell victim to a large-scale cyberattack involving the malware NotPetya. This attack began in Ukraine and quickly spread globally by exploiting a vulnerability in the Windows operating system. Hackers from the group Shadow Brokers had previously discovered and disclosed this vulnerability, originally identified by the National Security Agency (NSA) [36].

The NotPetya attack differs from conventional ransomware attacks because it did not primarily target financial extortion. Instead, it aimed to maximize the destruction of affected IT infrastructures. The malware not only encrypted files but also rendered entire hard drives unusable by overwriting the Master Boot Record (MBR). This action brought affected systems to a complete standstill and complicated recovery efforts significantly [21].

The impact on Maersk proved devastating. Within hours, all of the company's IT systems worldwide became paralyzed, leading to massive business interruptions: containers could not load, and communication between offices and terminals experienced total disruption. Maersk's global reach, as one of the largest logistics and transport companies in the world, amplified the attack's effects. In total, the company estimated the cost of the attack at up to 300 million US dollars, underscoring the scale and severity of this cyber incident [21].

This attack revealed not only the vulnerability of globally operating companies to cyber threats but also the dependence of modern logistics and transport systems on functioning IT infrastructures.

Analysis of the NotPetya attack on Maersk highlights the need for robust and adaptable cyber defenses that emphasize not only prevention but also rapid incident detection and response. In this context, frameworks such as the OODA loop and hybrid simulation models offer valuable approaches for improving cyber incident management. By integrating real-time data, detailed simulation analyses, and strategic decision-making, companies can significantly enhance their ability to manage cyber threats.

5.1   Observation of the Cyber Incident

In this phase, relevant data and information about the cyber incident undergo collection and integration. Sources include the following items.

- Security Information and Event Management (SIEM) systems
- Intrusion Detection Systems (IDSs)
- Computer Emergency Response Teams (CERTs)
- Common Vulnerabilities and Exposures (CVE) databases
- National Vulnerability Database (NVD)

Information gathered from these sources provides a comprehensive understanding of the current situation and forms the basis for the subsequent phases. By analyzing the malware and its distribution mechanisms in detail, Maersk traced the origin of the attack and implemented measures to stop its spread [36].

5.2   Orientation with Simulation

Once the information accrues, integration into a Situation Awareness Picture (SAP) occurs. Hybrid simulation models facilitate the simulation of different scenarios and help understand potential impacts. The SAP uses simulations to visualize the ongoing situation and deliver key information for prioritizing specific capabilities to resolve the incident. Challenges in this phase include integrating various data sources into the simulation models and managing the computational complexity associated with hybrid simulation models. Despite these challenges, integration provides a detailed analysis of system dynamics and helps decision-makers to adapt quickly to the current situation [15].

5.3   Decision-Making

In the decision-making phase, optimization algorithms, procedures, and stochastic methods facilitate the development and evaluation of possible courses of action. Decision-makers, often modeled as agents in the simulation, analyze the simulation output and make informed choices based on the developed strategies. This phase emphasizes rapid and informed decision-making to adapt to the dynamic and uncertain environment created by the cyber incident [7].

5.4   Implementation of the Decision

The final phase involves implementing selected measures to minimize the impact of the cyber incident. This phase includes the following items.

– Deployment of incident response teams
– Application of security patches
– Isolation of affected systems
– Communication with stakeholders

The measures derive from simulation outputs and strategic decisions made during previous phases. A feedback loop ensures continuous improvement by evaluating the effectiveness of the implemented measures and updating the simulation models accordingly [30].

5.5   Simulation of Attack Development in Logistics Processes

Simulating potential attack vectors in logistics proves essential for enhancing understanding of the associated threats. To this end, an attacker-defender model for cybersecurity in logistics management can serve as an effective tool. This model assigns a specific security level to the assets within a digital logistics network, indicating their protection needs in the event of an attack. Outsourcing logistics to 3PL companies often leads organizations to assume they can transfer the responsibility for managing cybersecurity risks to their 3PL partners. However, the effectiveness of this strategy varies, as the ability of 3PL to handle unpredictable and unexpected events differs significantly. The application of the OODA loop aids in this context through the following steps.

– Observing the development of the attack by collecting data from various logistics operations and processes
– Orienting based on the input data and modeling different attack scenarios to understand possible impacts
– Deciding on mitigation strategies based on simulation outputs
– Implementing the chosen strategies and seeking continuous improvement through iterative feedback integration

Disaster events such as cyberattacks typically feature critical resource restrictions. These restrictions represent an essential aspect of successfully managing such events, as they highlight the boundaries of the specific system. Therefore, close attention must focus on these restrictions when developing mitigation strategies. The emphasis of modeling disaster events lies in identifying vital resource bottlenecks, implementing relevant attack scenarios, and analyzing the impacts of specific scenarios on critical resources. Following the four steps of the OODA loop in modeling cyberattacks on logistics processes presents a promising approach in this context.

5.6 Summary

The integration of hybrid simulation modeling with the OODA loop provides a robust framework for responding to cyber incidents. This approach combines comprehensive data collection, detailed simulation analysis, strategic decision-making, and effective action implementation. Such integration enhances the ability to manage cyber incidents and mitigate their impact, particularly in complex systems like supply chains and logistics. By applying the OODA loop to simulation methods, organizations can strengthen their preparedness and response to cyber threats, ensuring better protection of digital assets and continuity of operations.

6 Discussion of Results

Logistics processes increasingly face targeting by cyberattacks. The approach of analyzing logistics processes through discrete events and actions, as well as interactions between defined agents, enjoys common usage in this field. Hybrid simulation models effectively represent complex systems such as supply chains, which can depict multi-agent systems. The capability to make decisions and adapt quickly to uncertain circumstances proves decisive in determining whether a cyberattack can undergo successful management. Thus, integrating elements of computer simulation into the military decision support concept of the OODA loop proves beneficial. The application of a strategic decision support tool, such as the OODA loop, in the battle against cyberattacks proves not only valuable but also vital for organizations active in the logistics field and beyond.

This study aimed to apply the OODA loop concept to the simulation approach utilized in the CONTAIN research project. The individual components of the simulation technique integrate into the elements of the OODA loop. Figure 4 and the associated explanations illustrate our intent to design a holistic protection approach based on the OODA loop concept and the applied simulation method. In this paper, this integration occurred theoretically to demonstrate how reactive methods extend by proactive strategies, ensuring optimal protection against cyberattacks while also managing them effectively when avoidance proves impossible.

Findings indicate that implementing effective cybersecurity processes at each company level closely links to understanding cyber defense as a continuous process enriched through experience and learning. Combining the OODA loop, which enables quick and effective responses to fast-changing circumstances, with the double learning cycle (referring to an organization's ability to learn and improve based on its actions and the underlying assumptions and patterns influencing those actions) establishes a broad foundation for a robust cyber defense strategy. Thus, we view the integration of these two concepts into organizational decision-making processes as a vital step toward profound protection against current and future cyberattacks.

As the Orient step of the OODA loop proves most critical for individual companies, sharing expertise within the EU serves as a valuable resource for organizations seeking to enhance their actions within this step. However, while the reporting obligations of the NIS 2 Directive can aid in establishing an early warning system, processing the available information and following the provided recommendations continues to challenge individual organizations. Thus, a coordinated European approach proves not only helpful but also necessary to equip organizations with the knowledge required to refine and advance their actions in the Orient phase. This approach results in better-informed decisions and actions, contributing to a more sophisticated overall cyber protection strategy.

Furthermore, situational awareness holds significant importance during the challenging Orient phase. In this paper, we suggest utilizing computer simulation to address this issue by developing a cyber threat scenario and conducting several model runs with varying parameter settings to analyze the success factors of effectively coping with a cyberattack, measurable through selected key indices. Moreover, simulation software enabling hybrid simulation modeling allows for the depiction of complex processes, potential capacity restraints, and resource bottlenecks. Therefore, simulation studies can effectively enhance situational awareness and advance critical applicable knowledge in the selected field, significantly contributing to informed decision-making during crises.

Thus, integrating simulation elements into the OODA loop decision support tool offers multiple benefits, as elaborated above. Nevertheless, applying the strategic OODA loop concept to the operative simulation approach presents limitations. Specifically, the operative level of the simulation approach entails a significantly lower level of abstraction and a higher level of detail. This limitation stems from the association of the strategic concept with a certain scope for implementation. For the simulation study in CONTAIN, this consideration requires testing in individual cases to determine the extent to which the OODA loop can integrate into the agents' scope for action and interaction for decision support.

7 Conclusion and Outlook

As outlined in the introductory section, the frequency and complexity of cyberattacks targeting supply chain networks continue to escalate. These attacks deploy a diverse array of tactics, ranging from phishing and malware injections to sophisticated social engineering schemes, posing significant challenges to the security of global supply chains. The interconnected nature of modern supply chain networks further amplifies the potential impact, creating ripple effects that disrupt operations across multiple sectors and regions.

Despite ongoing efforts to deploy technological solutions against these threats, a considerable gap persists in coordinating and executing preparation and response strategies. Traditional approaches often lack the agility and adaptability needed to counter dynamic cyberthreats effectively, underscoring the necessity for a more integrated approach to cybersecurity.

The current fragmented landscape, with its disparate tools and frameworks, hinders organizations from mounting a unified defense against cyberthreats.

Moreover, the reactive nature of many response strategies leaves organizations vulnerable to emerging threats, necessitating a shift toward proactive and pre-emptive measures.

This paper proposes combining two innovative methodologies, namely the NIST CSF and the OODA loop, to craft a simulation-oriented defense framework that addresses the evolving landscape of cyberthreats against supply chains. Integrating these frameworks enables organizations to leverage the strengths of both approaches to enhance cyber resilience and mitigate the impact of cyber-attacks.

This scientifically novel hybrid approach offers several notable advantages. First, it ensures comprehensive coverage of the core principles outlined in the NIST CSF while concurrently introducing a sophisticated tactical decision-making process, exemplified by the OODA loop. This decision-making framework, proven effective in defense and business domains, has earned endorsement from prominent authorities in the United States as a novel paradigm for organizing cyber defense initiatives.

Of particular importance, the emphasis on the Orient phase of the OODA loop presents a formidable challenge in practical implementation. Herein lies the pivotal role of a simulation-oriented strategy, which facilitates the integration of additional tools such as risk control measures and analysis of cascading effects. Hybrid simulation modeling provides a powerful method for raising situational awareness about potential critical aspects within systems, including potential capacity shortfalls and resource bottlenecks. By simulating various cyberscenarios, this approach offers a pragmatic means to refine and enhance the Orient phase, thereby strengthening overall cyber defense capabilities.

The simulation-oriented defense framework proposed here holds promise for deployment in cyber exercises, serving both as a structural component of such exercises and as educational material to prepare organizations for the nuanced complexities of incident handling in the digital age. Simulating realistic cyber threats and response scenarios enables organizations to enhance their prepared-ness and resilience, leading to more effective incident response and mitigation strategies. Within the KIRAS research project CONTAIN [26], an extended case study plans to test the practical viability of the approach.

In conclusion, the convergence of the NIST CSF and the OODA loop marks a significant step forward in developing a simulation-oriented defense framework for supply chain cybersecurity. By integrating these frameworks, organizations can bolster cyber resilience, improve their ability to anticipate and respond to cyberthreats, and ultimately safeguard the integrity and security of supply chains.

Acknowledgments. CONTAIN serves as the name of a bilateral German-Austrian research project. The authors acknowledge funding for CONTAIN from the German Federal Ministry of Education and Research (BMBF) (grant numbers 13N16581-13N16587) as part of the SIFO program, and from the Austrian security research funding program KIRAS by the Federal Ministry of Finance (grant number FO999902707).

Many thanks to Bettina Baumgartner from the University of Vienna for proofreading this paper!

References

1. Ainsworth, K., Aiken, K.: DP World Australia confirms employee data was stolen during cyber attack, warns of further freight delays ahead of Christmas rush (nov 2023), https://www.abc.net.au/news/2023-11-28/dp-world-australia-employee-data-stolen-cyber-attack-freight/103161588
2. Al-Mhiqani, M.N., et al.: Cyber-security incidents: a review cases in cyber-physical systems. Int. J. Adv. Comput. Sci. Appl. **9**(1), 499–508 (2018). https://doi.org/10.14569/IJACSA.2018.090169
3. Algarni, S.: Cybersecurity attacks: analysis of "WannaCry" attack and proposing methods for reducing or preventing such attacks in future. In: Tuba, M., Akashe, S., Joshi, A. (eds.) ICT Systems and Sustainability. AISC, vol. 1270, pp. 763–770. Springer, Singapore (2021). https://doi.org/10.1007/978-981-15-8289-9_73
4. Angerman, W.: Coming Full Circle with Boyd's OODA Loop Ideas: An Analysis of Innovation Diffusion and Evolution. Master's thesis, Defense Technical Information Center (2004). https://scholar.afit.edu/cgi/viewcontent.cgi?article=5087&context=etd
5. Argyris, C.: Organizational learning and management information systems. SIGMIS Database **13**(2-3), 3–11 (2012). https://doi.org/10.1145/1017692.1017693
6. Barbosa, C., Azevedo, A.: Hybrid simulation for complex manufacturing value-chain environments. Procedia Manuf. **11**, 1404–1412 (2017). https://doi.org/10.1016/j.promfg.2017.07.270
7. Bonabeau, E.: Agent-based modeling: methods and techniques for simulating human systems. Proc. Natl. Acad. Sci. **99**(suppl_3), 7280–7287 (2002). https://doi.org/10.1073/pnas.082080899
8. Boyes, H.: Cybersecurity and cyber-resilient supply chains. Technol. Innov. Manag. Rev. **5**(4) (2015). https://timreview.ca/article/888
9. Brailsford, S.C., Eldabi, T., Kunc, M., Mustafee, N., Osorio, A.F.: Hybrid simulation modelling in operational research: a state-of-the-art review. Eur. J. Oper. Res. **278**(3), 721–737 (2019). https://doi.org/10.1016/j.ejor.2018.10.025
10. Bundesamt für Sicherheit in der Informationstechnik (BSI): IT-Grundschutz (2021). https://www.bsi.bund.de/DE/Themen/Unternehmen-und-Organisationen/Standards-und-Zertifizierung/IT-Grundschutz/it-grundschutz_node.html
11. Cheung, K.F., Bell, M.G.H.: Attacker? Defender model against quantal response adversaries for cyber security in logistics management: an introductory study. Eur. J. Oper. Res. **291**(2), 471–481 (2021). https://doi.org/10.1016/j.ejor.2019.10.019
12. Cheung, K.F., Bell, M.G.H., Bhattacharjya, J.: Cybersecurity in logistics and supply chain management: an overview and future research directions. Transport. Res. Part E: Logist. Transport. Rev. **146**, 1–18 (2021). https://doi.org/10.1016/j.tre.2020.102217
13. Creswell, J.W., Creswell, J.D.: Research Design: Qualitative, Quantitative, and Mixed Methods Approaches, 6th edn. SAGE Publications, Thousands Oaks (2022)
14. Dykstra, J.A.B.S., Orr, S.R.: Acting in the unknown: the cynefin framework for managing cybersecurity risk in dynamic decision making. In: 2016 International Conference on Cyber Conflict (CyCon U.S.), pp. 1–6. IEEE (2016). https://doi.org/10.1109/CYCONUS.2016.7836616
15. Eldabi, T., et al.: Hybrid simulation: historical lessons, present challenges and futures. In: 2016 Winter Simulation Conference (WSC), pp. 1388–1403. IEEE (2016). https://doi.org/10.1109/WSC.2016.7822192

16. Europol: Internet Organised Crime Threat Assessment (IOCTA) 2024. Europol (2024). https://doi.org/10.2813/442713
17. Forrester, J.W.: Industrial dynamics. J. Oper. Res. Soc. **48**(10), 1037–1041 (1997). https://doi.org/10.1057/palgrave.jors.2600946
18. Ghadge, A., Weiß, M., Caldwell, N.D., Wilding, R.: Managing cyber risk in supply chains: a review and research agenda. Supply Chain Manag. Int. J. **25**(2), 223–240 (2020). https://doi.org/10.1108/SCM-10-2018-0357
19. Ghafur, S., Kristensen, S.R., Honeyford, K., Martin, G., Darzi, A., Aylin, P.: A retrospective impact analysis of the WannaCry cyberattack on the NHS. npj Dig. Med. **2**(1), 1–7 (2019). https://doi.org/10.1038/s41746-019-0161-6
20. Gkanatsas, E., Krikke, H.: Towards a pro-silience framework: a literature review on quantitative modelling of resilient 3PL supply chain network designs. Sustainability **12**(10), 1–25 (2020). https://doi.org/10.3390/su12104323
21. Greenberg, A.: The Untold Story of NotPetya, the Most Devastating Cyberattack in History (2018). https://www.wired.com/story/notpetya-cyberattack-ukraine-russia-code-crashed-the-world/
22. Howard, D.A., Jørgensen, B.N., Ma, Z.: Multi-method simulation and multi-objective optimization for energy-flexibility-potential assessment of food-production process cooling. Energies **16**(3), 1–27 (2023). https://doi.org/10.3390/en16031514
23. Huang, Y.: Modeling and simulation method of the emergency response systems based on OODA. Knowl.-Based Syst. **89**, 527–540 (2015). https://doi.org/10.1016/j.knosys.2015.08.020
24. Hübl, A., Altendorfer, K., Jodlbauer, H., Gansterer, M., Hartl, R.F.: Flexible model for analyzing production systems with discrete event simulation. In: Proceedings of the 2011 Winter Simulation Conference (WSC), pp. 1554–1565. IEEE (2011). https://doi.org/10.1109/WSC.2011.6147873
25. King, T.C., Aggarwal, N., Taddeo, M., Floridi, L.: Artificial intelligence crime: an interdisciplinary analysis of foreseeable threats and solutions. Sci. Eng. Ethics **26**(1), 89–120 (2019). https://doi.org/10.1007/s11948-018-00081-0
26. KIRAS: CONTAIN – Efficient Response to IT Security Incidents in Transnational Supply Chains (2023). https://projekte.ffg.at/projekt/4791800
27. van der Kleij, R., Schraagen, J.M., Cadet, B., Young, H.: Developing decision support for cybersecurity threat and incident managers. Comput. Secur. **113**, 1–15 (2022). https://doi.org/10.1016/j.cose.2021.102535
28. Kummer, Y., et al.: Facilitating resilience during an African swine fever outbreak in the austrian pork supply chain through hybrid simulation modelling. Agric. **12**(3), 1–17 (2022). https://doi.org/10.3390/agriculture12030352
29. Lella, I., et al.: ENISA threat landscape 2024 – July 2023 to June 2024 (2024). https://doi.org/10.2824/0710888
30. von Lubitz, D.K.J.E., Beakley, J.E., Patricelli, F.: 'All hazards approach' to disaster management: the role of information and knowledge management, Boyd's OODA Loop, and network-centricity. Disasters **32**(4), 561–585 (2008). https://doi.org/10.1111/j.1467-7717.2008.01055.x
31. Mandl, C.E.: Managing complexity in social systems – leverage points for policy and strategy. Manag. Prof. (2023). https://doi.org/10.1007/978-3-031-30222-0
32. Manky, D.: Cybercrime as a service: a very modern business. Comput. Fraud Secur. **2013**(6), 9–13 (2013). https://doi.org/10.1016/S1361-3723(13)70053-8
33. Marimuthu, S.K., Ben-Othman, J., Kalampatti Gopalasamy, S.: An investigation on wannacry ransomware and its detection. In: 2018 IEEE Symposium on Comput-

ers and Communications (ISCC), pp. 1199–1204. IEEE (2018). https://doi.org/10.1109/ISCC.2018.8538354

34. Melnyk, S.A., Schoenherr, T., Speier-Pero, C., Peters, C., Chang, J.F., Friday, D.: New challenges in supply chain management: cybersecurity across the supply chain. Int. J. Prod. Res. **60**(1), 162–183 (2022). https://doi.org/10.1080/00207543.2021.1984606

35. Morag, A., Maouda, I.: Understanding the evolving threat landscape – APT techniques in a container environment. Netw. Secur. **2021**(12), 13–17 (2021). https://doi.org/10.1016/S1353-4858(21)00145-8

36. Mos, M.A., Chowdhury, M.M.: The growing influence of ransomware. In: 2020 IEEE International Conference on Electro Information Technology (EIT), pp. 643–647. IEEE (2020). https://doi.org/10.1109/EIT48999.2020.9208254

37. National Institute of Standards and Technology (NIST): The NIST Cybersecurity Framework (CSF) 2.0. National Institute of Standards and Technology (NIST) (2024). https://doi.org/10.6028/NIST.CSWP.29

38. Parsons, K.M., Young, E., Butavicius, M.A., McCormac, A., Pattinson, M.R., Jerram, C.: The influence of organizational information security culture on information security decision making. J. Cogn. Eng. Decis. Mak. **9**(2), 117–129 (2015). https://doi.org/10.1177/1555343415575152

39. Pernkopf, M., Gronalt, M.: A simulation-based sizing approach for automated log yards. Simul. Model. Pract. Theory **104**, 1–15 (2020). https://doi.org/10.1016/j.simpat.2020.102123

40. Richards, C.: Certain to Win: The Strategy of John Boyd, Applied to Business. Xlibris (2004)

41. Schachenhofer, L., Hirsch, P., Gronalt, M.: How internet blackouts affect information flows in organizations – analyzing cascade effects and feedback loops. Int. J. Disast. Risk Reduct. **98**, 1–17 (2023). https://doi.org/10.1016/j.ijdrr.2023.104101

42. Shanthikumar, J.G., Sargent, R.G.: A unifying view of hybrid simulation/analytic models and modeling. Oper. Res. **31**(6), 1030–1052 (1983). https://doi.org/10.1287/opre.31.6.1030

43. Singer, J., et al.: Analysis of the impacts of the COVID-19 pandemic on the drinking milk supply chain in Austria by means of a business process modelling and System Dynamics approach. Die Bodenkultur: J. Land Manag. Food Environ. **72**(2), 73–82 (2013). https://doi.org/10.2478/boku-2021-0007

44. Sood, A.K., Enbody, R.J.: Targeted cyberattacks: a superset of advanced persistent threats. Secur. Priv. **11**(1), 54–61 (2013). https://doi.org/10.1109/MSP.2012.90

45. Tounsi, W., Rais, H.: A survey on technical threat intelligence in the age of sophisticated cyber attacks. Comput. Secur. **72**, 212–233 (2018). https://doi.org/10.1016/j.cose.2017.09.001

46. Urciuoli, L., Männistö, T., Hintsa, J., Khan, T.: Supply chain cyber security – potential threats. Inf. Secur. Int. J. **29**(1), 51–68 (2010). https://doi.org/10.11610/isij.2904

47. Værbak, M., Ma, Z., Demazeau, Y., Jørgensen, B.N.: A generic agent-based framework for modeling business ecosystems: a case study of electric vehicle home charging. Energy Inf. **4**(2), 1–26 (2021). https://doi.org/10.1186/s42162-021-00158-4

48. Verizon Enterprise Solutions: 2020 Data Breach Investigations Report (2020). https://www.verizon.com/business/en-gb/resources/reports/2020-data-breach-investigations-report.pdf

49. Vrabič, R., Erkoyuncu, J.A., Farsi, M., Ariansyah, D.: An intelligent agent-based architecture for resilient digital twins in manufacturing. CIRP Ann. **70**(1), 349–352 (2021). https://doi.org/10.1016/j.cirp.2021.04.049

50. Warren, M., Hutchinson, W.: Cyber attacks against supply chain management systems: a short note. Int. J. Phys. Distrib. Logist. Manag. **130**(7/8), 710–716 (2000). https://doi.org/10.1108/09600030010346521
51. Zager, R., Zager, J.: OODA Loops in Cyberspace: A New Cyber-Defense Model. Small Wars Journal (2017). https://smallwarsjournal.com/jrnl/art/ooda-loops-cyberspace-new-cyber-defense-model
52. Zhang, S., Shi, P., Du, T., Su, X., Han, Y., Chen, P.: Threat modeling and reasoning for industrial control system assets. In: 2022 IEEE Intl Conf on Parallel & Distributed Processing with Applications, Big Data & Cloud Computing, Sustainable Computing & Communications, Social Computing & Networking (ISPA/BDCloud/SocialCom/SustainCom), pp. 468–475. IEEE (2022). https://doi.org/10.1109/ISPA-BDCloud-SocialCom-SustainCom57177.2022.00066
53. Ziffer, D., Bamford, M.: Freight giant DP World recovers from cyber attack, but warns investigation and remediation is 'ongoing' (2023). https://www.abc.net.au/news/2023-11-13/dp-world-deals-with-impact-of-cyber-attack/103097658

Designing and Implementing an Educational Game for Cyber Planning Building on Cyberspace's Layers

Andreas Kornmaier(✉) ⓘ, Marko Hofmann ⓘ, and Ulrike Lechner ⓘ

University of the Bundeswehr Munich, Neubiberg, Germany
{Andreas.Kornmaier,Marko.Hofmann,Ulrike.Lechner}@unibw.de

Abstract. Cyberspace has become an integral part of many areas of everyday life. Consequently, there is a need to teach and incorporate cyber aspects into planning at the operational level and explain their impact on operational planning. This publication presents the design and implementation of the three layers of cyberspace in an operational context in a table top game as well as initial results.

Keywords: Cyberspace · Layers · Educational game · Operational planning

1 Introduction

Cyberspace has become an integral part of many areas of everyday life. NATO has also considered cyberspace as a domain of operations since 2016 [1]. In order to incorporate this fifth dimension into the planning and management of operations at the operational or strategic level, a minimum of understanding and knowledge of interrelationships within cyberspace and its interactions with the four traditional dimensions is required. In contrast, at the tactical level, detailed technical knowledge is required, as this is where the operational idea is implemented through actions.

The topic of cyber defense is addressed in tabletop and expert exercises as well as in board and card games [2–6]. Review of existing game concepts shows a wide range, from the defense of a company to the actions of states targeted by cyber attacks. The main focus of those games is to create understanding and thereby increase IT security awareness among the players. Although operational aspects are sometimes mentioned, the focus is on cyber defense measures, neither on the planning of cyber effects and the actions that lead to them, nor on the design of their integration into joint operations management. Consequently, there is a need for a game to teach and incorporate cyber aspects into planning at the operational level and explain their impact on operational planning. To satisfy this demand, we propose a serious game.

Our research interest is to design a serious game to facilitate the training of operational planners. The research contribution of this first publication is to

S. Zielinski et al. (Eds.): I4CS 2025, CCIS 2513, pp. 377–385, 2025.
https://doi.org/10.1007/978-3-031-94263-1_21

present the design, our implementation as a table top game focusing on the three layers of cyberspace (see Fig. 1) in an operational context for training purposes in the cyber domain, and initial results to verify the proposed prototype.

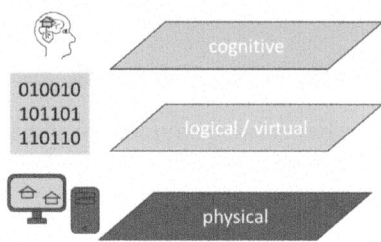

Fig. 1. Segmentation of cyberspace into its physical (e.g. hardware), logical/ virtual (e.g. software and data) and cognitive (e.g. perception of data representation) layers

This article is structured in the following sections. Section 2 summarizes the method used in our research. Section 3 describes the design of the game. Section 4 shares our initial results and our first assessments of these. The paper concludes in Sect. 5 with a way ahead.

2   Method

The design-oriented research approach of Hevner et al. [7] guides our iterative approach to design and evaluation. This paper describes the state of the game after pretesting and first play sessions in 2024. We report on the results of games so far.

The design of the game, as well as the interpretation of the players' considerations and the resulting outcomes, are based on the experience of the first author, who has over 10 years of experience as a specialist in IT security, hacking, and operational planning. The data generation and collection was fed on the one hand by observations being summarized in a structured way from notes being taken during the game by the first author acting as game master, and from secured game results; on the other hand, by a questionnaire the players were asked to complete after the end of the game. The questionnaire is comprised of a mix of questions from the Game Experience Questionnaire's Core Module [8], the Questionnaire on Motivation for Cooperative Playful Learning Strategies [9], and an article about the Development and Validation of Serious Games for Teaching Cybersecurity [10].

Every session's data have been evaluated and considered valid for application in the game and its environment or have started a refinement for the relevant aspects.

3   The Game

3.1   The Concept of the Game

The game familiarizes players with cyberspace's three layers and the interdependencies within and between the layers, promoting understanding, thinking, and inclusion of cyberspace in planning. Consequently, the game is an educational one. The game is designed for the operational level. Thus, the aspects of cyberspace have to be considered in a more abstract way and in the wider context of the operational mission. As this is a planning game, there is no opposing player involved. Rather, the opponent's actions are introduced into the game by way of event cards to which players have to react.

3.2   Target Group

The game can be used to train beginners as well as experienced planners and operators to consider cyber aspects and their benefits for the operational end state. It aims at training personnel to bring cyber aspects into mission planning on the operational level.

3.3   The Game's Hardware

The game comes with a tutorial/rule booklet, including an overview of the available cards, a scenario description (*Mission 1* and *2*), a scenario overview map, an IT-network plan, and cards.

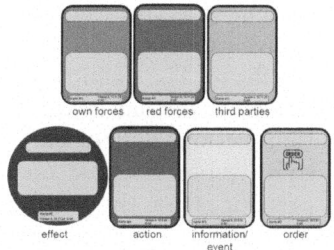

Fig. 2. Card types and their colors (top row used for entities)

The set of cards (see Figs. 2 and 3 as well as Table 1) comprises universally usable cards for entities, effects, and actions. Further cards provide scenario-specific information for the entities and escalation within the setting via information and event cards.

Adhesive blank sheets are provided for the players to amend - if needed - the set of effect and action cards, and to be attached to the entities with players' targeted element in one of the entities' layers (as can be seen in Fig. 4). For the game master, a memo pad to take notes is provided.

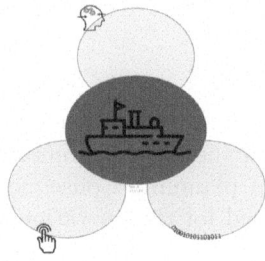

Fig. 3. Card for the entity of an *own ship* with cyberspace's layers in the adjacent bubbles. The bubbles represent the "entrance" via effect and action cards within the relevant layer.

Table 1. Card types and quantity

Card type	Number of different cards
entities (+ tutorial)	16 (+3)
effect	20
action	42
information/event	32
order	5

3.4   The Rules

The planning must be completed by the players within the allotted time. After analyzing the situation and mission objective, the players are free to plan effects and actions to accomplish the given mission. Players need to identify entities in whose layers they want to have effects. The main focus for the planning of effects and actions is on the entity's logical/virtual layer. The other two layers must also be taken into consideration: actions and/or effects can have effects within the logical/virtual layer and vice versa. At least one effect has to be planned in the logical/virtual layer (see Fig. 4) of the entities in order to achieve the mission objective. More effects within a layer are possible when they are aimed at different systems or elements in this layer. Due to interdependencies especially in the logical/virtual layer, effects in one entity can have effects in other entities.

Every effect has to be induced by at least one action (see Fig. 4). An action card cannot be placed without the respective effect card describing the desired effect.

3.5   The Missions

The game is divided into missions. *Mission 1* is in the category of *advance planning* (preplanned mission) and familiarizes the players with the scenario, the potential opposing actors, and the game mechanics. Building on this, *Mission 2* belongs to *crisis response planning* (contingency mission) as the situation

Fig. 4. A card for the entity *own ship* was amended with an adhesive sheet. The component to be targeted in the layer is written on the sheet by the players and supplemented with the cards for the intended effect and its inducing action.

worsens and players have to react. *Mission 2* is more complex in its structure, as more entities have to be included in the players' considerations.

3.6   Conducting the Game

In the beginning, the game master familiarizes the players with cyberspace's three layers and its dependencies within and between the three layers. This tutorial introduction uses a well-known and documented example a cyber operation: the real world's attack STUXNET [11].

The game master introduces the mission and the mission sheets are handed out. The players start with their analysis of the situation. They must first identify the problem and its elements within the layers of cyberspace and then solve it. Depending on their skills and level of knowledge, the players act independently, are guided by the game master with open questions, or are guided by specific questions and hints. Any gaps in knowledge or understanding of cyberspace, its three levels, and their dependencies can be addressed and closed directly by the game master. The reasoning and discussions of the players are interfered with by event cards introducing more information. The game master plays the cards depending on the speed of play, the proficiency, and knowledge of the players. This allows reacting to players' different experience and knowledge levels, distracting them with additional and partly misleading information for planning purposes. A flood of information and resulting stress as experienced in a real operational planning process, can thus be introduced to the players. The game master can slow down the play with additional event cards' information or advance the play to meet the scheduled educational time frame. The game master gives guidance by open questions and explains, when needed, relevant topics or gives examples. Thus, the players complete their learning experience with a success: effects being induced by actions to meet the mission objectives. Each mission's end is followed by a debriefing.

3.7 Debriefing

The mission's planning is debriefed by the game master in a moderated group discussion. He uses the notes being taken during the game to facilitate the discussion. The group discussion offers the game participants the opportunity to reflect on their individual experiences as well as the outcome of the game. They can transform these into newly gained experience and thus are more aware and critical in the real world of the facts experienced in the game environment. The group is able to reflect on the experience from different perspectives and to summarize the experiences from different perspectives. The group discussion in the debriefing is therefore a suitable means of evaluation. Suggestions for improvement and statements about the artifact are documented anonymously and summarized.

3.8 Questionnaire

After the end of the game, the players are asked to complete the questionnaire. The questionnaire's data is compiled in thematic clusters for evaluation and validation of the game and its design.

4 Results and Discussion

Our research interest is to design a serious game to facilitate the training of operational planners. The objective was to receive initial data for verification of the game logic of the proposed prototype and further feedback to direct the design research of the first author to further improve the game artifact.

Up to the date of this reporting, the game has been conducted in four sessions with a total of 26 participants; all of them have answered the questionnaires.

The questionnaires' clustered results are shown in Table 2.

The compiled data revealed that the majority of players enjoyed playing the game, immersing via the scenario into it. The scenario for the game is a fictional one, thus neither does security classification hamper or restrict its use for education and training purposes, nor do actual real-world political or security concerns limit or bias the players' approach to analyze and solve the given mission. Although the scenario is fictional, it is considered realistic, underpinning the relevance of this work. It immerses the players in it and transfers them into a state of flow. Hereby only a very small percentage felt distracted or negatively affected. Overall, they were positively affected by the game and assessed it as a valuable form of learning.

Table 2. Questionnaires' cluster results

Cluster	Percentage
Competence	83%
Sensory and Imaginative Immersion	90%
Flow	73%
Tension/Annoyance	13%
Challenge	58%
Negative affect	16%
Positive affect	94%
Clear objective	69%
Realistic, relevant scenario	79%
Improving skills	74%
Motivating	81%
Suitability for learning	81%
Game is valuable for player	85%

The aim of the game was evident to most of the players. This presumably can be increased by emphasizing more the game's aim in the introduction.

The players were highly motivated to apply their skills, improve them in this safe environment, and were encouraged to experiment with different alternatives, risking no real-world consequences. They were able to apply their competences to solve different missions' challenges. It was observed that the players identified in all play rounds the relevant entities and planned appropriate effects and those inducing actions to counter the given scenario situation within the given time.

The value for the *challenge* cluster suggests that for many, the game is not considered sufficiently challenging yet. However, it is important to point out that the last session was conducted with experts with years of experience in IT and planning. With further sessions in a teaching environment, the percentage for *challenge* will likely increase, because these groups usually are more heterogeneous in their training level. However, it is demanding to challenge every participant of the group adequately. Also, it should not be overlooked that this is a game for education and training, the focus of which is not on tricky tasks to solve, but on training the players.

Players' gaps in knowledge and understanding of cyberspace, its three layers and their (inter)dependencies as well as in procedures can be addressed instantly and thus be closed directly by the game master. Key to guiding the training audience to their learning success are the proficiency and experience of the game master.

The results show that the game design appeals to the players and almost all participants assessed playing the game as valuable for them. The majority of the players assess the game as suitable for teaching and training. The feedback implies that the artifact is a valuable tool for teaching the integration of cyber considerations and activities in operations planning and execution via the three layers of cyberspace. One IT expert stated that "the interconnection of the three levels becomes very clear through the game and thus contributes very well to insight."

The reason for the preliminary small number of participants in the four game sessions lies in the niche nature of operational planning within the cyber domain, where eligible and apt persons are scarce. However, the last session was conducted with 17 experts with years of experience in IT and planning. Their expertise substantiates the results. Nevertheless, further iterations are needed for a larger sample size to further substantiate the results.

The promising initial results and the valuable feedback allow to direct the design research to further improve the game artifact. From the designer's perspective, the game logic proved to be appropriate and the provided game material has served the players in the game according to its designed purposes. With segmenting cyberspace into three layers (physical, logical and cognitive) as basis for considerations in the operational planning, this game provides a novel contribution to cyber education.

5   Conclusion and Future Work

In this paper, we proposed a prototype of a fictional scenario table top game to teach and train planners to integrate cyber aspects in their operational plans.

The initial results are promising. From the designer's perspective, the game logic proved to be appropriate and the provided game material has served the players in the game according to its designed purposes. The data and feedback show that the game is a valuable form of training. The participants not only enjoyed playing the game, but also assessed it as valuable to them playing it. The scenario was valued as realistic by the players. This is underpinning the relevance of this work.

The received valuable feedback gives insights allowing to direct the design research to further improve the game artifact as a novel contribution to cyber education.

In the future, the first author will conduct subsequent sessions to further improve and substantiate the game artifact.

Acknowledgments. This work originates from the LIONS research project. LIONS is funded by dtec.bw—Digitalization and Technology Research Center of the Bundeswehr, which we gratefully acknowledge. dtec.bw is funded by the European Union—NextGenerationEU.

Disclosure of Interests. The authors Kornmaier and Hofmann have no competing interests to declare that are relevant to the content of this article. Author Lechner is a member of I4CS Program Committee.

References

1. North Atlantic Treaty Organization, NATO Cyber Defence (2020). https://www.nato.int/nato_static_fl2014/assets/pdf/2020/8/pdf/2008-factsheet-cyber-defence-en.pdf
2. Rieb, A.: IT-Security Awareness mit Operation Digitales Chamäleon. PhD thesis. Universität der Bundeswehr München, Neubiberg (2018). http://d-nb.info/1153067870
3. Long, D.T., Mulch, C.M.: Interactive wargaming cyberwar: 2025. Naval Postgraduate School, 11 (2017)
4. Röpke, R., Schroeder, U.: The problem with teaching defence against the dark arts: a review of game-based learning applications and serious games for cyber security education. In: International Conference on Computer Supported Education. In Proceedings of the 11th International Conference on Computer Supported Education (CSEDU 2019), pp. 58–66 (2019). https://doi.org/10.5220/0007706100580066
5. Association des Amis de la Réserve Citoyenne Cyberdéfense: Cyber Strategia (2016). https://trictrac.net/jeu-de-societe/cyberstrategia-1
6. Defence Science and Technology Laboratory: Cyber Game (2021). https://assets.publishing.service.gov.uk/media/61c3149d8fa8f54c17327a86/Easy_Access_IP_Cyber_Card_Game.pdf
7. Hevner, A., et al.: Design science in information systems research. MIS Q. **28**, 75–105 (2004). https://doi.org/10.2307/25148625
8. IJsselsteijn, W. A. , de Kort, Y. A. W., Poels, K.: The Game Experience Questionnaire. Technische Universiteit Eindhoven (2013)
9. Kulshrestha, S., Agrawal, S., Gaurav, D., Chaturvedi, M., Sharma, S., Bose, R.: Development and validation of serious games for teaching cybersecurity. In: Fletcher, B., Ma, M., Göbel, S., Baalsrud Hauge, J., Marsh, T. (eds.) JCSG 2021. LNCS, vol. 12945, pp. 247–262. Springer, Cham (2021). https://doi.org/10.1007/978-3-030-88272-3_18
10. Gaurav, D., Kaushik, Y., Supraja, S., Yadav, M., Gupta, M.P., Chaturvedi, M.: Empirical study of adaptive serious games in enhancing learning outcome. Int. J. Serious Games 9(2), 27–42 (2022). https://doi.org/10.17083/ijsg.v9i2.486
11. Falliere, N., Murchu, L. O.,Chien, E.: Symantec Security response W32. Stuxnet dossier. Version 1.3 (2010). https://nsarchive2.gwu.edu/NSAEBB/NSAEBB424/docs/Cyber-044.pdf

Cybersecurity Awareness Education by Making Ransomware Tangible Securely
The Beginning

Günter Fahrnberger[1]([✉])[iD], Maximilian Greiner[2][iD], Stefan Hofbauer[2][iD], Ulrike Lechner[2][iD], Andreas Seiler[2,3][iD], Judith Strussenberg[2][iD], and Philipp Wolf[4,5][iD]

[1] University of Hagen, Hagen, Germany
`guenter.fahrnberger@studium.fernuni-hagen.de`
[2] University of the Bundeswehr Munich, Neubiberg, Germany
`{maximilian.greiner,stefan.hofbauer,ulrike.lechner,`
`judith.strussenberg}@unibw.de`
[3] Lechwerke AG, Augsburg, Germany
`andreas.seiler@lew.de`
[4] University of Vienna, Vienna, Austria
`philipp.wolf@bmlv.gv.at`
[5] Austrian Armed Forces, Vienna, Austria

Abstract. Phishing techniques under the Massachusetts Institute of Technology Research and Engineering (MITRE) ATT&CK Framework, along with their offshoots Smishing, Spearphishing, and Whaling, remain prevalent despite widespread security awareness, facilitating ransomware attacks that encrypt data for impact. Ransomware threats expand from single to triple extortion, combining data encryption with threats of auctioning stolen data and launching Distributed Denial of Service (DDoS) attacks. Europol's Internet Organised Crime Threat Assessment (IOCTA) 2024 underscores the persistent risk of ransomware, a danger often underestimated by organizations. This research examines the security awareness gap, as typical end users and staff engaged in Information Technology (IT) rarely face ransomware incidents or gain hands-on experience with incident response. To address this gap, a safe, playful, and controlled environment enables trainees to interact with ransomware securely while exploring the encryption process and incident response strategies. A new research design assesses security awareness, with findings analyzed in the context of a walkthrough room named CONTAIN on TryHackMe, supported by a longitudinal study. The document concludes with a summary of results and recommendations for future work.

Keywords: Cybersecurity · Cybersecurity awareness · Cybersecurity education · Cybersecurity training · Incident response · Ransomware · Serious game

---

Note: Authors listed alphabetically by their last names, with equal credit given to all.

S. Zielinski et al. (Eds.): I4CS 2025, CCIS 2513, pp. 386–414, 2025.
https://doi.org/10.1007/978-3-031-94263-1_22

1   Introduction

Ransomware delivers its notice. What happens next? Would a user or a security professional recognize the threat and respond appropriately? Despite its prevalence, ransomware often feels abstract to both groups, mere users and security professionals. This research transforms the concept into a tangible experience. A serious game and interactive space on the TryHackMe platform create an environment where users explore ransomware behavior and practice strategies for containment and eradication. Prompts encourage both action and reflection. This hands-on approach provides education, training opportunities, and valuable insights based on data collected on ransomware awareness, threat recognition, and incident response.

The MITRE ATT&CK [39] Initial Access technique T1566 (*Phishing*) along with its variants *Smishing*, *Spearphishing*, and *Whaling*, continues to succeed despite widespread information security awareness. This exploitation path paves the way for the infamous MITRE ATT&CK Impact technique T1486 (*Data Encrypted for Impact*), a tactic frequently leveraged by ransomware. This type of malware has plagued the digital world by rendering critical data irretrievable. The threat has escalated from single to double and triple extortion. Single extortion relies on ransom demands after victims lose access to their data, leaving them with the choice to pay, restore from backups, or attempt decryption. Double extortion intensifies the pressure by threatening to leak or sell stolen data on the dark web if the ransom remains unpaid. Triple extortion introduces an additional layer of coercion, combining DDoS attacks with data auctions to further escalate demands. In the end, the attackers maintain control. As seen in recent years, Europol's IOCTA 2024 reaffirms the persistent ransomware threat, dedicating its entire second section on cyber-attacks to this escalating danger [11].

Apart from crimefighters, many organizations remain unaware of the full extent of the dangers they face, as highlighted in the publication by Greiner et al. [17]. Opinions differ as some consider themselves too uninteresting for Advanced Persistent Threat (APT) groups, while others assume that their defenses provide sufficient protection. However, one critical aspect often goes unnoticed: even security software like CrowdStrike fails to serve as a panacea against ransomware. Careless handling of credentials allows attackers to infiltrate systems undetected, using native Windows tools to effectively bypass security alerts. Reports on ransomware, along with surveys on risks and impacts, appear frequently, and warnings seem ever-present. Despite this, most users and only a handful of professionals have ever seen ransomware execute its encryption process or gained hands-on experience in managing a ransomware incident.

As a novel approach, this document addresses the security awareness gap by offering a tangible demonstration of ransomware in action. The literature survey in Sect. 3 highlights that existing research and electronic training rooms primarily emphasize threat detection, hunting, and mitigation. This work presents a training experience where trainees deliberately execute ransomware in a secure, isolated environment by intentionally clicking on a phishing link and observing the encryption process. The training leverages TryHackMe as a platform, providing a dedicated room for hands-on engagement. A survey assesses the effectiveness of this approach.

Section 2 outlines the research design, while Sect. 3 on related work provides evidence that this approach remains unexplored. As the centerpiece of this publication, Sect. 4 introduces the CONTAIN walkthrough room on TryHackMe, a well-known cybersecurity training platform, and presents a longitudinal analysis supported by initial and final questionnaires. Section 5 offers a detailed explanation of the study results based on CONTAIN. Finally, Sect. 6 summarizes the findings and proposes directions for future work.

2   Research Design

This study aims to raise awareness of ransomware threats, techniques, and mitigation strategies by designing a challenge on the TryHackMe platform that introduces key attack methods while emphasizing effective containment and defense measures[1]. The design and evaluation of the TryHackMe room align with the Design Science paradigm, as outlined by Hevner, with design and implementation alongside justification and evaluation serving as core research activities [21].

The TryHackMe room emerged through a collaborative exploratory process, leveraging the community platform's capabilities. Pre- and post-surveys assess its effectiveness in raising player awareness while integrating seamlessly into the gameplay experience. The evaluation process relies on individual player feedback and survey results. Key outcomes of this project include the TryHackMe room CONTAIN as a tangible artifact, refined design knowledge for developing security training on TryHackMe and similar platforms, and insights into ransomware awareness and the extent to which the game strengthens it.

The artifact resulting from the design and implementation activity consists of a room on the TryHackMe platform, featuring a scenario and ten tasks with 27 questions that players must answer to complete the room. The two surveys appear within the game as Task 1 and Task 10. Design and implementation took place between June and December 2024.

Data collection for the room took place between December 2024 and February 16, 2025. A total of 27 players entered the room, with 18 completing at least the first task, which included the survey. Only two players successfully completed the room, reaching Task 10. The SoSci tool facilitated the survey process. The questions explored topics such as education and current position, motivation for participation, and reflections on the room, focusing on insights gained from solving tasks, the perceived level of difficulty, and the use of additional resources during the problem-solving process. During the data collection phase, access remained limited to participants who either noticed a posting on the professional media platform LinkedIn, received an invitation, or discovered the room by chance.

To encourage participants to complete the survey, a flag needed to successfully finish the room appears at the end of the questionnaire. A flag represents

---

[1] https://tryhackme.com/.

a hidden string or token that participants must find and submit to earn points. Flags serve as proof of successfully solving a challenge.

3   Related Work

This section examines related work using a deductive approach, beginning with an overview of learning platforms. The focus then shifts to cybersecurity education before narrowing down to ransomware incident response education, which includes the TryHackMe room.

3.1   Cybersecurity Education Platforms

Numerous public initiatives attempt to raise information security awareness. This section highlights notable European, particularly German and Austrian, institutions and campaigns. One such initiative, European Cybersecurity Month (ECSM), takes place every October since 2013 [24]. Organized by the European Union Agency for Cybersecurity (ENISA) in collaboration with European Union (EU) member states, ECSM promotes cybersecurity awareness through events, training courses, digital campaigns, and informational materials, equipping citizens and organizations with knowledge about information security risks and best practices for safe digital engagement.

The German Federal Office for Information Security (BSI), serving as Germany's coordination office for ECSM, provides extensive recommendations and preventive measures against ransomware. These include a Top 10 list of key strategies for detecting and defending against attacks [41].

The Alliance for Cyber Security provides additional resources on the German side[2]. This initiative, launched by BSI and the industry association Bitkom, offers information, networking opportunities for companies and institutions, and training materials. For commercial enterprises, federal states and federal government police forces have established central cybercrime contact points[3]. These centers focus on preventive measures and serve as primary contacts in the event of a cyber incident.

Several initiatives in Austria focus on combating ransomware. The Austrian Institute for Applied Telecommunications (ÖIAT) operates the Watchlist Internet platform[4], which provides information on current threats and prevention strategies. The Austrian Federal Economic Chamber (WKÖ) runs a cybersecurity hotline[5], offering support to companies during cyberattacks. The Federal Criminal Police Office regularly shares insights on cybercrime and publishes prevention strategies, such as those outlined in the Cybercrime Report 2023[6]. Austria and Germany collaborate in the Counter Ransomware Initiative (CRI),

---

[2] https://www.allianz-fuer-cybersicherheit.de/.
[3] https://www.polizei.de/Polizei/DE/Einrichtungen/ZAC/zac_node.html.
[4] https://www.watchlist-internet.at/.
[5] https://www.wko.at/it-sicherheit/cyber-security-hotline.
[6] https://www.bundeskriminalamt.at/306/files/Cybecrime_Report_2023_WebBF.pdf.

an international effort to combat ransomware. This partnership enhances collective resilience, tracks attackers, and targets illegal financing structures behind ransomware operations. Both countries actively participate in annual CRI summits, working alongside other member states to develop and implement effective anti-ransomware measures.

Another valuable source of information comes from a website managed by law enforcement agencies, EU authorities and information security companies[7]. This platform provides decryption tools alongside essential information on ransomware threats. The German and Austrian Federal Criminal Police Offices contribute as supporting partners.

3.2 Cybersecurity Education Formats and Initiatives

As Yar et al. illustrate, cybersecurity education remains challenged by the rapid evolution of the field, while traditional academic programs struggle to keep pace with the growing demand for adaptation [43].

Ngambeki et al. present a comprehensive overview of cybersecurity education and training, highlighting the need to integrate practical workforce development with a strong knowledge foundation [33]. Hoachlander and Stewart underscore the importance of embedding industry knowledge and skills into the curriculum to better align education with real-world demands [22,38].

When teaching cybersecurity, the combination of knowledge, skills, and hands-on abilities remains essential. This perspective aligns with Yar et al., who highlight that many cybersecurity professionals prioritize practical experience over formal education [43].

Awareness serves as the central focus of many approaches, including the Unified Model of Security Policy Compliance. Other theoretical frameworks, such as deterrence theory and neutralization theory, explore the internal reasoning used to justify deviant behavior [37,40]. Serious games provide an effective method to improve cybersecurity awareness, offering significant potential to strengthen application-oriented information security knowledge [7,23,29,35].

Reviews and research of the literature conducted by [1–6,9,10,12,13,15,18–20,26,28,32,34,44] explore tabletop games, virtual games with various game mechanics, and multiple platforms for game creation. Many of these games remain inaccessible to a wider audience, often requiring moderation as part of a structured training experience. Capture-The-Flag (CTF) represents a widely recognized format with a strong competitive edge, primarily focusing on solving riddles, which often relate more to attack skills than to defensive or incident response skills. CTF formats tend to emphasize red team techniques, making them particularly valuable for penetration testers, while challenges designed for security experts or incident responders remain scarce. Escape room games foster social interaction, requiring a team to solve problems to escape a scenario, typically a locked room. Beyond solving puzzles or opening locks, essential soft skills such as teamwork and patience play a crucial role in incident response.

---

[7] https://www.nomoreransom.org/.

Mello-Stark et al. highlight escape rooms as an effective method in cybersecurity education, helping assess student learning while strengthening cybersecurity principles [31]. Many of these formats demand significant resources and commitment, whereas ransomware incident response training does not, particularly in formats that prioritize affordability and easy accessibility.

3.3 Ransomware Education

Various methods support ransomware education. Beyond traditional brochures and handouts from organizations like the BSI or law enforcement agencies, numerous digital platforms focus on different aspects of cybersecurity. Platforms such as TryHackMe (See Footnote 1), Hack The Box[8], Hack This Site[9], and ImmersiveLabs[10] offer interactive learning experiences, catering to people working in information security or preparing for a career in the field [27].

Podcasts have emerged as a valuable resource for understanding ransomware. Shows like *The Extortion Economy*[11] and *The Ransomware Files*[12] focus exclusively on ransomware, while *Darknet Diaries*[13], *Malicious Life*[14], and *Breach FM*[15] feature multiple episodes on the topic. The *Psychology of Cybercrime*[16] examines the psychological aspects of online crime, whereas *You are fucked - Germany's first cyber disaster*[17] delves into the ransomware attack on the German district of Anhalt-Bitterfeld and its far-reaching consequences.

Various serious games specifically address ransomware. The online game *Ransomware*[18] from G DATA CyberDefense AG features a series of interactive challenges that guide players through ransomware threats and effective response strategies.

The serious game *RansomAware*, developed by Butt as part of his dissertation, explores ransomware threats and mitigation strategies [8]. Furthermore, the Awareness Laboratory Small and Medium-sized Enterprise (SME) (ALARM) Information Security research project has created seven serious digital games covering key information security topics for Small and Medium-sized Enterprises (SMEs), including one specifically focused on ransomware[19].

---

[8] https://www.hackthebox.com/.
[9] https://hackthissite.org/.
[10] https://www.immersivelabs.com/.
[11] https://www.technologyreview.com/supertopic/extortion-economy/.
[12] https://pod.link/ransomwarefiles.
[13] https://darknetdiaries.com/.
[14] https://malicious.life/.
[15] https://breachfm.transistor.fm/.
[16] https://www.mark-thorben-hofmann.de/en/cybersecurity-podcast/.
[17] https://www.mdr.de/mdr-sachsen-anhalt/podcast/you-are-fucked/deutschlands-erste-cyberkatastrophe-hack-anhalt-bitterfeld-100.html.
[18] https://www.gdata.de/business/security-services/security-awareness-training/games.
[19] https://alarm.wildau.biz/.

As part of the German-Austrian research project CONTAIN[20], researchers developed several serious games, focusing on ransomware threats and incident response.

Operation Raven functions as a serious game designed for information security professionals in critical infrastructures, fostering discussions on processes and decision-making strategies to detect, contain, and eliminate ransomware threats [36]. *A Question of Security* offers a serious game experience for IT users without advanced knowledge, focusing on the mitigation of ransomware on mobile devices. Currently in development at the University of the Bundeswehr Munich, the game introduces practical strategies to handle ransomware threats. *Digital Detectives*, developed at the University of Regensburg, aims to inspire young people to pursue careers in information security [14]. Through interactive challenges, the game increases interest in cybersecurity concepts and problem-solving skills. *Hack dich nicht* adapts the well-known board game *Mensch ärgere dich nicht* for the freight forwarding industry. Designed to raise awareness of cybersecurity risks, the game presents industry-specific challenges and promotes best practices.

4   TryHackMe Room *CONTAIN*

The aforementioned games emphasize education and training; however, they do not provide hands-on experience of ransomware in action, a crucial element to fully understand this critical threat.

Since no room on the TryHackMe platform carries a similar name, we chose the title *CONTAIN* for two key reasons. Firstly, the project itself bears this name. Secondly, containing a threat represents a fundamental task in Digital Forensics and Incident Response (DFIR), a concept thoroughly explored within the room. This section outlines all components included in the room. The theme of the room *Demystifying Ransomware* refers to the hands on approach of the room and the goal to make ransomware tangible.

CONTAIN, like all TryHackMe rooms, consists of one or more tasks. The tasks within CONTAIN build upon the MITRE ATT&CK [39] and MITRE D3FEND [25] frameworks while aligning with the scientific goals of the project. The first task, outlined in Subsect. 4.1 features a questionnaire on an external website, which a player completes to obtain the first flag and earn points. Similarly, the final task detailed in Subsect. 4.10 involves a second questionnaire, leading to the last claimable flag. These questionnaires collect information from TryHackMe users regarding their background, knowledge and experience related to ransomware, as well as their evaluation of the room. The second task outlined in Subsect. 4.2 covers foundational knowledge about ransomware. Tasks 3 to 7, according to Subsects. 4.3 to 4.7, align with the MITRE ATT&CK framework [39], and tasks 8 and 9, detailed in Subsects. 4.8 and 4.9, follow the MITRE D3FEND framework [25].

---

[20] https://www.contain-projekt.de/, http://www.contain-projekt.at/.

4.1   Introduction

The first task of the CONTAIN room raises awareness among players about a scenario relevant to small business owners who depend on computer systems for daily operations. An individual inadvertently becomes a victim of a cyberattack due to a lapse in judgment while downloading software. The business owner, who needs to view a Portable Document Format (PDF) document for business purposes, attempts to install Adobe Acrobat Reader using a search engine to find a download link. However, the search results display a malicious website disguised as the official Adobe site, leading the individual to unknowingly download a compromised version of the software, which contains ransomware. Upon installation, ransomware activates and encrypts critical business files, rendering them inaccessible. A ransom note then appears on the screen, demanding a substantial sum of money in exchange for the decryption key needed to regain access to the files.

This event serves as a stark illustration of the risks associated with downloading software from untrusted or unverified sources. It emphasizes the importance of exercising caution when interacting with websites, particularly when downloading software, and highlights the potential consequences for businesses that rely on digital systems for essential operations.

As mentioned earlier, the task's conclusion requires players to roll up their sleeves and answer twelve questions from the following categories in order to claim their first flag.

- Sociodemographics
  - Gender
  - Profession
  - Current country of residence
  - How the player learned about this TryHackMe room
- Motivation
  - Motivation for participation
- Knowledge
  - Knowledge of threats
  - Confidence in dealing with ransomware
  - Understanding of ransomware
  - Effective protection against ransomware
  - Understanding of ransom notes
  - Typical distribution of ransomware
  - Common targets of ransomware attacks

4.2   Ransomware

In the second task, players explore different types of ransomware, notable campaigns, the ransomware attack lifecycle, and key mitigation strategies. A brief explanation of technical terms enhances understanding.

Following the room's theme, Demystifying Ransomware, this task applies the divide-and-conquer approach to break down ransomware threats into manageable components. Using the MITRE ATT&CK framework [39], players analyze an example ransomware attack, examining the tactics, techniques, and procedures employed by adversaries. This structured approach reduces ransomware complexity, aiding comprehension and defense.

Ransomware appears in several forms, each with distinct characteristics and impacts.

- **Encryptors:** These ransomware variants lock files on the victim's system, preventing access without a decryption key. Examples include the infamous WannaCry and CryptoLocker attacks. Encryptors cause severe damage by targeting critical data, disrupting business operations, and leading to significant financial losses.
- **Lockers:** Unlike encryptors, lockers block access to the entire system without encrypting files. This type of ransomware displays a full-screen message or window, restricting access to the desktop and applications. An example, Reveton ransomware, pretends to be a law enforcement notice demanding a fine for alleged illegal activities.
- **Leakware:** This type of ransomware threatens to publish or leak sensitive data unless the ransom gets paid. Leakware can prove particularly damaging to organizations handling confidential information, such as healthcare providers or financial institutions. The Maze ransomware group gained notoriety for using this tactic, combining data encryption with the threat of data exposure.
- **Scareware:** Scareware uses deceptive tactics to frighten users into believing their system has malware or critical issues requiring immediate attention. The ransomware demands payment for a supposed fix. Although scareware may not always encrypt files or lock systems, it can still cause panic and lead to unnecessary financial losses.

Attackers leverage various methods, like Ransomware-as-a-Service (RaaS), access brokers, and software vulnerabilities, to deploy ransomware. The RaaS model enables cybercriminals to purchase or rent ransomware tools from developers, lowering the barrier for launching attacks. RaaS operators often offer customer support and updates, making it easier for less technically skilled attackers to execute successful campaigns.

Access brokers represent individuals or groups that sell access to compromised networks, providing attackers with a foothold to deploy ransomware. Access brokers often exploit vulnerabilities or use stolen credentials to gain initial access. Attackers exploit unpatched software vulnerabilities to infiltrate systems and deploy ransomware. Keeping software up-to-date with the latest security patches proves crucial in preventing such exploits. Specifically, in the case of financially motivated ransomware, exploiting vulnerabilities in easily accessible systems proves lucrative, as these systems ensure a critical foothold within the target networks, such as firewalls, remote access gateways, or project collaboration tools.

Depending on the attacker's motivation, the profile of ransomware attacks ranges from widespread exploitation of easily exploitable victims based on a common vulnerability to high-value targets.

The MITRE ATT&CK framework [39] outlines key attack stages, offering a comprehensive view of the ransomware attack lifecycle.

- **Initial Access:** Attackers gain entry into the target system, often through the previously discussed deployment methods.
- **Execution:** The attacker uses various methods to execute malicious code, ranging from droppers and command-and-control tools to the ransomware payload itself.
- **Privilege Escalation:** Attackers aim to gain higher-level permissions to access more critical parts of the network and data.
- **Lateral Movement:** The ransomware spreads across the network, infecting additional systems and amplifying the overall impact.
- **Data Exfiltration:** In some cases, attackers exfiltrate sensitive data before encrypting it, using it to leverage ransom demands.
- **Final Encryption:** The ransomware completes the encryption process, presenting the victim with a ransom note demanding payment for the decryption key.

Organizations mitigate ransomware through e-mail filtering, patch management, network segmentation, Multi-Factor Authentication (MFA), and backup strategies. Early detection and response can significantly reduce the impact of an attack. Incident response teams should train to identify signs of ransomware, such as unusual file extensions, unexpected system behavior, and the presence of ransom notes. By following a structured approach and using frameworks like MITRE ATT&CK [39], organizations gain a better understanding of ransomware threats and implement effective defenses.

4.3   Initial Access

Initial Access as the third task refers to techniques that adversaries use to gain entry into a network or system. These methods often exploit vulnerabilities in exposed services or human behaviors. Common approaches include phishing, exploiting public-facing applications, and leveraging compromised credentials. Once attackers establish a foothold, they can move laterally and escalate privileges to deepen their access. By targeting weak entry points, adversaries bypass defenses, setting the stage for further exploitation. Effective mitigation of Initial Access requires strong security practices, such as patching vulnerabilities, MFA, and user awareness training to reduce attack surfaces.

Before this task imparts knowledge about initial access, the player should launch the attached Virtual Machine (VM) by clicking the green *Start Machine* button in the upper-right corner of the browser. The process takes approximately five minutes, during which the player should remain patient. However, staying proactive and perusing this task's text remains advisable. Next, the player connects to the TryHackMe network, either through a second VM, known as the

AttackBox, accessible via any browser, or by establishing a Virtual Private Network (VPN) connection. After connecting through one of these methods, the player uses the provided credentials and Internet Protocol (IP) address to access the CONTAIN VM. Tools like Remmina (Linux), xfreerdp (Linux), mstsc (Windows), or any preferred Remote Desktop Protocol (RDP) client facilitate this connection. Finally, the Windows screen appears, as demonstrated in Fig. 1.

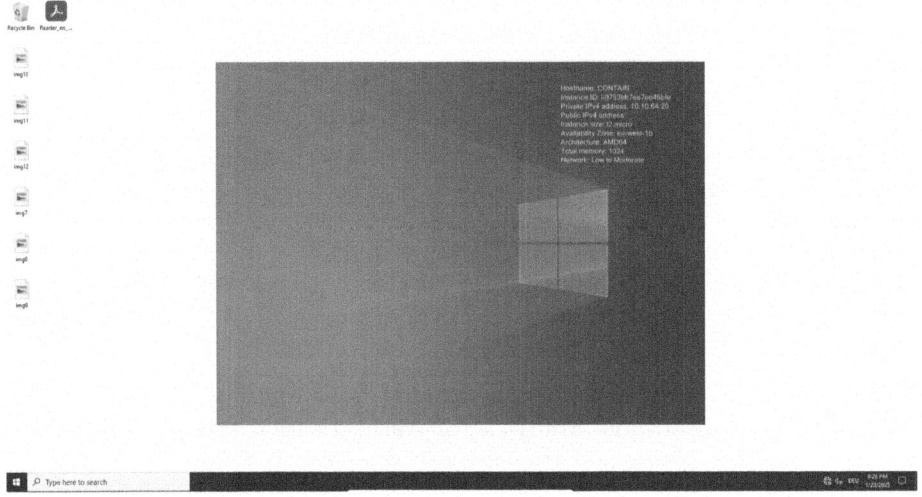

Fig. 1. Task 3

The conclusion of this task briefly outlines the well-known obfuscation methods used for artifacts intended for delivery during the Initial Access phase to achieve defense evasion.

4.4   Execution

The Execution phase of the MITRE ATT&CK framework [39] as the fourth task involves adversaries executing malicious code on a target system to achieve their objectives. This phase follows Initial Access and enables attackers to establish control, often using techniques such as command-line execution, scripting, and exploitation of trusted applications. Execution methods include PowerShell scripts, scheduled tasks, user execution (social engineering), and exploiting software vulnerabilities. Attackers may also leverage remote execution or built-in system tools to avoid detection. Success in this phase allows adversaries to deploy payloads, escalate privileges, or move laterally within the network, facilitating further compromise and persistence.

Upon bootstrapping the VM in the previous task, this task prompts a player to interact with it for the first time. The task description directs the player to execute a prepositioned executable file on the Windows desktop, designed to resemble an installer for the well-known Adobe Acrobat Reader. Both the name and icon imitate the genuine file, which remains publicly available, to mislead the user into running it.

In reality, the file contains the ransomware *ShinoLocker*. This educational malware serves two key purposes. Firstly, the corresponding decryption keys become available free of charge, allowing quick recovery of infected files without tedious ransom negotiations. Secondly, the infestation (and reversal) process unfolds visually for an affected user, as shown in Fig. 2. No other ransomware, to our knowledge, provides the same features. At this point in the walk-through, the ransomware encrypts the files and, in our case, the collection of photos on the Windows computer.

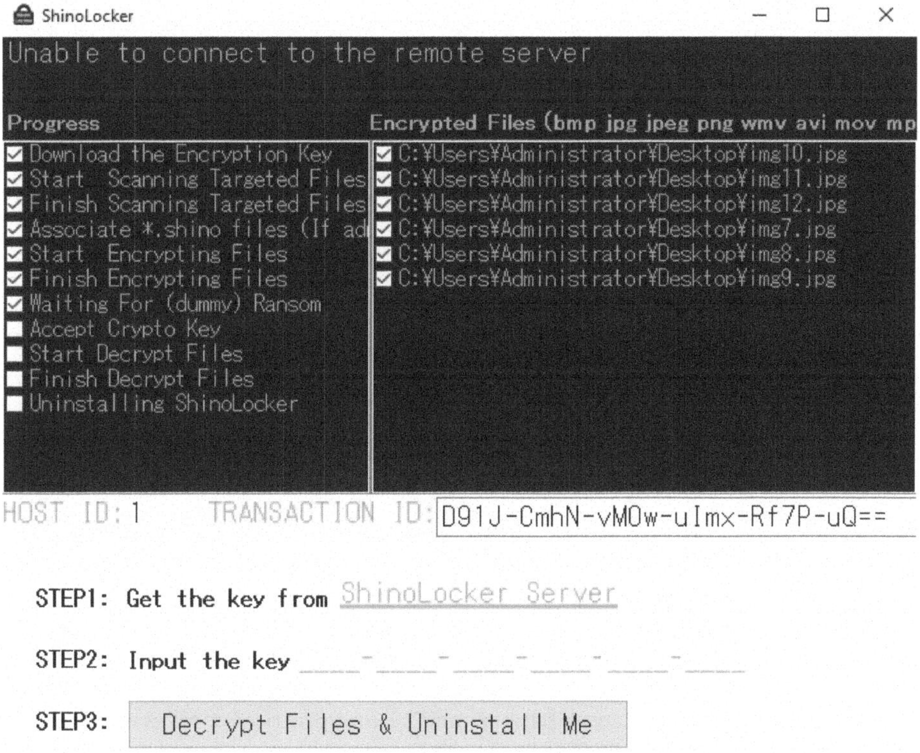

Fig. 2. Task 4

4.5 Lateral Movement

Lateral Movement as the fifth task involves techniques that adversaries use to access and control remote systems within a network. These techniques increase the danger of a ransomware attack, as attackers aim to infiltrate or encrypt particularly valuable information, IT assets, or information systems. Lateral Movement focuses on spreading throughout the network from the initial attack vector and the first infected system, gathering information about valuable and critical resources, and identifying methods to reach these systems.

Our TryHackMe room informs the player about Lateral Movement techniques. The content, based on the MITRE ATT&CK framework [39], recalls the initial scenario description and extends it. What happens when the attacker spreads across the network? The task then presents nine techniques of Lateral Movement: Exploitation of Remote Services, Internal Spearphishing, Lateral Tool Transfer, Remote Service Session Hijacking, Remote Services, Replication Through Removable Media, Software Deployment Tools, Taint Shared Content, and Use Alternate Authentication Material. The descriptions of these Lateral Movement techniques provide lightweight summaries of the MITRE ATT&CK framework [39], aimed at players with moderate information security backgrounds. The task questions focus on relevant and popular topics. For example, one of the questions asks which Lateral Movement technique uses Universal Serial Bus (USB) sticks.

This task in our TryHackMe room extends beyond what a regular TryHackMe customer can technically implement. Features like multiple Virtual Machines (VMs) and interconnected environments remain exclusive to TryHackMe employees. Designed as a narrative-style and informative task, it provides essential information on ransomware, its risks, and mitigation techniques. After the technically challenging work with the virtual engine and the survey, this task aims to maintain engagement without creating a roadblock. Keeping it lightweight ensures that all necessary information to answer the questions stays within the task text.

4.6   Command and Control (C2)

The sixth task describes C2 structures, classified under TA0011 in the MITRE ATT&CK framework [39], enabling attackers to communicate with compromised systems. These structures play a pivotal role in the operation of various types of malware, including ransomware, botnets, and Advanced Persistent Threats (APTs). By enabling remote command execution, data exfiltration, and sustained persistence, C2 structures serve as a cornerstone of modern cyberattacks. Understanding their architecture, functionality, and protocols proves essential for detecting and mitigating these threats. Although implementing such infrastructures with TryHackMe's toolkit would be feasible, limitations on VM resources led to the decision to include only a theoretical write-up on the topic. Despite their integral role in modern malware, these aspects remain a conceptual discussion rather than a practical exercise.

These C2 structures typically involve two primary components, first, command servers controlled by attackers to issue instructions, and second, compromised systems that carry out these commands. After an initial compromise (sometimes occurring months or even years earlier in the case of APTs), a system establishes a connection with the server. Authentication mechanisms, including encryption, ensure communication occurs with the attacker as originally intended. The server can issue commands that allow Lateral Movement (TA0008), Data Exfiltration (TA0010), or Persistence (TA0003) [39,42]. Attackers also utilize these established channels to monitor the activities of defenders and adapt their strategies dynamically.

C2 infrastructures exhibit significant variation in design. Centralized systems connect all compromised devices to a single server or redundant cluster, simplifying operations but creating a single point of failure. Decentralized Peer-to-Peer (P2P) models mitigate this vulnerability by enabling direct communication between compromised systems, reducing the reliance on a central server and complicating detection efforts. Domain Generation Algorithms (DGAs) facilitate periodic communication by algorithmically generating domain names, making detection more difficult due to frequent domain changes. Fast-flux networks enhance concealment by rapidly rotating IP addresses, often hosted on botnets, which mask the location of the command server and resist takedowns[21] [16]. Attackers often exploit widely used protocols to blend malicious traffic with legitimate communication. HyperText Transfer Protocol (HTTP) and HyperText Transfer Protocol Secure (HTTPS) remain popular choices due to their ubiquity and firewall-bypassing capabilities, with HTTPS offering additional encryption for greater stealth. Domain Name System (DNS) tunneling embeds instructions within DNS queries and responses, exploiting the typically unmonitored nature of this protocol. Other techniques include using the Simple Mail Transfer Protocol (SMTP) for e-mail-based C2 commands and employing legacy protocols like Internet Relay Chat (IRC) for simpler botnets [42]. Advanced attackers may develop proprietary protocols designed to mimic legitimate traffic, further enhancing their ability to evade detection.

To evade detection, attackers utilize advanced techniques. Encryption and encoding conceal C2 communications, while randomized beaconing intervals disrupt detection based on predictable patterns. Malicious traffic often routes through legitimate services such as cloud platforms, GitHub, or social media, mimicking regular activity. Polymorphic malware adds complexity by altering its code during each interaction, rendering signature-based tools ineffective [16]. Defensive measures target the detection and disruption of C2 operations. Monitoring network traffic for anomalies, including irregular DNS queries or unexpected HTTP requests, helps uncover malicious communication. Threat intelligence feeds identify known C2 servers, while Endpoint Detection and Response (EDR) solutions flag suspicious activities on endpoints. DNS filtering blocks access to malicious domains, and sinkholing redirects suspect traffic for further analysis. Regular patch management and system audits close vulnerabilities, preventing attackers from establishing C2 channels (See Footnote 21).

C2 infrastructures serve as a cornerstone of advanced cyberattacks, enhancing persistence, adaptability, and stealth. Cybersecurity professionals can improve their ability to combat and mitigate evolving threats by developing a deep

---

[21] https://www.zenarmor.com/docs/category/cyber-attacks.

understanding of these systems and applying layered defenses. As in previous tasks, implementing C2 structures exceeds what can be feasibly done on Try-HackMe, making this task primarily informative and narrative driven. Unlike Lateral Movement methods, this one emphasizes the variety and complexity of this attack phase.

4.7 Impact

Impact as the seventh task refers to techniques that adversaries employ to disrupt, manipulate, or destroy systems and data, resulting in significant consequences for organizations. These techniques aim to degrade the confidentiality, integrity, or availability of critical assets, with potential effects ranging from data corruption and loss to system shutdowns. Adversaries may also use Impact techniques to further the success of their attack, such as by hindering detection or response efforts. Understanding these techniques helps organizations develop strategies to protect assets, minimize damage, and enhance resilience against adversarial actions targeting key infrastructure components.

The selected educational ransomware, ShinoLocker, not only reflects its current development, but also allows configuration prior to initial access. To understand ShinoLocker's effect on the deployed TryHackMe VM, reviewing the chosen configuration for the TryHackMe box becomes essential. Figure 3 illustrates the default build options displayed when accessing the download link (See Footnote 22).

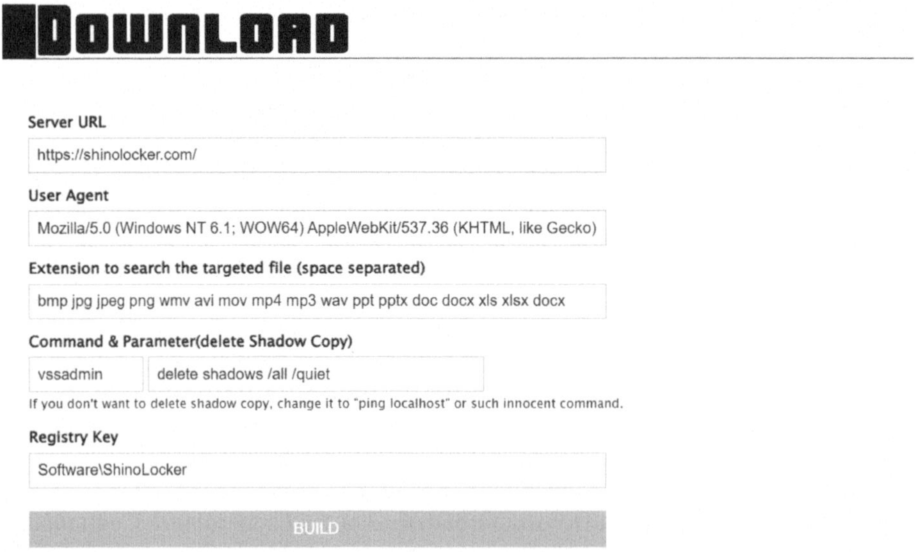

Fig. 3. Task 7

In addition to the server Uniform Resource Locator (URL) for retrieving the decryption key and an adjustable user agent for web-related actions, the third text field determines which file types ShinoLocker targets and decrypts in the executing user's home directory based on their extensions. To worsen matters, unless explicitly disabled, ShinoLocker secretly deletes all shadow copies of these file types by executing the command *vssadmin delete shadows /all /quiet*. Shadow copies, also known as volume shadow copies or Volume Snapshot Service (VSS) copies, function as a Microsoft Windows feature that creates backup snapshots of files or volumes, enabling recovery of previous file versions or entire volumes, particularly after accidental deletion, corruption, or modification. The fifth and final option defines ShinoLocker's registry location.

Beyond the ShinoLocker configuration, this task primarily explores the impact of a ransomware attack on a business or organization, concluding with relevant questions. As one of the hands-on tasks, it provides a tangible and immersive experience.

4.8   Detect

The eighth task covers ransomware detection and carries the title Detect. The Detect technique within the MITRE D3FEND framework [25] centers on identifying malicious activities across a network or system. It encompasses methods for monitoring, analyzing, and recognizing Indicators of Compromise (IOCs) or abnormal behaviors that indicate potential threats. Effective detection mechanisms depend on continuous monitoring, leveraging tools such as Intrusion Detection Systems (IDSs), network traffic analysis, and log aggregation. These techniques identify suspicious actions before they escalate into a full-scale breach. Detection strategies prioritize minimizing response times, facilitating swift mitigation measures, and reducing the overall impact of cyber threats on organizational assets and operations.

This task shifts the player from the victim to the defender role, advising how to mitigate the cyberincident rather than just suffer from it. For this reason, the well-known System Monitor (Sysmon) from Microsoft Sysinternals comes into play. Installed as a Windows service, Sysmon enhances default Windows event logs by providing detailed information about process creations, network connections, and file creation time changes. As a result, Sysmon helps identify malicious or anomalous activity while revealing how intruders or malware operate within the network (D3-PLA as per MITRE D3FEND framework [25]). Sysmon does not come automatically installed on Windows hosts. However, for the player's convenience, the room creators preinstalled the Sysmon service.

The task text advises the player on how to search for and find relevant Sysmon log entries to verify that ShinoLocker has successfully scrambled numerous files within the Administrator's home directory, including those on the desktop. Figure 4 depicts two exemplary log entries.

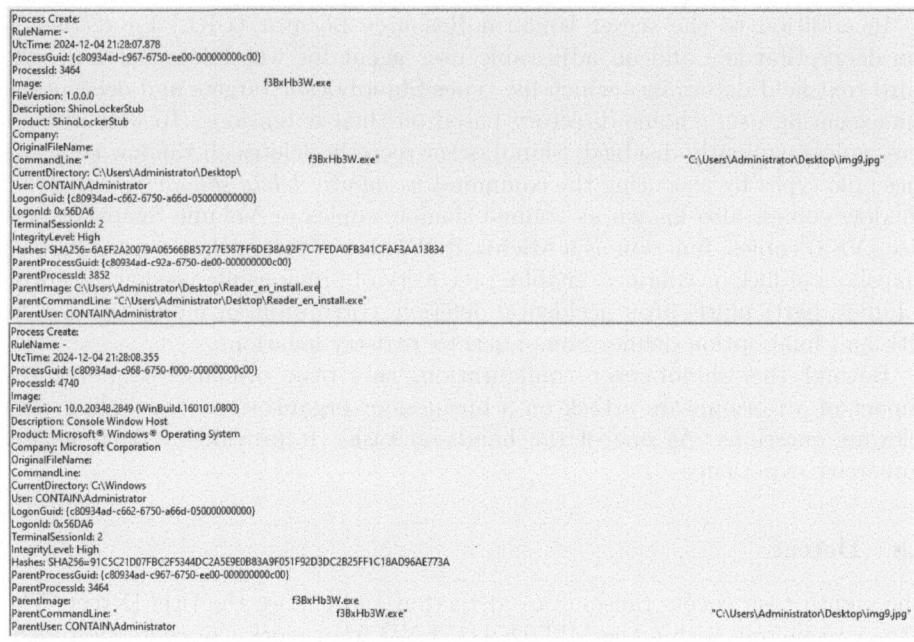

Fig. 4. Task 8

4.9   Restore

The Restore technique as the ninth task within the MITRE D3FEND framework [25] focuses on enabling recovery of systems and data after an attack. It emphasizes strategies that allow an organization to restore services, configurations, and files to their original state or a safe, operational state. This process may involve leveraging backup systems, using decryption tools, or applying patches to vulnerable systems. The goal remains to minimize downtime, reduce the impact of the attack, and ensure business continuity. Effective restoration techniques ensure resilience against future attacks, reinforcing the ability to recover quickly and effectively from cybersecurity incidents.

This task guides the player to restore the original files that ShinoLocker has infected. Fortunately, ShinoLocker behaves in a friendly manner, requiring no ransom and providing the correct decryption key free of charge. As a result, nothing prevents the player from following ShinoLocker's instructions by retrieving the correct decryption key[22], as Fig. 5 showcases, and starting the decryption of the affected files (D3-RF as per the MITRE D3FEND framework [25]).

To make this task more challenging for the player, they must handle the following situation without assistance: The ShinoLocker binary will delete itself after restoration (without retention in the recycle bin), and one file remains encrypted.

---

[22] https://shinolocker.com/.

STEP1: Get the key from ShinoLocker Server

STEP2: Input the key

STEP3: Decrypt Files & Uninstall Me

Fig. 5. Task 9

4.10 Conclusion

The tenth task covers the second questionnaire. While the first questionnaire aimed to gain an understanding of the players, their motivation, and their knowledge, the ten questions in the second questionnaire focused on their experience with the TryHackMe room.

– User experience
  • Rating of the room
  • Fun while participating
  • Use of the linked rooms
– Context
  • Experiences with ransomware
  • Reading the explanations provided
  • Sources for learning about ransomware
– Perceived usefulness
  • Helpfulness of the room
  • Most favorite task
  • Least favorite task

5 Results

Before delving into any results, let us recapitulate the TryHackMe room CONTAIN.

The techniques used in cyberattacks, according to the MITRE ATT&CK framework [39], show the level of sophistication and persistence of advanced threat actors. As the first major phase of an attack, Initial Access exploits vulnerabilities through phishing, credential theft, and compromised services. The hands-on labs in the TryHackMe room prove to be highly beneficial, reinforcing how adversaries gain a foothold and avoid detection. Through simulated attack scenarios, participants gain insight into the need for proactive security measures such as MFA and continuous system monitoring.

The Execution phase explains how adversaries utilize trusted applications and scripting to execute malicious code. An example of the way forward involves the educational ShinoLocker ransomware, which allows hands-on application of how execution techniques work in practice. By simulating real-world attack techniques, the exercises demonstrate the significant damage malware can inflict and the need for rapid detection and remediation. Strict application controls, along with endpoint monitoring and behavioral analysis, must detect and prevent execution attempts before they cause more serious damage.

Lateral Movement becomes one of the critical phases of an attack progression, allowing attackers to move across a network to reach high-value systems. The exercises note the use of common techniques, including remote service exploitation, lateral tool transfers, and internal spear phishing. These techniques help attackers maintain access and privileges, making early detection critical. This TryHackMe room emphasizes practical challenges, specifically how organizations can harden their defenses with network segmentation, access control policies, and monitoring unusual network activities.

In the discussion of C2 infrastructures, different approaches used by attackers to maintain persistence and exfiltrate data highlight the need for effective solutions. Current C2 strategies (such as decentralized P2P communication, protocol obfuscation, etc.) and their seriousness imply a search for high-level solutions. Finding ways to interrupt an adversary's means of control using network anomaly detection, DNS filtering, or endpoint monitoring becomes imperative for security teams. In general, the theoretical lesson demonstrates the difficulties in detecting and eliminating C2 channels while reinforcing good practices in cyber defense within the TryHackMe task.

Lastly, the remaining three phases of Impact, Detection, and Restoration focus on actions taken during a cyberattack and the post-cyberattack actions for mitigating and recovering the facilities. Key aspects of this process include knowledge of ransomware behavior, forensic analysis techniques, and restoration methods. With Sysmon integration for detection, as well as hands-on decryption exercises, we aim for participants to experience the entire attack lifecycle. However, TryHackMe exercises serve as a reminder of the importance of a layered security posture, where prevention, detection, and recovery mechanisms complement each other to protect organizational assets from ever-evolving cyber threats.

5.1   Design Knowledge

This subsection examines the design knowledge necessary to create the TryHackMe room within a collaborative setting. The author team, working on the CONTAIN research project, brings diverse backgrounds and varying levels of experience with TryHackMe. Some members have deep expertise and insight into what drives user engagement in solving a room. Understanding users, their backgrounds, and their motivations (whether driven by knowledge acquisition or reward points) plays a crucial role in designing an effective learning experience on this platform.

The design aims to balance several aspects. It should help players gain knowledge (and points), provide value for research by offering insights into the level of understanding of ransomware, and enhance skills related to handling VMs and encryption/decryption tools. The room design also needs alignment with TryHackMe's typical look and feel, including standard amounts of text, images, videos, and tools, while still representing the research program and its goals. Three key features define the design: first, the survey at the beginning, which earns a flag upon completion; second, a similar survey at the end; and third, the technical highlight, involving ransomware on VMs to allow players to see how ransomware functions and the resulting impact.

The design and implementation of this technical task demand more labor-intensive efforts and require an exploratory trial-and-error approach. While TryHackMe enjoys popularity within the community, the initial aim focused on participating in the annual advent event, only to reschedule later. During this busy period, TryHackMe's workforce faces challenges, and the team requires time to review and publish the room. It comes as a surprise to discover how many colleagues and friends already have accounts on the platform. Soliciting players and communicating the effort presents challenges and requires workarounds on social media to share the link.

The technical highlight of the CONTAIN room stands out in the design efforts. However, TryHackMe provides limited resources for the VM, resulting in slow execution and an unpleasant user experience. This design point will require further work in the future.

In addition, feedback from early users shows the need for clearer instructions and more guidance on troubleshooting the technical issues required by the course. Some players struggle to progress through the game because figuring out how to setup the VM proves difficult. Future versions could benefit from a step-by-step guide or interactive tooltips to assist the learning curve for new users.

Although the design already features quizzes and flags, introducing additional reward mechanisms such as time-based challenges or competitive leaderboards could further enhance player motivation and engagement.

Similarly, the design should also consider accessibility for users with varying levels of cybersecurity knowledge. Introducing tiered levels of difficulty or supplementary background reading could allow both first-timers and the more experienced players to gain from the room experience.

Finally, a structured feedback loop needs to be developed to iterate in the room based on the feedback of the players. This will allow for the collection of qualitative data from user comments and behavior analytics to adapt the learning experience to evolving educational needs.

5.2   TryHackMe Statistics

TryHackMe offers room creators a downloadable real-time table that includes all players, their correctly answered questions, and current scores. The number of itemized players meets or exceeds the number of participants in the questionnaires outlined in Subsect. 5.3. Players can skip the first and/or last task of the room, thereby bypassing one or both questionnaires. Naturally, such players cannot fairly complete the room without finishing both questionnaires and earning the points for the corresponding flags. Those who unfairly obtain the questionnaire-related flags from published write-ups or other players who have already obtained these flags contribute nothing to our research.

TryHackMe grants eight points for each correctly answered question in the so-called walkthrough rooms, including CONTAIN. With 27 questions in CONTAIN, a player can accumulate up to 216 points. At the time of writing this paper, CONTAIN remains under the status *submitted* due to a pending review and, therefore, acceptance. As a result, TryHackMe neither promotes CONTAIN nor counts the accumulated points toward a player's overall score. Consequently, we informed prospective players about CONTAIN through word-of-mouth recommendations and social media platforms like LinkedIn. Despite all efforts, CONTAIN has yet to attract the hundreds or thousands of players who typically engage with published TryHackMe rooms.

Despite these hindrances, a considerable number of players accessed CONTAIN, providing sufficient data for the first evaluation in this paper. As shown in Table 1, 31 different players had entered CONTAIN by February 16, 2025. On the one hand, the data reveal that most participants left all questions unanswered, thus missing the opportunity to collect fictive points. However, the maximum score indicates that at least one player obtained all 216 possible fictive points. The median reflects just four answered questions, while the mean hovers around nine. The standard deviation and variance highlight considerable volatility around the mean.

Table 1. TryHackMe creator statistics for CONTAIN

Statistic	Value
Count (n)	31
Maximum	216
Mean (μ)	72.77
Median	32
Minimum	0
Mode	0
Standard Deviation (σ)	77.85
Variance (σ^2)	6060.18

Figure 6 provides deeper insight into the score distribution. For example, it confirms the mode, with ten players having no points and only two players reaching the maximum score of 216.

In addition to the descriptive statistics intended for creators, each player can compare their room progress with those nine players who recently joined the same room. Figure 7 presents an anonymized snapshot of the ten most recent CONTAIN subscribers as of February 16, 2025.

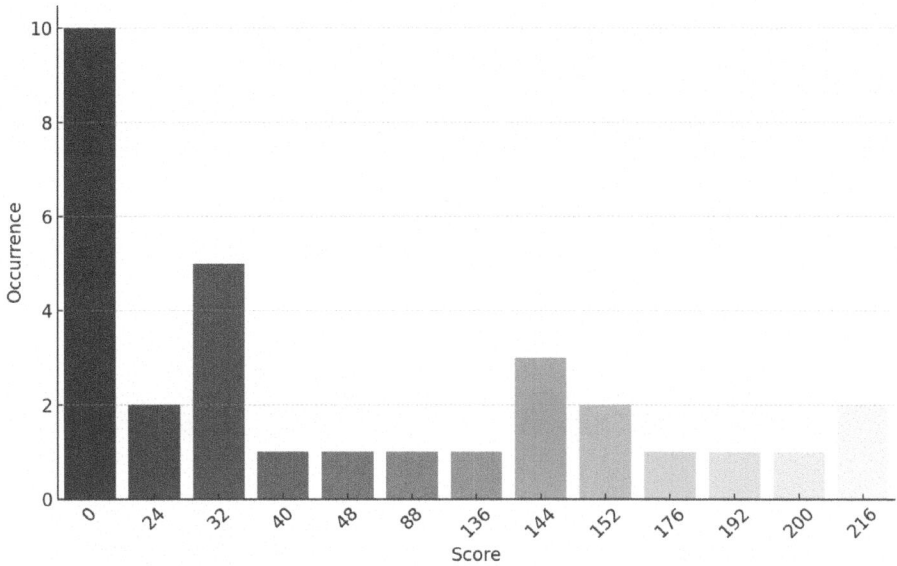

Fig. 6. TryHackMe creator statistics for CONTAIN

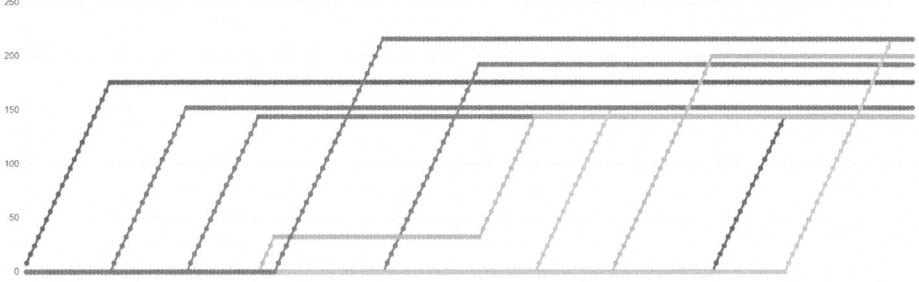

Fig. 7. TryHackMe player statistics for CONTAIN

5.3   Questionnaires

At the beginning of this subsection, we aim to get a picture of the 22 participants who completed the questionnaire.

- **Gender:** Male (18), Female (2), Other (2)
- **Profession:** Cyber/IT practitioner (12), Other (4), Student/Intern (4), Manager (2)
- **Country of residence:** Germany (18), Austria (3), Bahrain (1)

Most of the survey participants (n = 22) feel confident (n = 5) or moderately confident (n = 13) about handling ransomware. Two participants feel less secure, and two feel insecure. Although most consider themselves secure or at least moderately secure in handling ransomware, no participant selected the *very secure* option.

This self-assessment also appears in the results of the second questionnaire (n = 9). We asked participants how secure they felt handling ransomware compared to before the game. One participant reported feeling much safer, three felt somewhat safer, and five experienced no change.

Figure 8 provides an overview of the respondents' understanding of common ransomware attacks and protection measures against ransomware.

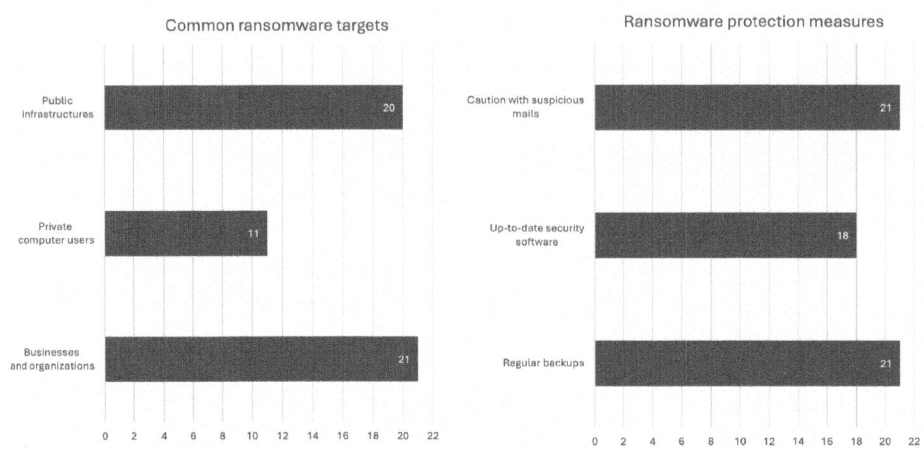

Fig. 8. Common ransomware targets and ransomware protection measures

21 respondents identified companies and organizations as common targets of ransomware, just ahead of public infrastructures, mentioned by 20 respondents. Eleven participants also named private computer users as targets of ransomware attacks.

When answering the question about measures that provide effective protection against ransomware, the respondents showed broad agreement. Increased vigilance with suspicious e-mails and links, along with regular backups, received recognition from 21 respondents as adequate measures. 18 of them considered the use of up-to-date security software an effective means of protection against ransomware.

The final survey (n = 9) provides the authors with information on the further development of the room while also reflecting certain challenges in its creation. The participants rated the difficulty of the room at an average of 2.22, corresponding to the level *easy*. The authors intentionally designed the room with this difficulty in mind.

Five of the players surveyed had no prior experience with ransomware. Three players encountered the topic through their work, and one player engaged with it as part of a private project.

The vast majority of the eight players read the room's explanations, while one player referred to them only when needing help.

We asked participants which resources they used to learn about ransomware. The responses included the BSI and the website NO MORE RANSOM (see Footnote 7). Additional sources mentioned include MITRE ATT&CK [39] and MITRE D3FEND [25]. The frequent references to the BSI come as no surprise. In the 2024 CONTAIN Monitor study, the BSI, its Austrian counterpart, and news sources accounted for 86.7% of the most frequently consulted information on ransomware [30].

The average rating of 2.44 out of 5 for the fun factor can partly be attributed to the room's status during the review phase, as indicated by feedback from testers we personally know. Playing the room requires the use of a VM, and the limited resources in its current state result in relatively long loading times.

For regular TryHackMe users, collecting points serves as an important motivation, which the room currently cannot support, as this feature did not serve as the intended focus at this test stage. The team communicated this limitation to the players. As a result, four participants in the initial questionnaire mentioned point collection as their reason for participating. Thirteen participants aimed to practice their skills, while six cited other reasons, such as curiosity, free time, or the authors' request to play the room.

6   Conclusion

The small number of responses (n = 22 in the initial and n = 9 in the final questionnaire) offers only a general indication rather than a statistically robust result. Once the room successfully passes the TryHackMe review process and gains official status on the platform, a broader base of players and the corresponding feedback should follow. Viewing the CONTAIN room as a regular room, alongside data collection and analysis, presents an important next step in our research. This initiative, as part of the research project, expands beyond the typical audience of professionals and security experts, reaching a less specialized target group of younger people, entrepreneurs, or individuals with limited access to education and training. Based on insights from design efforts and state-of-the-art literature, the CONTAIN room addresses a relevant gap in education and training methods. These factors justify the effort invested in this experimental design.

The interactive and hands-on format of the room played a key role in engaging participants and enhancing their knowledge of ransomware threats. Unlike traditional cybersecurity education methods, gamified environments offer playing experiences that allow players to test different attack and defense strategies in a controlled environment. This practice narrows the gap with dynamic knowledge and skills, making cybersecurity education more enriching.

Moreover, the possibility of inserting surveys into the room allowed us to gather useful information about participants' perceptions and learning. The responses suggest that numerous players became more aware of ransomware threats and how to prevent and mitigate them. These results align with previously published studies that indicate that interactive learning greatly enhances retention and the transfer of knowledge. However, wider participation in the TryHackMe community remains necessary to generate more definitive results.

During the implementation phase, a challenge involved the technical limitations set out by the TryHackMe platform. Occasionally, slower VMs and compute engines hindered the user experience. To ensure a smoother interaction, different deployments (or optimizations) in the room received preference. Improved responsiveness would significantly improve the user experience and keep players engaged in the session.

In addition, cybersecurity education programs such as CONTAIN emphasize the importance of ongoing adaptation in response to changing threats. Adversaries/malactors remain active and continuously evolve Tactics, Techniques, and Procedures (TTPs) in cyberspace, making operations and procedures around them dynamic by nature. As a result, educational tools must undergo periodic updates or adjustments whenever new threats intelligence or security strategy changes arise. The CONTAIN room could proactively evolve with future iterations, incorporating emerging attack vectors (e.g. Artificial Intelligence (AI) cyber threats, cloud security vulnerabilities, etc.) to maintain relevant content.

In summary, the CONTAIN room represents a major step toward more practical and effective cybersecurity education. Although challenges persist, early results highlight the value of hands-on, gamified training in raising awareness and readiness in cybersecurity. Observing which audience the room attracts once TryHackMe publishes it will provide valuable insights. During this first phase, we reached professionals and now aim to expand our reach to students, entrepreneurs, and staff from smaller and medium-sized companies that lack training resources.

As we move forward with this project, we will collaborate closely with cybersecurity professionals, teachers, and educational platform builders to refine the learning experience and ensure alignment with real-world cybersecurity training requirements. In addition, we aim to conduct a detailed analysis of the usefulness of our provided content.

Acknowledgments. CONTAIN serves as the name of a bilateral German-Austrian research project. The authors acknowledge funding for CONTAIN from the German Federal Ministry of Education and Research (BMBF) (grant numbers 13N16581-13N16587) as part of the SIFO program, and from the Austrian security research funding program KIRAS by the Federal Ministry of Finance (grant number FO999902707).

Many thanks to Bettina Baumgartner from the University of Vienna for proofreading this paper!

References

1. Alotaibi, F.F.G.: Evaluation and Enhancement of Public Cyber Security Awareness. Ph.D. thesis, University of Plymouth (2019). https://pearl.plymouth.ac.uk/secam-theses/214/
2. Alotaibi, F.F.G., Furnell, S., Stengel, I., Papadaki, M.: A review of using gaming technology for cyber-security awareness. Int. J. Inf. Secur. Res. (IJISR) **6**(2), 660–666 (2016). https://doi.org/10.20533/ijisr.2042.4639.2016.0076
3. Alotaibi, F.F.G., Furnell, S., Stengel, I., Papadaki, M.: Enhancing cyber security awareness with mobile games. In: 2017 12th International Conference for Internet Technology and Secured Transactions (ICITST), pp. 129–134. IEEE (2017). https://doi.org/10.23919/ICITST.2017.8356361
4. Angafor, G.N., Yevseyeva, I., He, Y.: Game-based learning: a review of tabletop exercises for cybersecurity incident response training. Secur. Priv. **3**(6), 1–19 (2020). https://doi.org/10.1002/spy2.126
5. Angafor, G.N., Yevseyeva, I., Maglaras, L.: MalAware: a tabletop exercise for malware security awareness education and incident response training. Internet Things Cyber-Phys. Syst. **4**, 280–292 (2024). https://doi.org/10.1016/j.iotcps.2024.02.003
6. Arachchilage, N.A.G.: Security Awareness of Computer Users: A Game Based Learning Approach. Ph.D. thesis, Brunel University, London, United Kingdom (2012). https://core.ac.uk/download/pdf/13641856.pdf
7. Bühler, M.M., Jelinek, T., Nübel, K.: Training and preparing tomorrow?s workforce for the fourth industrial revolution. Educ. Sci. **12**(11), 1–28 (2022). https://doi.org/10.3390/educsci12110782
8. Butt, U.J.: Developing a Usable Security Approach for User Awareness Against Ransomware. Ph.D. thesis, Brunel University London, London, United Kingdom (2023). https://bura.brunel.ac.uk/handle/2438/26661
9. Cone, B.D., Irvine, C.E., Thompson, M.F., Nguyen, T.D.: A video game for cyber security training and awareness. Comput. Secur. **26**(1), 63–72 (2007). https://doi.org/10.1016/j.cose.2006.10.005
10. Denning, T., Lerner, A., Shostack, A., Kohno, T.: Control-Alt-Hack: the design and evaluation of a card game for computer security awareness and education. In: Proceedings of the 2013 ACM SIGSAC Conference on Computer & Communications Security, pp. 915–928. CCS '13, Association for Computing Machinery, New York, NY, USA (2013). https://doi.org/10.1145/2508859.2516753
11. Europol: Internet Organised Crime Threat Assessment (IOCTA) 2024. Europol (2024). https://doi.org/10.2813/442713
12. Forero, C.A.M.: Tabletop Exercise For Cybersecurity Educational Training; Theoretical Grounding And Development. Master's thesis, University of Tartu (2016). https://core.ac.uk/download/pdf/83597547.pdf
13. Francia III, G., Thornton, D., Trifas, M., Bowden, T.: Gamification of information security awareness training. In: Akhgar, B., Arabnia, H.R. (eds.) Emerging Trends in ICT Security, pp. 85–97. Morgan Kaufmann, Boston, MA, USA (2013). https://doi.org/10.1016/B978-0-12-411474-6.00005-0
14. Friedl, S., Reittinger, T., Pernul, G.: From play to profession: a serious game to raise awareness on digital forensics. In: Ferrara, A.L., Krishnan, R. (eds.) Data and Applications Security and Privacy XXXVIII. DBSec 2024. LNCS, vol. 14901, pp. 269–289. Springer, Cham (2024). https://doi.org/10.1007/978-3-031-65172-4_17
15. Fung, C.C., Khera, V., Depickere, A., Tantatsanawong, P., Boonbrahm, P.: Raising information security awareness in digital ecosystem with games – a pilot study

in Thailand. In: 2008 2nd IEEE International Conference on Digital Ecosystems and Technologies, pp. 375–380. IEEE (2008). https://doi.org/10.1109/DEST.2008.4635145

16. Gardiner, J., Cova, M., Nagaraja, S.: Command & control: understanding, denying and detecting – a review of malware C2 techniques, detection and defences, pp. 1–38. arXiv (2015). https://doi.org/10.48550/arXiv.1408.1136

17. Greiner, M., et al.: Scared? Prepared? Toward a ransomware incident response scenario. In: Phillipson, F., Eichler, G., Erfurth, C., Fahrnberger, G. (eds.) Innovations for Community Services. I4CS 2024. CCIS, vol. 2109, pp. 289–320. Springer, Cham (2024). https://doi.org/10.1007/978-3-031-60433-1_17

18. Gutfleisch, M., Schöps, M., Sayin, S., Wende, F., Sasse, M.A.: Putting security on the table: the digitalisation of security tabletop games and its challenging aftertaste. In: ICSE-SEET '22: Proceedings of the ACM/IEEE 44th International Conference on Software Engineering: Software Engineering Education and Training, pp. 217–222. ICSE-SEET '22, Association for Computing Machinery, New York, NY, USA (2022). https://doi.org/10.1145/3510456.3514139

19. Hafner, L., Wutz, F., Pöhn, D., Hommel, W.: TASEP: a collaborative social engineering tabletop role-playing game to prevent successful social engineering attacks. In: Proceedings of the 18th International Conference on Availability, Reliability and Security, pp. 1–10. ARES '23, Association for Computing Machinery, New York, NY, USA (2023). https://doi.org/10.1145/3600160.3605005

20. Hart, S., Margheri, A., Paci, F., Sassone, V.: Riskio: a serious game for cyber security awareness and education. Comput. Secur. **95**, 1–16 (2020). https://doi.org/10.1016/j.cose.2020.101827

21. Hevner, A., Chatterjee, S.: Design science research in information systems. In: Design Research in Information Systems: Theory and Practice, vol. 22, pp. 9–22. Springer US, Boston, MA, USA (2010). https://doi.org/10.1007/978-1-4419-5653-8_2

22. Hoachlander, G.: Toward a New Framework of Industry Programs for Vocational Education: Emerging Trends in Curriculum and Instruction. Technical report, Institute of Education Sciences (1998). https://eric.ed.gov/?id=ED443969

23. Hofmeier, M.: Operation Digital Butterfly: Ein Serious-Game-basierter Ansatz zur Identifikation und Analyse von Intentionalen Bedrohungen durch Innentäter und Innentäterinnen (Malicious Insider Threats). Ph.D. thesis, University of the Bundeswehr Munich (2024). https://athene-forschung.unibw.de/148672

24. Kalenti, M., Biro, P.: ECSM 2023 campaign report ? Be smarter than a hacker. Technical report (2024). https://doi.org/10.2824/005990

25. Kaloroumakis, P.E., Smith, M.J.: Toward a Knowledge Graph of Cybersecurity Countermeasures. Technical report, Massachusetts Institute of Technology Research and Engineering (MITRE) Corporation (2021). https://d3fend.mitre.org/resources/D3FEND.pdf

26. Karagiannis, S., Papaioannou, T., Magkos, E., Tsohou, A.: Game-based information security/privacy education and awareness: Theory and Practice. In: Themistocleous, M., Papadaki, M., Kamal, M.M. (eds.) Information Systems, LNCS, pp. 509–525. Springer, Cham, Switzerland (2020). https://doi.org/10.1007/978-3-030-63396-7_34

27. Kjorveziroski, V., Mishev, A., Filiposka, S.: Cybersecurity training platforms assessment. In: Dimitrova, V., Dimitrovski, I. (eds.) ICT Innovations 2020. Machine Learning and Applications, LNCS, pp. 174–188. Springer, Cham, Switzerland (2020). https://doi.org/10.1007/978-3-030-62098-1_15

28. Labuschagne, W.A., Burke, I., Veerasamy, N., Eloff, M.M.: Design of cyber security awareness game utilizing a social media framework. In: 2011 Information Security for South Africa, pp. 1–9. IEEE (2011). https://doi.org/10.1109/ISSA.2011. 6027538

29. Lechner, U., Dännart, S., Rieb, A., Rudel, S.: Case Kritis – Fallstudien zur IT-Sicherheit in Kritischen Infrastrukturen. Logos Verlag Berlin (2018). https://doi. org/10.30819/4727

30. Lechner, U., Strussenberg, J., Hofbauer, S., Seiler, A., Greiner, M.: Monitor Resilienz angesichts von Ransomware: Einblicke in die Praxis. Technical report, University of the Bundeswehr Munich (2024). https://www.unibw.de/ wirtschaftsinformatik/monitor-contain

31. Mello-Stark, S., VanValkenburg, M.A., Hao, E.: Thinking outside the box: using escape room games to increase interest in cyber security. In: Daimi, K., Francia III, G. (eds.) Innovations in Cybersecurity Education, LNCS, pp. 39–53. Springer, Cham, Switzerland (2020). https://doi.org/10.1007/978-3-030-50244-7_3

32. Mettouris, C., Maratou, V., Vucčković, D., Papadopoulos, G.A., Xenos, M.: Information security awareness through a virtual world: an end-user requirements analysis. In: Zdravković, M., Trajanović, M., Konjović, Z. (eds.) ICIST 2015 – 5th International Conference on Information Society and Technology, pp. 301–306. Society for Information Systems and Computer Networks (2015). https://www. eventiotic.com/eventiotic/library/paper/135

33. Ngambeki, I.B., Rogers, M., Bates, S.J., Piper, M.C.: Curricular improvement through course mapping: an application of the NICE framework. In: 2021 ASEE Virtual Annual Conference Content Access, pp. 1–22. ASEE Conferences (2021). https://doi.org/10.18260/1-2-36889

34. Onduto, B.: Gamification of Cyber Security Awareness – A Systematic Literature Review. Master's thesis, University of Turku (2021). https://www.utupub.fi/ bitstream/handle/10024/152929/Onduto_Barack_Thesis_Final.pdf

35. Rieb, A., Lechner, U.: Towards a cybersecurity game: operation digital chameleon. In: Havarneanu, G., Setola, R., Nassopoulos, H., Wolthusen, S. (eds.) Critical Information Infrastructures Security, pp. 283–295. LNCS, Springer, Cham, Switzerland (2016). https://doi.org/10.1007/978-3-319-71368-7_24

36. Seiler, A., Lechner, U., Strussenberg, J., Hofbauer, S.: Operation raven. In: Phillipson, F., Eichler, G., Erfurth, C., Fahrnberger, G. (eds.) Innovations for Community Services. I4CS 2024. CCIS, vol. 2109, pp. 337–347. Springer Nature Switzerland, Cham, Switzerland (2024). https://doi.org/10.1007/978-3-031-60433-1_19

37. Siponen, M., Vance, A.: Neutralization: new insights into the problem of employee information systems security policy violations. MIS Q. 34(3), 487–502 (2010). http://doi.org/10.2307/25750688

38. Stewart, G., Rosemann, M.: Industry-oriented design of ERP-related curriculum – an Australian initiative. Bus. Process Manag. J. 7(3), 234–242 (2001). https:// doi.org/10.1108/14637150110392719

39. Strom, B.E., et al.: Finding cyber threats with ATT&CK^{TM}-based analytics. Technical report, Massachusetts Institute of Technology Research and Engineering (MITRE) Corporation (2017). https://apps.dtic.mil/sti/trecms/pdf/AD1107945. pdf

40. Sykes, G.M., Matza, D.: Techniques of neutralization: a theory of delinquency. Am. Sociol. Rev. 22(6), 664–670 (1957). https://doi.org/10.2307/2089195

41. Thubron, R.: Ransomware criminals use children's phone numbers to coerce payments from parents (2024). https://www.techspot.com/news/102905-ransomware-criminals-use-children-phone-numbers-coerce-payments.html

42. Yadav, T., Rao, A.M.: Technical aspects of cyber kill chain. In: Abawajy, J., Mukherjea, S., Thampi, S., Ruiz-Martínez, A. (eds.) Security in Computing and Communications. SSCC 2015. CCIS, vol. 536, pp. 438–452. Springer, Cham (2015). https://doi.org/10.1007/978-3-319-22915-7_40

43. Yar, M.A., Goh, H.G., Adnan, K., Gan, M.L., Ponnusamy, V.: Bridging cybersecurity education and industry demands: mapping and prioritizing curriculum guidelines. In: 2024 International Conference on Future Technologies for Smart Society (ICFTSS), pp. 188–193. IEEE (2024). https://doi.org/10.1109/ICFTSS61109.2024.10690269

44. Zhao, T., Gasiba, T., Lechner, U., Pinto-Albuquerque, M.: Raising awareness about cloud security in industry through a board game. Information **12**(11), 1–14 (2021). https://doi.org/10.3390/info12110482

Community Challenges

MAD-HOT: Mixed Rate DDoS Attack Detection in IEEE 802.15 4e/TSCH Networks Using Hoeffding Optimized Trees

Pradeepkumar Bhale[1(✉)], Darpan Maurya[2], Vaibhav Sodhi[2],
Tabish Farooqui[2], Harsh Singh[2], and Sonam Maurya[2]

[1] Department of Computer Science and Engineering, Indian Institute of Information
Technology, Design and Manufacturing, Kancheepuram 600127, India
pradeepkumar@iiitdm.ac.in
[2] Department of Computer Science and Engineering, Indian Institute of Information
Technology, Pune 411041, India
{darpan,vaibhav,Tabish,harsh,sonam}@iiitp.ac.in

Abstract. Internet of Things (IoT) is expanding rapidly as its use cases and technology advances. However, along with these benefits, IoT also faces many attacks. One of the most common and difficult-to-detect attacks is the DDoS attack and its variations (MrDDoS). Implementing security solutions in the IoT ecosystem is challenging due to resource-constrained devices. The proposed security solution, namely, MAD-HOT utilized the Hoeffding tree and placement strategies for MrDDoS attack detection with reasonable accuracy. The placement problem is formulated with a hypergraph and a game theory algorithm. Security module based on Hoeffding trees is the main classifier, along with many other classifiers for model training. Finally, for prediction, we have used logistic regression as the meta-classifier. Extensive experimentation on the Contiki cooja simulator shows that the MAD-HOT can best execute the balance between MrDDoS detection and energy overhead.

Keywords: Internet of Things (IoT) · Distributed Denial-of-Service (DDoS) · Mixed rate DDoS (MrDDoS) · Game theory algorithm · Hoeffding trees

1 Introduction

The *Internet of Things (IoT)* is growing exponentially and is becoming an irremovable aspect of our daily lives. IoT can be considered as a network of devices equipped with sensors, processing power, software, and various other technologies to facilitate communication and data sharing. Every device we see around us, from our smartphones to home appliances, can be considered as part of an IoT network [16]. However, as IoT becomes an increasingly integral part of our lives and given that it is still relatively a newer concept, it is evident that IoT poses significant security threats and challenges. Hence, there are various

© The Author(s), under exclusive license to Springer Nature Switzerland AG 2025
S. Zielinski et al. (Eds.): I4CS 2025, CCIS 2513, pp. 417–436, 2025.
https://doi.org/10.1007/978-3-031-94263-1_23

issues that need to be addressed and fixed when it comes to security within IoT devices. IoT devices have a lot of practical aspect including real-time data transmission, energy-efficient communication, and secure connectivity for applications like smart cities, healthcare, and industrial automation. As IoT networks grow in size and complexity, while handling increasingly larger amounts of data that may be sensitive and critical in nature, the need for much stronger security methods becomes more crucial than ever.

IoT devices are vulnerable to various network-related attacks, including Sniffing, Man-in-the-Middle(MitM), DoS and DDoS, Replay, Routing and Sinkhole attacks. In our paper we will primarily focus on DDoS attacks, specifically Mixed Rate DDoS attacks [7]. These attacks combine characteristics of both Low-rate DDoS as well as High-rate DDoS attacks making them more challenging compared to detection of traditional DDoS. While Mixed-rate DDoS attacks are not as stealthy as Low-rate, there fluctuating traffic patterns make them more difficult for an Intrusion Detection Systems (IDS) to identify them effectively.

In an IoT network, we consider three key aspects. First, the network operates on an IEEE 802.15 4e network, explicitly utilizing the Time Slotted Channel Hopping (TSCH) mechanism. TSCH is regarded as a combination of both Time Division Multiple Access (TDMA) as well as Frequency Division Multiple Access (FDMA) mechanisms. TSCH operates by transmitting data across multiple frequencies selected from a predefined frequency list while adhering to a synchronized schedule with designated time slots. If a packet is lost in communication between two devices, the packet is re-sent on a different frequency channel in the next available time slot. This approach ensures efficient channel utilization, minimizes interference, and enhances network reliability [27].

The second aspect is that the IoT network consists of heterogeneous nodes. This means that the devices in our network have varying characteristics in terms of hardware capabilities, communication protocols, energy resources, computational power, or functional roles. The third and final aspect is that the TSCH network [21] operates in storing mode, meaning that intermediate nodes maintain and store routing information locally rather than forwarding all packets to a central root node. This approach enhances routing efficiency, reduces network congestion, and minimizes dependency on a single point of failure, making it well-suited for large-scale Low power and Lossy Networks (LLNs).

We have trained and tested our ML model on three datasets, viz. IoT23 [11], CIC-DDoS [25] and WSN-DS [2] and obtained an average accuracy of around 0.98% among all the experiments which we have carried out. After analyzing this domain of DDoS attack detection, we have found that Decision Tree or the tree-based algorithms works best with the intrusion detection. So we have come up with an algorithm wherein we are using an ensemble ML model which combines Hoeffding Trees and Decision Trees with many other ML models as a base classifier for training of our Model from the dataset and the final prediction is performed with the Logistic regression classifier which we refer as the meta classifier for our algorithm. The promising results show that this approach works quite well and is also computationally sound when compared to heavy deep learning models, which the existing work has used till date.

The Hoeffding Tree, or Very Fast Decision Tree (VFDT), is an incremental machine learning algorithm that caters to streaming data [20]. Unlike traditional trees that function on decision datasets, Hoeffding Trees utilize batches leading to higher efficiency within real-time environments. This makes them learn more intelligently, it uses a Hoeffding Bound concept to decide when to split a node to keep the structure stable while new data is constantly being poured in which means that Hoeffding Trees are adaptable to large scale applications such as setting up security for IoT and intrusion detection systems where data inflow is unceasing and which requires immediate attention. Taking all these considerations into account(the three aspects of the TSCH network which we have explained in this section), we will also explore the optimal placement strategy for selecting the most suitable nodes to deploy our IDS. This selection process is crucial to ensuring effective threat detection while maintaining network efficiency and energy constraints. To achieve this, we will utilize a network simulator such as Contiki Cooja [26]. Additionally, we will implement a strategic algorithm to determine the ideal node placement in the network.

Section 2 of this paper discusses the related works. Section 3 describes the background of the IoT network attacks, IEEE 802.15 4e/TSCH networks, and Hoeffding trees. Section 4 implements our proposed approach (MAD-HOT) with the Contiki OS and Cooja simulator. Section 5 exhibits experimental results and analysis. Section 6 concludes the paper indicating the future direction.

2   Related Work

This section itemizes existing works in IoT networks and MrDDoS attacks. It also examines the attack detection methodologies used by these works. Each methodology has its benefits and weaknesses, as described in Table 1 below.

3   Background

3.1   IoT Network Attacks

In IoT networks, numerous attacks are possible. Such attacks may include DDoS attacks, Man-in-the-Middle (MitM) attacks, Replay Attacks, Eavesdropping or Data Interception attacks, Scanning or Probing attacks, Keylogging, WSN attacks like sinkhole, wormhole, black hole, and selective forwarding [6,8]. As this research work is based on DDoS attacks, the descriptions of these attacks are given below in detail.

High rate DDoS (HrDDoS) Attacks: In this attack, the attacker floods the victim system with network packets or garbage data in huge and bulky amounts, thereby wasting CPU computational power and time in handling these packets.

Low rate DDoS (LrDDoS) Attacks [4]**:** This attack is difficult to identify as attackers flood the network stream in small amounts at different times, which does not cause a major change in network traffic flow. The LrDDoS attack model can be described by three parameters, which are the off-time phase, on-time phase,

Table 1. Machine/deep learning approaches for IoT DoS and DDoS attack detection

Attacks	Reference	Methodology
DoS	M. Khandelwal et al. [15], An Ensemble Intrusion Detection Model for Internet of Things Network	An ensemble algorithm using deep neural network (DNN) and support vector machine (SVM)
	N. Moustafa, B. Turnbull, and K.-K. R. Choo [9], An Ensemble Intrusion Detection Model For Internet of Things Network	An ensemble algorithm which is made using the concepts of deep neural network (DNN) and support vector machines (SVM)
HrDDoS	Y. Li et al. [17], LSTM-BA: DDoS Detection Approach Combining LSTM and Bayes	LSTM and Naive Bayes approach
	N. Ravi et al. [23], Learning Driven Detection and Mitigation of DDoS Attack in IoT via SDN-Cloud Architecture	Proposed a novel mechanism named LEDEM (LEarning driven DEtection Mitigation) that detects DDoS using a semi-supervised machine learning algorithm and mitigates DDoS
	M. Saharkhizam et al. [24], An ensemble of deep recurrent neural networks for detecting IoT cyber attacks using network traffic	Approach integrates a set of long short-term memory (LSTM) modules into an ensemble of detectors. These modules are then merged using a decision tree to arrive at an aggregated output at the final stage
	F. Hussain et al. [14], A two-fold machine learning approach to prevent and detect IoT botnet attacks	Proposed a two-fold machine learning approach. In the first fold, they trained a state-of-the-art deep learning model. In the second fold, they trained another ResNet-18 model for DDoS attack identification to detect IoT botnet attacks
	G. Abdelmoumin et al. [1], On the performance of ML models for anomaly-based intelligent intrusion detection systems for IoT	They have focused on optimizing PCA and 1-SVM using hyperparameter tuning and ensemble learning approach
LrDDoS	A. Valdovinos et al. [22], A Flexible SDN-based Architecture for Identifying and Mitigating Low-Rate DDoS Attacks using Machine Learning	Used six machine learning (ML) models, namely Random Tree, REP Tree, Random Forest, Multi-Layer Perceptron (MLP), and Support Vector Machines (SVM), and evaluated their performance using the Canadian Institute of Cybersecurity (CIC) DoS dataset
	B. Liu et al. [18], TS-SVM: Detect LDoS Attack in SDN Based on Two-step Self-adjusting SVM	Two kinds of SVM approaches of self-adjusting are put forward in this paper
	N. Garcia et al. [12], Distributed real-time SlowDoS attacks detection over encrypted traffic using artificial intelligence	This paper describes an AI-based anomaly detection system for real-time detection of SlowDoS attacks over application-level encrypted traffic

and time interval, as shown in Fig. 1. In an off-time phase, no attack packet is sent. During an on-time phase, the assailant sends malignant messages. The time interval change phase maintains time among two successive attack packet generations.

Mixed rate DDoS (MrDDoS) Attacks [3]: This attack is a collection of both LrDDoS and HrDDoS attacks whose principal aim and objective is to maximize the negative impact on the target or the victim system. MrDDoS attacks have been developed to break the conventional attack detection strategies, but with proper study and an effective methodology, these attacks can be effectively detected.

3.2   IEEE 802.15 4e/TSCH Networks

IEEE 802.15 4e/TSCH is a technology that is used for the devices that are usually operated on batteries. In simple terms it is a low cost as well as low

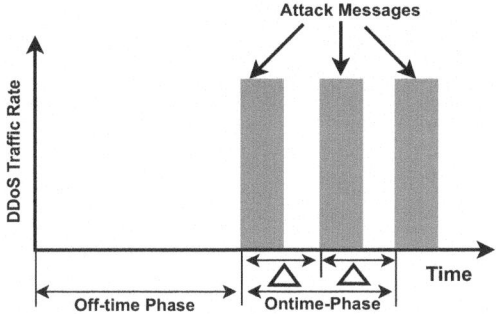

Fig. 1. Illustration of LrDDoS attack phases

rate data technology. The Time Slotted Channel Hopping (TSCH) is a protocol for the link layer of the IEEE 802.15.4-2015 standard. It is a highly reliable communication protocol in a low-power wireless sensor networks (WSNs). The traditional WSNs often suffer from High Packet Loss and network interference because of their use of a single-channel communication. TSCH can overcome these issues by introducing a time-synchronized communication with frequency diversity, which makes it useful for sensitive applications.

TSCH has a lot of use in smart buildings, environmental monitoring, industrial monitoring etc. What a TSCH network does it that it has specific predefined time slots, which makes sure that every device does data communication in these time slots only. Every device in the network strictly follows these predefined schedules, which makes sure there is no data collision, thereby improving the efficiency. Due to this behavior of devices it ensures that their energy and computational power is not wasted, which adds to the fact that it is very popular in battery operated devices where time and energy is a major concern. A TSCH network uses Channel Hopping in which a device can switch between multiple channels while working, this approach is quite uniquer than the traditional WSN networks and ensures that the interference from any other network like Bluetooth, Wi-Fi or any other private network is minimized. A TSCH network supports low-rate data communication, which makes it suitable for applications that do not require high throughput but which can demand high reliability.

A TSCH network operates on a Time-Frequency schedule which is duly noted by all the systems (end nodes) present in the network. Here, the protocol is that the network is divided into time slots, where each slot is designated for a specific communication task (which can be transmission, reception, or idle). This makes sure that only the designated nodes communicate at a given time, preventing any kind of packet/data collision. Each time slot uses are a different network channel which is called as a predefined hopping sequence. IEEE 802.15.4e/TSCH is a powerful MAC protocol which improves scalability and efficiency in low power lossy networks, by using time slotted protocols it ensures a decent network performance and thus TSCH networks are going to replace traditional WSN networks in the future. In Table 2 below, we give a comparison of TSCH with other MAC protocols.

Table 2. Comparison of TSCH, CSMA/CA, and TDMA protocols

Feature	TSCH (IEEE 802.15.4e)	CSMA/CA (IEEE 802.15.4)	TDMA (Time-Division Multiple Access)
Reliability	High (due to channel hopping)	Low (prone to interference)	High
Energy Efficiency	High (nodes wake up only during slots)	Moderate	High
Latency	Deterministic (depends on schedule)	Random (based on contention)	Deterministic
Scalability	High	Moderate	Low
Interference Resistance	High (multi-channel)	Low (single channel)	High

3.3 Hoeffding Trees

A Hoeffding tree is a special type of decision tree which is designed to handle and work with a bulky data smoothly. There is a problem in the traditional ML Tree algorithms which is that they require the full dataset in order to construct the logical prediction tree, but this is not the case with Hoeffding trees. An Hoeffding tree gradually learns from small chunks of dataset and build the prediction tree accordingly. This feature of an Hoeffding tree makes it a very good choice for areas where data is continuously generated, such as real-time fraud detection.

Hoeffding tree relies on a mathematical concept known as a Hoeffding bound which helps to determine whether is particular split in the tree branches is actually significant or not. This bound is derived from the Hoeffding inequality, which estimates how close the observed mean of a random variable is to its true mean given a number of independent observations. The Hoeffding bound ensures that with observations, the best attribute can be taken without the need to process the entire dataset. The bound is given by $\epsilon = \sqrt{\frac{\ln(1/\delta)}{2n}}$ where

- ϵ is the margin of error (confidence interval) for choosing the best split,
- δ is the probability of selecting the wrong attribute (Usually set to a small value like 0.05 or 0.01),
- n is the number of observations which is used to compute the attribute's merit (such as information gain or Gini index).

If the difference between the best and second-best attribute exceeds ϵ, then the best attribute is chosen for the split. To decide when to split a node, the Hoeffding Tree computes a metric such as Information Gain (IG), Gini Index, or Gain Ratio for each attribute like it's done in decision trees. The difference between the highest and second-highest attribute evaluation values, denoted as $G(A_1) - G(A_2)$, is compared with ϵ. If $G(A_1) - G(A_2) > \epsilon$, then attribute A_1 is selected for splitting. Otherwise, more observations are collected before making a particular decision. So this is how in brief a Hoeffding tree works. Some other benefits of using Hoeffding trees are:

1. **Time Complexity**: Traditional Decision Trees typically have an average time complexity of $O(n \log n)$. In contrast, a Hoeffding tree operates with constant time complexity, making it significantly faster.
2. **Memory Efficiency**: By storing only essential statistical features, a Hoeffding tree is much more memory-efficient compared to traditional tree algorithms.
3. **Scalability**: The Hoeffding tree algorithm is highly scalable, making it suitable for working in big data scenarios, such as IoT networks, where massive amounts of data are continuously generated.

Instead of restructuring the entire tree, the algorithm patiently waits until and unless it has seen enough examples before confidently making a decision about splitting a node. This overcomes the biggest drawback of the decision tree which is overfitting as if the dataset is huge using a normal decision tree will surely stuck into overfitting. Hence after considering all these factors we have chosen Hoeffding trees to play a vital role in our attack detection Model.

4   Proposed Solution

This section is divided into two parts. The IoT IDS placement strategy in Subsects. 4.1 and 4.2 describes the proposed IDS solution. MAD-HOT is used to detect MrDDoS attacks in IoT networks.

4.1   Proposed IDS Placement

Notation and Variables: Let K be the parameter controlling the uniformity of the hypergraph. The undirected tree graph is denoted as $G = (V, E)$, where V represents the set of nodes and E represents the set of edges. Each node v_i has an associated weight $W(v_i)$, which is inversely proportional to its contributed energy towards security . The binary variable $x(v_i)$ determines whether a node is selected for IDS placement. The function $\phi(v_i)$ represents the Shapley value function used for fair IDS allotment. The parameter β is introduced to balance the historical fairness in IDS selection. The timestamps t_0 and t denote the time of the last change in K and the current time, respectively. The optimization objective function Z represents the total cost associated with IDS placement. Finally, the set S consists of the selected nodes for IDS deployment.

We mathematically justify that $K0$ will range from K to $2K$ and derive bounds for Z. Bounding K in the Range $[K, 2K]$ The algorithm updates K dynamically using the function:

$$K0 \leftarrow \text{round}\left(K \cdot (1 + \text{mod}(\sin(\alpha)))\right) \tag{1}$$

Since the sine function oscillates between $[-1, 1]$, the expression $\text{mod}(\sin(\alpha))$ produces values in the range $[0, 1]$. This means:

$$1 + \text{mod}(\sin(\alpha)) \in [1, 2] \tag{2}$$

Multiplying by K, we obtain the bounds:

$$K0 \leq K \cdot (1 + \mathrm{mod}(\sin(\alpha))) \leq 2K \tag{3}$$

Thus, $K0$ is always in the range $[K, 2K]$, ensuring that the number of IDS placements fluctuates unpredictably but within a reasonable bound.By doing so we have a variable range of IDS at any time T. So attacker has some difficulty to guess the number of IDS nodes. Thereby not predicting the IDS placement and the network security increases.

To solve the fair IDS allotment problem we propose to use game theory as base. We use Shapley values $\phi(v)$ where v lies in the vertex set $G(V)$.Allocate IDS nodes in such a way that the marginal impact of each node's inclusion in the security framework is highest.IDS prevents biased and repeated IDS selection. It ensures that even if attacker provides wrong energy updates it cannot retain its IDS node position for long.

$$\sum_{v_i \in V} \beta(t - t_0)\phi(v_i)x(v_i) \tag{4}$$

The above equation illustrates about cumulative impact of each node's Shapley value-based contribution to the IDS selection process, adjusted over time. The function of the terms used are:

- β is a scaling factor that determines the influence of time on the IDS placement decision. Network manager decides it.
- $(t - t_0)$ represents the time elapsed since the last change in K, ensuring dynamic adaptation over time.
- $\phi(v_i)$ is the Shapley value of node v_i, quantifying its fair contribution to network security based on cooperative game theory.
- $x(v_i)$ is a binary variable indicating whether node v_i is selected as an IDS.

To refine the fairness and adaptability of IDS placement, we redefine $\nu(v_i)$ (Shapley function) as a linear combination of multiple factors:

$$\nu(v_i) = \lambda_1 \cdot T(v_i) + \lambda_2 \cdot H(v_i) + \lambda_3 \cdot U(v_i) + \lambda_4 \cdot R(v_i) \tag{5}$$

where:

- $T(v_i)$ represents the **traffic load** handled by node v_i, ensuring that the high traffic nodes receive appropriate monitoring.
- $H(v_i)$ represents the **historical IDS selection frequency**, preventing repeated selection of the same nodes.
- $U(v_i)$ represents **node uptime**, ensuring that nodes with stable operational histories are prioritized.
- $R(v_i)$ represents **resource availability and compatibility of resources** , allowing computational and bandwidth limitations.

Algorithm 1. IDS placement algorithm

Require: Algorithm for K-uniform Hypergraph creation from an undirected graph.

Require: Undirected tree graph $G = (V, E)$, parameter K.

1: Initialize variable α using the consensus mechanism of IoT nodes.

2: Define the Shapley function $\nu(v)$ for fair IDS allotment of nodes.

3: **while** true **do**

4:    Construct the K-uniform Hypergraph from the routing graph.

5:    Store timestamps t_0 (time of last change in K) and t (current time).

6:    Update K as:
$$K \leftarrow \text{round}\left(K \cdot (1 + \quad \text{mod}\left(\sin(\alpha)\right)\right)$$

7:    Solve the modified vertex cover optimization problem (see below) to determine the set S of nodes where IDS will be deployed.

8:    Solve the following optimization problem:
$$Z = \min \sum_{v_i \in V} (W(v_i) \cdot x(v_i)) + \beta \cdot (t - t_0) \sum_{v_i \in V} (\phi(v_i) \cdot x(v_i))$$

9:    Subject to:
$$\sum_{j \in E_m} x(v_i) \geq 1, \quad x(v_i) \in [0, 1]$$
$$\phi(v_i) = \sum_{S \subseteq V \setminus \{v_i\}} \frac{|S|!(|N| - |S| - 1)!}{|N|!} \left(\nu(S \cup \{v_i\}) - \nu(S)\right)$$

10:    Store IDS placement logs in edge storage.

11: **end while**

Here, $\lambda_1, \lambda_2, \lambda_3, \lambda_4$ are adjustable weights that balance the significance of each factor. By incorporating these parameters, the placement of the IDS shows fairness and robustness.

We have formulated the minimization problem specified above in the algorithm, denoted by Z. Here we give an approximate solution which is at most $2K$ time the optimal solution.

$$Z = \sum_{v_i \in V} W(v_i)x(v_i) + \sum_{v_i \in V} \beta(t - t_0)\phi(v_i)x(v_i) \tag{6}$$

$$Z \geq \sum_{\substack{v_i \in V \\ x(v_i) \geq \frac{1}{K_0}}} W(v_i)x(v_i) + \sum_{\substack{v_i \in V \\ x(v_i) \geq \frac{1}{K_0}}} \beta(t - t_0)\phi(v_i)x(v_i) \tag{7}$$

Next, we substitute $x(v_i) = \frac{1}{2K}$ for nodes in the solution set S since $2K$ is the worst case for K:

$$Z \geq \frac{1}{2K} \left(\sum_{v_i \in S} W(v_i) + \sum_{v_i \in S} \beta(t - t_0)\phi(v_i) \right) \tag{8}$$

Multiplying both sides by $2K$, we obtain:

$$2K \cdot Z \geq \sum_{v_i \in S} W(v_i) + \sum_{v_i \in S} \beta(t - t_0)\phi(v_i) \tag{9}$$

$$2K \cdot Z \geq W(S) \tag{10}$$

As seen above, the proposed solution is at most $2K$ times the optimal solution. By giving only a little extra energy, we can guarantee increased security.

4.2   Proposed IDS Solution

The proposed MAD-HOT security solution is structured into four key components: model description, model pre-processing, model training, and the final model. MAD-HOT operates a two-level stacked abstraction framework, as shown in Fig. 2, where various ML classifiers at Level 1 are incorporated with a logistic regression meta-learner at Level 2. This strategy provides a harmony of high performance and computational efficiency.

Model Description: Stacked Ensemble with Meta-Learner. We propose a two-level stacked generalization framework (Fig. 2) that combines diverse base classifiers at Level 1 with a logistic regression meta-learner at Level 2. This architecture is both high-performance and lightweight.

Level 1: Heterogeneous Base Models. Base classifiers provide complementary learning strategies:

1. **Hoeffding Tree (HT):** A streaming-optimized decision tree that uses the Chernoff bound for split decisions. It is highly efficient for large datasets. The information gain $IG(S)$ is calculated as:where $H(S)$ is entropy, and S_i are split subsets [20].
   The Hoeffding inequality ensures the quality of the split:

$$\epsilon = \sqrt{\frac{\ln(1/\delta)}{2n}} \tag{11}$$

with probability $1 - \delta$ (typically $\delta = 0.05$).

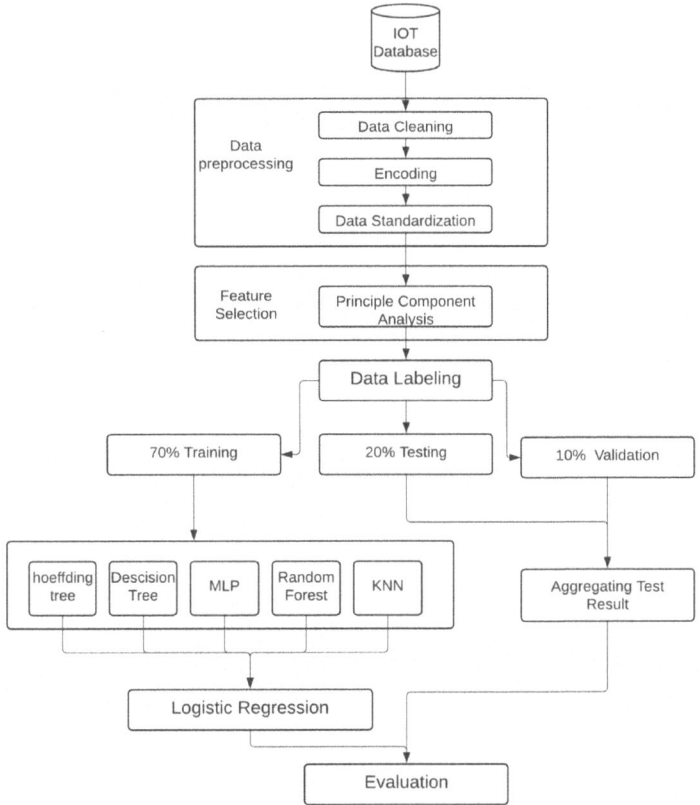

Fig. 2. Proposed methodology

2. **Decision Tree (CART)**: The Classification and Regression Tree (CART) algorithm is used with information gain minimization and post-pruning. The maximum tree depth is constrained to $d_{\max} = 10$.
3. **Random Forest (RF)**: An ensemble of 100 decision trees utilizing bagging and random feature selection ($m = \lfloor \sqrt{F} \rfloor$ features per split, where F is the total number of features) [5].
4. **k-Nearest Neighbors (kNN)**: An instance-based learner using $k = 5$ neighbors and the Euclidean distance metric. Features are standardized via z-score normalization [13, 19].

Level 2: Logistic Regression Meta-Learner. The outputs from the base classifiers form a meta-feature vector $\mathbf{z} \in \mathbb{R}^4$. A logistic regression model with L2 regularization is used for final predictions:

$$P(y = 1|\mathbf{z}) = \frac{1}{1 + \exp\left(-(\beta_0 + \boldsymbol{\beta}^T \mathbf{z})\right)} \tag{12}$$

The loss function optimized is:

$$\mathcal{L} = - \sum_{i=1}^{N} \Big[y_i \log(p_i) + (1 - y_i) \log(1 - p_i) \Big] + \lambda |\boldsymbol{\beta}|_2^2 \tag{13}$$

where $\lambda = 0.1$ controls regularization strength [13].

Ensemble Model for IDS Classification. To improve Intrusion Detection System (IDS) performance, we use an ensemble learning approach that leverages multiple classifiers. This method enhances predictive accuracy and robustness by aggregating decisions [10].

Let $f_1(X), f_2(X), \ldots, f_M(X)$ be the predictions of M base models on an input feature set X. The stacked ensemble model is then represented as:

$$\hat{y} = f_{\text{meta}}(f_1(X), f_2(X), \ldots, f_M(X)) \tag{14}$$

where f_{meta} is the logistic regression meta-learner. The total expected squared error of the model follows:

$$\mathbb{E}[(\hat{y} - y)^2] = \text{Bias}^2 + \text{Variance} + \sigma^2 \tag{15}$$

A stacked ensemble mitigates bias-variance trade-offs by:

- **Improving Accuracy:** Different classifiers capture distinct patterns in the data.
- **Enhancing Generalization:** Reduces overfitting through diverse learning strategies.
- **Handling Imbalanced Data:** Mitigates class imbalance issues common in IDS datasets.
- **Increasing Robustness:** Reduces the impact of noise and outliers.

Model Preprocessing. Before training, the dataset undergoes several preprocessing steps as follows:

- **Data Cleaning:** The dataset from **Syn-training.csv** is processed, with float-type columns converted to integers where applicable.
- **Encoding Categorical Labels:** Target labels are one-hot encoded for categorical value handling.
- **Feature Scaling:** Standardization using `StandardScaler`, ensuring zero mean and unit variance.
- **Dimensionality Reduction:** PCA retains 95% variance to reduce computational complexity.
- **Feature Selection:** `SelectKBest` with ANOVA F-test selects the top 25 relevant features.
- **Dataset Splitting:** The data is split into 80% training and 20% testing subsets.

Model Training. A structured approach is followed for training the stacked ensemble model as given below:

Training Protocol

1. **Base Model Training:** Two classifiers are independently trained:
   - **Decision Tree:** A traditional decision tree trained on the full dataset.
   - **Hoeffding Tree:** A streaming classifier, adapted to **scikit-learn** for compatibility.
2. **Meta-Feature Generation (Stacking Process):**
   - **5-Fold Cross-Validation:** The dataset is split into five folds, with models trained on four folds and predictions generated on the fifth.
   - This process ensures the meta-learner sees only unseen data predictions, reducing overfitting.
3. **Final Model (Meta-Learner):**
   - Logistic Regression with Stochastic Gradient Descent (SGD), learning rate $\eta = 0.01$, and 1000 epochs.
   - The model is trained on both raw features and meta-features from base classifiers.

This multi-layered strategy improves accuracy by allowing the meta-learner to correct individual base model weaknesses.

5   Experiments, Results, and Discussion

5.1   Performed Experiments

We have evaluated our model with three datasets, namely IoT23, CIC-DDoS, and WSN-DS. The experiments are performed while keeping Decision Tree and Hoeffding Trees as common classifiers in the ensemble model. That is both Decision and Hoeffding Trees are combined with classifiers like Random Forest, KNN, MLP, SVC one by one in the stacking classifier. And the final evaluation is done using Logistic Regression for all the experiments. The performance analysis of our algorithm will be based on these three datasets. This section is further composed into three subsections.

1. **Environment Evaluation:** This will discuss the environment in which the algorithm is running, that is, the total time and computational power associated with the algorithm. We also compare the total energy consumed in millijoules in Table 5 in results section below. The results when compared with existing approaches show that our algorithm is quite memory efficient.
2. **Performance Metrics:** Various Performance metrics like Accuracy(Acc), Precision(Pre), Recall(Rec), and F1-Score(F1) of the proposed methodology will be explained in this section.
3. **Result Comparison and Analysis:** The performance of our proposed approach will be compared with existing works in this section, which will explain the effectiveness of our algorithm.

5.2   Environment Evaluation

With WSN-DS Dataset: From the below Fig. 3, we can note that maximum computation reached is 20% of the CPU usage and the average CPU usage is around 14.6%. The total energy consumed is 5123.8 millijoules (mJ).

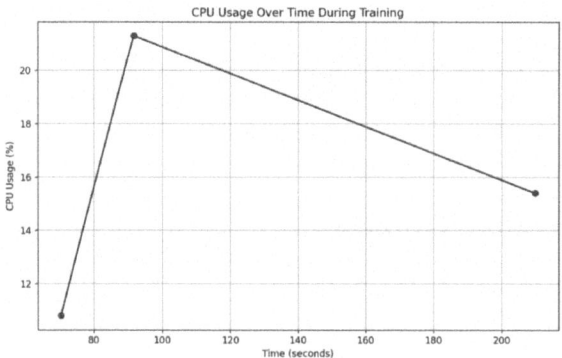

Fig. 3. Computational power versus time for WSN-DS dataset

With CIC-DDoS Dataset: From the below Fig. 4, we can note that maximum computation reached is 15% of the CPU usage and the average CPU usage is around 11.6%. The total energy consumed is 2186.48 millijoules (mJ).

With IoT-23 Dataset: From the below Fig. 5, we can note that maximum computation reached is 23% of the CPU usage and the average CPU usage is around 14.14%.The total energy consumed is 4853.24 millijoules (mJ).

5.3   Performance Metrics

The various performance metrics are defined in this section to evaluate the performance of our proposed solution:

1. **Accuracy (ACC)**: Accuracy measures how well the system distinguishes between actual attacks and normal traffic. It tells us what percentage of total network flows were classified correctly. The formula for accuracy is:

$$ACC = \frac{TP + TN}{TP + FN + FP + TN} \times 100 \tag{16}$$

where FP = Legitimate flow wrongly classified; FN = Attack wrongly classified; TP = Attack recognized accurately; and TN = Legitimate flow recognized accurately.

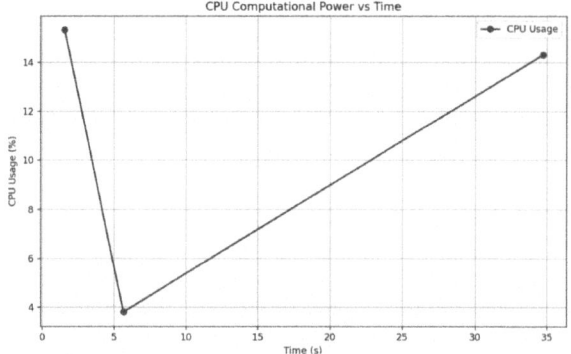

Fig. 4. Computational power versus time for CIC-DDoS dataset

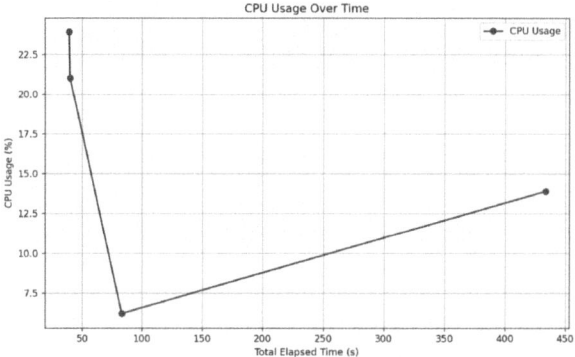

Fig. 5. Computational power versus time for IoT-23 dataset

2. **Precision (PREC)**: Precision tells us how many of the flows detected as MrDDoS attacks were actually attacks. It helps measure the accuracy of the system in identifying malicious traffic. The formula for precision is:

$$\text{PREC} = \frac{TP}{TP + FP} \times 100 \tag{17}$$

3. **Recall (REC)**: Recall measures how well the classifier detects actual MrD-DoS attacks. It shows the percentage of real attack flows that were successfully identified. The formula for recall is:

$$\text{REC} = \frac{TP}{TP + FN} \times 100 \tag{18}$$

4. **F1-Score**: The model's efficiency is measured by combining precision and recall into a single score. This score, known as the F1-score. It is computed using the harmonic mean of precision and recall, as follows:

$$\text{F1-score} = \frac{2 \times \text{PREC} \times \text{REC}}{\text{PREC} + \text{REC}} \times 100 \tag{19}$$

Accuracy. From the below Table 3 we can note that best accuracy is achieved by IoT-23 Dataset where Random Forest, KNN and MLP all giving same accuracy of around 0.99, while CIC-DDoS performed better than with WSN-DS Dataset (Fig. 6).

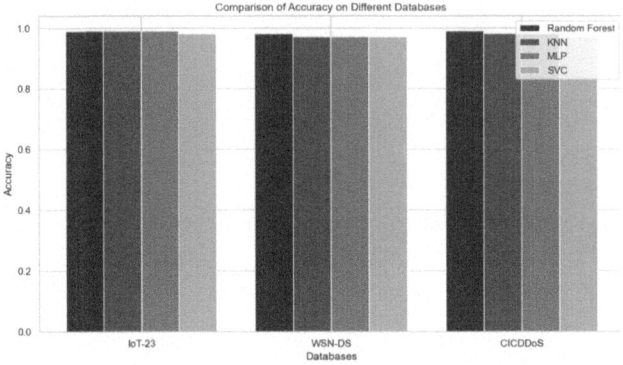

Fig. 6. Accuracy comparison of classifiers

Table 3. Accuracy and precision for different classifiers on various datasets

Accuracy				Precision		
Classifier	IoT-23	WSN-DS	CIC-DDoS	IoT-23	WSN-DS	CIC-DDoS
RF	0.99	0.98	0.99	0.99	0.99	0.98
KNN	0.99	0.97	0.98	0.98	0.98	0.98
MLP	0.99	0.97	0.98	0.97	0.98	0.96
SVC	0.98	0.97	0.97	0.98	0.98	0.97

Precision. From the above Table 3 we can note that best precision is achieved by CIC-DDoS Dataset in which Random Forest and KNN both give same precision of around 0.98, while IoT 23 dataset performed slightly better than WSN-DS (Fig. 7).

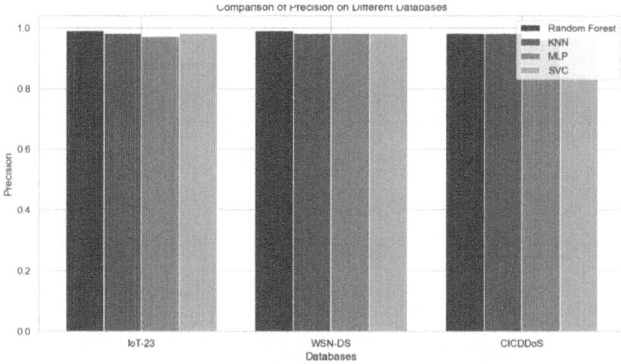

Fig. 7. Precision comparison of classifiers.

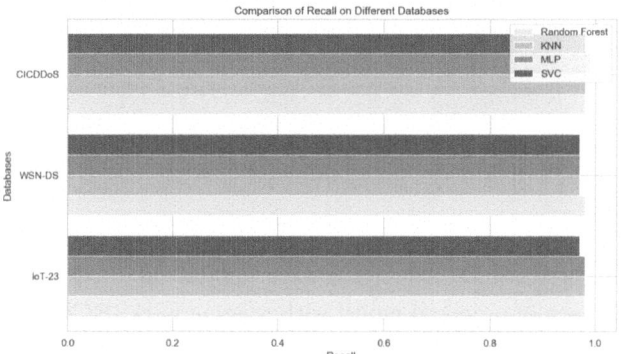

Fig. 8. Recall comparison of classifiers

Recall. From the below Table 4 we can note that best recall is achieved by CIC-DDoS Dataset in which MLP and SVC both give same recall of around 0.98, while IoT 23 dataset performed significantly better than WSN-DS (Fig. 7).

F1-Score. From the below Table 4, we can note that the best F1-score is achieved by the IoT-23 dataset. We can observe that almost all of the classifiers give the same F1-score of around 0.98. From the table, it is clear that the IoT-23 and the WSN-DS dataset are quite similar in performance when it comes to evaluating the F1-score (Fig. 9).

Result Comparison and Analysis. The below Table 5 tells us about the performance metrics of existing methods and compares them with our evaluated model. It is very clear from the table that our proposed approach is outperforming the existing methodologies.

Table 4. Recall and F1-score for different classifiers on various datasets

Recall				F1-Score		
Classifier	IoT-23	WSN-DS	CIC-DDoS	IoT-23	WSN-DS	CIC-DDoS
RF	0.98	0.98	0.98	0.99	0.99	0.98
KNN	0.98	0.97	0.98	0.99	0.99	0.98
MLP	0.98	0.97	0.99	0.97	0.98	0.97
SVC	0.97	0.97	0.98	0.99	0.98	0.98

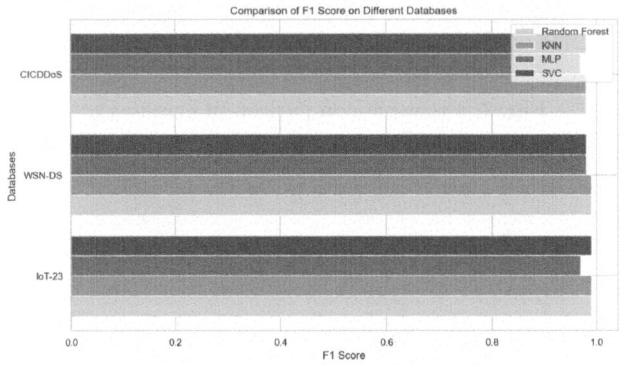

Fig. 9. F1-score comparison of classifiers

Table 5. Comparison of proposed model with existing work (**EC**: Energy Consumed, **Scalb**: Scalability, **Ligh**: Lightweight)

Ref.	Accuracy	Precision	Recall	F1-Score	EC(mJ)	Scalb	Ligh
[15]	0.80	0.60	0.60	0.60	N/A	No	Yes
[17]	0.96	0.93	0.92	0.95	6745	Yes	No
[23]	0.98	0.98	0.97	0.97	5128	No	No
[24]	0.95	0.94	0.93	0.94	12814	Yes	Yes
[14]	0.94	0.95	0.95	0.95	16439	Yes	Yes
[22]	0.99	0.96	N/A	0.95	10869	No	No
[18]	0.97	0.96	0.96	0.97	N/A	No	No
[12]	N/A	0.98	0.92	0.92	N/A	Yes	No
MAD-HOT	**0.99**	**0.99**	**0.98**	**0.98**	**4013**	**Yes**	**Yes**

6   Conclusion

This paper proposes a MAD-HOT security solution to detect MrDDoS attacks in the IoT ecosystem. In the most recent literature, deep learning models were used to detect attacks in IoT networks. However, it has a limitation in that it takes much time and computational power for attack detection. The MAD-

HOT approach has achieved better results than almost all experiments described in Sect. 2. We have also proposed an optimal IDS placement strategy for IoT networks. We have used three datasets, IoT23, CIC-DDoS, and WSN-DS, and got an average accuracy of 0.99, precision of 0.99, recall of 0.98, and an F1-score of 0.98. Additionally, the solution is highly scalable and lightweight. We carried out all the experiments using the Contiki cooja simulator. The promising results show that this approach works quite well and is also computationally sound compared to heavy deep-learning models that the existing works have used. Our future work will be driven into a deeper understanding of the behavior of a MrDDoS attack, thereby improving our solution's efficiency and scalability.

Acknowledgment. We thank the anonymous reviewers for their valuable feedback. This research work has been conducted under the SEED Grant from IIITDM Kancheepuram, Chennai, India for which the authors express their gratitude.

References

1. Abdelmoumin, G.: Rawat: on the performance of machine learning models for anomaly-based intelligent intrusion detection systems for the internet of things. IEEE Internet Things J. **PP**(99), 1 (2021)
2. Almomani, I., Al-Kasasbeh, M.: WSN-DS: a dataset for intrusion detection systems in wireless sensor networks. J. Sens. **2016**(1), 4731953 (2016)
3. Bhale, P., Biswas, S., Nandi, S.: An adaptive and lightweight solution to detect mixed rate ip spoofed ddos attack in iot ecosystem. In: 2018 15th IEEE India Council International Conference (INDICON), pp. 1–6. IEEE (2018)
4. Bhale, P., Biswas, S., Nandi, S.: LORD: low rate ddos attack detection and mitigation using lightweight distributed packet inspection agent in iot ecosystem. In: 2019 IEEE International Conference on Advanced Networks and Telecommunications Systems (ANTS), pp. 1–6. IEEE (2019)
5. Bhale, P., Biswas, S., Nandi, S.: ML for IEEE 802.15. 4e/TSCH: energy efficient approach to detect DDoS attack using machine learning. In: 2021 International Wireless Communications and Mobile Computing (IWCMC), pp. 1477–1482. IEEE (2021)
6. Bhale, P., Biswas, S., Nandi, S.: Effective injection of adversarial botnet attacks in IoT ecosystem using evolutionary computing. Internet Technol. Lett. **6**(4), e433 (2023)
7. Bhale, P., Chowdhury, D.R., Biswas, S., Nandi, S.: OPTIMIST: lightweight and transparent IDS with optimum placement strategy to mitigate mixed-rate DDoS attacks in IoT networks. IEEE Internet Things J. **10**(10), 8357–8370 (2023)
8. Bhale, P., Dey, S., Biswas, S., Nandi, S.: Energy efficient approach to detect sinkhole attack using roving IDS in 6LoWPAN network. In: Innovations for Community Services: 20th International Conference, I4CS 2020, Bhubaneswar, India, 12–14 January 2020, Proceedings 20, pp. 187–207. Springer (2020)
9. Choudhary, S., Kesswani, S.: An Ensemble Intrusion Detection Model For Internet of Things Network. Research Square (April 2021). License: CC BY 4.0
10. Dietterich, T.G.: Ensemble methods in machine learning. In: International Workshop on Multiple Classifier Systems, pp. 1–15. Springer (2000)

11. Garcia, Sebastian, M.J.: IoT-23: a labeled dataset with malicious and benign IoT network traffic. Stratosphere Lab., Praha, Czech Republic, Technical report (2020)
12. Garcia, N., Alcaniz, T., González-Vidal, A., Bernabe, J.B., Rivera, D., Skarmeta, A.: Distributed real-time SlowDoS attacks detection over encrypted traffic using Artificial Intelligence. J. Netw. Comput. Appl. **173**, 102871 (2021)
13. Hosmer Jr, D.W., Lemeshow, S., Sturdivant, R.X.: Applied Logistic Regression. John Wiley & Sons, Hoboken (2013)
14. Hussain, F.: A two-fold machine learning approach to prevent and detect IoT botnet attacks. IEEE Access **9**, 163412–163430 (2021)
15. Khandelwal, M., Gupta, D.K., Bhale, P.: DoS attack detection technique using back propagation neural network. In: 2016 International Conference on Advances in Computing, Communications and Informatics (ICACCI), pp. 1064–1068. IEEE (2016)
16. Laghari, A.A., Wu, K., Laghari, R.A., Ali, M., Khan, A.A.: A review and state of art of Internet of Things (IoT). Arch. Comput. Methods Eng. 1–19 (2021)
17. Li, Y., Lu, Y.: LSTM-BA: DDoS detection approach combining LSTM and Bayes. In: 2019 Seventh International Conference on Advanced Cloud and Big Data (CBD), pp. 180–185. IEEE (2019)
18. Liu, B., Tang, D., Yan, Y., Zheng, Z., Zhang, S., Zhou, J.: TS-SVM: detect LDoS attack in SDN based on two-step self-adjusting SVM. In: 2021 IEEE 20th International Conference on Trust, Security and Privacy in Computing and Communications (TrustCom), pp. 678–685. IEEE (2021)
19. Mahanta, K., Maringanti, H.B., Bhale, P.: Effective intrusion detection model using raptor optimized deep convolutional neural network. In: 2023 IEEE Guwahati Subsection Conference (GCON), pp. 1–6. IEEE (2023)
20. Muallem, A., Shetty, J., Biswal, B.: Hoeffding tree algorithms for anomaly detection in streaming datasets: a survey. J. Inf. Secur. **8**(4) (2017)
21. Oliveira, A., Vazao, T.: Low-power and lossy networks under mobility: a survey. Comput. Netw. **107**, 339–352 (2016)
22. Perez-Diaz, J.A., Valdovinos, I.A., Choo, K., Zhu, D.: A flexible SDN-based architecture for identifying and mitigating low-rate DDoS attacks using machine learning. IEEE Access **8**, 155859–155872 (2020)
23. Ravi, N., Shalinie, S.M.: Learning-driven detection and mitigation of ddos attack in iot via sdn-cloud architecture. IEEE Internet Things J. **7**(4), 3559–3570 (2020)
24. Saharkhizan, M., Azmoodeh, A., Dehghantanha, A., Choo, K., Parizi, R.M.: An ensemble of deep recurrent neural networks for detecting IoT cyber attacks using network traffic. IEEE Internet Things J. **7**(9), 8852–8859 (2020)
25. Sharafaldin, I., Lashkari, A.H., Hakak, S., Ghorbani, A.A.: Developing realistic distributed denial of service (DDoS) attack dataset and taxonomy. In: 2019 International Carnahan Conference on Security Technology (ICCST), pp. 1–8. IEEE (2019)
26. Velinov, A., Mileva, A.: Running and testing applications for Contiki OS using Cooja simulator. In: International Conference on Information Technology and Development of Education–ITRO, vol. 2016 (2016)
27. Vilajosana, X., Wang, Q., Chraim, T., Pister, K.S.: A realistic energy consumption model for TSCH networks. IEEE Sens. J. **14**(2), 482–489 (2013)

Intelligent Vehicle Detection System

Aahan Singh Charak📵 and Imran Shafiq Ahmad$^{(\boxtimes)}$📵

School of Computer Science, University of Windsor, Windsor, ON N9B 3P4, Canada
{charak,imran}@uwindsor.ca

Abstract. A steady increase in the number of vehicles on roads around
the world has increased the need for Intelligent Traffic System (ITS).
Vehicle detection, classification, and license plate recognition are essential for traffic analysis and ITS. License plate detectors are especially
helpful to the law agencies, as they assist in catching criminals and suspicious vehicles by recognizing license plates. Systems employing Artificial Intelligence (AI) utilize image classification and object detection
to monitor and analyze traffic on roads and highways. These systems
are powered by state-of-the-art neural network architectures (e.g., the
Convolutional Neural Network (CNN) for classification), which enable
accurate detection and processing of real-time traffic data. Most vehicle
monitoring systems, however, focus on only one aspect of vehicle tracking
at a time. For example, these systems may focus on detecting specific
attributes of a vehicle, such as vehicle's make, model, or color, often
ignoring the other attributes. This manuscript introduces a novel approach to vehicle monitoring systems, which involves focusing on all such
attributes simultaneously. We divide the Stanford Cars Dataset (SCD)
into groups based on the car's make, model, type, year, and color. Subsequently, we train a separate CNN classifier on each group to learn the
characteristics of each group. This allows us to study how each attribute
independently affects the classification accuracy of vehicle monitoring
system. Additionally, we also developed a license plate detector to complete our vehicle monitoring system. This provides a complete solution to
the problem of vehicle monitoring systems by incorporating all essential
components. Our vehicle recognition system achieves an average accuracy of 91.2% across all the different classification subtasks whereas the
license plate detection system achieves an accuracy of 93.46%.

Keywords: Vehicle detection · Intelligent transportation system ·
Automatic vehicle recognition · License plate detection · Computer
vision · Image classification

1 Introduction

The term Intelligent Transportation System (ITS) refers to collective use of
technology and information system to enhance the efficiency, safety, and sustainability of transportation networks. ITS includes a range of innovations, such as

S. Zielinski et al. (Eds.): I4CS 2025, CCIS 2513, pp. 437–452, 2025.
https://doi.org/10.1007/978-3-031-94263-1_24

automatic traffic management systems, real-time information systems, and self-driving vehicles. The primary objective of ITS is to improve transportation by making it safer, more efficient, and more accessible while minimizing congestion, emissions, and energy consumption. By exploiting advances in communication, sensors, and computing technologies, ITS delivers real-time data and feedback to drivers, operators, and decision-makers to optimize transportation network performance and enhancing the travel experiences. Additionally, integrating ITS with other smart city technologies is becoming increasingly vital for building sustainable and livable urban environments. In automated transportation systems, vehicle classification systems identify vehicles based on attributes such as size and weight, playing a critical role in ITS operations [32]. Automatic vehicle recognition (AVR) systems are a critical subcomponent of ITS and help provide enhanced and efficient traffic management through classification and detection of vehicles in real-time [32]. Artificial Intelligence (AI) is extensively used in AVR systems to classify vehicles through deep learning models [10]. AVR systems help with traffic management and reduce traffic congestion by providing real-time monitoring through the use of AI and Computer Vision (CV) techniques. CV based applications for such purposes are capable of detecting vehicles and identifying license plate text through deep learning [6]. In recent years, AI has become an integral part of the AVR systems and the future smart cities. It helps AVR systems in vehicles detection, classification, and efficient license plate detection and decoding. AVR systems also facilitate in detection of stolen vehicles as well as traffic violations through vehicle model recognition and license plate information. Some such systems are able to predict traffic congestions before it happens through real-time monitoring of vehicles and making important decision for smooth operations and flow of traffic [9]. AVR systems are also used for parking and toll collection [27] by classifying vehicles and charging accordingly.

An Automatic Vehicle Recognition (AVR) system consists of many different sub-components to detect license plate, vehicle make and model, its shape and color. Most existing systems focus on just one or a few of these components. For example, some systems may only detect the license plate while others may combine vehicle make and model detection. However, these systems lack the ability to provide full set of information to the ITS to make effective decisions. In this manuscript, we propose a complete system for vehicle detection and monitoring for efficient decision by the ITS and to detect and track vehicles of interest. The proposed system provides ability to detect not only make and model of a vehicle but also provides information about its color, shape and its license plate information.

Rest of this manuscript is organized as follows. Section 2 provides an overview of related work. Section 3 provides details of the proposed scheme and methodology. In Sect. 4, we provide details of experimental results and analyze its performance. Finally, Sect. 5 provides some concluding remarks.

2   Literature Review

The topic of vehicle recognition systems involves many subtasks such as its shape, make and model classification, and license plate detection & recognition. This section provides an overview of techniques and research relevant to these subtasks.

The process of vehicle make detection involves identifying its make from an image or video, such as whether a given vehicle is Hyundai, BMW, or another make. Vehicle make detection plays a crucial role in traffic management by identifying vehicle makes for better flow control and planning. For example, it can help restrict older or high-emission vehicle makes from entering low-emission zones in cities. This improves air quality and ensures that the environmental regulations are followed. In the security field, vehicle make and model information aids by tracking and identifying vehicles of interest, making the security systems more efficient.

Over the years, various methods have been explored to improve the accuracy of vehicle make classification. Badura et al. [3] proposed an image-processing-based approach for vehicle make detection. This approach involves image preprocessing, feature extraction, and classification using machine learning classifiers. In the experiments, authors correctly classified 30 different vehicle makes with an accuracy of around 75%. According to the authors, the system's efficiency was affected by factors such as poor visual image quality and low textural content of the vehicle brand.

Bularz et al. [4] used rear lamp features to identify the make of the vehicles. In this technique, the region of interest (ROI) is extracted from the original image, followed by binarization. The binarized image acted as an input to a convolutional neural network (CNN), which is used to identify the make of the vehicle. The author's approach achieved an average accuracy of around 89.2% on the test set. Additionally, similar methods are found in the early vehicle make detection research. Pearce et al. [22] used a feature detection technique called Harris corner strengths to extract features from the vehicle images. The extracted features were used to classify the make of the vehicles using machine learning techniques like the K-Nearest-Neighbor (KNN) classifier and the Naive-Bayes (NB) classifier. An accuracy of around 96% was observed but only on a dataset of 262 images.

Apart from machine learning and image processing-based methods, deep learning has also been used extensively to recognize make and model of the vehicles. Hassan et al. [12] used transfer learning to recognize the makes of vehicles in the Stanford Vehicles Dataset (SCD). Augmentation methods like horizontal flip, resize, shear, etc., are applied to the training dataset to increase the number of images. The ensemble learning framework used in the study obtained an accuracy of 93.96%. Komolovaite et al. [15] aimed to develop an updatable vehicle make monitoring system using transfer learning. Authors trained their model on two deep-learning architectures: EfficientNetV2 and MobileNetV2 and reported an accuracy of around 81.39% on the test dataset.

Broadly speaking, depending on body style, personal vehicles are classified into four different categories: car, minivan, mini truck and box truck. Within each category, there may be additional subcategories such as a car is further categorized as sedan, coupe, convertible, sports, etc. Type classification involves determining whether the vehicle in a given input image is in one of these main categories. This task is crucial, especially in surveillance systems, where the law enforcement agencies may identify and apprehend criminals based on their vehicle body style, especially when details about the make and model are incomplete.

Some early research in this field involved using machine learning to classify the type of vehicles based on their features. Kafai et al. [14] used a Bayesian Network for vehicle type classification. The authors extracted a feature set of rear lights and vehicle dimensions to develop a low-dimensional feature vector. The feature vector was used to train a Bayesian Network (BN) to classify the type of vehicle. Matos et al. [24] used a deep-learning-based approach involving neural network (NN) with conditional adaptive distance. The image-based features involved height, width, and fractal, which were used to train a NN. An accuracy of 69% was observed for the test dataset, which, according to the authors, was not feasible in real-world scenarios.

Tas et al. [29] proposed a CNN architecture that aimed to correctly classify vehicles in low-quality images. The images were captured through a standard camera installed far away from the regions of interest (ROI) like roads, highways, etc. According to the authors, despite not performing as well as the other state-of-the-art CNN models, the proposed solution provided several advantages, like being more lightweight and faster training times.

Color recognition systems involve determining the color of a vehicle from an input image. Vehicle color recognition is an essential element of ITS. It helps distinguish vehicles based on their colors, making it useful for identifying specific vehicles during incidents or violations. This is especially important when the make and model of the vehicle are difficult to determine from the image. However, it is a challenging task as weather conditions, lighting, and image quality severely impact the efficiency of the color recognition systems. Rachmadi et al. [23] used CNNs to classify the color of vehicles. The input images were converted to HSV (Hue, Saturation, Value) and CIELAB color spaces, in order to learn more color-based features from the input RGB (Red, Green, Blue) image. After that, the images were used to train a custom CNN architecture developed by the authors. An accuracy of as high as 94.47% was observed for the test set.

Apart from the general CNN architectures, some researchers proposed more complex architectures to solve the problem of vehicle color recognition. Fu et al. [8] developed a Multiscale Comprehensive Feature Fusion Convolutional Neural Network (MCFF-CNN) based on residual learning to extract color features from vehicle images. MCFF-CNN was used to extract the deep color features from the input vehicle images. These features were used as inputs to train a support vector machine (SVM). The architecture was found resulting in better performance compared to other state-of-the-art CNN networks. Hu et al. [13] proposed a color recognition method using a Smooth Modulation Neural Network with Multiscale Feature Fusion (SMNN-MSFF). SMNN aimed to extract features globally, and MSFF handled the long-tailed distribution problem in the dataset. The system could correctly recognize 24 different colors with an accuracy of 94.96%.

Vehicle model classification is a substantial part of AVR systems to keep the roads safe. For example, law enforcement agencies use it to track vehicles stolen or used in a crime. Overall, it makes the transportation system more innovative and efficient. Like other classification tasks, deep learning has been used extensively to solve the problem of automatic vehicle model recognition. Yu et al. [33] developed a CNN architecture called FF-CMNET for vehicle model classification. The FF-CMNET architecture consists of two branches to extract vehicle's upper and lower parts separately. According to the authors, both regions exhibit different feature distributions, so they helped to accurately identify the model of the vehicle. The authors were able to outperform other state-of-the-art research methods on a benchmark dataset called CompCars with the highest observed accuracy of 98.89%. However, the approach was found to be applied to a dataset which is consistently used in literature of vehicle model classification, with many approaches yielding high accuracy scores. The authors also stated that they intend to apply their approach to other state-of-the-art datasets in future work.

Most recent approaches in this field rely on attention mechanisms to solve the problem of vehicle model classification [34]. However, attention mechanisms often carry a computational burden. To handle the aforementioned problem, Gayan et al. [11] developed SIMSANET, a simple sequential attention network which efficiently balances complexity and accuracy using a sequential multi-kernel approach to extract multi-scale features. The model achieved remarkable accuracies across different benchmark datasets.

License Plate Detection (LPD) has been essential to automatic surveillance systems for decades, as it helps accurately identify vehicle owners through license plate information during emergencies like theft, accident, etc. LPD has also been widely used in automatic toll collection, parking payment, etc. to automatically withdraw specified amount from the attached financial institutions/accounts. Like the other tasks mentioned earlier, AI has extensively been used over the years for LPD. The earlier approaches involved image processing followed by neural networks, as seen in [16]. The authors describe the process in three steps: first, image quality is enhanced using image fusion; second, thresholding is applied to separate the license plate text from the background; and finally, neural networks are used for character recognition. The system was able to correctly recognize characters on license-plate with a probability of 95%. A comparative study of various automatic license plate detection systems can be found in [1]

Over time, deep learning was introduced to the License Plate Recognition (LPR) field. Selmi et al. [25] used two CNNs to achieve the task of LPR. The first CNN was used to identify between the plate and the non-plate parts in an image. The second CNN was used to recognize digits and alphabets on the license plate. A high F1 score was observed in the method proposed by the authors. F1 score is discussed in details in Sect. 4.

In recent times, YOLO-based license plate detection has become common. For automatic license plate recognition (ALPR) tasks, it has given excellent results [2]. The authors used YOLOV2 in the initial stages of their automatic license plate recognition (ALPR) pipeline. YOLOV4 is used later on along with data augmentation to develop a license plate detector. The authors achieved an average license plate recognition accuracy of 90.3%. YOLOV8 [26] has recently gained popularity due to the fact that it achieves high accuracy in many object detection tasks.

3   Methodology

In following subsections, we provide details of the dataset used and complete methodology of the proposed system.

Datasets: For our research, we mainly used two datasets. The first is the Stanford Vehicles Dataset (SCD) [17] for vehicle make, type, year, model, and color classification. However, since SCD does not contain annotated license plate information, to train the license plate detector (LPD), we used another dataset from Roboflow [7]. The Stanford vehicles dataset is a large dataset, developed for fine-grained vehicle classification. It consists of 16,185 images categorized into 196 classes. In our research, we divided the original SCD dataset into sub-datasets based on vehicle make, type, color, model, and year of manufacturing separately instead of classifying them as a single class (e.g., Acura Integra Sedan 2000). This approach provided us with more granular control over the classification process. By separating each feature, we are able to analyze each attribute independently and focus on specific aspects of the vehicles. This offers us a more detailed understanding of how factors like the make of the vehicle influence vehicle recognition. According to our exploratory analysis, this fine-grained approach has not been explored before, and it paves the way for studying vehicle classification without combining all the different attributes into a single class. Analyzing attributes separately rather than combining them into a single class allows us to study vehicle classification more precisely. The Roboflow dataset consists of 19,533 annotated license plate images from the Open Images Dataset [18]. The open images dataset is a large-scale dataset consisting of approximately nine million annotated images to train machine learning models. Additionally, this dataset also includes many annotated license plate images, which can be leveraged to train models for use in real-world scenarios.

Additionally, we created our vehicle color dataset from the original SCD, as it does not contain color categorization. We manually scanned the entire dataset and created our color dataset, consisting of 750 training and testing images. We ensured to include every dominant color in our dataset, and the colors for which the sample size was small (< 5 images) were discarded since a small sample may fail to provide meaningful insights for classification and analysis.

Figure 1 shows a sample of different vehicle makes, types, models, and colors from the SCD, thus showing the diversity and complexity of the dataset. This is important for training robust classification models that can handle real-world scenarios like poor lighting, low-quality images, etc.

Fig. 1. Sample images from the SCD dataset

There are mainly two main sub-tasks in which our methodology, which are:

- Vehicle detection. (e.g Acura Integra sedan 2007 red)
- License Plate Detection

Figure 2 summarizes our vehicle recognition system approach.

Vehicle Detection: For this sub-task, identifying the best performing CNN architecture was crucial to developing a good classifier. We tested many different CNN classifiers and found that EfficientNet [28] performed consistently well in all the classification scenarios. The main steps involved in this sub-task are as follows:

- Initially, the original dataset is divided into subdatasets based on the number of subtasks present. The original SCD is in the form of make, model type year (e.g., Audi Q3 SUV 2010). To study the classification of these factors independently, we separated the original dataset by make, model, type, and year. Additionally, we created a new vehicle color dataset from the original SCD, as there was no color categorization in the original dataset. After that, images were pre-processed to include augmentations like shear, zoom, rotation, etc. This helps to increase the accuracy of the trained models.

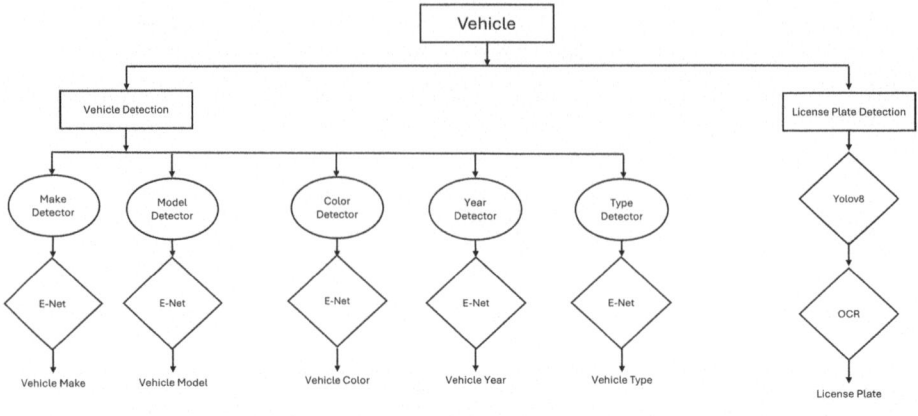

Fig. 2. Flow chart showing our vehicle recognition system.

- Now, for each different category, we trained a CNN classifier using transfer learning. CNNs are deep learning networks primarily developed for grid-based data structures like images. CNNs have the following key features:

  - **Convolutional Layers:** These layers mainly apply filters to the input image to extract features like edges, patterns and textural properties.
  - **Pooling Layers:** They help reduce the size of feature maps, thus making the model more efficient and preventing overfitting.
  - **Activation Functions:** The functions like Rectified Linear Unit (ReLU) introduce non-linearity in the network, allowing the network to learn complex functions.
  - **Fully Connected Layers:** These are simple linear perceptrons placed at the end of CNN architectures to classify the image.

- For selecting the optimal architecture, we tested a few state-of-the-art CNN architectures like ResNet, InceptionNet, EfficientNet, and MobileNetV2 using transfer learning. We found that EfficientNet (Enet) performed better than the other architectures, giving consistently higher accuracy for all the classification tasks. So, for our final training, we used Enet as our central architecture for transfer learning. Enet is a family of CNN networks designed to achieve high performance while being computationally efficient. Enet was initially developed to address the limitations of the previous architectures, which often relied on users manually tuning the depth and width of the network. Enet uses a compound scaling network to scale the network's dimensions uniformly. This allows the model to grow efficiently, increasing the accuracy without increasing the computational load. Enet uses depth wise separable convolutions, significantly reducing the parameters and calculations required to perform traditional convolutional operations. It uses the Swish activation functions, improving the gradient flow during training. The fully connected layers are also replaced with Global Average Pooling layers to reduce the number of parameters. As a result, Enet models are smaller and faster, making them ideal for deployment in environments with limited resources.

In our research, we used transfer learning on the Enet_B0 architecture, which consists of 13 layers, including the initial convolution layer, seven stages of Mobile Inverted Bottleneck Convolutions (MBConv), a Global Average Pooling layer, and a fully connected output layer. Transfer learning involves taking a large pre-trained CNN architecture, which is trained on a large dataset, to perform a different task on a new dataset. The middle few layers are frozen during the transfer learning process, and the dataset is trained on the final few layers. This makes the process faster, as we do not have to train the entire network, and it allows us to use the power of a large network on our custom dataset. In our study, five different Enets were trained for each classification task separately.

- Finally, we evaluated the performance of the trained classifiers on the respective testing sets.

License Plate Detection. For the task of training an efficient LPD, we took the following steps.

- First, we developed an object detector to accurately segment the license plate region from the vehicle image. For this, we use object detection using YOLOV8 via transfer learning. YOLOV8 is the latest version of the You Only Look Once (YOLO) family of object detectors. It is a real-time, deep-learning-based algorithm designed to detect objects, segment images, and classify tasks. The main characteristics of YOLOV8 are:
  - YOLOV8 supports multiple tasks like object detection, image segmentation and classification.
  - It also offers high accuracy on the benchmark object detection datasets as compared to the previous versions like YOLOV7.

  After training the license plate detection model, it was evaluated on some test images we sampled from the SCD.
- **Optical Character Recognition (OCR):** OCR is a technology that converts different types of text, such as printed, handwritten or scanned documents, into a machine-readable format. OCR is a combination of four main steps:
  - **Image Preprocessing:** Here, the input image is cleaned to improve text recognition accuracy. Techniques like binarization, skew correction, etc., are used at this stage.
  - **Text Detection:** This step involves finding paragraphs, sentences, etc., in an image. Modern OCR models generally use deep learning to improve text detection accuracy.

- **Character Recognition:** Character recognition step matches the text to patterns or uses machine learning to identify shapes and curves.
- **Post-processing:** Here, errors are corrected using a dictionary or a language model to double-check the recognized text.

In our study, we used PaddleOCR (POCR) [19] to accurately identify the text in the license plate image. POCR is a deep-learning-based OCR system. It helps identify text in images by using sequence-to-sequence-based deep-learning models. It is efficient, accurate and easy to use. We decided to use POCR in our study since in our experiments, we found it to be more accurate than traditional OCR systems. The presence of deep-learning models allows it to recognize text even in plates with complex backgrounds and/or low-quality images.

- Finally, we evaluated the license plate detection results on the sample dataset we created from the SCD, since the SCD does not has annotated text for license plates to verify results automatically. We manually took images with clear license plate text present and stored the respective license plates in an excel spreadsheet (.CSV file). After that, we used our LPD to extract the license plate text from the images and compared the automated results to the results we manually extracted to compare and obtain accuracy score.

4   Results and Discussion

For our research, the following metrics are used to accurately analyze the classification results for the vehicle recognition system we developed.

- **Precision:** It is the ratio of the correctly predicted positive observations to the total predicted positive observations.

$$\textbf{Precision} = \frac{TP}{TP + FP}$$

where:
- TP = True Positives
- FP = False Positives

- **Recall:** It is the ratio of correctly predicted positive observations to the total number of observations in the class.

$$\textbf{Recall} = \frac{TP}{TP + FN}$$

where:
- TP = True Positives
- FN = False Negatives

- **F1 Score:** It is the harmonic mean of precision and recall.

$$\textbf{F1 Score} = 2 \times \frac{\textbf{Precision} \times \textbf{Recall}}{\textbf{Precision} + \textbf{Recall}}$$

- **Accuracy:** It is the ratio of correct predictions to the total number of predictions.

$$\textbf{Accuracy} = \frac{TP + TN}{TP + TN + FP + FN}$$

where:
- TP = True Positives
- TN = True Negatives
- FP = False Positives
- FN = False Negatives

Table 1 shows the classification metrics we obtained for our vehicle recognition system.

Table 1. Classification performance metrics for vehicle recognition system

Classification Type	Accuracy	Precision	Recall	F1 Score
Vehicle Make	0.90	0.91	0.90	0.90
Vehicle Model	0.91	0.91	0.91	0.91
Vehicle Year	0.91	0.91	0.91	0.91
Vehicle Color	0.93	0.93	0.93	0.93
Vehicle Type	0.91	0.91	0.91	0.91

The system demonstrated consistent and high performances across all classification types. Vehicle color classification achieved the highest metrics with accuracy, precision, recall, and F1 scores at 93.0%, indicating its effectiveness in identifying vehicle colors. The remaining classifications achieved uniform strong metrics in the range of 90.0–91.0%, marking the robustness and reliability of the proposed system. Vehicle color classification tends to have higher metrics because colors are mostly distinct and visually separable compared to other features. Colors are less likely to vary within the same class and are easily distinguishable from different images, making it a relatively straightforward classification task.

Vehicle year classification also achieved a high accuracy of 91.0%. However, it can be challenging because older and newer vehicle models within the same make and models can look very similar. The design changes can sometimes be very subtle, such as door handle types, leading to slight dips in accuracy. For vehicle type classification, some classes can look very similar, like sedan vs coupe, where the subtle difference is that sedan has four doors and coupe has two doors. Such slight differences may cause a fall in accuracy scores. Figure 3 illustrates two common misclassification scenarios. In part (a), a red car is misclassified as orange due to its hue appearing slightly changed under the given lighting conditions. In part (b), a coupe is misclassified as a sedan, likely due to similarities in shape and proportion, which may have influenced the model's decision. Overall, the vehicle detection system achieves an average accuracy of 91.2%.

Fig. 3. Examples of cases where our AVR system may provide incorrect results (a) Red car misclassified as orange (b) Coupe misclassified as a sedan

For the license plate detection part, in addition to the two previously defined evaluation metrics, viz., Precision and Recall, we also use mean Average Precision (mAP) to measure the effectiveness of the LPD scheme as defined below:

Mean Average Precision(mAP) at IoU 0.5 (mAP@50): Mean Average Precision (mAP) is a metric used to evaluate the performance of object detection models. The mAP@50 is the mean of Average Precision (AP) scores calculated across all object classes, where AP is computed at an Intersection over Union (IoU) threshold of 0.5. IOU threshold score is the minimum overlap score required between the predicted bounding box and the ground truth box for the object detected to be considered a true positive. mAP is defined as:

$$\mathbf{AP} = \int_0^1 P(r)\,dr$$

where $P(r)$ is the precision as a function of recall. The mAP@50 is then given by:

$$\mathbf{mAP@50} = \frac{1}{N}\sum_{i=1}^{N}\mathbf{AP}_i$$

Here, N is the number of object classes, and $\mathbf{AP}_i$ is the Average Precision for class i.

Table 2 shows the evaluation metrics for the license plate detection task whereas Table 3 provides a comparison with other similar approaches in the cited references.

After that, OCR is used along with the trained license plate detector to identify the license plate text in the dataset accurately we made from the SCD. An accuracy of 93.46% is observed on our created dataset.

Table 2. Evaluation metrics for license plate detection

Metric	Value (Example)
Precision	0.98
Recall	0.96
mAP@50	0.98

The evaluation metrics for license plate detection show strong performance across all key metrics. The precision score of 0.98 shows that the model is highly accurate when predicting true positives with very few false positives. The recall score of 96.0% shows that the model can detect most license plates with very few false negatives. The mAP@50 score of 98.0% further shows the model's ability to detect license plates, as this metric measures average precision across different IOU thresholds. In a nutshell, the results indicate a highly efficient license plate detection system.

Table 3. Comparison of our approach to other state-of-the-art approaches on the SCD

Metric	[5]	[21]	[31]	[20]	[30]	Proposed Average Accuracy
Accuracy	89%	91.06%	84.6%	90.9%	86.79%	91.2%
Improvement	2.2%	0.14%	6.6%	0.3%	4.3%	–

Table 3 presents a comparison of our approach with existing methods on the SCD. The results indicate that our approach performs better than or at least competitively with state-of-the-art techniques, showing improvements in several cases. While some differences in the accuracy are marginal, the overall trend shows that our approach is effective. These findings align with prior research, reinforcing the reliability of our methods.

5 Conclusion

In this study, we developed a robust vehicle recognition system that efficiently classifies attributes such as make, model, color, and year, while also detecting text from license plates using a combination of object detection and OCR. By dividing the original Stanford Car Dataset (SCD) into sub-datasets based on individual factors like make, type, color, model, and year of manufacture, we are able to independently analyze the impact of each factor on the model's accuracy. This fine-grained approach is novel and offers new ways to explore vehicle classification without merging all the factors into a single class. We also created a dedicated vehicle color dataset from the original SCD to train a color detector and used an open-source dataset from Roboflow for license plate detection. Given the lack of license plate annotations in the original dataset, we manually selected a subset of images for analysis. Our system demonstrated high accuracy and consistency across various classification and LPD tasks. These results suggest that our approach provides a more reliable and interpretable vehicle recognition system by analyzing each attribute separately. Our approach also achieves better or at least comparable accuracy to the other state-of-the-art research in the domain of VRS. This method reduces complexity, allowing for a clearer understanding of each factor's influence on the system, and shows competitive performance with existing methods, with consistent improvements across different cases. Overall, the system is not only effective in classification and LPD tasks but also provides a new direction for future exploration in the field of vehicle recognition systems.

References

1. Ahmad, I.S., Boufama, B., Habashi, P., Anderson, W., Elamsy, T.: Automatic license plate recognition: a comparative study. In: 2015 IEEE International Symposium on Signal Processing and Information Technology (ISSPIT), pp. 635–640 (2015). https://doi.org/10.1109/ISSPIT.2015.7394415
2. Al-Batat, R., Angelopoulou, A., Premkumar, S., Hemanth, J., Kapetanios, E.: An end-to-end automated license plate recognition system using yolo based vehicle and license plate detection with vehicle classification. Sensors **22**(23), 9477 (2022)
3. Badura, P., Skotnicka, M.: Automatic car make recognition in low-quality images. In: Information Technologies in Biomedicine, vol. 3, pp. 235–246 (2014)
4. Bularz, M., Przystalski, K., Ogorzałek, M.: Car make and model recognition system using rear-lamp features and convolutional neural networks. Multimed. Tools Appl. **83**(2), 4151–4165 (2024)
5. Cynthia Sherin, B., Jayavel, K.: Effective vehicle classification and re-identification on Stanford cars dataset using convolutional neural networks. In: Proceedings of the 3rd International Conference on Artificial Intelligence: Advances and Applications: ICAIAA 2022, pp. 177–190 (2023)
6. Du, S., Ibrahim, M., Shehata, M., Badawy, W.: Automatic license plate recognition (alpr): a state-of-the-art review. IEEE Trans. Circuits Syst. Video Technol. **23**(2), 311–325 (2012)
7. Dwyer, B., Nelson, J., Hansen, T., et al.: Roboflow (version 1.0) [software] (2024). https://roboflow.com. Accessed 21 Feb 2025
8. Fu, H., Ma, H., Wang, G., Zhang, X., Zhang, Y.: Mcff-cnn: multiscale comprehensive feature fusion convolutional neural network for vehicle color recognition based on residual learning. Neurocomputing **395**, 178–187 (2020)
9. Gao, J., Shen, Y., Liu, J., Ito, M., Shiratori, N.: Adaptive traffic signal control: deep reinforcement learning algorithm with experience replay and target network. arXiv preprint arXiv:1705.02755 (2017)
10. Gayen, S., Maity, S., Singh, P.K., Geem, Z.W., Sarkar, R.: Two decades of vehicle make and model recognition-survey, challenges and future directions. J. King Saud Univ. **36**(1), 101885 (2024)
11. Gayen, S., Maity, S., Singh, P.K., Sarkar, R.: Simsanet: a simple sequential attention-aided deep neural network for vehicle make and model recognition. Neural Comput. Appl. 1–21 (2024)
12. Hassan, A., Ali, M., Durrani, N.M., Tahir, M.A.: An empirical analysis of deep learning architectures for vehicle make and model recognition. IEEE Access **9**, 91487–91499 (2021)

13. Hu, M., Bai, L., Fan, J., Zhao, S., Chen, E.: Vehicle color recognition based on smooth modulation neural network with multi-scale feature fusion. Front. Comp. Sci. **17**(3), 173321 (2023)
14. Kafai, M., Bhanu, B.: Dynamic bayesian networks for vehicle classification in video. IEEE Trans. Ind. Inf. **8**(1), 100–109 (2011)
15. Komolovaite, D., Krisciunas, A., Lagzdinyte-Budnike, I., Budnikas, A., Rentelis, D.: Vehicle make detection using the transfer learning approach. Elektronika ir Elektrotechnika **28**(4), 55–64 (2022)
16. Koval, V., Turchenko, V., Kochan, V., Sachenko, A., Markowsky, G.: Smart license plate recognition system based on image processing using neural network. In: Second IEEE Intl. Workshop on Intelligent Data Acquisition and Advanced Computing Systems: Technology and Applications, 2003, pp. 123–127 (2003)
17. Krause, J., Stark, M., Deng, J., Fei-Fei, L.: 3d object representations for fine-grained categorization. In: 2013 IEEE International Conference on Computer Vision Workshops, pp. 554–561 (2013)
18. Kuznetsova, A.: The open images dataset v4: unified image classification, object detection, and visual relationship detection at scale. Int. J. Comput. Vis. **128**(7), 1956–1981 (2020)
19. Li, Y., Zhang, D., et al.: Research and application of health code recognition based on paddle ocr under the background of epidemic prevention and control. J. Artif. Intell. Pract. **6**(1), 9–16 (2023)
20. Lu, Z., Sreekumar, G., Goodman, E., Banzhaf, W., Deb, K., Boddeti, V.N.: Neural architecture transfer. IEEE Trans. PAMI **43**(9), 2971–2989 (2021)
21. Nguyen, G., Chen, V., Taesiri, M.R., Nguyen, A.T.: Pcnn: probable-class nearest-neighbor explanations improve fine-grained image classification accuracy for ais and humans. arXiv e-prints, pp. arXiv–2308 (2023)
22. Pearce, G., Pears, N.: Automatic make and model recognition from frontal images of cars. In: 2011 8th IEEE Intl. Conf. on Advanced Video and Signal based Surveillance, pp. 373–378 (2011)
23. Rachmadi, R.F., Purnama, I.: Vehicle color recognition using convolutional neural network. arXiv preprint arXiv:1510.07391 (2015)
24. de S. Matos, F.M., de Souza, R.: Hierarchical classification of vehicle images using NN with conditional adaptive distance. In: Lee, M., Hirose, A., Hou, Z.-G., Kil, R.M. (eds.) ICONIP 2013. LNCS, vol. 8227, pp. 745–752. Springer, Heidelberg (2013). https://doi.org/10.1007/978-3-642-42042-9_92
25. Selmi, Z., Halima, M.B., Alimi, A.M.: Deep learning system for automatic license plate detection and recognition. In: 2017 14th IAPR International Conference on document analysis and recognition (ICDAR), vol. 1, pp. 1132–1138 (2017)
26. Sohan, M., Sai Ram, T., Reddy, R., Venkata, C.: A review on yolov8 and its advancements. In: International Conference on Data Intelligence and Cognitive Informatics, pp. 529–545 (2024)
27. Suryatali, A., Dharmadhikari, V.: Computer vision based vehicle detection for toll collection system using embedded linux. In: 2015 International Conference on Circuits, Power and Computing Technologies, pp. 1–7 (2015)
28. Tan, M., Le, Q.: Efficientnet: rethinking model scaling for convolutional neural networks. In: International Conference on Machine Learning, pp. 6105–6114 (2019)
29. Tas, S., Sari, O., Dalveren, Y., Pazar, S., Kara, A., Derawi, M.: Deep learning-based vehicle classification for low quality images. Sensors **22**(13), 4740 (2022)
30. Todescato, M.V., Garcia, L.F., Balreira, D.G., Carbonera, J.L.: Multiscale patch-based feature graphs for image classification. Expert Syst. Appl. **235**, 121116 (2024)

31. Touvron, H.: Resmlp: feedforward networks for image classification with data-efficient training. IEEE Trans. PAMI **45**(4), 5314–5321 (2022)
32. Van Cuong, N., Aziz, M.T.: Ai-driven vehicle recognition for enhanced traffic management: implications and strategies. AI IoT Fourth Ind. Revolut. Rev. **13**(7), 27–35 (2023)
33. Yu, Y., Jin, Q., Chen, C.W.: Ff-cmnet: a cnn-based model for fine-grained classification of car models based on feature fusion. In: 2018 IEEE International Conference on Multimedia and Expo (ICME), pp. 1–6 (2018)
34. Yu, Y., Xu, L., Jia, W., Zhu, W., Fu, Y., Lu, Q.: Cam: a fine-grained vehicle model recognition method based on visual attention model. Image Vis. Comput. **104**, 104027 (2020)

Challenges in Scaling Agile Frameworks and Ways to Address Them with Scaled Agile Framework (SAFe) and Scrum of Scrums (SoS)

Christoph Eigner[1] and Günter Fahrnberger[2]([✉])

[1] University of Applied Sciences BFI Vienna, Vienna, Austria
[2] University of Hagen, Hagen, North Rhine-Westphalia, Germany
guenter.fahrnberger@studium.fernuni-hagen.de

Abstract. Agile methods enhance flexibility and adaptability within organizations, excelling in small teams and projects. However, their effectiveness diminishes when applied to larger projects. This paper examines the challenges of scaling agile methods and explores scalable frameworks like the Scaled Agile Framework (SAFe) and Scrum of Scrums (SoS). Agile approaches align with the Agile Manifesto's values and principles, emphasizing iterative workflows, cross-functional teams, and continuous improvement. When extending agility across multiple teams or complex projects, challenges emerge, such as inter-team coordination and managing numerous stakeholders. SAFe ranks among the most popular frameworks for scaling agility, providing a structured multi-level approach with defined roles. Conversely, SoS adheres closely to Scrum principles, employing SoS meetings to align efforts between teams. These frameworks differ in their scaling strategies. SAFe adopts a structured, comprehensive method suitable for large organizations undergoing agile transformation, incorporating Lean Thinking and DevOps principles. It defines roles and processes that enable collaboration among sizable teams. In contrast, SoS offers a simpler, flexible approach, focusing on team coordination while staying true to Scrum fundamentals. SAFe proves advantageous for very large and intricate projects but presents challenges for smaller companies due to its complexity. SoS, while more scalable and simpler, may face limitations in massive projects. Both frameworks provide valuable strategies that can be tailored or integrated to meet project-specific needs, fostering agility within extensive structures. In conclusion, SAFe and SoS present viable solutions for implementing agility in large projects but also necessitate adaptations tailored to the specific context of each situation.

Keywords: Agile methods · Scaled Agile Framework (SAFe) · Scaling agile · Scrum of Scrums (SoS)

S. Zielinski et al. (Eds.): I4CS 2025, CCIS 2513, pp. 453–470, 2025.
https://doi.org/10.1007/978-3-031-94263-1_25

1   Introduction

Globalization presents businesses with several challenges, including rapidly changing market demands, increased competition, and the complexity of managing cross-border teams and operations. These challenges force businesses to stay highly adaptive and responsive to maintain a competitive edge. In the field of project management, agile methods offer a potential strategy for addressing these challenges, as they emphasize flexibility, collaboration, and quick decision-making. However, research shows that the benefits of agile practices can diminish in very large projects, where scaling and coordination across multiple teams create additional complexity [14]. On the contrary, in such cases, agile practices can sometimes lead to lower software quality or delayed completion. For this reason, adapting agile methods to large projects or enterprises becomes essential. Scalable agile frameworks support this need by providing structured approaches to maintain efficiency and effectiveness at scale [25].

Uludag et al. highlight reasons for the development of scalable agile frameworks in their study [26]. These frameworks aim to enhance the agility and adaptability of the organization or project, improve collaboration among agile teams working on the same product, and facilitate the coordination and synchronization of agile practices across teams.

According to Putta et al., companies expect that scalable agile frameworks will improve cooperation between teams, management of team dependencies, and transparency within the organization or project [18].

Research has already shown that the development and implementation of scalable agile frameworks also entail a range of challenges [9].

The aim of this paper revolves around summarizing challenges identified in the literature and analyzing, through specific scalable frameworks, how these frameworks provide solutions for overcoming these challenges. The focus includes examining the most popular scalable agile framework, the SAFe, alongside the SoS framework, which aligns most closely with original Scrum principles.

This paper addresses the main research question: *What challenges emerge when scaling agile methods?* and the sub-questions: *What approaches does SAFe offer to address these challenges?* and *What approaches does SoS offer to address these challenges?* The main research question focuses on identifying and systematically clustering the challenges encountered during the scaling of agile methods. The sub-questions explore the specific frameworks, SAFe and SoS, in terms of their approaches to tackling the previously identified challenges. Two distinct scaling approaches were selected to enable a comparative analysis of their methods for addressing these challenges.

The goal of this paper involves contributing to the advancement of understanding in scaling agile methods, an area attracting significant attention in recent years but still lacking exploration in many critical aspects. This goal takes shape through an extensive and rigorous literature review that not only compiles existing studies but also systematically processes them to reveal new insights and perspectives. While researchers have conducted several studies on scaling agile methods, this paper sets itself apart by offering a comprehensive analysis of the accumulated findings, identifying gaps, inconsistencies, and emerging trends that prior research has yet to address. By synthesizing the literature in a novel way, this study seeks to provide a more nuanced understanding of the challenges and opportunities in scaling agile practices across different organizational contexts. Furthermore, the methodology employed in this review incorporates advanced analytical techniques that go beyond simple aggregation, fostering a deeper, more critical reflection on the existing knowledge base. This innovative approach ensures that the review not only consolidates current knowledge but also lays the foundation for future research directions, thereby making a substantial contribution to the field.

To contextualize the challenges in agile project management, Sect. 2 provides a theoretical foundation. As agility forms a core element of the frameworks under consideration, an introductory overview outlines its key aspects. Following this, the concept of scalable agility, as defined in the literature and within this paper, receives detailed explanation. Section 3 introduces the two frameworks under examination. This presentation remains cursory, as an exhaustive description would exceed the scope of this paper. It aims to support understanding of the solutions discussed later in the work. After presenting these foundations, Sect. 4 first outlines the challenges reported in the literature regarding the scaling of agile methods. Section 5 presents the approaches to overcoming challenges provided by SAFe and SoS, with reference to the chapters that offer an overview of the two frameworks.

2   Related Work

This section begins by introducing agility and agile practices as central concepts. Building on this foundation, the discussion then explains what scaling agility entails. This section concludes with an overview of the two frameworks, SAFe and SoS.

2.1   Agility

The Agile Manifesto, serving as the theoretical foundation of the agile movement, defines the following four core values [10].

– Individuals and interactions over processes and tools
– Working software over comprehensive documentation
– Customer collaboration over contract negotiation
– Responding to change over following a plan

These values find support in twelve principles that enable flexible, customer-focused, and continuously improving software development in agile projects.

A central characteristic of agile methods involves iterative workflows, with product increments developed in short cycles known as sprints (see Fig. 1) [21].

This contrasts with the linear process of traditional methods and allows for continuous adaptation of the product to the evolving needs of customers [15].

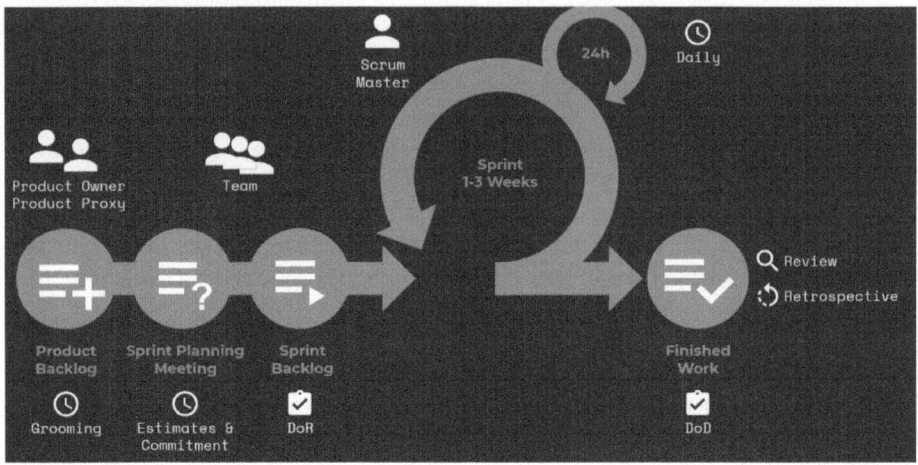

Fig. 1. Sprints in agile work

Teams in agile projects function as self-organizing and multidisciplinary units, granting greater autonomy and enhancing the ability to respond quickly to changes [21]. This contrasts fundamentally with the rigid hierarchies and clearly defined roles found in traditional teams. Regular retrospectives further promote continuous improvement, which often lacks in traditional models.

2.2   Scaling Agility

The term *large-scale agile* lacks a clear definition in the literature [4], with its meaning varying depending on the context [7]. A common factor used to determine whether a project requires scaled agility involves the number of teams participating. Dingsøyr et al. propose a three-tier classification: small-scale projects (one team), large-scale projects (between two and nine teams), and very large-scale projects (ten or more teams) [8].

Rolland, on the other hand, describes large-scale projects based on the literature as projects involving a higher number of external experts in addition to the existing team members [20]. This means the level of multidisciplinary collaboration exceeds that of regular projects. Furthermore, according to Rolland, large-scale projects generally involve more stakeholders and feature stronger integration with the existing IT systems of the client company.

In this paper, scaled agility refers to projects where at least two agile teams collaborate on a shared project.

Overview of Scalable Agile Frameworks. Several scalable agile frameworks exist to address different needs. According to Turhan et al., organizations most frequently adopt SAFe, Large-Scale Scrum (LeSS), Disciplined Agile Delivery

(DAD), and Scrum@Scale (S@S) [25]. Camara et al. also recognize these frameworks as the most popular choices today [4].

A brief overview of the frameworks not covered in this paper follows.

- **DAD** serves as a framework covering the entire product lifecycle, from conception through the initial phase, implementation phase, and ultimately the post-delivery phase [3]. Unlike other frameworks, DAD primarily utilizes well-known agile methodologies, such as Scrum or Kanban. DAD offers four different lifecycles, each adaptable to the product's requirements. These lifecycles share a goal-oriented approach, rather than a prescriptive one, emphasizing the agile nature of the framework.
- **S@S** serves as a framework rooted in the Scrum framework [2]. Based on these principles, two cycles form the Scrum Master Cycle, responsible for how the system should be implemented, and the Product Owner Cycle, responsible for what should be implemented. Unlike simple Scrum, a team size of four to six people gets recommended. When multiple Scrum teams exist, a SoS team should form to coordinate the Scrum teams. Scaling can extend so far that, with several SoS teams, a Scrum-of-Scrum-of-Scrum (SoSoS) team can form to coordinate them. Product Owners can scale similarly to the Scrum cycle. The equivalent to SoS lacks a specific name, but leadership of this group refers to the Chief Product Owner (CPO). The highest level of this framework designates the top Scrum team as the Executive Action Team, and the Product Owner team as the ExecutiveMetaScrum.
- **LeSS** does not focus on scaling the existing elements of Scrum but rather scaling the ideas and mindset behind Scrum [13]. The emphasis lies on ensuring that the entire team or teams take responsibility for the entire end product, not just parts of it.

2.3 SAFe

One of the two frameworks analyzed in this paper, SAFe, stands as the most well-known and popular scalable framework, making it also the most researched framework [11]. The first version of the framework was released in 2011 and underwent several revisions since then. This paper refers to the current version, 6.0, of the framework.

SAFe consists of seven core competencies, a spanning palette with eight elements, a foundation with five pillars, and can be divided into three areas (Essential, Large Solution, and Portfolio). In the SAFe framework, beyond the Scrum roles, additional roles exist, along with practices beyond familiar agile practices like Kanban and project backlogs, which vary depending on the area. Figure 2 provides an overall overview of the SAFe framework.

The Seven Core Competencies. The seven core competencies (see Fig. 3) essential for the application of SAFe will be described first.

Each core competency comprises three dimensions. The following itemization provides only a brief overview.

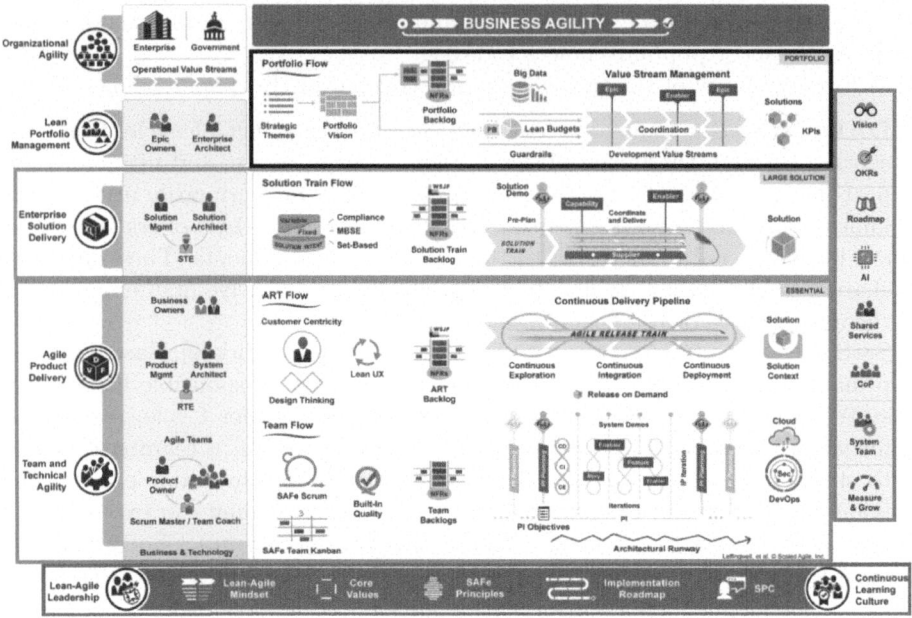

Fig. 2. SAFe overall overview [22]

- **Team and Technical Agility** highlights the necessity of agility within the framework.
- **Agile Product Delivery** refers to a user-centered approach for continuously defining, creating, and delivering valuable products and services.
- **Enterprise Solution Delivery** outlines the application of lean-agile principles and practices across the entire spectrum of the world's largest and most complex software applications, networks, and cyber-physical systems, spanning initial specification and development to deployment, operation, and continuous evolution.
- **Lean Portfolio Management** focuses on aligning strategy with execution, achieved through the application of Lean principles and systems thinking.
- **Organizational Agility** requires enterprises to adapt rapidly to address challenges and seize opportunities presented by today's fast-evolving markets.
- **Continuous Learning Culture** can be defined as a set of values and practices that encourage individuals and the organization as a whole to engage in an ongoing process of knowledge acquisition, skill development, performance improvement, and innovation.
- **Lean-Agile Leadership** emphasizes that the introduction and success of Lean-Agile development, along with mastering the competencies that lead to business agility, ultimately depend on the actions of leaders.

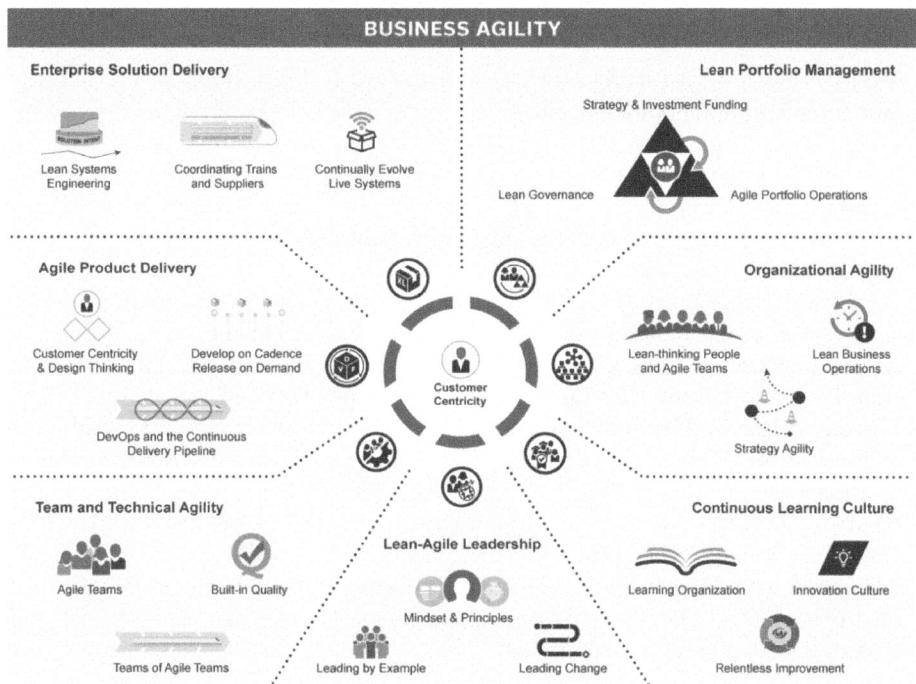

Fig. 3. SAFe core competencies [22]

Foundation of SAFe. The foundation in the red-bordered rectangle in Fig. 2 relies on the previously outlined core values of lean-agile leadership and a culture of continuous learning.

The following itemization briefly describes each component of the foundation.

- **Lean-Agile Mindset** draws from the concepts of the Agile Manifesto and Lean Thinking.
- **Core Values** of the SAFe framework include goal orientation, transparency, continuous improvement, and respect for individuals.
- **SAFe Principles** rely on ten principles that integrate agile methods, lean product development, DevOps, and systems thinking.
- **Implementation Roadmap**, provided by SAFe, guides the transformation into a lean-agile technology company, representing a significant change for many organizations.
- **SAFe Practice Consultant (SPC)** serves as a change agent, combining their knowledge of SAFe with intrinsic motivation to improve enterprise software and system development processes.

Spanning Palette. The spanning palette in the turquoise-bordered rectangle in Fig. 2 represents a range of artifacts and values that may be relevant for a specific agile team in the context of a large solution or portfolio perspective.

A brief description of each component of the palette follows.

- **Vision** describes a future view of the solution to be developed, considering customer and stakeholder needs.
- **Objectives and Key Results (OKRs)** serve as parameters to compare portfolio strategy and organizations, measuring improvements within the company.
- **Roadmap** displays planned Agile Release Trains (ARTs), development value streams, and milestones over a defined period.
- **Artificial Intelligence (AI)** as outlined by SAFe, shows the context where its use may bring benefits.
- **Shared Services** represent the specialized roles necessary for ARTs or Solution Trains but cannot be fully assigned to a specific train.
- **Community of Practice (CoP)** represents an informal team within the context of an ART or organization that shares practical knowledge in one or more areas.
- **System Team** represents a unique agile team that helps build and utilize the continuous delivery pipeline.
- **Measure and Grow** represents how portfolios evaluate their process toward business agility. The three SAFe measurement areas (Outcomes, Flow, and Competence) receive consideration."

Levels

- **Essential Level** (see the green-bordered rectangle in Fig. 2) includes the team flow and the ART flow. This level contains all elements necessary to enable solutions in a scaled agile environment. Each ART flow can include between five and fifteen agile teams.
  - **Team Flow** characterizes the work of agile teams in short iterations (sprints) with direct customer feedback [12]. These teams follow Scrum or Kanban practices to quickly respond to changes.
  - **ART Flow** means that ARTs coordinate and plan program increments across multiple teams. ARTs consist of several agile teams working together to deliver incremental value. This level ensures synchronization among all teams, working toward common goals.
- **Large Solution Level** (see the orange-bordered rectangle in Fig. 2) applies to very large and complex development projects that require multiple ARTs. It coordinates the work of several ARTs and delivers solutions that a single ART cannot provide [12].
- **Portfolio Level** (see the black-bordered rectangle in Fig. 2) enables the strategic alignment of business goals. It includes lean portfolio management, which ensures that investments align with corporate strategies. Here, budgets get managed, and significant strategic projects crucial to the organization's long-term goals receive prioritization. These large and complex initiatives significantly contribute to realizing the company's long-term vision [12].

2.4 SoS

SoS, a concept for scaling Scrum, closely follows the original Scrum concept and extends it.

When more than one team exists, each team should select one or two representatives (usually the Scrum Master and a representative from the technical team) to participate in SoS meetings (see Fig. 4). These meetings serve to synchronize interacting teams [19].

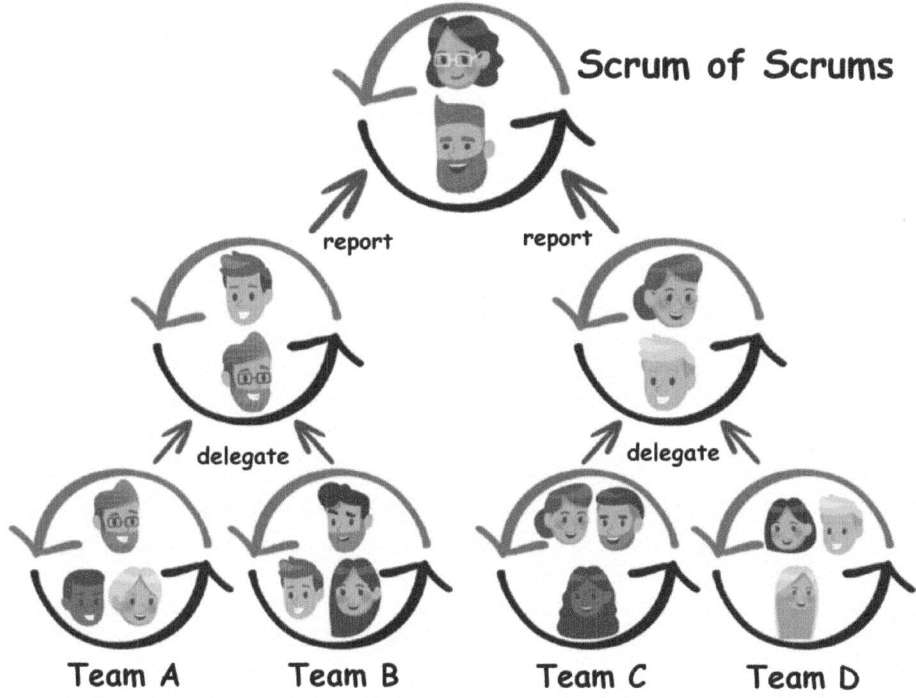

Fig. 4. SoS [6]

In the frequent meetings, the teams' representatives share their progress, next steps, and obstacles. The discussions focus on improving coordination between teams and clarifying responsibilities. Unlike the daily Scrum meeting, the SoS meeting addresses the following questions.

– What has your team done since we last met?
– What will your team do before we meet again?
– Does anything hinder or slow down your team's work?
– Will your team soon be providing work for another team?

In SoS meetings, no solutions get sought. These get worked out in the sub-teams. A separate backlog for SoS helps manage cross-team concerns. The frequency of SoS meetings gets decided by the team and can vary depending on project size and complexity. This scaling method allows for more than two levels, such as a SoSoS meeting, if the project size requires it. This process reflects the agile philosophy of collaboration, continuous improvement, and adaptability.

3   Challenges in Scaling Agile Methods

This section will now highlight the challenges identified in the literature that arise when scaling agile methods and applying scaling frameworks.

3.1   Implementation

Change. For successful implementation of such a framework, employees and organizational structures must exhibit readiness to embrace the change. A distinction arises between general readiness for change and the willingness to adopt the chosen framework specifically [5]. Resistance often accompanies changes, presenting a significant challenge [18].

Additionally, a specific challenge involves fostering openness among employees toward the chosen framework. Without this openness, implementing the new framework becomes difficult. Agile scaling typically applies to large projects or organizations, where an existing culture already prevails. Introducing a new framework requires altering this culture, which proves to be a highly demanding task [9].

Understanding New Roles and Responsibilities. Agile work represents a well-defined concept, often perceived as intuitive and easily understood by practitioners. However, scaling agile methods introduces new roles and alters familiar responsibilities and workflows. Understanding these new roles and distinguishing them from one another presents a significant challenge, primarily for team members but also for clients [5,9].

Several frameworks provide extensive resources to simplify their application for practitioners. However, research highlights challenges in translating theoretical concepts into practice, as the terminology often feels overly abstract. This abstraction can result in differing interpretations of identical concepts across various teams [5]. Similarly, Edison et al. observed difficulties in defining new roles and responsibilities in several case studies examined [9].

3.2   Challenges at the Team Level

Communication Among Teams. Projects requiring the scaling of agile methods often involve a larger number of teams collaborating on a single product. These teams need to maintain effective communication within their own groups. As team sizes grow, challenges related to communication and coordination tend to increase. Additionally, communication between teams emerges as a critical factor for the success of such projects. According to Theobald and Schmitt, inter-team communication also represents one of the key challenges when scaling agile methods [24].

Collaboration across different locations and time zones further complicates coordination and communication [16]. This factor becomes particularly important, as the State of Agile Report indicates that 80% of surveyed companies work with geographically distributed agile teams [4].

Knowledge Transfer Between Teams. In addition to general communication, knowledge transfer between teams presents a significant challenge [20]. Coordinating many teams increases the risk of information loss, especially in asynchronous communication [1].

Beyond information loss, the knowledge transfer itself can be challenging, as it may not be sufficient to simply pass on information [20]. Often, the information must be translated into the *language* of the other teams to ensure that the knowledge can truly be understood and applied effectively. This requires an understanding of the specific contexts and workflows of each team, making communication and collaboration even more critical in large-scale agile projects.

Transparency for Teams. As the number of teams grows, maintaining a high level of transparency for all employees becomes increasingly challenging [9].

Coordination of Teams. The increased number of teams also makes coordination more difficult. This mainly involves the synchronization of different teams [17]. Agile teams work at their own pace, which brings challenges in synchronizing and integrating work results [1].

With multiple Scrum teams, responsibility diffusion can occur with user stories if responsibility does not lie with individual developers [9].

3.3 Agility Versus Structure

Scaling agile methods brings a higher degree of structure compared to traditional agile work, creating challenges when transitioning to scaled agile practices [20]. However, structure plays a crucial role in enabling agility, just as agility supports the effectiveness of structure.

Preserving Developer Autonomy. Developers today feel accustomed to a certain level of autonomy in their work methods [9]. Autonomy in scalable frameworks poses a significant challenge. Thus, the structure of frameworks competes with the familiar autonomy of agile work. Frameworks can reduce the autonomy of individual teams, leading to frustration and decreased motivation. The direct, straightforward communication style in small Scrum teams may not easily transfer to planning meetings in scaled frameworks, causing important information to be lost due to fear of criticism.

Handover. Scaling up can lead to so-called *handovers*. This refers to the need for additional coordination and informational meetings in decision-making processes due to the involvement of multiple teams, making the workflow less straightforward and resources less effectively utilized compared to unscaled agile work.

Additionally, the time developers need for consultations with management increases, leaving less time for their core task, development. This slows down the value creation process and can negatively impact developer motivation. Cross-team tasks can cause internal team tasks to suffer or be executed reluctantly.

3.4   Adapting the Framework to a Company

Scalable agile frameworks often fail to adapt to the organization, with a one-size-fits-all solution applied instead [5]. This leads to interference with the existing (agile) organizational structure, requiring changes. The structure frequently undergoes constant adaptation to external circumstances, and the added factor of change presents a challenge.

The one-size-fits-all approach poses a challenge, as it does not always work well, with different projects or teams having varying needs [23]. This can lead to less flexibility across the organization, inadequate communication, and a limited ability to respond to change.

4   Approaches to Overcoming Challenges

This section presents the coping strategies of the two frameworks, SAFe (see Subsect. 2.3) and SoS (see Subsect. 2.4), for the identified challenges. The two frameworks get compared for each challenge. The structure of this section follows the one used in Sect. 3 outlining the challenges.

4.1   Implementation

- **SAFe** provides a road map for implementing the framework (see Fig. 5). This guides the gradual introduction of the complex SAFe framework into the company or project through workshops and so-called *change agents*. The approach ensures that all new roles and responsibilities get understood, with experts available to offer support in case of uncertainties.
- **SoS** scaling poses minimal challenges for companies or employees already working in an agile manner, as the scaling relies on familiar mechanisms and roles. This typically results in fewer issues regarding uncertainties about new roles. Consequently, Scrum-of-Scrums provides no dedicated support to address this challenge.

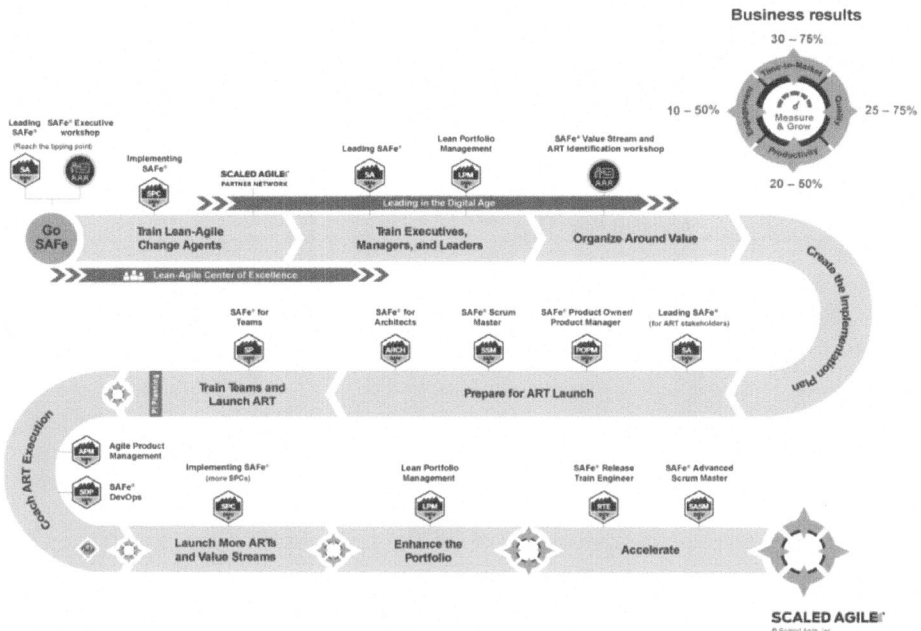

Fig. 5. SAFe implementation roadmap [22]

4.2   Challenges at the Team Level

Communication Among Teams

– **SAFe** At the essential level of SAFe, teams work as agile as possible (drawing from Scrum and Kanban). This approach aims to keep communication and coordination within teams straightforward. SAFe ensures communication through various mechanisms, including Program Increment (PI) Planning, which occurs regularly and brings together all teams within an ART (see Fig. 6). This meeting enables the definition of shared objectives and the creation of a synchronized plan for the next PI. PI Planning establishes a common vision and promotes communication and collaboration across teams.

– **SoS** Communication within teams remains unaffected by scaling. Communication between teams occurs through the SoS meeting. The number of participants stays small by involving representatives, enabling effective and open dialogue. Representatives can change depending on the current issue, fostering broader interaction among team members compared to SAFe, which prescribes fixed roles that typically remain unchanged within the project [19]. However, SoS provides only the SoS meeting as a communication tool. Additionally, a predefined structure guides the meeting. This creates a risk of overlooking perspectives, as participants, heavily influenced by their team's tasks, may lack an objective, external viewpoint.

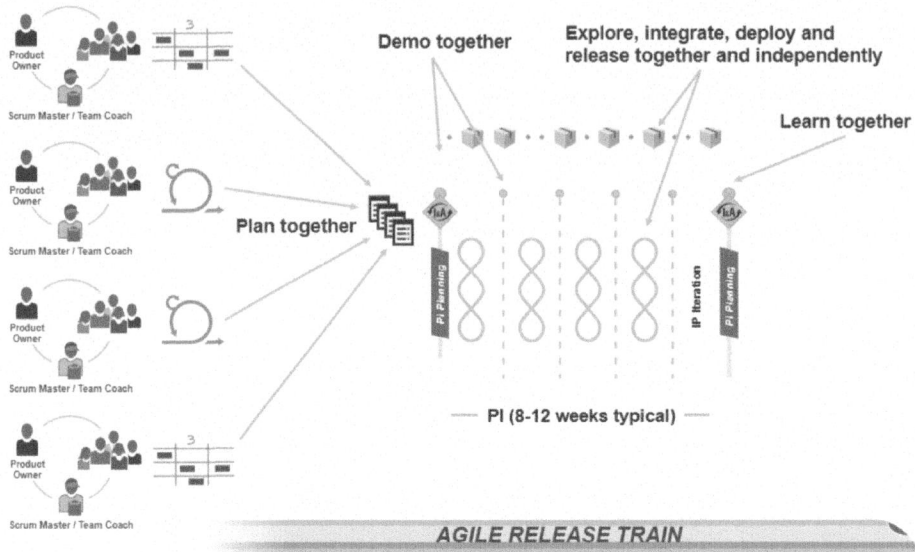

Fig. 6. SAFe ART and PI Planning [22]

Knowledge Transfer Between Teams

– **SAFe** A central foundation of SAFe lies in fostering a continuous learning culture. This principle spans all areas of SAFe, aiming to make insights accessible to everyone. Specific measures to achieve this goal embed within all SAFe mechanisms, though practical implementation often proves challenging.
– **SoS** In SoS, potential knowledge transfer occurs only during the SoS meeting, where technical representatives, for instance, can exchange information. However, this remains an implicit process, which can lead to knowledge asymmetries across the project, particularly within this framework.

Transparency for Teams

– **SAFe** Transparency in SAFe relies on ARTs, where all team representatives come together to plan and reflect collectively. Additionally, the initial roadmap aims to enhance transparency by clarifying information and decision flows within the project or organization.
– **SoS** In SoS, Scrum Masters ensure transparency by relaying insights from the SoS meetings to their teams. The structure remains straightforward, minimizing uncertainty regarding points of contact or decision-making processes within this framework.

Coordination of Teams

- **SAFe** SAFe relies on clearly defined roles and processes to ensure coordination between teams. Roles such as the Release Train Engineer (RTE) focus on aligning team efforts and achieving program objectives. The RTE serves as the primary coordinator, assisting teams in removing obstacles and adhering to the plan.
- **SoS** In the SoS framework, the SoS meeting handles cross-team coordination. Due to the immediacy of the meeting, coordination can occur easily. However, this introduces the same risk as with communication: since the representatives come from their own teams, their perspective on coordination may be influenced by the interests and priorities of their team.

4.3   Agility Versus Structure

- **SAFe** The SAFe framework imposes a high degree of structure. However, it aims to maintain a high level of agility within individual teams, granting each agile team the authority and responsibility to manage its own work. This approach seeks to strengthen team member autonomy. Nevertheless, it must be noted that a clear shift toward structure occurs, compared to the agility seen in non-scaled agile work. One of SAFe's core principles, the lean-agile mindset, seeks to minimize *handover* as much as possible.
- **SoS** In SoS, the original agility remains largely intact, with agile teams working in their familiar way [19]. However, the autonomy of individual teams gets reduced through shared synchronization in the SoS meeting. The challenge of handovers gets addressed by allowing SoS meeting participants to decide how frequently the meeting occurs, ensuring optimal use of project participants' resources.

4.4   Adapting the Framework to a Company

- **SAFe** offers different levels where the framework can be applied to a project or organization, providing a certain degree of adaptability. On the other hand, SAFe prescribes many roles and processes that bring significant change to the company or project, with some being indispensable.
- **SoS** The autonomy in designing the SoS meetings lies with the participants, allowing for adaptation to the participants or the organization. However, SoS offers only one form of expansion, leaving little room for other types of extension.

5   Discussion

This paper demonstrates that scaling agile methods presents several challenges. In addition to introducing a new framework with new roles and responsibilities, the change itself poses a challenge. Specific challenges, particularly in scaling agile methods in large projects, mainly lie in the coordination and communication between teams. To deliver high-quality products within the set timelines, well-organized communication between teams becomes crucial, allowing for synchronized work and preventing dependencies that could negatively impact progress. Agile workers must relinquish some autonomy during scaling, as tasks and schedules require global coordination. This inevitably reduces agility within the scaling process, potentially affecting motivation and results if perceived negatively. Additionally, scaling often requires team members to allocate resources for coordination and communication, presenting a challenge to keep this process lean, ensuring minimal resource loss while enabling team members to focus on their core tasks effectively.

The two frameworks examined in this paper for scaling agile methods differ significantly in their approaches, allowing them to address the respective challenges in distinct ways. SAFe offers a complex, well-thought-out framework that manages coordination and communication between teams through new roles and constructs, thus maintaining a focus on the overall project. SoS, as an extension of Scrum, effectively handles the challenge of preserving the autonomy and agility of team members. Overall, scaling agile methods requires consideration of both the needs of the employees and the project's context to best tackle emerging challenges. The frameworks provide guidelines that must always be adapted to the specific organization to enhance agile practices and avoid becoming rigid rulebooks that offer no real value.

This paper provides an overview of the challenges in scaling agile methods as discussed in the referenced literature. However, since it does not constitute a systematic review, it cannot be considered an exhaustive overview.

It becomes evident that no universally accepted definition of agile scaling exists so far. Therefore, other works may exist that do not align with the definition chosen in this paper but still present additional challenges and insights.

Furthermore, this paper considers only two frameworks. The selection relies on the popularity of SAFe and the proximity of SoS to the Scrum model. This choice warrants critical examination. SoS forms part of several developed frameworks for scaling agility and also serves as a component of SAFe, meaning the consideration and comparison of these two frameworks cannot be equal.However, the significant difference between the two frameworks offers a valuable point of comparison, with a very complex framework (like SAFe) compared to a comparatively simple one (such as SoS). Both frameworks aim to solve similar problems. Therefore, this paper offers a contribution by providing companies and/or project managers with a foundation for decision-making.

In addressing the research question and describing the fundamentals, it becomes clear that, at least for SAFe, providing a comprehensive representation within the scope of this paper proves difficult. Therefore, for future work, focusing on specific aspects of the framework would be more effective, allowing for a deeper representation and analysis of the framework.

A comparison of additional frameworks would have exceeded the scope of this paper but presents an interesting approach for future work.

In summary, it can be stated that the research question holds significant relevance, making further research in this area desirable. Particularly, the tension between autonomy and structure in frameworks for scaling agile methods plays a crucial role in employee satisfaction, presenting an important avenue for future research.

Acknowledgments. Many thanks to Bettina Baumgartner from the University of Vienna for proofreading this paper!

References

1. Abbott, M.L., Fisher, M.T.: Scalability Rules: Principles for Scaling Web Sites, 2nd edn. Addison-Wesley Professional, Boston (August 2016)
2. Alsaqaf, W., Daneva, M., Wieringa, R.: Do the scaled agile practices from s@s help with quality requirements challenges and if so, how do they do it? In: Fill, H.G., van Sinderen, M., Maciaszek, L. (eds.) Proceedings of the 16th International Conference on Software Technologies – ICSOFT, pp. 441–452. SciTePress (July 2021). https://doi.org/10.5220/0010514304410452
3. Ambler, S.W., Lines, M.: The disciplined agile process decision framework. In: Winkler, D., Biffl, S., Bergsmann, J. (eds.) SWQD 2016. LNBIP, vol. 238, pp. 3–14. Springer, Cham (2016). https://doi.org/10.1007/978-3-319-27033-3_1
4. Camara, R., Marinho, M.: Agile tailoring in distributed large-scale environments using agile frameworks: a systematic literature review. CLEI Electron. J. **27**(1), 1–51 (2024). https://doi.org/10.19153/cleiej.27.1.8
5. Conboy, K., Carroll, N.: Implementing large-scale agile frameworks: challenges and recommendations. IEEE Softw. 36(2), 44–50 (2019). https://doi.org/10.1109/MS.2018.2884865
6. Dalton, J.: Scrum of Scrums. In: Great Big Agile: An OS for Agile Leaders, pp. 227–228. Apress, Berkeley, CA, USA (December 2018). https://doi.org/10.1007/978-1-4842-4206-3_53
7. Dikert, K., Paasivaara, M., Lassenius, C.: Challenges and success factors for large-scale agile transformations: a systematic literature review. J. Syst. Softw. **119**, 87–108 (2016). https://doi.org/10.1016/j.jss.2016.06.013
8. Dingsøyr, T., Fægri, T.E., Itkonen, J.: What is large in large-scale? A taxonomy of scale for agile software development. In: Jedlitschka, A., Kuvaja, P., Kuhrmann, M., Männistö, T., Münch, J., Raatikainen, M. (eds.) Product-Focused Software Process Improvement, LNCS, pp. 273–276. Springer International Publishing, Cham (2014), https://doi.org/10.1007/978-3-319-13835-0_20
9. Edison, H., Wang, X., Conboy, K.: Comparing methods for large-scale agile software development: a systematic literature review. IEEE Trans. Softw. Eng. **48**(8), 2709–2731 (2022). https://doi.org/10.1109/TSE.2021.3069039
10. Fowler, M., Highsmith, J.: The Agile Manifesto (August 2001). https://www.drdobbs.com/open-source/the-agile-manifesto/184414755
11. Gustavsson, T., Berntzen, M., Stray, V.: Changes to team autonomy in large-scale software development: a multiple case study of Scaled Agile Framework (SAFe) implementations. Int. J. Inf. Syst. Project Manag. **10**(18), 29–46 (2022), https://hdl.handle.net/11250/3055543

12. Knaster, R., Leffingwell, D.: SAFe 5.0 Distilled: Achieving Business Agility with the Scaled Agile Framework, 1st edn. Addison-Wesley, Boston (July 2020)
13. Larman, C., Vodde, B.: Large-Scale Scrum: More with LeSS. Addison-Wesley, Boston (April 2016)
14. Lee, S., Yong, H.S.: Agile software development framework in a small project environment. J. Inf. Process. Syst. **9**(1), 69–88 (2013). https://doi.org/10.3745/JIPS.2013.9.1.069
15. Meyer, B.: Agile! – The Good, the Hype and the Ugly, 1st edn. Springer, Cham (April 2014). https://doi.org/10.1007/978-3-319-05155-0
16. Morrison-Smith, S., Ruiz, J.: Challenges and barriers in virtual teams: a literature review. SN Appl. Sci. **2**(6), 1–33 (2020). https://doi.org/10.1007/s42452-020-2801-5
17. Paasivaara, M.: Adopting SAFe to scale agile in a globally distributed organization. In: 2017 IEEE 12th International Conference on Global Software Engineering (ICGSE), pp. 36–40. IEEE (May 2017). https://doi.org/10.1109/ICGSE.2017.15
18. Putta, A., Uludağ, O., Hong, S.L., Paasivaara, M., Lassenius, C.: Why do organizations adopt agile scaling frameworks? a survey of practitioners. In: Proceedings of the 15th ACM / IEEE International Symposium on Empirical Software Engineering and Measurement (ESEM), pp. 1–12. ESEM '21, Association for Computing Machinery, New York, NY, USA (October 2021). https://doi.org/10.1145/3475716.3475788
19. Qurashi, S.A., Qurashi, M.R.J.: Scrum of Scrums Solution for Large Size Teams Using Scrum Methodology. arXiv pp. 443–449 (August 2014). https://doi.org/10.48550/arXiv.1408.6142
20. Rolland, K.H.: Scaling across knowledge boundaries: a case study of a large-scale agile software development project. In: Proceedings of the Scientific Workshop Proceedings of XP2016, pp. 1–5. XP '16 Workshops, Association for Computing Machinery, New York, NY, USA (May 2016). https://doi.org/10.1145/2962695.2962700
21. Rubin, K.S.: Essential Scrum: A Practical Guide to the Most Popular Agile Process. Addison-Wesley, Boston (July 2012)
22. Scaled Agile: SAFe 6.0 (April 2024). https://scaledagileframework.com/
23. Tendedez, H., Ferrario, M.A.M.A.F., Whittle, J.: Proceedings ACM Human-Computer Interaction
24. Theobald, S., Schmitt, A.: Dependencies of agile teams – an analysis of the scaled agile framework. In: Paasivaara, M., Kruchten, P. (eds.) Agile Processes in Software Engineering and Extreme Programming – Workshops, LNBIP, pp. 219–226. Springer, Cham (2020). https://doi.org/10.1007/978-3-030-58858-8_22
25. Turhan, Y., Buehrle, D., Herzwurm, G.: Developing a taxonomy for agile scaling frameworks. In: Proceedings of the 7th ACM/IEEE International Workshop on Software-Intensive Business, pp. 40–47. IWSiB '24, Association for Computing Machinery, New York, NY, USA (April 2024). https://doi.org/10.1145/3643690.3648239
26. Uludağ, Ö., Putta, A., Paasivaara, M., Matthes, F.: Evolution of the agile scaling frameworks. In: Gregory, P., Lassenius, C., Wang, X., Kruchten, P. (eds.) Agile Processes in Software Engineering and Extreme Programming, LNBIP, pp. 123–139. Springer, Cham, Switzerland (2021). https://doi.org/10.1007/978-3-030-78098-2_8

Author Index

A

Ahmad, Imran Shafiq   437
Ahmed, Junaeid   269

B

Banerjee, Pradipta   330
Bhale, Pradeepkumar   417
Biermann, Jan   307
Böhme, Thomas   126
Brandauer, Christof   115
Bub, Udo   144

C

Charak, Aahan Singh   437

D

de Kok, Willem   189
Dewangan, Bhimendra   36
Dorfinger, Peter   115

E

Eichler, Gerald   94
Eigner, Christoph   453

F

Fahrnberger, Günter   23, 353, 386, 453
Farooqui, Tabish   417
Feld, Sebastian   3, 189
Fong, Jackie   231

G

Goodridge, Lawrence   231
Greiner, Maximilian   307, 386
Großmann, Marcel   269

H

Haghighi, Sepinood   231
Hirsch, Patrick   353
Hofbauer, Stefan   386
Hofmann, Marko   377

H

Hofmeier, Manfred   251
Hrestic, Razvan   251

I

Iosif, Andrei-Cristian   289

J

Jokela, Sami   144
Jouyandeh, Farzaneh   231

K

Kölle, Michael   63
Kornmaier, Andreas   377
Krieger, Udo R.   269
Kubek, Mario M.   126
Kuikkaniemi, Kai   144

L

Lähteenoja, Viivi   144
Langner, Gregor   353
Le, Duy Thanh   269
Lechner, Ulrike   251, 289, 307, 353, 377, 386
Lesan Pezeshki, Kiana   231
Linecker, Stefan   115
Linnhoff-Popien, Claudia   63, 209
Lüke, Karl-Heinz   94

M

Mansky, Maximilian Balthasar   63
Maurya, Darpan   417
Maurya, Sonam   417
McDaniel, Emma L.   126
McKay, R. Michael   231
Mikler, Armin R.   126
Moradian Zadeh, Pooya   231

N

Ng, Kenneth K. S.   231
Nüßlein, Jonas   209

O

Oancea, Rares Adrian   189

P

Papp, Attila   144
Pechler, Orin   159
Petersen, Sobah Abbas   330
Pham, Quynh-Lan Nguyen   330
Phillipson, Frank   79, 159
Pinto-Albuquerque, Maria   289
Pokharel, Shiraj   126
Porter, Lisa A.   231
Preßler, Wesley   51

Q

Quirchmayr, Gerald   353

R

Riesel, Kevin   307
Rohe, Tobias   63
Royer, Denis   94

S

Sabatelli, Matthia   189
Sadeghi, Sarvnaz   231
Schachenhofer, Larissa   353
Schauer, Stefan   353
Seidel, Patrick   51

Seidenfad, Karl   307
Seiler, Andreas   386
Singh, Harsh   417
Sodhi, Vaibhav   417
Soucie, Kendall   231
Srinivas, M.   36
Stein, Jonas   63
Strohmeier, Felix   115
Strussenberg, Judith   307, 386
Subramanyam, R. B. V.   36
Sünkel, Leo   63

T

Tong, Yufeng   231
Turpeinen, Marko   144

U

Unger, Herwig   126

V

van der Linde, Stan   189

W

Wolf, Philipp   353, 386

Z

Zielinski, Sebastian   209

The manufacturer's authorised representative in the EU is Springer
Nature Customer Service Centre GmbH, Europaplatz 3, 69115 Heidelberg,
Germany. If you have any concerns regarding our products, please
contact ProductSafety@springernature.com

Printed and bound by CPI Group (UK) Ltd, Croydon, CR0 4YY
27/04/2026
02097845-0011